Talbot Mundy,
Philosopher of Adventure

Talbot Mundy, Philosopher of Adventure

A Critical Biography

BRIAN TAVES

McFarland & Company, Inc., Publishers
Jefferson, North Carolina, and London

ALSO BY BRIAN TAVES
AND FROM MCFARLAND

*P.G. Wodehouse and Hollywood:
Screenwriting, Satires and Adaptations* (2005)

OTHER WORKS BY BRIAN TAVES

The Jules Verne Encyclopedia

Robert Florey, the French Expressionist

*The Romance of Adventure:
The Genre of Historical Adventure Movies*

Frontispiece: Publicity photograph of Talbot Mundy in 1936 (Library of Congress).

LIBRARY OF CONGRESS CATALOGUING-IN-PUBLICATION DATA

Taves, Brian, 1959–
Talbot Mundy, philosopher of adventure : a critical biography / Brian Taves.
    p.   cm.
Includes bibliographical references and index.

ISBN 0-7864-2234-3 (softcover : 50# alkaline paper)

1. Mundy, Talbot, 1879–1940. 2. Authors, English — 20th century — Biography. 3. Adventure and adventurers — Great Britain — Biography. 4. British — Foreign countries — History — 20th century. I. Title
PR6025.U66Z895   2006   823'.912—dc22   2005020109

British Library cataloguing data are available

©2006 Brian Taves. All rights reserved

*No part of this book may be reproduced or transmitted in any form
or by any means, electronic or mechanical, including photocopying
or recording, or by any information storage and retrieval system,
without permission in writing from the publisher.*

On the cover —*foreground*: Talbot Mundy (Ames Collection);
background: artwork from *King — of the Khyber Rifles*

Manufactured in the United States of America

*McFarland & Company, Inc., Publishers
Box 611, Jefferson, North Carolina 28640
www.mcfarlandpub.com*

To Dick and Betty Ames
and
W. Emmett Small
for sharing their memories of Talbot Mundy
and for their years of encouragement as I wrote this book

Table of Contents

Preface   1

   I. From Wanderer to Writer, 1879–1913   5

  II. The Yasmini Conundrum, 1913–1921   24

 III. War and Its Colonial Impact, 1916–1919   46

 IV. From Jerusalem to Jimgrim, 1919–1921   60

   V. Journey West, 1921–1923   89

 VI. The Masters, 1923–1926   112

VII. The Ancient World, 1924–1928   132

VIII. Four Failures, 1926–1929   151

 IX. New Faith, 1928–1931   168

   X. Lost Trails, 1931–1937   189

 XI. An Audience of Millions, 1936–1940   212

XII. Legacy   240

Appendix A: Books by Talbot Mundy   261

Appendix B: Chronological List of Original Publications of Talbot Mundy's Work   262

Chapter Notes   273

Index   297

Preface

Preconceptions of empire adventure portray it as a genre that uniformly celebrates the hegemony of white imperialists and Western culture, at best with a minor, patronizing glimpse of Eastern "exoticism." Countless studies have relied on the example of Rudyard Kipling as the model of such literature during the late 19th and early 20th century. However, there was a significant counter-example, largely overlooked: an Anglo-American writer who also achieved wide popularity. While writing for the same readers and within a similar framework, he was not only overtly anti-colonial but also championed Eastern philosophy and culture.

Talbot Mundy (1879–1940) spanned the interval between Victorian classicism and the modernist era, writing 45 novels, most of which appeared in multiple editions during his lifetime. Mundy's short stories and novels have been translated into many languages, including Armenian, Danish, Dutch, French, German, Hindustani, Hungarian, Japanese, Norwegian, and Swedish. Equally well known in his time were short stories and serials in magazines, and he penned 156, including essays and poems, in addition to hundreds of radio scripts. Working within the genres of adventure and fantasy, he used as his settings the contemporary colonial locales of Africa, the Middle East, and especially India and Tibet. Mundy's writing reflected his own youthful years roaming these regions and his firsthand observations of occult teachings. His spiritual interests led him to explore a wide variety of faiths, and he became especially involved in theosophy.

Mundy was more than a writer of diverting tales; through his literature he was engaged in a lifelong discourse on philosophy and religion. Long before Eastern religious ideas became diluted and mainstream under the label "New Age," he effectively translated such ideas as karma and reincarnation into a Western idiom in such classic tales of India as *King — of the Khyber Rifles* and *Om — The Secret of Ahbor Valley*. These and other stories of Lamas and Tibet, such as *The Devil's Guard*, *Black Light*, and *Old Ugly-Face*, situate Mundy as one of the first prominent genre writers to chronicle such teachings from a sympathetic, understanding viewpoint. They paved the way for an acceptance of new literary norms, as epitomized by James Hilton's *Lost Horizon* (1933). From 1925 to 1936, Mundy changed literary expectations again when his Tros of Samothrace saga of imperial Rome departed from conventional portraits of Caesar and Cleopatra to offer a feminist, anti-imperial critique of the foundations of Western thinking. Mundy's books continue to find new readers; 25

titles, including two published for the first time posthumously, have been issued over 50 times in the 65 years since his death.

My principal goal has been to investigate an important author who will need to be acknowledged in future studies as one who flourished despite defying all the "rules" supposedly dictated by the genre and publishers of his time. Yet these deliberate decisions also kept Mundy from the bestseller status achieved by authors like Sax Rohmer, who framed the East as an "other" and menace to the West. Joseph Conrad provides the closest parallel to Mundy — a major adventure author sharing philosophical concerns, but without the religious overtones so vital to Mundy. This sensibility, and Mundy's hopeful conclusions, also placed him outside the realm of the bleaker currents of literary modernism represented by Conrad's "heart of darkness."

In this critical biography, I regard as worthy of attention not only novels, but also other, more often neglected texts. These range from short stories and serials for magazines, to the lengthy letters magazines often carried from Mundy to his readers, introducing his tales or discussing various historical and occult topics. I also include Mundy's writing for film and radio, along with adaptations of his work by others, revealing the different ways the media have handled his texts for a mass audience. The importance of reconstructing his four years of radio scripts extends beyond questions of literary merit. Not only do the scripts represent a huge share of his writing; they reached an audience beyond the possibilities of prose — millions of daily listeners. Few novelists have ever had the opportunity to relate their stories to an audience of that size. Only by thus grasping the entire Mundy oeuvre can one gain an accurate and full understanding of the author: what he produced, his cultural impact, and how he was perceived by the consumers of his work.

In exploring Mundy's life and ideas I generally follow the chronology of his writing. I conclude by tracing the evolution of his critical reputation and offering my own evaluation of why his writing has proved to have enduring value to readers. The first complete chronological listing of Mundy's published writing is offered at the end, in Appendix B. I tracked down and read all of Mundy's often elusive periodical publications, in a myriad of libraries and institutions, and with the help of collectors.

I traveled to the various locales where Mundy resided in the United States and England, walking in his footsteps to better understand the man, thereby uncovering a variety of local resources which have helped to fill gaps in his life story. These have ranged from the Hammersmith, London, neighborhood and Rugby School of his birth and youth in England; from New York City to Norway, Maine; from Reno, Nevada, to San Diego, California; from Manchester, Connecticut, to Anna Maria, Florida. Significant archival resources have been provided by New York Supreme Court records; the court records and attendant newspaper publicity surrounding Mundy's attempted 1923 divorce in Reno, Nevada; the Theosophical libraries in Altadena and Point Loma, California; the Bobbs-Merrill and Curtis Brown papers at Indiana University; the J. Lloyd Eaton Collection at the University of California at Riverside; the Rose Wilder Lane papers at the Herbert Hoover Presidential Library; the Library of Congress; the Charles Scribner's Sons papers at Princeton University; the Fox and Universal scripts at the University of Southern California; the University of California at Berkeley; the *Jerusalem News* at the Boston Public Library; the Anna

Maria Historical Society; the Arthur Sullivant Hoffman papers at Pennsylvania State University; the Academy of Motion Picture Arts and Sciences Library; the British Film Institute; the Wincenty Lutoslawski letters; the Nicholas Roerich Museum; and most notably the private collection of Richards Ames, Mundy's stepson by his marriage to his wife Sally. I have had complete access to the Ames papers, and am especially grateful for the unfailing kindness and patience of his widow, Betty Ames. (Upon her death, the papers were donated to Indiana University, joining the letters of Mundy to those of his publishers and agents.)

Most of these sources were unknown until found during the research for this book. No one previously seems to have comprehensively looked into Mundy's writing for film or radio, although the limited resources on the latter medium have long been in existence. By contrast, the Thomas H. Ince papers (relating to Mundy's 1923 employment in Hollywood) did not become available until 1998. The manuscript of Mundy's film treatment of *Rung Ho!*, entitled *Fifty-Seven*, only emerged for a brief time in the 1980s, in the hands of a series of dealers, before it was abruptly sold (after my own examination for this book) to an unknown collector, rather than an archive.

I first began reading Mundy when I was in high school, and I realized that he was an author meriting serious interest. When I began university studies, I was able to locate many rarer Mundy stories; at the same time, I discovered the dearth of information about him. Beginning the research that would eventually culminate in this book allowed me to receive firsthand the recollections and insights of many who knew Mundy, including his widow Dawn and stepson, along with Emmett Small, Robert Lloyd Davis, Jan (Trimble) Zilliacus, Rodney Mundy, Charles Curtis, and Charlotte Loring White. An essay I wrote about Mundy, one of the first significant studies on him, appeared in 1985. Mundy's ideas significantly inflected my 1993 book *The Romance of Adventure: The Genre of Historical Adventure Movies*, and the research for that book in turn suggested much of the approach utilized here.

I am grateful to many fellow Mundy enthusiasts who have provided encouragement as well as assistance in uncovering hitherto unseen materials, including Richard Minter, James W. Thompson, Howard D. Snively, Steven T. Miller, Brian Emerich, Kathleen Arc, R.T. Gault, Frank Webb, Mark Jaqua, and Stephen Michaluk. Others who have assisted include Michael Morris, Paul Dobish, and Janina Lutoslawski. Doyce Nunis published my first article on Mundy in *Southern California Quarterly*. R.T. Gault, Pervin Mistry, and especially Malcolm Henderson provided their own comparative reactions to readings of Mundy books. Translations of essays on Mundy in Italian (in 1944 by Claudio Montalbano) and in French (in 1970 by Jacques Bergier) were provided by Lucy Rapillo and Evelyn Copeland, respectively. William K. Everson facilitated my detailed examination of *The Black Watch* with a loan of his print of the film. John McLaughlin of Book Sail allowed me to examine the manuscript of *Fifty-Seven* during the time he owned it. Doug Due and especially Fred King provided a vast resource regarding *Jack Armstrong*. I am grateful to Henry King, Frank Rosenberg, Walter Doniger, Harry Kleiner, and Ivan Goff for a series of interviews and letters that permitted telling the story of the filming of *King of the Khyber Rifles*.

And to one more, who has heard endlessly about this project, just as she has listened with love all my life — the person to whom I owe eternal gratitude, my mother.

"That as an anvil is the earth; and as a smith's sledge is a destiny, that shapes us to an end far different from our beginning. So it may be that this interval, between a birth and death, is but a visit to a workshop of the gods, where resolution heats us and adversity descends on us as hammer-blows, reshaping us for purposes we are not able to perceive."
—"From the Diary of Olympus the Physician,"
by Talbot Mundy in *Queen Cleopatra*

I

From Wanderer to Writer, 1879–1913

Like many adventurers of his time, Talbot Mundy chose his own name. His was not the name given at his birth, nor was it a pseudonym. The adoption of a new name allowed him to create a fresh persona that liberated him from the constraints of the past and the class into which he was born.[1] He chose, created, and lived by this identity for over half his life, selecting the surname of distant cousins over that of his parents.

He was born on April 23, 1879, as William Lancaster Gribbon, Lancaster being the maiden name of his mother, Margaret.[2] The place was London, 59 Milson Road in the Hammersmith district, a spacious, two-story home that is still standing.

At the beginning of Mundy's writing career, he used the first and middle names of his father, Walter Galt Gribbon, as a pseudonym for magazine material of secondary quality he wrote to increase his income. The elder Gribbon was the son of a barrister, an Oxford graduate, church layman, and Tory, who wore a monocle and was an accountant in the City of London Wool Exchange. Within two years the family grew to include a younger brother, Harold, nicknamed "Guppie," and later a sister, Agnes Margaret, known as Daisy. All three siblings, in common with their father, would die from complications relating to diabetes. Nonetheless the two brothers were a physical contrast: Talbot was tall, big, and broadshouldered, while Harold was short and roly-poly.[3]

As a child, Talbot was dismayed by many of the daily sights of his country that would have seemed normal to most lads of his age.

> I once heard the whole argument for vivisection compressed into a sentence by a Cornish fisherman, who was skinning eels alive. They were squirming horribly, and I protested. The fisherman looked at me with honest blue eyes, shifted his pipe to the other corner of his mouth, went on with the skinning and answered:
> "Lor' bless ye, boy, they *like* it!"[4]

In Talbot's "education," of equal importance to his schooling were, he once wrote, "The gardener. A governess who had false teeth. Several excellent dogs.... The wide world," including a number of non-whites, especially Chinese and Blacks.[5]

Mundy's upbringing illustrated the failures of strait-laced, restrictive Victorian society and the public school system. "We send our little children to school, children who are natural comrades, and there set them to working for rewards, marks, honors, prizes—for every empty and worthless bauble that shall foster a spirit of rivalry."[6] A spate of critical teachers destroyed Talbot's self-esteem with punishments permanently etched into his consciousness. He was enrolled, as he recalled, in "a school at Guildford [in Surrey] where an inferiority complex was regarded as righteous and yelling was the medium of instruction — a rattan cane, the method of stirring affection."[7] In school, he was doubtless assigned, among other works, *Caesar's Commentaries*, volumes whose authority his novels would vigorously challenge, but in these early years "I was cruelly punished if I dared to form a judgement of my own."[8]

Helped by his family connections, Talbot talked himself into Rugby at a late stage in his schooling, after his 14th birthday, winning a special scholarship rather than the standard examination.[9] A small, rather dingy town that remains even today little more than a train depot, Rugby hardly satisfied a young man already dreaming of "get rich quick" schemes and adventures in far-away places.

Harold followed his older brother at Boxgrove School in Guildford and then Rugby, his success providing a source of disadvantageous comparison as Talbot failed to live up to the family's expectations. There was no love lost between Talbot and his father or mother; parental figures are largely absent from his fiction, or malicious on the rare occasions when they appear. His pious parents intended him for the church or the law, both of which he regarded as evils he was determined to avoid.[10] After the death of his father, "I quit thinking out conundrums [and] deserted algebra and Rugby, age sixteen," ending his formal education.[11] After a few weeks spent working for a newspaper, he responded to the family's disillusionment with an alternative they never contemplated.[12] He left home and took the first major step toward becoming an adventurer. (Some of Mundy's character must have been shared with his sister who, after ten years of marriage and three children, was to run off with another man and begin a second family.)

Talbot counted his money, found out the distance it would take him, closed his eyes and jabbed at random with a point on a map to determine precisely where he would go. It was the town of Quedlinburg in central Germany. Two days later he arrived with five shillings and a fox-terrier, but without the portmanteau carrying his clothes, which had been lost by the railroad. He encountered a mechanic who spoke some English and drove a traction engine that towed circus vans. Talbot was to do the work, take the blame if anything went wrong, and sleep under the engine regardless of the weather, while his boss drank himself insensible as often as possible.

Nonetheless, Talbot regarded the job as a good one, and enjoyed the company of the circus. One day, however, the mechanic became more than ordinarily drunk and savagely killed Talbot's dog, resulting in a bitter fight that left Mundy with a ready antipathy toward all things Teutonic. He explained later, "When I quit I had money in my purse. I wrote a piece about my travels with that traction engine and sent it to England to a publication called *Answers*. Much to my surprise my story was accepted and soon after sending it I was richer by two guineas."[13]

Then his luck turned; he was often hungry while trying for any job, including working on a farm in the Harz Mountains. After an absence of a year, the 17 year old secured a job on an English estate. "'High farming,' high church and old port and all that went with that life — pheasant shooting, fox-hunting and so on. Fed up."[14] The pattern had been set for his life; roving always, Talbot never settled for much more than a few years at a time.

Heading for a government job in Baroda, India, his first sight upon disembarking from a steamboat "was a bullock-cart loaded up with corpses — legs and arms sticking out from every side of it, and a fetid mixture of flies and aroma floating up above."[15] He was not disconcerted; the shocking sight only confirmed this foreign land's strange allure. He spent most of the next fifteen months in a minimum temperature of 112 degrees in the shade, fighting plague, cholera and famine, as thousands died. One of his first experiences with the failure of colonialism came when a commission decided that the famine was caused by ancient farming methods and plows which were little better than a forked stick. Steel plows were imported and distributed to the peasants, but they left the new implements to rust, believing "that for inscrutable reasons their rulers had tried to burden them with foreign difficulties in addition to their own — which, they reasonably argued, already were enough." Progress in technology, Talbot realized, could not jump ahead of the state of men's minds.[16]

His principal relaxation was pig-sticking, and he explained its attraction in a 1911 article entitled "Pig-sticking in India." Similarly, he enjoyed lounging in the club that attracted white men from throughout the district; he admired such men at the time, but as he matured he would criticize these centers of imperialist sentiment.

Overwork gave him a case of malaria, and with his earnings, Talbot returned to England, happy to loaf in a more pleasant climate. He happened to meet Rudyard Kipling during a rainy February holiday in Brighton, spending four hours talking of British soldiering and life in India, Malaysia, and Africa.[17] Only 13 years Talbot's senior, Kipling was already famous. Talbot found that "six months of Europe are enough for anybody at one time...," and he soon wanted to return to India, having only seen one small portion of it.[18] This time, Mundy left as the occasional correspondent for a London newspaper firm, probably the *Daily Mail*, optimistically believing that his career as a famous war correspondent was underway. He was to cover an uprising by the Mahsudi, the dominant tribe in South Waziristan, near the Khyber Pass. The commander of the British forces was also a newcomer, less than eager to have a reporter pointing out his errors, and forbade anyone leaving the lines. However, when Mundy's persistent prodding caused him to be told to go to hell, he took this as permission.

Mundy did acquire some information, but on his way back to camp at midnight was heard by a Ghurka picket, who fired intermittent volleys at the rock Talbot hid behind. Wet and shivering with cold, not until the next morning could the Ghurkas recognize him as part of their own force. The general pumped him for information, then censored his dispatches out of existence and ordered him back to the base for disobeying orders. Whether anything of Mundy's was actually published at the time is doubtful, but over the next month he acquired experience that he would subsequently exploit in fictional form. While the Mahsud blockade was as close as Mundy came to the Khyber, readers more familiar with the region assured him he accurately reflected the area's ambiance, geography and atmosphere.

Rajputana, to become one of his favorite settings in his fiction, was also the locale of his first mystical encounter with a guru. As later chronicled in his article, "Mystic India Speaks," his concerns were decidedly more worldly, because he was being blackmailed by a beautiful woman to whom he had written a number of indiscreet letters. Faced with a choice between marriage or a lawsuit, his decision was demanded the next day. Beneath a tree on a mountain, he met an older man on a mat, accompanied by some meditating pupils. The guru asked Talbot to join him, and already knew the purpose of his midnight climb. He taught him that "beauty is a dimension of spirit," and they absorbed and contemplated the moonlit view, becoming one with it, hoping beauty would provide a miracle. At daylight the guru and Talbot separated, with Talbot still perplexed, but at his bungalow an Indian lawyer was waiting to return the letters. The lady had decided that Talbot was merely "a victim of his own too chivalrous emotion."[19]

Mundy's portraits of the lamas in such books as *Om* and *Old Ugly-Face* would be drawn not only from imagination and theosophical teachings, but also from such chance encounters as he began to learn about the Indian occult teachings.[20] Soaking up the impressions of the people who knew India best, both white and native, it began to dawn on his "rather idly curious mind, that virtue is neither racial, national, nor even international, but universal; and that possibly lots of Western theories are wrong."[21]

Talbot had several contract jobs directing Indian laborers, learning to speak Pishtu and Hindustanee.[22] He traveled on foot and horseback, wandering the northern boundary of India. He went far to the north, to Kashmir and Ladakh on the west, along the lower ranges of the Himalayas from West to East, past Darjeeling, Sikkim, and the Brahmaputra River (known as the Tsangpo in Tibet), as far east as Assam, where he learned about elephants.

Apparently, the colonial government grew suspicious of Mundy, for he left India to give "them time to forget me," traveling to China and the Straits Settlements, today Penang, Malacca and Singapore on the Malaysian peninsula. He took a trip up the Persian Gulf on a tramp steamer captained by a black; the ship broke down half way, "and then I really did know what — was like."[23]

The Boer War interrupted his plans in October 1899, and he promptly joined a group forming a volunteer cavalry regiment. He vividly described, in anti-heroic terms, the misery of the subsequent fighting.

> The picnic consisted for the most part of lying in the rain and being fired at, or lying in the scorching sun and being fired at. The rations were usually dead trek-ox or dead horse, dry biscuit, nice green water to wash it down with, and as a general rule no salt. There was no smoke to speak of, but every now and then you could see a flash somewhere on the hillside in front of you, and sometimes the man next to you would give a short sudden sob and lie very still. Or then again, sometimes he would sit up and scream, and go rolling over and over in agony. When the ground wasn't wet it was swarming with vermin, and most of the men who weren't shot went sick either from the vermin or the flies or the bad water or else exposure.[24]

An English army officer visiting the *Adventure* office in 1911 remembered Mundy carrying dispatches under fire at Colenso, a battle fought on December 15, 1899.[25] Mundy refused to elaborate on the experience at the time, and never did boast of displaying any bravery, although he did continue to mention his Boer War service in nearly all his later reminiscences. He recounted being wounded "before the relief of Ladysmith" at the close of February, which ended his service, with sufficient experience to gain a mastery of military backgrounds for his early stories.[26]

He was back at home to celebrate his twenty-first birthday, and remained at least through early June, 1900.[27] He returned to India from 1900 to 1902 when some of the previously mentioned experiences may have occurred. While working in India as a merchant, he met Kathleen Steele, the daughter of a London banker. Back in England, on January 31, 1903, Talbot and Kathleen were married, and they took a home in Cape Town. By July, Talbot was in financial difficulties, and sent Kathleen back to England, promising to follow.[28] He never did; an arrest warrant for debt had been issued, and he was only one step ahead of the law. Although occasionally they corresponded, for the remaining five years of the marriage they never saw one another, and he was in no position to support her or to ask her to join him.

He went before the mast on a big steel merchant sailing ship, then was shanghaied onto a "hell-ship," where a brutal mate contended with the sea in the effort to shorten his life. "We were short-handed, fed on offal that would not be good for pigs, ill treated, struck, sworn at, overworked all the time, housed in a fo'castle that was swarming with rats and vermin, deprived of any kind of privacy, and, in fact, treated like animals. Only animals are never worked so hard."[29] Talbot traveled through the waters of Polynesia and the Antarctic and, together with Charlie, a comrade, jumped ship when it docked in Sydney, leaving their kits and wages behind. Without qualifications, jobs, or money, they had to either walk or go back to sea, so they tramped some 500 miles, receiving the scant hospitality afforded "sun-downers."

Penniless in Brisbane, Talbot and Charlie secured positions as stokers on a comparatively pleasant small tramp steamer to Hobart, Tasmania. Charlie remained, but Talbot sailed on a three-masted vessel, "bumping bluey"—carrying a form of Australian eucalyptus known as blue-gum piles for a new pier at Delagoa Bay. However, the crew became ill from being fed bad salt fish, and all jumped ship at Laurenço Marques in late 1903. Mundy fictionalized the voyage and the first days ashore in the 1918 *Adventure* short story, "Oakes Respects an Adversary," recounting a near-crazed skipper, Antarctic blizzards, wet sails, ice, adverse winds, and manning the clumsy pumps for days on end. In the story, conditions ashore are even worse than on the ship; without a job or money, a man is jailed, after which he is either shipped back to sea, or sent at the point of a gun to boss slave labor.

This was the ignominious beginning of Mundy's longest and most confused odyssey, one that would carry him throughout nearly the entire eastern length of Africa. Laurenço Marques was part of Portuguese East Africa in what is today the southernmost part of Mozambique. He later described it as the most lawless place in the world, "'where a man was fined only ten pounds for killing a white, and only a pound or two for a black.'"[30] In addition to "Oakes Respects an Adversary," it also became the setting for his stories "America Horns In," "Jackson Tactics," "Heinie Horns Into the Game," and the serial *Solomon's Half-Way House.*

Destitute in a dreadful climate, Talbot succumbed to a fever in the swamps of the Umbuluzi River. When he recovered, he found a good job on a big estate up the Limpopo River at Chai-Chai in Gazaland. However, by Christmas he was ill again, this time with East Coast fever, a malignant form of malaria. A Portuguese trader lent him a bungalow in which to die. When the visiting local doctor, Leal, began to help himself to his belongings, Talbot's black servant, Samaki ("Fish"), interfered, and Leal threatened to implicate him in Talbot's death, expected the next day. Instead of simply fleeing, Samaki returned at midnight with a native doctor, and made the nearly delirious Talbot swear to not reveal his treatment. While the doctor danced and hummed a monotonous refrain, four women smeared "quantities of vile smelling greasy stuff" that made Talbot feel like he was being burned alive. However, as daylight came, the pain ceased, and the liquid was sponged off. A few hours later, the fever was gone, and by evening Talbot's appetite returned; on New Year's Day he had completely recovered. The doctor refused Talbot's offer of payment, sent via Samaki, instead making him swear to secrecy.[31]

The railway to Lake Victoria had just been completed, and Talbot heard overrated reports that British East Africa was booming and decided to get his share. He left at the end of January, 1904, on the steamer *Bundesrath* for Zanzibar and Mombasa (the ship eventually figured in "A Transaction in Diamonds," "Heinie Horns into the Game," and "The End of the Bad Ship *Bundesrath*.") As documented in his 1925 article, "On the Trail of Sindbad the Sailor," the country offered little wealth except in game, but he was "one of the comparatively early birds who helped to find it out."[32] He would later chronicle his illegally shooting elephants, in his articles "Elephant Hunting for a Living," "Random Reminiscences of African Big Game" and "The Things Men Fear." At the time, Mundy reflected the conventional belief among his fellow hunters that the law protecting elephants could not be enforced, and that if the white man abstained, the native would take all the plunder.

Talbot hired a servant just out of jail, named Kazi Moto ("Work like hell"), assembling a safari in the hope of locating the legendary buried ivory hoard of Tippoo Tib. However, the terrain and its inhabitants—from lions to tsetse flies to reported cannibals— proved too formidable. He fictionalized the journey in his 1918 autobiographical novel, *The Ivory Trail*, and in a 1937 *Jack Armstrong* radio serial, altered to successfully find the ivory; Kazi Moto appeared in both tellings.

Talbot reported shooting more than fifty lions, but he did not reflect on the ethics of the life of the hunter until almost two decades later when he came to better appreciate nature. He chronicled some of these experiences in his articles "Elizabeth," "Ready Rhino," "Baboons," "Some True Stories About Wild Animals," "Random Reminiscences of African Big Game," and the published speech "Of Wild Animals in Africa."

Talbot also regarded hunting as a sport, which he once defined as "warfare against one's own inherent limitations, not the least of which is fear in one form or another." Overcoming this became a driving force behind his travel and adventure, as vividly described in two key articles, "Random Reminiscences of African Big

Game" and "The Things Men Fear." "As a child, I was in terror of a barking dog; to me, a horse was a thing of horror; and a ride, even in the front of my father's saddle, a strong arm holding me, was torture." He was so afraid of his own self-criticism that he found it easier to force himself into dangerous situations, than to know the difference between common sense and cowardice; he once killed a horse he was riding rather than avoid an impossible jump that a more sensible man would not have tried. When shooting elephants, he knew that if fear froze him, he and not the elephant would be killed. "The only way I know of overcoming fear is to face it again and again, [wearing it down,] until at last it loses some of its power to numb the nerves and freeze thought."[33]

He once discussed his fear of heights with a Catholic priest, Father Brandsma, who convinced Talbot to accompany him on a climb up Mount Kilimanjaro, although he had no interest in mountaineering. Within a thousand feet of the summit and with three miles behind him, fatigued but far from the limits of endurance, Talbot felt himself unable to go on. A rope around him made him safe, and he still had his footing, but he was in a mental funk and could not make himself obey. "People who have never felt that kind of fear cannot have the remotest conception of how numbing it is...."[34] Brandsma was unable to shame, bless or tempt Talbot to continue, so resumed his own journey to the top, then found on his way back down that Talbot was afraid to leave his ledge. Brandsma only succeeded in getting him down the mountain by finally forcing Talbot to laugh at his fear and reestablish his sense of the ridiculous.

With the proceeds from the safari with Kazi Moto, Talbot acquired a herd of 4,000 cattle that bore the brand of an official entitled to only own two, who, admiring Talbot's nerve, later employed him.[35] With British officials on his trail, he decided to drive the herd across the border into German East Africa. Near Shirati, on the eastern shore of Lake Victoria, a band of fierce Masai fought Talbot and his men, taking the cattle. He received a wound in the right leg from a spear dipped in gangrene, and later it took seven men to hold him down while the wound was cauterized with stems of grass heated in a fire. "They were wonderfully loyal and brave to do it, for the treatment is frightful torture;" afterwards, the men left, taking their loads in lieu of pay, recognizing that their employer was now without any other way to compensate them.[36]

Talbot and Kazi Moto began a walk to the nearest doctor, 200 miles away in Muanza, where the Germans were inhospitable. Talbot had developed black-water fever, and he was placed in a rat-filled shed where he was expected to die. Kazi Moto stole food for him, and the doctor made brief visits. After a few days, Talbot heard the doctor order a sergeant to bring the chain-gang to dig his grave, and bury him doubled-up.

> Up to that time I had not particularly wanted to get well; I had neither money nor prospects and was feeling much too ill to care, and I haven't the least doubt that if he had said nothing I would have died either that day or the day following. But I hated the man so, and was so utterly disgusted with his treatment of me, that I made up my mind to disappoint him, and from that minute I began to get better. When the chain-gang came with a sack to tie me up in I was sitting up with the aid

> of Kazi Moto. Two days later I leaned on Kazi Moto's shoulder and walked out to have a look at the grave; I was so weak that I very nearly tumbled into it.... I sat there for about an hour, thinking; and at the end of it I pushed some dirt down into the grave as a sort of concrete sign that I had buried the old wanderlust at the bottom of it and would try henceforward to put my garnered knowledge to some use.[37]

In that country he walked as far south as Lakes Tanganyika and Nyasa. After "trekking about" in German East Africa, Talbot realized that he could not make enough to live on, and took passage on a dhow for British territory. Talbot then traveled as far as present-day Uganda to the Ruwenzori Range, on the northeastern border of the Congo. According to W.R. Foran, a former poacher, colonial official and later a writer himself, Mundy was back in the British colony in late 1904, raising money as "Sir Rupert Harvey, Baronet," and was arrested and sentenced to six month's hard labor.[38]

Later, Talbot did road work and was appointed town clerk of the frontier village of Kisumu, on the northwest shore of Lake Victoria and situated almost exactly on the equator. He would later recall one of his duties.

> I was once a government official, in a country where the native wore no clothing. In the name of civilization and religion — that is to say, for the sake of the cotton mills of Manchester, the missionaries' disgusting sexual emotions and the arbitrary ethics of the reputedly easily scandalized Lord God (in whose presence it is also said, however, that our souls stand naked) — word went forth by high authority that nakedness must cease. It was an ultimatum.
>
> So it fell to my lot to devise a garment that should fulfill the minimum requirements of alleged decency, while imposing the least possible economic hardship.... I invented a small goatskin apron, furnished with suitable strings to be tied around the wearer's waist.
>
> And on the first of the month they obeyed the law. They came in thousands to market, those hitherto sinfully naked and yet singularly moral and unvicious people.... They were rather proud of their clothing. It was new — amusing. Not one of them but wore a ten inch apron, and some were larger. But every man–Jack and woman–Jill of all those thousands had the apron on behind![39]

He saw two campaigns and mastered several of the local languages, including Zulu, Swahili, Kavirondo, and Lumbwa.[40]

His work took him as far north as Kapsabit, in the Nandi highlands, the last outpost of British settlement. He often went canoeing at night on Lake Victoria, observing the hippopotami, and he served as a sort of best man in the Kavirondo wedding of his headman, Ngozi.[41] Incidents in this period are recounted in his article "Watu." Talbot tried to make time for writing, but the climate was unhealthy and depressing, with temperatures usually above 100 degrees.

In his later article "A Jungle Sage," and elsewhere, Mundy chronicles how he continued the investigations begun in India into indigenous "magic." Talbot quickly discovered that few whites, especially missionaries, had studied the subject, and fewer still had the opportunity to, since the magicians themselves regarded questions as proof of enmity.

Talbot became well acquainted with Oketch, a member of the Kakkamegga Kavirondo tribe. Oketch, of Nilotic origin, resided near Mount Elgon and was over seven feet tall and said to be 300 years old. Talbot compared the height and appearance of the confident "maganga" to the Pharaoh Rameses, and chiefs and headmen treated him respectfully. Oketch had a low opinion of white men and resented their new customs.

When Talbot shot a rogue elephant that had been destroying the villages, the behemoth fell on top of him, breaking ribs, a collar bone and right shoulder. No European doctors were within a hundred miles, so the bearers took him to Oketch. His wives provided fresh sheets to reduce the fever before he set Talbot's bones by touching the nerves with his fingers, "until the muscles drew the bones into place."[42] Talbot was then tied so that he could not move, without use of bandages or splints, and remained nearly immobile for a month. Oketch kept Talbot's mind cooperating with him during every waking moment, and later x-rays would reveal the excellence of Oketch's handiwork, with only a shoulder that dislocated easily.

Not long afterward, a local drought was used by authorities to force Mundy to arrest Oketch. But he was not abiding by the rules of the white colonial system. "I protested — a bit explosively, I don't doubt — and flatly refused to do any such thing" and complaints were promptly made to the governor in Nairobi. So Talbot had to gather eight native policemen who were equally reluctant to act against Oketch. He ordered them to bring their rifles but no ammunition, traveling with his terrified men to Oketch's village, where Talbot explained the predicament, offering to defend Oketch through the proceedings. Oketch's response was to say, "White man, if I make the rain come, will you go away and leave me?"[43] Even Talbot doubted the promise, but within ten minutes, out of a cloudless sky and after months of drought, a storm came, followed by torrents of rain.

Mundy regarded Oketch as a sort of high priest. "Magic, after all, whether or not superstition causes one to resent the word, is relative to the ignorance of the individual confronted by it."[44] Oketch frankly admitted that there were two reasons for keeping his methods secret: the difficulty in expressing his knowledge into words, and the power that secrets give the holder over others. Neither Oketch nor Talbot believed in the supernatural as such. Even Oketch's knowledge had limits; he was baffled by smallpox and to him Talbot's watch was magical.

By this time, Talbot had become involved in affairs with women from different local tribes, causing a scandal that lost him his job. He did not accept the colonial tabu or the pretense of its inviolability; throughout his oeuvre there is a motif of not only sexual contact, but also romantic love and marriage between the races, and those of mixed background.

Now that he was momentarily settled, and with his health back, he contacted Kathleen, explaining that he had adopted the name "Thomas Hartley," sometimes going by "Lord Hartley." He had learned some cynical lessons from a former Montana sheriff who had fled the law, as later related in "The Sayings of Hell-Fire Smith Done Into Polite English." In a May 1907 letter, he acknowledged that he had been unfaithful to Kathleen and urged her to divorce him. He cooperated with the subsequent proceedings, which entailed taking testimony in Nairobi to prove a charge of adultery, a charge essential for most divorces in this era. When the decree came through, a year later, he had also been named in another divorce trial.[45]

Mundy had been guiding a number of hunting expeditions, with the help of Kazi Moto, and on one of these, they made the acquaintance of the rambunctious, quarrelsome Rupert Cecil Craven and his party. His wife, 35-year-old Inez Broom, was regarded as one of the most beautiful women of her day, attributed to her Spanish grandmother. She had once been named as co-respondent in the notorious Chandos-Pole divorce of 1899, when her unchaperoned life made her a centerpiece of English gossip. She had left home at age 19, and became known as a daring cross-country rider who smoked and drank brandy; she described herself as a respectable but "unconventional sort of person." Inez and Rupert had been married in April 1898, and the Cravens naturally used their family influence to vindicate Inez in court—unsuccessfully.[46]

Ten years later, when Inez met Talbot, the Cravens's marriage, which had begun so inauspiciously, was crumbling; in the subsequent divorce suit, Rupert Craven would have to admit that he was as guilty of adultery as was his wife. Inez left her husband at the beginning of 1908 and moved in with Talbot, as both were receiving their respective divorces. Inez went to London to finalize her divorce, then returned to Talbot in Africa. Shortly afterward, the man born William Lancaster Gribbon adopted a new name for the final time, Talbot Chetwynd Miller Mundy, and asserted he was the illegitimate son of the Earl of Shrewsbury.

Inez and Talbot married in a town near Mombasa at the end of the year, and by then the repercussions of the scandal had again cost him his job.[47] After he recovered from a near fatal fourth bout with black water fever, the couple decided to leave Africa for Europe and London. Ashamed of the embarrassment her eldest son had caused the family, Talbot's mother, who died four years later, eliminated him from her will after a final gift of a portion of her husband's estate.

The money given by the family was quickly spent, since Inez was accustomed to a considerably higher standard of living than Talbot could provide, and his prospects were not favorable. Friends and relatives turned their backs on the couple, and Talbot's efforts to resume his career as a newspaper correspondent were fruitless. His wife's drinking was becoming a matter of growing concern. Active in the women's suffrage movement, on one march she took an axe and smashed the windows of a newspaper office where Talbot held a menial position.[48] With the future bleak, the couple gathered the last of their resources and headed for America aboard the White Star liner *Teutonic*.

Disembarking in New York City on September 30, 1909, the Mundys had their remaining funds, a British £100 note, turned into American currency, about $500. Without friends or much knowledge of the city, Mundy started to walk, and having a vague recommendation in mind, happened to head south into the perilous district near the East River. He found a kitchen and bedroom in a tenement three flights back at 503 East Fifteenth Street, and word spread in the neighborhood that the "green" Englishman and his wife were worth the risk of robbing.

Carrying his money on him, the next day Talbot began to search for employment at a newspaper on Park Row, saying he was formerly connected to the London

Mail. Three men called at the Mundy apartment, asking for a Mr. Franklin. In and out several times, they demanded and sent for beer. Inez thought this was odd, but they looked tough, and in fear she agreed when they insisted she join them in a drink.[49] When her husband returned, she asked him to take the men away, and the men wanted Talbot to join them for a card game; it seemed the only way to get the men out of the house, despite Inez saying her husband didn't drink.[50]

Shortly afterward, two of the men returned, without Talbot, one of them asking if he could "treat" Inez, and upon her refusal, grabbed her watch.[51] The shrill blasts of an English police whistle attracted a detective to the agitated Inez standing in front of the building in a bathrobe.[52] The tenement was roused, but the man had escaped.

Talbot failed to return, and just before midnight, a night watchman found him lying unconscious not far from his rooms, in the vicinity of East 19th Street between Avenues B and C.[53] He was bleeding, with his skull apparently fractured and his jaw broken. His pockets empty, money and watch gone, he was immediately taken by ambulance to a public ward of nearby Bellevue hospital, with a death certificate already signed. Later that night, Mundy recovered long enough to send police to his wife.

At the tenement, police and reporters were surprised to find a woman unexpectedly beautiful and cultured, and the Chandos-Pole case had not been forgotten. "Former Mrs. Craven in Poverty Here," noted the *New York Times*, "Assault on Her Husband Reveals the Plight of the Once Noted English Beauty." Reporters next located her in a dingy First Avenue saloon, smoking cigarettes and drinking brandy and seltzer, dressed in clothes that badly needed mending, saying "with a sudden incoherent gust of earnestness, 'But don't you say anything about Rupert; — I love him — I love him as deeply as ever.'"[54] That afternoon, Talbot regained consciousness to the clamor of the press, eager for a death-bed interview.

Despite the deep depression in his skull, the next day Talbot was propped up with pillows on a cot in a public ward, his head swathed in bandages. He told his story in more detail. "I took a small glass of beer. It must have been drugged, for I remember nothing after that other than being conscious of receiving a heavy blow."[55] One of the newspapermen seemed kinder than the rest, and tried to make Talbot a little more comfortable. He only recognized a man he dubbed "the red-headed reporter."

Suspects were quickly arrested, and Inez came to see Talbot briefly on Saturday. Lying in his cot, Talbot could see the daily closing of the morgue that expected him. Yet, as the weeks went by, his condition improved, and he began to hope that he had again cheated death.

His tribulations as an immigrant, however, had only begun. When his skull plates finally healed, but with his jaw still in a wire brace, he was released from Bellevue. His first stop was a tailor to clean his blood-stained clothes, on the promise of a future payment. On November 7, Inez began legal proceedings against the New York Herald Company for their story entitled "'Lady Mundy' on Trail of Robbers," which claimed she had gone to search for the men who robbed her husband the day after the crime. The suit, filed with the assistance of attorney James F. Egan, claimed the article was "false and defamatory," and that she "was injured in her reputation to" the sum of $100,000.[56] The Mundys had to wait until February 11, 1910 for a response, and meanwhile became objects of charity, "applicants for and the recipients of alms from a number of individuals and benevolent organizations...."[57]

In applying in November to the New York Association for Improving the Condition of the Poor, the Mundys were referred to St. George's Society of New York, an organization to give relief to indigent natives of England. In December, the Mundys turned to them and claimed that they were virtual paupers. Cunliffe Owen, an officer of St. George's Society, decided that the case fell under the law that excludes aliens who are likely to become a public charge from entry into the United States. In January, Owen and other officials of St. George's gained information leading them to believe that the Mundys had falsely presented their previous personal histories and antecedents.

At the end of January, Talbot entered the Metropolitan Hospital on Blackwell's Island, where the two smaller fingers of his right hand, which had become cut and infected, were amputated. (He would later enjoy saying that the fingers were lost during an attack by a lion, while he was serving as an African Territorial Governor.)[58] As a result of the charges by the St. George's Society, the case had been referred to the Department of Commerce and Labor. Talbot and Inez were arrested, and ten days later taken to Ellis Island and imprisoned until March 10. There, the Mundys would later charge they "suffered great mental and bodily distress" and were "compelled to associate with and remain in the company of persons of the lowest and vilest character, some of whom suffered from loathsome and unclean diseases," as described in a subsequent lawsuit.[59]

The Mundys were the subject of hearings before several Boards of Special Inquiry at Ellis Island, and compelled to answer questions "of a most humiliating, insulting and revolting character," based on Owen's allegations.[60] Mundy was charged with being "an Englishman by birth and ... the subject of many vicissitudes of fortune in different parts of the world; [who] arrived ... with a woman whom he represented to be Inez Morton Mundy, his lawful wife...."[61] The Mundys had to employ counsel to defend themselves against the government's charges, costing $500. At the end, the Department of Commerce and Labor determined that there was no evidence to sustain the charges. In the subsequent suit filed on the Mundy's behalf by Egan against Owen, the Mundys charged Owen with "falsely, wickedly, maliciously and without reasonable or probable cause therefor, and conspiring with others to do so," seeking $50,000 in damages.[62]

Inez and Talbot had already been on the verge of separating when they headed for New York, and by February 1912, divorce papers had been filed, with a final judgement on October 14. By then Inez was a well-known New York suffragette, whose drinking interrupted several marches. By early 1913 she was admitted to Bellevue, suffering from alcoholic hallucinations.[63] Mundy scarcely saw Inez again, but she lived for another quarter century, and, still paying alimony, he always referred to her simply as "Craven."[64]

After the lawsuit against Owen, Mundy lacked the money to press the case, and spent the next months of 1910 in desperate straits. Without skills, friends, or recommendations in a strange city, he wandered for days, looking for work. He took any job that was offered, holding it until fired — which happened quickly. With his last nickel, he bought a Sunday paper, and on at least one night used it to cover himself while he slept on a Central Park bench.

Hungrily walking down a street, as he later told his wife Dawn, he "was looking in a restaurant window, and 'the red-headed reporter' came up on his elbow, and said, 'What happened to you? You look like you need a cup of coffee.'"[65] "The red-headed reporter," whom Mundy now knew as Jeff Hanley, was one of the journalists who had covered his tumultuous initial days in the United States. An Irish Catholic, Jeff took Talbot to his apartment, a flat already shared with two or three other men — but there was room for one more. This was the turning point for Mundy in America; as he later said, I "Was very fortunate in meeting the sort of American who makes you glad you are alive, and in making friends with some of them, who persuaded me to try my hand at writing stories."[66]

Mundy already had the intangible gift of the story teller, and those who knew or heard him were unanimous on this fact.[67] Near the end of Mundy's life, author Wyatt Blassingame wrote that "Mundy was a great raconteur who had more stories to tell and told them better than any man we've known. Such yarns as the time in the Boer War when, bearing dispatches, he jumped his horse over a hedge and landed in a general's picnic lunch. He had wit, and drama, and made the right pauses, and talked almost better than he wrote."[68] As Dawn would recall, "He was a very good conversationalist. He was fun — that's what you can't get from reading the books, probably.... He was a grand guy — you would have liked him. Whether the stories he told were true or not, it [sic] always made people happy and laugh."[69]

Jeff procured a typewriter for Mundy, and encouraged him to go ahead and teach himself to write, by dint of practice to make up for his lack of formal training. Autobiography was the first mistake to go by the wayside, as Talbot learned that readers wanted a plot. "I would pound out stuff on the typewriter, and Jeff would come home, look my stuff over, say it was rotten, which it was, and make me go ahead doing more of it."[70] After some three months, Mundy had a manuscript he was ready to present; within three days, it was sold by an agent, who paid him the $60 remittance in weekly installments of $10.[71]

The first story was "A Transaction in Diamonds," published at the end of the February, 1911 issue of *The Scrap Book*, a pulp magazine. Motivations and characterizations are weak, yet Mundy's later writing style is very much in evidence, much more than in many of his subsequent short stories over the next few years.

In between checks for writing, Talbot took any job that was available. He was night cook in a station restaurant until he was fired when the food burned; he drifted upstate, doing chores and milking cows on a farm in such towns as Pawling, New York.[72] Among his roommates with Hanley and others during this time was Sinclair Lewis, then barely making ends meet as a copy reader for New York publishers, and the two became close friends; Lewis was about to become assistant editor of *Adventure*, a position he held through its first years and the formative period in Mundy's writing.[73]

The August 1911 issue of *Adventure* marked the first appearance of the type of narrative to form Mundy's reputation for colonial adventure in the Kipling tradition, "The Phantom Battery." Yet it is hardly a paean to the military; officers are unsure what to do when the Sepoy mutiny breaks out, while their British enlisted men are, without exception, rum-swilling, foul-mouthed scoundrels, who had to be kept in order by the fiercest kind of discipline.

Together with "The Phantom Battery," "Sentence of Death" and "An Offer of Two to One" in *The Scrap Book* share a tone reminiscent of Edgar Allan Poe, although all three emerge from different generic contexts. Mundy also revealed a skill for light, humorous stories with a series in *All-Story*: "The Lady and the Lord," "Kitty Burns Her Fingers," and "Vengeance is Kitty's," and "Kitty and Cupid," remaining fresh and diverting to the end.

During this first year, Mundy was producing a range of stories notable not so much for themselves as for how much they diverged from his later oeuvre. He would even turn out a quantity centering on the race track and boxing. Throughout his life, Mundy was an avid fan of boxing, and often attended the bouts at Madison Square Garden.

A four-year series of ten stories in *Adventure* about pugilist Billy Blain began with "The Goner?" in the February 1912 issue. His bouts are described in vivid, convincing detail, foreshadowing Mundy's approach in later, far more sophisticated books, such as his use of the Roman arena in novels of the ancient world. Mundy had a winning series character in Blain, at once simple, honest, unwavering, but a skillful fighter who has seen life from the highs and the lows, and the stories are engaging reading, even to a non-sports enthusiast. Further chronicles of Blain allowed Mundy to sometimes have two stories in a single month's issue of *Adventure*, since he wrote about Blain under the pseudonym Walter Galt (although some of the stories were reprinted in England under the Talbot Mundy by-line). Boxing was not the only sport to concern Mundy: another was horse-racing, with "Making £10,000," a short story in the April 1913 issue of the illustrated slick paper magazine *McClure's*, and "The Guzzler's Grand Prix," in the May 1913 issue of *Adventure*, Mundy's longest story up to that time.

Mundy's association with a particular genre and magazine crystallized when a notice accompanying his "The Blooding of the Ninth Queen's Own" in the December 1911 issue of *Adventure* introduced him as an author who had travelled the world and had many dangerous experiences. The magazine was looking for fresh talent, and they realized his potential with the second story they bought from him. Designed for "intelligent readers," *Adventure* would come to be regarded as the most distinguished and literary magazine in its genre and class, attaining a reputation as "The *Atlantic Monthly* of the pulps." Circulation reached 300,000, including Theodore Roosevelt and subscribers that included "many a lawyer, statesman, physician, [and] college professor...."[74] *Adventure* was published in issues of about 200 pages from 1910 until it finally expired, all but unnoticed, in the early 1970s. Arthur Sullivant Hoffman (1876–1966), who helmed *Adventure* for its first 17 years, sought to reconcile the elemental urge for action stories with sophistication, realism, and artistic story-telling.

Adventure promised to take as many such stories as Mundy could write, allowing him to concentrate all of his energies on the genre, leaving behind uncertain subject matter for other journals.[75] Despite being just a novice writer, Mundy's stories had what the Hoffman termed "tremendous punch."[76] Hoffman became not only a literary mentor during Mundy's formative years but also a trusted friend, who did not necessarily agree with Mundy, but appreciated his speculative turn of mind. For four years, from 1912 through 1915, nearly every issue of *Adventure* contained something by Mundy, sometimes two pieces in a single issue, first with short stories, then novellas, and eventually with serials. In the years to come, Mundy was well aware of the enormous contribution he had made to the magazine's success.[77]

Hoffman was intensely concerned with the image of manliness that *Adventure* projected, and believed the magazine's mythology, that his authors were real adventurers, members of his "writer's brigade," bringing stories fresh from the earth's far corners with the tang of authenticity. Mundy adjusted to the archetype his editor desired, that an author must have lived the type of stories he writes. However, manliness was not the same as masculinity or brawn, but a passion for seeing and understanding all of the Earth. (In its early years, *Adventure* sought equal appeal to female readers, with fashionable women frequently gracing its covers.)

While the source of adventure literature goes back to legends and folklore, such writers as Sir Walter Scott, Alexandre Dumas, W.H.G. Kingston, Sir Arthur Conan Doyle, Baroness Orczy, Captain Marryatt, Robert Louis Stevenson, Rudyard Kipling, Joseph Conrad, and H. Rider Haggard codified conventions of the genre that appealed to the imagination of an industrial society (Haggard, Orczy, and Sabatini all appeared in *Adventure*). As medieval knightly exploits became dated, and Europe came to dominate nearly all regions of Africa and Asia, contemporary overseas military activity enlarged the genre's range, accented by a natural curiosity about the world's far horizons and newly-discovered or settled lands. Adventure became the literary expression of advancing Western civilization.

In adventure, characters are usually two dimensional, and indigenous peoples are often situated as the ally or adversary of the white hero, or a victim whose plight requires his rescue. Adventure was portrayed as an experience that sought to enlighten and uplift, with colonies supposedly ruled not for self-interest, but out of an altruistic desire to bring peace and justice. Instead of encountering legitimate striving for self-determination, the genre portrayed the adversary as indigenous tyrants, religious fanatics, or rival imperial powers. Maintaining order, the empire builder's goal in the genre is not so much conquest as to promote long-term peace. Taking up "the white man's burden" in the empire adventure is presented not as the exploitation it was, but as a form of service by the white imperialist. It brings the advantages of Western civilization through the suppression of disease, slavery, or such indigenous rituals as suttee or the murderous sects of Kali or Thuggee.

Rather than casting the hero as a forthright jingoist promoting expansionism, empire becomes a by-product of the adventurer's desire to live in remote lands on the edge of civilization. While offering many racist undercurrents, and more mythic than factual in its setting, colonial adventure was popular and became more than simply propaganda because it served as one of the principal avenues for presenting knowledge of distant lands and foreign cultures (however warped) to curious and receptive audiences. Adventure luxuriates in appealing, romantic locales, or faraway

Mundy merits his first magazine cover: *Adventure*, February 1912, for "The Soul of a Regiment." (Courtesy Brian Emerich collection.)

places, the colony becoming an adopted country, a place of opportunity for wealth and status impossible to realize in the hero's homeland. Hence, colonial adventure heroes are those individuals who best understand and adapt to the land in which they live, adjusting to the unique circumstances of the culture and bringing together people of all races.

This was the generic background Mundy first utilized, and gradually subverted, as he became a regular writer for *Adventure*. His early aptitude was demonstrated by "The Soul of a Regiment" in the February, 1912 issue of *Adventure*, Mundy's first magazine story to mark him as a writer to watch and to merit a cover illustration. The style itself is some of the most compelling of these early years, as exemplified by the first paragraph. "So long as its colors remain, and there is one man left to carry them, a regiment can never die; they can recruit it again around that one man, and the regiment will continue on its road to future glory.... So although the colors are not exactly the soul of the regiment, they are the concrete embodiment of it, and are even more sacred than the person of a reigning sovereign."[78]

The story tells of the First Egyptian Foot, with certain attitudes emblematic of the time and the genre. The fellaheen, accustomed to Arab cruelty and Turkish misrule, find Sergeant-Instructor William Stanford Grogram treats them like men for the first time in their lives, and they especially enjoy it when he dances for them one day. Recognizing the need for a band, but refused by a colonel who disdains natives, Grogram buys them three fifes and a drum, teaching the only music he knows, "God Save the Queen" and "The Campbells Are Coming."

"The Soul of a Regiment" has an engaging three-act structure, veering toward mystery in the middle portion, with the seeming disappearance of the First Egyptian Foot among the doomed forces dispatched to put down the Mahdi's revolt. Nonetheless, rumors begin to emerge from the desert of four natives playing vaguely British tunes on the fife and drum, with a dancer who is a feringhee — a pork-fed, infidel Englishman whose perceived insanity is the only passport among the Dervishes.

Three years later, in Cairo, at the annual polo tournament presided over by "the Sirdar" (General Kitchener, unnamed in the story), the festivities are interrupted by the entrance of five men from the desert. Grogram, ragged, dirty, barefoot, scarcely more than a skeleton, and clad in only a loin-cloth and tattered tunic, identifies them as the First Egyptian Foot before the reviewing stand. Fumbling with his tunic, Grogram pulls forth the colors, blood-soaked and torn, from around his whipped and wounded body — and falls dead. The scene memorably combines colonial spectacle at its peak with the rawest evidence of courage and sacrifice.

Hoffman said "The Soul of a Regiment" sent chills down his spine, and when he wrote that the story moved him to tears, many other readers also admitted as much.[79] "The Soul of a Regiment" is a spare, eloquent chronicle of elemental survival, a model of simplicity and stirring sentiment that embodies the belief in seemingly impossible fortitude. At the end, Grogram's body will be compared to that of a mummy; earlier in the story he himself had suggested the parallel with his men as mummies of Nile mud. Hence, Egyptian and Englishman become one in their service and ordeal for the colors.

"The Soul of a Regiment" is a masterpiece of its kind, and was hailed as Mundy's greatest short story, and is the most often reprinted. It has the distinction of being issued on its own in a special limited edition in 1925, due to Colonel Franklin R. Kenney. However, the martial, patriotic tone robs the story of the timeless appeal of tales less redolent of the prevailing perspective of the times.

Adventure presented fiction but had a practical side as well, sponsoring historical debates, an expedition to Abyssinia, and the founding of the American Legion. In late 1912, a meeting of two world wanderers in Hoffman's office led to the formation of The Adventurer's Club, of which Mundy was a charter member. Mundy also wrote articles which were becoming more sophisticated, no longer using the reportorial style of a "how to" guide, such as in "Single-Handed Yachting." His biographies for *Adventure* of William Mayes, T.C. Ansell, and arms merchant Francis Bannerman demonstrated that Mundy dealt equally well with a man he detested, such as Bannerman. "The Closed Trail of William Walker" is one of Mundy's rare, straightforward historical pieces. Couched in terms typical of the admiring portraits of such men, each section has a heading which seems predictable in words if sarcastic in tone. Mundy gradually undercuts the "great man" framework to reveal Walker's flaws and corruption with an ambivalent approach to the entire imperialist scheme.

During 1912, eighteen stories and four articles by Mundy appeared, and by the middle of that year, his stories began to be sold to such English magazines as *The Strand Magazine*, *The Grand*, *London Magazine*, and *Cassell's Magazine of Fiction*. Often the titles of the stories were changed, and both the name Talbot Mundy and Walter Galt were used interchangeably on by-lines. Nearly all the British journals edited Mundy's work, sometimes severely, so the American appearances of his work must be regarded as the authoritative texts. Mundy's growing success as a popular author was also demonstrated in 1912 by the fact that two of his short stories were adapted to motion pictures, with the two films representing opposite poles of Mundy's writing — yet were the most faithful screen versions of his stories ever produced.

For Valour was based on a story of the same title which had appeared in the January 1912 issue of *Adventure*. One of Mundy's lightest stories for the magazine, it was his first to include a major romance, but it also displays the dubious attitude toward courage that would become typical of his later works. The Boer War was then a popular subject for the screen, and the Edison company produced *For Valour* in the Bahamas under the direction of J. Searle Dawley. By July, the one-reel picture version was ready for release in the United States, appearing in England in September.

The second of the 1912 films, *The Fire Cop*, released November 30, was based on one of the tales written for *The Scrap Book* a year earlier. "The Fire Cop," appearing in the October 1911 issue, resembled many of Mundy's military stories with its emphasis on courage and how a man who fears that he may be a coward finds redemption. In late 1912, the Selig Polyscope Co., turning out five films a week, produced a series with narratives including fire scenes. The film avoids the tragedy of Mundy's original for the conventional cinematic "happy ending;" Brannigan is home once more, rocking the cradle. *The Fire Cop* offers some real tension in the fire scenes, and manages to convey, if with less force, the crisis of courage that Brannigan undergoes. As the earliest surviving Mundy movie, it holds up well nearly a century later, and is a reasonable approximation of the story.

1913 was a similar year for Mundy as 1912, with fourteen pieces published, most appearing for the first time in *Adventure*. Simultaneously, the length of his work began to grow from an average of 8000 words to as long as 35,000 words, a short novel.

Each of Mundy's early stories for *Adventure* utilize archetypal military formulas to explore the myths of adventure, its sacrifices, achievements, and fellowship. The themes typically involved sacrifice, either of regiment ("The Phantom Battery," "The Soul of a Regiment," "The Queen — God Bless Her!"), self ("The Chaplain of the Mullingars," "Honor," "Rabbit," "At Maneuvers"), or another ("In Winter Quarters"), in the name of duty and honor. Together with a continual emphasis on Tommy Atkins, Mundy explores those abstract, almost spiritual qualities that attract men to become involved with the regimental unit and identify their individual and collective future with such an entity. The poverty of the background of Tommy Atkins, the essential humanity of all successful officers, and the ultimate equality between them and enlisted men, pervades all of Mundy's stories from the beginning. In "The Payment of Quinn's Debt" and "Three Helios," colonial adventure provides an arena in which a man can pick himself up from failure to proudly make a new life. Settings ranged from the Peninsular War ("In Winter Quarters"), India at the time of the Sepoy Mutiny ("The Phantom Battery," "The Man Who Saw"), the Afghan frontier ("The Chaplain of the Mullingars," "Honor"), the Crimean War ("The Blooding of the Ninth Queen's Own," "The Queen — God Bless Her!") Khartoum ("For Valour," "The Soul of a Regiment"), up to the Boer War ("The Cowards," "Rabbit," "Three Helios"). Ironically, the various British empire locales and the sameness among them would be very different from Mundy's later, far more vivid portrayals of particular lands, especially India.

After several youthful false starts, within two years, by Mundy's 34th birthday, he had proven himself a successful commercial writer in a number of genres, from sea stories to humor to romance, before settling on his metier. "I claim to be nothing but a lineal descendant of the old-time story-teller, who spun his yarn and passed the hat round. Nowadays it is the editor who passes round the hat, and he is rather more particular than the old-time capper used to be; but the effect is just the same. The public pays, and the public calls the tune."[80] While Mundy's initial short stories clearly reveal the need to tailor his compositions to the marketplace, once his reputation was established, he spent the rest of his career determined to avoid its constraints.

II
The Yasmini Conundrum, 1913–1921

Talbot Mundy's early short stories and first novels evidenced steadily greater literary skill. Although his first book was a historical novel, it was with the creation of his most important female character, Yasmini, that Mundy's narratives reveal his true forte. She reflected the feminism that would, uniquely, inflect his adventure writings, as well as the traits he would value in his own spiritual teachers and spouses.

Gradually Mundy's stories were increasingly set in India, from beyond the Afghan frontier on the west, to Tibet on the east. The country had become a focus of the adventure genre after the Sepoy Mutiny of 1857, as fiction became one avenue for Western cultural understanding of how a supposedly primitive Eastern nation had nearly expelled the white imperial presence. Unlike Africa, a continent where the emphasis remained on exploration, India was recognized for its highly developed and structured civilization, with established systems of government and religion. Mundy found in India a land where indirection and subtlety surrounded even the most prosaic actions, and he delved beneath the surface to the underlying beliefs, realities, and the character of India's people. This was not just an evaluation among white critics, but Indians as well.[1]

After "The Phantom Battery," Mundy wrote a series on 1857 which explored the cooperation between English and Indians. In "The Man Who Saw," the Englishman Michael Blackmore may not quite be, as his name implies, a blackamoor, but this nonconformist lives between the worlds of British and Indians. He gains advance warning of the coming rebellion when he learns that his Hindu mistress has compelled the native leaders to promise to save him. He personally rescues his unit, despite the disbelief of officers. *Hookum Hai!* and "For the Salt Which He Had Eaten," were reprinted in the 1920 Mundy hardcover omnibus, *Told in the East*. *Hookum Hai!* ("It is an order!") is often eloquent within its generic bonds, with a fakir warning of the coming anarchy and bloodshed before Sergeant Bill Brown, Juggut Khan and a handful hold onto their roadside base, then selflessly rescue British women hidden in a nearby captured fort.

Mundy began another short story in this vein which, on Arthur Hoffman's advice, was expanded into Mundy's first novel. Scribners quickly agreed to publish *Rung Ho!*, even before the acceptance by *Adventure* in August. A 371 page book, it painted a rich canvas on an epic scale, full of vivid supporting characters and mingling episodes and subplots, all of which unify to achieve the climax. Both "For the Salt Which He Had Eaten" and *Rung Ho!* chronicle how a 21-year-old Englishman is shepherded to manhood by an aging Indian warrior who had eaten of the British salt and served their father. The Indians support imperialism, not out of loyalty, but out of a selfless belief that the alternative, a return to feudalism, is worse. Together, Englishman and Indian are the best of both East and West, Christian and Mohammedan, a union that proves necessary for all to succeed.

Each chapter of *Rung Ho!* opens with a poem (signed "T.M." in *Adventure*, an appellation dropped in the book), and the first verse reflected the book's concern with intrigue and rivalry among the religious and secular realm — whose only goal in common is power over the city of Howrah in Rajputana.

> Howrah City bows the knee
> More or less to masters three,
>   King, and Prince, and Siva.
> Howrah City pays in pain
> Taxes which the royal twain
> Give to priests, to give again
>   (More or less) to Siva.

Mundy views both the Maharajah and his conspiring younger brother Jaimihr, as well as the priests, as "representative of all the many cancers eating at the heart of India."[2] By contrast, the motto of Ralph Cunningham's father was "For the Peace of India," the book's title in serial publication in three parts in *Adventure*, from February-April 1914.

Mahommed Gunga ensures that Ralph encounters the full force of entrenched British jealousy and obstinacy. "It was not considered decent for a boy of twenty-one to do much more than dare to be alive. For any man at all to offer advice or information to his senior was rank presumption. Criticism was high treason. Sport, such as tiger-shooting, was for those whose age and apoplectic temper rendered them least fitted for it. Conservatism reigned: 'High Toryism, sir, old port, and proud Prerogatives!'"[3] The principal subplot concerns the McCleans, the Reverend Duncan and his daughter Rosemary, and their unsuccessful missionary work in Howrah. Mahommed Gunga plans for everything except the meeting between Ralph and Rosemary, who is simultaneously attracted to him yet bridles at the thought of turning to this youth for comfort or guidance.

Rung Ho! was hailed critically, winning Mundy instant comparison with Kipling, who was no longer regarded as in his prime. Within two months, some 2500 copies had been sold domestically, and the book had gone into a second edition, with a total of 4000 printed, on which Mundy earned a 10 percent royalty.[4] By November, arrangements were being made with Cassell's in England (a house which had already brought out some of Mundy's short stories in their magazines) for publication of the novel in Great Britain.[5]

Sudden hardcover success came as a surprise to Mundy, surpassing any expectations he could have held. He had matured rapidly as a writer, advancing from articles to short stories to novelettes to a serial and novel in less than three years.

Even at this early stage in Mundy's writing, one of the most distinctive features began to appear. Many of his works, particularly those that were the most important, would include proverbs or verse before each chapter. They were sometimes credited to sources mentioned in the novel, such as the songs of Yasmini or Fred Oakes in *The Winds of the World* or *The Ivory Trail*, or to characters, such as "Book of the Sayings of Tsiang Samdup" (*Om*), "The Diary of Olympus" (*Queen Cleopatra*), "The Book of the Yogi-Astrologer Ram-Chittra Gunga Singh" (*Black Light*), "The Sayings of the Druid Taliesan" (*Tros of Samothrace*), and the logs of Tros in *Tros of Samothrace* and *Purple Pirate*. Occasionally the novel did not mention the source in any way, such as "the books of Noor Ali" in *Full Moon* or the "Sayings of Tsiang Samdup" in *The Devil's Guard*. *Rung Ho!*, *Cock o' the North*, and a number of magazine novelettes include unattributed verse. A mix of poetry and sayings is to be found in *King—of the Khyber Rifles*, *Hira Singh*, *The Eye of Zeitoon*, *Guns of the Gods*, and *Om*.

Mundy was especially proud of his poetry, and hoped for a collected volume.[6] By the 1920s, however, Mundy had turned largely to prose as this prefatory material before chapters became increasingly didactic. In 1923, he outlined their purpose.

> From the dawn of recorded history, men have always sought to coin short phrases that should be imperishable guides of conduct — brief, indisputable interpretations of the Higher Law.... Proverbs are the oldest crystallizations of human thought, and some of them are diamond-hard, reflecting the fires of Truth in whatever light, from whichever angle they are studied.[7]

This element adds a measure of profundity that transcended the fictional narratives, becoming Mundy's single most direct tool for injecting philosophy into his stories. In 1934 he would describe them as fragments "of the Ancient Teaching," containing nothing original save his phrasing of them.[8] For their part, readers often best remembered these sayings, and many accepted the temptation to believe that these "sources" were real.[9] Moreover, even outside of the "sayings" Mundy has an epigrammatic sensibility, with frequent pauses for momentary disquisitions or pronouncements on various topics, a tendency that adds interest to even his minor work.

His discipline and approach to his writing were nearly always the same, working seven hours a day, six days a week.[10] An incredibly early riser on a daily basis, he would awake at three or four a.m. and place five sheets of paper with four carbons between them in the typewriter and go to work. His wife Dawn would recall, "He said you have to see it, hear it and smell the whole area before you can put a word on paper. You have to know where you are at — where you are going…. Its got to be in front of your eyes."[11] At such times his concentration placed him in another world for hours on end. Dawn noted, "If he became stuck for a word or phrase, he'd flop on a davenport for ten or fifteen minutes, eyes closed — then abruptly back to the typewriter — passage completed."[12] Talbot would continue until he was exhausted or had written himself into a corner, from which a night's rest usually extricated him. Elmer Davis's son recalled one unusual occasion: "One of Mundy's stories I remember dealt with his getting around a block ... in writing one of his books. At any rate, Mundy couldn't think what to write next when, after whatever invocation may have been involved, a lama he had known (at least some kind of monk) materialized in front of the blank wall and dictated to him a number of verses or couplets. These turned out to be fitting headings for the chapters of the book and guided the plot."[13]

Mundy never composed a written outline in advance; as Dawn remarked, "The story created itself, as he went along, and they were much better when he did that."[14] As he explained in 1916, "I should be sorry to burden myself with an unnecessary yoke by stating in advance what my next book is to be about." Although at one point Mundy could rapidly write a novelette clean through over a long weekend and sell it Tuesday morning, that proved, he said, "nothing except the kindness of editors and the patience of the public."[15] As he began to write longer, more involved works, they required careful, patient development, discarding early drafts and plots to rework entire manuscripts, until not only the writing was smooth but also connected to overarching themes.

The portrait of Mundy first published in magazines as he gained fame.

The first of Mundy's grand character sagas was "Dick Anthony of Arran," an eight part series of separate novelettes, united around the exploits of the hero, which ran monthly in *Adventure* from August 1914 through March 1915. They told of a Scottish gentleman fighting Russia in Iran, but he is too shallow and stereotyped to sustain the series; the diverse supporting characters are considerably more interesting. As in the Jimgrim Arabian stories, Dick Anthony leads Middle Eastern rebels against colonialism. Like Tros of Samothrace, Anthony is an independent spirit, forced by the scheming of others into actions that place him at the center of events. Mundy had never tried so hard on a project, rewriting and discarding plots, contemplating the direction of his chronicle as he skied in the Maine woods, taking twice the time a single long serial would have required. Nonetheless, despite the concentration of energy, the effort was beyond his ability at the moment; "Dick Anthony of Arran" is an ordinary, flawed work only interesting for the flashes that reveal Mundy's future direction. The plot becomes highly repetitive after the third installment, and "Dick Anthony of Arran" sprawls without any of the unity or interest later found in the Tros stories. Unfortunately for Mundy, World War I began as the series was appearing, and with Russia, now an ally of France and England, having been denounced for her imperialism

The August 1914 cover of *Adventure*, illustrating *Dick Anthony of Arran—The Sword of Iskander*, showing the hero and his Russian nemesis. (Courtesy Brian Emerich collection.)

in the stories, Cassell's asked Mundy if they could cancel the contract for British publication. Mundy agreed, not wanting to force the stories upon them, and, as he noted sarcastically later, they never subsequently accepted one of his stories.[16]

After so many male-centered stories for *Adventure*, it is not surprising that Mundy turned increasingly to writing about female characters, but this was more than a change of pace. The first woman to figure as the central character in a Mundy series had been Kitty Crothers in the amusing series of four 1911 *All-Story* short stories. They told of the various entanglements and vicissitudes of a self-absorbed, good-hearted. not-so-young widowed actress, who is independent from both the men and women around her. The first person narrator is himself a writer, not taken too seriously by the vivacious Kitty (she describes him as a "nonentity," in an obvious analogy to Mundy himself).[17]

The Kitty stories provide the first indication of the gender equality and vivid feminine characterizations Mundy would create. Two years later, Mundy united feminism and his fascination with India in the greatest character in all his writing, the remarkable, matchless Yasmini.[18] Yasmini is devious, manipulative, and always surprising, like Kitty, but on a different scale, since Yasmini is scheming to carve an empire.

Yasmini first appeared in two *Adventure* novelettes in early 1914, "A Soldier and a Gentleman" and "Gulbaz and the Game," and figures prominently during the next two years in *The Winds of the World* and *King— of the Khyber Rifles*. *Guns of the Gods*, written from 1919 to 1920, is a reminiscence of her youthful climb to political power. In her final appearance in *Caves of Terror* (1922), she has descended from politics to become an evil seductress and head of a house of gambling and intrigue, yet still dreams of world dominion.

The idea for Yasmini's character was born around 1900, while Talbot was standing amidst the crowded traffic of Bombay, and saw a closed carriage in which the wives of wealthy Indians go out into the city.

> Suddenly the horses plunged and tried to bolt; the coachman, with a rein wrapped round his waist, exerted all his strength; the carriage lurched, and the front wheel struck the curbstone within three feet of me. The shock jarred the door, which swung open.
> I believe there were three women in the carriage, but I had eyes for only one of them. She was unveiled; she had golden hair; she was dressed in diaphanous silks of the color of early morning in the hills; she seemed to me, in that sudden moment, to be lovelier than any pictured woman I had ever seen; and she was amused—she was tickled to bits by the scandalous fact of being seen by alien eyes. She laughed gayly [sic], and I can hear her laughter now, it was so merry and full of mischief. I had hardly time to raise my hat before one of the huge footmen jumped down from his place behind the carriage, shoved me violently backward, slammed the door, jumped back to his little platform, yelled to the coachman — and the carriage drove away. That was all I ever saw or knew of her....
> Perhaps if I had known about her any facts whatever, I might have been so hampered by those facts as to have made her tame, implausible and valueless as a heroine of fiction.[19]

In the first chapter of *Guns of the Gods*, Mundy supplies Yasmini with a biography. Her father was a Rajput, Maharajah Bubru Singh, making her kin to all the great families of Rajputana. Her mother was a Russian, Sonia Omanoff, compelled to marry him by the Czar as part of his country's plans for the sub-continent. Her husband's nephew succeeded to the throne, while Yasmini was reared "by her mother with tales of Western outrage and ambition, and well-schooled in all that pertained to her Eastern heritage by the thousand-and-one intriguers whose delight and livelihood it is to fish the troubled waters of the courts of minor kings."[20]

Unlike most Eurasian characterizations of the era, Yasmini's racial background is an asset. "She is of the East and West, very terribly endowed with all the charms of either and the brains of both. Her quick wit can detect or invent mercurial Asian subterfuge as swiftly as appraise the rather glacial drift of Western thought; and the wisdom of both East and West combines in her to teach a very nearly total incredulity in human virtue. Western morals she regards as humbug, neither more nor less."[21] She is impelled by a daring and mischievous spirit, enjoying thrills and plots for their own sake, and her audacity and cleverness make her endlessly fascinating.

Her gender is a source of power. Yasmini relies on her knowledge of Indian customs and unique position with other women, who admire Yasmini's determination to break out of the molds of both Indian and British culture. She has an uncanny "gift for reading men's hearts [that] has been her secret and her source of power first and last."[22] Enthrallingly beautiful and sensuous, Yasmini gained exquisite dancing skill from her Russian background. "Every move she ever made was poetry expressed ... as no man had ever yet seen woman."[23] While she bewitches men who come near her, she has no need or use for a man, unless he is part of her goals or shares her outlook. Her first love had been a success in *Guns of the Gods*, but her inability to be happily united with Athelstan King does not frustrate or doom her, and she continues her plotting, this time in opposition to him, in *Caves of Terror*.

Yasmini is a complex character, a very human mix of emotions and motivations. She unhesitatingly has any man executed who threatens her secrets. Her intoxication with power impels her to many foolish actions, and she becomes consumed in the downward spiral brought about by her thwarted ambition. In the words of Gulbaz, "The Game has swallowed her alive.... She can not draw back, and she knows it, and she dare not try."[24]

"A Soldier and a Gentleman" relates her attempted vengeance upon Gopi Lall, when the corrupt police are unwilling to capture the notorious local dacoit. The army is called in, and in typically oblique fashion, Mundy alternates between four separate plot strands that eventually all lead to Gopi Lall and Yasmini.

Initially, Yasmini appears as a mysterious secondary character, who has inhabited, with her ladies, an old palace in a deserted city in the jungle. Mundy presents Yasmini from both the Indian and the Anglo perspective, as members of each race try to determine who she is and her motivations. When she is attacked by Gopi Lall, he is killed by a well-intentioned English captain, robbing Yasmini of her own plans for Gopi Lall's fate.

Yasmini explains the unique trauma that she suffered at Gopi Lall's hands, which left revenge as the only honorable option left to her. Gopi Lall assassinated her husband, a maharajah and the only man she loved, in such a way as to implicate her and force her to flee her homeland in disgrace. In addition he killed one of her favorite handmaidens, sending her the woman's severed head as a gift (presaging a key incident in a later Yasmini tale, *King— of the Khyber Rifles*).

Yasmini turns out to be a woman of integrity, rather than a temptress. Mundy succeeds in the goal of his last chapter, which "has no verse or title to head it, but which leaves the reader with a feeling that he would like to read some more of Yasmini." And, seemingly, Yasmini has equally taken hold of Mundy, as a characterization that quickly grew on him.

The second story, "Gulbaz and the Game," lacks the suspense of the first, and is more conventional, as Yasmini secures vengeance upon the country which mistreated her mother. As a result of the scheme in which she aids secret agent Gulbaz, the visiting Grand Duke is lured to her nautch where he becomes so intoxicated as to sign a document supporting an uprising. Delivered into British hands, it gives the diplomatic leverage to prevent Russia from interfering in India, so that a period of peace follows. "Gulbaz and the Game" seems hastily composed, and it was so insignificant in Mundy's mind that within six years he had forgotten it.

As the Great War dragged on in Europe, Mundy's curiosity could not be slaked by newspaper reports of the effect it was having on India, and he let his imagination roam. As he explained, "The censorship had shut down tight; there was no knowing what was happening, and nobody with any sense could believe the scraps of news that did reach the United States."[25] Sikh militants led the failed Ghadar uprising in February 1915, and by October of that year, a German delegation had arrived in Kabul to foment an Afghan invasion through the Khyber Pass as part of a large-scale Moslem Holy War.[26] Yet, despite small mutinies, India was remarkably peaceful, although there were often as few as 15,000 Englishmen, without artillery, remaining to control a nation of over 300,000,000.[27] The factors eliciting loyalty to the regiment or Raj, and how it unites men of different races and ethnicities, was already in the forefront of Mundy's 1857 stories, and it would dominate *The Winds of the World* and *Hira Singh*, and was mentioned in advertisements for *King, of the Khyber Rifles* in *Adventure*.

The title of *The Winds of the World* signifies both the literal temple in which the climax will take place, as well as the house (also revealed in "Gulbaz and the Game") where Yasmini entertains, creating "a clearing house of underground political information from every corner" attracting plotters and their conspiracies— knowledge she labels "the winds of the world."[28] As in "Gulbaz and the Game," Yasmini's songs run in verse at the head of each chapter; she devises them herself and rarely sings the same song twice.

As Mundy's second novel, *The Winds of the World* is poised delicately at a crossroads in his work, between past and future concerns. On the one hand, *The Winds of the World* invokes Mundy's previous subject matter, particularly the mix of Indian and British in the army, but also looks forward to the themes that would increasingly come to dominate Mundy's writing, with the key characters of Colonel Kirby, Ranjoor Singh and Yasmini accenting this dichotomy. Kirby is a typical military man, but unique for the esteem and trust in which he holds his Indian officers. Ranjoor Singh points simultaneously to the Anglo-Indian and military axis dominating

An early British book edition dust jacket showing Yasmini.

Mundy's previous stories, as well as toward the increasing emphasis on indigenous characters and the secret service. Yasmini also foregrounds the latter aspect, and the degree to which intrigue becomes uppermost in Mundy's depiction of India.

The Winds of the World is set in the days just before and after the mobilization of August 1914, with the menace provided by German spies who offer to supply the Sepoys with arms to rebel against the British when war breaks out in Europe. Ranjoor Singh and Yasmini are contrasts: he is straightforward and disdains guile, while she revels in it, finding his scruples annoying. Yasmini is ostensibly an espionage agent for the British, but in a forecast of the task she would undertake in *King— of the Khyber Rifles*, works only on her own terms, and freely plays tricks on the government men. To deceive and entrap the Germans, as Ranjoor Singh learns, requires that a noble warrior sacrifice his pride by going undercover, appearing treacherous to the British and his own squadron, "Outram's Own."

Yasmini is astonished at Kirby's belief in Ranjoor Singh; she had heard of such regard by a Indian "for a native, or for an Englishman, but never before by an Englishman for a native."[29] She responds cruelly to such esteem. Pretending Ranjoor Singh is in her power, she tells Kirby and another officer to kneel before her to beg for his life, and to celebrate her dominance, pours enough musk in their hair so that all may know of her deed for days to come.

Through his narrative construction, Mundy interrelates the several threads of the stories of Yasmini, Kirby, Ranjoor Singh, and "Outram's Own." The first and last third of *The Winds of the World* (Chapters 1–4 and 10–14, coinciding approximately with the three-part serialization in *Adventure* from July to September 1915) concentrate on Ranjoor Singh's pursuit of a murderer when one of his men is killed. The middle third of the book shifts viewpoint entirely, to concentrate on the British perspective, and Colonel Kirby's determination to continue to believe in Ranjoor Singh. This portion is structured around the mystery of whether the Sikh officer is still alive, while the last third reveals what happened, resuming the Indian perspective. By implication, only through the latter viewpoint may the mysteries of India be understood.

The novel ends patriotically, with the Sikh arriving to join his regiment in France just in time to lead them into their first battle. In retrospect, the elements of espionage, intrigue, and the military never thoroughly mesh, and the clichéd Germans click their heels and are easily deceived. Nonetheless, critical reaction was decidedly positive, and while the ingredients were old, Mundy's overall brew had a fresh and unique flavor.[30]

By the close of *The Winds of the World*, Yasmini had already predicted the future for Ranjoor Singh in *Hira Singh*, and her own as well. "You shall run away to fight men you never quarreled with, and I will govern India!"[31] While *The Winds of the World* was a timely story of loyalty to the empire, *King— of the Khyber Rifles*, finished less than a year later, recycled many of the same ideas, showing Yasmini in her greatest bid for power. The new book probed much deeper, to the most remote portions of India, a more imaginary realm where the only British are solitary intelligence agents.

Many of the themes and characters Mundy would elaborate in *King— of the Khyber Rifles* had also been adumbrated in the otherwise unmemorable *The Letter of his Orders* in the September 1913 number of *Adventure*. Dispatched with only Indians to accompany him, Sigurd Fitzalan Rodrick of the secret service must defuse a potential outbreak that could divert Lord Roberts's flank during his march to Kabul. When first confronted, Rodrick is revealing his medical skill in bandaging one of his men, and the fact that many Orakzai Pathans need such attention prevents Rodrick from being killed at the outset, a motif that would become central to King's impersonation of a "hakim." While still accepting the imperial, Kiplingesque ideology of Anglo nobility triumphing over indigenous peoples, ultimately it is the Indians of the secret service who first sow divisions among the rebellious tribesmen, then compel military intervention. These unnamed sons of India who labor anonymously are the preservers of the empire, and while Rodrick is foregrounded in the narrative, he is ultimately their tool. Hence, Mundy's perspective already contains the seeds of its own contravention, to shortly flower in the more mature, overtly anti-colonial period of his writing.

King — of the Khyber Rifles, as Mundy's third novel, is the first work to reveal the unique talent and archetypes that would emerge throughout his oeuvre. Mundy imagines a set of incredible places, situations, and characters, using all of the imagination of which he was capable at the time across such topics as the army, the secret service, a powerful woman, hidden caves, secret wisdom, a mad mullah, war, and indigenous peoples. All these elements had appeared separately in previous Mundy tales, but in this, his longest novel to date, they are woven together in a single powerful narrative. *King — of the Khyber Rifles* has attained a certain classic status through his arrangement of these plot elements into mythic form.

It was the book's title which came first to Mundy's mind, rather than the tale; "I remember I had not the least idea who King was or what the story was going to do with him."[32]

> I remember sitting in the dark and seeing the throat of the Khyber Pass at sunset — gloomy, ominous, mysterious, lonely, haunted by the ghosts of murdered men and by the prowling outlaws who live by the rifle and shun the daylight. As if the word were almost spoken in my ear I heard "Death roosts in the Khyber while he preens his wings." It seemed a good line, so I made a note of it. Then, dimly silhouetted by the light of the low moon, a small group of horsemen, with overcoat collars turned up to their ears, appeared to ride into the picture. They vanished up–Khyber. Why? I had no more idea than you have. But the story had begun; one of the riders was probably King, whoever he might be; so I wrote that part of it and called it Chapter One. However, I was wrong; several chapters took their place ahead of it....[33]

The qualities of *King — of the Khyber Rifles* were almost instantly recognized. Mundy's magazine publishers, the Ridgway Company, quickly realized that he had written a novel with a potential to secure a far wider readership than his stories in *Adventure*, and published it in one of their other magazines, *Everybody's*, a slick-paper illustrated monthly whose name indicated the hoped-for audience. The serialization of *King — of the Khyber Rifles* extended over a period of nine months, from May 1916 through January 1917, and was such an immediate success that by August 1916 Mundy received a check from *Everybody's* for an extra $1000.[34]

Charles Scribner's Sons, publishers of *Rung Ho!*, turned down the new book, probably because, unlike *Rung Ho!*, *King — of the Khyber Rifles* focused on the fantastic instead of the historical. Mundy's agent, Paul Reynolds, then turned to Bobbs-Merrill, who would publish all but two of Mundy's books over the next fifteen years. The hardcover version, published in mid–November 1916, proved as popular as the serialization; Bobbs-Merrill kept it a high sales priority into the spring of 1917, despite an inept advertising campaign that labeled the book "a peach of a story."[35] By the beginning of 1919, Mundy told the *New York Times* that 15,000 copies of *King — of the Khyber Rifles* had been sold.[36] The book has remained nearly continuously in print in all the years since its first publication, and was also widely translated, including editions in such languages as Danish, Norwegian, and Hungarian. The title properly includes a dash or comma; the *Everybody's* version and the British book edition used a comma, while the book edition in the United States used the dash. However, many covers, dust jackets, reprints, and references to the book simply treated King as a word rather than a name, amplifying the noble or royal implication of the alliteration.

The unusual name of Mundy's hero, Athelstan King, is an inversion of the name and title of the tenth century ruler who became the first Saxon to govern all of England. Creating the English civil service, King Athelstan established legal codes and led a victory over an alliance of Norse, Scots, and Strathclyde Britons invading England. Like his namesake, Mundy's hero saves India from a foreign invasion brewing in the Khinjan Caves beyond the Khyber, which Yasmini hopes to lead.

Mathematics is the key to King's character; he relies on its logic and immutability to both govern his actions and resist Yasmini. He also studies medicine for relaxation, allowing him to adopt the disguise of the Indian physician ("hakim"), Kurram Khan. The very first page describes King, "and a hundred like him," as "picked from British stock and taught" by India, born and reared there, and of a line who are also buried there.[37] The country is as much his own as if he belonged to her indigenous races. Like Yasmini, with her background of both Russian and Indian ancestry, but reared in India, King is also a child of the country, despite being of English blood.

King is ready to lay down his life to preserve the peace of India, although, like many Indians, he serves British colonial rule. Indeed, the opening poem facing Chapter One, a portion of Mundy's "Song of the Indian Secret Service," pointedly notes that the mission of the service is to be "the pullers of roots of ruction...." (This poem has been omitted, probably inadvertently, in many reprints, such as those published posthumously by Grosset & Dunlap and Donald M. Grant.)

Anchoring King's support is the balance of power, preventing India from becoming a new front in the Great War.[38] Yet, from the outset of *King — of the Khyber Rifles*, Mundy demonstrated his increasing habit of reversing the imperialist presuppositions of colonial adventure. In a situation reminiscent of the suspicion of Ranjoor Singh in *The Winds of the World*, King and his unknown secret service activity are regarded as abandoning his regiment when it goes to fight in Europe.

Unlike most previous chroniclers of British India, Mundy takes his hero well beyond the territorial and spiritual realms of English control. King provides a surrogate for the white, Western reader into a land far beyond their knowledge or domain, where all characters and power are in the hands of Moslem Indians. King's adventure in the Khyber Pass and Khinjan Caves is at once both a patriotic mission and a journey of metaphysical discovery, an initiation. While this motif runs throughout Mundy's work, seldom is it so concrete as in *King— of the Khyber Rifles*.

Such experiences are a physical and mental trial, dividing hero from villain, as Mundy noted in his theosophical article, "Hope." "Not hearing that Hope which is the Soul's voice singing of the Universal Purpose, [the lowest criminal and the vilest sensualist alike] are deceived by the counterfeit voice that echoes in the empty caverns of the lower self, where envy and suspicion and all Truth's opposites hold sway, in darkness."[39] The hero emerges transformed when he survives a series of temptations, dangers, and ordeals. Hence, although King's character is revealed in his actions, they are as much psychological as external, making him an unusually complex hero for an adventure novel.[40]

It is no accident that Mundy describes the door that leads into Khinjan as resembling a tombstone. To penetrate the "Hills" and Khinjan Caves, King must proclaim that he has slain an infidel, and announces that it was an English officer, Athelstan King. This metaphorical murder of his real self, in favor of his new identity as Kurram Khan, becomes all the more profound when he is handed the severed head of a white officer to show the crowd as evidence of the deed.

King learns that his mission has unintentionally helped to cause of the death of his own brother. Shortly after meeting with Athelstan, Charles King had been killed by one of Yasmini's enemies, who had kept his head as a trophy, but Yasmini's men had stolen it. Hence the initiation turns into a trauma: not only has King horribly learned of his brother's death, but he is expected to throw the head to the mob of Hillmen. King resolves the dilemma by the dangerous tactic of throwing the head over a nearby cliff into a waterfall. Yasmini distracts the crowd from its disappointment by dancing for them. Nonetheless, King wonders whether she planned the entire incident, and he endangers his mission to maintain an even higher loyalty than that of the secret service, the loyalty to his family.

The presentation of King's brother, Charles, probably has much to do with how Talbot regarded his own brother, with whom he had some communication since moving to the United States. After Talbot had left his family behind, Harold had been inspired to become a soldier by watching the military procession at King Edward VII's funeral in 1910. By the time Talbot wrote *King— of the Khyber Rifles*, Harold had become an officer in Burma and India, and his relationship with his older, "black sheep" brother remained problematic, with only intermittent contact until the last decade of Talbot's life. For his part, Talbot often feared that Harold had died fighting in some far corner of the world, without the opportunity for reconciliation. Similarly, King's brother is a shadowy, almost unknown figure, seen only occasionally in his life, and with whom his affection is largely unspoken.

Within the Khinjan Caves, Yasmini has discovered the sleepers, a legend known to the hillmen as "the Heart of the Hills," the remarkably well-preserved corpses of a forgotten Roman warrior and the woman who inspired his brief conquest of the East. Their physical resemblance to Yasmini and King is uncanny. Throughout *King— of the Khyber Rifles*, Yasmini's temptation to take the place of the sleepers has been foreshadowed in descriptions of King as having typically Roman features. Yasmini hopes to use the legend of the "Heart of the Hills" to convince the hillmen that

By TALBOT MUNDY, Author of RUNG HO!

KING; OF THE KHYBER RIFLES

Imagine India for a background — the India of grandeur, cruelty, charm, nobility and treachery all commingled: the India of teeming streets and magic palaces, of troops entraining and stifling journeys, the India of scorching plains and windy hills, the India immemorially old and ever new, the India of war-stirred intrigue and secret service, the India of mystery, mystery mystery.

Imagine a story written with power, with invention and the thrill of perilous adventure in the unknown. Throw over it the elusive, intangible spell of a strange and enchanting woman.

And you have some idea of what this book presents.

Illustrated by Joseph Clement Coll. $1.35 net

THE BOBBS-MERRILL COMPANY, Publishers

Mundy himself provides the model for Athelstan King, reclining here with Yasmini in one of Joseph Clement Coll's illustrations for *King—of the Khyber Rifles*.

she and King are reincarnations of the dead pair, ready to resume their conquest. In this way Mundy also begins the theme of reincarnation in his writing, while not yet suggesting his actual belief in the phenomenon. Through a magical crystal, King and Yasmini are able to see events in the lives of the "sleepers." Previously, Yasmini has read King's thoughts, yet Mundy handles both these fantastic elements in a restrained, spare, and realistic manner.

In the test of wills between Yasmini and King, he maintains the greater self-mastery. Both are reluctant to admit their increasing love for one another, which would compromise their respective missions. Just as Yasmini has been unable to kill King, despite his interference in her plans, King is barely able to resist her spell. He is unable to harm her and indeed hopes for a conclusion that will allow him to serve her.[41] Only the actual romantic scenes fail to convince, as in Chapter XIV. The last page almost hints at a sequel ("...chances for intrigue are almost infinite, given such a combination as King and Yasmini and a love affair"), but there is no sense that they have a final, lasting commitment to each other, and marriage is never mentioned.

The book ends by quoting the saying, "'A man and his promise — a woman and intrigue — are one!'" The irony and lack of resolution, and Mundy's refusal to provide an expected outcome, give the novel added strength. There can be no surrender into the arms of the other for either King or Yasmini. King cannot be said to have triumphed over her, because to preserve the status quo is a far different task from Yasmini's dream of reviving an empire. As well, as Mundy points out in the concluding lines of the book, King has promised to be her "loyal servant" should she join the British cause, and he is not one to quibble. Hence, even in defeat Yasmini retains her imperiousness, while in victory King retains his dignity and humility.

The Times Literary Supplement, and other critics, believed such other predecessors as John Buchan, Seton Merriman, and most importantly, Sir H. Rider Haggard, needed to be mentioned to describe the new blend Mundy was creating.[42] Although some of the experiences of King and Yasmini resemble those of Ayesha, "She-who-must-be-obeyed," in Haggard's *She*, and its prequel *Ayesha*, the style and interpretation are different. Both Haggard and Mundy use a white man's journey to a remote area, where both Ayesha and Yasmini reside in underground caves. Unlike Ayesha's other-worldliness, and ties to ancient times, Yasmini is no superwoman who has overcome mortality to live on through the centuries. Instead she is a 20th century woman, whose dreams would only be possible in the present and whose interest in the past is the power it can give her today.[43]

Mundy's style is elliptical and oblique, in a natural rather than affected manner, with numerous arresting juxtapositions, such as his summation of the Khyber as "haunted after dark by the men whose blood-feuds are too reeking raw to let them dare go home and for whom the British hangman very likely waits a mile or two farther south."[44] The book is also full of telling details that add a sense of authenticity, despite the likelihood that they came largely from Mundy's imagination. For instance, the opening paragraph of the final chapter conveys setting, motivation, character, teaching, and knowledge all at once. "Four thousand men with women and children and baggage do not move so swiftly as one man or a dozen, especially in the 'Hills,' where discipline is reckoned beneath a proud man's honor. There were many miles to go before Khinjan when night fell and the mullah bade them camp. He bade them camp because they would have done it otherwise in any case."[45] In this complex interweaving, the reader learns simultaneously about hillmen, India, and the weakness of the leadership of Yasmini's rival, Mohammed Anim, a fanatical, over-confident mullah nicknamed "Bull-with-a–Beard."

Throughout *King — of the Khyber Rifles*, Mundy turns conventional assumptions and metaphors on their head to reveal new perspectives, spanning the political to the sexual realm. All of the unexpected reversals and multiple roles of the hero and heroine add depth to both the plot and the leads. This reaches its apex with a major character, Rewa Gunga, who early in the novel King had anxiously suspected of being one of Yasmini's past or present lovers. Instead, Rewa Gunga is revealed as Yasmini herself in disguise. Just as Yasmini had been hired by the British to defuse a rebellion she was leading, and King went into Khinjan as an Indian, now Yasmini is disclosed as one of her own supporting characters.

The narrative is well-planned and carefully written, although some of the book is overwritten, repeating plot points in a manner typical of a novel that first appeared as a magazine serial. Regrettably, Mundy is unable to find a conclusion fully consonant with a storyline that has become steadily more amazing. After the soaring fantasy of the sleepers, the novel returns to a more mundane tone, causing a certain let-down to be inevitable; not until later stories would Mundy find unexpected climaxes to equal the preceding narrative.

Reviews of *King — of the Khyber Rifles* were positive both among the critics writing for periodicals in the major cities, as well as in newspapers in the outlying regions. For instance, the *Grand Rapid News* noted that, whatever the foundation of the story, "The reader believes it all true as he turns the pages, and to the last word feels that a story of the inner India is open to him. It is here that the highest art of the fiction writer is felt."[46] In the words of the *Philadelphia Post*, Mundy "gives us the atmosphere of India which he evidently knows from personal association and which most of us think of only in terms of Kipling, but he outdoes that writer in the wealth of his imagination, the creation of weird situations and the manner in which he brings the tale to a climax."[47]

Guns of the Gods, Mundy's last novel centered around Yasmini, was mentioned as early in 1918. It was planned as a sequel to *King — of the Khyber Rifles*, to include not only Yasmini but also King and Ranjoor Singh. These preliminary ideas changed markedly, and the book, intended for *Everybody's*, was rejected and was not actually published until serialization in five biweekly issues of *Adventure* from March to May of 1921. There it was rated the year's sixth most popular serial.[48] Book publication in the United States and England occurred in the following months; several British publishers were interested, and Hutchinson finally decided to take up the option, and brought the book out in November, five months after Bobbs-Merrill's edition. *Guns of the Gods* would later be translated into French, Italian, and other languages, although Mundy remarked to a friend that the volume sold "nicely, but no better than that."[49]

While not as imaginative or unforgettable as *King — of the Khyber Rifles*, *Guns of the Gods* is the most literary work of Mundy's early years, a far more even and perfectly developed novel that lacked the flaws that had marked portions of his earlier works. An introduction to the Italian translation indicated the complexity of Mundy's achievement, noting the story was "rendered with a light hand and a rare communicative effectiveness," the narration assuming "intense dramatic rhythm ... always pervaded by a fine ... humor."[50] Mundy successfully avoids his weaknesses and highlights his strengths, especially in the portrayal of Eastern thinking, power politics, and convincing, strong women characters. Enchanting descriptions of the vivid Indian landscape superbly capture the sense of magic endemic to the most entertaining Western imaginings of the East, while at the same time maintaining a sense of realism and authenticity; one contemporary critic commented that "some of the descriptive passages are as fine as anything in contemporary romance."[51] The *Boston Herald* reviewed the book with an eight stanza poem of its own, an appropriate compliment since the poems between chapters of *Guns of the Gods* are among Mundy's best verse.[52]

Pivoting around a woman in the "man's" realm of power politics, the novel is as rich in character as action, even to including an elephant, Akbar, with a craving for alcohol. The central people are all women, making this one of Mundy's most thoroughly feminist works; men are secondary, or villains. To illustrate his theme of the power of women to rule India, Mundy wrote a newspaper article, "A Land Where Romance Reigns," to accompany publicity for *Guns of the Gods*, which he hoped might be used as a preface in a second edition.

Like Yasmini's introduction as Rewa Gunga in *King—of the Khyber Rifles*, she first appears in *Guns of the Gods* dressed as, and imitating, a man, a sign of her refusal of all limitations on the position of her sex. She ultimately succeeds in the quadruple goal of deposing a maharajah, gaining a husband, setting her husband and herself on the new throne, and finding the riches to secure their position. To accomplish these goals, she capitalizes on the yearning for old customs—not the modern directions with which she is identified. Yasmini revives the ancient tradition of a princess choosing her consort to promote her political aims, enabling her to select the brave and wise Prince Utirupa Singh, who has a lesser claim to the throne.

Yasmini's struggle for power is made all the more audacious by giving her two antagonists, one representing indigenous despotism, the other the power of the British occupation, and showing the similarities between the two. The incumbent maharajah, Gungadhura, is the man who had succeeded Yasmini's father on the throne of Sialpore, and had been given his position by the British because of their distrust of Yasmini's Russian mother. Gungadhura is an unfit and spendthrift ruler, who is paralleled with the official British government representative, Rupert Samson, a despicable self-promoter, who studies Julius Caesar as the best road to power.

In contrast to Gungadhura and Samson, Mundy enhances the positive aspect of Yasmini by making a motif of her virtue and chasteness. While she is an adventuress in all other senses of the word, her charms do not include sexual favors, and she is also truly in love with Utirupa. Yasmini will be a loving wife, while also his political equal.

The white heroes are, significantly, an American couple, Dick and Tess Blaine. Although Tess's role in *Guns of the Gods* was originally conceived in early 1918, more than a year before he met Sarah Teresa Ames, the character was ultimately modeled after the widow with whom Talbot was falling in love as he wrote the novel. Tess Blaine's husband, Dick, was named for Mrs. Ames's son, and the union of Tess and Dick Blaine is depicted as an ideal of love and affection, like that of Yasmini and Utirupa. By contrast, Samson attempts to make Tess his mistress.

Dick and Tess become friends and allies of Yasmini, feeling an instant camaraderie. While ostensibly telling the story as heard from Yasmini, Mundy makes Tess her confidant and the other principal character, contrasting women of different races and goals. Tess's expected sympathies gradually change; for instance, she is surprised to find herself rooting for the Rajputs, lead by Utirupa, in a polo game with the English.

An added variable and further motivation for the political machinations is the search for the lost treasure of Sialpore, the reason Dick Blaine has been hired by Gungadhura. The Maharajah, together with Samson and the local priests, are all pursuing in their own way the same objective, to loot the country. The priests want the treasure for the temples and their own use, Samson hopes it will go to the British and help win his promotion, and Gungadhura desires it to continue his own profligate lifestyle. Only Yasmini desires the money for the country's good, and when she realizes it is on British territory, tricks Samson into a land trade that places it in Indian hands.

Yasmini and her ambitions are far more sympathetic than the ambivalent role she had served in *King— of the Khyber Rifles*. As Yasmini tells Tess,

> Men taught me this and that thing, and I have always reversed it and believed the opposite. Why do men teach? To make you free, or to bind you to their own wheel? The English teach that English ways are good for the world. I answer that the world has been good to England and the English would like to keep it so! The pundits say we should study the philosophies.... Why? To bind me to the wheel of their philosophy, and keep me subject to them! I say philosophy is good for pundits, as a pond is good for frogs; but shall I be a frog, too, and croak about the beauties of the mud? The priests say we should obey them, and pray, and make offerings, and keep the religious law. I say, that religion is good for priests, which is why they cherish it, and add to it, and persuade foolish women to believe it! As for the gods, if they are anything they are our servants![53]

Mundy thereby conflates British imperialism, patriarchy, and church dogma as part of one hegemonic system that results in the simultaneous colonizing of both non–European countries and women.

Guns of the Gods also has a melancholy note, its frame indicating it has been written after Utirupa is dead. *Caves of Terror* was in a very different and much bleaker vein, with the occult theme of *King— of the Khyber Rifles* becoming primary. The characters provide continuity, with Athelstan King again undermining the political plans of Yasmini, but with different motives. "I've been working for [self-government] ever since I cut my eye teeth.... So has every other British officer and civil servant who has any sense of public duty."[54] He has become an outcast by leaving the army to investigate the supernatural in India, and the man who once resisted such mysteries has become a credible aspirant. By contrast, Yasmini's search for occult knowledge is strictly to enhance her doomed, obsessive dream of conquest. Although "there was absolutely nothing between him and her except his own obstinate independence," she also can not accept a man who will not assist in her ongoing schemes.[55]

Before writing *Caves of Terror*, Bobbs-Merrill had been interested in more Yasmini stories, including expanding "A Soldier and a Gentleman" and "Gulbaz and the Game" to book length. However, none were forthcoming, and the reason becomes understandable considering the progression she underwent when the stories are placed in the chronology of her life. In *Guns of the Gods*, the narrator — writing after the events in *King — of the Khyber Rifles*—comments how, over the years, Yasmini has become a harsher person. The admiration aroused by her daring is now overwhelmed by the impossibility of sympathizing with her actions. Her evolution suggests that Mundy did not create her with greatness in mind, but her character grew upon him as a model of feminist strength and power. Eventually, perhaps, he found her ruthless ambition too disturbing, and he finally turned upon her.

Yasmini could only be exceeded in Mundy's imagination by a historical reflection of one of the most powerful women of all time, Cleopatra, and indeed the opening of *Guns of the Gods* had made precisely this comparison. Yasmini's career trajectory resembles Mundy's portrait of Cleopatra: from youthful discovery of wisdom and creation of her own destiny, including political power. However, excessive ambition and doomed love-affairs lead to failure and downfall. Mundy imposes much of the model of Yasmini upon Cleopatra, seeing both as full of contradictions, and of a land of which she was only partly a native.

Feminist views infused Mundy's literature, depicting, in a manner that was highly unusual for the time and genre, female characters who seldom occupy traditional roles. Frequently they are the leading players in his stories, ambitious, likeable, out-thinking and dominating men. In addition to other Eastern women like Sankyamuni in the Ben Quorn saga, and Arsinoe in *Purple Pirate*, are women of the West who have moved to, or been reared in, the East, such as Elsa Burbage and Nancy Strong in *The Thunder Dragon Gate* and *Old Ugly-Face*, or Samding in *Om* and Amrita in *Black Light*. On occasion, Mundy compared women of two cultures in a single novel, such as Gloria and Maga in *The Eye of Zeitoon*, and Henrietta and Wu Tu in *Full Moon*. Western women appeared in a more traditional Eastern adventure setting, like Rosemary in *Rung Ho!*, the Ranee in *Cock o' the North*, and Joan Angela Leich, the modern 1920s woman of *The Mystery of Khufu's Tomb* and *The Hundred Days*. Even the more conventional American women of the melodramas *East and West* and in particular *Her Reputation* have an unusual degree of independent spirit. Yet, Mundy was never to exceed Yasmini or Cleopatra in his literature; even such female sages as Samding, Amrita, and Nancy Strong were philosophers, rather than leaders of warriors.

As his life and writings make clear, Mundy never felt either threatened by or resentful towards women, and was a lifelong believer in full and complete equality between the sexes.[56] This was recognized by associates at the time; a Christian Science practitioner who had treated Rosemary found Talbot to have "a high opinion of women" and commented that he treated "them well in thought and deed."[57] Moreover, he was aware of society's constraints upon women, as he revealed to Rose Wilder Lane.

> I don't remember how I got appointed to a "secret" committee of "investigators," solemnly invited by the mayor to report on the sex situation. Maybe I "horned in," being hugely curious. In that year (1924 or 1925) there were seventeen high school girls of fifteen years or older, who had babies, and I "interviewed" 'em all. They were swell. I didn't find one who didn't genuinely want to keep her baby. And I couldn't find one brace of parents who would even think of "standing for it." I thought the parents were swine — chuckle-headed hypocrites and cowards. All the babies, of course, went to institutions, most of 'em at the tax-payers' or charitable subscribers' expense. And all the girls but two were "sent away to stay with relatives." Two or three of them, of course, were sub-average girls; but the others were better stuff than anything I have seen in any other country in the world. Not one of them could be persuaded or bullied into giving the boy's name. And they all gave the same reason, although in not nearly the same words. It amounted to:
>
> "He hasn't guts enough to stand the gaff and take it. Poor thing, why worry him?"
>
> They elected to "take it" alone. But they were pretty helpless, poor young devils, in the face of their parents' stupidity.[58]

Yet Mundy could also see the other side of the equation; as the humorous Chullunder Ghose proclaims, "Women are fools in a number of ways, including that they think a man is worth their trouble."[59]

In the political realm, Mundy knew the importance of the rise of women to elective office. He praised fellow Christian Scientist Nancy Astor for the basic but overwhelming changes rendered by her presence as a member of Parliament.[60]

Yasmini's qualities are reflected in many of the women who were influential in Mundy's life, including several of those he married and subsequently divorced. Yasmini and his vision of Cleopatra shared a character arc with Mundy's perception of two of his wives, Inez and Rosemary: attraction and initial glory, followed by eventual hubris and downfall. In particular, Mundy was probably at first intoxicated with Inez Craven's beauty, nobility, liberated lifestyle, and dedication to equal rights for women, but eventually found her to also be vindictive and self-destructive.

Talbot was drawn to Rosemary Strafer by her artistic talent and strong spiritual beliefs. Although Yasmini is ostensibly based on a briefly-seen woman in India, the period of her rise in Mundy's pantheon takes place precisely at the time of his esteem and affection for Rosemary; just as Talbot and Rosemary are finished as a couple by 1922, so has Mundy dismissed Yasmini as unworthy in that year's *Caves of Terror*. Meeting in New York City, Talbot and Rosemary wed in Connecticut on August 21, 1913, although his entire capital at the time was a mere $100.[61] He was much in love with his new bride, who was age 40 to his 34, the same difference as that between Inez and Talbot.

Harriette Rosemary Strafer (1873–1935) was born (and would die) in Covington, Kentucky, one of five children. She spent much of her youth in Ohio, studying at the Academy of Fine Arts in Cincinnati, and from 1890–1899 working for the Rookwood Pottery Co. in the city as a decorator and miniature painter. She left Cincinnati for New York in 1899 to pursue her studies, which also took place in Paris. Mundy was fond of saying, in a statement revelatory of their relationship, that she "is a far better painter of pictures than I ever dare hope to be writer of stories. I claim that as proof of good sense, and of ability to recognize a good thing when I see it."[62]

Mundy with wife Rosemary, 1914.

Rosemary Mundy, as she became known, was an ardent Christian Scientist, who had joined the church in 1904 and would remain a member until her death. Christian Science was a new movement, the most rapidly expanding and influential denomination of its time, indigenous to America and founded in the year of Mundy's birth, 1879. Under Rosemary's guidance, Talbot became a believer, joining in 1914; although he withdrew in 1922, it remained an important influence. (Even Arthur Hoffman had Christian Science sympathies, although never a member.) Talbot's experiences with the healing powers of native "magic" had also convinced him that there was more to health than Western science could explain.

This new strand of religious thought was intriguing, both for its basis in the Anglicanism Talbot had been reared in, and for its lack of the ordained clergy, ritual, and sacraments that he had rebelled against. Women were predominant in the church as officers, and it was one of the few denominations that did not reflect patriarchy.

Christian Science was founded by a woman, Mary Baker Eddy, whose book *Science and Health* Mundy studied. In *I Say Sunrise*, Mundy eulogizes the two individuals who most impacted his thinking in his chapter, "Two Women"—the primary thinkers discussed in the volume. These women to whom Mundy looked for philosophy, Eddy and Helena Petrovna Blavatsky, echoed the will and intellectual force he vested in Yasmini, and Cleopatra.

> Mrs. Eddy and Madame Blavatsky were contemporaries. It would be almost impossible to imagine two women who less resembled each other personally. But there is no historical record of two contemporary women who rendered humanity a greater

service, each in her own way. Apparently, and certainly on the surface, opposites, they worked like Titans to the same end—the release of human consciousness from its dungeons of illusion. Both of them were utterly unselfish women. Neither of them (all the criticasters to the contrary notwithstanding) cared "one whoop in hell" for worldly success, personal profit, or for anything whatever but to do their full duty by the faith that was in them. Both of them aroused the wanton malice of every selfish publicist who saw a chance to make some money by personal vilification.

One of his attractions to both Christian Science and the Theosophical Society was the fact that each had been founded by women. As he wrote, "Every vested interest on earth is in league against women who assume the leadership that men believe should be theirs."[63]

Mundy clearly identifies Christian Science for its impetus for gender equality, indicating how this aspect of it attracted him. He credits Eddy with breaking down the distinction in prayer between the genders, lauding her for interpreting the Biblical phrasing to mean "Our Father-Mother-God, all-harmonious."

> She perceived that the idea had been, so to speak, born into human consciousness, and that no human expedients, no human law nor custom could prevent the idea of equality of the sexes from becoming a fact in human experience. So she named the idea. No one possibly could genuinely pray to or be conscious of a Father-Mother-God, without presently becoming conscious of the equal genius and equal rights of men and women. Hers was a terrific blow aimed straight at the heart of prejudice.... She gave the idea of the equality of men and women a prodigious impetus, whether they know it or not.[64]

Mundy's involvement with the leader of the theosophical movement that he actually knew personally, Katherine Tingley, again was with a woman of vision and unusual organizational ability.

Yasmini and Cleopatra, Eddy and Blavatsky, Tingley, and at times Inez and Rosemary, were Mundy's measure of the ideal woman: charismatic, intelligent, and independent. While failing to find an enduring paradigm of Yasmini's best qualities, Mundy's search was lifelong, and many of the women he followed, loved, or created shared these characteristics.

III

War and Its Colonial Impact, 1916–1919

By 1916, Talbot Mundy had discovered his metier as a novelist with the creation of his most vivid character, Yasmini, and the introduction of fantasy and intrigue in adventure stories of India. However, rather than pursuing this theme, he concentrated on the topicality of the Great War, along with the longstanding Teutonic and Turkish menace in various parts of the world.

While writing *King—of the Khyber Rifles*, Mundy was on his own probationary period awaiting American citizenship, eager to prove to his Yankee neighbors that his British background was not a drawback. In 1914, he had taken out papers and at the end of 1916 became naturalized, noting his gratitude for the friendship he found and the opportunity to start his life anew. He later wrote, "The more I see of other lands, and the more I enjoy them, the better I like the U.S.A.—which I regard as the silliest, kindest, shrewdest, most tolerant and intolerant, most ignorant and best informed, most corrupt and incorruptible, meanest and most generous, least comprehensible, and much the most amusing, comfortable and contenting country in the world."[1]

He wrote a pair of stories on the theme "of a decent feller's version of what U.S. citizenship means, at least to him."[2] Told in the first person, the style of "Peter From Paradise Bend" and especially "The Real Red Root" are oblique, contemplative, and indirect, with frequent parenthetical digressions. Mundy found the stories enjoyed by every person to whom he read them and believed that "Peter From Paradise Bend" was "far the best I ever wrote."[3] Yet, both were rejected by every editor in the business, and only sold (for $500 apiece) when Mundy answered an advertisement in the Author's League Bulletin from *The Crescent*, a monthly published to small circulation by the Shriners, although Mundy was never a member. He hoped to write a third story to complete the trilogy believing "they would make a very good little-sized book," but Bobbs-Merrill had minimal interest.[4]

"The Real Red Root" indicates that, by the late 1910s, Mundy desired to move in new directions from the formulaic storytelling that dominated even his novels. A number of incidents are autobiographical for Mundy, or nearly so, criticizing the Boer War, imperialism, the British civil service in India, and modern safaris where "personally conducted millionaires and poisoned bait became the vogue."[5] "The Real Red

Root" travels from Africa to India to the United States, relating a series of encounters with an iconoclastic American who influences the narrator to change his life. In fact, it is the American, Dan Ivan, who is more like Mundy, trying to explain his ancestry in various ways, and possessed of a vision and quirky altruism that gets him expelled from the colonies. The motivation for "Peter From Paradise Bend" is a variation on the theme "you can't go home again," but with a slightly different twist; what's past is past.

Ironically, despite Talbot having quickly become one of the top writers for *Adventure*, upon their first meeting, he and editor Arthur Sullivant Hoffman had taken an instant dislike to one another that lasted for two years. Finally it transformed into a close friendship during a weekend camping trip to Maine in the summer of 1913. Arriving at night, Talbot awoke the next morning, took a deep breath, and announced "This is God's country! I'm going to live here!"[6] *Adventure* writer Hugh Pendexter came down from the coast sixty miles away to join them over the evening fire, convincing them that his town of Norway was the best place to settle.

Tucked away in a valley in the southwest part of the state, Norway is situated some fifty miles directly north of the coastal city of Portland, and not quite as distant to the New Hampshire state line. Amidst the center of the heavily forested, mountainous Oxford Hills, the region is dotted with hundreds of ponds, brooks, and lakes. Moving to Norway, Talbot explained, was "partly because I like the climate and partly because the people in the village make no attempt to take me seriously."[7] The center of a farming community, Norway had a population of 3000, together with a bank, a shoe factory, a lumber yard, a hotel, and a movie theater showing films twice a week. Churches were ubiquitous; the Christian influence surrounded Talbot, and it is little wonder that his interest in mysticism would not flower until he lived in different environs.

In Norway, Talbot approached civic duties with his usual enthusiasm. When America entered World War I, his eyesight rendered him ineligible for service at the front, so he joined the local public safety committee's vigilance department. By April, chafing under the committee's inactivity, Mundy met with some neighbors at Henry Foster's Main Street Clothing Store, including Pendexter, photographer Vivian Akers, and retired lumberman Fred Cummings. Mundy pointed out that crops, enlistments, and bond purchases all needed to be markedly increased, and if the work was to be done, they could not wait for the committee.

The farming problem centered around the fact that although more could be planted, not enough manpower was available at harvest time. So Mundy and his friends canvassed Norway, going from house to house, convincing men to pledge whatever time they could spare to work on the farms—for pay and Uncle Sam, and to beat the Kaiser.

There had long been animosity between the farmers and the townspeople, so Mundy decided to overcome the ill feeling by becoming the envoy to the rural areas. After a six A.M. breakfast, according to a reporter, he drove out in "his big black car, hatless, with his chestnut hair blowing about and his face all on fire with enthusiasm."[8] When Mundy told farmers that they must raise more, they demurred, pointing out that with so many men having left to fight, help would be scarcer than ever. However, his pledges indicated that he and his friends would supply the men needed.

Harvest time came, and with their cars ready, Mundy and his friends answered the farmer's call for men. The organizing work was rigorous; Mundy was up by three a.m. and picking up the workers an hour later, taking them home by moonlight. Finally demand outstripped the supply of men available, and as disaster loomed, the Norway shoe factory was convinced to temporarily shut down, releasing thirty-five more men who willingly worked on the farms for lower wages. Two more weeks of frantic work, and the crops were in; Norway had doubled its amount of land under cultivation in 1917 to 10,000 acres.

After calves were sold for veal, rather than being raised for the beef Europe needed, Mundy was determined to save Norway's pigs from a similar fate. To allow them to grow into bacon, ham and pork, Mundy revived the practice of keeping extra pigs by small farmers and families that owned a bit of land around their homes. For those who could not afford the pig's upkeep, Mundy promised shares in the pig's ultimate sale to other neighbors who would pay a portion of the cost of feed. Soon people far from town, including Arthur Hoffman, owned an interest in Norway pigs, and many of the sponsors received snapshots of their pig in various stages of growth. Hoffman explained in "The Camp-Fire" section of *Adventure*, "The humorous phases of this pig stunt are one of its best 'selling' assets. I've sold several pigs for Mr. Mundy chiefly by reason of the laughs and chuckles these city men got out of owning a pig and having a photograph of it to put up over their desks as a sort of continuous chuckle and a subject for jovial and more or less witty conversation.... It's a laugh, but it's also patriotism."[9] During the summer, 138 pigs were raised this way, and the plan was adopted by New Hampshire and other parts of the country.

Mundy helped Pendexter to exceed Norway's quota of enlistments, convincing men that they were needed in France. During the Liberty Loan drive, Mundy assured many others they could afford to buy bonds by buying more for himself than his budget would allow. He wrote a poem and newspaper articles to sell the bonds, and discovered he could entertain the men in nearby camps with his stories of elephant and lion hunting.[10] A January 1918 article in *Everybody's* magazine cited Norway as an example for the nation to emulate and chronicled Mundy's special efforts (summarized in *The Norway Advertiser*, February 15, 1918); in response, Mundy wrote a piece entitled "Patriotism and the Plow-Tail" for *Everybody's* June issue, pointing out the simplicity of his system.

Following Hoffman's advice and after the publication of *Rung Ho!*, Mundy's output of short stories had diminished considerably, with only a handful written from 1914 to the end of the 1920s. Mundy's preferred form became novelettes and novels that could be serialized, 60,000 or 90,000 to 200,000 words, respectively.[11] Although by 1916, he had almost given up short stories, his work in this form was receiving recognition in the volume of the year's *Best Short Stories*, particularly his first publication in the prestigious *Saturday Evening Post*, "Sam Bagg of the Gabriel Group," in the March 11 issue. Among Mundy's best literary works to date, this was a tale inflected by World War I, but primarily concerned with the impact of British Protectorate rule on a small Pacific island. After 18 years of duty, managing without any visible signs of British support, 48-year-old governor Sam Bagg wonders about what he has accomplished, and if the changes he has brought will endure, including a self-governing council. He feels isolated, but not only by race; the island's previous ruler had been Bill Hill, semi-literate son of a "half-breed" trader who is still known as "Chief" and maintains a harsh shadow regime ready to replace Bagg. Matters come to a head when, instead of the expected British ship, a German steamer stops at the island; Bagg, in his isolation, had not even known there was a war between England and Germany, and none of the police or others he has trained stand by his side. The Germans tell the indigenous people that the British no longer control the Gabriel Group, and the islands are too small for their interest. With complete self-government, the locals kill Hill — placing his head on a pike — and ask a surprised Bagg to take over as king.

Bagg, educated at Rugby and a veteran of famine relief in Baroda, India, is also a self-portrait of what Mundy would have hoped to accomplish had he continued in colonial government. Bagg makes no attempt to mold indigenous beliefs to proper Christianity. Mundy has clearly reached a median point in his attitude toward imperialism: he sees the war as marking its finish, although there may be a need for a continued colonial presence in the transition to self-government. This same sentiment would be reflected in his next novel, *Hira Singh*.

From the outset of World War I, England was strongly supported by India, and her enormous population was considered an inexhaustible source of manpower. The logic of the time expected that the empire would be willing to sacrifice for the overseas defense of the very country that colonized them. Within the first year, 100,000 of India's troops were in Europe fighting with the Allies against the Germans and Austrians. There was a widespread Indian assumption that participation in the war would be rewarded with increased autonomy and eventual independence. (When no fundamental change in British rule was forthcoming after 1918, the sense of betrayal fueled the growing independence movement, and there was no rallying to the British cause in World War II.)[12]

Censorship prevented the press in England from publicizing the valor of the troops from India, so Mundy believed that fiction could best relate their exploits to English and American readers. He turned away from the "oriental" flavor and plots of German-led espionage within India of *The Winds of the World* and *King— of the Khyber Rifles*. The idealized, chivalrous Sikh Risaldar Major Ranjoor Singh of *The Winds of the World*, who returns in *Hira Singh*, is an overt manifestation of India's loyalty, exemplifying the pride of the Sikhs that makes them willing to fight alongside the English in a European war. The purpose of *Hira Singh* was established in the book's subtitle (often eliminated in reprints): "When India Came to Fight in Flanders."

Each of the eight chapters is a phase of the story, ending with a phrase looking forward to the next portion, yet with a reportage style reminiscent of a newspaperman's version. The war brings together men of many different faiths, whose prejudices do not change but who manage to work cooperatively. Of one Englishman, Hira Singh noted, "He understood wherein our Sikh prayer differs from that of Islam. Yet he refused to believe I am no polygamist. But that is nothing. Since then I have fought in a trench beside Englishmen who spoke of me as a savage; and I have seen wounded Germans writhe and scream because their officers had told them we Sikhs would eat them alive. Yes, sahib; not once, but many times."[13]

Hira Singh makes no effort to conceal the poor tactics and failures of British command, although saluting the bravery of the men involved; only the first battle is an unqualified success. Both of the white commanders of Outram's Own are quickly killed, Colonel Kirby and Captain Fellowes, leaving the Sikhs to rely entirely on themselves. The distrust and doubts sown about Ranjoor Singh's allegiance because of his undercover work recounted in *The Winds of the World* persist, since his unique knowledge of the German language makes him their negotiator. Two hundred and fifty-three of the Sikhs are captured when a charge into German territory carries them beyond reach of their Anglo allies, and they spend the spring and summer of 1915 in a German prison camp. They are sent to Turkey for their propaganda value, the Sikhs meanwhile planning to return to the Allied side if they can get close enough to the battlefield at Gallipoli.

Ranjoor Singh's plan for a return across Asia to India is so daunting and apparently impossible that he dare not even mention it to his men before their escape. As the Sikhs cross the ravaged Turkish countryside, Mundy depicts the land, barren of animals or relics of farming. Turkish atrocities are graphically depicted, along with the temptation felt by some of the Sikhs to succumb to the war's dehumanizing effect. The Turks and Kurds, traditional enemies, rather than fighting on behalf of their ostensible German allies, have allied against the defenseless Armenians. When Ranjoor Singh's men see such sights as Armenian children skewered on Turkish lances, he turns their weary minds away from simply escaping to doing all they can to disrupt the Turks.

During the spring of 1916 the Sikhs conduct guerilla-style operations against the Turks, and are believed to be Kurds; in turn they tell the Kurds that they are the advance party of victorious Allied soldiers, inciting the Kurds they encounter to attack the Turks for plunder. The Sikhs pursue the unseen General Wassmuss, a German "Lawrence of Arabia" in Kurdistan, who directs the uprisings in the region. In the climax, Ranjoor Singh's men stop a German plan to set up a radio station in neutral Afghanistan to broadcast false propaganda of their victories on the Western front. Crossing over 3000 miles through Turkey, Persia, and Afghanistan with incredible heroism, resource, and endurance, Ranjoor Singh and the Sikhs remain disciplined, with ultimately 133 returning of the 800 who left India over two years earlier.

The sole European by whom the Indian's behavior is measured, both ethically and as fighting men, is that of the German Fritz Tugendheim. He places self-interest above loyalty to his fellow countrymen and is forced to comply with the Sikhs so thoroughly as to seal his prospective fate at the hands of his countrymen. His own best hope to avoid execution is to reach a British prison.

Hira Singh was originally serialized in four parts from October to December 1917 in *Adventure* as *Hira Singh's Tale*, a title retained for British book publication by Cassell & Co. the following June. The American edition from Bobbs-Merrill was delayed still further by wartime publishing conditions, and did not appear until September 1918, with the result that many journals in the United States did not review it until after the Armistice, when the novel's timeliness had been lost. For the American book edition, Mundy added a preface explaining the genesis of the novel. Elmer Davis (1890–1958), formerly of the *Adventure* staff, had sent Hoffman a small *New York Times* clipping from July 1915, suggesting he forward it to Mundy; the article related how a group of Indian troops escaped in Turkey and traveled across Asia to return to their home.[14] Despite the unlikelihood of finding more than other second-hand accounts, the book's preface claims Davis helped him track down the hero of the incidents, and the book was dedicated to Davis. (Although Davis and Mundy subsequently lost track of one another, their friendship resumed at the end of the 1920s when Mundy returned to New York, and it would then last until his death.) Mundy completed the framing of the American text with an explanatory opening set in a convalescent camp in India, written in a distinctly reportorial style; the British and *Adventure* versions had only included a closing with Hira Singh completing his story to an interviewer.

There are many authentic details: the landing at Marseilles; the Indians going into combat on their first full day at the front; trained cavalrymen thrust into a conflict where their primary skills as lancers and swordsmen had little value; the operations of Wassmuss; and Germans establishing wireless stations in the East to broadcast propaganda.[15] Nonetheless, there are clear textual indications that *Hira Singh* is fiction. Casting immediate doubt on the sense of realism created by the added introductory material is the fact that Mundy situates his own pre-existing character, Ranjoor Singh, in a role that would have been filled by an historical personage. *Hira Singh* begins at the very point where *The Winds of the World*, written two years earlier, left off, making *Hira Singh* a sequel. Mundy's novel also alters a number of significant facts as given in the *New York Times* clipping, which recounted how a hundred Indian troops had arrived in Kabul, after marching a mere four months from Constantinople. Captured in Flanders, they had been sent to Turkey in the hope they would join their fellow Mohammedans, but instead they had escaped. Mundy relates the saga of an entire squadron, but made up of Sikhs rather than Mohammedans—increasing the odds against them, as Mundy explained in his preface—whose journey took years rather than months. Indeed, the entire story in the *New York Times* may have been apocryphal; no other mentions of this feat has been found, and in reviewing Mundy's book, *The Times Literary Review* in London noted that the story of a detachment of troops engulfed in Flanders who reappeared at the Khyber was "among the many rumours that have been circulated during the war...."[16]

The ostensible basis in contemporary fact may have been a device to make palatable to publishers the exclusive concentration on a story about, and told by, Sikhs. Although written for British and American readers, the book, as more clearly expressed by the original title, *Hira Singh's Tale*, is remarkable for its complete adoption of the Indian viewpoint. In the framing introduction at the Sikh cantonment, the reporter indicates he briefly met Ranjoor Singh, who was on his way back to the front, and had directed him to get the story from Hira Singh, who has taken a bullet through the ankles and is hence available to recount the story. The journalist spent days with Hira Singh, sharing his lunch, and fetching him water, while listening to his story; "To have tried to tell the tale otherwise than in Hira Singh's own words would have been to varnish gold." Mundy retains the Indian narrator's voice, cadence, and grammar, with his penchant for Sikh aphorisms paralleling Mundy's own style. Nearly the whole book is told in this voice, resembling a verbal history, with the repetitions and digressions that are typical of speech, all of which does not make for smooth reading. (Even the synopses appearing before each installment in the serial publication in *Adventure* were written as if by Hira Singh.) At the same time, Mundy never veers into dialect, a trait that would become such an irritating aspect of many of his contemporaries writing colonial fiction.

Mundy was well aware of how distinctive *Hira Singh* was, in these ways as well as in others, as revealed in a letter sent to his publishers as the American reviews were coming in. "It is written on a subject that has not been touched by anybody else. It breaks all the rules for success: there isn't a woman in it; it is told from the first person singular by a colored man; it is told from a view-point not by any means the general public's."[17] The novel provides another demonstration of Mundy's ability to convincingly place himself in the mindset of another culture.

Two of Mundy's short stories for *Adventure* had also focused on issues of race and prejudice, most notably "The Damned Old Nigger," told entirely from the perspective of an African. The title is intentionally ironic because the hero is the superior in all respects of the Englishman who gives him the racist label. Although Mundy disdained "A Drop or Two of White," it explored the tripartite divide in the colonies between white, black, and mixed.[18]

The first years of the marriage between Talbot and Rosemary were happy ones, but soon there were growing strains. The Mundys and the Hoffmans were frequent guests of each other or took vacations together. Hoffman explained that Rosemary's "conduct and demeanor ... were such that we looked forward to their visits with dread and invited them to our home as little as was barely decent in view of our friendship for [Talbot], thus seeing far less of him than we wished."[19] Rosemary was invariably overbearing, insisting on dominating the conversation. "Her mind worked almost entirely without logic, sequence or order; she exercised no restraint in following its impulses and considered her smallest whim sufficient ground for making him and everyone else near her give up whatever they were interested in to listen to her." Talbot was unable to talk without being constantly interrupted by Rosemary, "disputed as to inconsequential details, having the conversation taken out of his mouth by her for endless and empty dissertations of her own, or having the topic of conversation completely changed by her." Others were amazed by the forbearance Mundy displayed, always treating Rosemary with patience, courtesy, and endless affection, his self-control containing any display of irritation.[20] Hoffman added that as soon as Talbot was away, Rosemary habitually complained about his actions to the wives of his friends, marring the couple's visits.[21]

Mary, Arthur Hoffman's wife, noticed that Rosemary, within a year of their marriage, "would leave all responsibility and practically all work to [Talbot] for every detail of their life, yet would interrupt his writing on the most trivial excuse." By 1918, Mary added, Rosemary demanded that Talbot wait on her "hand and foot" and "do all her thinking for her."[22] Arthur Hoffman added that, "my business for some twenty years having been to deal with writers and being a writer as well as editor myself, I know from experience of hundreds of cases that no writer can go through what [Talbot] went through without suffering from frayed nerves, constant interruptions and too many demands upon his time. That his work did suffer from such demand and interruptions I do know from personal observation...."[23]

Rosemary was jealous of his friendships with others, especially women — even her own sister, becoming indignant when Talbot permitted her sister to steer their launch on the lake instead of asking her to do it.[24] The sister was unmarried and a teacher in a Michigan college, and Talbot urged her to resign and live with them, although in fact the Mundys were not able to provide for her. Rosemary urged her to keep her position, but described Talbot's gallant gesture as that of "a very generous man, and was always trying to please and make others happy."[25] Hoffman said that "I know of no provocation or cause whatsoever that [Talbot] could have given [Rosemary] for even the slightest jealousy."[26] However, Rosemary called Talbot a "born flirt," an appellation he deeply resented although he may have deserved; in the words of his last wife, he was fond of "women, particularly if they were good looking and intelligent ... and the attraction was mutual."[27] Alice Chambers Mann, who was verging on her 20s when she knew Mundy distantly at Point Loma, studied Mundy's writings and was mildly smitten when they met, recalling him as handsome with a magnetic personality.[28]

Norway had an active Christian Science community, with a church, reading room, and guest speakers, and Talbot organized services and testimonials. Rosemary's rigid religious views were at the heart of much of their incompatibility, and religious disputes were frequent. Throughout their marriage, Talbot maintained he had never carried a point in an argument.[29] As he wrote, "There is one other matter I must raise, because it underlies the whole trouble ... I stand on the ground where I dare to claim my right to interpret Mrs. Eddy's writings and the Bible as the light is given to me individually, and will accept no second-hand instruction, if I can help it."[30]

Norway as a town and region had little impact on Talbot's writing; only his article, "Shooting Foxes," discussed fox-hunting and hounds in Maine. The oppressive insularity began to weigh on Rosemary, and soon it would tell on Talbot as well. Intellectual stimulus was minimal except in the small artistic colony of "characters," including most prominently Mundy himself, and Vivian Akers, along with his more traditional fellow author Pendexter. The Mundys moved several times around Norway, living in a cottage on Lake Pennesseewasee, then moving to town and renting some rooms. Talbot had a building remodeled as a studio for Rosemary, but she complained of the dearth of local subjects.[31] He bought her books on all types of art, including Japanese, and she did remain active as a painter; in late June, 1917, she visited Boston to exhibit her work.

She was often deeply depressed, and Talbot would later claim she frequently spoke of suicide, and once disappeared for several hours, causing him to fear she had carried out her threat.[32] As Mary Hoffman noticed, Rosemary wore down Talbot's affection, and his patience and gentlemanly consideration "given during the early years of their married life through real affection, became visibly a restraint he imposed on himself — a duty carried out."[33] Talbot came to realize that he and Rosemary were temperamentally incompatible, with neither having any peace of mind when they were together, and both doing their best work when they were apart. At the beginning of 1918, the Mundys began to live a portion of the year in New York, taking an apartment on Fifth Avenue that would quickly become their new permanent residence.

He had seldom used Africa as a setting outside of short stories of the Boer War, but he knew the continent even better than he did India. He wanted to paint an accurate portrait, as he had seen it, giving the stories the most autobiographical tone of any of his writing. They reflected the esteem in which he held the land, its culture, and its people, but also the frequently disillusionment of his experiences there. Delagoa Bay, Laurenço Marques and Chai-Chai, capital of Gazaland, along the Limpopo River, areas Mundy had travelled in, were the locales in "A Transaction in Diamonds," in the February 1911 issue of *The Scrap-Book*; the series "Oakes Respects an Adversary," "America Horns In," "Jackson Tactics," "Heinie Horns Into the Game," and "The End of the Bad Ship 'Bundesrath,'" in the December 3, 1918, January 1, 1919, February 18, 1919, March 18, 1919, and April 18, 1919 issues of *Adventure*, respectively; and *Solomon's Half-Way House*, a four-part serial in the Canadian biweekly *Maclean's* from August 15 to October 1, 1934. Although composed over a span of nearly a quarter century, all of these told essentially the same narrative, only sometimes changing character names.

"Oakes Respects an Adversary," "America Horns In," "Jackson Tactics," "Heinie Horns Into the Game," and "The End of the Bad Ship 'Bundesrath'" formed the beginning of the "Up-and-Down-the-Earth-Tales," eventually also comprising two long novels and another three novelettes. The saga moves gradually north through eastern Africa, the Portuguese, German, and British sectors; and finally skirts parts of Arabia, ending in Turkey. Set before World War I and written in the first person, these works comprise a saga centering on the fortune hunting of three characters.

Premier among these is Lord Montdidier (pronounced Mundidger, nicknamed Monty) and Earl of Kirkudbrightshire, a middle aged bachelor and unrepentant member of the English old order, quite well aware that he is one of a dying breed. He hopes to replenish the family treasury, expended over centuries as the family served the military, leaving his hereditary estates heavily mortgaged.

Slightly older is his lifelong friend, Frederick Joliett Oakes, another English bachelor of a similar build, weighing 240 pounds. Oakes is distinguished halfway through the opening series of stories by his sometimes irritating passion for the concertina, using it to accompany songs of his own devising composed on the spot. He is fluent in a dozen languages and full of humor. He explains his philosophy this way.

> A hunter hunts, a fisherman fishes, a ship's captain masters the elements. A true adventurer adventures, not specializing so much as embracing all occupations in the one.
> So, you see, I've been soldier, lawyer, hunter, fisherman — you'd be surprised how often a fisherman! — ship's captain on occasion — everlastingly at war with the elements and chance — and I've buried too many good and true men not to have a slice of parson in my make-up.... To me, adventure is life, and life is a succession of adventures. Monotony is death, and the only death.[34]

The narrator (presumably occupying Mundy's role for those stories based on his experiences) joins them, and by keeping him unnamed, this novice outsider doubles as the entry point for the reader into the adventurous existence. In his early 20s, the narrator at first is just a hired associate, hero-worshipping his older comrades, but becomes a full-fledged member after a deed of bravery on behalf of all.

William Simpson Yerkes, often called "America" by Oakes, is added to round out the group. No enthusiast for autocratic government, whether in the colonies or accompanied by nobility, Yerkes has to learn respect for Monty, who refuses to allow any questioning if he is to be the leader.

The four men cooperate harmoniously in their mutual effort to find the wealth all need but which Monty's estates most demand. They follow the classic pattern of Dumas's three musketeers, with the narrator as the initiate d'Artagnan. Monty, Oakes, and Yerkes bring together diverse levels of society in a social mix that dismisses differences of class and caste as each individual must prove himself worthy. Valorous and humane, fulfilling the obligations of duty and selflessness is as much their goal as the search for wealth. They adhere to a chivalric sense of honor, and a knightly apotheosis is ultimately achieved, especially by Monty, in the final book of the series, *The Eye of Zeitoon*.

The African portion of the saga reached its pinnacle in *The Ivory Trail*, originally titled *On the Trail of Tippoo Tib* in its six-part *Adventure* magazine serialization from May to July 1919. Mundy explained to Bobbs-Merrill that the new stories were reminiscent, an account that only he could tell. While always exciting and well written, the treasure hunt is a long, sprawling epic, hastily written in a frantic, successful "effort to subscribe for (and pay for) more Liberty Bonds than any mere author ought to be asked to take."[35]

Most of the characters are based on people Mundy knew, from international criminals to the drunken settler Brown of Lumbwa. The aging great hunter Frederick Courteney Selous appears under the name of F. Courtney, singled out for his gentleness.[36] He advises that Mount Elgon, with its unexplored caves, some inhabited by cannibals, are just the location Tib would have chosen to hide the ivory. Selous was probably a childhood hero of Mundy's, having also been at Rugby for two years nearly three decades earlier, and was already a legend by the time Mundy arrived in the continent. Unlike Selous, Mundy saw no need to hide the name of the loyal and courageous guide Kazimoto. The Greek, named Georges Coutlass in the novel, had in fact met a much less merciful death in German East Africa than Mundy provided in the book, and swore so profanely that Mundy had to cleanse his mouth at the request of Bobbs-Merrill.[37]

Possibly the beautiful, arrogant temptress and German agent, the treacherous Lady Isobel Saffren Waldon, is inspired by Inez Broom Craven. She is a sad but entirely selfish figure, exploiting others, even to having her Syrian maid appeal to Coutlass's rough affections.

At the conclusion of "The End of the Bad Ship 'Bundesrath,'" Monty, Oakes, Yerkes, and the narrator resolve to go after Tib's treasure. They travel to Mombasa, Nairobi, Kikuyu, Lumbwa, Lake Victoria, Muanza, Ukerewe, and Kisumu, before arriving at Mount Elgon — all places Mundy knew personally.

In Chapter 4, they meet Brown of Lumbwa, a settler who becomes a companion, a friend but never a member of the trio. His drinking is constant but he is also a man of courage; assisting him when his cattle are stolen becomes the catalyst for a long detour amidst the blight of German misrule of East Africa. Following the pattern of Mundy's wartime fiction, the book becomes as much a denunciation of Germany as an adventure in Africa. A court practicing "good, sound German law that knows no fear or favor, but governs all alike" becomes a mass of bloody beatings, men and women writhing under the whip.[38] As Brown explains, in the British courts the blacks are treated with leniency because they often do not understand the law, and both races can be condemned for a crime against the other; but in the German court only the African may be guilty, with a hanging preferred. The Germans seek to elicit local fear; Oakes and his friend's first sight of such "justice" is seeing the lashing of a black who begged for money after the commandant had made his daughter pregnant.[39] The Teutons turn the same cruelty on each other only as a psychotic game; one officer challenges a fellow German to see who can submit to the most lashes, and relishes the flogging and his victory.

Today *The Ivory Trail* is more than an entertaining adventure, serving as an autobiographical testament of colonial conditions on the continent at the turn of the century. For the first time, Mundy's anti-imperial sentiment becomes an important theme: the indigenous peoples derive nothing but suffering from their status, although Mundy does find British rule preferable to that of Germany, which seeks to conquer the continent as a stepping-stone toward the next European war.[40] There is questioning of the beneficence of any imperial offerings. Approaching Elgon, the narrator comments that "In every direction were villages, of folk who knew so little of white men that they paid no taxes yet and did no work—marrying and giving in marriage—fighting and running away—eating and drinking and watching their women cultivate the corn and beans and sweet potatoes—without as much as foreboding of the taxes, work for wages, missionaries, law and commerce soon to come."[41]

Some *Adventure* readers accused Mundy of propaganda. Fred Fleischer of the "Ask Adventure" staff took it upon himself to discover if Mundy's depiction of German practices in Africa was truthful or elaborated—and found them documented in German sources.[42] The magazine's readers who had also been in Africa wrote in to "The Camp-Fire" to attest to the truth of the background and conditions as Mundy presented them, and his presentation was praised by the *New York Times* as vivid, detailed, and entirely convincing.[43]

From the perspective of almost a century later, Mundy's own attitude toward the Africans was hardly free of racism, but was certainly enlightened and he unquestionably respected black humanity. Mundy clearly resented white supremacists, whether ignorant or evil, respectively, as shown in the characterizations of Brown and the brutal German imperialist Schillingschen—who tortures animals in the name of science. Mundy was also reflecting a convention of the empire adventure genre, dominated by the widespread perception of the uncivilized, unmapped "dark continent," while frequently portraying Arabs, Indians, and Asians in a better light.

The colorful descriptions of Africa and the land and animals are beautifully written. Abundant detail adds a further sense of authenticity, and the novel reflects the sweep and grandeur of the locales and people. Beyond the fictional aspects, these elements give the book a documentary flavor in describing Africa at the end of the 19th century, such as the wildlife entering Nairobi during the night in Chapter 5. In the verses and the book generally, Mundy recognized the need for wildlife conservation, and the most memorable are the songs of the game reserves, as in this excerpt from the prelude to chapter 6.

> But who can the paleface people be with red meat appetites
> Who ruled anew what Noah knew — that animals have rights?

Reviews of *The Ivory Trail* were many and favorable; the *Chicago Daily News* labeled it the best new book of the season.[44] Ironically, Constable, Mundy's English publishers, would hold back the book's appearance for over a year, and it was his last book that they handled.

The team of Monty and his friends moved their fortune hunting to the Red Sea, Egypt, and Syria, respectively, in *The Shriek of Dûm*, *Barabbas Island*, and *In Aleppo Bazaar*, which Mundy correctly regarded as no more than three ordinary potboilers. The final "Up-and–Down–the–Earth" book was nearly the length of these three novels combined, and echoed the eastern trans–Asian trek among vile Turks and Kurds of *Hira Singh*. Like *The Ivory Trail*, *The Eye of Zeitoon* was set prior to the conflict, it reflected ongoing Turkish oppression of Armenia. During April 1915, the Turks had ordered the deportation of the Armenian population to the deserts of Syria and Mesopotamia, resulting in the murder or starvation of up to 1.5 million. With the defeat of Turkey, the independent Republic of Armenia had been established in mid–1918, but only survived until late 1920, when it was annexed by the Soviet Army.

The Eye of Zeitoon grew out of an involvement with the Armenian relief movement when Mundy authored a May 1919 article for the *New York Times*, "America as Protector of Armenia," in favor of the United States accepting Armenia as a League of Nations mandate. He argued that England and France succeeded in colonial rule through ceding to Islam the religious and ethical realm; were they to try to create a Christian nation surrounded by Mohammedans, it would be considered a wedge that would start a religious war. By contrast, America was regarded as having no territorial intentions in the region, and was respected as having only entered World War I to safeguard democracy. Today, however, with the political immediacy past, *The Eye of Zeitoon* reads less for its social content than as a serious and durable historical curiosity among adventure novels.

The title character in *The Eye of Zeitoon*, Kagig, is a leader of his people and veritable "father" of his country, who watches out for their interests and is hence their "eye," in addition to being a colorful character in his own right. Zeitoon was, in fact, one of the regions where the 1915 Turkish attacks against the Armenians began, forcibly relocating them to non–Christian regions; in the book Mundy makes it a stronghold unconquered by the Turks, to which Kagig urges his fellow Armenians to flee and make their last stand.[45]

Abandoning fortune hunting to aid the weak and oppressed, Monty and his friends hire Kagig as their guide into Armenia, hoping foreign presence may deter bloodshed — while Kagig plans to use the four as potential hostages. The long journey overland to Armenia, the first two-thirds of *The Eye of Zeitoon*, is too long and unfocused, but the last third of the novel is intense, gripping, and memorable, recounting the arrival in Zeitoon and its defense. As a privy councillor, Monty hopes to secure attention for the Armenian cause, and discovers his forebear's castle in Zeitoon itself. Besieged inside by the advancing Turks, he flies the Montdidier arms, since there is no Armenian flag. It is a course of action that, should he survive, could mean trial in England, but Mundy compares Monty to Byron in Greece. Recognizing that he, like the castle, is an anachronism, Monty lays down his life in a noble and selfless sacrifice, willingly placing himself under Turkish gunfire and burning the ancestral fortress to win a victory. Monty is laid to rest in a nearby family crypt where the Montdidiers from crusader times were buried.

A group of adventurers can be broken up by death or marriage, and the foursome of the "Up-and-Down-the-Earth" experience both. Most memorable of the characters of *The Eye of Zeitoon* are the females; the Armenian women fight proudly beside their men, and regard it as a historical prerogative. Yerkes's weakness for, and appeal, to the "fair sex" has landed Monty and Oakes in some tricky situations, and in *The Eye of Zeitoon* he loses some of his innocent idealization of the opposite sex. Underlying the political conflict in the novel are two very different women. One is the intrepid American college girl, Gloria Vandermann, who eventually wins his heart. Similar to Grace Vandam of *Barabbas Island*, Gloria is as courageous as any of the men, refusing to be "rescued," proud of her wound gained in fighting, and as determined to aid the Armenian cause as her Western companions. One of the factors attracting her to Yerkes is his acceptance of gender equality. The other woman is young Maga Jhaere, lovely and wild. Near-savage in some ways, barefoot, wielding a knife and gun, she breaks horses, dances like a force of nature, and has a bloodthirsty streak. She is rabidly jealous of Yerkes and Gloria, but turns out to be Kagig's wife, an Armenian rather than a gypsy. Their relationship was kept secret so she could engage in espionage — one of the novel's least credible developments.

Mundy wrote *The Eye of Zeitoon* for both political and commercial reasons, not only because it was a cause he believed was just, but one he thought would attract a wide readership. He hoped to sell a hundred thousand copies, accepting "inside information" from the head of the Armenian National Committee that President Wilson and the congress were going to support aid to Armenia.[46] Nonetheless, in the novel, Yerkes recognizes that his nation is unlikely to come to Armenia's defense, or even to defend an American imperiled there.

The Eye of Zeitoon was serialized (as *The Eye of Zeitun*) in the magazine *Romance*, a Ridgway companion publication to *Adventure*, ostensibly to hasten publication but possibly also because of Hoffman's sensitivity to the propaganda charges aired in "The Camp-Fire" against the previous "Up-and-Down-the-Earth-Tales." (Mundy had actually expected the book would be serialized in the magazine *Asia*, mostly devoted to nonfiction, which would have provided a new, more serious audience, appropriate for this novel.) *The Eye of Zeitoon* was translated into Armenian for a Boston ethnic newspaper, *Hairenik*, and certainly had an impact within that community. However, despite Mundy's Armenian contacts promising sales of up to 25,000 copies of the book, in the first three months only 9,000 copies were sold after March 1920 publication by Bobbs-Merrill.[47] *The Eye of Zeitoon* was widely applauded for its message, but the timeliness of the novel was not entirely an advantage; it was turned down by a number of publishers in England (where *The Ivory Trail* had not yet appeared) "on the ground that it gave anyone the blues just to hear the word 'Armenia.'"[48] All of Mundy's personal charm was required during his stop in London in January 1920 when arrangements were made with Hutchinson. Published there in October, sales of *The Eye of Zeitoon* were dismal at first, but Hutchinson persevered and would henceforth handle all of Mundy's books in England.

By 1920, Talbot Mundy was a novelist with five books to his credit that had achieved critical recognition. He had a range of experience of the world, but only with further travel and encounters with new types of thought in the next few years would his background fully emerge with the important books to come. The war and its aftermath had caused him to take up topics that would divert him from discovering the central themes of his oeuvre.

IV

From Jerusalem to Jimgrim, 1919–1921

Several factors impelled Talbot Mundy to undertake the only one of his journeys on which complete and detailed documentation survives, through correspondence, personal diaries, and reminiscences from a variety of sources. He headed for the Middle East, the center of post-war chaos, and won the respect of participants on all sides. His subsequent writings about the region were widely read over the next fifteen years, portraying the rationale for Arab independence to tens of thousands of readers in the United States and England. The trip also transformed his personal life through a romance that would lead to a fourth marriage.

The Middle East was a part of the world of which he had only a tantalizing glimpse in his youth, having visited the Persian Gulf at least once on a tramp steamer nearly two decades earlier. The area's local traits interested him, and had figured in three magazine stories, "The Pillar of Light," "An Arabian Night," and "MacHassan Ah" (all of which he would choose to include in his 1939 anthology, *The Valiant View*).

In July 1919, Mundy sought the tranquility to finish *The Eye of Zeitoon* at the White Mountains Camp in Tamworth, New Hampshire, a Christian Science resort 100 miles southeast of Mundy's former home in Norway. There he briefly met an attractive widow, 33-year-old Sarah ("Sally") Teresa Leach Ames and her son, 14 year-old Richards ("Dick") Ames. Although they only knew each other for about ten days at the camp, Talbot and the Ames made a distinct impression on one another.

Sally was the youngest of seven sisters of an old New England family, and had been born on January 31, 1886, in Fairfield, Connecticut, and now lived in Boston. She was a few inches over five feet, with blue eyes and brown hair.[1] A month after turning 18, she had taken a trip to Arizona where she met Alonzo Garcelyn Ames, 15 years her senior and recovering from tuberculosis. After a whirlwind courtship, Alonzo and Sally married on June 29, 1904. Their only child, Richards, was born the next year, on May 30, and the family moved to New York in June 1906 where Ames worked as a businessman until his death in 1915.

Years later, Dick remembered that summer. "There were a few private 'cabins' (cottages) on the property. Mrs. U.G. [Ulysses Grant] McQueen had one and T.M. had another. Mother and Mrs. McQueen (Mrs. Mac) were friends, and that is where she met T.M. Rosemary Mundy, to my knowledge, had not been there, perhaps ever."[2] McQueen was, Dick said, "the sort of woman who was a doer and loved to organize."[3]

Another resident was William Denison McCrackan, known as "Billy Mac," and his wife. Professor McCrackan was educated at Yale and Heidelberg, and for nearly two decades was an officer of the Christian Science church or related organizations. For a time, McCrackan became an older, respected eminence in Mundy's life, in whom he recognized greater intellect and education. He also proved to be a man of considerably more rigid and less sophisticated political and religious beliefs than Mundy.

World War I had an almost religious impact on the Holy Land, seeming to mark the fulfillment of ancient predictions. Jerusalem was in Christian hands for the first time since the Crusades, after 700 years of Moslem rule. The material and spiritual needs of the city's inhabitants prompted McCrackan to feel a calling to go there. The coming winter was expected to be especially severe for the 70,000 inhabitants, and the price of food was skyrocketing; there was little local industry, and tourism would not resume until the League of Nations mandates restored a stable government.[4] Sally wanted to go also, as did Dick, although his age made it uncertain whether he would be permitted.

McCrackan offered their services to the British Military Administration, acting unofficially and paying their own expenses.[5] Special permits were still required for all travel in the region, and the only practical way for individuals to obtain visas so soon after World War I was to form what they called the Anglo-American Society of America, a branch of a London group of the same name founded by various nobles and notables.[6]

Mundy's prestige, and involvement with the American Committee for Armenian and Syrian Relief, impelled McQueen, McCrackan, and the Ames to convince him that he had an important role to play in their plans. Within days they met in New York, and Talbot was elected president of the Anglo-American Society, McCrackan as vice-president, Sally Ames as secretary, and even young Dick was an officer as well. (Shortly thereafter, Mrs. Fred Gatling of New York City and an individual named Dittemore joined the board, which was planned to eventually comprise ten people, divided evenly between men and women.) Having gathered some $10,000 worth of used clothing, McCrackan, McQueen, and the Ames departed on the *Caledonia*, a ship that had some two decades earlier twice carried Mundy to India. Talbot then returned to Tamworth, where he remained until September.

McCrackan, McQueen, and the Ames arrived in Jerusalem on September 7, 1919, and were cordially received, becoming members of the Joint Advisory Committee for Relief of Jerusalem, presided over by the mayor and military governor.[7] Sally suggested publishing the first English language daily (except Sundays and holidays) following the war; the idea of a regularly scheduled newspaper was a novelty.[8] Up-to-date information, even for Europeans and Americans, was incredibly rare. Within weeks of proposing the idea to British authorities, McCrackan began editing *Jerusalem News* on December 9, the anniversary of the allied takeover of the city. The one page paper, printed on both sides, was priced at one piastre, about five cents an issue, and distributed by a bookseller in the Jaffa Road.

Jerusalem News was to be an impartial newspaper, distinct from the irregular propaganda sheets from the various factions of conflicting races and religions.[9] However, others regarded this vaulted impartiality as one more form of propaganda, and they may not have been entirely wrong. McCrackan failed to realize his own bias, since he regarded the British authorities as misunderstood and unappreciated by Moslems, Jews, and indigenous Christians.[10] On numerous occasions, when deciding items to include in *Jerusalem News*, McCrackan consulted General Edmund Allenby's Occupied Enemy Territory Administration (O.E.T.A.), which governed the entire territory west of the Jordan River and up to Damascus, including Syria, Palestine, Egypt, and Mesopotamia.[11]

McCrackan arranged for *Jerusalem News* to be printed on the press of the Syrian Orphanage, founded by Germans and now run by the American Near East Commission. On the grounds was the half-empty Hornstein house, awaiting disposition, and McCrackan secured a lease. With a tower on one side, and a balcony on the second floor with a marvelous view, encompassing Mizpah, Ramallah, and the hills of Judea, the house was considered a wonder for having stoves, a cistern, and — especially — a bathroom.

Some of Sally's letters home were published as articles in various newspapers. Relief work was her primary activity, and she led one of the delegation's major achievements, the Jerusalem Laundry, providing employment for 40 of the city's destitute women, many of them war widows.

Talbot was uncertain of his own departure for Palestine, and he and Sally corresponded to keep each other up to date, quickly revealing a relaxed and confidential tone. After six months, Sally's letter of January 14th was headed "Jerusalem and waiting for you ... I'm mighty glad if my letters have been a comfort and help.... I would like to be having this trip with you and seeing all the wonderful things along the way again. I have a feeling we'll all go to India ... I never dared think we would see you in *six months* time, but here you are on the way.... You'll be the best kind of a Christmas present ever...."[12]

Mundy reveled in his position as president of the Anglo-American Society and used the title in writing letters to the editor reporting on the group's efforts in Palestine to the New York newspapers. Nonetheless, there was no assistance to be found as he strived to establish chapters in all 50 states.

On November 22, 1919, Mundy was invited aboard the royal yacht *Dolphin* for a reception for the Prince of Wales, then touring the United States. He was the last to speak to the Prince, telling him, "Your Royal Highness, on behalf of the Anglo-American Society it gives me great pleasure to congratulate you on the fact that the British occupy and administer jurisdiction in the city of which your ancestor, David, was King." In response, Mundy said, "the Prince of Wales smiled and said it was to him, too, 'gratifying, deeply gratifying.'"[13] Two years later, Mundy would write several letters to "The Camp-Fire" section of *Adventure* arguing that the ancestors of those now known as Anglo-Saxons were the descendants of the Ten Tribes of Israel. When the Babylonians took Jerusalem, the eldest surviving daughter of the line of David fled to existing colonies at Isaiah's "Islands of the Sea," landing in 583 B.C.[14]

Rosemary did not support Talbot's involvement in the Anglo-American Society, and was suspicious of the relationships among the members; Mrs. McQueen lived amicably apart from her husband. Arthur Hoffman's wife, Mary, had noticed how Rosemary attempted to set limitations around Talbot's action and ideas: "Being extremely self-centered, she left him no independence of expression or action while she was within reach of him."[15] Even as he had tried to adjust to her convictions over the years, she often disapproved when he associated with other Christian Scientists.[16] After one especially bitter argument, Talbot told her their marriage was "through." He would write to her that "When it comes to opinions, my own is as good as yours, or anyone's."[17]

Rosemary's father had lost all of his wife's money, except their home, and her mother had to teach school to support them and finally achieve financial security. Her father had tried to leave, but her mother, believing that marriage was a sacred bond, strove to hold the family together in a manner that made it difficult for Rosemary to break away from them. As a result, Rosemary was keenly susceptible to anxiety over Talbot's finances and believed she needed to maintain their marriage despite all adversity, just as her mother had done.

Talbot did not conceal Rosemary's opposition in his letters to Sally. She responded sympathetically, saying "Don't you ever feel my protecting thoughts go out to you? Don't you suppose I can guess at all the hell you have gone through for this Delegation."[18]

Talbot hoped that the separation of his trip would heal the marriage with Rosemary, and wanted her to meet him in Europe on his return trip, and made plans accordingly. On a trip to Indianapolis to arrange for the publication of his next book, he secured a $1350 advance from Bobbs-Merrill to cover immediate expenses on the promise to try to merge the three *Adventure* novels, *The Shriek of Dûm*, *Barabbas Island*, and *In Aleppo Bazaar*, into a single volume (although the task would stump him). Mundy received additional credit, and Bobbs-Merrill was to send Rosemary, who would be staying with friends, a check for $300 a month through May (when he planned to return). The advances were not unreasonable, considering that *The Ivory Trail* had already earned over $1600 in royalties.[19]

Mundy and Mrs. Gatling then each put up $5000 to send a printing press and enough paper to supply an eight-page daily for a year. He also bought an electric power and lighting plant, and the equipment it would need; two room-houses in sections to erect; and camping and other outdoor supplies.[20] He would also take seeds, groceries, kitchen devices, books to sell on England and Israel, and enough books donated by friendly publishers and a friend named Beauchamp to start a small lending library.

Together with Gatling, Mundy formed "New Earth News, Inc." with himself as vice-president and chairman of the executive committee, taking a dominant and expensive interest in establishing the firm. The purpose was to spread good news, combing the world for proof that life has become a little better today than it was the day before. By the time Mundy reached the Middle East, "New Earth News" had offices in New York, London, Rome, and Jerusalem to sell his own exclusive letters and those of other special correspondents to the newspapers, including the *Christian Science Monitor*. Initially, any profits were to go to Gatling as compensation for her financing, and she was to make publication arrangements with newspapers in Mundy's absence. With her lack of experience, the "New Earth News" was doomed to fail, and by December 1920 Mundy had acknowledged as much to Bobbs-Merrill.

Talbot departed on January 3, 1920, and one of his fellow passengers was Lord Dunsany, with whom he spent considerable time, later writing an article lauding his plays for *Jerusalem News*.[21] Talbot spent two weeks in London; he had not seen the city of his birth in over a decade, and was disappointed. A month later, he expressed pro–Labor government sentiments in an article on contemporary England he wrote for *Jerusalem News*. Mundy criticized those who disparaged the working man's ability to properly use his increased income and praised the quiet awakening he recognized in England, noting the studied carelessness of ceremony, increased social mobility, and a quickly-accepted falling of class barriers.[22]

Joining the local Anglo-American Society, and visiting his British agent, Curtis Brown, Mundy was invited to speak at some of the London Christian Science churches. He secured an introduction to Nancy Astor, who, like Talbot, had been reared as a devout Protestant. In 1914, after a severe illness, she began to seriously examine *Science and Health*, and soon became a believer. Talbot spent a day with Viscount and Lady Astor, and although religion may have brought them together, Talbot was most drawn to the politics represented by the couple. "Viscount Astor seems to be one of the finest "democrats," I have ever met — a perfectly splendid fellow, utterly different from Dunsany, who walks and talks and acts like a man in armor. Not that Dunsany isn't splendid, for he is all that. But Astor shows one what the aristocrat can become, and how he need not disappear. The world can be levelled upward."[23]

Talbot rendezvoused with another new member of the delegation, Miss Mary Virginia Blandy, a Southerner most recently from Boston who was a fellow Christian Scientist and was to teach a kindergarten in Jerusalem. As they proselytized on the final leg of the journey, Mundy had such luck as to prompt him to write Rosemary "that there is no room left for doubt as to *Who* sent me...." He did have some time for sightseeing, especially some of the areas reminiscent of the Roman empire and New Testament times.

> Never saw so many priests in one place in all my life.... But I never went near St. Peters, nor inside a single church — unless you count the catacombs that I found time to visit late this afternoon. There a shriven little Friar lied to me glibly about ancient history, and ended by giving me plenary absolution and total remission of all my sins forever, in return for a fraction less than fifty cents (U.S. money). I thanked him, and we parted on excellent terms. He could curtsey to an image of the Virgin better than any dancing master ever I saw. A nice little Friar he was, who believed most of the lies he told me.[24]

He spent a day in Alexandria, but found it lacking traces of Cleopatra. From Egypt he travelled by rail, crossed the Suez Canal, through towns like Ludd that were still dominated by military encampments from the war.

Talbot finally arrived in Jerusalem on February 5; the rain was coming down incessantly, and four days later three feet of snow blanketed the city.[25] By the time he and Blandy moved in, Hornstein house contained ten people, the six of the delegation, along with an Egyptian cook, a teen-age maid, and two other servants.[26] Blandy was to share a room with Sally, while Talbot was given a dark room that he compared to a dungeon, which had to be whitewashed to destroy the bugs and chicken lice.[27]

He was immediately put to work assisting with the daily publication of the *Jerusalem News*. The press room was dark and cold on those winter days, illuminated only by oil lamps as the last proofs were corrected.[28] Mundy immediately turned out a number of articles, most but not all of them signed. The paper eagerly announced his recent impressions of travelling through England and Italy, as well as a series of authentic animal stories of his experiences of hunting big game.

The hard work on the newspaper and the snow-bound weather had kept Talbot and Sally in close proximity. Only a week after he arrived, Talbot realized that he was in love. On February 13, he wrote her two letters in two envelopes, one inside of the other. The first letter indicated that the second included a check for $2000, to make certain that circumstance would never force Sally into an unwilling marriage, or leave her and Dick destitute. He asked her as a free woman to follow her intuition as to whether to open the second letter, indicating it contained a truth that she could now only partly guess.

Sally was also falling in love with Talbot, and opened the second envelope, not for the check (which she never cashed), but to learn of his feelings for her. He wrote to her of a vision that he had back in New York, which he had prayed over, knowing it was improper for a married man to carry emotions beyond friendship for another woman. The only answer, he felt, was that he must wait, and although he could not tell how it would happen or how long it would take, in the end it would be his privilege to make her happy. He also knew that she might regard his past mistakes as disqualifying him, and he indicated he would accept whatever course would make her happy, even if that meant marriage to someone else. However, whenever he would find himself free, he pledged to hasten to ask her to marry him.[29]

She accepted, and Talbot immediately wrote to Rosemary, asking for a divorce, basing his request primarily on their growing overall incompatibility.

> I know and appreciate how hard you have tried to live on terms with me. It is likely your task was impossible because of my own too obvious shortcomings. No doubt whatever I am to blame for not having spirit enough to face again that doctrine of fear that seems to possess you. It is too intangible, and too vast for me to overcome, at any rate at close quarters. I believe I am doing the best thing for you as well as for me in insisting on this step, for you will know where you stand at any rate. You seem never to have been able to believe in my fidelity, for you have always mistrusted me on every possible occasion, and on occasions, too, that no one else could have guessed were possible. I believe you will be actually happier knowing that the most has happened. I know that I am…. I want you to forgive me for all my faults and thousands of omissions, and to "loose me and let me go," as I do you.[30]

She should not have been surprised, since her criticism of his trip had continued in her intermittent letters to him. Yet he had also been unfailingly solicitous and loving in his correspondence during the month of his absence.

She adamantly resisted any divorce as they exchanged a long series of letters back and forth in February. His resolve was not only personal, but because of their religious incompatibility. He could no longer pretend to accept what she regarded as dogma. "Your brand of Christian Science has too sharp teeth to it, and that it makes any sort of partnership with you merely a long-drawn struggle to survive.... Freedom from that terrible mental espionage and criticism, extended for a few weeks, has done its work. It is difficult to catch again the bird that has flown free. In this case it is impossible."[31]

Both Talbot and Rosemary indicated they had prayed and quoted Mary Baker Eddy in their letters to support their respective positions. Rosemary refused to recognize the finality of Talbot's decision, seeing it as part of their ongoing evolution together. She insisted that she had changed during their time apart, and vowed that she had made many resolutions, among them "never to restrain your impulse, but just to love, love you knowing that God is taking care of you all the while.... This terrible blow and suffering surely have done their work, and I can never be just—the same. I *must* be better. I know I have made great mistakes, but I will never make the same mistakes again, and as you say *fear* was at the bottom of it.... I can't find today any resentment in my thoughts.[32] He expressed his continuing respect, indicating he expected her future would "likely be brighter and more useful than mine, although I shall not wander idly." He asked his lawyer to make the best financial arrangements possible and to give her all property free of debt, although he indicated he would not pay Rosemary alimony into the indefinite future.[33]

When the weather improved, Talbot began to see some of Jerusalem and found it to be "a city of frauds, faith, fanaticism, and sudden death."

> All ancient history beckons.... To right and left roofed passages, and darkness lit at intervals by feeble lamp-rays. Here and there the shadow of a Sikh on guard, silent, all observing, mindful of his duty—and eleven rupees monthly, less deductions for his family in India. Greeks, Jews, Arabs, Levantines, brush by you, fitting less awkwardly by dark into the ancient molds. Then coffee-shops, where men in red tarboosh talk politics by candle-light, and spies listen. Snatches of song in Arabic. Melancholy 'cello music, by a Jew from Chicago or somewhere. Explosive bursts of quarrelling. Silence.
>
> Narrower and narrower the street grows, until in places you can touch the walls with either hand. Through key-hole arches you can peer down dark courts and passage-ways, where mystery reigns. A door opens; a man in Arab robes steps out; stands for a moment as if conscious of the picture; disappears.[34]

Sites and legend quickly grew into ideas for stories. For instance, the Dome of the Rock, where Abraham is supposed to have offered up Isaac, includes a cavern underneath where David, Solomon, Elijah, and Mohammed are said to have prayed. The cavern floor sounds hollow, but digging in search of ancient treasure or holy documents is forbidden because Moslems believe that beneath the Dome is a hole reaching directly to the center of the Earth, through which the souls of the dead emerge once a week.[35] The next year, in *Under the Dome of the Rock*, Mundy's second Middle East story, German and Arab plotters tunnel under the dome in an attempt to dynamite it and blame it on Zionists, to ignite a religious conflagration.

Sally and Talbot at the Damascus Gate, Jerusalem, on Sunday, March 21, 1920. (Courtesy Richards Ames Collection)

Jews were a minority, outnumbered by both Christians and Moslems; although tolerated, further Jewish immigration to the Holy Land under the terms of the Balfour Declaration was widely opposed locally.[36] In order to settle in Palestine, Jews needed the support of the British government, a presence that, in turn, blocked Arab independence.[37] Talbot was not a Zionist, nor were Sally and Dick, views that were typical of British and Americans at the time.[38] Mundy was free from prejudice, as demonstrated in two early stories, "Payable to Bearer" and "The Gentility of Ikey Blumendall," although, like many of his contemporaries of English birth, he had a consciousness of Jewish identity that allowed him to occasionally indulge in stereotyped remarks.

During the preceding fall, the Society had rapidly became part of the British social scene in Jerusalem, and the officers, many of them scarcely in their twenties but already aged by their wartime experiences, appreciated the company of Dick's young and unattached mother. As Dick recalled, upon Allenby's taking of Palestine, everything owned by Czechoslovakians, Hungarians, Austrians, Turks, Germans— their homes, offices, and business, "with their breakfasts on the table"— had been closed with His Majesty's seal. "That had never been inventoried, the chap who was public custodian of enemy property, of which this was all a part, felt an accounting should be made. So he appointed me his deputy, at the age of 14, gave me two Tommies, enlisted men, to help, whenever there was any heavy lifting to be done."[39]

In mid–March, McCrackan left for Cairo, and in his absence, Mundy took the editor's place on *Jerusalem News*, and wrote Bobbs-Merrill that "at present it doesn't quite pay its way," but he had hopes the paper would develop into something bigger.[40]

The only salaried employees were the four typesetters, one of whom knew a bit of English. The press was run by a gasoline engine that habitually began to sputter when printing was about to begin in the afternoons.[41]

As Talbot explained to the head of Bobbs-Merrill, "I've got pretty well carte blanche from the administration (personal to me) to go where I like, see what I like, and write what I jolly well please."[42] The confidence in Mundy was probably based on his British origins, and turned out to be misplaced. Any reader of his recent work would have noticed the increasing tendency toward anti-imperialism; perhaps authorities were simply relieved that Mundy did not have any strong feelings on Zionism. This was to be expected of an adventure writer; questions of faith were secondary to the interest in an indigenous movement for freedom from foreign rule, in this case that of the Arabs.

Mundy became intensely interested in events to the north. Feisul had been declared King in Syria after Arab forces took Damascus near the end of World War I, in accord with his understanding of promises in exchange for Arab military help. He had been willing to allow a single temporary mandate, but France and England were both eager for permanent territorial acquisition. The unusually severe winter snowfall in the region had cut off all communication between Damascus and the West at the end of the month, and during this isolation Feisul capitulated to nationalist pressure to be proclaimed King of an independent Syria, to include Palestine.[43] A day later, in Jerusalem, a demonstration in support was held on March 8; the British were alarmed and such public gatherings were banned.[44]

With exciting events happening on a daily basis, Mundy was eager to visit Damascus. On March 12, he departed Jerusalem via train by way of Haifa, a roundabout route but the only one available given the rail lines of the time. Mundy intended to sell reports of his trip to the *New York Times* (instead, they hired another analyst, more experienced in Arab affairs), and planned his own reportorial "coup," an interview with Feisul. During this initial trip, Mundy made preparations for a meeting with Feisul, and after his return, Mundy was summoned on March 20 for an appointment with Allenby, and received a permit to travel to Damascus again. Mundy later wrote of having been "in Damascus while Feisul was playing that losing hand," and his impressions would be fictionalized a year later in his novel, *The King in Check*.[45] He described the interview with Feisul as a meeting with "the most gallant leader of his race since Saladin," the only man who could unite the Arabs.

> When he came he took your breath away.... He was both [dignified and stately], yet he wasn't either. And he didn't look like a priest, although if ever integrity and righteousness shone from a man, with their effect heightened by the severely simple Arab robes, I swear that man was he.... Rather tall and thin ... with a slight stoop forward from the shoulders due to thoughtfulness and camel-riding and a genuine intention not to hold his head too high, he looked like a shepherd in a Bible picture, only with good humour added, that brought him forward out of a world of dreams on to the same plane with you, face to face — understanding meeting understanding — man to man.[46]

Mundy said, "I heard the whole story from his own lips of the Arab share in the great war, of the Allies' promises, and of how they had been broken after the armistice, when Arab friendship didn't look quite as necessary as it did when the promises were given. We talked for hours, but he never once complained on his own account. He is an Arab patriot first and last, with no other aim than to see his nation self-determined and ruled by a government of their own choosing."[47]

In addition to talking with Feisul, Mundy spoke with a number of his associates, but noted with concern the number of treacherous men in Feisul's camp, a fact the leader was already cognizant of; their conspiracies would form some of the basis of *The King in Check*. Mundy secured written proof of the friendship and trust of Feisul that would prompt the editor of *Adventure* to note that "under Feisul's personal letter [Mundy] went safely into parts of Arabia where no English letter could or would have protected him."[48]

By April 4, Feisul's position was crumbling due to the refusal of France and England to recognize his kingdom, combined with the dissension of some within the Arab community.[49] Feisul accepted the ultimatum of a French mandate and demobilized, but the French army continued to advance, and by the end of July, had attacked and taken Damascus.[50] Arab forces were routed, and Feisul and his cabinet escaped into British territory. Hoping to ease resistance to its own rule, in May 1921, England sponsored Feisul as king of the country recently renamed Iraq (the former Mesopotamia), in a government granted independence in 1932.

On March 11, Talbot and Sally attended their first dance together. By the end of the month, their commitment was made more tangible as he shared and co-authored the entries in her diary and scrapbook. Throughout their time in Jerusalem, Sally and Dick Ames did much sightseeing, and after his arrival Talbot increasingly joined them. They visited the sea of Galilee, Mizpah, Hebron, Jericho, Bethlehem, the Garden of Gethsemane, and other areas reminiscent of the Bible and ancient Rome. On April 2, they received an invitation from the Grand Mufti to witness the procession of the feast of Nebi Musa, in which Moslems march to the reputed burial place of Moses near the Dead Sea. They left on Saturday, April 4th, travelling by gharri, until arriving at the Governorate, where they were cordially received for Sally's sake by Captains Champion, Bailey, Crossley, and Pavey. The next morning, Easter Sunday, they breakfasted at the Governorate, and Champion provided the threesome with a police escort to Abraham's Tomb, and were more overwhelmed by the genuine feeling of history than any of the holy places seen so far.

Although Easter began peacefully, it was known as the season for rioting, with the risk of collisions between the various processions celebrating Moussa, Passover, and Easter.[51] With political demonstrations banned, religious celebrations now became an avenue for protest.[52] On Easter morning, the crowds attracted by the ceremonies of the feast wanted to show solidarity with Feisul and became inflamed by anti–Zionist orations. In the morning of April 6, with Jerusalem full of British soldiers, Arabs tried to enter through the Damascus gate but were fired upon, and some houses were burned.[53] During dinner, Talbot, Sally, and Dick learned of what occurred, but Champion and Bailey had known since morning, and this was a reason one or the other of them had quietly accompanied the Mundy-Ames party.

Fresh reports came in, and soon a telephone call prompted the officers to discuss setting up a machine-gun should the local rioters attempt to storm the

At the Hebron Governorate, Easter Sunday, April 4, 1920, Captains Pavey and Bailey, Sally dressed in full Arab regalia, Mundy, and Dick Ames. (Courtesy Richards Ames Collection)

Governorate, which soon happened. Talbot wrote of the events that followed in the journal. "About half-way through dinner a mob came up-street in pitch darkness, chanting Arab seditious-patriotic stuff, and growing in numbers as it ran. Champion and Bailey went out to meet it, came back ostentatiously to light cigarettes, and then strolled out, smiling and casual, to face the mob. Crossley went to the telephone. Never saw anything finer than the way the thing was handled."[54]

After a day of wild rumors in Jerusalem, the rioting resumed. After retaliations by an armed Jewish group, the Moslem police took sides with their coreligionists, and the entire responsibility was given over to the military. Indian troops under British officers disarmed the police and kept the casualties to only two dozen with one killed. The worst features of the rioting, according to the *Jerusalem News* report of April 7, were "two cases of rape of Jewish women, and the wounding of some Jewish children," both the type of action apt "to lose for the Arabs all public sympathy whatever for their case."[55]

Meanwhile, after a final lunch at the Governate, Talbot and the Ames left Hebron in the afternoon under Bailey's instructions. He gave Talbot a loaded pistol "and advised me to use it at the least excuse, but nothing happened until we reached Jerusalem and the bayonet of a British sentry thrust into the carriage from the shadow of the city wall took a button off my waistcoat."[56] Back in Jerusalem, they were held up seven times before arriving home, where they learned that Blandy saw the beginning of the riots "but was none the worse for it. An altogether enjoyable trip, and about the most interesting yet," as Talbot summed it up.[57]

Talbot, Sally, and Dick found a city where machine guns commanded all strategic points, a squadron of airplanes was in the air, and roads were blocked. At the end of three days, nine had died, divided almost evenly between Moslems and Jews. Mundy was one of the few given permission to report on the events, and on April 6 he had been issued a pass to enter and leave the city at any time by the Military Governor.

Events continued to move at a rapid pace, and Mundy had the opportunity to assist in preventing the eruption of trouble on another front. On the morning of April 8th, the Military Governor of Jerusalem and its district, Colonel Ronald Storrs, asked Mundy into the Governorate. Storrs was essentially a diplomat, eager to keep in contact with all sides, although as a result he was trusted by no faction.[58] First, Storrs wanted him to write an article in the *Jerusalem News* pointing out the difficulty in increasing the military presence in the city without causing further friction. Second, he desired that Mundy, as an American, would visit the Grand Mufti. The Mufti intensely admired America, and as an Englishman who had become a citizen of the United States, Talbot Mundy was in a unique position. The Mufti had previously visited the Society's delegation in an amicable manner.[59] Moreover, the Mufti was impressed with the "sayings" in Mundy's books, and their apparent insight into his faith caused him to innocently ask Talbot where he had studied the inner teachings of Al-Islam.[60]

The Mufti had been appointed to his position after his father's death in 1908; the position had been held continuously for over two hundred years by members of a family that traced its lineage back to the time of the Prophet Mohammed. The office was primarily an honorary one that advised the local Governor on Moslem law and could be called upon to settle disputes. Cultivating the art of getting along with whomever was in power in order to maintain the family prestige, the Mufti had cooperated with the Turks, and was now on such good personal and political terms with British that they added the term Grand to his title.

During the riots two British officers had made the mistake of forcibly searching the Mufti's home. In addition, on April 9, five men in British uniform, thought by some to be Zionists in disguise, had approached the Mufti's house and fired at his son.[61] The Mufti was incensed, and Storrs hoped that Mundy might "say what I could to pour oil on the very troubled waters."[62]

Late that same afternoon, Sally and Talbot called on the Grand Mufti and were immediately received, although they had to wait a half hour for Mahmoud Husseini, the translator, to arrive. Talbot recounted the episode in his journal.

> I told the Mufti we were there to express our profound sympathy for him in his difficult position. He asked just what we meant by that. I answered that certain Government officials had told me of the terrible indignity that had been put upon him, and that it had come to my knowledge how unintentional the affront had been; that orders given out at a critical moment had been misinterpreted by an overworked, and possibly too enthusiastic junior who knew little or nothing of the true circumstances, and that knowledge of what had happened reached the Military Governor too late for him to make the instant apology that might otherwise have sufficed to remedy the mistake. I added that while I had no connection of any kind with the British Government, I hoped that as Americans we might be permitted to

express to him our independent view of the situation, in the hope that our friendly offices might encourage him toward taking a statesmanlike attitude. I added that I felt perfectly sure that he is a great enough man not to permit any feeling of personal resentment to govern his actions, but the predicament called for more than that. The British officials had, in my opinion, made a terrible mistake while acting from the highest sense of public duty. They — the British — were in the difficult position of trying to serve and protect all impartially, but of being blamed by everyone for everything that went wrong. What is needed, therefore, is not more recrimination, not another brand added to the fire, but the quality of forgiveness. The Mufti listened very patiently all this while, saying hardly a word, but thinking and nodding. I went on to the point that the great men of the world are those who could forgive most. If he had much to forgive, then that was his great opportunity. That while other men might talk, he could prove himself to be the servant of God by forgiving instead of harboring offense. That forgiveness, at this crisis, would accomplish more than armies. That he who forgives has God on his side. That as the head of the Moslems it was his opportunity to set an example of magnanimity that would take effect far and wide.

The Mufti answered by thanking us for having come to talk with him, and for our friendly offices. The Moslem religion, he said, inculcates forgiveness of one's enemies. It is well known, he added, that if a man should commit a murder, the victim being a Moslem, and the offender should go to the family of the victim and ask pardon, that pardon would be granted. He went on to say that although he had lost his father and several relatives and many friends through sufferings caused by the war, and had experienced more than the usual share of trouble, he had never been so stricken down and crushed by all the rest together as by this affront, not only to a family that has always stood first in the land, but also to the whole Moslem community. He excused himself for being human. As a human being he could not in a moment overcome the nervous condition of grief and depression in which we found him. But, he added, he so far recognized the truth of our message to him that he would, and does forgive the offenders entirely. The interview was brought to a close by expressions of gratitude on our part to him for having so graciously received us, and a very gentle response from him. The whole interview lasted about three hours, including interruptions.[63]

For once, Talbot had undertaken and accomplished a mission worthy of one of his own heroes.

In June, Sally and Talbot visited Cairo and the Great Pyramid, while Dick stayed behind in Palestine, packing for the return trip home. McCrackan had written to Sally in May that he was grateful for the way they took on the burden of the *Jerusalem News*; "The paper looks well and we are grateful...."[64] However, with McCrackan's return to Jerusalem in June, some of the tensions resurfaced that were bound to occur with two leaders of the group, Mundy as president of the Anglo-American Society, and McCrackan as vice-president of the Society and head of the delegation. To Talbot, McCrackan demanded and hogged "all the privileges and freedom on earth." McQueen seemed to be jealous of Sally, believing that "she had too easy a life."[65]

Jerusalem News had already ceased publication, the last issue appearing on June 8th, six months to the day after it began, in recognition of the transition from a military to a civil administration. McCrackan believed that the delegation had been strictly for war relief, and he and McQueen were eager to return home. Talbot, Sally,

Sally and Talbot strolling through the Garden of Gethsemane, May 1920. (Courtesy Richards Ames Collection)

Dick, and Virginia Blandy disagreed that their work had been rendered abruptly superfluous. The discord grew into a horrendous clash of wills on both a political and deeply personal level that made it impossible to continue.[66] Talbot seemed to regret much of his efforts and actions, and wrote Rosemary on June 26th that "This foolish 'delegation' thing with its silly little newspaper went to pieces several days ago, and the delegation members are returning home by different routes—at least one of them disillusioned."[67] Blandy decided to remain in Jerusalem until the laundry was turned over to a local relief committee, and a stone seat was placed on David's Tower to commemorate the Society's work.[68]

The divisions were shown in McCrackan's book, *The New Palestine*, published in 1922. Much of it was composed of articles written for other periodicals as well as the news reports of *Jerusalem News*, and he chose not to mention the Anglo-American Society, and the involvement of Mundy or the Ames. Blandy rates merely the briefest notice, and only McQueen is given significant attention. An introduction to the volume by Lord Bryce reflected its support of England's League of Nations mandate over the area; McCrackan believed in England's supposed manifest destiny to develop the "backward races" of the world.[69] McCrackan continued to travel, dying suddenly of heart disease in New York on June 2, 1923.[70]

An equally pronounced divergence only became public in 1995, when the activities of Talbot's brother Harold were revealed with the posthumous publication of his memoir, *Agents of Empire*.[71] He became a significant backer of the growing Zionist movement, both politically and as a cause which could serve the plans for British colonial dominion. Harold perceived the Arab revolt against Ottoman rule as a negligible contribution to the Allied military victory in World War I, and disparaged the Arabs as a people and their cause: he was with the British delegation at the Versailles Peace conference.

At the beginning of August, Sally and Dick had begun travelling back to New York. Sally visited her sister, Fanny (Mrs. Harry Stevens), on a farm in North Platte, Nebraska, while Dick enrolled in Blackstone Military Academy in Virginia. Meanwhile, on May 7, Mundy had asked Bobbs-Merrill to discontinue payments to Rosemary. By June, Talbot's letters to Rosemary had taken on a new tone, and he acknowledged that he had wronged her. Talbot met Rosemary upon his return from Egypt aboard the *S.S. Patria* into Newport, Rhode Island, September 23. The reunion was a short one, however, and after a single night and a day, Rosemary left for New York. He visited her there for a couple of days, before leaving for the last time.

Talbot moved into "The Willows," a boarding-house on Huguenot Avenue in Staten Island, the first of many ocean front areas where he would live. The location was idyllic, with close proximity to Manhattan for necessary trips into town to call on publishers. Otherwise, the Huguenot Park area was quiet and felt far removed from the metropolis, with a heavily wooded region stretching for miles inland. Talbot had a room which gave him a beautiful view straight out to sea, with "the waves on the beach ... playing obbligato to the frogs," all framed by willow trees.[72] The beach was a mere hundred feet away, looking out toward the Atlantic with the New Jersey shoreline bareline visible to the South.

During these many months, he had written to Sally almost every day, and received responses nearly as often. His love was unselfish; he urged her to come visit whenever she chose, and not to tailor her life to his. Sally visited, and she, Dick, and Talbot spent the Christmas holidays together. Talbot was now sending Dick $2 or $10 with every letter for pocket money, and Dick already regarded him as a virtual stepfather.

The Willows, Staten Island, where Mundy boarded while writing the Jimgrim Arabian stories, and where Sally and Dick Ames later joined him, still stands today. (Photograph by author)

Sally had been helpful in Talbot's business matters and had penned several letters for him to Bobbs-Merrill, where she was introduced as his secretary. Although he never discussed Sally with the Hoffmans, he was pleased to be able to tell her that after their meeting they immediately liked her and were not in the least surprised at his desire to marry her.

After a lonely winter and spring, in mid–April Sally moved into another of the rooms at "The Willows." They planned a summer job for Dick, investing so he could set up a business catching lobsters in the bay to sell to the local hotels, which paid far better wages than the hourly jobs. However, when Talbot bought a 28 foot motor boat in July, named the *P.H.M.* for *Poor Honest Man*, Dick found its lure impossible to resist. Talbot was not in the least annoyed at the appropriation of his boat or the fruitless investment he had made in a dory and lobster traps.

Tormented over how to proceed with Rosemary, Talbot even withdrew his request for a divorce in January 1921. However, he also indicated that he did this because it was his interpretation of the Golden Rule, so he probably hoped she, in turn, would give him his freedom. By summer, Talbot was firmly telling Rosemary that there would be no reunion, and to send all letters care of his lawyer. He sent her a check for $400, but otherwise during the following two years she would maintain herself on a small bequest she received upon the death of her mother.[73]

Mundy on Staten Island, 1921, while writing the Jimgrim Arabian stories. (Courtesy Richards Ames Collection)

Meanwhile, business circumstances had been unfavorable immediately upon Mundy's return to America. There were many notes of outstanding debts to be met on a nearly monthly basis to a variety of individuals and organizations from whom he had borrowed money to make the trip.

Mundy had been urging Bobbs-Merrill to publish a book of eight to ten of his short stories, with new poems between. However, volumes of short stories were always hostage to a variable marketplace that swung back and forth between indifference and approbation, and such books seldom were given much promotional effort by the publisher. Finally, to hasten a new Mundy book on the market in the long interim between *The Eye of Zeitoon* and *Guns of the Gods*, Bobbs-Merrill produced a short Mundy anthology, appropriately entitled *Told in the East*. While well reviewed in the United States, British publishers rejected the book because of the poor sales of *The Eye of Zeitoon*—which in turn discouraged publication of other books of Mundy short stories. *Told in the East* barely earned the author $450 in royalties.[74] The inclusion of *Hookum Hai!* and "For the Salt Which He Had Eaten" in *Told in the East* were understandable, since they were generic stories of India of the type that secured Mundy's fame, but combining them with the light-hearted "Machassan Ah" seems a strange decision, unless a change in tone was desired. A far wiser choice would have been "The Soul of a Regiment," the one story that alone might well have substantially increased the sales of *Told in the East*. Although Hoffman had often saluted the phenomenal popularity and reputation of "The Soul of a Regiment," and the way it was sought and treasured by countless readers, Mundy's book publisher failed to understand the success and potential of this tale.

With no more advances from Bobbs-Merrill forthcoming, the need for quick cash forced Mundy to return to writing pulp stories for *Adventure*, rather than books. Fortunately, *Adventure* was preparing to increase publication from two to three issues a month in October 1921, and new contributions from Mundy were welcome. Despite all the personal turmoil and change in Talbot's life, he wrote busily, and for nearly a year made ends meet by living from one *Adventure* check to another.

Instead of being serialized, these brief, fast-paced novels would appear in their entirety, comprising just under a third of that particular issue, in the manner of *The Shriek of Dûm*, *Barabbas Island*, and *In Aleppo Bazaar*. Dick recalled, "T. was very faithful, turning out a 50,000 word novelette for Arthur Hoffman every 23 days."[75] Mundy wrote at a pace of some ten pages a day, with little time for revision, often turning in the work to *Adventure* within days of its completion, starting the next one a day or two later.[76]

Probably because Mundy had a ready market for such output, he did not write a factual book on his travels in Palestine, as did McCrackan. He only authored one brief article, "Oh, Jerusalem!," in the April 1921 issue of *Delineator*, which was later rewritten and expanded as "Jerusalem" for the February 1923 issue of *The Theosophical Path*. Nonetheless, the background of his time in the Middle East was drawn upon to create an entirely new cycle in his fiction.

The series would eventually comprise eleven stories of the Middle East, chronicling the exploits of a new hero, James Schuyler Grim, known as "Jimgrim:" *The Adventure at El-Kerak*, *Under the Dome of the Rock* (combined in book form as

Jimgrim and Allah's Peace), *The "Iblis" at Ludd, The Seventeen Thieves of El-Kalil, The Lion of Petra, The Woman Ayisha, The Lost Trooper, The King in Check, A Secret Society, Moses and Mrs. Aintree,* and *Khufu's Real Tomb* (published in hardcover as *The Mystery of Khufu's Tomb*). In apparent reference to the Lawrence of Arabia myth, Mundy notes that the ability to lose oneself in another culture is not rare. What is truly exceptional is the ability to function equally well in one's own culture as well as another, and this is Grim's gift, to move back and forth with ease between his identities. His transformation is instantaneous: "Grim doesn't have to pretend to be an Arab; he is one as soon as he puts the costume on — thinks, speaks, looks, and acts as if he had been born somewhere east of the Red Sea, with the only difference that he knows more than all the Arabs put together about the white man's view of things. It won't be until a few millions of us on both sides get that gift of Grim's, and learn to see both sides at once, that East and West will ever really meet."[77]

Mundy asserted that Grim was a real person, and provided him with a pedigree: he is an American, proud of his citizenship, who has been recruited by British army intelligence to be an independent secret agent because of his knowledge of Arab life. He had twice made the pilgrimage to Mecca, "on one occasion overland, and once by train."[78] "Decorated by five governments and trusted, as a rule, by all of them," he was probably the first American to be commissioned in the British Army without pretending to be a Canadian; he fought behind Lawrence, and is now on "special duty."[79] Mundy asserted that all the stories about Grim were founded on fact, and that in exchange for information that he could fictionalize, he was under oath not to reveal Grim's real identity.[80]

Although Mundy explicitly disavows Lawrence as *the* prototype of Grim in the stories, Thomas Edward Lawrence was an archetypal figure so central to the time that he unavoidably influenced Mundy. During the fall of 1919, Lowell Thomas had begun to publicize Lawrence in a series of illustrated London lectures, generating myths of his wartime deeds, many of them wrongly attributed. Lawrence was widely talked about during the time Mundy was in the Middle East, and although Dick Ames believed that the two men had met, probably such an encounter never took place, because Lawrence was in England at the time.[81] Feisul himself had impressed upon Mundy the importance of Lawrence to the cause, as the man who, Mundy wrote, "had proved himself capable of bridging the division between East and West and making possible the dream of Arab independence."[82]

Mundy used the public fascination with Lawrence and the legends already growing up around his deeds to provide a variation on the myth with a separate characterization, sufficiently similar to benefit from Lawrence's popularity, but different enough so that he would not seem to be merely following in his wake. The success of the Jimgrim stories reflected the public thirst for a continuation of such deeds in the changing Arab world, "where every colonial disturbance" was credited to Lawrence, who had meanwhile disappeared from public view.[83] Moreover, the stories were received in the context of this phenomenon; as Mundy was writing, Lawrence re-emerged, becoming an important advisor and diplomat when Winston Churchill took over the Colonial office. In the 1930s, *Jimgrim and Allah's Peace* was published in book form with both the American and British dust jacket illustrations

The American dust jacket for *Jimgrim and Allah's Peace* in the mid–1930s recognizes its relation to the Lawrence of Arabia legend.

evoking images of Lawrence. The inside flap for the American edition went so far as to announce that "If T.E. Lawrence of Arabia had chosen to continue as a British officer in the Near East, he would have been involved in this kind of adventure."

Whatever the actual derivation of Grim, he was also likely a composite. He may be Mundy's conception of an Americanized Lawrence, and the added strengths such a figure would have had, without the problems created by Lawrence's British nationality. Since Mundy claimed that the model for Grim had twice made the pilgrimage to Mecca, he may have been conceiving of a modern-day Sir Richard Burton, whose

Mecca and Medina he described at the time as "awfully good reading, and perfectly priceless as far as I'm concerned."[84] Over the next decade, Grim evolved toward political and philosophical dimensions that likely far outdistanced any original person, following a trajectory similar to H. Rider Haggard's Allan Quartermain, who became steadily more involved in paranormal experiences.

The Jimgrim stories begin as straightforward adventures in turbulent post-war Palestine. In the traditional colonial pattern, Grim discovers outlaw plots and alone or with a small command prevents rebellions from gaining momentum. Rather than adopting his point of view, Grim is presented externally, through Ramsden, a "heavy siege-gun of a man," and a tower of moral and physical strength.[85] The name, Jeff, was surely taken from the redhaired reporter, Jeff Hanley, who took Mundy in after his arrival in America and encouraged him to start writing.

Ramsden becomes a steady companion, not only assisting Grim but also providing balance as a more humane, unpretentious man. He is a surrogate for the reader, a fellow initiate to whom Grim's talents and surroundings are surprising at first. Ramsden is, in effect, the Dr. Watson to the cerebral, wily Sherlock Holmesian nature of Grim. Since Ramsden is a man of ordinary intellect, Mundy's use of him eliminates the philosophical interjections or asides that are possible when Mundy writes in the third person. All of the teaching must come through what is described or explained by other characters, and as a result the stories often seem less literary, although more accessible to general readers.

Each Jimgrim story was complete in itself, and followed by another tale that was less than a true sequel because the original premise expanded while recycling characters and introducing new ones along with gradually changing settings. Grim acquires a larger group of companions—including Ramsden, Narayan Singh, Jeremy Ross, Meldrum Strange, Athelstan King, and Chullunder Ghose—some of whom, like Ramsden, Strange, King, or Ghose, had been, or would become, lead characters in stories of their own.

Feisty Jeremy Ross is an amusing characterization who supplies needed humor in *The Lost Trooper*, *The King in Check*, *A Secret Society*, and *The Mystery of Khufu's Tomb*. A juggler, trickster, and amateur magician, he is as adept as Grim in adopting Arab disguise but is less serious of purpose.

Under the Dome of the Rock introduces one of Mundy's most marvelous characters, Narayan Singh, who was to become a regular companion of Grim on all his remaining adventures, until his death in *The Devil's Guard*. A fierce warrior and magnificent swordsman, supposedly he was based on a friend of Mundy's, probably one of the Sikhs utilized by the British, because of their religion, as impartial policemen in Jerusalem. Unlike the loyal Sikhs of *The Winds of the World* and *Hira Singh*, this new character is deeply subversive of the loyalties they upheld. Mundy once quoted a letter to *Adventure* readers from Singh's prototype, saying he "'prays daily that full madness may descend on all the politicians, so that their inflictions and abominations may increase to the point where men rebel at last, and act like men, and slay the devils.' Narayan Singh rather believes in slaying as an antidote for most things.... He thinks more of the notches on his saber than of the medals. A truculent, incredulous, amazing man, of peculiar tact at times, and of cast-iron friendship always."[86]

The participation of women is minimal. In *The Lion of Petra*, *The Woman Ayisha*, and *The Lost Trooper*, the wily Ayisha, harkening back to the Yasmini prototype, hopes to ensnare Grim, but is instead married to the Arab chieftain Ali Higg. The passionless Grim remains single for the same reason that Sherlock Holmes did, because his intellect sets him apart from ordinary men. As well, as Grim's character trajectory becomes increasingly occupied with spiritual powers, a love interest would have distracted from the high calling that required leaving earthly desires behind.

The fellowship among members of Grim's band is never simply that of sidekicks, military-style comrades, or "soldiers of fortune." There is none of the inevitable sense of elitism that infused some of the relationship with Monty in the "Up-and-Down-the-Earth-Tales." Grim's band proceed on a basis of equality, mutual respect and friendship that span differences of intellect, race, nationality, religion, wealth, and background. While serving initially under the British flag, Ramsden is independent from the outset, and by the conclusion they are all freely working for Feisul and the Arab cause. They are never seeking simply wealth; on one occasion in which they have it, in *The Lost Trooper*, it is turned over to help Feisul, and in the other, *The Mystery of Khufu's Tomb*, it is placed into a special fund.

While acceptable fictional types, enjoyable as characters, the primary purpose of Grim's followers is to serve as representatives of different aspects of the entire modern colonial system. The group was a significant expansion from the "Up-and-Down-the-Earth-Tales," which had been geared toward the pre–World War I era and composed of three Englishmen and one American, and led by the nobleman Monty. Mundy would not repeat the mistake of using four characters who were outwardly similar. The new group is representative of the post-war and post-colonial world, with all vestiges of the class system gone. Symbolizing the new dominance of the United States in world power is the leadership of an American, Grim. He manifests the importance of the Anglo-American alliance, and the fact that the United States has become the dominant partner in the English-speaking world. He also makes clear that the destiny of the United States lies, not in a permanent partnership with the colonial policies of Europe, but with movements for national independence. Ramsden embodies the raw strength, vitality, and natural wealth of the United States. Grim's group were also more international than those in the "Up-and-Down-the-Earth-Tales," including not only Ross, a member of the dominion, but also many Arabs and Indians. Some *Adventure* readers accused the magazine and Mundy of anti– or pro–British propaganda, so the implications for global politics were recognized by contemporary readers.[87]

Grim made his debut in *The Adventure at El-Kerak*, which appeared in the November 10, 1921, issue of *Adventure*. The next installment was issued exactly one month later, and was entitled *Under the Dome of the Rock*. When these were collected in hardcover over a dozen years later as *Jimgrim and Allah's Peace*, the 1933 British edition used the original magazine version, while the partly rewritten version published in the United States in 1936 muted the pro–Arab sentiment. *Under the Dome of the Rock* is one of the best of the early works, with the characters and setting fresh. The quality remains high in the following story, *The "Iblis" at Ludd*, which appeared in the January 10, 1922 issue of *Adventure* (and was only published posthumously in book form, together with *The Seventeen Thieves of El-Kalil*, as *Jimgrim and the Devil at Ludd* [1999]).

The next three stories, published monthly in *Adventure* from February 20, 1922, form an outlaw cycle, beginning a slight but noticeable downturn in quality. The first of these is the shortest and weakest, and appeared in book form only in England (in 1935) during Mundy's lifetime. The title characters in *The Seventeen Thieves of El-Kalil* are the colorful bandit Ali Baba and his band of sixteen equally lawless sons, operating in the area better known today as Hebron. The story is written with an amusingly self-conscious recognition of its Arabian Nights antecedents

The Lion of Petra and *The Woman Ayisha*, first appearing in the March 20 and April 20, 1922 issues of *Adventure*, saw wider book distribution a decade later, but were unfortunately not bound together although they form companion pieces. *The Lion of Petra* was published in book form in England in 1932, and in the United States the next year. *The Woman Ayisha* was published in book form in England in 1930 but was issued the next year in the United States bound together with a story of India, *The Hundred Days*, related only by also featuring Grim and Ramsden. *The Lion of Petra* and *The Woman Ayisha* were of interest because of the lively characterization of the chieftain Ali Higg, the title character of *The Lion of Petra*. Higg has taken advantage of local political confusion to become a power in Jordan, and Grim goes after him by gathering his own group of cutthroats. Higg's position is complicated by a love affair with the tempestuous Ayisha, opposed by his wife, Jael Higg, whose intellect he relies upon. (At this time, Talbot and Sally had adopted two much loved but fly-bitten airdales named Jael 1st and Jael 2nd.) In the next installment, *The Woman Ayisha*, Grim keeps the peace between two rival chieftains, Ali Higg, the Lion of Petra and Ben Saoud the Avenger, of Abu-Lissan, by arranging for Ben Saoud to marry Ayisha, who had been divorced by Ali Higg. The title character in *The Lost Trooper* (published in the May 30 issue of *Adventure*, and only in book form in England, in 1931) is Jeremy Ross, who in his desert wanderings found a gold mine. He cedes control to Feisul, described as an Arab "George Washington."

Far superior to these last few novels was the climax of Grim's Palestine adventures, *The King in Check*, published in the July 10, 1922 issue of *Adventure*. The novel was widely reprinted in book form in England at the time of Feisul's death in 1933, and the next year in Canada and the United States. While the edition published in the United States presents one literal conception of the title, a chessboard, on its dust jacket, the British edition was far more faithful, showing an idealized portrait of the Arab leader.

The magazine series had drawn the reader into the web of the adventure before revealing that it led not to supporting imperialism, as in most such colonial tales, but Arab independence. Mundy had initially muted his own political viewpoint, although glimpses were apparent from the outset, for Grim believed that the British betrayed the Arabs after World War I.[88] After a few stories, he rejects England, whom he had always served in his own manner anyway. "I'm dead set against outside interference. If I could have my way, there'd be no meddling in foreign lands. Each to his own affairs is my creed."[89] Hoffman wrote in "The Camp-Fire" in response to accusations of a pro–British bias in a way that indicated Feisul's cause found a welcome home with *Adventure* and its readers. "Throughout the series *Grim*'s main aim and that of his comrades is to put Feisul at the head of an independent Arabia. A perfectly American idea. To *Grim*, and to Mr. Mundy, England's control there should be only temporary, a step on the way to independence. Nor does Mr. Mundy fail to state the fact that England as well as France rankly broke its war-time pledge to Feisul...."[90]

The King in Check was the most explicitly political novel of the series, indicating how Mundy merged fact, his own experiences, and tales he doubtless heard. The book describes a stroke of intrigue moving from Ludd to Haifa to Damascus, as Grim, assisted by Narayan Singh, Ramsden, and Ross, save Feisul from conspiracies in Syria. He emerges in the last three chapters of *The King in Check* as a character, lifting the book into the realm of the historical novel rather than genre fiction. Grim finds that Feisul is ready to be a martyr; he becomes the catalyst to save the Arab leader during the battle, as Mundy reveals the means of Feisul's escape to vindicate his reputation.

Mundy refused to say how much of the story was true, but noted that the description of Feisul was drawn from their meeting in Damascus, an incident he recounted in a letter to *Adventure* readers that was quoted again in advertisements when the novel was later published in book form.[91] Mundy said that Feisul had given him permission to use him as a character in a story. He praised Feisul: "He is like good wine that needs no bush; you can't say enough in his praise, or overdraw the man's impressive manliness, any more than you can overstate the meanness of the method used to get rid of him."[92]

Mundy shifted from interaction with desert tribal leaders and the struggle for independence to take Grim to a new area, Egypt. Mundy had experienced it as a land of almost as much unrest as Palestine, and rife with riots, conspiracies, and assassination plots, full of chicanery, where only "graft and privacy" are sacred.[93] The populace supported self-determination, and believed the United States would oppose England's sovereignty.[94]

With *A Secret Society* in the August 10, 1922 issue of *Adventure* (never published in book form), Grim and Narayan Singh leave the British military, since service in it is no longer commensurate with their aims. They form the firm of Grim, Ramsden, and Ross, a group of altruistic mercenaries. A new character is added, Meldrum Strange, an American billionaire who looks like General Grant. He offers to subsidize Grim, Ramsden, and Ross, and when they are convinced of his beneficent intentions, they decide to join with him. He further rounds out the group by introducing the new economic class of multinational finance.

The first stage in the cycle concluded with *Khufu's Real Tomb* in the October 10, 1922 issue of *Adventure*, which was republished in 1933 in England and in 1935 in the United States as the book, *The Mystery of Khufu's Tomb*. (An inexplicable note was added with the copyright notation for the hardcover version: "This novel appeared in less than three issues of a magazine under the title *Khufu's Real Tomb*.") The imaginative high point of the Middle Eastern adventures, it was written and first published before the Egypt-mania that greeted the discovery of the tomb of Tutankhamen at the end of 1922, and afterward the novel was not published in book form because Bobbs-Merrill believed the market was saturated with Egyptian stories.[95]

The Great Pyramid had made a profound impression on Mundy, and as he wrote many years later in a letter to Wincenty Lutoslawski, he had been able to visit in a unique way. "I once spent a night, alone, in the so-called King's Chamber of the Great Pyramid. The experience was indescribable. It left me so convinced that that chamber—in fact the entire pyramid—was built as a Place of Initiation that the contrary would have to be demonstrated before I would believe otherwise. I have no proof. But I know. Or I believe I know."[96] Mundy wrote that, unlike the other pyramids, the Great Pyramid was never meant as a tomb, but is the most scientific building in the world. "The more you study what is known of the Mysteries of the ancient Egyptian priests, the more it appears possible that the Great Pyramid was a symposium of their knowledge, stated, as it were, in code with the idea of preventing any but initiates from understanding, yet at the same time of preserving the secrets for all ages to come."[97] He was influenced by *A Miracle in Stone*, by Joseph A. Seiss, D.D., and recounts an old legend recalled from his Baedeker's *Guide Book of Egypt*. Herodotus, who arrived a thousand years after the death of Khufu, heard reports that an underground passage connected the Nile with a great tank underneath the pyramid. Although the pyramid's altitude compared with that of the Nile made this demonstrably false, the second part of what Herodotus reported might have been true: Khufu was buried in an unknown spot away from the pyramid, in a place surrounded by water and connected by a tunnel to the Nile.

Mundy begins the story with an amusing chapter titled "Which Is a Kind of Preface," providing a revisionist history of Khufu, Egypt, and the tombs of the Pharaohs. This humorous disquisition reveals that Pharaoh's motives' were readily understandable in the most modern terms, and dismisses the views of such contemporary historians as Flinders Petrie that the national discipline required for such an endeavor would have been beneficial for Egypt. His satirical opening distinguishes *The Mystery of Khufu's Tomb* from its rivals, such as the Egyptian stories of Sax Rohmer, which generally keynoted action from the outset. Khufu, Mundy notes, must have been the richest Pharaoh in history to have paid for the Great Pyramid's construction.

> [Khufu] was a calm, proud, confident-appearing man, with an obvious sense of his own importance and a smile that seemed to say: "Carry on, boys, What's good for me is good for you." Being city-folk, he had them all in one place where they had got to listen. Spell-binders laid the argument on thick in one direction; in the other the overseers laid on the lash; and the minstrels, who were the equivalent of the daily Press in those days, praised all concerned.
>
> But right here I'm going to be called in question by the Egyptologists unless I hasten to explain. It will be said with a certain amount of surface truth that the Egyptians who laboured at building the Pyramid were peasants on vacation. Work ceased to the fields when the Nile had overflowed, and they were kept out of mischief by thoughtful superiors, who provided wholesome amusement with educational value that incidentally promoted trade. When the Nile receded at the end of three months, those who had survived the education were permitted to return home and go to work in the fields again, in order to raise crops, with which to pay the taxes, that should keep the ball a-rolling and Jack-Pharaoh's pyramid a-building again next season. That is what the text-book writers will assert....

Sally and Talbot at the Great Pyramid of Gizeh in June 1920. (Courtesy Richards Ames Collection)

The peasantry — the real Egyptians, that is, who lived on Main Street and paid taxes or were whipped — were no more impressed by that theory than they are by the Sermon on the Mount to-day. The had a more pragmatic, Nile-mud point of view. They wondered, just as they do to-day if anyone propounds a theory to them, whether there is money in it. It was obvious to them that there was. There was their money in it. Every Pharaoh, and every high official who got buried, had as much of the tax-money as he could scrape out of the treasury buried with him for his use in the next world. The dwellers on main street, preferring this world to the next, and having toiled in the sun for twelve hours a day to earn that money, did some good, plain, Nile-mud thinking; and the result was what you might expect.

It can't have been long before the insurance companies, if there were any, who underwrote burglary risks on mausoleums went out of business. It got so that a Pharaoh's mummy was hardly set stiff before the boys were out with pickaxes to break the door down and get the treasure out of the vault. It was no use putting a guard before the door, because you can always bribe the guard in Egypt, anyhow, and the guard, being peasants in uniform, would be quite as anxious to get their share of the loot as anybody else. No doubt a few got caught and hanged, or flayed alive, or whatever was considered suitable for that offence in those days, but the number of kings' and noblemen's tombs that were not broken open and robbed was zero, and that was all about it. The cash went into circulation again.

So succeeding kings and noblemen took thought.... It was decided that secrecy would solve the problem.... Undertakers' helpers came cheap, so they were all killed and shipped along with Pharaoh to be useful to him in the next world. The mausoleum was underground, out of sight, in an unfrequented spot, and the sand was tidily arranged on top to look as if nothing but the desert wind had every ruffled it. The living nobility breathed again.

But all they had accomplished was to add a sporting zest to what had hitherto been humdrum certainty. The boys had to go prospecting now, and there's no doubt whatever they found the loot, getting away with it all the more profitably because there were no expensive imported guards to be bribed....

Things had reached the point where Pharaoh and his friends didn't know what the rising generation was coming to, when who should ascend the throne but Khufu, otherwise known as Cheops. He went through the usual process of removing his predecessor's signature from all the public monuments in order to call attention to his own omnipotence, and then proceeded to entertain a distinguished stranger....

"Suppose I show you a real idea," he suggested. "If I draft out a plan by which nobody will ever find your real tomb, Khufu, will you give me the contract for the job?"

The plans were produced, and they were marvelous. No doubt there was a cost-plus-basis contract attached with red tape and sealing-wax. Pharaoh signed that, and for thirty years the laborers—the tax-payers that is—of Egypt toiled at the building of what they were told was to be the largest and most magnificent tomb the world had ever seen.

Meanwhile, very secretly and quite a long way off, other workmen were digging the real tomb; and it was into the real one, when Khufu died, that his body and most of his treasure were smuggled, although the public funeral was held at the base of the Great Pyramid, while the population stood around and cursed the tyrant who had forced them to build such a mausoleum for his bones.[98]

By casting his descriptions of the pyramid's secrets in modern slang, Mundy effectively counterpoints the majesty of the subject as well as potential objections to his explanation of its secret. (The book is ostensibly narrated by Jeff Ramsden, although including passages in the words of Narayan Singh, effectively alternating the point of view.)

The Mystery of Khufu's Tomb begins in Nevada with the delightful Joan Angela Leich, daughter of a wealthy California rancher. She had bought an apparently worthless stretch of sand in Egypt and is now pressured to sell it at a substantial profit, by a group of suspicious buyers that includes Aintree and Zegloush. The pursuit of buried treasure in *The Mystery of Khufu's Tomb*, although treated differently than in *The Ivory Trail*, has many themes in common with the earlier book. To Grim, Khufu's treasure is a problem of colonial politics. If the British learn of the treasure, they will not grant independence to Egypt, and rebellion will break out; yet without the British, a civil war will erupt between those fighting to get the fortune.[99]

Grim and Joan Angela's men discover the underground tomb and treasure of the Pharaoh Cheops on her land, hidden in a cavern flooded by the Nile. A harrowing scene describes their first exploration in the walled tunnel connecting the underground burial site to the tunnel, through a passage where no men, or outside light, have been for thousands of years. On board a duck punt, with the noise of their motor echoing in the tunnel, they are surrounded by blind crocodiles, with scales grown over their eyes because of the darkness. The grate connecting the tunnel with the Nile admitted only the smallest fish, and keeps them from escaping once they have grown.

The Jimgrim stories achieved immediate success in *Adventure*; their readers' poll of 1921 stories rated *Under the Dome of the Rock* the second most popular complete novelette.[100] *Khufu's Real Tomb* and *The Lost Trooper* were the third and fourth, respectively, most popular complete *Adventure* novels of 1922, according to the readers' poll for that year (while another Mundy tale, not involving Grim, was the single most popular novel, *The Gray Mahatma*).[101] By fall 1922, Hoffman was telling Talbot that he was leading the list of the favorite writers for *Adventure*, as shown by reader's votes, by double the vote of the runner-up, Hugh Pendexter.[102] The stories gained even greater popularity when they were published in book form between 1930–35. Unfortunately, they appeared out of sequence, weakening the series from a literary viewpoint, since much of the characterization and political development was created cumulatively through a chronological narrative progression. Consequently, the flaws of the novels became all the more noticeable, and 1930s critics were harsh in their judgement, assuming the books to be among Mundy's recent work, not from nearly a decade earlier. By the time the original Tros of Samothrace *Adventure* series had achieved bestseller status as a single volume, most of the Jimgrim Arabian series had already been published as separate books, precluding the possibility of compiling them together a similar manner as Tros.

Ironically, despite the role of Bobbs-Merrill in financing Mundy's Palestine trip, the series for *Adventure* was only reprinted in book form after Mundy had switched to a new publisher in the 1930s. Bobbs-Merrill did not believe the 50,000 word length of the Grim novels for *Adventure* was sufficient for a book, and regarded the sales prospects of a two-in-one or three-in-one volume as dubious. They urged Mundy to take many of the ideas from his series and turn them into a single first-class novel in the spirit of *The Ivory Trail*. "I propose to make it a brand-new story, beginning in Jerusalem and ending up in Constantinople, with an incident or two in Cairo on the side, but to incorporate in it several whole pages—possibly even whole chapters— from the Jimgrim stories that appeared in *Adventure*. It will be a rather long book,— as long as *Ivory Trail*—otherwise I can't crowd the story in. There will be some poetry, in the form of alleged translations of imaginary Arab songs, and one or two songs by the Sikh, Narayan Singh, something after the fashion of the Vedic Hymns."[103] By April 1922, Bobbs-Merrill felt sufficiently confident to predict fall publication of *On Jimgrim's Beat* to Hutchinson.[104] However, the speed of turning out the material for *Adventure* robbed Mundy of the energy for a quality novel, and writing on two tracks proved impossible. Another part of the problem was that *On Jimgrim's Beat*, while built on the type of incidents that made the series popular in *Adventure*, had to appeal to a wider audience, with E.M. Hull's *The Sheik* in everyone's mind. "Jimgrim shall have a most delightful girl to get his goat and, finally, his hand and heart, and all that kind of thing. (I'll wager they won't stay married long, for all that.)"[105] (The union sounds similar to the unsuccessful one between Yasmini and King offered at the end of *King— of the Khyber Rifles*, with two strong-minded individuals and conflicting beliefs and loyalties.) As late as 1925, with Bobbs-Merrill pressing Mundy for a novel quickly, he would again propose boiling six of the novelettes into a 100,000 word book.[106]

In future years, Mundy only returned occasionally to Arabian settings, although the depictions were never the same. An offshoot of *The Mystery of Khufu's Tomb* and his Cleopatra series was a modern story of her tomb, the novelette *One Egyptian Night* in the May 1929 issue of *Everybody's combined with Romance*. Mundy wrote two more stories of the Red Sea, both of them evocative of his first stories set in the region, but disappointingly weak, "Red Sea Cargo" in 1933, and the posthumously published *Odds on the Prophet*. Renewed rioting in Jerusalem in 1936 inspired a new espionage tale of a female spy which appeared in two different versions, first as "The Princess," then re-written as "The Piping Days of Peace."

The impact of Mundy's Jerusalem trip was less in a specific long-term change — the early Arabian cycle of Jimgrim stories was relatively shortlived — than in commencing a process that would soon induce alterations in all aspects of his life. This mid-life adventure came at a time when Mundy was reaching his literary maturity and was best able to absorb the rich variety of new impressions that the Middle East made upon him. It was also this trip, and meeting Sally Ames, that would contribute to his decision to move west, which would in turn bring about his encounter with the Theosophical Society.

V

Journey West, 1921–1923

Leaving New York on October 7, 1921, Talbot Mundy began to travel westward through his adopted country for the first time. He loved the American energy and spirit he reported finding bubbling up everywhere.[1] Other motives also lay behind the journey: Mundy had become almost obsessed with the idea of making good in the movies, and he needed to secure a divorce from Rosemary in order to marry Sally.

Going to San Francisco, he met Sally for a side trip to the Grand Canyon, then settled in Reno in rooms at 64 Washington Street. Nevada permitted comparatively easy divorces, and the many individuals residing in the state specifically to meet the six-month residency requirement were a key part of the state's growing commerce. Local lawyers had a flourishing business, and during the 1920s a thousand divorces were typically granted annually.[2]

As fall turned into winter in Reno, Talbot quickly settled into a routine, writing nearly continuously, beginning in the morning, still in his nightshirt and dressing gown. He would resume again in the afternoon, finishing up the day reading by the stove, although sometimes he was up past midnight.[3] As he told Bobbs-Merrill, "I would work longer if I could stand up under the strain. But six hours on a story leaves me feeling like a flat tire."[4] Thanks to the wintry weather and the conservative nature of the town, there was little to distract him. "Reno is one of those places where they eat at 6 P.M. and get to bed as soon as the movies are out," as he noted in *The Mystery of Khufu's Tomb*.[5]

Writing 19 novel-length stories in the 28 months from 1921 through the end of 1923, Mundy largely recycled characters in various combinations, usually in association with James Schuyler Grim and his band. The reason was practical: turning out such a large series of novels in a short period, Mundy needed as many characters as possible, and had little time to develop new ones.

Simultaneously, Mundy also returned to settings in India. To provide a sense of continuity in the transfer of Grim, Ramsden, and Ross from Arabia, Athelstan King joined the group in *Caves of Terror*, *The Nine Unknown*, and *The Hundred Days*, with his final appearance opposite Cotswold Ommony in *Benefit of Doubt*. However, King is no longer such an insightful or convincing character as he had been in *King — of the Khyber Rifles*. Only in his initial return, *Caves of Terror*, is he the lead; in the subsequent stories, he is secondary, becoming essentially redundant. Whereas he is established in *Caves of Terror* as the logical character to penetrate the mysteries of Tibet, Mundy chose instead to make Grim the Eastern initiate, giving him many of King's characteristics. The reason was clear: King would always have the status of a former colonial official, linked with the Khyber Rifles, while Grim was a new, independent American hero.

Caves of Terror was a landmark in Mundy's career, fully revealing his incorporation of fantasy to facilitate the presentation of Eastern philosophy. Precisely what caused him to veer into this new mode is unknown; his discovery of theosophy was still more than a year in the future, and previous hints of the occult had only been a secondary theme, as in *King — of the Khyber Rifles* and *The Mystery of Khufu's Tomb*. Mundy had begun to read about the occult since his return from Jerusalem, and with his library in storage, he bought new books during his travels.[6] Although financial limitations precluded any more overseas travel, his curiosity was hardly satiated, and he also had intriguing correspondence. As he told William C. Bobbs, "I have several invitations to go to India and be shown things that the rest of the world hasn't seen, and would go and spend two years in India and China if I had my way; but the necessity of grinding out *Adventure* novelettes at the rate of one a month prevents at present."[7]

The shift represented a fundamental departure from Mundy's previous writing. Such works as "The Soul of a Regiment," *Rung Ho!*, *The Winds of the World*, *Hira Singh*, and *The Eye of Zeitoon* belong to the time before the disillusionment of World War I changed literary conceptions of heroism, military ethics, and colonialism. Adventure has a logic of limitations, whose situations no matter how unlikely still could be true. Fantasy is not its extension, but its antithesis. Adventure, taking place in the past or present, remains within the physically possible despite improbability or unlikelihood, while in fantasy the characters exceed human reach through access to supernatural forces. The violation of the bounds of physical reality are fantasy's motif and narrative highlight, as the larger-than-life hero undergoes mystical experiences. These range from the gods in the tradition of Homer and Greco-Roman mythology, to the genies and magic found in the Arabian Nights—making fantasy ideal for Mundy's new focus on occult forces in India and Tibet.

Caves of Terror originally appeared under the title *The Gray Mahatma* in the November 10, 1922 issue of *Adventure*. Despite deviating from the norm in *Adventure*, the story was readily accepted, readers voting it their favorite novel of the year, and such approval may have encouraged Mundy to continue in this vein.[8] The first publication in book form was a softcover by Doubleday in 1924, under the new and more dramatic title, *Caves of Terror*, a title retained for hardcover publication in England by Hutchinson in spring 1932. It was never otherwise published in the United States as a book until 2001.

While reuniting King and Yasmini for the only time after *King — of the Khyber Rifles*, *Caves of Terror* simultaneously links King with the recent Jimgrim novels by having Meldrum Strange send Jeff Ramsden to work with him. However, at the center is the figure represented by the original title, *The Grey Mahatma*. This is the first of Mundy's fantasies centered on a Westerner's quest for indigenous magic, and using a sage-like Indian priest. He is absolutely unsentimental about human life, but is also intensely human, wisdom not having robbed him of friendliness, "the common touch," or a sense of fun. A man of both East and West, he holds a Ph.D. from Johns Hopkins University, but found no man in the United States worthy of trusting with the rudiments of Indian science.

Caves of Terror offers Mundy's vision of the Inferno as the Grey Mahatma leads King and Ramsden through hellish caverns where the secret science of India is practiced. These become not only literal, but a series of Dante-esque steps into a phantasmagoric region, as the Mahatma reveals to King and Ramsden practices never before seen by Western eyes. They see the Indian religious philosophy in its totality, both its vast possibilities, and its pitfalls, leading to self-torture.

Caves of Terror becomes a fictional explication of Mundy's belief "that, while many of the native magicians are frauds and charlatans, some of them really possess 'occult' powers that truly come under the heading of magic — in the sense that science has not yet explained them or explained them away."[9] Superstition serves merely to protect the secrets, from both the uncomprehending eyes of the ignorant masses or the interference of colonial governments. There are limits even to the Mahatma's powers, and he has unwisely allowed Yasmini to learn of their sciences, an error for which the uncompromising Nine Unknown have condemned him to death. Nonetheless, his death, while agonizing, will serve a scientific purpose, because they need a subject of his wisdom to discover how much newly-mastered cosmic pressure can be withstood.

The Mahatma believes India and the entire East are emerging from the end of Kali-Yug, the age of darkness. For Yasmini this implies that India, rising from the shackles of colonialism, can use her secrets to harness the power of mob violence and subjugate the West. For Mundy, King, and the mystical Grey Mahatma, the close of Kali-Yug has a more positive meaning, Indian independence and freedom. King has been chosen to carry this message to the United States. The Mahatma unselfishly refuses to be saved by King and Ramsden, or by Yasmini for her own purposes, and together King and the Mahatma dash her plans for conquest.

Caves of Terror is one of Mundy's most unconventional works, both for its relative brevity (barely novel length) and the self-effacing manner in which it deals with profound questions. The tight structure is part of what makes it so perfectly formed and highly disciplined, with each chapter a movement in the drama. A multi-layered work, like an Edgar Allan Poe story, the surface emphasis on morbid thrills covers a deeper meditation on the mysteries of life. *Caves of Terror* is also unforgettable through its picturesque, highly visual, almost surrealistic style, and is one of Mundy's most unusual and extraordinary novels.

There was other evidence of his increasing absorption in esoteric beliefs. Mundy wrote the first of four long letters over the next year to "The Camp-Fire" column in *Adventure*, initially inspired by a letter from I.D. Langley about Mundy's theory of the location of the Ark of the Covenant in *Under the Dome of the Rock*.[10] Mundy argued that the ark was hidden for safe-keeping, and remains so, predicting it would one day be found near Mount Tara. Soon he was receiving many personal letters from *Adventure* readers, with others going to "The Camp-Fire," asking for more information or commenting on the subject.[11] He also endorsed esoteric theories on the lost tribes of Israel.

This thread would be amplified in the later debate on the purposes of the pyramid of Gizeh after the appearance of *The Mystery of Khufu's Tomb*. In response to a letter, Mundy indicated that he placed greater reliance on ancient over modern science, but had since been introduced to Fred J. Dick (Mundy only identified him as a member of the Institution of Civil Engineers, rather than, by that time, a fellow theosophist). Dick's essays on the Maya antiquities in Guatemala had convinced him the Great Pyramid was even older than previously guessed, far before Khufu's time.

> I think the men who built it were the keepers of the ancient Mysteries, whose science was all bound up with astronomy, of which they knew much more than we do. If I am right, then the so-called sarcophagus in the "King's Chamber" used to be filled with water for the final ceremony of the initiation. The aspirant, having completed his course of trials (which were tragically fierce), stepped into it, was immersed, and stepped out again "reborn."
>
> I think the Pyramid was closed up, and made as inaccessible as possible, at the time when the Mysteries fell on evil days and were no longer observable, perhaps because of invasion of the country, or because of royal jealousy, or for any of a thousand possible reasons.
>
> In all likelihood the hierophants intended to resume the celebration of the Mysteries at some future date, which, however, never came. The sacred nature of the building of itself would serve to prevent forcible intrusion until, in course of centuries, such legends as Herodotus set down accumulated and were accepted as fact.[12]

Mundy's beliefs, and his approach to religion and history in general, were transforming quickly.

On Christmas day, 1921, Talbot thought lovingly of how much he wished Sally were with him in Reno.[13] He even tried to give up his nearly lifelong smoking habit for her, although he ultimately failed. She was planning her second visit, and would be arriving in two weeks. Sally would help, as always, with his writing and correspondence. As Talbot told her,

> Somehow or other, when you are with me, although you don't do much of the actual story writing, the work gets done better and quicker.... When you're with me, I can talk things over with you, and they grow and grow in my mind. It isn't even that you actually make suggestions (although when you do they are always good ones) but my thoughts seem to marry yours, and to increase and multiply amazingly. I never seem to lose by telling you anything. When you tell things to some people they seem like wild beasts that take them away from you ravenously. You hand the thought back to me all improved and rounded out, although I daresay you are quite unconscious of the process.[14]

She also assisted organizing his finances, which were, as always, a problem. The novels for *Adventure* remained the basis of his income, bringing in about $2000 each, and he was only spending $200 a month.

Sales of Mundy books were slow. Talbot felt that part of the reason was that the existing promotion plans for his books were failing. As he related, there might also be other tacks to use in describing his books. Other publishers had invited him to their list, including Houghton Mifflin, and most recently Doubleday, who wanted Mundy to join their house and its magazine, *Short Stories* (to which he contributed in the 1930s). As they wrote,

> Your knowledge of the lands of which you write, and your unique handling of the subject matter places your books in another category; in our judgment your books should be treated seriously, not only as works of art and splendid fiction in themselves, but as a genuine contribution to knowledge.[15]

Mundy hoped to derive additional income from a popular edition of his novels, which might raise his value in the motion picture market.[16] Bobbs-Merrill first discussed the possibility in the fall of 1920, but not until early 1922 was the deal concluded. Finding that Grosset & Dunlap would not commit to a date for issuing the volumes, Bobbs-Merrill went to their primary competitor in such publications, A.L. Burt Company.

Burt was uncertain whether Mundy's books would sell well enough, but finally agreed to publish eight Mundy titles in two years, including six by June of 1923. 70,000 books were to be printed, earning Mundy an eight cent royalty on each, with half to be paid within four months, and the other half eight months from printing. The first six titles appeared in January of 1923, with new dust jackets that Bobbs-Merrill prepared. These were *Rung Ho!*, *King— of the Khyber Rifles*, *Hira Singh*, *The Winds of the World*, *The Ivory Trail*, and *The Eye of Zeitoon*. Later the same year, *Guns of the Gods* and Mundy's forthcoming movie tie-in book, *Her Reputation*, would round out the original eight, although Burt claimed to Bobbs-Merrill that the books were not selling well and no further printings had been made.[17] (*Told in the East* was not included.) In subsequent years, after the success of *Om— The Secret of Ahbor Valley*, Burt reprinted *The Nine Unknown*, *The Devil's Guard*, *Cock o' the North*, and *Black Light*, usually a year after their publication by Bobbs-Merrill. The arrangement was eventually carried over when Mundy's books began to be published through Century in 1931, continuing into 1936, shortly before Burt went out of business.

Burt was not the only publisher of reprints of Mundy's books in the mid 1920s. Ten of his books—all of those published through 1924 with the exception of *Her Reputation*—were published by McKinlay, Stone and Mackenzie in special bindings labeled "Masterpieces of Oriental Mystery." The publishing company was an affiliate of the Hearst journal, *Review of Reviews*, and the books had an extensive sale, primarily through mail order. The edition was capped with the unique publication of a version of *Om— The Secret of Ahbor Valley* featuring a frontispiece portrait of the author. Mundy received a one-and-a-quarter cent royalty from each of these volumes, but their value was also, like the Burt popular edition, in bringing his name before a wider book-buying public in the United States.

Similar efforts were underway in England. By early spring, 1922, Hutchinson was interested in building the sales of Mundy's works, and sought to issue his earlier titles in cheap form. By 1925, Hutchinson had published all of Mundy's novels to date, with the sole exception of *Rung Ho!*.[18]

Mundy and Dick Ames driving toward Reno from San Francisco, June 1922. (Courtesy Richards Ames Collection)

In the spring of 1922, having fulfilled the six-month Nevada residency requirement, Talbot moved a short distance across the state line to Truckee, California, where Sally was living. In July, "stewing at 6000 feet above sea level," Mundy made official to Bobbs-Merrill what he had been hinting at for months.[19] His new manuscript was a serial he had sold to *Adventure* entitled *The Nine Unknown*, from a story idea that went back to 1912.

He was uncertain of the quality of the new work. "I'm sending you this *Nine Unknown* as a make-shift, driven by shame to show you that I haven't forgotten my friends and my obligations to them. Hoffman didn't want a serial, but I crowded him and he agreed.... Quite likely you'll denounce the thing when you have read it. You may do that without offending me. I've done my best, but that doesn't mean you're bound to be done to. Use your most impartial eye when reading.... Maybe you'll be satisfied with *The Nine Unknown*. Lord knows. I like some parts of it."[20] After waiting nearly five full months, Bobbs-Merrill finally indicated their rejection, at least partly because of Mundy's ready acceptance, as well as the novel's lack of a romantic element.

Over a year later, however, after the five-part serialization of *The Nine Unknown* in *Adventure* during March and April of 1923, Bobbs-Merrill changed their mind. They finally published *The Nine Unknown* in book form in March of 1924, with Hutchinson bringing it out in England in June of the same year. Talbot's reservations about the story continued even then; he wished he had time to rewrite it all, and did the last few pages to provide a clearer ending. In an innovation, Bobbs-Merrill provided each chapter with a small illustration of a scene of India at its beginning. Their fears from a commercial perspective proved well-founded; the book initially sold poorly.

Unlike the Arabian adventure Bobbs-Merrill had expected, *The Nine Unknown* was a new story of India in the vein of *Caves of Terror*. Mundy wrote that, "*The Nine Unknown* reaches the fringe of a mystery, which I know to exist, but which many people seem to find it to their interest to say does not exist."[21] Although written before Mundy learned of theosophy, *The Nine Unknown* indicates his early belief in its precepts.

The number nine holds a special significance in Mundy's work, appearing not only in the book's title, but later as part of "The Nine Books of Noor Ali," sage-like quotations Mundy devised in *Full Moon*, written a dozen years later. Like the Grey Mahatma in *Caves of Terror*, King, Grim, and their companions also believe in these nine wise Masters, a secret society that has existed since the time of Atlantis, helping to better the destiny of mankind.

Just as *Caves of Terror* had turned Athelstan King from an empire adventurer to an investigator of the occult, so did *The Nine Unknown* transform Grim and Ramsden. Even such former skeptics as Ross are becoming intrigued by mysticism; he wants to learn the Indian rope trick. The international cast of characters had to change as well, as Grim moved thematically toward the occult, and geographically into the Far East. Joining Narayan Singh is a new Indian character, Chullunder Ghose, and a host of his fellow countrymen in support.

Disappearing gold is believed to be hoarded by the Nine to end Kali-Yug (here, darkness and capitalism), but later discovered to be used in alchemy as a virtual form of atomic energy, and in one scene to irradiate and cleanse the Ganges for its many pilgrims. Some of the hidden books of the Nine have been taken and could be used to create untold destruction in the wrong hands; there is a rival order, trying to acquire the knowledge of the true Nine to create wealth.

There are many faults with the structure of *The Nine Unknown*. Too much of the plot revolves around a repetitive and violent series of captures, escapes, and skirmishes, with little explanation of the more fantastic incidents.[22] The book contains a multitude of various incredible ideas, pulp-fashion, in search of a theme, one Mundy will shortly find in *Om*. The team of heroes, King, Grim, Ramsden, Ross, Ghose, and Narayan Singh, proves unwieldy from the outset; there is an excessive number of significant characters for the reader to follow.[23]

Many individuals, from Jacques Bergier to Mundy's stepson, Dick Ames, have valued *The Nine Unknown* as deeply meaningful and revelatory, full of esoteric insight and one of his finest efforts. In the words of Bergier, *The Nine Unknown* is a perfectly-written work. "All mysterious India appears in it, and the adventures of the personages provide quite admirable character studies as well."[24] However, this reader must confess that, despite four readings, *The Nine Unknown* remains the most shallow and least satisfying of Mundy's fantasies.

A finer literary achievement, but one which is far less unique in its content, paired Grim and King in a pure adventure. Initially titled *Mohammed's Tooth* when it first appeared in the December 10, 1923 issue of *Adventure*, it was later published in book form as *The Hundred Days*. Unlike *The Nine Unknown*, *The Hundred Days* returns to the pattern of having Jeff Ramsden provide the narration. In *The Nine Unknown*, Mundy had mixed King and Grim, which resulted in leaving the reader uncertain as to who the leader was, and also diminished Grim. In *The Hundred Days*, King is usually kept separate, leading a group of Waziri that support Grim and Narayan Singh's activities, thereby leaving him off-stage for the bulk of the narrative. Singh is the only additional male supporting character.

The heroine of *The Mystery of Khufu's Tomb*, Joan Angela Leich, returns to resolve her possible romance with Ramsden. Mundy makes a rare attempt to realistically explore the relationship between the sexes, despite the fact that the adventure genre's formulas generally militate against such characterizations.

One of Mundy's most vivid female creations, Joan Angela is convincingly real and three-dimensional. She emerges just as Mundy expunged a previous archetype, Yasmini, from his heroic pantheon in *Caves of Terror*. Jeff, who has known Joan Angela since her childhood, provided the opening description of her in *The Mystery of Khufu's Tomb*.

> She's tall—maybe a mite too tall for some folks' notions—and mid–Victorian mammas would never have approved of her, because she's no more coy, or shy, or artful than the blue sky overhead. She has violet eyes, riotous hair of a shade between brown and gold, a straight, shapely little nose, a mouth that is all laughter, and a way of carrying herself that puts you in mind of all out-doors. I've seen her in evening dress with diamonds on; and much more frequently in riding-breeches and a soft felt hat; but there's always the same effect of natural-born honesty, and laughter, and love of trees and things and people. She's not a woman who wants to ape men, but a woman who can mix with men without being soiled or spoiled. For the rest, she's not married yet, so there's a chance for all of us except me. She turned me down long ago.[25]

Her determination and fearlessness allow her to take her place with the men as an equal, while still eliciting their chivalrous intervention.

The Hundred Days begins as King, Grim, Ramsden, and Narayan Singh are helping to secure the Northwest frontier against unrest during the visit of a prince. To their surprise, Joan Angela Leich is also in the area, and she is abducted by a local chieftain for ransom money needed by his impoverished tribe. As King, Grim, Ramsden, and Narayan Singh swing into action to rescue her, a picturesque, sometimes grueling account ensues. She proves valorous, not only tending the wounded but taking her own share in the bloodletting.

Providing a sobering and human background is the virtual dissolution of the friendship between Ramsden and Joan Angela. The difficulty stems from two causes. One of them is summed up by Narayan Singh: "A man sees himself in a woman, and the more he loves her the worse the vision shocks him."[26] For Narayan Singh, the sight of his weakness has made him look no more at women; for Ramsden, it causes him to feel unworthy.

When Ramsden tries to conceal her at the bottom of a well before another attack, she misconstrues his motives completely. He is unable to believe or forget that she could suspect him of such a base action. Even when she apologizes and asks him to marry her, he declines, just as he had once also asked her to marry him and she refused. Despite the obvious love they do have for one another, Ramsden knows it is not the love that forms the basis for a marriage. As well, he is acutely aware that he is middle-aged, while Joan Angela is 26 and wealthy; he knows that somewhere there is a man who will be a better match. The renunciation, of course, also allows Ramsden and Grim to continue their association.

Unlike most of Mundy's books, *The Hundred Days* is less concerned with strategy, and is instead an account of almost non-stop action, with minimal pause for reflection. The narration is written with unusual denseness, filled with such descriptions as "Crags like glistening teeth arose in irregular rows and curves out of silvery mist that seemed to float on a coal-black sea."[27] This style is both the novel's strength, and weakness if judged by literary standards. As the London *Times* noted in an appropriately serious review, "A genuine gift of style, and a power of sustained vigorous narrative place this story ... in a higher category than the everyday thriller.... But Mr. Mundy seems scarcely to realize that vigour needs the contrast of restraint to make it fully effective. The pace throughout is set too fast."[28] However, for such a chronicle to be so vividly written is no small achievement. Stories of action are indeed the staple of pulp fiction, but neither in plot or wording is *The Hundred Days* simple. It retains the necessary metaphysical dimension for a story of survival; typically, Chapter X beings with a brief disquisition on the persistence of humankind's lower nature.

Mundy believed, with more than adequate reason, that *The Hundred Days* was deserving of book publication. He could easily have added additional background to the brief introduction of the main characters that had sufficed for *Adventure* readers familiar with Grim's saga. *The Hundred Days* was finally published by Century together with one of the Jimgrim Arabian stories, *The Woman Ayisha* (an odd combination), advertised as "Two thrilling novels for the price of one." In England, the novel had been first published in book form a year earlier, as a separate volume, where the title was first switched from *Mohammed's Tooth* to *The Hundred Days*.

In Reno, Talbot renewed his acquaintance with the man who was his best friend for twenty years, the red-haired Laurence Trimble (1885–1954). Today, Trimble has his own star on Hollywood Boulevard, between Ivar and Vine, for creating the first films with canine stars, beginning what would become a major dramatic film genre long before Rin-Tin-Tin or Lassie. In the words of Trimble's daughter Janet, "Larry was intrigued by his [T.M.'s] foreign adventures and T.M. was intrigued with Larry's communication with animals, especially wild animals. They were both interested in the occult."[29]

Larry, like Talbot, had to overcome fear as a child, and was terrified of dogs until he realized that it was his own fright they sensed and made them regard him as dangerous.[30] During the early years of Larry's film career, he and Talbot had met in his native Maine, which Larry had used as a location since 1910, and still regarded as his home. Trimble wrote and directed films in many genres, including three films from Rex Beach novels from 1917–20 for Goldwyn release. This made him a natural to film Mundy's stories, which he wanted to do.

Larry was separated from Janet's mother, and over the years became romantically involved with many of the women with whom he collaborated on films. Larry's daughter Janet recalled that her memories of Talbot went back to listening to his stories as a 4 year old in 1916. Dick Ames was not the first child Talbot had a hand in rearing; Janet remembered that "He had so much to do with my growing up. Instead of consulting a mother, Larry consulted T.M. on just about everything to do with me.... I rather think that I substituted for the children he did not have.... [Yet] I wouldn't say he was very interested in children."[31]

By 1920, Larry planned to make the first feature-length movie to headline a dramatic canine actor. His partner was screenwriter Jane Murfin (1893–1955); as Talbot noted, she had "the cash and was a sure-fire business woman."[32] Larry found the perfect dog, able to take instruction, and to think. During World War I, the 115 pound Etzel von Oeringen had carried medical supplies at the front, but had also been trained to jump over any six foot adversary, or kill with them with his fangs. Larry changed Etzel's name to Strongheart and taught him how to play for the first time.

Brawn of the North, the second Strongheart vehicle, was adapted by Murfin from Trimble's story, which he also directed, with the team as producers. In February, March, and April, 1922, Trimble and Murfin were filming in the area of Bridgeport in the high Sierras, near Reno, with "seventeen huskies and a pack of honest-to-God timber wolves."[33] Talbot assisted with their training, such as going into the wolf cage "as part of the wolf's education. D'you get that? Her education, not mine."[34]

Trimble's appeal to an animal's rational instincts, and desire to be friendly, understood and appreciated, were highly unorthodox for the time, and from him Talbot learned much about nature. The music of the wolves was described by Trimble as their "evening hymn," and Talbot saw Larry lead them in their howls by sitting "near to them and rendering a wolf solo so perfectly that they could not resist the inclination to sing the chorus."[35]

Such spectacles made Talbot wonder about the place of man in nature, and the conventional interpretations of the relationship, in a manner that would reflect his personal experience and the tenets of Eastern philosophy. To Talbot, animals had just as much soul as his fellow men, as exemplified in the animals depicted in his fiction, and the pets that were always a part of his life. His animal characterizations were always expert, whether Quorn's elephant Asoka or the canine Trotters in *Guns of the Gods* and Ommony's Diana, regarded as entirely plausible for her species by Trimble.[36]

Larry also believed that animals could read human minds in another direction, as recalled by Dick, who was visiting. "Up in this cottage, Larry put a choke collar on Etzel, and had him down by his chair, and T. was over here and I was over here. Larry said to T., 'I'm going to think some thoughts about you, very bad thoughts, and Etzel is going to dive for your throat. I'm not going to let him get there....' So we went on with our conversation and all of a sudden Etzel just took off, straight for T.'s throat. With a choke collar, of course, he didn't get there. That was a piece of the occult: thought transference."[37]

After spending time with Larry, Mundy returned to writing about a character, Cotswold Ommony, who first appeared in a January 1914 *Everybody's* magazine short story, "Burberton and Ali Beg." The character was based on a man he had met in Bengal around 1897–98.

> The tales he told at night, in his little bungalow surrounded by the forest that he loves more than anything else on earth, were the most absorbing I ever heard. He is something of an astronomer, knows animals and trees as some men know arithmetic, and dreaded, as I remember, only one thing — retirement to London on a miserable pension....
>
> He believed in reincarnation, although not of men's souls into the bodies of animals. He used to say it was ridiculous to suppose that sixty or seventy years could teach a man much; and equally ridiculous to imagine that the Universe could have any use for a blackguard or a fool. Therefore, according to him, logically a man must come back to earth again and again in different bodies to learn common sense, and incidentally to face punishment for past offenses and mistakes. And the same with animals. "That's why I like 'em," he used to add.[38]

In his incarnation as a hero of full-length novels, Ommony comes to reflect not only these traits, but others that Mundy borrowed from Trimble. Most obvious is the addition of Ommony's large and remarkably intelligent dog, Diana, inspired by Strongheart. Ommony "believed that on their plane, in their degree, the trees have souls and life and consciousness...."[39] The forest shelters an aboriginal race of junglis, the remnants of a people who were conquered and proscribed thousands of years earlier. Ommony is the first man outside of their tribe to learn their language and culture. Thin, naked, the junglis become Ommony's friends, providing information (although work is usually the province of the women of the tribe), as both seek to keep their wooded sanctuaries safe.

Ommony is a significant step farther removed from the British colonial tradition once represented by Athelstan King. Ommony sympathizes openly with the rebels and their desire for independence. He carries out his job less out of love for his fellow countrymen than for the protection of the forest he guards as a preserve.[40] Yet this was also a formula that would become increasingly prevalent in post-colonial adventure: finding a continued place for the Anglo, this time as part of the effort for conservation in these countries.

After the crescendo of fantasy with *Caves of Terror* and *The Nine Unknown*, Mundy's thoughts shifted back toward adventure to fictionalize a fresh rebellion in India, much as he had done with the Jimgrim Arabian stories. *Benefit of Doubt*, first published in the December 10, 1922 issue of *Adventure*, and its follow-up, *Treason*, in the January 10, 1923 number, actually formed one single work on the Moplah uprising in Malabar. They were received in that sense in England; the critic for the *Times Literary Supplement*, noting the background, incorrectly faulted the book from a factual standpoint, saying "the local colour and conditions are hopelessly incorrect."[41] An area which had historically been the scene of several previous revolts was declared peaceful by a District Superintendent in May 1921. However, by August, and through early 1922, British control broke down in the most serious rebellion since 1857.

Although sympathetic, the Moplah's own motives are far from pure. In the absence of British rule, they hope to massacre as many Hindus as possible, and forcibly convert the rest to Islam, seizing their property and women, a process that occurs at regular intervals in the region and is one of the risks of living there. Hindus, Mundy points out, live in Moplah country just as people live on Vesuvius, profiting during the quiet years even as they know the dangers. The Moplahs were in fact abandoned by Gandhi's Congress and came to be regarded as an example of Moslem violence and religious fanaticism.

Benefit of Doubt begins 25 years earlier, as the boys Mahommed Babar and Athelstan King are sworn to friendship, after Cuthbert King saves Babar's father from a beating at the hands of an Englishman. Now, "the famous Athelstan King," formerly of the Khyber Rifles, visits Ommony.[42] Hunting with King and Ommony, Babar steps backward before an oncoming tiger, an act of either bravery or cowardice. However, when he loses his footing, King shoots the animal. Babar flees, believing that the Englishmen displayed a lack of confidence in him that belied their friendship, proving indeed that men of different races could never truly be brothers.

Babar, although he would have once liked to stand with his British friends, is also a pious Moslem who owes money to Hindus and believes the time has come for their death. Babar chooses to be a rebel, knowing his fate and believing that the revolt will fail, but knowing that under his command the fewest atrocities possible will occur. Babar is an ambiguous revolutionary; Ommony is often perplexed by his actions, keeping faith even when Babar does not always seem to be a man of his word.[43] In a "Camp-Fire" letter introducing *Treason*, Mundy pronounced both men to be rebels, and each guilty of treason in the conventional sense.

Although *Benefit of Doubt* and *Treason* were filled with strong incidents, due to the format of being broken into two ostensibly complete magazine novels they do not effectively mesh into a single book. A single longer treatment of the theme with continuing characters rather than new ones in each part would have been vastly more successful. Internal dramatic flaws, and a lack of continuity, such as introducing a major character like King and then eliminating him from the second part, keeps the work from reaching a more enduring level. Instead, Mundy seems to have realized King was superfluous and Ommony much more interesting, giving it the feel of a work-in-progress. At the same time, Mundy adopts a more introspective writing style; of all his non-philosophical books, *Benefit of Doubt* and *Treason* are the richest in asides and digressions. They are written into the text, like plain speech without verse, such as "Misfortune is not a cause, but the result of mistakes and misuse of opportunity."[44]

Babar (spelled Baber) makes a final appearance in Mundy's magazine novel, *The Wolf of the Pass*, for the May-June 1936 issue of *All Aces*. His background is changed; the Moplah rebellion is placed during World War I, as an uprising on behalf of the Turks, but Baber is still a leader who loses because he will not tolerate looting. He surrenders to an Irishman, General Rory Shane, who, rather than take him prisoner, secures his oath to be a friend of the King henceforth, despite personal opinions. *The Wolf of the Pass* continues in the present, amidst religious violence, as the Moslems fear being overrun by the Hindu majority should the British leave India. Baber is frustrated that his oath to Shane binds him to support the King's Hindu politicians when he needs to lead his own people. In a surprise ending, it is not Baber who makes a sacrifice to uphold British authority, but Shane, who dies at Moslem hands. Baber keeps the peace by taking the blame, disappearing on the pilgrimage to Mecca. It is a fitting end for one of Mundy's most noble characters, in a creditable novel that is absorbing if not quite truly memorable.

The Ommony series declined substantially in quality. *Diana Against Ephesians*, which appeared in the August 10, 1923 issue of *Adventure*, is a satire directed against missionaries, in an Indian state where the Resident is addicted to morphia. As in Mundy's earlier derision of hypocritical religious figures, *Moses and Mrs. Aintree*, the results are again second rate. *Diana Against Ephesians* is as insignificant as *The Marriage of Meldrum Strange*, a satirical attempt at role reversal, which Mundy facetiously called "an immoral story."[45] Mundy scorns Strange for his materialism, but does not denounce him, and Strange and Ommony engage in a contest of wills. The besetting sin of both men is their pride, Ommony through his self-confidence and belief in destiny, and Strange in his confidence in the power of his wealth, riches that are scorned by Ommony. Ommony then behaves selfishly as Strange courts his sister, and is fooled by her and Chullunder Ghose into blessing the marriage. Published in the October 10, 1923 issue of *Adventure*, it only appeared in book form in England, published by Hutchinson in 1930. *Benefit of Doubt*, *Treason*, and *Diana Against Ephesians* were collected, nearly a decade after their appearance in *Adventure*, into a single book with the preposterously inappropriate title of *Jungle Jest*, a title which also belied the factual focus on the Moplah rebellion.

Talbot told Dick Ames that he was weary of producing a new novel every few months and wanted a rest. By the beginning of October, 1922, he and Dick had moved to San Diego to spend the winter months. San Diego was conveniently close to Hollywood, yet distant in character from the Los Angeles metropolitan area. Talbot rented a beautiful home at 2030 Homer Street in Loma Portal, a high-class residential subdivision on Point Loma.[46] As Dick recalled, "We lived together; mother was back east.... We had only one car, so he rented a Lancia for me. We had a butler, a very nice one."[47] By early winter, however, Talbot told Bobbs-Merrill he was "almost frantic with discouragement."[48] He was depressed over the ephemeral nature of his recent writing, and a lack of new ideas. However, the long anticipated call from Hollywood was about to come.

After Talbot Mundy turned over movie rights to his work to Bobbs-Merrill just before leaving for Jerusalem, they often heard film ideas as often as once a week, but none came to fruition. Looming over the attempt to sell Mundy's stories to the movies was the simple fact that the genre of most of his stories, adventure in colonial lands, was yet to become a cinematic formula, and not until the last years of Mundy's life would films with such subject matter begin to proliferate. Ironically, Talbot's sole period actually working in Hollywood coincided with the making of one of the decade's few features set in India, *The White Panther* (1924), with a character named Yasmiri who falls in love with an English officer at a fort near the entrance to the Khyber Pass. Despite Mundy's anger, Bobbs-Merrill advised him that claiming a "copyright violation" would be more costly than would prove worthwhile, especially since it was made by a low-budget producer, Phil Goldstone.[49]

In 1919, producer Thomas Ince joined with a number of fellow independent filmmakers to form Associated Producers, and two of his partners expressed interest in filming Mundy's works in 1920. George Loane Tucker took an option on *King — of the Khyber Rifles*, and J. Parker Reed considered another Yasmini novelette, *A Soldier and a Gentleman*. Mundy was first contacted in February 1921 by Ince, believing that Mundy novels of his original stories produced for the screen would give them literary value as book tie-ins and allow advertising in bookstores and libraries. During the 1910s and 1920s, it was common practice to publish reprints of established novels when they were filmed, as well as new novelizations of plays and original screen stories brought to the screen.

By early January 1923, Ince signed Mundy to write a novel of standard size and length based on the motion picture *News*, which would also be known as *The Devil's Own* (a title Mundy and Bobbs-Merrill may have remembered two years later when *Ramsden* was retitled *The Devil's Guard*) before finally being entitled *Her Reputation*. Shooting had taken place from November 2, 1922, to January 2, 1923, on a budget of $166,421, including $21,680 in overhead.[50] At a length of seven reels, or 6,560 feet, *Her Reputation* could last anywhere from 76 to 93 minutes, depending on the projection speed.

Because of the haste required to finish the book in time for it to benefit the release of the film, a mere six weeks were allocated for Mundy to write it, at the studio, at a salary of $250 per week. The author had to arrange for its publication by Doubleday, Page, & Co., Bobbs-Merrill, or a firm of equal stature by April 1.[51] Fortunately, Bobbs-Merrill was amenable to the arrangement, and an elaborate exploitation campaign was planned to pique interest in readers who would read the book and want to see the movie.[52] In the Ince studio's publicity journal, *The Silver Sheet*, and in the trade press, Mundy's addition to the Ince staff was touted as an event that brought cultural prestige to the company.

The author of the scenario of *Her Reputation* was Bradley King, who earned a weekly salary equivalent to what Mundy was receiving, together with a $1500 bonus for each original story.[53] Mundy's assignment was strictly to write the book, and he had precious little time for that (considering he would be writing a book twice as long as the *Adventure* novels, each of which usually required close to a month to complete). His contract stipulated that it was up to him to negotiate privately with King as to how author credits would be given on the book, and whether they would share the royalties, which were reserved for the authors, rather than the studio.[54] Ironically, although the scenario preceded the book, the official movie credits give the novel by Talbot Mundy and Bradley King (in that order) as the source, which had to appear in advertising at 10 percent of the size of the title. Most reviewers misspelled either Talbot Mundy's first or last name (indeed, his contracts with Ince had spelled his name "Talbott Monday").[55]

Her Reputation became the only completed film on which Talbot Mundy worked in Hollywood. Told in 680 shots, the plot was far afield from his usual themes. At the office of the *San Francisco Tribune*, John Covert Mansfield (played by Winter Hall), remains embittered by the faithlessness of his own wife two decades earlier. His associate, the elderly, slightly disheveled "Dad" Lawrence (James Corrigan), is more understanding of human nature. Mansfield cables ace reporter Clinton Kent

Title lobbycard for *Her Reputation*.

(Brinsley Shaw) to get the an interview with Jacqueline Lanier, who has become the latest news sensation.

At the Louisiana plantation of philanthropist Don Andres Miro (Eric Mayne), wedding festivities are underway for his marriage to his convent-reared ward Jacqueline (May McAvoy). Fiery young Jack Calhoun (Casson Ferguson), furious that Jacqueline is unattracted by his protestations of love, shoots Andres, then turns the gun on himself. Although a witness, Kent senses a story and believes that a "scoop" is more important than the people concerned. In flashback, Miro is revealed to have been the last of an old Spanish family, with a short time to live, with the marriage to have been in name only, so that Jacqueline could inherit his estate.

However, the newspapers of America trumpet Kent's saga of a sensational double killing into front-page news, filled with speculation calling Jacqueline a "vamp." Heartbroken and penniless, she flees, accompanied by her faithful duenna, Consuelo (Louise Lester). Meanwhile, Kent, called back to San Francisco, turns the task of getting the interview over to Sherwood Mansfield (Lloyd Hughes), son of the tycoon, who was covering the floods.

When the Mississippi River surges over the levees, Jacqueline finally finds refuge on top of a barn, and meets Sherry, also marooned. Jacqueline arouses Sherry's protective instincts, although he was brought up with his father's distrust and bitterness for women. After three days, they are in love, with their time in the barn shown in a series of flashbacks as Sherry later begins to comprehend her identity. When they are rescued and taken to a relief station, Jacqueline finds Consuelo with the Cervanez family, entertainers who had performed at the wedding ceremony. Señora Cervanez (Eugene Besserer), her son Ramon (George Larkin), daughter Pepita (Jane Wray), and a pet monkey named Charlie, are traveling to their next engagement, in San Francisco.[56]

As the partner of Ramon, Jacqueline loses her identity dancing under a mask in various nightclubs, and finally becomes the rage at an elegant venue in San Francisco. Kent, back in the city, sees her performance and tells his suspicions to Mansfield, and to Sherry as well. Dad succeeds in meeting Jacqueline, and becomes convinced of her innocence. To save them from further press coverage, Dad puts Jacqueline and Consuelo in his car and tells her to drive to his mountain cabin for safety.

On the way, Jacqueline stops at the *Tribune* and tells Mansfield that Kent's new story will besmirch not only her, but someone they both love. Mansfield sends her away contemptuously, after giving Kent's story the go-ahead. Fast driving on the mountain roads leads to an accident for Kent, and he is rescued from the flaming wreck of his car by Sherry. Awakening painfully in the cabin, Kent is touched by the love between Jacqueline and Sherry, and begins to believe that something might be more important than "news," but still feels obligated to defend his story.

When Mansfield arrives at the cabin, Sherry defends Jacqueline to his father, and he berates Kent for not verifying his story before it went to press. The forest fire caused by Wahl's car wreck parallels the confrontation between father and son, and flames topple the telephone poles moments after Mansfield telephones his newspaper to cancel the second exposé of Jacqueline.[57]

Her Reputation has acquired an unjustified low repute of its own among Mundy's writing, both because of the disdain he later felt for the finished product, and its distinction from his usual genre. As Dawn Mundy recalled, "He only mentioned it once, and that was with the utmost disgust. I don't think I've ever read it.... I probably had the impression from Talbot that [Bradley King] was just some scenario worker."[58] However, such estimations of *Her Reputation* are wrong.

Few novels originating as movie tie-ins had the literary merit of *Her Reputation*, and fewer still had a writer of Mundy's stature adapting the screenplay to prose. King is credited coauthor on the British edition (retitled *The Bubble Reputation*), and on the original Bobbs-Merrill edition, but not the A.L. Burt reprint. Mundy wrote in the introduction to the American editions that King "detected, tracked, ran down and caught the idea for the story—a much more difficult thing to do than those who have never hunted such elusive game will ever guess. She trained it to perform...." Years later, considering a collaboration with Rose Wilder Lane, he recalled his earlier experience. "You would certainly be easier to work with than she was, because you don't 'think' in terms of tabloid scare-heads."[59]

From a fast moving scenario, Mundy has added abundant detail and incidents, including supporting characters, and fleshing out in human terms those who do appear, filling in their nature and motives. He emphasized some themes over others, while originating a few himself, such as Jacqueline's maturation and growing strength. Mundy added a vast measure of complexity, depth and texture to the story that enriched it considerably and made *Her Reputation* worthy of treatment in novel form. The dialogue is unusually frank and realistic, for instance containing more swearing than any other Mundy novel except *Old Ugly-Face* (published 17 years later), and which would have been unsuitable for a movie in the 1920s.

Although the movie does not survive, scripts do, so it is possible to chart how closely the novel and the film resemble each other. Some scenes apparently reproduce what was on the screen exactly, from the evidence of photographs and summaries, such as the confrontation with Ramon after Sherry recognizes Jacqueline dancing. Since Mundy wrote the book himself, the divergences from the film likely reflect his own preferred interpretation. Other differences may reflect composing from an initial script, rather than a completed movie; reporter Clinton Wahl of the novel had his name changed to Clifford Wahl in the script, then finally altered again to Clinton Kent on screen. There are also changes in narrative technique; the movie uses numerous quick flashbacks, providing a sense of parallel action. The book follows a strictly chronological narrative development, achieving alternation of viewpoint and changing the pace by using Mundy's split narrative pattern, with characters meeting, separating, and re-merging, sometimes covering the same events from different perspectives.

While the movie opens in the newspaper office in San Francisco, with the initial events at the wedding having occurred, the book begins with preparations for the wedding. The circumstances leading up to it are carefully constructed by Mundy, allowing more detailed study of the character of Don Andres Miro, his sister, and Jack Calhoun. Jack, having already destroyed 20 women, notices Jacqueline, and, in the words of her duenna, "saw a flower and craved to pluck it!"[60] By contrast, King's scenario had described Calhoun as not villainous, simply suffering and "unbalanced by the force of his desire."[61] The book's important character of John Miro, who bridges the cultural contrasts between the courtly Southern beginning and the dangers of San Francisco, is entirely absent from the film and script drafts. Consequently, rather than John, in the film it is Dad who rescues Jacqueline from the cafe and drives her away. (However, the movie did not then have the book's excessive coincidence of the Cervanez family leading Jacqueline to the city that is also home to one of the Miro family.) Mundy's conclusion is uncompromising, with Wahl raving lurid accusations about Sherry and Jacqueline. In the movie, Wahl feels remorse, while the fire is entirely eliminated in the book.

The strength of *Her Reputation* is that its plot and central themes seem immediate and first-hand, as indeed they were; perhaps Ince's assignment of Mundy to the project was not so accidental. There is a clear sympathy in the portrayal of Jacqueline Lanier as a woman wronged by the press and its scurrilous pandering to the basest instincts. It reflects the resentment Mundy clearly felt for the coverage of his own first divorce from Kathleen, for both of Inez Craven's divorces, and his mugging upon arriving in New York City. Mundy considers both journalists, and their readers, in the words of Dad, "a rotten lot of vultures raising a stink with our claws and wings in the sewer! And the public's worse — it likes to see it — pays money for it! Wahl would crucify that girl, if the law would let him, and the public would go broke buying ringside seats! To hell with the whole dirty business!"[62] Although Jacqueline knows the power Wahl has over her, she is determined not to submit, even if it requires the ultimate sacrifice. "She would like to prove to him that he *could not* destroy her with his lies; and yet she knew he could! She knew that if Wahl discovered her, and told who she was, and wrote more lies about her in the papers, she would run — run — run — perhaps even kill herself."[63] Thus the underlying motif, of how an innocent person could be smeared, was one that Mundy could express with a passion and conviction appropriately projected onto his characters. This theme also highlights Jacqueline's transformation from dependence and naiveté into a self-reliant woman.

Mundy was at work at the Ince studio from January 15, remaining at least four months, through May of 1923.[64] In addition to creating a novel from Bradley King's scenario, Mundy's contract called for him to write an original story for which Ince would own the film and dramatic rights, with Mundy paid $250 per week for not more than 12 weeks, even if the task took longer.

He was assigned to script an adaptation of Henry Wadsworth Longfellow's book-length poem *Evangeline,* a love story of a young couple separated when the French Acadians who had long settled in Nova Scotia are ordered relocated before the French and Indian Wars. Just months earlier, Ince had filmed a story of the Acadian's modern Alabama descendants, *Scars of Jealousy.*[65]

Evangeline was not produced, and Mundy was assigned to a third American story, to which he would once more own the book rights. This time the subject was to be conquest of the west, on which Ince was planning an epic historical film.[66] Talbot had long had the typical European interest in the American West, and had written two stories ("Nothing Doing" and "A Temporary Trade in Titles") and an article ("The Sayings of Hell-Fire Smith Done Into Polite English") for *Adventure* using standard Western characters. Keenly aware of the western's popularity and sales, Mundy had considered writing a novel of the genre a year earlier. He had been asked by Larry to write a tale "of Virginia City and the Comstock — Fortyniner Stuff," to initially appear as a story, then be made into a movie which Trimble and Murfin would produce.[67]

Ince also signed Courtney Ryley Cooper (1886–1940) to write a western incorporating buffalo hunts, a book which had to be finished in two months, with a slightly more generous contract than Mundy had been given.[68] This became *The Last Frontier,* published in October of that same year by Little, Brown, and the book incorporated historical characters such Wild Bill Hickok, General Custer, and Buffalo Bill Cody. *The Last Frontier* was the western Ince ultimately decided to film, although it was not actually completed until after the producer's death.

Like *The Last Frontier,* Mundy's novel, entitled *When Trails Were New,* incorporated historical figures, Abraham Lincoln and Jefferson Davis. Lincoln is depicted as already a wise judge of character and natural leader of men, although Mundy is not able to make of him more than a singularly colorless figure.

While *The Last Frontier* uses a more traditional, post–Civil War period of western history, *When Trails Were New* is set in the Wisconsin woods of 1832, with conflicts among the settlers and Indians against a background of the Blackhawk War. Mundy maintained that he had thoroughly researched all available sources.

Mundy composed in the literary style of James Fenimore Cooper, using as his model the Leatherstocking tales: *The Deerslayer*, *The Last of the Mohicans*, *The Pathfinder*, *The Pioneers*, and *The Prairie*. Like Natty Bumppo, Mundy's hero, Louis d'Arras, is a true pioneer, a woodsman like Cotswold Ommony who has lived compatibly among the Native Americans. Despite being a Bumppo-style noble loner, who lives on the frontier, d'Arras is unable to avoid contact with his own race. D'Arras's best and most trusted friend is, like Bumppo's Chingachgook, an Indian, Blue Heron. He is a Sac, who will eventually die in the defense of Louis's bride, Daphne. Like Bumppo and Chingachgook, d'Arras and Blue Heron are drawn into the clashes between whites and Native Americans, defending individual whites but not taking sides in the broader question of settler versus Indian. Mingling between white and Native American is portrayed as natural; one of Louis's friends has had a squaw, Running Caribou, for 20 years, to whom he is gruffly devoted, and she is equally faithful, despite the frequent peril in which her position places her. There is full equality of the sexes on the frontier, with Daphne and Running Caribou able to match any of the male characters.

The villain of *When Trails Were New* is the white gun-runner Sully, and it is only whites like him who cause conflict with the Indians. Sully is determined to have Daphne, but Louis had to make a vow to the priest that married them to avoid shedding Sully's blood. The newlyweds must separate when the wars with the Indians begin, and most of the narrative follows their subsequent adventures in alternating chapters.

There is some overlap in plot as Mundy provides an omniscient perspective. Each group learns what has become of the other, finally reuniting for the denouement. Unfortunately, this pattern becomes so mechanical and repetitious that it turns tiresome. A further drawback is poor character delineation. Sully is disappointing, a blustering bully with an ungovernable temper who seldom displays the promised strategic sense that would make him convincingly menacing.

When Trails Were New contains an unusual amount of violence for a Mundy work, a result of his attempt to depict the savagery of the frontier. Whites and Indians scalp one another at every opportunity, and at the fort where Daphne formerly lived, a bloody massacre takes place that leaves it burnt and in ashes. Daphne, returning after the massacre, saves the infant child of her best friend shielded by her mother's dead, charred, and scalped corpse. Believing Louis died in the attack, Daphne adopts the child, a surge of maternal feeling striving to replace the husband she believes died in the massacre. This section, Chapter 15, is the most moving of the book, one of the few occasions Mundy is able to use Western conventions to advantage.

When Trails Were New was unquestionably one of Mundy's worst stories, demonstrating both his inexperience and disdain for the genre. He would later describe it as "disgusting ... my last effort to write down to standards with which I have no sympathy."[69] Mundy did not complete *When Trails Were New* before he left the studio; the concluding two chapters are in the form of a summary of the historical events and how they impacted the characters, the minimum necessary tacked on to make it publishable. *When Trails Were New* did not appear in print until over four years later, and was first serialized in *Argosy All-Story Weekly* from October 27 through December 1, 1928 (with an introductory letter to magazine readers). The only book publication took place in England by Hutchinson in 1932.

Mundy had already left the studio by the time *Her Reputation* and the novelization were released on September 3, 1923 (the book was published in England in November). The movie won wide plaudits from reviewers as a melodrama with sentimental appeal and plenty of action. The acting of the entire cast was praised, as were the settings, costumes, photography, and John Griffith Wray's direction, especially the spectacular flood and fire scenes.[70] However, the movie was slightly less profitable than expected, grossing $201,048 after just over five months.[71]

The plot of *Her Reputation* does not sound original today, but it was in its time. A prologue showed the development of human communication, from cavemen to the invention of the printing press and the modern industry of the "news—usually truthful—yet sometimes vicious and distorted." According to studio publicity, Ince challenged the "Fourth Estate" to find one scene which was not accurate as to newspaper production. Mundy, in his introduction to the American edition of *Her Reputation*, said "fellow newspaper men" should "recognize the friendly and entirely sympathetic illustration of the way in which the mighty and far-reaching power of the Press occasionally is abused by individuals."[72] Their words did not go unnoticed, causing consternation in some parts of the journalistic community.

Just as in 1941, when *Citizen Kane* offered a fictionalized biography of a yellow journalist inspired by William Randolph Hearst, and found the press responding in hostile fashion, a milder version of the same reaction was accorded *Her Reputation*. After a positive review in *Variety*, two weeks later the journal ran another review, which, while rare, happened on occasion in this era, and revealed that journalistic sensitivities had been aroused.

> *Her Reputation* seems like propaganda against the newspaper profession. If it isn't directed against the entire press of the country, it is at least a slap to the "yellow" journalist and their methods of ruining the lives of "innocent" ladies.
>
> And in the making of the picture the producers have shown an admirable disregard for newspaper methods, for they have based their whole theme on the assumption that any newspaper in the country can print anything it likes about anybody and get away with it. They forget that there are laws of libel and that nine-tenths of the papers in the world go to a great deal of trouble to verify any questionable story....
>
> To those who are wont to look upon newspapers as instruments through which scandals are created all will be well and the picture will prove a delight.[73]

Within a year the movie and the book's damning of the journalistic profession had reverberations in the lives of both Ince and Mundy. In November 1924, Ince visited the yacht of William Randolph Hearst, and died days later, officially of heart failure from acute indigestion. Rumors that Ince had been shot by Hearst led to an official investigation, and in his death Ince suffered from just the same type of sensationalism as had been the subject of *Her Reputation*.

Mundy was also about to experience anew the ravages of the press on his own reputation; he had finally filed for divorce on April 17, 1922 in the courts of Washoe County, where Reno was located. Hearing after hearing was held, depositions were taken in eastern states, and there were demands for support money and attorney fees.[74]

To contest the divorce, Rosemary moved from New York to Reno in June 1922, and supplemented her income by painting. On October 1, 1922, Talbot secured a loan against his life insurance policy in order to pay Rosemary $1,102.34, his first payment to her since a check for $400 in the fall of 1920.[75] Not until March 24 of the next year, 1923, was the case taken up again; Talbot sent her a check for $50, when she wrote to him saying she was without funds, his first knowledge that the previous fall's check had been spent.[76] Her answer on April 9 denied receiving community property, and also denied all of Talbot's allegations about her jealous behavior and the inability of the two to accomplish their respective work in their marital life. She claimed he had abandoned her on January 3, 1920, when he left for Jerusalem. Citing ill-health since February 1922, she demanded $400 a month for her support during the legal action, $500 to secure legal depositions on the east coast, and $2000 for attorney's fees, and said that Talbot had a large income and was well able to pay.[77]

He pointed out that magazine and book publishers had rejected some of his recent writings as not up to standard, which he blamed on the strain of the pending legal action. He stated he was unable to pay the amounts Rosemary requested, offering her $50 a month and $150 for legal fees, adding she was capable of earning large sums for her artistic work.[78] On June 13, Rosemary wrote Talbot, pleading for a reconciliation. It was too late.

The case finally began on Monday, August 20, 1923, before Judge George A. Bartlett, lasting for the next four full days. The trial quickly turned into the most publicly humiliating week of Talbot Mundy's entire life.[79] Those who followed such events, the "Reno divorce colony," were well represented, and by the end of the proceedings the courtroom was filled to capacity with spectators.[80] Reporters actively covered it as a celebrity event, describing Mundy as a well-known novelist, short story writer, and scenarist, and Rosemary as a nationally-known portrait artist.[81]

On the first day, Talbot took the stand, spending it entirely under questioning, and described ten years of nagging and fault-finding that began shortly after the couple married. Her complaining and baseless jealousies often interfered with his work, and Rosemary had destroyed his peace of mind after the first month of their marriage. He added that she tried to offend him in every letter, although he had not kept them, since he had sought to calm her fears by promising her he would not show her letters to anyone else.[82] Hence, he could not match the battle for exhibits she created, since she had kept letters from him. He blamed religious differences for most of their disagreements, saying he found it impossible to subscribe to the teachings his wife believed.[83]

Early in the afternoon, Rosemary's lawyer, Sam W. Belford, began the cross-examination. Belford placed in evidence 22 letters Talbot had written to Rosemary during their separation, most of them during his trip to Jerusalem. In the words of one reporter, the many letters to Rosemary were "gems of literary effort, and in several instances there were terms of endearment within the epistles."[84] Mundy had seemed prescient when, in a short story authored eleven years earlier, he had written that "A man's love-letters make disgusting reading, and for that reason they ought to be sacred, if for no other."[85] This was the defendant's tactic: using Talbot's own words against him, undermining what he said in the trial.[86]

A new element was added when Belford charged that Talbot went to Jerusalem with a former secretary, who had later visited him in Reno for a time. Talbot tried to defuse the issue by claiming that Mrs. Ames was chaperoned by her mother in Reno, although in fact Sally's mother had been dead many years.[87] However, the second defense tactic was now clear: exposing Talbot's love for Sally, which he was determined to keep private. He did have the deposition of Ruth (Mrs. C. Theodore) Herman, a woman who had known Talbot at the residences he had stayed in Reno. She indicated that she had no suspicions that Talbot had any unusual relationship with Mrs. Ames, who was described as his secretary, and whose son had shared a room with Talbot.[88] Belford forced Talbot to reveal his previous two marriages, but he claimed he married Inez Craven when he was informed that he had only a short time to live and she needed his name to return to England.[89]

Rosemary next took the stand, and was described by one reporter as making "a splendid witness on direct examination...." Her age, now 50, clearly older than Talbot, helped her project an impression of dependence which she exploited. Another of her lawyers, James T. Boyd, led the questioning. She denied they had ever had any serious disagreements in the early years of their marriage, or in Norway, and said they had got along amicably at all times. She said that she was not jealous of his actions, such as his trip to Jerusalem, saying "I always trusted him and believed in him."[90] She concluded by stating that this feeling had not changed.

The fraying of their marital relations from her opposition to the Jerusalem trip, evident from Talbot's letters that Rosemary had entered in evidence, was not reported.[91] Both Talbot and Rosemary showed a touch of sentimentalism and were guarded in their answers to questions, speaking only words of praise for the other, and the attorneys tried to maintain the atmosphere of comity.[92] Talbot was careful to avoid any statement that might reflect upon the character of Rosemary, and she had only praise for the man who was trying to divorce her.[93] However, this civility only rebounded to her benefit, allowing her to deny all of Talbot's claims.

Returning to the stand, the next tactic of the defendant was to paint Talbot as a religious fanatic, following his admission that, in addition to his religious disagreements with Rosemary, he was on the verge, at one point, of becoming a "fanatic."[94] Although she admitted religious disagreements, she said they were never major, but then proceeded to paint them in just such a manner. The Jerusalem trip was inaccurately described as made with former members of the directorate of the Christian Science Church, who founded *Jerusalem News* without the sanction of church officials, a move she claimed led to a court battle. Mundy's increasing interest in the occult was also used against him, and a 20 cent book, entitled *Curious Causes*, by W.A. Redding, subtitled "Explains many curious and valuable things of great benefit to the people," was entered as evidence.

She spoke of Talbot one day making "violent protestations of his love for her," but after meeting with members of the expedition returned embittered at his wife. On one occasion he offered to give up the church for her, then shortly thereafter wanted to give her up for the church. To indicate her attempt not to offend him, some of her letters to Talbot were then read into the record, including one detailing her feelings about his request for a divorce. In sum, according to the press report, Talbot "was not himself, she said. She was not afraid of anything he might do, but afraid of the influence others had over him."[95]

Shortly thereafter, Boyd began his opening argument, waxing "eloquent and sarcastic" at times, according to one reporter.[96] He emphasized the religious factor in the couple's split, and said that Talbot and a woman in Norway, Maine, had concocted a scheme to bring about the second resurrection at Jerusalem. No immediate decision from the bench was expected, but Judge Bartlett surprised onlookers by announcing he would study the action until the first of the week and announce his decision on Monday.[97]

Even before the verdict, the worst of the trial and publicity was not yet over. Saturday, the *Nevada State Journal* printed a report that Talbot expected to sign a contract with the London *Times* and leave the country for India shortly after the judge's ruling.[98] The next day, Talbot denied it completely, and the story was palpably false.[99] However, the damage was done; the report paralleled the characterization of Mundy that Rosemary's lawyers had created in the courtroom, and was well calculated to incur the Judge's ire.

And indeed Judge Bartlett ruled against Mundy on August 27, saying he had failed to sustain his charges of desertion, but that Rosemary had proved it. She was entitled to a divorce if she wanted it, but since she had only asked for separate maintenance, this was awarded, with Mundy ordered to pay $75 a month. The court also reserved the right to increase the amount as soon as it was shown he could pay more, but the Judge indicated that testimony demonstrated that Talbot was in straightened financial circumstances. Talbot was also required to pay $250 to Rosemary's lawyers in addition to the amount already allowed. The decision, in effect, barred Talbot from bringing a divorce action in any other state, with any future action having to take place in Washoe County.[100]

By Autumn 1923, all Mundy's hopes and plans were destroyed. After waiting over three years, he could still not marry his beloved Sally. He was broke and had not written a book that was well-received, even one he felt proud of, since 1920. Only one restorative came to mind: the theosophical community at Point Loma that he had discovered the previous fall.

VI

The Masters, 1923–1926

Talbot Mundy's move to the western United States proved to be the single most important action of his adult life with his discovery of Theosophy in Point Loma. The overwhelming bulk of his writings while in regular contact there (late 1922 through early 1928) were exceptional works, some of them masterpieces: *Om — The Secret of Ahbor Valley*, *Tros of Samothrace* (the length of three ordinary novels), *The Devil's Guard*, *Caesar Dies*, *W.H.*, *The Red Flame of Erinpura*, *Queen Cleopatra*, and the twenty-four articles for *The Theosophical Path*. At no other time in his career, either before or after, was Mundy able to sustain so consistently high a standard for such an extended period.

In the America of the 1920s, the loudest voices in religion were arguing over fundamentalism and modernism as the only alternatives. Not until the late 1930s would "Shangri-La" become a popularly accepted myth, but for prior decades the vanguard movement of Theosophy provided an intellectual base for promoting the alternative of the wisdom of the East. The word "theosophy" derives from the Greek for "divine wisdom," designating a way of thought speculating on God and the universe grounded in either mystical insight or analysis and comparison of various religions and philosophies.[1]

The founder of Theosophy was the Russian-born writer Helena Petrovna Blavatsky (1831–1891). During her youth she travelled through Europe, Asia, and Africa, and claimed to have penetrated Tibet. Arriving in the United States, Blavatsky began the Theosophical Society in New York in 1875. Her first book was *Isis Unveiled* (1878), and her second was the massive, multi-volume *The Secret Doctrine* (1888), subtitled "the synthesis of science, religion and philosophy." Blavatsky set forth three central principles: the revival of the lost mysteries, reincarnation, and the existence of the "Masters." These were radical assertions in an era characterized by the smugness of European colonial activity, but no movement was more influential in introducing Eastern thought in America.[2]

After Blavatsky's death in 1891, the Theosophical Society began to split between factions in India, England, and America. The largest group had its headquarters in Adyar, India, and was led by Colonel Henry Steele Olcott and Annie Besant. The American branch was under William Quan Judge, who was succeeded upon his death in 1895 by Katherine Tingley (1847–1929). She took the Theosophical Society in an entirely new direction, envisioning "an ideal community which would also serve as the Society headquarters and a place where the Theosophical way of life could be realized."[3] The cornerstone was laid in 1897, and construction of buildings and facilities soon followed. It survived for 40 years, with a school and university; industries and agriculture; and a large colony of practicing artists and scholars attracted by the value placed on music, dance, drama, literature, philosophy, and archaeology.

By the 1920s, the community was at the height of its fame and success, with some five hundred residents.[4] Tingley was a well-known figure in San Diego, respected despite the fact that she promulgated beliefs well outside of the contemporary religious norm.[5] Because of its sources in the "ancient wisdom," the headquarters was never regarded locally as a cult, although it was recognized as different from the mainstream faiths of the time.[6] Attracting many prominent callers, Point Loma was a spot where East truly met West.

The search for such teaching may have been part of the reason Talbot traveled to the west coast. He told Boris de Zirkoff, an early Tingley follower, that a man whom he did not describe "in the Orient told him that he had taught him all he could teach; that if he wanted to learn more along the lines of occultism, he should go to California, where his next Teacher was."[7] With Mundy's resignation from the Mother Church of Christian Science in 1922, he was open to a new faith, one more appropriate to his life's experience as well as his writing. Dick Ames suggested, "*All during the Sally period T.M. was exposed to a great deal of selflessness, spirituality, kindness, conscious or sub-conscious insight, and on many, many occasions I knew about, of clairvoyance and actual psychic phenomena. Many, many influences were new to him in addition to* [Tingley]."[8] While Theosophy did not initiate this direction in Mundy's writing, he encountered the Society at just the point in his own development when it helped him add a new depth to his fiction, supplying an intellectual dimension that clarified his own ideas. He was not the first writer to be influenced by Theosophy; it had provided a widely recognized inspiration for such figures as George W. Russell (AE), W.B. Yeats, and other writers and poets of the Irish literary revival of the late 19th and early 20th centuries. In Kenneth Morris, Point Loma had a historian and fiction writer who had already won modest acclaim.

Unlike Talbot's conversion to Christian Science, which had occurred because it was already the religion of Rosemary at the time of their marriage, and his subsequent experiments in spiritualism at the instigation of friends, Talbot discovered Theosophy by himself. Sally accepted Theosophy for Talbot's sake, but without reluctance, having also given up Christian Science. On New Year's Day, 1923, Mundy was admitted to membership in the Theosophical Society, which he would retain until his death. At the end of the month, Sally joined as well; Dick Ames never became an adherent of Theosophy, and Talbot respected his independent thought.

Prior to the fall of 1922, Mundy explained, he "had never seen a copy of *The Secret Doctrine* ... nor ever read a copy of *The Theosophical Path* or any of the *Theosophical Manuals* until the magic of Blavatsky's pen stirred in me something deeper and more challenging than I had known was there and capable of being stirred. And

At the Ince studio, 1923 from left: Katherine Tingley, Mundy, Thomas Ince, and actress Margaret Livingston. (Courtesy Richards Ames Collection)

I remember the bewilderment of all the knowledge crowded into her immortal book...."⁹ Tingley's was the ideal teacher for Talbot, and she was crucial in bringing him into the Theosophical fold. Seemingly ageless at 75 years old, she was like the typical heroine of Mundy's fiction: with a charisma that captivated and overwhelmed her male followers, she was a woman of immense magnetism and energy, whose intuition more often than not wisely directed her decisive nature.¹⁰

He found the Tingley interpretation of Blavatsky's books gave meaning to his personal contact with the East, confirming impressions he had long had, but only vaguely understood; for example, he had believed in reincarnation even while in Africa.¹¹ Mundy would later say, "What I have learned from Katherine Tingley is much the greatest and much the sublimest and most wonderful science that I have ever found anywhere; and I can never sufficiently express my gratitude for having met her and having been privileged to be taught by her."¹²

In turn, Tingley was impressed with Mundy and his depth of character and abilities, recognizing a man whose talents, properly developed, could turn him into a formidable champion of the cause. A deep friendship sprang up between them, despite the vast difference in age. They shared in common a searching background, with obscure, rebellious early years and unsettled private lives; both had three marriages and two divorces by this time. She was not naive about Talbot, and saw his weaknesses, protectively forbidding the young women who worked at the headquarters from even speaking to him during his residency.¹³

Tingley was aware that Talbot, after the Reno trial, was financially strapped and discouraged. She hoped he could write the great novel he was capable of, and believed it might prove to be a theosophical work, given the overtones of some of his previous novels. To this end, in the fall of 1923 she invited him to take up residence as a guest in her two-story home, the society headquarters, "Wachere Crest" (which still stands today). Through the spring he occupied a room in the northwest corner of the second floor.

The setting was conducive to his work. The colony had something of the feel of a cloister, with uniformed guards at the iron gates normally admitting only authorized guests. On a typical day at the Theosophical community, a light wind scattered through the well-ordered trees gathered from many lands. The sun shone over the nearby Temple of Peace and the Homestead (or Academy), with their imposing colored glass-domed structures, while in other directions were the circular Spalding House, and the Greek Theater, all centered around the Tingley residence. The avenue between the Homestead and Greek Theater was lined with pepper trees, eucalyptus groves, palm trees, and pines.¹⁴ Only a few hundred feet away from the main cluster of buildings, wave upon wave of the Pacific Ocean pounded against the steep straight cliffs. In afternoons, Talbot and his Airedale pup would get some exercise and occasional inspiration by walking down to Mission Beach, with sea-gulls for the pup to chase.¹⁵

Only one special companion was lacking, and soon she, too, moved to San Diego. Talbot thought of her every morning. After a seven o'clock breakfast, his morning routine would continue as he walked, with a vigorous stride and bounding step, down the open stairs at the back of the Tingley house. He crossed about ten feet of

View of Lomaland, with the amphitheater of the Greek Theater at left, the Egyptian Gate in foreground, Katherine Tingley's two-story home in the center, and in the background, the circular Temple of Peace, and at right the larger Homestead, both topped by glass domes.

yard to another small building, where Gottfried de Purucker and Mrs. Tingley's private secretary, Iverson L. Harris, lived. A public telephone could be reached from outside at the corner, and every morning Talbot promptly made the same call. He would dial, and upon receiving the response, would almost shout, "Good morning, Sally! Hello!" Talbot spoke with such exuberance that he could be heard through the windows by a young Theosophical student, Emmett Small, then living in No. 10 room in the southwest home.[16]

Point Loma was a sanctuary of learning and philosophy that enriched Mundy's writing, and made up for some of the formal education he had missed. Theosophy became his university, providing an intensive education in higher thought through an immersion in lectures, plays, and the classics of ancient times and of the East. The impact would be evident not only in the growing Theosophical content of his novels but in his new interest in writing non-fiction as well as his decision to challenge the legacy of Shakespeare and Shaw in *W.H.* and *Queen Cleopatra*.

Gathered at Point Loma were companions whose model provided a further impetus to Talbot's intellectual development. In 1923, Tingley appointed him to her

September 10, 1923: Guests and Point Loma luminaries gather to observe a solar eclipse. From left, Reginald Machell, Mundy, Sven Hedin, Captain J.F. Anderson, Swedish viceconsul Nils Malmberg, J.H. Fussell, Kenneth Morris, and Winfield Scott. (Courtesy Richards Ames Collection)

cabinet, a position of honor that involved advisory and supportive duties. Membership enhanced his opportunities to meet and form friendships with the inner circle of Tingley's intellectual group. It was a sign of the respect given Talbot despite his newcomer status, since cabinet positions were usually reserved for veteran Theosophists. Mundy placed himself in the context of the older leaders with due deference but without any sense of inferiority.

Many members had been with Tingley since she had taken over the Society in 1898, and some had been personal pupils of Blavatsky in London, including F.J. Dick and Reginald Machell.[17] Machell's mystical artistry was adapted to portals, arches, doorways, and furnishings to create an inspiring harmony of style. Two particular Mundy friends among the members were Joseph Fussell and Dick. Fussell had been with Tingley from the beginning, her best pamphleteer, and would arrange to have *Om* reviewed in Masonic publications. Mundy regularly attended cabinet meetings, and remained in contact even when he was away; he only resigned after Tingley's death in 1929.

Talbot joined privately held studies of H.P. Blavatsky's *The Secret Doctrine*, led by Gottfried de Purucker (1874–1942), under Tingley's direction. The classes began on January 4, 1924, and were held once or twice a week. The sessions would begin simply with the lighting of incense at the altar and the sound of a gong, as Purucker would address his "Fellow-Students of the Ancient Wisdom."[18] Tingley believed no one was better qualified than Purucker to interpret *The Secret Doctrine* and his work was both a commentary upon, and expansion of, *The Secret Doctrine*. He had met Tingley in Switzerland 1902, just as the Society was at a crisis point, when she had been told that the spot she wanted to buy at Point Loma was government property. Purucker was not only American-born, a Theosophist, but also a former resident of

San Diego who was familiar with Point Loma and knew that the land she wanted was just north of the government portion and indeed available.

Outside of the cabinet, another friend of Talbot's was the Hungarian Maurice Braun (1877–1941), who came to the United States at age four, already showing the skill of a painter. He came to San Diego in 1909, and established a reputation for his landscapes, especially for his warm, bright, and colorful rendering of Western scenes. He credited Theosophy with sharpening his insight into nature and the realization that beauty was the language of art, which was in turn to serve the divine powers of humankind.[19]

The impact of the cabinet, the sessions led by Purucker, and the other intellectual influences of Point Loma were readily evident in the long series of articles and poems Mundy contributed to *The Theosophical Path*. The study of religion and philosophy had given Mundy the desire to pen such studies of his own, which he had begun even before taking up residence. The first appeared in the August 1923 issue, and subsequently one would be featured in nearly every monthly issue through the beginning of 1926. These articles would be collected posthumously in the 1995 anthology *The Lama's Law*, edited by Mark Jaqua for Isis Books.

Mundy's articles formed an increasingly thematic and original series of essays attempting to distill his entire philosophy into a few pages. At the heart of all of these was the view that "this earth-life is but an incident in an eternal chain of lives," a belief in reincarnation and karma.[20]

> The fallacy, that the Psalmist's three score years and 10 are the sum-total of a man's experience, is at the bottom of the ignorant delusion that a man may do wrong and not pay for it in full. There is no escape through death's door, because death is no more than a period between two lives, and we return to earth again to face in naked justice the effects of all we did or left undone.
>
> Precisely there is where the churches fail. They preach the Sermon on the Mount, but teach that men may not revisit scenes of earth-experience or meet again in justice those whom they have loved, neglected, wronged. They lull the conscience of the race to sleep with fables of vicarious salvation, and invent a death-bed remission of sins to disguise the sheer injustice of the doctrine.[21]

Rejecting such a belief he found to be profoundly liberating, giving purpose and motive to existence. "No more crawling on our knees to an imagined God to beg for favors or implore forgiveness! The remission of our sins becomes our own affair! We wipe them out, henceforth, by standing up and facing consequences, proving, by the way we meet those consequences, that a portion of life's lesson has been learned."[22]

The quality of these articles varied, both within each individual essay and among them. Although clearly part of a projected series, there was much repetition. Sometimes the internal complexity of the articles was virtually self-defeating. Often his style veered toward an excess of rhetorical questions, one following on the heels of another, becoming overblown and strident. The articles were clearly the work of a novice in the area, not nearly as well defined or organized as the chapters that would eventually comprise *I Say Sunrise*. Yet Mundy wrote with singular vigor and clarity, and there were many unique and stirring passages that reflect the Point Loma milieu.

In the Theosophical Society, Mundy was immediately recognized as one of their most popular, persuasive, and charismatic public speakers.[23] His British accent was a reminder of his English origins, and his powerful voice created a drama enjoyed by listeners.[24] He was called upon to make numerous addresses, although it was not a task he enjoyed. Many of these speeches lasted over an hour, on occasions varying from the informal to the ceremonial, and he was best in extemporaneous forums, as was Tingley. He could be especially entertaining by cleverly sprinkling his speeches with his reminiscences of India and other lands that would have a special appeal to Theosophists because of their inclination toward all things Eastern.

Several conferences on world peace brought global attention, and at one of these, the Parliament of Peace and Universal Brotherhood convened by Tingley from July 16–27, 1923, Mundy was a featured speaker. In his speech, later reprinted as the article "Universal" in the January 1924 issue of *The Theosophical Path*, he reversed his support of the League of Nations in favor of Tingley's belief that universal brotherhood was the first necessity.

He spoke to the youth as well, and particularly the boy's groups in the Society, including the William Quan Judge Theosophical Club of Lomaland, of which he was made an honorary member.[25] For youth he had also written a reminiscence of Africa entitled "Some True Stories About Wild Animals" for the May 1924 issue of *Raja-Yoga Messenger*, the Point Loma magazine for children.

Mundy's public reputation at Point Loma was established not only as a speaker, and in his writing for *The Theosophical Path*, but in participation in the community's dramatic presentations, which he reviewed for *The San Diego Union* newspaper. The most renowned plays at Point Loma were those presented in the Greek Theater, the first built in America. These productions created Tingley's world-wide reputation for unique dramatic presentations; probably she had been a member of a travelling stock company in her 20s.[26] The plays were either Shakespearean or ancient Greek, but usually with a new musical score composed by such Point Loma luminaries as Rex Dunn.[27] As many as 2500 spectators—performances were always sold out—could attend the temple of open Greek architecture that made up the stage.

In November, 1923, Talbot took part in *The Aroma of Athens*, a combination of pageant and symposium that was performed by members of the Theosophical Society from time to time from 1911 until Tingley's death. Tingley had originated the composition, relying on Theosophist scholar Fritz Sage Darrow in the preparation of the script. The result sought to present the ancient wisdom as enunciated by Blavatsky upon the problems of the day, through a dramatic presentation. Athens is portrayed in the Periclean glory of the final day of the truce with Sparta in 431 B.C., and at the climax, Socrates predicts a new Athens will arise in the West. In between songs and dances, many of them magnificently performed by the Raja-Yoga children, there are imagined discourses between many ancient notables, including Euripides, Thucydides, about the true, the good, and the beautiful.[28] During the 1920s, the part of Apollo was performed by Purucker; Reginald Machell was Phidias; Iverson L. Harris, Sr., was Pericles; and Herbert Coryn was Socrates.[29] That year, Tingley took the part of Aspasia, and the performance took place in San Diego's downtown Isis Theater, the first time she had been on the stage since 1900.[30]

Sadly, no record exists of Talbot's role, although he did have a speaking part, and he made a memorable impression on one of the Point Loma children watching a rehearsal. "I remember him standing and I can still hear his sonorous voice, but I do not know whom he represented. On completing his part he raised his right hand and I saw only two fingers... The actors of the Symposium sat in a semicircle again and I remember Dr. Wood, Talbot Mundy and Mr. Neresheimer sitting there in their Greek costumes and with a lot of make-up on their faces."[31] Sally also appeared in local dramatic productions, and she and Talbot attended the classical concerts in the Rotunda of the Raja Yoga Academy.

Meanwhile, Talbot was hard at work on *Om*. His idea was simple yet overwhelming: to write a novel about the Masters who formed such a centerpiece of Theosophical thinking, and make their teaching the thematic centerpiece. He would use this pattern in two subsequent novels written at Point Loma, *The Devil's Guard* and *The Red Flame of Erinpura*, and later in *Black Light* and *Old Ugly-Face*.

To Mundy's reading public, the Masters involved a complex set of beliefs that would be foreign in many ways. The Masters are highly evolved adepts who have attained advanced powers and labor on behalf of the enlightenment of humanity. When the Masters emerge publicly, some are rulers, teachers, and philosophers. Buddha, Jesus, and Confucius are regarded as a mighty triad of ethical teachers, who taught openly to the multitudes. In this way, Theosophists regard Jesus as one of history's most prominent "Masters," rather than the Christian belief in a literal son of God; Abraham, Moses, and Solomon are also regarded as Masters.

Because their learning may become a dangerous possession in the wrong hands, and its misuse could have disastrous consequences, it is up to the Masters to entrust it only incrementally to selected individuals. Such figures are usually reviled as imposters, because none can discover the source of their knowledge; according to Theosophical belief and her own assertion, H.P. Blavatsky was one. Mundy summed up his own beliefs about the Masters.

> I am reliably informed that at this present time the home of the Masters is in Tibet, that country being difficult of access and affording them the opportunity they need to think and move and have their being in an undisturbed calm, beneath whose unruffled surface they persist in pauseless effort to induce into the world high thinking and its consequences, purity of living; since through purity alone comes true enlightenment.
>
> But this may give a false impression of them. They are manly men, not meditative fakirs. Except that they are human they resemble not at all the popularity pursuing "swamis," self-styled "mahatmas" or "yogis" who posture on rocks for the plaudits of ignorant people — or who cross the Atlantic to pocket the dollars of fools. They do not advertise. They shun the fawning adulation of the mob as sedulously as they keep aloof from its vindictiveness and passion. To them, I have been told, all forms of selfishness appear ridiculous, since selfishness contains its own destroying agent, and to them there is no profit under the sun except in benefiting others.[32]

By March 1924, Mundy had completed his new book and submitted it to Bobbs-Merrill and *Adventure*. To Mundy's surprise, Arthur Hoffman accepted the story, and the magazine's whole staff was enthusiastic, which the author regarded as a marvel. As Hoffman wrote, "Before going on it is only fair to say this. I not only read the story word for word, but I also tried all along to understand what it is all about, which meant I had to lap up an awful lot of esoteric stuff that was all new to me."[33] Bobbs-Merrill had far fewer reservations, but believed that it was too long and preachy.[34]

In *Om*, Mundy created his most distinctly literary book, surpassing earlier novels by exhibiting a maturing skill in choice of language, plot structure, theme, and depth of character. Although in later years Mundy may have matched *Om*, he probably never exceeded its standard; it is his strongest fictional statement of philosophy, with the sole exception of his last novel, *Old Ugly-Face*. Not only was *Om* written with greater care, it was meant to be taken more seriously. Mundy authored a long letter in the October 10, 1924 issue of *Adventure* to introduce *Om* to readers (reprinted in the February 1925 issue of *The Theosophical Path*), emphasizing the reality of the Ahbor Valley, its inaccessibility, and his reasons for believing in the "Masters."

Although working titles included *The Crystal Jade* and *The Ringding Gelong Lama*, the far more esoteric title of *Om* was eventually selected. The serialization in *Adventure* from October 10–November 30, 1924 and British book edition were called simply *Om*, and the subtitle, *The Secret of Ahbor Valley*, was added for American book publication. The title, *Om*, has a tripartite meaning. First, it signifies the famous mantra; "'Om' is part of an ancient Buddhist chant (Om mani padme hum)," as Dick Ames noted, translating as "Hail, jewel in the heart of the lotus!"[35] Second, *Om* was an abbreviation for the title character, Cotswold Ommony. Together, both meanings symbolize Ommony's transformation as a European who adopts the ways of the East and is initiated into its mysteries.

In *Om*, adventure, drama, humor and an unusual philosophy are blended expertly, revealing a multi-layered, perplexing India full of picturesque cities, regions and customs, and beneath it all a stratum intimating the supernatural. These aspects are portrayed authentically and sympathetically, through Mundy's facility for expression, incident, and atmosphere, as the reader feels the very pulse of India.[36] The verisimilitude of the descriptive portions wins acceptance for the teaching and philosophy.

Om opens with a fascinating panoply of India, as a seemingly inevitable series of bizarre incidents grow into a tempest on the streets, triggering an accidental roadside pile-up — a vivid, materialized depiction of the same Karmaic law of cause and effect that also governs the souls of Mundy's characters. In such ways, moments of danger become transformed into opportunities to create destiny.

As one who thinks the British should leave India, Ommony is an outcast from his race. Ommony is also known as a believer in indigenous magic, who has encountered a mysterious, broken piece of jade that reflects its observer's thoughts. He meets a lama, Tsiang Samdup, and Samding, his chela (student), which confirms his desire to seek the mysteries of which he has learned so many tantalizing fragments, as well as solve the disappearance of his sister into the inaccessible Ahbor Valley two decades earlier.

These threads grow into the subplots along Ommony's journey. The elements fuse into Ommony's discovery of a philosophy, labeled here as "the middle way," to credibly explain that most profound of questions, the mystery of life. Like Theosophy itself, the middle way eclectically incorporates the best of both philosophy and religion, avoiding the pitfalls of extremes. The middle way proves to be not only a philosophy Samdup practices, but also a material road for secret communication, a type of "underground railroad." Secret paths in India open, close and change constantly, through which the travelers pass furtively from town to town.[37] It is only these scenes, some of which seem rather protracted and slow, that cause the pace of the novel to sag during the long trek in the center of the book.

Unlike some Mundy books, in *Om* characterization is a strength, with a fascinating array of vibrant, authentic individuals splashed across its pages. As San Diego critic Austin Adams wrote, Mundy's *Om* more than withstood comparison with Joseph Conrad, ranking *Om* alongside E.M. Forster's *A Passage to India*, finding that Mundy paints "his portraits of real people ... almost as convincingly...."[38] Mundy spins an endless web of incredibly diverse Indian characters, all equally vivid and arresting—whether the wise Samdup, the bloodthirsty and duplicitous Dawa Tsering, the Sikh double agent, or the nervous but knowing merchants Chutter Chand and Benjamin.

The final chapters, set inside the Ahbor Valley as Ommony hears Samdup's remarkable story, become Mundy's essay. The jade is revealed as actually part of a scientific instrument made by the savants of a long-forgotten race, to reflect the best and worst traits of whomever looks in it, "a mirror for the soul...."[39] After facing this trial of self-revelation, Ommony is sent out into the world once more to face his destiny. As Mundy wrote in the proverb facing chapter 2 of *Om*, "He who would understand the Plains must ascend the Eternal Hills, where a man's eyes scan Infinity. But he who would make use of understanding must descend on to the Plains, where Past and Future meet and men have need of him."

Ommony's own striving is rewarded with a trust: his companion traveling back to India will be Samding, revealed to be his niece, the daughter of his late, long-lost sister. Samding has been protected and reared all these years by Samdup as foster-father and teacher.

Since Samding was born in the Ahbor Valley, its people exact the price of Samdup's life when she departs, a sacrifice the Lama willingly makes because he has intentionally tricked them. In this way he hopes to avoid the karmaic consequences of evading his lie to the Ahbors. Or, as Mundy had put the same idea in one of his articles, "Another's Duty is Full of Danger," for *The Theosophical Path*, "the occult law, that what is due eventually must be paid; with interest, if we delay the payment...."[40] In accepting his unavoidable death sentence, the Lama Samdup follows an example set earlier by the Gray Mahatma in *Caves of Terror*.

Ommony is now to become Samding's chela, assisting and protecting her. However, Samding is not, as some interpretations have suggested, a "savior," but merely a wise teacher, one of many who will be needed to convey Eastern wisdom to the West. In her, East and West synthesize without clash or disharmony, and contrary to Kipling the twain must and shall meet. In *Om* both cultures must be brought together, and Samding has the unique combination of a Westerner reared in the

East — qualifications Mundy hints will be required for the wisdom of the East to be transmitted to the Occidental world.

Samding is a woman, like Mundy's teachers, Blavatsky, Tingley, and Mary Baker Eddy. Similarly, the visit in the novel to the mission school at Tilgaun is clearly modeled on Tingley's own Raja-Yoga principles of education in the society's academy at Point Loma. Many Point Loma Theosophists thought they recognized the inspiration of Tingley's own teachings in Samdup's sayings and character.[41] Mundy acknowledged the debt when he wrote to Tingley, "What wisdom [Om] contains was learned from you, and its unwisdom is my own. Without your teaching, patience, and encouragement I could not have 'imagined' either the wise old Lama or his chela."[42]

Not only did the teachings Mundy learned at Point Loma inspire Samdup, but also the lamas he had met while in India. When asked about the "Masters" in *Adventure*, Mundy would reply that he believed he had once met such an individual who, however, naturally would not admit to that identity.[43]

In Samdup, Mundy vastly enlarges the archetype of the Grey Mahatma who had appeared in *Caves of Terror* two years previously. The Ringding Gelong Lama of *Om* is far more likable, wise yet whimsical, compassionate, perceptive, humble, a man of incomparable serenity even when facing death.[44] In the words of the Lama, "Drama is the way to teach.... By allegories, parables and illustrations men learn easily what no amount of argument will drive into their understanding."[45] Ommony, in disguise, follows Samdup as he leads a theatrical caravan toward Tibet, performing small plays wherever they go. Ommony plays a series of roles: those he performs on stage, together with the identity of the Bhat-Brahmin actor he assumes in the vain hope of concealing his presence from Samdup. Similarly, Samding wears male clothes to facilitate her passage through India. The British police only understand enough of Samdup's play to claim it is seditious.

Not only is this a reflexive analogy on Mundy's part for the role of his own tales as conduits and illustrations for teaching philosophy, it is the most successful form he ever devised to convey abstract ideas in a comprehensible and practical manner — while still managing to entertain. The inspiration for Samdup's technique surely came from Katherine Tingley's own theatrical background and the plays which Mundy was attending, reviewing, and participating in while writing the novel.

Mundy's strategy proved fruitful: he "succeeded brilliantly in making philosophy the very life-blood of a most absorbing story...."[46] More effectively than in any of his other work, *Om* strikes a delicate, unique balance between the descriptive, the narrative and the didactic, while still retaining the guise of the storyteller. For *Adventure* readers and other laymen, *Om* could serve as pure entertainment or an introduction to Eastern thought, providing escapism mixed with Theosophy for the unsuspecting. For Theosophists, on the other hand, *Om* is a reaffirmation and fictionalizing of their teaching in novel form. *Om* becomes a journey that can be oft repeated and never leaves the reader unaffected, a novel which, perhaps more so than any other by Mundy, richly rewards re-reading.[47]

Between each chapter are philosophical poetry and proverbs, some of which had previously appeared in *The Theosophical Path*; many were credited to the "Book of the Sayings of Tsiang Samdup." The sayings themselves are rich and sometimes obscure, changing in meaning for the reader over time; like the Jade of Ahbor, they give the impression of never quite staying the same.

Writing such a book as *Om* was a risky venture for Mundy; he chose to diverge from the conventional commercial formulas. In a letter to his publisher, he described it as "soaked with sound philosophy and stirring mystery, plus dangerous adventure."[48] Bobbs-Merrill was concerned by such a statement. "Everything about it sounds bully except that it is 'soaked with philosophy.' That gives the wary publisher a bit of a chill, because he knows how the common peepul [sic] run away from brain stuff unless it is so well covered with sugar that they don't know it for medicine."[49] Probably only a writer of Mundy's established stature could have succeeded in taking such a story as *Om* to widespread popularity and publication.

In *Om*, more strongly than in any of his previous fiction, Mundy firmly established the literary pattern of looking to the East, not only for exoticism, but for wisdom and an alternative mode of living superior to Western habits. Mundy crystallized the archetype of the Westerner who quits the dissatisfying colonial life to search for wisdom. In this way *Om*, and later Mundy works such as *The Devil's Guard*, *Black Light*, *Full Moon* and *Old Ugly-Face*, reinvigorated and revitalized fantasy-adventure literature.

Mundy resented his book being called a "second *Kim*" by Hoffman and critics; the 1926 A.L. Burt edition, using one of the Bobbs-Merrill dust jackets, designed vaguely along the lines of Machell's work, contained an endorsement from Gertrude Atherton: "strikes me as being the most interesting and important novel about India since Kipling's *Kim*." Mundy's interpretation of a lama is totally different from that of Kipling, and indeed *Om* is arguably the better work, and certainly the more timeless.[50] The Lama in *Kim* is fundamentally a passive, impractical figure, hardly a "Master"—in Mundy's words "as untrue to life, as stupid, effete, impossible and missionary-ignorant (to coin a phrase) as a character could be.... [*Om*] is the only piece of fiction ever written that gives a true view of the inner, that is esoteric philosophy of the Lamas, and a real inkling of who the so-called Mahatmas [Masters] really are."[51]

Although proud of his work, Mundy expected *Om* to be criticized outside the Theosophical community for its favorable portrayal of Eastern ideas. Even Hoffman had wondered about the advisability of publishing this new story with its implicit denial of the dogma of Western religions. He felt obliged to issue a strong preliminary disclaimer to *Adventure* readers, nodding to Christian sensibilities by indicating he in no way endorsed Mundy's views, adding that there was no intention of starting a religious debate in the magazine's pages. "This magazine is in no way sponsoring the opinions he offers. If you don't like them settle it with him, not with the magazine or with me personally, and don't think for a minute that Camp-Fire is going to use any of its time or space for arguments pro and con. No religious discussions at our blaze."[52] Talbot had similar anxieties.

However, Hoffman's concern and those of Mundy himself proved unnecessary. *Om* was published in book form in November 1924 in the United States by Bobbs-Merrill—where it began its third edition after several months—and in England at the beginning of January 1925, and went into a second edition before the end of the month.[53] By February, 1925, only a few months after its publication, thanks to Mundy's status as a local celebrity in southern California, *Om* became a regional best-seller, with sales of nearly 750 copies in the first six months.[54] Readership was not limited to sales; by mid–1925, the librarian in San Diego told Talbot that she had 25 copies of *Om* but still could not keep up with demand.[55] Mundy received offers to dramatize the play for city audiences. The novel was also popular abroad, where it was soon commercially translated into such languages as French, German, and Slav, under the titles *L'Oeuf de Jade*, *Om, das geheimnis des Abhortales*, and *Abhora ielejas nos lepums*, respectively.[56]

Critics in both England and the United States were enthusiastic. A typical mainstream review of *Om* appeared in the *Manchester City News*: "The volume contains a wealth of Oriental lore, and is the product of a well-stored and scholarly mind. Those who want philosophy and ... a work of fiction entirely out of the common may be safely commended to this work.... The Lama's impressive teachings produce a deep impression.... Mr. Mundy has produced a literary and philosophical masterpiece."[57] During 1925 and beyond, *The Theosophical Path* joyfully reprinted excerpts from the stream of praise *Om* received in letters and reviews from around the globe.[58]

Theosophists quickly took *Om* to heart, since it perfectly expressed their deepest beliefs in a popular context.[59] Tingley was vigorous in her praise, saying *Om* contains "a genuine and powerful message of Brotherhood. In the wise utterances and quaint sayings of the old Lama, the book marks a new epoch in the history of fiction."[60] The journal's December 1924 issue contained Gottfried de Purucker's perceptive and ecstatic review, emphasizing the novel's psychological power. *Om* was equally hailed by Theosophists around the world. Theosophists on the European continent immediately began translating it into a number of languages, including Dutch and Swedish, under the titles *Om — Het Geheim van de Ahbor Vallei* and *Aum, Ahbordalens Lemlighet*, respectively.

There were hundreds of more personal testimonials. Even during serialization, and for a year thereafter, Mundy was deluged with up to seventeen letters a day from *Adventure* readers praising the story as his best yet. These were thoughtful letters, written on a par with the professional reviews of the book.[61] Over a third of the letters asked where they could obtain a copy of "The Book of the Sayings of Tsiang Samdup."[62] Mundy took advantage of the situation to write an article for the January 1925 issue of *The Theosophical Path* entitled "An Answer To Correspondents." He asked, "Has the world gone mad, that it accepts my book? Or is it waking up?"[63]

Among those who spoke highly of *Om* were Alice Roosevelt Longworth, a regular Mundy fan, daughter of former president Theodore Roosevelt and wife of the Speaker of the House of Representatives.[64] California's Progressive Senator Hiram Johnson quoted from the book in a Senate speech in the capitol, and a letter from Sally prompted a note from Johnson praising *Om*.[65]

Despite the support of readers and critics, Mundy was ultimately disappointed when *Om* did not become the commercial breakthrough to reach a mass audience. Nonetheless, in the years to come the book has achieved a classic status evident by its frequent reprinting, with steadily increasing popularity.[66]

Within barely a month after the publication of *Om* in book form, Mundy had received more than 800 letters asking for a sequel.[67] The favorable reception prompted Katherine Tingley to call on him to provide one, and he promised to try, later deciding to provide instead a new, hopefully better work.[68] Within less than a year, he had authored another Indian novel, and submitted it in August 1925 to his publishers.

Mundy continued the experiment begun with *Om* of reading aloud selected passages freshly written to family and fellow theosophists such as Kenneth Morris. Using appropriate dramatic flourishes, he wanted to gauge reactions and listen to comments, incorporating or rejecting them according to his story-teller's instinct. As Dick Ames recalled, "The 'Sayings of Tsiang Samdup,' and all the manuscript[s] ... were read to us (Sally and me) at the breakfast table.... Sometimes we suggested changes or additions—sometimes accepted, sometimes not. *All* this before K.T. ever saw it."[69]

Hoffman was not enthusiastic about the new novel, but Bobbs-Merrill believed that since it contained more action than *Om* it might not be so much over the heads of the masses. The company suggested the book might be enriched by including Tsiang Samdup's sayings before each chapter, as in *Om*.[70] Although Samdup is not a character, his commentaries are thematically connected to the subsequent action.

The new novel ultimately was serialized in *Adventure* in five parts from June through August of 1926, under the title *Ramsden*. The British book edition was taken directly from that text, so it lacked Samdup's sayings, as well as modified chapter headings in the American edition. There was also a discrepancy about the title, Bobbs-Merrill desiring one that was stronger, as Mundy explained to a correspondent. "*Ramsden* came out last September in England, published by Hutchinson's. The United States publishers, who are nothing if not United States American, changed the title to *The Devil's Guard*. It didn't do them or me or the book or the readers any good, but they still think they ought to be praised for their remarkable ingenuity."[71]

For *Adventure* readers, Mundy wrote a long, four page letter for "The Camp Fire," setting his novel in a context of East-West religious thinking and the attractions different individuals feel for good and evil. At this time, Mundy wrote, he had reached a stage where gun-play, love affairs, flappers, and treasure seekers no longer intrigued him. "But I am more than ever interested in adventure, and I see vast realms in which to go adventuring if any of you care to come with me. I can promise you excitement. I will guarantee to make you think, if you will go the distance."[72]

The Devil's Guard is actually a follow-up to *Caves of Terror* and *The Nine Unknown*, continuing the exploits of Grim, Ramsden, Narayan Singh, and Chullunder Ghose in India. While the use of these familiar figures is in one sense largely a convenience, with Ramsden returning as first person narrator, Mundy wisely reduced the number of Western characters to two, matched with two Indians. The British press noted Mundy's new distribution of nationalitites, and he was castigated by the critic for the London *Times Literary Supplement*. "Mr. Mundy's party of explorers consists of two Americans, assisted by a Bengali, a Sikh policeman, and two Jews.... The general impression is that the United States is gaining ground."[73]

Both Indians see beyond the occupation of their land, each undercutting imperialism in their own way. Narayan Singh accepts his mortality, believing this life is one of many, and he has reached his limit in this life; Ramsden believes he may be marking time in this life between a past and future life in which he had, and will, again, achieve greatness. By contrast, Ghose complains.

> What am I but a babu—failed B.A.? Should I have sat down and have said "yes, sahib, yes, sahib" to every alien Jack-in-office who could order me, because he had a white skin, without knowing the thousandth part of what I know? Should I have said "yes, sahib" to the hypocrites and "yes, sahib" to the fools and "yes, sahib" to the men who grow rich while I am supposed to be grateful to them for the right to swallow the dust they make?... And is it my fault that the world is no oyster for a failed B.A. with a brown skin and no capacity to be a hypocrite?[74]

Yet he also recognizes Grim and Ramsden as the only white men who never thought of him as anything but their equal.

Narayan Singh, the fighting man *par excellence*, represents the best of India's past, even under British rule, while Ghose is a man of its future, actively resenting colonialism and looking to the new India. At the climax of *The Devil's Guard*, Narayan Singh will be killed, because he must die just as will old India, despite its virtues. Ghose sums up the differences between them.

> Sahibs, I was jealous of that Sikh. I loved him. He was a fighting fool, as sure to go off as a stick of dynamite. I was afraid of him. I hated his way of sitting by a fireside with that little hone and sharpening his saber. But I would give all I have to be able wear such blinkers as he wore, and to have such firmity of purpose. Firmity of purpose—ah! To understand too much and see too much is my infirmity, since I see all around a thing. I see absurdities, were other men see only opportunities for valor. Sahibs, knowledge is a dreadful handicap. I envied that man Narayan Singh his blindness; he could not see the absurdity of things, and so he died a hero. But I fear me I shall die in bed, which is of all abominations the least tolerable because it is the essence of expectedness and almost any fool can do it.[75]

Grim continues the evolution begun in *The Nine Unknown* into a steadily more occult, mysterious character. He is further distanced from imperialism; in *The Devil's Guard*, he is identified as having been part of the Younghusband expedition, but "got himself into disfavor by ignoring the military problems he was there ostensibly to help clear up, and studying exclusively those apparently insignificant odds and ends, that, he maintains, are 'the guts of things.'"[76]

The Devil's Guard is a curious novel, often stunning, full of contradictions, more of a metaphorical adventure into the soul than a fantasy, a direction taken explicitly a few years later in *Black Light*. Unlike *The Nine Unknown*, which had lacked essential thematic unity, *The Devil's Guard* is a literary achievement that is both a powerful fantasy and a revelation of occult teaching. *The Devil's Guard* actually goes further into the specific mysteries at which *Om* concluded, as befits a product of the time of Mundy's deepest involvement in the Theosophical movement.

In *The Devil's Guard*, Mundy carries the search for the teaching of the "Masters" from the Indian setting of *Caves of Terror* and *The Nine Unknown*, and the

Himalayan plateaus where *Om* left off, through a grueling journey into Tibet. Grim, Ramsden, Chullunder Ghose, and Narayan Singh follow a summons for help from a former schoolmate and mining partner of Ramsden, Elmer Rait, who turns out to be as treacherous as his name, with its resemblance to "rat." They are caught in the middle as a battle between good and evil rages amidst rockbound monasteries, in encounters with powers both apparently supernatural and simply barbaric. The search for Rait also becomes a quest for the wisdom of Sham-bha-la, which he was trying to reach.

Many have searched for Sham-bha-la, and it has remained one of the most prominent myths of the East, a fabled kingdom consecrated to the teachings of the Buddha's disciples. The residents are the Masters and their initiates, who preserve the ancient wisdom on written manuscripts in a language older than Sanskrit. They have renounced violence and refuse to take a life under any circumstances — hence their inability to save Narayan Singh from death at the hands of Rait. These individuals make up the secret White Lodge; the Dalai Lama and the Tashi (or Panchen) Lama are the trusted outer representatives. Grim, Ramsden, Ghose, and Narayan Singh encounter an actual Master, Lhaten, who has the ability to appear whenever and wherever needed. He tells them that no true discovery can be made when profit or selfishness are the motivations, the reason many others have failed to find Sham-bha-la, and why the altruism of the "hope, faith, perseverance, and true friendship" of Grim's band make them so formidable.[77]

In *The Devil's Guard*, "everything is evolving into something else."[78] The two Americans, Grim and Ramsden, and two Indians, Narayan Singh and Ghose, are all men in various stages of evolution, each striving upward as best he can from the different plateaus he has reached. Ghose claims the whites have stolen India, and, after Grim has been accepted to Sham-bha-la, believes they will now rob his land's spiritual heritage as well. However, Ghose proves fearful of Sham-bha-la, and the changes it will bring in the way he sees the world. Unwilling to abandon his illusions and false sense of reality, Ghose will return to India, escorted by Lhaten, while Grim and Ramsden go forward to Sham-bha-la.

Ramsden writes the story of their journey, since he is not yet bound to secrecy until he actually enters Sham-bha-la, with the manuscript to be taken by Ghose to a friend in the West (obviously a reference to Mundy himself, and his publishers). This is the novel that we have been reading; as in *Hira Singh* and *W.H.*, Mundy uses such a framing device to remove the novel from the fictional realm. At the same time, Ramsden closing the narrative as the men come to escort him into Sham-bha-la gives the story the abrupt ending of a dream. Indeed, much of *The Devil's Guard* reads like an extended dream, in parts a nightmare — a bizarre, surrealistic realm where souls are governed by psychic forces. As Ramsden notes, the high altitude of Tibet tends to make dreams and waking thought equally vivid and sharply edged. Incidents based in actual dreams, hypnotism, and fantastic events are so frequent that the reader is forced out of his conventional view of the world, just as Grim and Ramsden will lose their illusions upon entering Sham-bha-la.

The Devil's Guard also shares with *Caves of Terror* and *The Nine Unknown* the theme of contending forces of good and evil, the one completely opposite the other in methods as well as goals, to explain the presence of misery in the world. Why, if the "Masters" exist and they have their reputed power, do they not banish evil from the world? (Mundy never invokes a divine presence in his fiction.) Why does evil seem as strong a force in the world as good? And since evil clearly exists, what attracts men to it, and how do they acquire their power? Mundy offers an answer, which in some ways is analogous to the Christian belief in a universe where God and the Devil coexist as opposites. *The Devil's Guard* becomes a meditation on evil's palpable presence, which demands it be recognized as a separate force in order to be understood.

While Mundy draws evil and good in sharp contrast, the two may exist side by side. Monks fight among themselves, members of the Black and White Lodge, Red and Yellow Hats, respectively, often living in the same monastery. In this way Mundy also explains how institutions have both good and evil impact. What is true of an institution is also true of an individual.

Various types of black magic are used by members of the Black Lodge, failed initiates who are akin to the kali-worshippers of India or the Bible's fallen angels. Envy, hatred, and impatience caused them to be excluded from the White Lodge, and in turn they use the knowledge they did learn for ill. These fiendish human devils, known as dugpas, oppose the Masters's efforts and deify evil. Dugpa literally means sorcerer, but it also implies more; they represent the forces opposed to the power of good, and are energetic, intelligent, and far-seeing, just as Satan, in the Christian tradition, is supposed to be clever. Through the influence of dugpas, and their ability to manipulate temptations, Mundy found a more satisfying explanation for the dark deeds that occur than the teachings of psychology. He suggests, and demonstrates in the narrative, that dugpas are often able to superimpose their will, and such transferences account for the sudden criminal outbursts of apparently sane people.

By contrast, the Masters's only authority comes from within, not from outside, and the proof of their authority is in its consequences.[79] One distinction, Mundy noted in his letter to *Adventure* readers, was "that those who grope their way toward the higher planes of good, refuse to accept power over those who follow them; although they insist on obedience from those whom they consent to teach, they insist on its being freely given, in order that the individual may himself accept the full responsibility for every step he takes, without which — if the theory is true — there is no character improvement.... The dugpas, who are said to be the students of the law of evil, use the opposite procedure. Their intention is to get, and then to keep control, of all who come within their clutches."[80] Certainly Mundy is defining a phenomenon that would include modern cults holding their adherents in a slavish thrall.

As the Bobbs-Merrill reader had noted, while *The Devil's Guard* lacks the inherent literary dignity of *Om*, Mundy intended to convey the ideas of *Om* in a more popular format, employing the style of a thriller. As the *New York Herald Tribune* reviewer commented,

> More than a corking adventure story of eerie wanderings.... It is a sort of philosophical epitome of human experience, set in a frame of adventure.... One of those satisfying books that you like to lay aside and then pick up again to re-read. It has been a long time since I read a book that gave me more genuine pleasure.... The book is notable for the words of wisdom that precede each chapter.... These bits of

philosophical common sense are alone worth the price of admission. Then, too, Mr. Mundy has drawn three remarkable characters—Jimgrim, Chullunder Ghose and Narayan Singh, that noble Sikh warrior, who lived by the sword and died by the sword.... It is a fascinating and beautifully written yarn, by all odds the very best thing that Mundy has ever done.[81]

Yet at the same time, the occult mysticism of *The Devil's Guard* may seem strange to the reader unfamiliar with its lore, just as *Om* required an acceptance of its didactic tone. Although generally well received by reviewers in the United States, and highly regarded by Theosophists, *The Devil's Guard* was not reviewed in *The Theosophical Path*, and thus denied the official stamp of approval received by *Om*.

Mundy's final story of the Masters written at Point Loma was *The Red Flame of Erinpura*, first published in the January 1927 issue of *Adventure*, and issued in book form in England by Hutchinson in 1934, but never in the United States. *The Red Flame of Erinpura* begins without any foreshadowing of the mystical turn it will take, and even by its conclusion hardly seems recognizable as occult, instead following the traditional outline of the adventure genre. Without abandoning the literary style of *Om*, *The Red Flame of Erinpura* presents a "master" in a more camouflaged manner, and perhaps as a result, or because of the comparative scarcity of Mundy stories in *Adventure* at the time, *The Red Flame of Erinpura* was selected as the magazine's fourth most popular novelette of 1927.[82]

This is the first story in which Chullunder Ghose takes the lead, having previously appeared only in the company of other Mundy heroes. The plot device of a corrupt Indian ruler seeking hidden wealth on his land, that had already formed the background for *Guns of the Gods*, is again used, except in this case the "buried treasure" is a deposit of oil, probably inspired by Mundy's own growing interest in oil in Mexico. (The idea may also have been derived from the presence of oil in Assam, one of the Indian provinces Talbot had visited in his youth.) Mundy portrays the acquisition of wealth as part of the adventure he was simultaneously writing about and trying to live at the time.

Two competing firms from the United States arrive in Erinpura in the wake of rumors of oil deposits. On the one side is the hero, John Duncannon, drawn to the daughter of his competitor, Deborah, a typically modern and fearless girl, to whom life, action, and accomplishment have an almost identical meaning. She begins thoroughly disrespectful of mysticism and Ghose, nor is she afraid to ride on horseback with the serpentine Rundhia, although such conduct shocks the British officers, "adepts to a man in the art of erecting social barriers" between Englishman and Indian.[83]

Against this background the primary theme emerges with the character of the Gnani or "Knower." Like the grey mahatma in *Caves of Terror* and Tsiang Samdup in *Om*, but unlike *The Nine Unknown* and *The Devil's Guard*, the Gnani appears in *The Red Flame of Erinpura* as a principal character. The Gnani represents the tradition of Rajputana, a land Mundy notes was civilized when Britons were fighting the Wars of the Roses and burning witches, and that has absorbed Western science without losing respect for the Ancient Wisdom.[84]

The Gnani seems to appear and disappear almost at will, with the stealth of an animal in the wild, and is able to know another person's thoughts and to examine their character. The government dislikes him, but is afraid to interfere. The British administrator is a typical colonial adventurer, content merely to prevent friction, without any of illusion that he is bringing enlightenment or progress. He wanted to meet the Gnani, but proves a scold during their encounter. Mundy maintains the anticolonial tone with another Resident who proves an unimaginative incompetent during a crisis and tries to commit suicide.

By contrast, the Gnani's wisdom is held in trust for all, and the answers he gives, to those seeking advice, serve the general good.[85] Although he has spent years trying to prevent the secret of the oil deposits in Erinpura from being discovered, the Gnani realizes it is no longer possible. The Gnani knows that if the local princes or wealthy Indians get control of the oil, it will simply worsen an already bad autocracy: If the British gain control, it will likely lead to revolution. A foreign concession, which could be controlled and prevented from acquiring political power, would have the least evil outcome. For the first time, Mundy involves one of the Masters directly in a political situation, perhaps again a reflection (and personal justification) of his own activities in oil development in Mexico.

Although the length of one of Mundy's short novels that he had written intermittently for *Adventure* during the last eight years, *The Red Flame of Erinpura* is a far more diffuse and richly textured work than most of its predecessors of that format. Rather than relying on action, as in *The Devil's Guard*, interest in *The Red Flame of Erinpura* is maintained through characters, introducing them during incidents, then returning to them at later points in the narrative. In this way, *The Red Flame of Erinpura* fails to qualify as a literary achievement to the degree of *Om* or even the later, more generic Ghose novel, *"C.I.D."* Similarly, *The Red Flame of Erinpura* lacks the strong thematic insight and purpose of *Caves of Terror* and *The Devil's Guard*, although it is far superior to *The Nine Unknown*. Nonetheless, within the limited length, Mundy has succeeded in producing an unexpectedly high quality work, intended for, and deserving of, the American book publication it failed to receive.

With these three books, *Om*, *The Devil's Guard*, and *The Red Flame of Erinpura*, Theosophy had its most direct influence upon Mundy's writing. He created a new model of the Eastern fantasy-adventure, one that foregrounded Eastern characters and Eastern teaching in a way that made them credible and convincing. He did this while simultaneously maintaining, and even enlarging, his following in *Adventure* magazine and popular literature. Theosophy would next impact a different kind of story, in a less obvious manner, as Mundy undertook to explore and re-shape another genre, the historical novel.

VII

The Ancient World, 1924–1928

Talbot Mundy was about to enter the middle period of his stay at Point Loma. Even as his stories of the East became steadily more enveloped in fantasy, he began writing in a diametrically opposite genre, historical fiction. Infusing it with the theosophical perspective, Mundy quickly proved as adept in telling history as he was in the stories of India that had long been his specialty. The most important of Mundy's historical works are the five dealing with ancient Rome, *Tros of Samothrace*, *Caesar Dies*, *Queen Cleopatra*, *Purple Pirate*, and *Roman Holiday*. Along with these came another, set in Elizabethan England, *W.H.— A Portion of the Record of Sir William Halifax*, a minor masterpiece forgotten today.

Mexico, a country Talbot had not hitherto visited, was about to become important in his life. In the summer of 1922, Mundy was one of the three top vote-getters (with Edgar Young and Arthur O. Friel) in a poll of *Adventure* magazine readers to elect members of a committee to establish an "*Adventure* expedition." He accepted, but like many of the others nominated, lived too distant from New York to be involved in planning. Southern and Central America, including Yucatan, were the most popular proposed destinations; Asia and Africa lagged well behind, and Talbot began to think of setting a story in the region. Meanwhile, Arthur Hoffman took a trip to South America in the spring of 1924. Thoughts of Mexico took on a more concrete purpose: Talbot had learned that he could obtain the divorce he was determined to get that had been denied him in Reno, with a residency in Mexico of only six weeks. After several months of planning, the timing seemed right when Hoffman insisted Talbot make a trip to New York City no later than mid–May 1924. After visiting Bobbs-Merrill's offices, Talbot and Sally left for Yucatan on June 11, expecting to return in less than two months.

On July 18, having satisfied the Yucatan residency requirement, Talbot finally secured the divorce from Rosemary denied him in Reno nearly a year before. The next day, he and Sally were married. By July 30 he was back in New York, and a month later was leaving for San Diego via Canada.

The two years from mid–1924 through mid–1926 would mark the height of Mundy's success and renown at Point Loma, and Sally was an important factor. As usual, money was a problem when Talbot wed Sally, although Talbot had never made less than $10,000 annually for years past.¹ The Mundys first action upon returning to San Diego was to buy a large old frame house in the center of two fenced-in acres on a hill overlooking the harbor and the Pacific. The front faced on Warrington Street, on the northwest corner of Wildwood, and adjoined the estate of the Seftons, one of the leading families of the area. Near the Theosophical Society headquarters, on the highest part of Point Loma, the area was originally called the Cliffs, the site of some of Katherine Tingley's early work with education and children in 1899. Mundy purchased 6.5 acres of the Point Loma estate from her for $20,000 (with a down payment of $5500), with the surrounding 4.5 acres to be sold off at a later date. It appeared to be a good buy—although later appraisals cast some doubt.²

However, because of its age, there was much work to be done on the home. As Dick recalled, "We remodeled it, and 'T' had a studio out in back.... Sally had an aviary, probably 150 birds."³ The home was converted from a pioneer house into a stately colonial type, more in keeping with the predominating houses below with their Spanish and Moorish design. During the expensive and extensive alterations, the Mundys occupied one of the residences at the Theosophical headquarters. However, Talbot, Sally, and Dick would remain distinctive for retaining civilian dress, not adopting the uniforms typical of many other society members.

To pay for the home and renovations, Mundy began a series of novelettes of ancient Rome that would eventually comprise the book, *Tros of Samothrace*, requiring that he begin every day with six to nine hours of writing.⁴ Writing one novelette a month netted $2500 each. By the new year, 1925, Mundy was working on the sixth novelette in this series. Even with that new income, and Sally's advice, Talbot soon found himself living beyond his means again.

At the beginning of April, 1925, the Mundys moved into their new home, which they decided to name "Tilgaun" after the gateway to the Ahbor Valley in *Om*. When visiting the Society grounds, he always turned down the comfort of a ride in an automobile for the mile-and-a-half distance from the Headquarters to Tilgaun, saying "I'll walk," and heading off with a vigorous stride and bounding step.⁵ Dick lived with the couple, and shortly after the Mundys moved in, Sally's niece, Helen "Peggy" Stevens, joined them to work as Mundy's secretary through 1928.

Although Dick had lived with Talbot prior to the marriage, this was the first time Talbot, Sally, and Dick lived together, the only such familial period in Talbot's adult life. Dick recalled, "It was a very happy time really.... We got on beautifully, and those were very good years indeed. He and Sally seemed to be very happy." He found his stepfather as "a hell of a guy, in all regards.... I was fortunate to know him at his absolute best."

> T.M. was a spoiler, he had a Pierce-Arrow, and a driver for mother. I had the first Chrysler roadster delivered to the city of San Diego, and that was some automobile. I was arrested for doing 80 through the city of La Jolla. T.M. liked it so much he got the next model, which was a 72. Once in a while, when I wanted to be very swanky indeed, I would take the driver, when mother wasn't using him, and put him in the rumble seat, typically English. T.M. thought that was great, he liked that idea.

Sally and Talbot, newlyweds, at home in Tilgaun. (Courtesy Richards Ames Collection)

Talbot was generous to a fault with his family and Theosophical friends, despite Sally's occasional good-natured lectures on his extravagance.[6] The Society's members knew that appearances belied his circumstances.

Talbot was an indulgent stepfather and Dick led a carefree life. "My home away from home [was] at the Coronado Hotel, with the [United States Navy] officers and their wives, etc. Quite often, the whole bunch of us would prefer to go out to the house, which was a long drive from Coronado, particularly if one has missed the last ferry, at one in the morning, which I did very often indeed. They'd like to come out to the house, sit on the fireplace, on the floor, and talk with T.M. or listen to him tell stories."[7] Talbot found these conversations equally invigorating, as he reminisced to Rose Wilder Lane. "This new generation excites me, too. It's the only hope we have, but it seems a good hope to me. In California I used to get them up by the dozen to my house and sit with them around the fireplace until long after midnight, learning things. I liked the girls best; most of the boys seemed rather brash, and as full of undemonstable [sic] assumptions as I am.... The modern California high school girl is the most marvelous thing in the world."[8] There was a penalty for Dick's many late nights. Waking to the alarm of a Little Ben clock, T.M. "got up at the crack of dawn, he had to turn out 50,000 words every 23 days, go out to the studio and come in for breakfast. Many is the time I could have strangled him, because maybe I had gotten in at four from La Jolla, and he'd come in at a quarter after six, and say 'All right, come on, get up and have some tea with me. Quit this nonsense, you'll get bedsores.'"[9]

Larry Trimble also became involved with the Theosophical Society, and Talbot introduced him to Tingley. Tingley and Trimble liked one another immediately, and Trimble eventually became a Theosophist, at least partly out of his admiration for her.[10] At Talbot's suggestion, Larry's daughter Janet enrolled in Tingley's Raja-Yoga boarding school in 1923, where the tuition was up to $2000 per year.[11] Dick laughingly referred to Larry as "The Man Who Came to Dinner," a popular play about a dinner guest who virtually moved in with the family. As he explained, Larry "came down for a weekend and stayed three years and brought quite a number of dogs," so the necessary kennels were added to the property.[12] In 1926, Larry's own last two films were released, and another frequent guest was Mundy's *Her Reputation* collaborator, Bradley King, with whom Larry was having an affair.

Two unusual Mundy books appeared at this time, both reprinting stories whose length had hitherto precluded book publication. Doubleday, Page & Co. finally followed up on its December 1921 attempt to lure Mundy to their list when he was invited, in April 1924, to add his name to a new publishing endeavor, paperback books. Although the 15 cent books paid only a half cent royalty on each copy sold, there were other benefits, most notably a large advertising campaign with other well-known popular authors, many of whom also wrote for *Adventure*. Length was another unusual factor; 30,000 words was desired, allowing material generally otherwise impossible to publish in book form.

Mundy accepted the offer against Bobbs-Merrill's advice. Chosen was *The Grey Mahatma*, seemingly the least likely candidate for publication for the desired youthful audience; it was labeled on the cover "a book for boys." The title was changed to *Caves of Terror*, and it became number 62 in a paperback series from Garden City Publishing Company. Despite the setting in India, the cover showed a pyramid and a palm tree, to remind readers of Mundy's recent popular magazine series on the Middle East.

In 1925, Mundy was flattered when an enthusiast arranged for a book edition of his 1912 short story, *The Soul of a Regiment*, to be printed in San Francisco. Hoffman had also selected it as one of eighteen short stories from his magazine's files to be reprinted in an anthology, *Adventure's Best Stories—1926*, published by George H. Doran Company.

For theosophists, the interest in Talbot Mundy shown by Tingley and the Society had, by this time, seemed more than justified. In 1925, *Om*, described as "profound truths in the guise of vivid and fascinating fiction," was placed on the "Book List of Standard Theosophical Literature" appearing monthly in *The Theosophical Path* for the next four years, preceded only by the writings of H.P. Blavatsky and Katherine Tingley.[13] The reprinting of "The Soul of a Regiment" and "The Pillar of Light" in *The Theosophical Path* provided further demonstration of the Society's willingness to discern Theosophical significance in popular literature—a policy unique to Tingley's leadership. In this she followed the lead of Blavatsky herself, who in the last months of her life composed five theosophical stories, posthumously collected as *Nightmare Tales* and illustrated by current Point Loma resident Reginald Machell.[14]

By 1925, Tingley's second book had been completed, to be entitled *The Wine of Life*. Three initial reviews were presented side-by-side in the January 1925 issue of *The Theosophical Path*, written by Mundy, Kenneth Morris, and Gottfried de Purucker. Mundy's review was selected for the honor of appearing as the preface in the book, thereby passing over other prominent and more senior members of the Society in favor of the individual most likely to be known to a wide range of readers. Just as Tingley had become Leader of the Theosophical Society at a time when she was a comparative newcomer to the movement, she readily gave priority to a relatively junior member because of her belief in the contribution he could make to the cause.

After Mundy's return from Yucatan, he wrote seven pieces for *The Theosophical Path* during the remainder of his residence at Point Loma. Among the Tingley-favored political cause on which Mundy spoke out included opposition to vivisection, expressed in reviewing William J. Long's book, *Mother Nature*, for *The Theosophical Path*, and many of his articles there also made clear his long-held opposition to colonialism.

"As to Capital Punishment" appeared in the December 1925 issue of *The Theosophical Path*, and revealed that Mundy was influenced by the social theory of crime, as well as Theosophical teachings. Both had an impact on the other, and early Theosophists had been involved with prison reform activities, as had Tingley herself before assuming leadership of the movement. Mundy wound up the article with a reminiscence of a man whose execution he had to oversee as a colonial officer, and who gradually came to accept the idea of learning from his mistakes in future lives, allowing him to face death with an impressive dignity.

As with capital punishment, Mundy's social views had been shaped before coming to Point Loma. During the winter of 1921–22 in Reno, Talbot and some friends tried an holiday experiment. Having seen "the hoboes in midwinter crawl out from under the freight cars ... frozen, full of hate against society, and as bitter as rabid animals," Talbot, who had gone hungry himself on many on occasion, had first-hand experience of their emotions. "Midnight; no money; a row of bright restaurant windows in view. The prospect — arrest at daybreak, no breakfast, and a 'floating order' from the magistrate." So Talbot and others tried handing a dollar to each of the hoboes who passed. "We said nothing. The hoboes said nothing. They lit out for the ham-and-egg shops over the way. But the change in the hobo's frame of mind, as he discovered there was someone who thought enough about him to stand there at midnight and give him a dollar without any strings attached, was magical. You could feel it, see it, understand it. A potential murderer turned into a man with a human appetite."[15]

Mundy not only discussed his views in *The Theosophical Path*, but also expressed them in the pages of "The Camp-Fire" in *Adventure*, with a letter on hunger as the cause of crime. He believed that any nation with food enough for everyone should be ashamed that anyone went hungry.

> Hungry men grow bitter against society.... They become tramps and hoboes because of a mental condition produced by lack of food and friendship. Food and friendship (nothing else) will cure that condition in them.

> Friendship without the food is hypocrisy. Food without the friendship (as in prison) is a temporary stop-gap that may keep the victim alive but does nothing to reduce the underlying cause of social hatred.

Mundy was not naive, indicating that at first such "unearned" gifts would be taken advantage of, and the beneficiaries would refuse work. However, he concluded, "The craving for independence that is part of the secret of the tramp's condition, would assert itself along new lines."[16]

A new focus was about to emerge in Mundy's fiction. Shortly after deciding to spend the winter in San Diego, in October 1922, Talbot had an interesting meeting, as he related to Bobbs-Merrill. "Four elderly gentleman personally unknown to me, but each with a world wide reputation, called on me after dinner and remained until midnight trying to persuade me to write a series of books dealing with ancient history; their point of view apparently is that my books have stressed the quality of manliness; their suggestion was that I should, through the medium of fiction, trace as it were the growth of manliness on down the pages of history, beginning in India's dawn and ending at last in the United States."[17] Just a month later, Hoffman made the same suggestion; ancient history was popular in *Adventure*.[18] The sights Mundy had seen on his trip to Jerusalem, with the visits to Rome and Egypt, doubtless provided other ideas, and Sally had a personal interest in ancient Egypt.

With his background and interest in the Bible, by 1922 Talbot considered a story based upon its themes and characters.[19] The Bible was not the only holy text that intrigued him; in 1926, in another letter to "The Camp-Fire," Mundy indicated he hoped some day to write a story in which Mohammed of Mecca should be the hero, providing his viewpoint and writing sympathetically, although he indicated that this by no means meant he was a Mohammedan.[20]

Another influence derived from Kenneth Vennor Morris (1879–1937), who was Point Loma's preeminent historian and a sometime author of fiction and poetry—although his output, and the audience it reached, never approached that of Mundy.[21] Both Mundy and Morris were friends who commented on the work of the other in *The Theosophical Path* and privately.[22]

Morris became saturated in Druidic lore, wrote Celtic poetry, studied and interpreted Chinese poets, and was dedicated to Eastern thought, mastering Brahmanic and Buddhistic philosophy.[23] Morris was an early champion of the notion of history operating in identifiable rhythms and tides, with events of a certain nature governing any period, a view which caused him to be regarded by many authorities as a dangerous iconoclast. Mundy himself was a skeptic of history as written, as he explained to *Adventure*. "Much of the best fun in the world is digging out old myths and discovering that they are much more nearly true than anything recorded in the 'highbrow' history books."[24]

Morris told Mundy of Irish and Welsh legends regarding the Druids, including one which inspired him to write an episode of the abduction of the king's wife by Caesar.[25] Morris's *The Fates of the Princes of Dyfed* (1914) uses Druidic rituals and a high priest named Taliesan, although Morris relied far more on legend and fantasy than did Mundy. Similarly, Mundy also makes Taliesan a key character in *Tros of Samothrace*, and the book version included sayings prefacing chapters attributed to him. Taliesan was an actual bard of Wales in the 6th century A.D., whose lore descended from pagan–Celtic myth.[26] This name also shared the first three letters of Mundy's adopted first name, Talbot — and he would use the name Taliesan again for a high priest, this time in Tibet, in 1939 while writing the radio show *Jack Armstrong, the All-American Boy.*

Mundy transferred the motifs of adventure into the setting of ancient Rome, emphasizing the struggle between freedom and tyranny — self-determination against imperial domination — as a timeless historical pattern, no less than in his contemporary adventure novels like *The Eye of Zeitoon* and *The King in Check.* He gradually focused on a revisionist, theosophical interpretation of Cleopatra and her age. It was a result both of his fascination with strong women who undertook leadership, and by the theosophical belief that she was one of the last of her dynasty to be initiated into the wisdom and knowledge of ancient Egyptians. He quickly came to believe that traditional views of Caesar were overrated, ignoring his lack of spiritual vision; while Cleopatra, although corrupted by Caesar's materialism, was far more noble than most accounts would have us believe.

This magnum opus, ultimately spanning thirteen years and three volumes, was never actually completed. Eventually the work centered not only on Cleopatra, and Caesar, but also a fictional character, Tros of Samothrace. The saga begins by examining Caesar through Tros's eyes as he thwarts the would-be invader of Britain (*Tros of Samothrace*), then to Caesar as he saw himself and is loved by Cleopatra (*Queen Cleopatra*), and finally Cleopatra's decline, as viewed by Tros and Cleopatra's younger sister Arsinoe (*Purple Pirate*).

Tros was planned as a supporting personality, and his initial adventures were written frankly for income. However, Tros grew into a character of Odyssean dimensions, an explorer and philosopher whose own story turned into be an unexpected near-masterpiece with immense, enduring popularity.[27] Tros's story took shape throughout 1925 and through early 1926 in the pages of *Adventure* as an epic serial, composed of seven novels, all of which appeared as complete, separate works, except for the last, which was the longest and hence was serialized in three parts.[28]

Tros is the daring captain of his trireme, and the son of Perseus, an initiate of the mysteries of Samothrace who was murdered by Caesar. Tros fights back by helping to repulse Caesar's invasion of Britain. Tros joins the early British King, Caswallon (an actual person called Cassivellaunus by the Romans), who with his psychic wife Fflur is trying to unite the island's acrimonious tribes. Guided by Tros, Caswallon turns back the invasion; at another point, Tros destroys Caesar's fleet during a storm off the British coast. Some of these incidents were inspired by the tales told by Pruen, a geography instructor at Boxgrove school who taught Talbot and his brother Harold.[29]

Tros of Samothrace is full of delightful, vibrant supporting characters: Conops, Tros's one-eyed first mate; the intriguers Gwenhwyfar and Skell; Olaf Sigurdsen, whose Northmen become Tros's esteemed crew; Olaf's sister Helma, who becomes Tros's wife but is killed by Caesar; Caswallon's nephew Orwic, an ally of Tros; Rhys, a treacherous Briton, and Nepos, keeper of the Roman arena. There are numerous battles and murders, together with incidents of conspiracy and loyalty, as Tros struggles to build his advanced ship, the *Liafail*, and aid the Britons against Caesar. (The name, Liafail, referred to the coronation stone Mundy had written about in 1923 to "The Camp-Fire," originally used in the throne of the Biblical King David, reputedly now the "Stone of Scone" in Scotland.)

Bold and crafty, like a true adventurer Tros wants to avoid fighting, but circumstances draw him into it, forcing him to battle the injustice around him. A warrior philosopher and navigator, Tros represents the adventurers and explorers, who value chivalry, honor and freedom, and will outlast Rome. However, Tros is no reckless swashbuckler, mercenary or fortune hunter; his opposition to Caesar is more than revenge. Unlike many of his powerful contemporaries, Tros has a highly developed, almost modern moral sense, and he is labeled a pirate only by his Roman adversaries. Although he makes use of guile, Tros is a man of conscience who is monogamous and loyal, despising the treachery and treason he sees all around him.[30]

Although a hero, Tros is aware of his limitations, wise enough to be influenced by the esoteric religious thought of Samothrace, but not wise enough to qualify for initiation, lacking his father's ability to follow his vision without diversion. Tros's theology is that of an adventurer: "The gods despise a man who prays. They help men who make use of opportunity."[31] Instead, Mundy dwells on a more occult form of religion, the mysteries. Mundy asserts that both the Samothracians and the Druids had their foundation in the same ancient wisdom from which theosophy arose, the same mother religion from which all others are derived. This concept provides moral grounding as well as facilitating the narrative. As the *New York Times* critic wrote, "Mr. Mundy has chosen, with great fictional plausibility, to connect the two and to ascribe to the higher Druid priesthood and to the Samothracian initiates a knowledge of the laws of nature, a power of divination and a super-wisdom that help his tale along mightily."[32] Mundy utilized the fact that the Druids seem to have believed in life after death, reincarnation, and the transmigration of souls. He spelled out the contrast in theosophical terms: "Caesar loathed the Druids (who were an order—and a very high one—of the Mysteries) because his own private character and life were much too rotten to permit his being a candidate for initiation. In all ages the first requirement for initiation has been clean living and honesty."[33]

Caesar and Tros are drawn as the antithesis of each other, spiritual opposites; Tros represents the waning influence of the ancient mysteries, which Mundy proclaimed "were based on the theory of universal brotherhood," a key theme of Tingley's theosophical teaching.[34] Caesar represents militarism and treachery, and understands, according to Tros, "that where the wisdom dwells, freedom persists and grows again...."[35]

Through Morris and others, Theosophy helped to inspire the unconventional approach to history Mundy took with his heretical and unflattering portrait of Caesar in his novels. Other works Mundy cited for ideas were the volumes of Tacitus, Plutarch, Suetonius, and Gibbon on Rome; Gilbert Stone, *Wales, Her Origins, Struggles and Later History, Institutions, and Manners*, Giles's *Gems of Chinese Literature*, *Irish and Welsh* legends regarding the Druids, and B. de W. Weldon, *The Origin of the English*. Mundy wrote for readers of "The Camp-Fire" in *Adventure*, "In studying Caesar, I have tried to take the attitude of jury. I began with a strong prejudice in his favor, and have ended — after reading everything about him I can find — with a verdict of guilty on all points and a rider to the effect that he seems to have been the ablest, most charming [and] dangerous cynic who ever lived."[36] Mundy often pointed out that much historical estimate of Caesar is based on literal acceptance of his own *Commentaries*, taking him at his own evaluation with little allowance for propaganda. Accepting that "Caesar came a little nearer to greatness than any other military conqueror," Mundy indicated the Tros stories were "not an attempt to debunk Caius Julius Caesar.... There is nothing to be gained by trying to reduce all human nature to an average dead-level of drab stupidity, but it does pay to discover how the clever opportunists mislead fools.... We still worship our Caesars...."[37]

Mundy believed that Caesar's materialism and lack of spiritual awareness had adversely affected all of the subsequent cultural institutions that had come to idolize him. The implications for the foundations of modern Western civilization was recognized by readers of *Adventure*. Writing in "The Camp-Fire," Mundy explained, "The purpose of the Roman empire was to make life comfortable for the Romans and to keep other people out of mischief [and it] was conducted on principles diametrically opposite to those taught by all the world's really great philosophers." He blames Rome for imperialism and its destructive impact. He notes that England similarly justified its rule of India by making the land apparently incapable of self-government, then trying to ease the resentment of conquest by offering defeated peoples a place within the empire. "Here, today, is the net result of Roman theories — war, mistrust, rancor, suspicion, hatred, misgovernment, and a world not half so civilized as China was two thousand years ago."[38]

Although the Tros stories were very popular, they were the most controversial Mundy ever wrote, and many readers in the 1920s were shocked by his defiance of tradition and anti-classical views. There was a storm of protest during the serialization of the initial Tros stories, lasting almost a year, and a vast correspondence in Adventure debated the merits of Mundy's case until enough letters were printed to be considered for publication themselves in book form; it was the largest such confrontation ever in any pulp.[39] These letters, particularly those of Elmer Davis, indicate that Mundy's theosophical beliefs were known yet almost completely ignored as a basis of argumentation; readers quarreled directly with Mundy's conclusions more than the underlying philosophy that led to them. Readers and contributors included not only subscribers but authors and professors, and the debate was widely followed by a literary community that respected *Adventure* as falling outside the purview of "mere pulps."[40] Newspapers editorialized on the contention, and Mundy himself wrote five long letters introducing and defending his series.[41]

Eventually a consensus formed, cautiously siding with Mundy. The Tros series was able to be critically acclaimed because it combined adventure with the unusual twist of a distinctly revisionist spirit — permitting the tales to be respectable within the intellectual community as well as enjoyable diversion. Davis was typical: after having vigorously opposed Mundy, he later came around to accepting his position. In retrospect, Davis wrote, "His characterization of Caesar has been sharply attacked, but he was writing of Caesar as he looked to the people Caesar had conquered, a view somewhat different from that of even his political enemies in Rome. At any rate his

Caesar comes to life, as do the other historical figures in these stories; but better yet is the total picture, the sense that gradually pervades the reader of how it must have felt to live in the late Republic or the early Empire."[42]

The saga is a vast, sweeping, spectacular panorama, full of detail, with its principal setting in Britain, although the final part of the saga, *The Messenger of Destiny*, takes Tros directly into Rome itself, from the Vestal Virgins to the Arena. It is told in an energetic, dynamic style, full of dash and gusto, that still conveys both the feeling of the time and the authenticity of the characters as history and fiction blend naturally.[43] Mundy reverses the traditional reverential, historicized language, using narration and dialogue that partake equally of a modern idiom, by endowing his characters with contemporary motivations and moods.

Bobbs-Merrill completely overlooked the quality of the series, despite the incredible publicity, saying that the requirements of *Adventure* "have served to make your stories so prevailingly masculine as to limit greatly the extent of your book public."[44] "For both your sake and ours there must be no more *Nine Unknown*s. Your books should be written with book publication mainly in mind, not be made-over magazine things turned out under pressure to meet the demands of that magazine's peculiar public; should represent your best in characterization, cohesive plot and atmosphere. Then we'll have a chance, a fine chance, because your best is so awfully good."[45] The company had definite preconceptions; a love story was regarded as a crucial selling point. "Romance is what your readers want from you and when you have given it to them as in *King of the Khyber Rifles* they have nobly responded. When you have stuck simply to adventure they have not been so numerous or so enthusiastic."[46] Yet, while Bobbs-Merrill was urging Mundy toward literary work, their bias rendered them unable to perceive those very qualities in much of his work originally conceived for magazine publication, especially from the mid 1920s forward.[47]

Finally it was a fellow writer, Rose Wilder Lane, who convinced Talbot in the 1930s to renew the attempt to publish all the Tros stories in book form. Lane believed all seven original novels should be published together as they had been written, convincing Mundy that the tome should be kept essentially intact. She wrote,

> You re-created for us in those stories a period in history which is very dim, which no one else has so vividly resurrected. Your Cleopatra book — I do, truly, beg you to forgive such impertinence!— is a good piece of work; I read it through with great interest; I admire and like it — but it hasn't the quality of the Tros stories. You overcame the staleness of your theme; that is an achievement. But too much of your skill — craftsmanship, imagination, everything that makes the artists— was spent in doing that. You made a good book; it is impossible for anyone to make a fresh book, an entirely vivid, living book, out of Cleopatra. Shaw didn't do it. It can't be done.... No reader has any fresh spot in the retina, for a book about Cleopatra. But it is impossible not to look for the first time at the scenes, the characters, the background, of your Tros stories. That selection gave you, not a handicap, but an opportunity. All the qualities you have as a writer came into action, freely. And the readers' minds, unhampered by prejudice, by anticipations or by stale connotations, were also free to appreciate those qualities, to receive the impressions you produced by those qualities.... The result — as I have long been saying to the publishers I've

stirred into inquiring about book-publication of the Tros stories—is in my opinion not only by far the best thing you've done, but by far the best thing that has been done in your field.[48]

D. Appleton-Century and Hutchinson, with success publishing the earlier Jimgrim Arabian novels from *Adventure* as separate books, were ready to follow Lane's suggestion in 1934, and Talbot dedicated the book to her. As a result, the novels were collected with very little revision, primarily adding connective passages and inserts of philosophy, sayings to preface each chapter attributed to the Druid Taliesan and Tros's log. The tremendous length of nearly a half million words, 950 pages, proved to be no drawback, but perhaps even an advantage in drawing attention and sales, and the *New York Sun* placed *Tros of Samothrace* among the finest historical romances of the last two decades.[49] The enormous critical and commercial success, among the greatest ever achieved by a Mundy book, has endured in popular reprints over the years, and *Tros of Samothrace*, has remained one of Mundy's most celebrated works since his death.

By 1934, *Tros of Samothrace* encountered none of the resistance faced during serialization in *Adventure*. The tempest it aroused opened the way for further revisionist novels of Rome. For instance, Mundy's interpretation of the Roman Empire had been first advanced eight years prior to Robert Graves' series on the Emperor Claudius.

Tros of Samothrace has also been hailed in a way Mundy did not intend. The mythical underpinnings, such as the interaction between the Druid and Samothracian mysteries, have served as inspiration for many subsequent fantasy works. Largely ahistorical, concentrating on the hazy line between legend and magic, they lack Mundy's emphasis on the factual backdrop of Roman domination. So too, such writers usually did not have Mundy's restraint, with Tros's fallibility, humanity, and philosophical bent replaced by Conan-style superheroes.[50] Indeed, in the mistaken interpretation of the Tros stories as fantasy by many publishers and later writers, *Tros of Samothrace* and *Purple Pirate* received the most attention, while *Queen Cleopatra* was often overlooked or belittled because of its unmistakably historical nature. However, examination of all three novels together, along with Mundy's other tales of the ancient world, *Caesar Dies* and *Roman Holiday*, indicates the paramount importance of history in all of these stories of the ancient world. More than simply Tros's adventures, Mundy explored the uses to which he could use the historical genre.

When *Tros of Samothrace* was in book form it acquired another sort of timeliness not evident during its original serialization. Mundy's theme of liberty subverted by those who would increase their own power had a topical resonance beyond history in the 1930s. Fritz Leiber has suggested that contemporary readers saw in Tros's battle against Caesar's designs of conquering the world an analogy for the contemporary increase in militarism and the necessity to fight the steadily growing threat of fascism.[51] Mundy was aware of this relevance; in his foreword to the British edition of *Tros of Samothrace* in 1934 he noted that both Lenin and Hitler were following in Caesar's footsteps by trying to destroy through propaganda the old belief in spiritual values.

Mundy's study and knowledge of the ancient world was not limited to the time of Julius Caesar and Cleopatra. He revealed the depth and extent of his grasp in *Caesar Dies* (originally published as *The Falling Star* in the October 23, 1926 issue of *Adventure* and in England in book form by Hutchinson in 1934, although it did not appear in America until offered by Centaur as a paperback in 1973). *Caesar Dies* portrays a much later period, the last months of the Emperor Commodus in 192 A.D. Commodus is cruel and maniacal, bordering on complete insanity. Commodus has split his character into three distinct personas: himself, a shadowy double who is assassinated, and Paulus, the premier warrior-athlete in the arena, the role in which he finds his greatest satisfaction.

Nonetheless, by comparison with the self-serving schemers and hypocrites around him, Commodus is at least openly and honestly reprehensible in his brutality. His physician, Galen, remarks that Commodus "has the fear, the frenzy and the resolution of a splendid animal. We have only cowardice, the unenthusiasm and the indecision of base men. If we had the virtue of Commodus, no Commodus could ever have ruled Rome for half a day." Subtitled "An Episode without a Hero," *Caesar Dies* reveals that the falling star seen shortly before Commodus's murder is not only for him, but nearly all those around him. As Galen notes, "All conspirators resemble rats that gnaw and run, until one rat at last discovers himself Caesar of the herd by accident."[52]

Commodus's Christian mistress, Marcia, is a realistic portrayal, avoiding the religious pitfalls to which such a characterization is susceptible in most ancient world tales. This was a new theme in Mundy's stories of Rome; previously he had avoided the traditional use of the setting to portray the rise of Christianity. Most venal of the characters is Pertinax, Commodus's successor, who goes along with his assassination while constantly assuaging his conscience with delays and doubts, indecision and irresolution, finally forcing others into committing the murder.

Caesar Dies is the anatomy of one of Mundy's favorite subjects, a *coup d'etat*, in this case based on actual history. Just who is going to die as the characters gamble with destiny, and how, and the identity of the nearly-accidental assassin of Commodus, are told in a denouement that combines the best of suspense with historical recreation. Each chapter resembles a scene in a play, constantly increasing in vividness the portrayal of Rome. Elmer Davis was especially enthusiastic, saying that Mundy had "captured the essential quality of everyday life in Rome better than any other writer we have ever read."[53] While inspired, *Caesar Dies* falls just short of the classic status the Tros series achieves; there are, for a novel of this short length, perhaps too many central characters: Commodus, Marcia, Galen, Pertinax, his mistress Cornificia, the outlaws Sextus and Norbanus, the gladiator Narcissus, and Bultius Livius.

Following *Caesar Dies* came a work of similar length, also focusing on actual historical characters, but one with a very different setting. In the midst of his writing on ancient Rome, Mundy had a sudden inspiration for a change of pace — that impelled him to pen one of his most brilliant and unusual novels. This was *W.H. — A Portion of the Record of Sir William Halifax*, a swashbuckler of Elizabethan England that reflects several influences

However, this experiment proved discouraging when publication became unexpectedly difficult, especially for a volume of this calibre. Completed by June 1928,

Mundy offered *W.H.* to Bobbs-Merrill along with his first revision of *Cleopatra*. Although praising *W.H.*, the company wanted to defer it until the expected interval before a sequel on Antony and Cleopatra.[54] *W.H.* finally appeared as a four-part serial, *Ho for London Town!*, in *Argosy All-Story Weekly* from February 2 to February 23, 1929. Book publication by Hutchinson occurred in England at the beginning of 1931 under the original title, *W.H.*, and it quickly went into a second edition. Bobbs-Merrill continued to postpone publication, and ultimately *W.H.* was not published in book form in the United States until 1953, when it was issued under the title *The Queen's Warrant* as one of the volumes in a two-in-one Universal Giant paperback.

In *W.H.*, Mundy allows his sense of humor full sway. This was a trait he seldom lost, even in the most trying situations, and it was constant in his letters and conversations with friends and associates. He had the gift of being able to laugh at his own foibles, and regarded solemnity as "the mark of pompous and self-satisfied ignorance."[55] It was Talbot's humor that kept his philosophical pronouncements from ever becoming pretentious; he could laugh about his interest in the ancient world, speculating that in an earlier incarnation he "was probably one of the pimps who sold out the women on the Wall in Alexandria, and then pocketed the money."[56] This awareness of his own limitations and failures kept Mundy from having anything in common with, for instance, L. Ron Hubbard, a fellow pulp author who established a religion of his own, Scientology.

Mundy inscribed a copy of *The Ivory Trail* in March 1928 to Amy Lay Hull (1876–1958), a well-known New York actress specializing in historical roles. His poem perfectly captures the self-effacing side of Mundy, acutely aware of his own flaws and limitations.

> You speak of me as wise!
> You view with mocking eyes
> My diffident disclaim.
> I say it all the same:
> Such things as I have done
> Were principally fun;
> Mere impulse and a gest [sic]
> For mischief did the rest
> I know no royal road
> To owleate abode
> Of Pallas in the skies
> So—"wonderfully wise"?
> Oh Amy Lay Hull Scherr,
> I only wish I were![57]

Among his previous work, only the four 1911 "Kitty" stories in *All Story* could be accurately described as humorous writings.

W.H. also reflects Mundy's education in the classics, along with his iconoclastic interpretation of history. He had a long interest in Shakespeare, and theosophical admiration for the playwright was pronounced at Point Loma and went all the way back to Blavatsky's writings.[58] In *W.H.*, Shakespeare himself is a character, and occupies a pivotal role. Mundy frequently intersperses adapted excerpts from

Shakespeare's plays and poems and places them in the conversation and pronouncements of his character.

W.H. begins on a parodic note, with an editorial recounting the discovery of an aged manuscript in a house in Bloomsbury. The tone of this note, admitting that what follows may be a hoax, sets the tenor of the book.

> Such learned authorities as have seen the document are unanimous in denying its historical value, on the reasonable ground that its author is otherwise wholly unknown and his statements are at times apparently in conflict with recorded facts....
>
> The manuscript is therefore hardly sacrosanct, since men of such authority and learning have denied it credit; it has accordingly been edited, its more archaic phrases being rendered into modern English, and for words that have dropped out of common use or whose meaning has changed in the course of centuries, more modern words have been substituted to convey the writer's apparent meaning. Many phrases, also, have been modified or totally omitted out of deference to modern taste — a taste that would have seemed inexplicable in the days of Good Queen Bess.
>
> Due to dampness, rats, and the indifference of the workmen who came on the manuscript, some pages from the beginning and from the end are missing or so damaged as to be undecipherable, but the remainder is clearly written in an upright hand that certainly suggests its author may have been the man of character he represents himself to be.[59]

Despite the supposed modernization of language, the first sentences give the feel of the style to follow, the amusing effect enhanced through the first-person narration. "So I made up my mind I would leave Brownsover for good and all, for it offended me that such a coney-catching louse as Tony Pepperday should own my father's mansion. But I will say this for the chuff: ill-favoured caitiff though he was, he had gift of self-advancement.... There was not a horn-book printed that could teach him anything."[60] *W.H.* is strewn with such archaic language, and written in a style wholly different from all of Mundy's other stories, demonstrating his ability to transform his authorial voice into a vocabulary and cadence appropriate to the time and place. He becomes immersed in Elizabethan speech and slang as much as the dialects that helped give a sense of atmosphere to his stories of India and the Middle East.

Before turning into a swashbuckler, *W.H.* begins as a picaresque tale, as young William Halifax rides forth to London to make his fortune in the Queen's service, hoping to return and claim his beloved, Mildred Jackson, for his bride, although she is an heiress and Pepperday's ward. Upon disarming a highwayman, Jeremy Crutch, Halifax takes a stolen gimcrack — in a typical Mundy touch, it resembles the Indian god Ganesha — that he later learns is a sign of Mary Stuart's coming rebellion against Elizabeth.

The first friend Halifax encounters on the road to fortune, as he passes Stratford, is "Will" Shakespeare. The title, *W.H.*, and the initials of the hero, derive from the frequent allusions to an unnamed and mysterious friend to whom Shakespeare dedicated the sonnets and other works. He is depicted as roistering, lecherous, and ale-guzzling, but a wise and skillful storyteller. At the time Halifax meets Shakespeare, he is fleeing his wife, Ann Hathaway. "Ann, so he said, unlike good wine, was hardly mellowing with age. She loved to sit in church o' Sundays and quote sermons at him all the week, so that he knew by heart so many sins it would take a lifetime to commit the half of them. For himself, he better loved to rest him merry and to write such airy nothings as imagination conjured into words, whereas Ann tolerated no such nonsense, as she called it, in the house, but used his scribbled sheets to light the oven fire."[61] In the year Mundy sets his supposed meeting with Halifax, Shakespeare was 21 and his wife was eight years older, and they had their second and third child.

Otherwise Mundy's account is perfectly plausible. Halifax reveals that Shakespeare's ability to entertain a landlord or their wife helps to pay the bills—just as Mundy had told tales in his travels in Australia and elsewhere. The Will whose initials are W.H. and the Will whose last name is Shakespeare are both projections of a third Will, the man born William Lancaster Gribbon and known as Talbot Mundy. Halifax is an adventurer, hunting for prestige, position, and fortune; Shakespeare is reflective, a philosopher, poet, and pacifist, one who thinks of life in broad strokes that Halifax seldom comprehends. Both men are romantics, but the outcomes are opposite. Halifax hopes a profitable and happy marriage to his beloved Mildred may establish his social position. Shakespeare is involved in a hectic, day-to-day escape from Ann's stern ways, preferring to spin yarns by which to seduce willing women.

Like Mundy, Halifax is an alumnus of Rugby, who learned by the stick, "and if the frequent soreness of my hams from caning is the measure of my scholarship, then few youths ever set forth better versed in Latin...." Shakespeare tells Halifax that none ever heard of Brownsover "until they started Rugby school—and such a poor school, and poor scholars, that a pair of barns was reckoned good enough."[62] Shakespeare addresses Halifax at one point as Willy, the nickname given young William Lancaster Gribbon in his youth.[63] That Mundy should present Shakespeare as a sort of alter ego is not surprising, since according to some calendars, both shared the same birthday, April 23. He certainly endows Shakespeare with such marital woes and age difference as he had known, particularly with Rosemary.

Shakespeare appears primarily in the first half of *W.H.*, and only occasionally thereafter, as the humor is lessened. The year is 1585, a time rife with political conspiracies, when the Catholic Mary of Scotland is still the logical successor to the throne, and the pope has excommunicated Elizabeth and promised eternal salvation for anyone assassinating her. A possible Romanist revival was checked by the identification of Catholic interests with those of Spain, equating Romanism with treason against the nation, not just the monarch and Church of England. Although Halifax is one of the few Mundy heroes whose religious beliefs are conventional in the period, the setting also allows Mundy to express his own strong anti-papal sentiment through Halifax's first-person testament.

Shakespeare and Elizabeth are not the only actual individuals of the period to be offered; Lord Burghley, the Earl of Leicester, Sir Francis Drake, and John Hawkins, among others, are also major characters. The fictional and real characters become indistinguishable, the deeds of all mingling into a single, virtually seamless whole. Like many Mundy heroes, Halifax proves adept at intrigue and forcing others to reveal their knowledge to him for his own use and advancement. For instance, note the following exchange between Halifax and the agent Benjamin Berden before the arrest of Stiles, when he learns the meaning of the gimcrack.

> "I see," he said, "you are already chief adviser to Lord Burghley, so I pay you my humble respects. But are you aware that Joshua Stiles is plotting to deliver the Queen of Scots from Tutbury?"
> It was news to me, but I was no such lack-wit as to let him know it.
> "So far you shoot middling straight," I answered.
> "And have they told you that the green thing in the red box, that you showed to Phelippes, is the Queen of Scots' own talisman that the Lords in Council have been hunting for these many months? The sight of that thing was to warn the disaffected men to hold themselves in readiness. It has been sent around the country, and the Council has heard of it scores of times, but none knew who the leaders are, nor how ready they are."[64]

Elizabeth rewards Halifax by allowing him to serve her further and thereby gain his own glory, and he ultimately judges her "the greatest and the bravest monarch, though the meanest mistress, who ever in all history has saved a half-rebellious country from its foes. I give her all the credit; since, without her mastery and meanness, I believe the land had fallen of its own internal bickerings."[65] Elizabeth becomes a figure similar to other Mundy heroines, from Tingley to Cleopatra.[66]

W.H. is a lively, amusing fiction which superbly conveys the flavor of its time. Densely written, *W.H.* is a complex, richly-textured work that exceeds the bounds of its genre and deserves wider reputation. The greatness and success of his Roman novels had been no fluke for Mundy, and *W.H.* provides evidence that he could have achieved more by concentrating on historical tales, a perspective expressed by Morris.[67] Mundy's historical fiction was well ahead of its time; just as the Rome of Tros prefigured Robert Graves, *W.H.* foreshadowed the parodic adventure tales of the 1960s and beyond, such as the Flashman series of George MacDonald Fraser.

After becoming side-tracked on the Tros serial for *Adventure*, in 1925 Mundy finally began *Queen Cleopatra*. Eventually it was to become his last novel written under the Point Loma influence. Mundy believed *Queen Cleopatra* could not be rushed, and it required more re-writing than any previous project. It took far longer than anticipated, considering that he paused while writing the book to turn out other volumes. As he explained to his publishers, "Do you realize what writing *Cleo* means? How much digging into the history of her day? How much checking up of references, to make absolutely sure that the sensational novelty of the fiction-treatment won't lay me open to ridicule? I have a version (or will have, when it's finished) that will upset even [historian Arthur] Weigall; and there won't be one tiny opening for the criticasters to exploit."[68]

The manuscript of *Cleopatra* gradually grew to epic length, and, for a time, Mundy expected *Queen Cleopatra* to be 200,000 words, some 750 pages in length. He was worried about whether a work of that size could be serialized, or even fit between the covers of a single book, and might require two volumes. The company replied that they foresaw no maximum length, so long as the wordage was of sufficiently high quality, and the book was finally reported finished in August 1927.

Meanwhile, other fictional works appeared on the Egyptian queen, depriving

Mundy's project of some of the originality it might have had. Not until June 1928 did the readers at Bobbs-Merrill have Mundy's complete 174,000 word manuscript of *Queen Cleopatra*, where the principal criticisms were that the work was overwritten. They wanted to cut the sayings and claimed that conversations developed into essays and the mystical philosophy overemphasized. Hutchinson had a similar reaction, refusing to publish the novel at its submitted length because of the low price at which fiction books were sold, 7/6d. Mundy was bitter, as he later told Rose Wilder Lane.

> My description of Cleopatra was unfortunately edited, castrated, peeled, perverted, disinfected and reduced to its lowest possible common denominator in obedience to the editor of *Adventure*, who bought it "as is." Later, he resigned and [it was rejected; then] *McClures* "bought" the *Cleopatra* serial, but they, too, changed their editor. They hadn't paid me, and they took care not to. And by that time E.M. Barrington came out with her "Laughing Queen" in *Delineator*. Nothing left then but book publication. And I was too discouraged, and too broke to rewrite the book. It sold poorly.
>
> Someday I believe I will have another fling at Cleopatra, rewrite the story and continue it to the end.[69]

In barely a month's time, Talbot cut more than the 40,000 words that Bobbs-Merrill had requested, to 125,000 words, although even then some of Bobbs-Merrill's readers complained of its length and theosophical content.[70]

Inspired by his willingness to depart from accepted doctrine and offended by the dramaturgical interpretations of Shakespeare and especially Shaw, Mundy deliberately invited comparison with them. Mundy's interpretation also differed from that propounded by a novelist whose work was more akin to his own, H. Rider Haggard. Haggard's *Cleopatra* had appeared in 1889, recounting the later portion of Cleopatra's life after Caesar's death. However, to Haggard, Cleopatra is cruel, ready to use her seductive wiles and beauty to any end that will keep her in power, looting her country's temples, priests, riches and tradition for her own whim and glory.

By August 1925, in light of the enormous debate the "Tros" series provoked in *Adventure*, Mundy was proposing the inclusion of a lengthy Shavian-style introduction in *Queen Cleopatra*, and corresponded with the playwright in 1928. As Mundy wrote, "Shaw has done Julius Caesar so discerningly that there is no hope of doing him better, except in a few minor details; but Shaw's Cleopatra is a joke."[71] However, all that remains of the preface idea is a brief but sage-like philosophical piece placed in the words of Cleopatra's physician, Olympus. The diary of Olympus was imagined by Mundy, but Plutarch had mentioned having seen it.[72]

Mundy's image of Cleopatra is far from the wanton opportunist etched by many authors. He was as sure of her intelligence and courage as he was of her morals. In his novel, she is a patriot, yet also wily and manipulative in her determination to save Egypt at all costs, even her own integrity.

She opposes her wit to the ruthless Caesar as she waylays him into a sojourn in Alexandria. Her youth and brilliance fascinate him. Tempted to share her reverence for the teachings of the ancient religious tradition, he ultimately despises the Mysteries,

Hierophant of Philae, and physician Olympus. When she tries to convince Caesar of the potential divinity within himself, and the immortality of ideas, he, like the rabble of Alexandria, misunderstands her to mean that he is a god, above other mortals.

She begins to lose her spirituality and is ultimately corrupted in the struggle: "His thought, under Cleopatra's influence, was groping upward, just as hers, under his influence, was descending and losing its way."[73] Her efforts go beyond matching her feminine, Eastern mind to the task of saving Egypt; Caesar and Cleopatra do fall in love, and she comes to believe that he has the potential to be a beneficial, civilizing force on the world.

Queen Cleopatra provides a larger conception of Caesar, more detailed than in *Tros of Samothrace*. Caesar still represents and personifies Rome and its omniverous decadence. However, in Egypt, Caesar is at the height of his power and skill, revealing some of his traits that compel Cleopatra and even Tros to become his reluctant allies. There is sympathy for Caesar in his final years and months as he displays his hubris and vanity, with age and the enormity of his ambition to be a king of the world proving more than his match as destiny inevitably closes in on him.

Queen Cleopatra follows the first series of Tros stories in narrative sequence but is a separate entity, not requiring knowledge of its predecessor, and Tros is a supporting character who takes a back seat to history, nearly disappearing in the middle of the novel. Caesar still despises and is amused by Tros's scruples, but the Samothracian remembers that while Caesar is master of the Roman world, he is not master of Tros. The novel features not only Caesar's assassination, but a parallel occurrence with the murder of Pompey, which Mundy portrays superbly, especially in Chapter 13. Here, Mundy steps out from conventional prose narration to offer a short playlet on Pompey's burial—perhaps a hint of the play he once hoped to write from the book.

Caesar's own assassination is ironically witnessed by Tros, who had the greatest reason to kill the murderer of his wife and father, but who refused to kill an enemy simply for revenge; he sees Caesar's murderers as a cowardly, selfish group. The entire final section in Rome, from Cleopatra's arrival to her flight following Caesar's assassination, is among the best of all Mundy's writing. Elmer Davis commented, "Take the murder of Caesar; in Appian and Plutarch and even Shakespeare it is just a fact of history, one of the things one learns. When Mundy does it, you are there, looking down at the corpse in the empty Senate house.... And to have the courage, in the funeral scene, to steal "Friends, Romans, countryman—" and the tact to stop right there."[74]

Among the other intriguing characters in *Queen Cleopatra* are the stylish Mark Antony, the devoted Charmian, and the sportsman and artist Apollodorus. One weakness of the novel is the overdrawn characterization of the perpetually childish, egotistical and hysterical Ptolemy, while Cleopatra's equally devious and ambitious younger sister Arsinoe preserves both her own life and her dignity. Mundy captures the barbaric, fickle Rome and Egypt, especially Alexandria, with its restless citizenry teeming with rumor and superstition, and each conflicting class jealous of the other's prerogatives. The *Daily Telegraph* described it as "episode after episode in vivid splendour of word painting," as quoted on the dust jacket of the Hutchinson edition. *Queen Cleopatra* was Mundy's last book to be reviewed in *The Theosophical Path*, and from April to September 1929 the novel joined *Om* on the magazine's list of recommended reading.

Queen Cleopatra was finally published by Bobbs-Merrill in February 1929 with an abstract dust jacket containing the overblown slogan "The Love Story of the Woman Who Sent Imperial Caesar Mad;" if a popular edition had been issued, it would have substituted the pictorial dust jacket showing the Egyptian monarch that Hutchinson used for their publication of *Queen Cleopatra* in March of 1929.[75] *Queen Cleopatra* met with a mixed critical reaction, and sold well during its initial months, but subsequent sales did not reach expectations.[76] (Harry Marks published a specially bound edition of 265 autographed copies, with a frontispiece of the author, which quickly sold out, and hoped to issue other Mundy books, but it remained the only novel so treated.)[77]

With the book failing to receive the anticipated approbation, or serial publication, along with the difficulties publishing *W.H.*, Mundy abandoned historical novels for the moment. Not until *Tros of Samothrace* appeared in book form did he realize that the saga of Cleopatra could be more popularly continued as an adventure with Tros in the foreground, rather than as a supporting character, as in *Queen Cleopatra*. *Queen Cleopatra* would gain its greatest popularity in later years, when the other books in the Tros series began to be reprinted and with a series of paperback editions in the 1960s.

The study of Egypt and the contemplation of the mythology surrounding Cleopatra gave Mundy the idea for a story of modern Egypt that partook of some of the spirit of *The Mystery of Khufu's Tomb*. *One Egyptian Night* (echoing the title of his earlier *Adventure* story, "An Arabian Night"), was a magazine novel written for the May 1929 issue of *Everybody's combined with Romance*, detailing a plot to fake Cleopatra's tomb. A reenacted pageant along the Nile, combined with the secret service and its airplanes patrolling the ageless land, searching for a desert bandit and a lost tomb, together summon the mystique of both ancient and modern Egypt. As one character in *One Egyptian Night* wisely notes, Cleopatra, unlike Ramses or other rulers of Egypt, is too vivid a historical personage to imagine her bones in a museum exhibit.

Mundy would seem to have achieved a potential permanence and status as a Point Loma resident, as an official of the Theosophical Society, and as an author who had won notice for branching out into entirely new genres. Instead, the seeds had already been planted that would take him far away from Point Loma, leaving the organization he had joined and his home behind. His writing would never again reach the stature it had during these years.

VIII

Four Failures, 1926–1929

Although the reception of *Queen Cleopatra* was not living up to Mundy's hopes, other possibilities seemed to offer important new markets. The first major motion picture was to be made from one of his stories, and the *Saturday Evening Post* solicited a novel. A business venture even promised the possibility of wealth.

Mundy had become widely known and respected not only at the Theosophical colony, but in San Diego proper. Although earning a respectable living by his writing, Talbot still yearned for greater financial security, one that would enable him to concentrate on turning out his best work, rather than primarily magazine material.

Thoughts about finances were also in Talbot's mind when Dick Ames's twenty-first birthday made it time for the family to seriously contemplate his future. As Dick recalled,

> T.M. wanted me to find a business of my own choosing, and to my liking, and he would finance it. Through some San Diego friends I met three men — among them the later "con" man. These were very agreeable people, and each *seemed* to have been successful in his own right. They were older than I, but younger than T.M. San Diego and La Jolla real estate was the announced objective of this activity. I took them home (Tilgaun) for dinner, and T.M. became so enthused about the project that he determined to take a "mental vacation" for a short time only, and then I would move into his spot when he returned to full time writing.[1]

Their initial capital was based on a small inheritance Dick had received from his father, along with the money that Sally had helped Talbot accumulate.[2] Sally and her relatives also became investors.

By the beginning of 1926, the business was gradually consuming steadily more of Mundy's time, and after three months the Sindicato de Desarrollo Liafail, S.A. (Liafail Development Syndicate) was officially established, Talbot giving it the name of the ship captained by Tros of Samothrace. Sally soon found that she had no control over Liafail, despite the fact she had better business acumen than her husband, while Dick had too much respect for his stepfather to question his business decisions.[3]

Initially, Liafail secured 23 prominent business corners, including part interest in the Isis Theater, where so many of Tingley's plays and speeches had been given, and options on *The San Diego Union* newspaper, and the San Diego Railway. The holdings were further diversified when they bought control of Airfan Radio Corporation and radio station KFSD. KFSD had been launched by the Theosophical Society at a time when radio was a new and untried medium, and the station's broadcasts included lectures by Gottfried de Purucker from 1927–1928, his first public appearances.[4] Talbot may have hoped that, if Liafail were a success, it would benefit the Society's solvency (certainly KFSD was already helping to publicize its "message"). Cabinet meetings had made Mundy aware of Point Loma's increasing financial difficulties, now that Tingley was past eighty years old.

Soon the prime mover in Liafail was W.H. (Bill) Black, a local promoter with an idea sure to appeal to Mundy's adventurous instincts: drilling for oil in Mexico. Europeans had first realized the commercial value of oil in Mexico in 1826, with the first well drilled in 1869, but not until after 1900 did the commercial possibilities become apparent.

Finding oil was still a matter of luck and grit; discovery of surface seepage was considered the best clue to an oil deposit, and geology had only begun to be used to locate oil deposits by the 1920s. The subject had already captured Mundy's imagination; a couple of years earlier he had spent $100 for a share in the Torrey Pines Oil Company. His character, Jeff Ramsden, was an engineer, and in Mundy's 1918 story, "Oakes Respects an Adversary," Mundy had written, "But it's as prospector for minerals that an alert adventurer finds his widest field; and as free-lance writer that he can best keep in touch with opportunity, or feather an empty nest. These are my two chosen standbys."[5] Six long years after his trip to Jerusalem, Mexico represented an opportunity for fortune and adventure, while not requiring that he leave behind the life he had established in San Diego.

Louis Iaeger, one of the first to join the Syndicate, was chosen as Liafail's president. Frank Arrington became treasurer, and Mundy the secretary. Bill Black brought in W.H. Lyne as a director of Liafail; Lyne had vast experience as Field Superintendent for the Texas Company, with a reputation for being able, practical, and a man of integrity. He was convinced Liafail's site would open one of the world's great oil fields. The majority of independent geological surveys were also in favor of drilling.[6]

Iaeger was fluent in Spanish and favorably known to the Mexicans. He secured a lease of 47,000 acres of lower California, which ran for 25 years, and in perpetuity if oil was developed. The concession consisted of 20 miles of Pacific Ocean coast, extending nine to ten miles inland.[7] The land was on a subdivision of the ranch "Ex-Mision del Descanso" near the city of Tia Juana.

Mundy and his partners realized that, although Liafail could continue financing from the United States, it would be wiser politically to have Mexican investors as well. Abelardo Lujan Rodríguez, Sr., Governor of Baja California (and formerly a general during the Mexican Revolution, and future Mexican president from 1932–34), was invited to share in the enterprise. He and his friends bought a two-fifths interest, and promised cooperation and protection for the endeavor. Another local partner was Mariano Escobedo, wealthy landowner, hotel and restaurant owner in and around Tia Juana; by May 1927, he became president of Liafail.[8] A third party was Mexican President Plutarco Calles himself. Liafail became the first company to apply for a permit to operate under the new Mexican oil law, and to prove that it was fair and workable, the government made favorable terms, with a total royalty of 15 percent.[9]

Mundy himself went to Mexico City to negotiate with the Mexican government. Dick squired Calles's daughter Alicia during their visit, and he was not the only one who enjoyed being away from home. As Dick noted of his stepfather, "He was over-sexed, we knew that," and added, "I don't know, but I have a good idea that he was not faithful to Sally on several occasions."[10] In fact, Talbot and Sally had already been having marital problems; her personality could get on the nerves of those around her, as her daughter-in-law would later recall.[11]

Mundy was neglecting the tasks the Theosophical Society hoped he would undertake. Every few years, Tingley led a Theosophical "crusade" overseas, and planned a lecture-tour of Europe in the spring and summer of 1926. The party of six was to include such veterans as Purucker, and Mrs. Spalding, but for the first time Mundy was included in the roster.[12] By the next month, *The Theosophical Path* announced that half the members of the group would not join until later. Mundy was detained in Mexico on business, but planned to join Tingley in Germany before the end of May.[13]

In the July issue of *The Theosophical Path*, Tingley announced her disappointment with Mundy, after three months of delays, saying "We are all waiting to hear from Mr. Mundy. He is one of the great factors in this caravan of ours. We cannot move until he comes, and then when he does come, the caravan will move on."[14] Despite the scolding, Mundy was labeled a "beloved Comrade" in the descriptions of the birthday festivities held July 6 at the Lomaland Headquarters for Tingley in her absence. Ultimately failing to join Tingley, this public imbroglio marked the start of Mundy's fading in the Theosophical firmament.

By late 1927, 30 shares were remaining in Liafail's treasury, each representing 1/500th of the whole Syndicate, and selling for $1500 each. The price was expected to go up shortly when oil was struck.[15] Other companies were searching for oil in the same general area.

A drill site was chosen in the center of the lease, about 30 miles below the border and two miles inland. Liafail procured the best rotary rig obtainable, installed the machinery, and hired a crew. As Lyne had forecast, at 640 feet the drill struck oil sand, and continued, through pockets of gas, which seemed to assure a profitable field. Talbot was spending an increasing amount of time at the well, and adapted to the necessary task of writing while at the drilling site, although his productivity was down.

Then problems arose: the drill encountered a "cap rock" of uncertain depth. The drillers had to use up to two sets a day of Hughes hard rock bits, at about $100 each. Each of the bits was only drilling about 10 inches of hole, and in addition to their own cost, the expense of pulling up the drill pipe to replace them was very high.[16] The situation was tantalizing; in Dick's words, "T. was enthused, and Bill reinforced that enthusiasm. 'By god, T., here it is, we've got, we can see it, have it tested.' Who's to say whether one more set of cones or bits would penetrate — who's to say — it could be another 30 feet or it could be another three inches, nobody knows, and of course that kind of bait kept him going."[17] The expenses of further drilling became prohibitive.

Mundy searched for more investors to keep drilling, making several business trips to New York in his frantic efforts to stave off bankruptcy. With no more shares to sell, he sent a three page solicitation to those who had written him about his stories, inviting them into the venture, explaining the risks and possible benefits, selling off five-acre sub-leases for 85 percent of the oil at $250 each.[18] He gradually brought into Liafail a steadily larger group of his own friends, including Arthur Hoffman and Elmer Davis, who believed it offered him the chance to become a millionaire.[19] Only Bobbs-Merrill rejected Mundy's offer outright, privately questioning his financial judgement.[20]

As 1928 dawned, matters grew even worse. The Seftons and other wealthy neighbors around Tilgaun had insisted that the whole area be paved. Property owners were assessed to pay for the paving. The paving bill was $65,000, and the mortgage was $68,000. Mundy was in no position to afford the paving, and only a very wealthy person could purchase Tilgaun with this huge lien upon it.[21]

One more disillusionment, the final blow, remained. Talbot had trusted his partner Bill Black for more than two years, even as threats of foreclosure proceedings were in the offing. Then he discovered that he had been defrauded. As Dick recalled, "All of a sudden it developed that things weren't all that they should be.... Sally had collected a bunch of checks made out to Bill Black, no note for this, for that, for anything ... just Bill Black ... and it all came to naught."[22] Since February, 1926, through June, 1928, about 150 checks had been made out to Black personally, in sums up to $6000 on one bank account and $4000 on another account, without any notation, and no collateral or security.[23] Mundy had been swindled. As Dick explained, many years later, "Bill was an out and out crook, a very bad one."[24]

All the investments of Sally, Talbot, Dick and their friends came to naught. The failure of the well, the looming paving bill for Tilgaun, and the betrayal by Black, coming in quick succession, combined with Mundy's own instability, prompted him to leave.[25] In Dick's words, "That was when T.M. went to New York, and I never saw him again.... He couldn't stand it, he couldn't face it. It was complete failure, and he didn't like failure. I guess he had quite a number."[26] The humiliation of bringing financial ruin upon Sally and Dick weighed too heavily upon him to effect a reconciliation, despite their willingness to accept his return, nor could he live in a community where the disaster would be known to all.

Mundy left Point Loma for New York in June 1928, and the next month he and Sally officially separated. An undated fragment of one of Talbot's surviving letters to Sally may give a hint of his farewell. "We have learned a tremendous amount together, you and I. If you had only taught me the beauty and delight of human love, that would have been much; but you have taught me a great deal more. And I know I have taught you some lessons."[27] Talbot left Sally with nothing save Tilgaun, which was already worthless because of the paving lien against it. Later that year, he gave her $4,000, a third of the profits of the sale to Fox of the movie rights to *King — of the Khyber Rifles*, and more than double the amount he kept from the sale after his advances from Bobbs-Merrill had been discounted.

For a number of years, Sally continued to hope for his return, remembering the man who had ardently courted her for four years. Like Talbot, her religious quest took her in many unusual directions, including Yoga, spiritualism, and Ernest Holmes's Church of Religious Science, but she seldom remained with any particular faith for more than a year. In the 1930s, she came to know many people in the film world, and made her living by selling them French essence perfumes.[28] In 1932, Sally wrote Talbot regarding the sale of some of his earlier magazine stories to friends in the movie business. His new agents, Brandt & Brandt, told her a sale was agreeable for almost any amount, since the agency was only handling his recent books, and that any sales which she secured would be on a 50 percent basis.[29]

After Mundy's death, Sally became reconciled to the part she had played during an important and tumultuous decade in his life. While in her eighties, in the late 1950s, on several occasions she visited Boris de Zirkoff, an early Tingley follower, expressing to him the "genuine affection and regard" she felt about Talbot.[30] Sally died of cancer on November 20, 1963.

Dick retained many warm memories of his stepfather, although they never communicated again. He was married and divorced twice before his fortunate third marriage to Betty, with whom he remained to the end of his life in 1984. He became a successful businessman, guiding new inventions to a market. Betty urged Sally to publish many of Talbot's letters in a volume to be entitled simply *Sally*, but instead she took the advice of a friend to burn most of them, in order to attempt to better put the past behind her.

Mundy may have also been induced to leave Point Loma by the lure of a new love. This was a tall, slender brunette, 24 years Talbot's junior, who was then named Theda Conkey Webber. Theda said she and Talbot first met during a visit he and Sally made to Scarsdale, New York in the late fall of 1927. Talbot and Sally accompanied Larry Trimble and his girlfriend, Troy Sefton, to the home of Troy's sister. Mrs. Webber, seven months pregnant and uncomfortable at meeting new people in such a condition, was asked by the neighbors to play the piano, and Talbot was impressed with her music.

The Mundys returned to California, but Larry and Troy stayed on with her sister. Weeks later, the Webbers' child was born, and died after less than a month. The Webbers spent many evenings with Troy and Larry, where he psychoanalyzed, interrogated, cross-examined, and challenged them.[31] The young couple, who had already experienced marital difficulties due to their divergent goals, began to talk more and more of divorce. Meanwhile, Larry revealed that the Mundy marriage, which had seemed serene, was in fact rocky.

Theda asked Troy to join her for a weekend at the Connecticut shore to get away from her husband. Troy in turn asked Larry to join them, and, according to Theda, the Mundys were again in town. Sally insisted Talbot join the trio, claiming he had been working too hard and needed some relaxation, and probably believing that Talbot's philosophy might help the young woman who had lost her child and was facing divorce. Initially, Theda was reluctant. "My conservative New England background reared its head momentarily, but as Talbot Mundy strode out of the hotel, tall, broad-shouldered, salt-and-pepper hair blown by the wind, his smile was so disarming that all resistance vanished."³² As Troy and Larry were a couple, this threw Theda and Talbot together. Soon they began to discuss religion; she had searched in vain, certain only that her Congregational Church background had not answered many of her questions.³³ "We stopped at a little inn, where there was a bridge. It was full moon with the moonlight shining on the water. Somehow Talbot and I had walked out and he started to talk his philosophy to me, as we stared up there at the night. It was all a revelation to me. I had never thought that way…. I had tried everything: Christian Science, all those things, and none of them was what I was looking for. What he told me absolutely boggled my imagination. That was the thing I remembered: he was teaching me that night."³⁴ Theda and Talbot realized they were in love two days later, but upon their return from the weekend, the Mundys departed for California.

Just as Talbot had fallen quickly in love with Sally, and his love grew during their long period apart, the situation may have been similar when he spent his first weekend with Theda. Larry was clearly playing a role in guiding the prospect of a new romance for his old friend, and he had certainly told Theda enough to intrigue her. Although she must have known of the financial calamities that drove him from California, instead she feigned ignorance of Liafail and chose to believe that he had left Sally and came to New York for one reason only, his love for her.³⁵

Mundy seems to have told the story of his meeting with Theda in "Speed," a short story for the May 5, 1935 issue of This Week. Set in eastern Africa, Jim O'Neill's friend, Harry Humboldt (for Harry read Larry Trimble), tells him he will marry a woman he met eight days ago, and he intends to propose the next evening. In the crucial passage, Mundy offers his philosophy of marriage as Harry tells Jim,

> "I've rushed too many women and been rushed by too many not to know a good one when I see her. The better they are, the less it pays to give 'em time to think. Take 'em by storm. They love that, and it makes 'em behave like human beings. They're all savages at heart, the same as we are. If a girl likes you and you show some speed, she'll surrender in no time at all."
>
> "And later?"
>
> "Oh, a good one sticks. They find us out, of course. They learn we're not perfect, any more than they are. But it's 50-50. When the bloom has worn off, people get along together, provided she's the right woman.
>
> "And if she isn't?"
>
> "The divorce court. Why not?"³⁶

The heroines, just as Mundy and Trimble match Jim and Harry, are Ann Gilkeson and Vera Denby — Theda Webber and Troy Sefton. Ann is a writer, whose books have been rejected, just as Theda was an unpublished composer. Having just received a new rejection, Ann does not wish to meet Jim and Harry, just as Theda wanted to avoid meeting Mundy and Trimble. Jim also aspires to be a writer, but regards his one effort as unworthy; Ann tells him to burn it and write a better one, advice Mundy had been given when he began to write. Jim falls in love with Ann while they have dinner, and tells her the next day. She accepts him before Harry reveals that he deliberately introduced Ann and Jim, mistakenly believing Jim needed lessons in speed.

The first step in commencing Theda and Talbot's relationship was for them to join Larry and Troy on a vacation, for six weeks, on MacDonald Island, an island Larry owned along the St. Lawrence River near Gananoque, Ontario, Canada. The island contained two houses, and Talbot's house was little more than a shack, but it was situated along a placid, cool, and isolated lake, providing an idyllic environment for revisions of *Queen Cleopatra* from late July through August. By September, Mundy's library and manuscripts were arriving in New York, and Larry and Troy had decided to go back to California, so it seemed time to take the next step.[37]

Theda and Talbot found adjoining lodgings on the outskirts of Greenwich Village, just off Fifth Avenue, in an old brownstone at Five East Ninth Street, with his apartment on the third floor, and hers in the basement. Theda's divorce became final in the fall, and she legally changed her name to Dawn Allen. From almost the beginning of their relationship, Talbot would introduce her as a talented, up-and-coming musician — just as, 15 years earlier, he had eagerly touted Rosemary's ability as a painter to his associates. Talbot initially envisioned his relationship with Dawn as not only love, but a great creative collaboration.

On MacDonald Island, the idea to combine Dawn's music with Talbot's writing had been born. In a blend to be entitled *A Drama with Music*, she sought melodies to accompany his verse and philosophical ideas. The couple also sought to create a musical element in his books, an ingredient as unique as the poems and sayings that frequently introduced each chapter. At the beginning of February, 1929, Mundy wrote to Bobbs-Merrill, energized by the idea of being the first to have songs in the books along with the music that accompanies them, believing the two elements would help sell one another, also increasing the possibility of sheet music and movie sales.[38] However, since Bobbs-Merrill was not in the sheet music business, they responded cooly.

While a piano accompanied the couple on nearly all their subsequent moves, only two surviving examples of Dawn's songs survive, both in a romantic style. "In Some One's Heart," published as an appendix in the American edition of *Cock o' the North*, is an other-worldly melody to match lyrics in Chapter 23, as sung by the heroine to inspire her hillmen going into battle. Requiring a skillful singer and musician because it incorporated several shifts to very high notes, the song was added to the repertory of Madame Ernestine Schumann-Heinck. Another composition, "Horse-Song of Caesar's Arab Cavalry," was later inserted in Dawn's own hand-written form in a special edition of *Queen Cleopatra*. A hymn to Allah, it is rather absurdly placed here, and must have been retitled and designed for another story, since Islam only came into being more than half a millennium after Caesar's death. For about a year Dawn devoted her time to the songs and *A Drama with Music*, and Mundy even had his attorney prepare a formal contract for the collaboration, yet in fact their relationship was primarily personal, not professional. Dawn recalled: "I didn't have the education and I knew it. That was the only argument we ever had. He said, 'You can do it if you want to — anybody can.' He could write because he wanted to. But I knew that I lacked the technical knowledge. I had gone so far in my music work, up till 21, studying, writing with my teachers, but I hadn't gotten what I needed and I knew it."[39] Mundy regretted that she did not continue; nine years later he would say to Wincenty Lutosławski, "Dawn is a musician, but she has disgracefully abandoned her music in favor of working with me."[40]

Mundy reinvigorated his reputation in New York City and among the literati at his favorite hotel there, the Algonquin. Frequent companions included Konrad Bercovici, Norman Bel Geddes (a guest lecturer at the Master Institute); Charles G. Clarke; Mr. and Mrs. Elmer Davis; Leslie Grant (a Theosophist, Jungian and Rorschach analyst—despite the contradictions—who was a teacher of Theosophy; Natacha Rambova had been one of her pupils) and her husband Major R.T.M. "Rex" Scott (a British writer of thrillers and a book on Rasputin, who had been a frequent contributor to *Adventure* and Chairman of the New York section of the American Society for Psychical Research), and others from the arts and theater. From their discussions Mundy wrote two bellicose letters to *The New York Times*, one humorously modifying a Davis proposal to permit the city to have a triumvirate of mayors, each revolving around one another like twin suns. Mundy was also fascinated by the American gangsters, and wrote a number of letters to the editor on the subject.[41]

He realized after two years largely lost to the Liafail disaster that a return to writing was his only possible source of income. Beginning in October 1928, until 1931, Mundy had short stories, novelettes and serials appearing virtually every month in either *Adventure*, *Argosy*, or *Everybody's Combined with Romance*, and he had requests from four other magazines.[42] First, he dusted off *When Trails Were New* and *W.H.*, selling them to *Argosy All-Story Weekly*. However, this was the only old material; his other work was fresh, but fortunately, as he told Bobbs-Merrill, "I suffer from a flux of words."[43] First was a series for *Adventure* from 1928–29, of Ben Quorn in India: "The Wheel of Destiny," "The Big League Miracle," "On the Road to Allah's Heaven," "Golden River," "A Tucket of Drums," and "In Old Narada Fort." The Quorn saga then switched from the pages of *Adventure* to *Argosy All-Story Weekly* with the serial *Asoka's Alibi* in 1929, followed by a non–Quorn serial, *By Allah Who Made Tigers*. The same year, two novelettes, *One Egyptian Night* and *Flame of Cruelty*, appeared in *Everybody's Combined with Romance*. In addition to this fiction were four articles for *The Theosophical Path*; "An Author's Characters" for *The New York Times*, and "Random Reminiscences of African Big Game" for the *Saturday Evening Post*. In late 1929, *Adventure* serialized *Cock o' the North* and published the short story "Consistent Anyhow" in 1930. *Argosy* serialized *The Affair at Kaligaon*, and *Black Light* was published by Bobbs-Merrill without serialization. As 1931 loomed, *Adventure* serialized the novel *Jimgrim* as *King of the World*, and published the short stories "Black Flag" and "The Man on the Mat," while *Argosy* serialized *The Elephant Sahib*. (What became of *Down and Bugle Blast*, on order by *Adventure*, is uncertain.)[44] Frantically hurrying to complete one novel by New Year's Day, 1930, Mundy reported to Bobbs-Merrill that he was up by 4 A.M. with a pot of cigarettes and a kettle of strong tea, continuing until bed-time, with hardly a pause for meals, often going without shaving or getting out of his pajamas.[45]

Reader's polls had long showed that Mundy was one of, if not the most popular author in *Adventure*, but relations were growing strained. Mundy even treated with enormous facetiousness a long questionnaire on how successful author's produce their work that Hoffman submitted to Mundy and others, later collected for publication by Bobbs-Merrill at the end of August 1922 as *Fiction Writers on Fiction Writing*. Although Mundy could not afford to pass up the income *Adventure* offered, for years Arthur Hoffman had not scheduled Mundy's serializations so that Bobbs-Merrill could publish the books at the desired time. Hoffman waited nearly a full year after accepting *Ramsden* before it appeared in *Adventure* in the summer of 1926, delaying Bobbs-Merrill's desired publication in spring of that year. In England, Hutchinson, who was enthusiastic about publishing the book, was equally frustrated.[46]

However annoying these matters were, when the situation changed, it soon became worse. In 1926, *Adventure* had cut back from three issues a month to two, along with a more spacious type face that offered at least 20 percent less wordage, resulting in a drop in the need for contributions. Later that same year, the magazine's owner, the Ridgway Company, was sold, and by mid 1927 Hoffman had departed. Five editors had succeeded him by 1934. Mundy gradually departed from the magazine's fold, as more of his material appeared elsewhere, often in the pages of competitors of *Adventure*, especially *Argosy*, an equally prestigious ten cent pulp weekly.

While unwilling to take any less than the pay he received from *Adventure*, Mundy hoped to finally crack the slick paper magazine market. However, he knew there were obstacles; he did not want to write short stories, preferring novelettes or serials, 60,000 or 90,000 to 200,000 words. "It is quite obvious that my stories are different from those usually published in the current magazines and there might be some difficulty in getting editors to consider them. The matter needs tactful and foresighted handling."[47] At the time there were over a hundred pulps, 13 large circulation slick paper fiction magazines, and additional literary magazines and women's magazines. Bobbs-Merrill approached others such as *Collier's* and the Hearst journals, but without success.

The *Saturday Evening Post* was the leader, selling at five cents an issue and printing some 250 short stories and 25 serials annually, paying between $7500 to $50,000 apiece for the latter, depending on the author's name.[48] However, it wanted writers whose appeal was universal, and longtime *Post* editor George Horace Lorimer was notoriously xenophobic. He preferred the "yellow peril" school of oriental fiction, so opposed to Mundy's enlightened tone.

Nonetheless, late in 1928, the *Saturday Evening Post* asked Mundy to write them a serial at a price that made him "woozy in the head."[49] Completed by the beginning of 1929, this became the 90,000 word novel, *Cock o' the North*, which was okayed chapter by chapter, with Mundy proudly telling Bobbs-Merrill, "believe me, I am getting away with murder."[50] It was accepted in March by Thomas Costain, who wanted more Mundy stories for the magazine, and had tentatively approved the plot of what was to become *Black Light*. Mundy exulted to Bobbs-Merrill that they "*Are Even Going to Run the Poems!*"[51] However, at the last moment, after agreeing on the price, Costain was overruled by Lorimer.

Mundy instead sent it to *Adventure*. He owed them a novel, since before his departure, Hoffman had bought *Queen Cleopatra*, as Mundy later told Rose Wilder Lane.

> They put in a new man, named Anthony Rudd, "who knew not Joseph." He hated my stuff anyhow, and hated me more; and he hated to pay 10 cents a word, and to find such a nick in his budget lying waiting for him in the ice-box. So he put up a bleat.
> With a feeling of generosity, of which I am now thoroughly ashamed, I volunteered to take the story back and replace it with other stories.[52]

Trying not to be bitter, Mundy believed that perhaps he should have offered *Cock o' the North* to *Adventure* in the first place. "It is part of my creed (although it is sometimes very difficult indeed to believe it) that nothing ever happens to us—and particularly no disaster happens to us that is not our own fault, though we may have to dig very deep indeed to discover what is wrong."[53]

The new novel was not serialized until October 1 to December 1, 1929, in five biweekly parts. *Adventure* insisted on the title *The Invisible Guns of Kabul*, which Mundy regarded as "absurd," since there was nothing either invisible about the guns nor was the story set in Kabul.[54] Choosing the book title became a major difficulty, and the British edition, published by Hutchinson, used Mundy's original working title, *Gup Bahadur*. *Cock o' the North* referred to a leader of the hillmen of the Northwest frontier of India, and was the title of a popular military song of the period.

Cock o' the North was not one of Mundy's philosophical or fantasy novels that might have understandably aroused Lorimer's ire, thereby providing an even stronger indication of how hopeless was Mundy's desire to become a *Post* writer. The novel was based on current events in 1928, when Afghanistan was plunged into civil war because of a tribal revolt. These events, and their impact on India, intrigued Mundy, just as the effect of World War I on India had caused him to write *King—of the Khyber Rifles*. Indeed, the new book reworked much of the narrative, character, themes, and incidents of *King—of the Khyber Rifles*, but without its fantastic overtones and mythic symbolism.

Instead of Athelstan King, Mundy creates a more complex, ambiguous hero, Angus "Gup" McLeod, a man who describes himself as "a loaded gun" torn by the experience of World War I.[55] Unlike Mundy's typical bachelor heroes, Gup once knew but has now lost a personal purpose in life; his wife had possibly "foreseen the earthquake nature of the coming change in him," and ran off with another man, by whom she eventually "had three babies and a bank account."[56] Gup's quiet rebellion is finally manifested in a determination to study politics, exchanging views with men of all convictions. As a result, the British government grows suspicious, regarding Gup as a likely Bolshevist, rather than one who believes "it's the isms and osophies that have us hog-tied."[57]

Cock o' the North reverses the respective strength and weaknesses of *King—of the Khyber Rifles*, and this is ultimately its failure. Although Gup is a more vital character than Athelstan King, Mundy simultaneously undercuts the balance by replacing the vibrant Yasmini with a weaker female lead, who lacks her predecessor's wisdom and audacity. Like Yasmini, the Ranee is famous for her dancing and singing, but it is as a former actress beloved by the soldiers, Lottie Carstairs. Lottie left the theater after meeting the ruler of Jullunder, when something greater than love ensued between them, a partnership of ideas to make his state prosperous and well-governed. When her husband died, she refused to bribe a vindictive Englishman, the aptly named Glint, to remain on the throne, and he saw to it that she was replaced. Glint seeks to destroy both Gup and the Ranee, trying to make Gup appear to be guilty of conspiring with her. Having a British imperialist as the primary force for evil sets much of the tone toward the English presence in India, despite Gup's loyalty.

She justifies her aim of creating a kingdom in the hills, from which to invade

India, as the necessary first step before Indian independence. The Ranee can become a virtual Joan of Arc because her primarily female advisors use military tactics to plot their strategy, but she still needs the presence of a strong male leader to win the support, ironically, of the Moslem women. The Ranee believes that Gup's alienation from his government and race will make him receptive to an invitation to become the commander-in-chief of her army, but he feels an inherent patriotic and human obligation to help preserve the peace of India.

In *Cock o' the North*, like *King— of the Khyber Rifles*, an Englishman rides north in a spiritual and geographical journey, beckoned by a woman ambitious to rule. *Cock o' the North* is its predecessor's equal as seemingly impregnable rocky caverns provide a lair and a symbolic, initiatory journey for Gup to traverse. The raw material of cyanide has always been present in the sands of the cavern; a nearly-mad Russian scientist is using it to manufacture poison-gas. The skeletons of a scouting party of Alexander's army are still to be seen, killed before they suspected its presence.

Gup is instantly antagonistic toward the Ranee's closest advisor, Harriet Dover, the "first woman Secretary of State who has ever lived."[58] He discovers that her weakness is an obsession against men's alleged superiority, mention of which robs her of her brilliance and self-control. Mundy's first major characterization since *Rung Ho!*, in 1914, to use the first name of former wife, Harriette Rosemary Strafer, creates a woman who resembles his own impression of her: initially impressing with her talent, but dismaying as she becomes narrow-minded and vindictive.

Unlike the denouement of *King— of the Khyber Rifles*, *Cock o' the North* turns far more political during a summit when Dover tries to betray the Ranee to the Afghan Amir. Gup succeeds in both stopping the Amir's invasion and spiking the Ranee's plans by summoning her army prematurely to defend the very land it was sworn to destroy. *Cock o' the North* ends with a clash of armies, with, again like *King— of the Khyber Rifles*, the caverns blown up.

Initially, the novel shows great skill and appears to be an unfolding masterwork, especially with the character of Gup. However, the story gradually crumbles as the unconvincing Ranee and her relationship with Gup take center stage. In her Eastern garb and position, the Ranee reminds Gup of one of the ancient Egyptian rulers, but behind the veneer he still sees the Lottie idolized on stage. In Gup, Mundy offers a man who loves the Ranee in his own way, and serves what he believes are her best interests. The growing love between these two strong characters is simply not believable; unlike Yasmini, the Ranee surrenders too quickly to Gup for a woman who has invested much of her life in plotting to win an empire. Mundy may have found this transformation of her character necessary if he was to achieve the promise of wedding bells that he decided to give the novel and which he knew his publishers—and Hollywood–wanted, not the ambiguous denouement of *King— of the Khyber Rifles*.

Like much of Mundy's quality work, the chapters in *Cock o' the North* were prefaced with brief poems, and he believed they were his best verse. In fact, however, the poems were significantly lower than his standard, lacking clarity, perhaps because most were about love, and intended as songs. The Ranee's background as a former star of the English music-hall would have eased the adaptation of *Cock o' the North* for a movie, or the stage. Such plans would not have been out of place in 1929; the popular use of sound technology had just revolutionized motion pictures, and the musical had already been combined with adventure in *The Vagabond King* and *The Desert Song*, both also released in 1929 and based on popular stage hits.

Indeed, in addition to selling a novel to the *Saturday Evening Post*, one of the primary purposes Mundy may have had in writing and revising *Cock o' the North* was the fact that Hollywood was at last set to make a major movie from *King— of the Khyber Rifles*, starring Victor McLaglen as King. In October 1928, despite it being a tumultuous time in the industry, Fox had bought *King— of the Khyber Rifles*, with Mundy receiving a badly needed $15,000, most of it immediately used to pay off debts, including years of accumulated advances from Bobbs-Merrill.

If the movie was successful, Mundy hoped for a follow-up, with McLaglen again in the lead, and *Cock o' the North* reconceived *King— of the Khyber Rifles* along lines that would better suit a McLaglen vehicle. Today it is difficult to imagine McLaglen as King or Gup, since he became associated with drunken, comedic (and eventually hammy) performances after winning an Oscar as Best Actor for playing a weak-minded traitor in *The Informer* (1935). However, in 1929 his persona was considerably different; at age 42, he was still young enough for a heroic, romantic lead, and capably played in a number of empire adventure roles, *Beau Geste* (1926), *The Lost Patrol* (1934), *Under Two Flags* (1936), and *Gunga Din* (1939). Recasting Yasmini as a Western woman in the East, rather than one of mixed racial ancestry, was Mundy's response to Hollywood's inability to positively portray a woman of the East. Ironically, the result of Mundy's efforts to write for McLaglen was that the two stories were regarded as too similar for *Cock o' the North* to be filmed.[59]

The Black Watch is one of the most unusual, even bizarre, commercial movies made during the early years of sound movies. Although *The Black Watch* is hardly faithful to the novel, it also has more resemblance than any other version considered or made. It belongs to a time when the empire adventure, or adventure of any type in the colonies, had yet to be formulated as a cinematic genre; *The White Panther* one of the few such pictures set in India. On the screen, India was still treated more as melodrama than adventure.

On December 30, 1928, Douglas Z. Doty offered a Continuity Outline, placing King in the "Black Watch," the first introduction of the key idea preserved in the final screenplay. Rewa Gunga, now a British spy, is no longer a persona assumed by Yasmini, but a separate character, presumably because the androgynous combination was regarded as too complex, or unusual, for audiences to fathom.

A new writer, John Stone, was placed on the project, and on January 17 he completed a new Continuity Outline. Here King acquires an amusing Moslem companion who kicks Hindus, Mohammed Khan, lifted from another Mundy novelette, "For the Salt Which He Had Eaten." Fox had also bought the rights to *Told in the East* along with *King— of the Khyber Rifles*.

Until this point, the movie had been planned as a silent, but now the decision was made to film it in sound, and a new writer, James Kevin McGuinness, was brought in for additional changes and the writing of dialogue. His version of January 25, 1929, gave King a brother, Malcolm. It was McGuinness's inept dialogue

In *The Black Watch*, Mundy's single character becomes two: Myrna Loy as Yasmini and Roy D'Arcy as Rewa Gunga. (Autographed to the author by Miss Loy)

which would especially vex Mundy, and even *Variety* speculated that *The Black Watch* might have been more effective as a silent, since the dialogue is often unbelievable.[60]

With McGuinness as supervisor, the movie became the second talking picture for his friend John Ford, assigned to direct and produce; he had already become one of the leading filmmakers in Hollywood. After production, the change of the American release title was made from *King of the Khyber Rifles* to *The Black Watch*, while the original title was retained in the United Kingdom. Mundy did not object, but he was probably one of the few in the picture's audience who entered already knowing about the Black Watch; today they are best known for their work as British ambassadors of goodwill, performing bagpipe music and routines for appreciative audiences at home and abroad.

Dawn and Talbot attended the opening night in New York, May 22, when *The Black Watch* played to a full house at $11 a seat. Dawn recalled that at the conclusion, "Talbot turned to me and let off what he felt about the people in the picture, and right in the row in front, we were in about the third row, there were three actors, and they turned around! I'll never forget that — he was so angry. It was a travesty of the book."[61] Mundy promptly wrote an eight page letter to Bobbs-Merrill and their Hollywood agent giving his views on the picture, full of invective, both frank and amusing. He also wrote, for public consumption, an article, "An Author's Characters," for the June 30 issue of the *New York Times*, to publicize the movie; it was a detailed account of how he came to write *King — of the Khyber Rifles*.

After a foreshadowing toast to "the King," Donald King is summoned by the War Office and told that since he knows Pushtu and Hindustani like a native, he must prevent a holy war about to be incited by Yasmini, a goddess to the troublesome hillmen. The assignment requires King leave the regiment alone, under a cloud, apparently transferring to the Khyber Rifles to avoid service at the front, leaving his younger brother Malcolm (David Rollins) to carry on the family name in this war. Only after twenty four minutes does *The Black Watch* finally shift to the center of action — "Peshawar — on the northern frontier of British India — near the Khyber Pass" — but the movie is never convincing in conveying the Indian locale.

One of those at prayer is Risaldar Major Mohammed Khan, who announces "For all the violence I have displayed toward my fellow men, Allah forgive me." He promptly shoves a nearby man, causing a disruption, and repeats the line after every violent act to comedic effect. Officially deemed too old, Khan is glad to join King for a secret mission, having served King's father forty years earlier: "having eaten thy salt, and thy father's salt." Khan is the only type in the entire film that is redolent of Mundy, and as played by Mitchell Lewis, is perhaps the best acted individual as well. Mundy commented that he was excellent low comedy, "farce at the right moment and not overdone. He had the only good lines in the picture and the only good part. Wanted more of him and so did the audience."[62]

Held in as much contempt by local citizens as he was by the Black Watch, King deliberately becomes a drunkard and renegade, but he wins the admiration of the beautiful Yasmini (Myrna Loy), partial to "stalwart men." On the screen, Rewa Gunga (overacted by Roy D'Arcy) is her oily aide, a power-hungry dandy.

Finally, with more than half the film over, the narrative is about to reach the Khyber pass; only two-thirds of the film is set in India, and 40 percent in the hills — versus nearly all of Mundy's book in both. Even at this point, the movie destroys the mood by cutting back to the Black Watch fighting in the muddy fields of Flanders, with the men taunting Malcolm that his brother is a slacker.

Rather than Mundy's emphasis on the indigenous people, in *The Black Watch*

Mohammed Khan (Mitchell Lewis), lifted from "For the Salt Which He Had Eaten," and Donald King (Victor McLaglen) form an Anglo-Indian partnership against Yasmini in *The Black Watch*.

it is on the Scots and the World War I subplot. The scenes in England serve as a framing story, grounding the excursion into an Asian culture by showing details of another foreign tradition, Scotland, one less strange to the audience, and one of their own race. The arrangement of scenes attempt to make India more comprehensible, through showing her similarities and contrasts with Scotland.

King, in local costume, has joined a caravan led by the mullah Harrim Bey (Walter Long), the representative of a foreign power, presumably Turkey, who has supplied Yasmini's men with ammunition to attack the British. As Mundy noted, "It did not go to pieces until they began to pretend to use my material. Then it became worse than awful, and the last reel was the worst thing I have ever seen."[63] The mystical portrayal of the Khinjan caves given by Mundy is replaced in the film with a cacophonous din of loud prayer and fighting men that resembles Madison Square Garden gone mad. When newcomers are brought forward, King needs a sponsor, and Yasmini appears in soft focus, dressed in a slinky, diaphanous dress to recommend him. However, Bey and Gunga urge that King wrestle for their sport, replacing the wrenching initiation in the novel with a scene Mundy called "stupid beyond belief."[64] Yasmini then announces that "Virgins will dance for your desire"; unlike the book, she performs no dances of her own in the film, and the tawdry presentation cheapens the manner in which she mesmerizes the imagination of her followers.

Gunga is ready to "talk, we three, of glory, of wealth, and power," but Yasmini wants to speak of something else, because King's presence has changed her dreams. Yasmini, whose face is milk-white against dark hair, brows, nostrils, and medium lips, appears tall and thin, in contrast to her dark-skinned waiting women. She reveals to the surprised King that she is white, a descendent of Alexander the Great, who took a wife in the hills. She relates a prophecy that when a woman of Alexander's line shall find the mate ordained to rule these tribesman, the conquest shall be fulfilled. She is also lonely; "It is sweeter to be a woman to one man than a goddess to thousands," the opposite of the sentiments of Mundy's heroine.[65] King's restrained response is to wander to the other side of the room, saying "It can't be," despite his growing love for her. All of the scripts and the final film demonstrate that a woman like Yasmini was something that the filmmakers simply could not understand; publicity termed her role "a she-devil who aspires to a throne and domination of India."

Gunga, lurking outside to kill King, is pushed over a cliff by Khan. King's men remove their native robes to reveal British uniforms, assembling their machine guns in a critical spot overlooking the cavern, bottling up the hillmen, and setting the stage for a struggle that is small and obviously budget-conscious (the film was made for $400,000).[66] Yasmini, dressed in angelic white, says "Thou hast triumphed," and is shot by one of her own; King lifts her away as his men's machine guns spray the cavern.

King goes to Yasmini's room where her maids have placed her dying body. In the moving death scene, the best of the film, the couple are clearly in love. She tells him, "It was for thee, Donald! My head has rested on thy breast. My lips have burned on thine. Henceforth — no other woman's lips can kiss thee — but thou will be reminded of me. Thy memory of Yasmini — will never die." Khan, standing nearby, has been looking respectfully to one side with his men. His hand is seized by King, clenching his teeth, telling him bitterly to deliver the message "The job is finished — King."

The final sequence parallels the opening, returning to a dinner of the Black Watch, their numbers thinned around a smaller table, on New Year's Eve. The Colonel announces King has won the D.S.O. for his service in India and has been promoted to Major; Malcolm approaches, wounded, as the brothers are reunited. Outside other, typical civilian Scots also share a drink, and the movie closes with the line, "Happy New Year!"— although released in May 1929.

McLaglen turned out to be far more capable in his role than Loy was in hers, particularly in the dialogue scenes. In their second film opposite one another, McLaglen and Loy are a physical contrast, the boyish, innocent, burly King versus the feminine Yasmini, the tempter and the aggressor. They are far superior to the two principal villains, Bey and Gunga. Loy's makeup and physique could have facilitated a role as both Gunga and Yasmini, adding greater complexity to the piece, and broken the sexism with which the role was endowed. Ford choose Loy in the role of Yasmini, and while she projects some of the sensuality, she never embodies her strength of character. She looks too young and innocent, despite speaking in stilted, regal tones.

Ford's direction won critical praise for its visual and auditory artistry, but not its narrative sense. The style nullifies the adventurous elements, preventing *The Black Watch* from becoming the spectacle it might easily have been, instead emphasizing emotions, drama and the frustrated love story; the largest number of extras go into the scene in the London railroad depot. The entire movie is deliberately overdone, from the pacing to the acting.

Publicity emphasized McLaglen's starring role; secondary appeals were Ford's reputation and the novelty of sound. The film was moderately successful, with an estimated gross of $800,000.[67] However, it clearly demonstrated Hollywood's difficulty in adapting Mundy to the screen.

Mundy's dreams of a popular movie adaptation, of becoming a contributor to the *Saturday Evening Post*, of business success and a happy marriage to Sally, had all failed to come to fruition in the span of a single year. As close as Mundy came to a mainstream commercial breakthrough in the 1920s, it remained elusive; his reputation was secure, but his readership, while large, never expanded beyond a certain audience. Gone was the confident figure with the rising reputation who had been so effective a spokesman for the Point Loma Theosophical Society only a few years before. In his place was a man who had been compelled by financial need to return to more traditional stories for the pulp magazine market, whose height of critical recognition had passed. Yet, despite failure, Mundy's religious curiosity would prove to be unwavering, and he still had many unusual tales for his readers.

IX

New Faith, 1928–1931

The changes in Talbot Mundy's life that led him to return to New York City, and to begin life with the woman who became his fifth wife, Dawn, had other results. First, he became involved in an extended investigation of spiritualism, which impacted his novel *Black Light*. Second, he joined another theosophical organization, this one headed by Nicholas Roerich. Finally, signing with a different agency, Brandt & Brandt, took Mundy to a new publisher and changed his critical reception.

Departing Point Loma had hardly ended Talbot's interest in religion, and in New York he resumed his friendship with Natacha Rambova (1897–1966), a stunning beauty with a taste for the exotic and mystical. To those who did not know her or looked at women through sexist stereotypes, she might have seemed cold. However, men like Talbot, who were not so intimidated, thought highly of her, and found a talented, intelligent, and friendly woman who liked to laugh.[1] Born Winifred Shaughnessy, her parents divorced and her mother married perfume magnet Richard Hudnut. She took the name Natacha Rambova after joining a Russian dance company in her youth, and then became a designer on the artistic movies of Hollywood actress-producer Alla Nazimova, who had visited Point Loma. Through her, in 1920 Natacha met Rudolph Valentino, who was not yet a "star." The two fell in love, but their marriage was sundered by Hollywood pressures, and in 1926 the couple divorced.

A year earlier, Natacha's mother, who had been a Mormon, a Catholic, an Episcopalian, and a Christian Scientist, joined the Point Loma branch of the Society, and the daughter followed her lead. Natacha took the theosophical perspective as the basis for her own studies in Oriental and ancient philosophies and myths from Tibet, India and Egypt. She had great respect for Mundy's theosophical novels, and in later years would introduce them to such scholars as Mircea Eliade.

Spiritualism was fashionable at the time, and Sir Arthur Conan Doyle would die in 1930 after dedicating the last thirteen years of his life to the subject. Natacha first experimented with séance phenomena in 1922.[2] In 1925, she met George B. Wehner (1890–1970), a medium for writers and show business people. Wehner proudly noted that he shared H.P. Blavatsky's birthday; his father had been close to her in his youth, but later quarreled with her. Wehner claimed Blavatsky as one of his important spirit guides, before he realized her true identity; he believed that she had learned more in the afterlife since the statements against mediumship during her Earthly existence. His primary control, however, was a boisterous Indian, White Cloud, who spoke in classic pidgin English, and sang songs in his own tongue.[3]

Wehner's first séance with Natacha, her mother, singer Donna Shinn Russell, and several filmmakers had proved successful, and Wehner was hired to conduct séances twice a week for Natacha and Mrs. Hudnut. Natacha returned to New York in mid 1927, a year after Valentino's death. Dawn immediately modeled herself on Natacha, in her fashion, hair style, and her decision to adopt a new name. Natacha prepared a cover design for *Queen Cleopatra* that was rejected by Bobbs-Merrill, who also turned down Talbot's attempt to interest them in her book on Valentino.[4]

Wehner was now in New York, and Natacha suggested Talbot and Dawn join her in the serious study of spiritualism, in particular trance mediums. Spiritualist elements had already appeared in *Om* and *The Devil's Guard*, and it was compatible with Talbot's many psychic experiences. As Dawn recalled,

> Another thing he could do, believe it or not, he could read palms. He used them as a focal point; I think he was psychic to that extent, that he'd meet people, and when a lot of people were gathered together, he could use it as a conversation piece — but he could hit the truth! One time — he wouldn't read my palm, he absolutely refused — he had been reading two or three and everybody was having a beautiful time, so I just stuck my hand in front of him — I was standing in back of him, and he said "No way — no!" It was interesting — he could do things for other people, but he refused to do it for me, which was probably logical; a physician doesn't treat his own family.[5]

Dawn proved susceptible to frightening psychic visions, relating these experiences in a manner that emulated Talbot's story-telling ability; for instance, in one she glimpsed Talbot in a previous incarnation, as an ancient Egyptian.[6] Talbot was more than willing to accept what she said; he thought artists were more sensitive to the feel of a place, intently observing what others fail to notice, experiencing vibrant, inexplicable but undeniable sensations.[7]

For months, from fall into winter, Talbot, Dawn, Natacha, and a court stenographer gathered regularly one night a week with Wehner. Talbot, Dawn, Natacha, and Wehner quickly became a limited group when it was discovered that guests with even the most subconscious skepticism would ruin the occasion. There were discussions of "life after death," with the dead, including a voice that credibly identified herself, by teaching, choice of words, and personality, as Blavatsky. On one memorable evening, they seemed to make contact with Mary Baker Eddy, whom they believed healed Natacha's attorney, who had been seriously ill in the hospital.

Mundy assisted Wehner by trying to interest Bobbs-Merrill in his autobiography in October 1928, indicating his belief that it was the first book about spiritualism actually written by a medium, in comparison to the vast number of books seeking to expose and discredit spiritualism.[8] When Wehner found a more literary publisher than Bobbs-Merrill, Horace Liveright, his book was entitled *A Curious Life*, and Mundy wrote an introduction. Admitting there were frauds in the field, as in all areas, and that some had abused their gifts for profit, Mundy nonetheless argued that spiritualism had not been treated without prejudice. "At least nine-tenths of the allegedly scientific 'tests' of psychic phenomenon made by the opponents of Spiritualism have been made under conditions so grossly unfair as to make their production and proof problematic, if not impossible. For instance: if we should challenge a great artist to paint a picture under our hostile gaze, clothed in uncomfortable garments of our choosing, in a place of our selection, in an atmosphere of suspicion, would it be logical or just to brand him as a 'faker' if he should generously accept the challenge but produce a mere 'daub'?... Or would a surgeon agree to perform a major operation under such conditions?" After an assault on ignorance and skepticism, condemning those who closed their minds to new thinking and prefer the ease of ignorance and ridicule, Mundy introduced Wehner to readers as a gentleman without reproach.[9]

During these experiments in spiritualism, Mundy had maintained contact with the leadership at Point Loma. The founders of the Theosophical Society itself at one time had spiritualist inclinations, which were later regretted, and although sometimes referring to such phenomenon, it is officially rejected by Theosophy. (Christian Science is also opposed to spiritualism, with Mary Baker Eddy teaching that the dead do not remain separate entities but are all part of one great spirit of God.) News of Mundy's latest predilection was a subject of concern and added to the unlikelihood that he would "return to 'where he really belonged.'" Dawn noticed the "long, persuasive letters" urging him, in the strongest possible terms, to come back to Point Loma, in the belief, she said, "he was on the dark road to—well, I don't know, we'd better say oblivion."[10] Chief among these correspondents was Gottfried de Purucker. One of Mundy's replies was a copy of *A Curious Life*, inscribed: "This book is so important that it can't be ignored. It is either true or false. I vouch for its author's integrity of statement and of motive, but of course I am not qualified to interpret what it actually means. I believe you should review the book, but—in the name of all that's honorable, don't do so without 'taking thought.' Then, either praise or denounce it publicly—but give your reasons."[11]

In the spring of 1929, Katherine Tingley departed for a European tour. As she stopped in New York, Talbot arranged for her to meet Dawn, an occasion she vividly recalled. "He took me—Gottfried de Purucker didn't know about this—but he took me to meet Katherine Tingley. I was scared to death, from Connecticut, and very unsophisticated. I knew he was doing it, and afterwards he told me he wanted to see whether she approved of me or not, and she did. She was very gracious to me. He was very fond of Katherine Tingley."[12] Her renewed contact with Mundy prompted him to again become a contributor to *The Theosophical Path*, and from April to September he was given first place among the list of contributors appearing at the end of each issue. The first of his new articles for *The Theosophical Path* was appropriately titled "I Have Risen," an Easter piece that concentrated on the theme of facing death without fear. "Spiritual Man is Eternal: There Are No Dead!" concerned Saint Paul's dictum that we die daily. It reveals Mundy's belief that anyone could alter their person and possibilities through the process of daily rebirth, not unlike the process of reincarnation—change and revitalize as he had on many occasions. One incarnation of Mundy's existence had indeed died when he fled Point Loma in the shame of bankruptcy, but he had risen again in renewing his career and his life once more since his arrival in New York City. These complex articles demonstrated new influences and a new style, and highlight his debt to Christianity asserting itself.

That same spring, Mundy decided to emulate Tingley and take a trip to Europe, which would also be his first since 1920, with Dawn accompanying him. The goal was ostensibly to convince his British agent that some of his early 1920s *Adventure* novelettes should be the next book publication in England. Wehner accompanied the couple; Talbot was curious to observe his reactions, since he had reported observing numerous psychic phenomena during his trip to Europe with Natacha three years earlier. They toured London, then went on to Rome via Paris, seeing the churches and the ruins.

They discovered that the *cloaca maximus*, the main sewer of ancient Rome, a dungeon into which prisoners had been tossed, corresponded to one of the visions that Dawn had in New York. In the very same spot, Talbot felt himself strangled and nearly fainted. Neither was part of what the other saw, and they believed they had had brief glimpses into lives centuries past, at different times, but in the same place. Later Mundy elaborated to Rose Wilder Lane. "I think I must have been one of Tros' contemporaries—probably Bath-house John in a dive near the public wharf of Alexandria; or perhaps, if that wasn't the particular incarnation in which I earned some of the slaps I have received in this one, a priestling of Serapis. Anyhow, I'm on the way up. I have vague half-memories at times of having pulled an oar in a Phoenician galley, and of having reached the coast of Britain."[13] After Naples, they drove up the coast of Italy, through Monte Carlo, Nice, and visited Natacha's mother at her chateau. Wehner, who had taken a side trip to Switzerland while Dawn and Talbot were in Italy, rejoined them for the voyage back to England.

On July 11, six weeks after suffering a fractured leg in an automobile accident on her European tour, Tingley died in Germany. Although she had not officially named a successor, Purucker was the obvious choice, and he was ready, with letters to the general membership outlining plans for the future and asserting endorsement by the Masters.[14] His other main concern was the looming debts, mounting to nearly $1,000,000. Drastic economies were necessary, and members who could earn their living outside of the colony were encouraged to do so.

Between Purucker and Talbot there was respect, but none of the close fellowship that had preserved his esteem for Tingley. Despite having served Tingley faithfully, Purucker was not a believer in gender equality, and urged that the Theosophical Society choose a man as his own successor, predicting that women would remain handicapped by misconceptions in leadership roles for centuries to come. After Purucker became Leader, *The Theosophical Path* took on a much more erudite tone, and Mundy wrote only one more article, for the November 1929 issue, "Three Signs of the Times: Kenneth Morris—Flinders Petrie—Spengler." Purucker moved the organization toward a more academic style, which placed a lower priority on the popular fiction and secular appeals that were so central to the Tingley era, and which Mundy could provide. Moreover, his possible contributions had changed too; by the end of the decade Mundy no longer had the virtually guaranteed outlet in *Adventure* magazine for nearly anything he chose to write.

Mundy's association with the Theosophical Society was meteoric: he came into prominence very quickly, stayed a few years, and then was gone. This was probably inevitable; he came to Point Loma at the very end of its peak years, just before a decline set in.[15] There was never any possibility that Mundy would become the pillar of theosophy for which Tingley doubtless hoped: a writer in the mold of Kenneth Morris, only with Mundy's ability to reach a mass audience. His wanderlust, unsteady private life, and financial instability kept him from occupying a leading, long-term position. Moreover, he was ill-suited for such a role, unable to constrain his creative freedom or submerge his individuality to doctrinal constraints. As Dawn Mundy observed, "He started out at the bottom and went up through it until he got out at the top.... I think he sort of went through things, and then looked for something else."[16]

During the limited time of his own active involvement in the society, Mundy proved that it was possible to fully and palatably integrate the offbeat philosophy of a minority, avant-garde religious group into popular works of fiction and still maintain a wide readership. Through his writing, the Eastern notions that were the basis of theosophical beliefs had their best chance to be favorably received without the instant, out-of-hand ("heretical") rejection that would likely be the result of a straightforward, unconcealed presentation to a largely Judeo-Christian audience. With Purucker's failure to continue using him as an active contributor, the Theosophical Society lost its best opportunity to disperse its concepts to a large audience and have any hope of wide acceptance. Just as Mundy departed, so did the other great writer of fiction at Point Loma, Kenneth Morris, who was encouraged to leave the community to make his own living outside and help rebuild the lodges in his native Wales, where he taught and edited a Welsh Theosophical magazine. Nonetheless, Mundy remained a favorite writer of theosophists, with his *Theosophical Path* articles and "sayings of Tsiang Samdup" still reprinted in contemporary theosophical journals.

Leaving Point Loma did not end Mundy's involvement with the movement, and he began to be active in a new type of Theosophically-oriented institution, on the opposite coast. Returning to New York in September of 1929, Dawn and Talbot gave up their leases in Greenwich Village and moved uptown, taking a two-year lease at the Master Building, a 29-story apartment hotel at 310 Riverside Drive. The low-rent apartments were available to artists, singers, actors, musicians, and scholars pursuing universal harmony through art and culture.[17] This complex, with unique architecture, opened on October 17 at a ceremony that attracted a crowd of thousands. Talbot took an eighteenth floor apartment, while Natacha joined them, moving into a suite three floors above. Here Dawn could continue her music studies, while Mundy began writing *Black Light*.

The first three floors of the building were known as the Nicholas Roerich Museum, filled with his paintings. The Hall of the East contained an exact replica of a Tibetan Library, with commentaries on religious scriptures, books in Tibetan on philosophy and religion, morality and ethics as taught by Buddha, complete with a shrine.[18] The Master Building was designed as not only a skyscraper that would serve as a cathedral of art, but to serve as headquarters to several organizations. To promote

The Master Building in New York City still stands today.

greater American familiarity with international art, in November 1921 the Master Institute of United Arts had been founded, to bring all the arts under one roof, with classes in music, painting, sculpture, architecture, ballet, and drama, and lectures, concerts, and exhibitions, based on the belief that art would unify humanity. Eight months later, an international art center to promote understanding among all peoples, Corona Mundi (Crown of the World) was established.

Nicholas Roerich (1874–1947), founder of the Master Institute and Corona Mundi, was a Russian expatriate painter of Oriental art, an explorer, and author of many books. Roerich saw a museum as a dynamic abode, a home of the muses, and in the Master Building he had created a small-scale version of Point Loma.[19] Unlike Tingley, he was more of a figurehead, seldom actually visiting New York, but his principles guided the activities. His own spiritual philosophy incorporated elements of Buddhism, Hinduism, pantheism, and Russian Orthodoxy, believing in the fundamental unity of spiritual teachings. He had joined a Russian branch of the Theosophical Society before World War I, and, like Mundy, his vision of the East was that of a Westerner, reared in Christianity, adopting a culture.

Roerich was one of those who had benefitted from the education available in the turn-of-the-century years in Czarist Russia. He lauded reform in Russia, but lived in Finland at the time of the Revolution and did not take sides, believing it had made some improvements, and saw Bolshevism as having some elements in common with Buddhism, earning him suspicion in both Russia and the United States.[20]

In 1929, Roerich was at the peak of his fame, having just been nominated for the Nobel Peace Prize. Fascinated with the East from childhood, he and his wife Helena studied Indian literature and philosophy (she authored the first full-length Russian translation of *The Secret Doctrine*). He became convinced that ancient Slavic and Indian culture, as well as Native American tribal customs, shared common origins, and feared that much of the vestiges were being lost under British colonialism. *The Devil's Guard* had revealed Roerich's influence, since at the time he was traveling from India north to Mongolia. Before setting out, he lived for a time in Darjeeling, at the moment when the Tashi Lama's flight from Tibet was considered an event foreshadowing the era of Shambhala, with war and the fall of kingdoms. Finding this supposed secret valley in the Himalayas became one of the unspoken goals of his journey, just as in the book the search is the ostensibly secondary but actually true goal. Among the myths Roerich found evidence for was that Jesus traveled to Kashmir after his resurrection and taught until his natural death; Mundy added a chapter heading to the American publication of *The Devil's Guard*, mentioning a manuscript in the handwriting of Jesus.[21]

Some five years after Mundy wrote *The Devil's Guard*, the aftermath of Roerich's expedition directly involved him. Roerich's interest, coming from a Russian, annoyed those in the colonial offices, coinciding with long-standing fear of Russian espionage in India. They believed that his expedition was now serving Soviet aims, prompting a request for the Tibetan government to detain him. The expedition had to spend the winter living in summer tents at 15,000 feet, amidst subfreezing temperatures, denied food, fuel, and medicine. All letters were seized and communication forbidden, and 90 animals perished and five men died.[22] There was also hostility from armed robbers, but Roerich nonetheless had the opportunity to mix with all levels of men, from lamas to the fiercest tribes, and found evidence of Jesus's teaching in that land.

Finally returning to India, the Roerichs found themselves under surveillance, while Helena Roerich's health was in decline from the winter conditions. In May 1929, Roerich and his sons left for Europe and the United States to contact scientific institutions, but then was denied permission to return to India, despite Madame Roerich's condition, for the next year and a half. Meanwhile, a secret probe in the United States had begun to examine if the Roerich Museum was a Bolshevik organization, but no evidence was found and the results were transmitted to authorities in India.[23]

With the situation at a hopeless impasse, the Roerich Museum sent Mundy to London to try to convince the British authorities to grant permission. As in his mission to the Grand Mufti, and in setting up favorable contracts for Liafail with the Mexican government, Mundy proved adept at a task that required tact, boldness, and acumen. Dawn recalled, "He walked in where angels fear to tread. He got up into the high important people—he knew he had to see important people and he saw them. How he was able to do it was just unknown. He was not a diplomat, not in the American government, or in the secret service or anything. He called one night and said, 'Roerich will be in India tomorrow,' and he was. So he had some sort of ability to charm people into doing what he wanted them to do."[24] The entry was by a roundabout way; in November, 1930, Roerich won a visa from the Governor of Pondicherry, a French colony in South India. Subsequently, Roerich settled in Kulu, where he founded a Himalayan Institute, never to leave India again.[25] Mundy's mission took 15 days, and Dawn was only mildly annoyed when he returned with a "striking brunette" that he had met on the boat, and who stayed with them for six weeks before proceeding to her own destination.[26]

Shortly after Talbot, Dawn, and Natacha moved into the Master Building, George Wehner also rented an apartment there, and the weekly sessions devoted to the study of trance mediumship resumed. Seances would typically begin with recitation of the Lord's prayer, and the singing of hymns, until Wehner dozed off and went into the trance state. Entering the trance, the medium would seem to fall asleep, his abdomen would swell, and he might bang his head uncontrollably on the chair.

While Wehner might fall into a trance almost immediately, he might awaken after a few minutes, conscious that the connection had failed. He compared a seance to a telephone connection, with himself like a battery, partly dependent on the receptivity of the group, with disruption caused by skeptics or movement. Some sessions proved uneventful, such as one attended by Elmer Davis and recalled by his son.

> I also remember one winter afternoon when he took Dad and me down to the Roerich Institute on Riverside Drive to attend a seance. I have some quite clear visual images from that afternoon—the late winter sun going down over the Palisades, the room on the top floor of the institute where the seance was held—and the room itself in its darkened state. My recollection is that there were about 10 people there altogether. During the seance there were a number of noises (of course the room was completely dark) but no significant occurrences. As the disappointed

group filed out some time later into a sort of anteroom or lobby up there we overheard some people complaining of the presence of the skeptics. How they knew we were skeptics I can't imagine. Surely, neither of us said anything about it.[27]

On other occasions, the trances would continue for hours.

In an unconscious medium state, Wehner introduced Talbot's brother Harold, late a much-decorated English general in Egypt. The morning after Harold's second "appearance," a letter arrived. Although Talbot had not seen Harold's writing for fifteen years, he immediately recognized the penmanship. Harold was very much alive — he had become Chief of Staff to the commander of British forces in Constantinople, then in 1928 was given command of the foreign service battalion of The King's Own in India. Subsequently, Talbot, Dawn, and Natacha tried to keep Wehner conscious, with sometimes violent and inexplicable results. Supposedly possessed by the spirit of a suicidal man, Wehner tried to jump to his death, and once nearly carried Dawn over a balcony.

Besides much twitching and jerking in the near darkness on Wehner's part, succeeding seances frequently offered music. Wehner, who had taught and studied harmony in Michigan, repeated the music he heard from the spirits, while inhabited by the spirit of a dead musician. Dawn, who had been born with near perfect pitch, recognized they were melodies of extraordinary beauty and clarity. She was assigned to transcribe these melodies, and found there were a total of fifteen or twenty of them. Subsequently, Dawn worked out the tunes on the piano, preparing them for voice, while Wehner added words to the music for songs. At the beginning of 1929, he had also been part of Dawn's efforts to create *A Drama with Music*.

Subsequently, Natacha arranged for the music to be performed publicly in a recital, with Dawn at the piano accompanying singer Donna Shinn Russell. Although Dawn gave Wehner all credit for the music as well as the words, one morning not long afterward he viciously accused her of trying to steal his music. As a result, both Talbot and Dawn promptly and irrevocably severed all contact with him, which also ended most of their interest in spiritualism. Years later, Dawn would recall that because of Wehner, *A Curious Life* was the only book she ever threw away. She recalled their surprise at the way he turned: "He was so vicious, maybe he was controlled by something, anyway that was what Talbot and I wondered."[28] In future years, Mundy spoke against forms of spiritualism ever more directly. One character in *Old Ugly-Face* remarks, "'Physical prostitution would be better than [a trance medium]. A prostitute, after all, gives no more than her body to be defiled by strangers. But a medium's *soul* is at the mercy of every devil and fool who chooses to misuse it. The very least you will become, unless you wake up, and stay awake, will be a sort of radio receiving set employed by mischievous and godless liars.'"[29]

By the end of 1929, Mundy was frantically hurrying to complete his new novel, eventually entitled *Black Light*. With high hopes, Mundy believed the book would be readily adapted to stage and screen, and filled with songs and music destined to be hits.[30] None of these performance aspects were achieved, and the book itself elicited a disappointing response. When Bobbs-Merrill received it at the beginning of the year, they promptly made two demands: that the 123,500 word book be cut by one-fifth and eliminate the swearing by the hero.

No magazine serialization ever took place, and again the *Saturday Evening Post* rejected the book. Like *Queen Cleopatra*, *Black Light* neglected to include the action ingredients that would appeal to the generic-minded pulps and other fiction magazines, and because this was such a lucrative supplement to the comparatively meager income of book royalties, Mundy never again disregarded this element until he could rely on his *Jack Armstrong* contract for support. By the time Mundy's revisions were completed, in June, Bobbs-Merrill declared themselves satisfied, and *Black Light* was published in the United States and England in October, 1930. Sales were respectable; in its first six months, the book sold some 4500 copies in the United States and Canada, earning its author $1250 in royalties.[31] Reviews varied in their estimation, but in general were mixed, particularly toward the occult aspects; notices of the book in subsequent years have retained the same divided view.

Many of the poems and particularly the sayings between chapters are in a different style than other such Mundy work. The sayings are "From the Book of the Yogi-Astrologer Ram-Chittra Gunga Sahib," and in many cases are virtually essay-length, frequently commencing and closing with the phrase, "I am a Yogi, I sit at the feet of Wisdom." Subjects covered include virtue, love, wisdom, critics, the soul, reincarnation, motherhood, evolution, imagination, karma, prisons, science, spirituality, materialism, astrology, science, the laws that govern the universe, whether there is a god, and the clash of different cultures despite their underlying unity. All make explicit the debt his literary and religious thinking owed to teachers of all faiths, most notably mixing the words of the Bible and Jesus into an Eastern context, urging Westerners to understand the teachers of their own culture before turning to Eastern faiths.

Whereas the sayings in his other books generally have a single topic, those in *Black Light* typically cover several ideas, one running into another, demonstrating the linkage and interdependence between them. For instance, after a saying facing Chapter 9 where the Yogi is unable to convince a western scientist that his watch bears the same relation to the cosmos as does the Yogi's astrology, Mundy leads the topic in a new direction in the saying preceding Chapter 16.

> If I, who observe the stars as you, it may be, observe signposts on the road, inform you that to-morrow this or that will happen — and it happens — you say it is accident. But is it accident when you, who read the road-signs in a language that perhaps I cannot read, inform me that in an hour we shall come to this or that place — and we come there? Nay, say you, that is knowledge won by understanding from experience. We are again in agreement, but without consistency: your one and one makes two, you say, but mine do not.
>
> And when I say you have lived at least a hundred thousand lives in this world, you answer, How then can I not remember some of them? To which I say, Take pen and paper; write all that you remember of your doings day by day in this present life; can you recall a tenth part, or a hundredth? Nay. Then how shall you remember former lives? But you answer, I have a diary. I can read that and remember.
>
> You have a better diary, wherein is written all your history; and not of this life only, but of all your lives. It is you yourself. And I, who know a little of that language, read in that book that you are, a few humiliating reasons why you cannot read it.[32]

Regrettably, Bobbs-Merrill decided, on the basis of length, not to include the sayings in their edition of *Black Light*.[33] The American edition of the book suffered by this excision, since, as always, the inserts between chapters were key to setting the tone of the story, enriching its meaning. Only in the British edition published by Hutchinson, and in Hutchinson's reprint in the Mundy omnibus volume, *All Four Winds*, were readers able to experience the full richness of *Black Light*.

The original title of *Black Light* was *The Man from Jupiter*; the hero, the young American Joe Beddington, is heir to the Jupiter Chemical Works. The Yogi, and later the story's heroine as well, initially call Joe "Man From Jupiter," from having read the astrological impact of Jupiter in his face when they first meet. (Mundy then believed in astrology; he had the noted astrologers Evangeline Adams and Iris Vorel check Dawn's horoscope with his own, just as he had with Dick and Sally years earlier, and Dawn and Talbot's configurations were pronounced startlingly similar. Later, however, he would lump astrology with stage-magic and patent medicines as unscientific.)[34] *The Man from Jupiter* was probably dropped as too redolent of science fiction, while the new title, *Black Light*, referred to a magical state, at the end of the novel, that the Yogi induces upon each of the main characters.

The writing style is extremely literary, more formal than was typical; gone is the breeziness and often breathless tone of many of his stories. *Black Light* was planned with great care, composed to perceptively build up character and incidents that foreshadow developments brought to a resolution later in the story. Certainly the Roerich Museum had provided Mundy an intellectual atmosphere unrivalled since his creation of *Om* while residing at Tingley's home in Point Loma.

Mundy's other tales of "Masters" had a strong element of action and suspense, and emphasized the fantastic from the outset, while it only appears at the end of *Black Light*. Nor is *Black Light* moved forward by a journey or travel, with all the events instead confined to a single Indian village (near Nepal) which is, to all initial appearances, rather ordinary. Indeed, *Black Light* is a morality play, without the intrigue or intricate plot line of many of Mundy's other narratives.[35]

Instead, Mundy seeks to merge the dual ingredients of the psychic and psychological. In a way, Mundy has written his own version of *A Passage to India*, the recent E.M. Forster novel that some reviews had compared to *Om*, in that *Black Light* describes the effects and changes that a trip to India has on a small group of Westerners.[36] Unlike previous novels, Mundy presents a familial situation, of a very disturbing nature, and offers a full-fledged romance as a principal element.

Joe Beddington is a new type of hero for Mundy. He is a 28 year old, living under the iron rule of his mother. Joe's mother is a woman who has learned to ruthlessly manipulate governments and defraud labor with the same skill with which she keeps her son subject to her will. Whether she had a precedent in Mundy's life, and was based on his own mother, or one of his wives, is impossible to determine, although the vitriol in her portrayal encourages such an interpretation.

A more likely explanation than such a personal inspiration is that Mrs. Beddington is intended to represent domination of any sort by one person using others for their own ends. Mundy uses classical allusions in describing her, explaining that she is a symbol, to be overcome.[37] Unfortunately, the prosaic Freudian formulation, with its requisite and necessary rebellion, seems trite for modern readers. It is a weak base for the wisdom teaching that Mundy imbues throughout the novel and detracts from the other, more unusual aspects of the narrative.

Black Light uses some of the same basic plot elements of *Om*, such as the search for a young white woman. This time, instead of a relation, the woman is Amrita, the daughter of Mrs. Beddington's bridesmaid. Just as in *Om*, with Samding, the niece of Ommony reared by Samdup, Amrita is an ideal, combining Western ancestry with birth and training in the East. Like Lottie Carstairs in *Cock o' the North*, Amrita is a heroine of extraordinary musical ability, who sings songs of her own composition, in English, possibly as part of Mundy's plan to use Dawn's music and his lyrics in a dramatization of the story. Some of the lyrics are given as poems between chapters, with one, preceding Chapter 19, distinctly evocative of the earlier composition, "In Some One's Heart."

Similarly, there is an American schoolteacher in India, Annie Weems, reminiscent of Hannah Sanburn in *Om*, who runs a mission school accepted by both whites and native priests, and who, like Sanburn and Samding, has cared for Amrita since childhood. Since *Black Light* was written during a time of official fraternizing among theosophical organizations, the first name may have been intentionally chosen as a friendly gesture, since it calls to mind Annie Besant, longtime Tingley rival and leader of the Theosophical group based in Adyar, India.

While the harsh portrait of Mrs. Beddington goes against Mundy's usual favorable treatment of willful women characters, she is contrasted with Amrita and Annie, women who are both wise and strong-minded, especially Amrita. Amrita's parents died at birth, and she has been reared by native priests, wisely, outside of the western influence. She can read people's auras, know their mood, nature, and intentions (another clairvoyant skill with a theosophical origin, most prominently associated, for once, with the Adyar branch). This may also be influenced by George Wehner; his control, the Hindu Priest Ami, discussed the elementary spirits of fire, their colors and shapes, and the colors of auras emanating from individuals—resembling some of the visions described in *The Devil's Guard* and *Black Light*.[38] Even when Joe was still in New York, 'Rita tells him that his soul came to her and told her to wait, that he was coming, at a time when it would resolve both their difficulties—Joe with his mother, and 'Rita's with Poonch-Terai, who wants to force her into his harem.

Like most of Mundy's sages outside of Tsiang Samdup, the Yogi-Astrologer Ram-Chittra Gunga Sahib is a man the reader may admire, but one who it is difficult to like. *Black Light* is the first time Mundy presented an Eastern sage as a Yogi, the practice of which was condemned in *Caves of Terror* and *I Say Sunrise*, but *Black Light* may have been different in this regard because the Roerichs believed in the Indian philosophy called Agni-Yoga.[39] The Yogi has largely removed himself from society, and accepts the fact that his wisdom cannot be understood by most of the searching souls around him. He knows better than to interfere with destiny, and so cannot prevent evil, but continually appears at all the crucial times when he is truly needed.

'Rita is the first girl to interest Joe, and uncertainty coupled with fascination and the mystery of her mind and learning soon cause him to fall in love. Mrs. Beddington tries to convince Joe that 'Rita is not the daughter of her bridesmaid, but instead the Eurasian offspring of a soldier and a prostitute, who is promiscuous with soldiers and participates in temple orgies. Mrs. Beddington threatens Joe that if he persists in his love for 'Rita, she will disinherit him, and when the Indian government learns he is destitute, he will be deported (as perhaps happened to Mundy himself). Joe's sense of filial duty is finally overwhelmed by his mother's treatment of 'Rita.

Mrs. Beddington's gossip goes beyond besmirching the reputation of 'Rita, turning into action. Mundy links her with the misrule of the Maharajah Poonch-Terai, whose plans to abduct 'Rita she endorses. She also uses colonial power, attaching herself to a spineless British official, Cummings, who is all too eager to sell himself to her in return for a life of dominated ease. The materialism and greed she elicits contrast with the Yogi's benign spirit, representing opposite poles of humanity.[40]

Within the sanctuary of the temple, the Yogi gathers the principals, while an unseasonal storm rages outside. The Yogi tells them they have challenged destiny and he demands judgement. Strangely the doors lock, and pistols jam. In the subsequent five chapters the characters together experience the black light the yogi creates. Only Mrs. Beddington and Poonch-Terai are fearful; the others yearn for the experience.

Through the black light, in absolute darkness, whether eyes are open or shut, each sees their own life in intimate review. Each judges themselves, seeing as much of their own guilt as their soul allows. Poonch-Terai wants to both rape 'Rita and force her to use her psychic knowledge to help him gain dark powers that the priests have forbidden him. His more powerful mind has captured the will of Amal and Chandri Lal to give both of them murderous intent, but Chandri Lal has revenge. During a brief interlude in the black light he slips in and sets his remaining cobra on Poonch-Terai, who is found dead at the end of the black light experience in a perfect instance of karmic retribution.

In this way, the bad and misguided receive visions of their misdeeds, repent and are made whole again (in the case of Mrs. Beddington), or are punished (Poonch-Terai), with the wisdom of the Eastern sage directing events.[41] The black light has weakened Mrs. Beddington's resolve, and given Joe the strength he needs to finally end his mother's dominion. Nonetheless, the final evaporation of her will after the encounter with the black light is not entirely credible, and the last chapter is regrettably one of the weakest, despite the fact it was rewritten at Bobbs-Merrill's instruction.

Complex, ambitious, and only sometimes successful, *Black Light* is still one of Mundy's deepest and most rewarding novels. It is a story rich in fascinating philosophy and rewarding teaching, although these elements are not as noticeable as usual, particularly because of the mix of the Yogi's pronouncements combined with Joe's hesitant internal monologues. However, the frequent brilliance of *Black Light* is undercut by fatal narrative flaws and clichéd situations that keep it from being great. Delicately balanced between profundity and an excess of stereotyped characters, some sections of the book sadly fail to keep up the standard. Despite Bobbs-Merrill's dictum that Mundy cut the novel, there is still substantial repetition of many of the philosophical ideas. Nonetheless, *Black Light* is one of Mundy's most worthwhile and daring novels, representing an occasion on which he discarded some of his usual tendencies and created one of his most memorable, if still imperfect, works.

Mundy returned to the pages of *Adventure* with his first short story in a dozen years in the February 1, 1930 issue with "Consistent Anyhow," a tale that frankly and convincingly proposed reincarnation and working through the errors of former lives as a determinant of destiny. Using an informal retrospective first-person tone, Mundy told of two schoolboy chums whose lives and fate are intertwined. There are also a number of autobiographical elements. "Consistent Anyhow" is unique for opening at Rugby, as Tommy Knott and the narrator are "birched" for disobeying the rules together. Talking with a kindly matron afterwards, Tommy tells how a gypsy told him that in a former life he had killed his own best friend for the sake of authority. He is haunted by the story of how Sir Francis Drake hanged his friend Doughty. Meanwhile, the narrator has a recurring vision of three small ships of obvious Elizabethan rig at sea in distress. Tommy believes that the only explanation for dreams and visions is that they are memories, possibly from a past life. At last they quarrel, because Tommy insists that a friend obey him, but suddenly realizing what he has done, Tommy dashes in front of his friend and takes a deadly stone from a mob. At Tommy's funeral, his friend once more sees the image of the three ships that has punctuated their years together, and now sees, as in a dream, Tommy in armor, leading himself to a tree to be hanged. "I don't know how I recognized them, any more than I can find words to explain how clear it seemed that they were Drake and Doughty, and at the same time Tommy and myself."[42] *Adventure* advertised its content boldly, noting below the title: "Do you believe in Reincarnation? The Strange Tale of a Youth Who Seemed Endowed with the Spirit of Sir Francis Drake."[43] Mundy's next short story in the magazine, "The Man on the Mat," was equally profound, investigating existence and illusion in the context of a guru's teaching about mass and individual hypnosis on Mt. Abu.

In the year after returning to New York, Mundy's income ranged from $2200 to $9800 a month, yet his financial troubles remained.[44] By the end of 1928, Talbot was located by a lawyer for Inez Craven and notified that he was delinquent in alimony payments. By early 1929, attorney Thomas F. MacMahon was handling all of Mundy's legal affairs, having no confidence in the author's business ability, as Talbot himself admitted to Bobbs-Merrill.[45] In contrast to the strong income Mundy received from the magazines at this time, his books earned just over $3700 in royalties from Bobbs-Merrill from the beginning of 1929 to mid 1930.[46] In June of 1929, D.L. Chambers of Bobbs-Merrill, who handled Mundy matters, had a breakdown and was out all summer.[47] Throughout the 1920s the company had not done well with his novels, and few copies of *Cock o' the North* had sold.[48] The cuts Bobbs-Merrill had demanded in *Queen Cleopatra* and *Black Light* were also vexing, and Mundy could maintain that they would have been better received had they been published as written — as was the case with his best-received book, *Om*. Some years later, his character Sir John Bobbs in *Old Ugly-Face* was perhaps a jab at his former publisher, described as representing "civilized and scientific Christianity — the spirit of the Ten Commandments, slightly edited in favor of His Majesty the King — iodine — soap and water."[49] Other publishers had indicated their interest in having Mundy on their list, most

TALBOT MUNDY

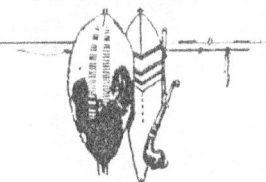

Has been to hell and back several times. Starting to roam the unfrequented places of the world at 17 . . . 'officially' reported as dead of a poisoned spear wound in German East Africa . . . later again 'certified' dead in Bellevue Hospital, New York City, knocked on the head by gangsters. In the interim . . . England, Germany, India, Tibet, Assam, Burma, South Africa, broke in Cape Town, Australia before the mast on a windjammer, Africa, Northern Abyssinia, Congo Free State, East Africa, The Near East . . . over-Jordan to Damascus, Mexico, Yucatan, Europe . . . Then Mundy took his pen and began to write. Little wonder that same pen never misses fire. His "King of the Khyber Rifles" has long been a classic adventure novel. He holds the record for reprinting in ADVENTURE . . . his "The Soul of a Regiment" having been reprinted four times . . . and still requests for more.

 YOU and WE have long known the magic of Talbot Mundy's stories . . . have long known the secret of his being a major name among the fiction writers of two continents. Your FRIEND no doubt has often wondered, when he has seen your nose buried deep in the pages of ADVENTURE, just what all the attraction could be . . . his wonderment is merely because he does not KNOW. Let's inoculate him with the lively bug that has bitten us. Write his name and address below, tear off the coupon and mail to ADVENTURE, 161 Sixth Avenue, New York, N. Y. We will mail him a FREE copy and start him on the trail.

• • •

Name

Address

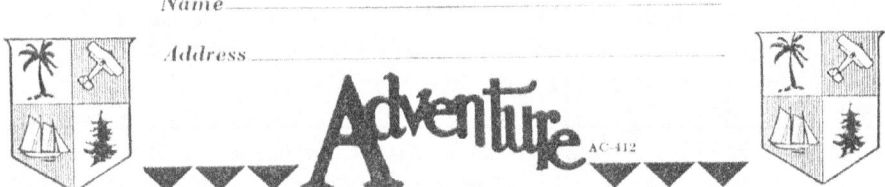

Ad in *Adventure* promoting the magazine through Mundy's popularity. (Courtesy Brian Emerich Collection)

recently Putnam, whom Talbot had visited to promote the books by Wehner and Rambova.

Despite Dawn's comparative youth, she was as strong-willed as any of the women with which he had been associated, and at this point she began to influence his financial arrangements. Elmer Davis's son recalled that, by nature, she "had a not unpleasant practical side."[50] With a caution verging on suspicion toward publishers, agents, and producers, she convinced Talbot that, with Hoffman's departure from *Adventure* and its changes in management, an American agent was essential to assist in magazine sales.

Mundy had already briefly used another agent, George Bye, who had unsuccessfully handled the rights to *W.H.*, much to the displeasure of Bobbs-Merrill.[51] Back in 1926, the literary agency of Brandt & Brandt had introduced themselves to Talbot by selling German translation rights to *Om* for 30 pounds.[52] By the fall of 1928, Mundy linked up with the firm, remaining with them until the end of his life — the longest relationship Mundy maintained with an American agency. His previous experience had not been encouraging; Mundy's first agent, Paul R. Reynolds, was a very formal Bostonian who had been in the business since the 1890s and confined himself to working out contracts. Once Mundy had initially put short stories behind him, and had found the necessary magazine market and secured Bobbs-Merrill as his regular book publisher, he dealt directly with them, having little need for Reynolds, especially considering the 10 percent fee he charged.

Carl Brandt had a reputation for winning good prices and contracts for his clients, and the firm oversaw Mundy's commercial, financial needs.[53] Carl became a good friend of the Mundys, and helped them out of financial difficulties. He was in his late thirties when they met in 1928, a kindly, self-made man who suffered from periodic bouts of alcoholism.[54] Significantly, Mundy never dedicated any of his books to Carl Brandt, but he did dedicate *Old Ugly-Face* to the agent in Brandt's office, Collier Young, who arranged his *Jack Armstrong* contract.

Although Mundy was an established author, he was also at a turning point when he joined the firm. After Hoffman, Bobbs-Merrill and Point Loma, Brandt & Brandt became a fourth major influence on Mundy's writing, one very different from those that had fostered the author's artistic development and reputation for quality. Another of Brandt & Brandt's clients at this time, John Marquand, bluntly wrote that Carl's "mind was on nothing except commercial literary profits and he never possessed the slightest artistic feeling and was almost wholly devoid of any literary background."[55] As Marquand wrote, Carl "seems to feel that a publishing house is a kind of sausage machine to which the author-agent throws a lot of manuscripts, the use of which has been exhausted elsewhere."[56] Carl precipitated Mundy's break with Bobbs-Merrill, based on their disinterest in reprinting much of his magazine material, which Carl believed other companies would be interested in issuing.

Early books such as *Guns of the Gods* and *The Eye of Zeitoon*, although initially unsuccessful in England, were still selling appreciably.[57] Hutchinson had agreed to begin issuing in book form some of his magazine stories written earlier, some of which Mundy sold outright.[58] The result of the deal was that Hutchinson began to publish as books many of Mundy's magazine novelettes and serials which had not appeared on that side of the Atlantic. With the urgent need to ready the novelettes for Hutchinson, and after a disastrous experience with a stenographer who put material out of sequence, Dawn soon found herself making the transition from piano to typewriter. These books were popular, and most were issued in several editions, with sales, according to Hutchinson's own catalogs, averaging between 5,000–10,000 copies per title, with a high of 17,000 for *King— of the Khyber Rifles*. However, Mundy found he received little royalties, and his only income was derived from Hutchinson's advances.[59] Carl and Talbot sought an American publisher who would prove amenable to what Hutchinson had begun — a plan which would necessarily have to entail ending Bobbs-Merrill's option on Mundy's next book. They soon found one in a new publisher specializing in Oriental fiction, The Century Co., shortly to become D. Appleton-Century.

Carl was enthusiastic over *Black Light*, but after seven months of effort, he was unable to find a magazine that would accept it for serialization. At the same time, while Mundy was receiving suggestions for revisions of *Black Light* from Bobbs-Merrill, he was convinced to sever his ties with the company. Only two years earlier he had been talked out of the same course, but now, with the sale of movie rights for *King— of the Khyber Rifles* to Fox, he was finally out of debt to them. On January 24, 1930, Mundy wrote Bobbs-Merrill, informing that he could not agree to a new contract on the same terms as the old one, particularly considering the manner in which the royalties were figured (10 percent of list price minus 50 cents) and the 50 percent split on the sale of movie rights. He offered to absolve them of any obligation to publish *Black Light*, but Bobbs-Merrill insisted on going ahead and completing *Black Light* as their next, and as it turned out final, Mundy book.

In mid–February, 1930, Bobbs-Merrill heard that Talbot's British agent, Curtis Brown, had arranged for a commissioned book to be written for another publisher, without telling them. In 1927, Robert McBride published a successful book, *Genghis Khan, the Emperor of All Men*, by Harold Lamb, who specialized in Asian history, and since 1917 had authored for *Adventure* a long and popular series of historical stories of Khlit, the Cossack, set in the time of the Mongols. McBride then became interested in the possibility of a book on Kublai Khan, and when he met with Curtis Brown in London, Mundy was one of the authors suggested by the agent. Certainly given Mundy's treatment of Caesar and the Roman empire in the Tros books, his selection to write of another empire and its leader was an understandable choice. After hearing McBride's "ideas as to how the book should be written," and "the terms he was prepared to pay," a contract had been signed between Mundy and McBride.[60] This was not a new interest; in 1921 Talbot had mentioned to Bobbs-Merrill that "I would like immensely to tackle China, but can't afford to go there just yet."[61] To Bobbs-Merrill, the action amounted to "raiding another publisher's list," particularly for an author who they regarded as having been shown "exceptional generosity" and "for whom we have done so much in the way of personal accommodation."[62] Brown pointed out that they had sold a number of Mundy stories in England that Bobbs-Merrill had not published. After all the heated words, this turned out to be right; Century would sell more of Mundy's books than had Bobbs-Merrill. Curtis Brown remained Mundy's agent in England, while the Kublai Khan book was never written, and Mundy never published with McBride.

As a result of the new arrangements with Hutchinson and the switch to Century, a number of Mundy's 1920s novels began to appear in hardcover, commencing in 1930. (All were originally from the pages of *Adventure*, with the exception of *When Trails Were New* and *W.H.* from *Argosy*.) *The Hundred Days*, *The Woman Ayisha*, *Jungle Jest*, *The King in Check*, *The Mystery of Khufu's Tomb*, *Jimgrim and Allah's Peace* and *Tros of Samothrace* were all issued by Century, generally after their publication by Hutchinson, with the series concluding in 1936. (Burt continued to publish the popular editions of all these Mundy novels even after the change from Bobbs-Merrill to Century.) Considerably more Mundy titles appeared in hardcover form in England than in America, since Hutchinson issued five more titles, *The Marriage of Meldrum Strange*, *The Lost Trooper*, *When Trails Were New*, *The Red Flame of Erinpura*, and *The Valiant View*, a volume of short stories. Three additional Hutchinson titles, *Caesar Dies*, *The Seventeen Thieves of El-Kalil*, and *W.H.*, would not appear in book form in the United States until after Mundy's death. Between 1930–35, Hutchinson published an astonishing total of 22 Mundy titles, issuing a fresh volume on a quarterly basis, an output only made possible by drawing on the magazine material written as much as a dozen years previously.

Most of the 1920s works that finally received book publication in the 1930s appeared largely as they were found in the original magazine version, with little if any re-writing. Certainly it was not literary merit that justified reprinting many of these stories; some were frankly second rate. This saturation policy flooded the market with nearly every post–1920 Mundy manuscript the publishers could get their hands on, cashing in on the author's name with little concern for its future. With so many books of variable quality, their reception changed. Potential sales were exploited and maximized, ruining much of Mundy's critical reputation. From 1930, when Hutchinson and Century began to also publish Mundy's new books, neither they nor critics distinguished between the onrush of older material and his new novels: *Jimgrim, C.I.D.*, *The Gunga Sahib*, *Full Moon*, *Purple Pirate*, *The Thunder Dragon Gate*, *East and West*, and *Old Ugly-Face*. No longer was Mundy a writer whose progress and development could be charted by new book publications, and he came to be regarded as one who was sacrificed quality for quantity, treading the ground he already knew without advancing into new areas. A *Times Literary Supplement* comment reflected the impression conveyed: "Mundy seems to be in a fair way to rival Mr. Edgar Wallace.... Novels stream from his industrious pen. This, perhaps, is a pity; Mr. Mundy would probably do better work if he did a little less work."[63] Yet, at the same time, there was a single, positive exception to the impact of this policy, the gathering of the Tros *Adventure* novels in hardcover as a single, epic historical novel.

The first new Mundy novel published by Century, *Jimgrim*, diverged from his usual genres of adventure and fantasy to enter for the first time the domain of science fiction — where advanced technology makes the story possible. The new genre was appropriate for what became Grim's last exploit, overcoming the wicked Dorje, who plans to make himself "king of the world." The basis may have originated in a 1926 symposium on Atlantis in the "Camp-Fire" section of *Adventure*; one letter, from R.E. Briggs, suggested the subject to Mundy as the basis for a story, and indeed *Jimgrim* was first mentioned in *Adventure* back in 1928.[64] Not until November 1930 to February 1931, however, did it appear as a seven part serial in *Adventure*, as *King of the World*, and it was then published in book form under the more ambiguous title *Jimgrim*, with portions of Chapters 2–6 rewritten to eliminate the hero's wealthy sponsor, Meldrum Strange. Century's dustjacket showed a menacing hooded figure (presumably Dorje) gazing down on a globe, a design used on the most common cover of the book and continued henceforth in all the publisher's yellow-covered Mundy novels. A tripartite division of the novel into "The Reincarnated" (Chapters 1–13), "Messiah of Tinsel" (Chapters 14–34), and "The Uncrowned" (Chapters 35–41), was apparently first added in a 1953 paperback reprinting retitled *Jimgrim Sahib* and retained in the 1968 Avon softcover.

In the words of Nicholas Roerich, the name "Dorje derives from the unconquerable sign of lightning, traditionally held in the hand of Buddha."[65] With the inadvertent help of Benjamin from *Om* and *The Devil's Guard*, Dorje has discovered the scientific secrets of Atlantis amidst the Gobi desert. (Curiously, none of H.P. Blavatsky's theories on the subject are used, and Atlantis itself is given only minimal reference). Dorje has new weapons: silent guns, deadly but untraceable gas, an antigravity airship, and what sounds eerily close in its effects to the atomic bomb, except that it is powered by surrounding electricity. In the words of one reviewer, "The frequent glimpses of new scientific horrors make the cycle of combat extremely fascinating, intricate and unique."[66] By the conclusion, the secrets of Dorje's power are lost as surely as the means by which men built the pyramids; "when a man like Dorje taps a new vein of the infinite resources of the universe, he leaves our ablest scientists as ignorant as cave-men gaping at a radio receiving-set." In this way the novel was an explication of Mundy's traditional theme "that we know no more, comparatively, than the ancients did; their ignorance of what we know was probably not greater than our ignorance of principles they understood."[67]

Grim's fate is similar to the leader of another heroic group in one of Mundy's sagas 10 years earlier, Monty in *The Eye of Zeitoon*, who sacrificed his life in the Armenian cause. Both heroes die defending civilization against barbarism, in a battle representing humanity's striving for good. To finally compete with, and defeat, Dorje, Grim must sacrifice himself by taking soma, a mysterious, addictive Indian drug that nearly eliminates the need for sleep and heightens mental powers before ultimately destroying them. In a moving climax, Grim destroys Dorje's base, while his companions are left to a melancholy return across Tibet after raising a simple funeral cairn to their friend.

Grim is assisted by the enigmatic Baltis, whose jealous twin sister is also killed, and one of the two may have been among Dorje's spouses. Baltis has been reincarnated many times, as the Queen of Sheba (whose name was Baltis, still a common name today in the region where she once reigned), a dancer in Cleopatra's court, and as Anne Boleyn. She believes she was associated with Grim in many of his previous lives, as a Roman, as a general of Genghis Khan, and as the commander of Clive's army in India, but he spurns her offer of a partnership. Eventually she relinquishes him for an aviator who is the reincarnation of D'Artagnan, Henri de la Fontaine Coq (Dr. Henri La Fontaine was actually the name of a Nobel Peace Prize-winning Belgian jurist who had visited Point Loma), and they fly off in Dorje's ship, perhaps to the moon.

There is a serious, underlying concern in this astonishing plot, as revealed in the preface to the first edition, a prophetic essay reprinted from the original letter introducing the story to *Adventure* readers—the only time one of his "Camp-Fire" letters was so used. Mundy explains in this document the longing that was arising for a "king of the world," and the historical context in which such urges and legends have appeared before.

> Given distance and sufficient mystery, people always are determined to believe in a superman; and if the superman has any genius he gets away with it—until they find him out. That was what Alexander, Caesar and Napoleon counted on. To-day, in many more than one civilized and educated country, the cry goes up for a dictator—someone in whom to believe, who shall impose obedience where unity of purpose is not. If they only had new weapons, those dictators, they might very likely beat us into mass-obedience—until we learned a new way to rebel.... If a beast like Dorje should possess such weapons.... Civilization ... would lie ... "belly upward...." There has been plenty of propaganda. The first man who takes advantage of it ... will score at least some staggering successes; he will smite civilization in its Achilles heel—its vanity.[68]

Jimgrim is, in fact, an examination of a conspiracy whose techniques and methods forecast the rise of Adolf Hitler and Nazi fascism. In the novel, Mundy sarcastically notes the many unimaginative officials who see communism as the source of every possible threat, making clear his own conviction that greater dangers exist from another source. With its science fiction elements *Jimgrim* is, as noted by Jacques Bergier, timely and immediately relevant to a world entering a decade of crisis, and Mundy considered titling the story *Next Week* to emphasize its topicality.[69] The narration is also distinctive, not only by Mundy's usual tactic of ostensibly telling real events, but relating them in retrospect, as the true story behind a time of global tumult and mysterious events.

Dorje is a super villain, and the novel is cast in the mold of Sax Rohmer's "Dr. Fu Manchu" stories, with a seemingly endless series of thrills low on probability but vividly imagined. What sets the book apart from others like it is the use of Eastern myths of coming rulers and knowledge, rather than Western fears. Dorje is ethnically ambiguous and does not represent the racial threat of Rohmer's "yellow peril." His lisp even hints at a German accent; he is a fascist version of Fu Manchu by way of Nietsche's Superman.[70] Mundy may also have used some of the ideas for the biography of Kublai Khan commissioned by Robert McBride earlier in the year. Mundy suffused Dorje's thinking, his hubris, megalomania, and the enormity of his ambition to be a king of the world, with many of the characteristics appearing in his historical interpretation of Caesar that had occupied so much of his thinking in the 1920s. Mundy also highlights the parallel between Caesar's ends and their modern counterparts, making Dorje and Jimgrim in fact a contemporary version of the earlier attempt to rule the world chronicled in the Tros books.

Mundy was not pleased with the book; the inscription copy he gave to Elmer Davis and his family on St. Patrick's Day, 1931, said "May they never write a worse book—nor I, either."[71] It is the type of book some authors label as "entertainments," described by the *Times Literary Supplement* as "an uncommonly well-constructed and cleverly-written 'thriller,' swift in action, packed with incidents, and sufficiently puzzling to keep the reader's intelligence alert."[72] On that level, *Jimgrim* is one of Mundy's most exciting novels, although it does undeniably sag in the middle, with the strongest portions involving Baltis, Vasentasena, and Dorje himself, as the would-be king of the world is defeated in a riveting whirlwind climax.

After almost three years together, Dawn had already had a profound influence on Talbot Mundy. She was well regarded by Talbot's friends; as Elmer Davis's son recalled,

> I remember when Dawn came on the scene (as far as our household was concerned) and her striking looks—ivory complexion, white turban, and bright red nails. These trivial details don't sufficiently bring out how good-looking I thought she was.
> I remember my mother being impressed one time in Mason's Island [after 1932] at how Dawn took off her turban after dinner and came out to the kitchen to help mother wash the dishes, dipping her beautifully varnished nails right in without a qualm. My parents liked both of them.[73]

She learned, through the occult interests that Rambova shared with Talbot, and imitating Rambova's sense of fashion, how to appeal simultaneously to his fascination with beauty and the mysterious. Just as Inez and Rosemary helped inspire Yasmini, Dawn may be the source for the characterizations of preternaturally wise young women, often with clairvoyant powers, who populate Mundy books in the 1930s, such as Amrita of *Black Light*, Arsinoe of *Purple Pirate*, and Elsa Burbage of *The Thunder Dragon Gate* and *Old Ugly-Face*.

By the spring of 1931, Dawn and Talbot had lived together for nearly three years, but friends and their surroundings were changing. The Roerich Museum was unable to pay the mortgage on the Master Building, and Natacha was sorry to see Svetislav Roerich leave the city to join his father in India.[74] She was planning to move to Europe. Natacha prompted Talbot to ask Dawn to join him on a trip to Yucatan to secure a divorce from Sally, to add a marriage to the proceedings.

Learning he had already met the residency requirement in the neighboring state of Campeche, the divorce was granted there at the end of July on the grounds of incompatibility. Talbot declared Sally was difficult to get along with; she was not represented at the hearing. Shortly afterward, Talbot and the judge crossed to the other side of the room, where witnesses awaited the wedding. Dawn recalled, "Talbot was very quiet, very serious. His eyes held mine throughout the ceremony, when he put the ring on my finger and kissed me, his eyes were misty. Companion, friend, lover, teacher, and now husband, he was all these to me, and for all time would continue to be."[75] Returning to Merida, the couple celebrated with acquaintances, then returned on the next voyage of the *Morro Castle*, with a brief stopover in Vera Cruz. Back in New York, Talbot finally met Dawn's father, Frank Conkey; Talbot had already met her mother, Florence.

In a few short years, Talbot Mundy's organizational affiliations had changed markedly, from Point Loma to the Master Building. These activities maintained his commitment to theosophy, despite his dabbling in spiritualism. Mundy stories were again frequently appearing in a range of pulp magazines, and his books were becoming primarily known as entertainment, not literature.

X

Lost Trails, 1931–1937

During the last nine years of his life, Talbot Mundy became a true maverick, without the dogma of the Christian Science Church, or the influence of the Point Loma Theosophical Society, the Master Building, or spiritualism. However, he also missed the education in philosophical and religious concepts provided by these organizations and schools of thought. His stories went in several very different directions, from the political machinations of *The Gunga Sahib* to the fantasy of *Full Moon* and the historical adventure *Purple Pirate*. As well, Mundy continued the tendency evident since 1928 to rewrite and recycle ideas from earlier work. This, along with the simultaneous hardcover publication of many of his earlier magazine stories, kept him from achieving the literary recognition he had won in the 1920s.

A new series about the Criminal Investigation Division in India shifted his generic appeal to the thriller. The treatment was far from heroic; in a later Mundy novel he would comment that the initials C.I.D. stand for "Confidential — indiscreet — dirty."[1] These tales, commencing with relatively simple short stories, soon grew to novelette and then novel length. While highly variable in quality, they were notable for the richness of their character detail, most featuring the characters Larry O'Hara or Chullunder Ghose.

Ghose's odyssey became one of Mundy's most cohesive character sagas, portraying the entire arc of his rise and fall. Some of Mundy's earliest tales had mentioned characters very similar to Ghose. In *The Letter of His Orders*, a babu in the secret service is named Sita Ram, while in *The Winds of the World*, a similarly-named but different character, an obese Bengali clerk and failed B.A., provides comic relief. The occupation and physiognomy of these first two individuals named Sita Ram (yet another Sita Ram in *Guns of the Gods* is entirely different) became, eight years later, Chullunder Ghose. Beginning as support in a number of novels from 1923 on, Ghose was featured in *The Marriage of Meldrum Strange*, *The Nine Unknown*, *The Devil's Guard*, and *Jimgrim*. Ghose first appeared outside the company of other Mundy stalwarts in *The Red Flame of Erinpura*, and he would evolve into Mundy's most brilliant male characterization.

Ghose is a sly, streetwise, cunning scoundrel, a classic artful dodger, trickster, and exhilarating liar. He was known as a babu, a word which initially meant an educated Hindu, such as a government clerk, but also signified a comical Indian figure who garbled the English language and classical allusions. "He possessed a prodigious stomach, wore a very brightly colored turban and the graceful Bengali costume which displayed one huge thigh. He had a small black cotton sunshade and a silver-mounted cane...."[2] Despite his Falstaffian proportions—some 300 pounds—Ghose is agile and strong, a man of lightning thought and action.

The travels with Grim were only part of Ghose's varied past. "I have been wayside conjuror—secret service agent—salesman of spells and potions—twice to the United States as lecturer on magic—twice deported on the ground of too hot competition with the native clergy—twice to Tibet—twice around the world."[3] He failed his bachelor's degree from Calcutta University through an excess of knowledge. "The babu could talk nine languages and think in terms of quantum; drunk or sober, he could quote Kant, Einstein, the Mahabharata, Shakespeare, and Plato with equal humorous familiarity."[4] His views on religion are cynical and lacking in spirituality, despite his experiences in Tibet with Grim. He even pays a Mullah to pray for him—or so he was promised—although he is a Hindu.

As he emerges as a protagonist in his own right, Ghose tirelessly conspires to raise himself from the alleys of India through the Criminal Investigations Division to become prime minister of a native state. Scheming, ambitious, humorous but wise, he is fearful but not cowardly. Ghose always remains the manipulative presence, the catalyst behind the narrative—the spider busily spinning his web of circumstance and reaction that will serve the results he desires.

He transforms himself felicitously from one role to another, alternately wearing the mask of a fool to deceive his enemies or cynically disarm his friends. "Am cosmic gigolo—a member of the Rogues' Racket Club. Its coat of arms is five aces. The motto is *suave qui peut*, which is French for a new one is born every minute."[5] Ghose serves the function of both sage and a clown, pointing out the more ridiculous aspects of society and culture, and is a connoisseur of irony, absurdity and the law of improbability—but "a sense of humor is a bad thing for a failed B.A., in a country ruled by white man's burden bearers."[6] Mundy clearly enjoys writing about this character, using a breezy, amusing style (despite the deeds of intrigue), and the enthusiasm is infectious. Ghose was popular: his presence was prominently advertised in the cover art of the dust jackets in both England and the United States on the three novels in which he is the lead, *The Red Flame of Erinpura*, "*C.I.D.*," and *The Gunga Sahib*.

The Ghose saga begins strongly with "The Babu" in the October 1, 1931 issue of *Adventure*. Initially, Ghose shares the stage with O'Hara, their secret service collaboration establishing a personal bond that ties them closer together than O'Hara with the British. Ghose uses O'Hara's American fiancée, Phoebe Barron, to assist in saving O'Hara; he has nearly been killed in an elaborate plot to play on the cupidity of a bandit leader, Akbar Sayyid. The journey into the underworld where O'Hara and Ghose operate uses Phoebe as an outsider to provide a surrogate for the reader's viewpoint. She initially distrusts the babu, just as she had once hated the Irish before meeting O'Hara.

"The Babu" had an unusual subsequent publication history. It was rewritten and retitled "Milk of the Moon," for publication in the April 30, 1932 issue of the British magazine, *The Passing Show*. This version was reprinted in the September 17, 1938 issue of *Argosy*, and again appeared, this time retitled "Impudence is Art," in the English journal *Britannia & Eve* in May 1939. The different titles of a story originally entitled "The Babu" were probably a result of this being the first of a number of stories about this character, necessitating a change to a more specific title to avoid confusion. The two versions provide an opportunity to see how Mundy rewrote a work.

The revised version highlighted Ghose's importance and displaced O'Hara to the periphery. However, the richness of "The Babu" had depended in large part on the dynamics of three equally significant characters, Ghose, O'Hara, and Phoebe (renamed June Sedgely in the "Milk of the Moon" revision). At the same time, the revision no longer succeeded as well in introducing Ghose. Instead of O'Hara having been truly wounded in a bungled operation from which Ghose will both extricate him and allow him to learn from his mistake, crucial aspects of the climax are changed. Unlike Phoebe, a nurse, June only pretends to be one, as part of a plot to deceive Akbar Sayyid into lowering his guard so that he may be captured. Equally important is to keep Sayyid from killing dancer Milk of the Moon when he discovers she is a British spy, by having her pretend to stab O'Hara. The changes are both less credible and rob the story of the uncertainty that provided memorable tension.

The novelette ironically titled *Chullunder Ghose the Guileless* first appeared in the March 1, 1932 issue of *Adventure*, and was later reprinted in Mundy's anthology *The Valiant View* under the title *Innocent, Noncombatant and Guileless*. O'Hara is no longer present; Mundy does not feel the necessity of supporting Ghose with a European character. At the request of a friend, a white sergeant, who is to be hanged for having murdered an officer who insulted him beyond endurance, Ghose arranges for a prison break that will allow his friend to be shot in a much more manly fashion — while fighting. There is no alternative to the sergeant's final end; karma, and military law, enforces the sergeant's inevitable payment for his crime. Ghose must scurry around town, conning various criminals into actions, betrayals, and intentional counterplots, utilizing their avarice and desire to take advantage of him. All Ghose's plans finally fit together like pieces of a puzzle, the notes of an orchestra, or a chemical reaction.

Ghose's exploits then shifted to novel form. "*C.I.D.*," Mundy's new book for 1932, was, as the title indicated, primarily an entertainment, and is most important as a signpost and transition toward the most significant Ghose novel, *The Gunga Sahib*. Nonetheless, "*C.I.D.*" is expertly crafted, composed with great skill and only minimally indebted to genre formulas.

The dissipated rajah of Kutchdullub has mortgaged his state and all its possessions for more than they are worth, relying on British departure to allow him even greater possibilities for exploitation. This starting off point was one Mundy used before and after, but each time offering a distinct resolution: in *Guns of the Gods* and *The Red Flame of Erinpura*, and later in *The Gunga Sahib* and *East and West*.

In the jungle, a sect of Kali-worshippers gathers amidst ancient ruins and uses a man-eating tiger in their ritual sacrifices. The beast also feeds off of the local population of Kutchdullub, and the spendthrift Rajah refuses to kill it, because that would require submitting to the priestly perogative of granting him an expensive religious cleansing ritual. As usual, Ghose is surrounded by a panoply of characters who become — intentionally or not — players in the drama as he orchestrates a new order from the chaos. These include a young American doctor researching cataracts who runs the only public clinic (the other doctor is a Sikh), whom Ghose sets up to kill the tiger. As a visitor to Kutchdullub, unfamiliar with local traditions, his intervention would be accepted as not causing a sacrilege.

The book also demonstrates why Chullunder Ghose became a favorite Mundy character: his chronicles lent themselves to abundant amusing dialogue as a vehicle for narration. Each chapter begins by establishing the setting and mood — often blended with some light philosophy — of a different locale or character. Consequently, the story is told in pieces which the reader must sort and organize; episodes not only jump between plot threads, but take elliptical leaps, rather than following a sequential, connected order–which also enhances the suspense. Many of the connecting incidents that would be usually recounted in other ways are elided altogether. Rather than advancing the story in a straight line, each chapter highlights various specific incidents, not only switching locale but characters as well. As the omniscient narrator sums it up, "it was like a dream directed by a humorous, fat showman."[7]

The British are represented by two polar opposites. The intemperate resident, a member of the old school, is Major Eustace Smith, 54 years old. He loathes having to deal with business before eleven in the morning and is unwilling to take any action lest it complicate his retirement, only three months away. His philosophy of government is simple: minor issues, such as the marauding man-eater, are a nuisance; major issues are anathema. Smith reads Edgar Wallace and believes that Gandhi will lead to communism. One ironic result of Chullunder Ghose's efforts is to win Major Smith a thoroughly unmerited ribbon. Smith despises Hawkes, who represents the better side of the Anglo-Indian tradition. A retired sergeant, Hawkes (who previously appeared in a different context in *Black Light*) has stayed on in India, taking a position with the local government in order to support his mother and sisters in England.

"C.I.D." is one of the few Mundy novels to invoke the Thuggee cult, although it was one of the most typical conventions of the empire adventure genre. Mundy depicts the capture of Hawkes by the Kali priestess, who then allows him to observe a voluntary sacrifice to the man-eating tiger. Two of Ghose's agents have infiltrated the sect, however, and manage to save Hawkes and contain Thuggee. Mundy uses Kali as a metaphor, a manifestation of the latent potential for evil in humankind, whatever its form — "Moloch-worship, the fire of the Inquisition, and a hundred other horrors, are only new names for a basic madness that is older than history" — a particularly timely and apt observation in 1932.[8]

The secret service, Mundy shows, is no less a sect, completely ruthless, proceeding regardless of consequences, and occasionally murdering. One of the C.I.D. agents learned his crime lessons in Chicago; Ghose knows that the trials and temptations to which he puts potential inductees may overwhelm, and lead them to lives of crime. Nonetheless, like the two parallel nine unknowns in his novel of that title,

Ghose and the C.I.D. is hardly comparable to the Thugs, but a necessary antidote to such evil, operating separately from constables or soldiers.

The next Ghose novel, *The Gunga Sahib*, was unusual for having been rewritten from an earlier series. In the latter part of 1928, Mundy had become fascinated with the idea of a homely Philadelphia taxi driver, an anti-hero named Ben Quorn who is self-educated on five cent books. Quorn is drawn to India: "Why did he like elephants? There was nothing in Freud or Jung or Adler about elephants. And why did elephants like him? There was nothing in natural history to explain that."[9] Then there was the strange birthmark on his forehead, in the same place as a Hindu castemark. When Quorn reads in the newspaper's help wanted section of an opening for the only white man allowed in the obscure Indian state of Narada, he applies, and is accepted.

Narada is a frankly mythical border state, unsullied by modern "progress," which only needs to be liberated from the artificial, foolish constraints of the past. Without a train station, Narada is sufficiently isolated for its people to work out their own destiny during the absence of the British Resident and the colonial presence he represents. Rather than becoming a substitute for British influence, Quorn, the outcast from his homeland, progressively loses his own identity in the culture and superstitions of Narada.

Quorn's odd face and strange eyes, which had made people avoid him in the United States, had the opposite effect in Narada, where he resembled the character in a wall carving depicting the ancient story of the Gunga sahib. He fulfills part of the legend when he rides the mighty pachyderm Asoka through the city when the beast is enraged by the Maharajah's mistreatment, Quorn's smashed helmet resembling a turban.

Quorn is one of the few persons entirely loyal to the untraditional young Ranee, Sankyamuni, who has read Kant, Mencken, Ring Lardner, and Eleanor Glyn, and listens to jazz. She scandalizes Narada by going without a veil and refusing to stand on pride or ceremony, although she remains chaste. Like Yasmini in *Guns of the Gods*, the Ranee is trying to secure her throne and her own husband, with the help of local whites, but Sankyamuni lacks her predecessor's charisma. Sankyamuni's ambitions are opposed at every turn by the conspiracies of unholy priests and their use of hypnotism.

In the view of the local citizenry, the Ranee, Asoka and Quorn sufficiently resemble the fabled Gunga Sahib to be the reincarnated fulfillment of the prophecy. This upsets the priests, who are not prepared for a miracle to happen in their time; "they prefer miracles that are said to have happened, somewhere else and long ago."[10] Nor is Quorn himself pleased; but he gradually comes to realize that his portrait was indeed "carved in stone on a wall in the public market place a thousand years before [he was] born," and accepts the challenge that destiny has set for him.[11]

The Quorn series began in *Adventure* on November 1, 1928, and six tales just under two dozen pages in length appeared at two to four week intervals through February 15, 1929: "The Wheel of Destiny," "The Big League Miracle," "On the Road to Allah's Heaven," "Golden River," "A Tucket of Drums," and "In Old Narada Fort." The saga begins quickly, with Sankyamuni winning much of her freedom from purdah, and establishing herself as her father's successor. Although the stories began by emphasizing the mystical aspect as each character fulfills the legend, this element was soon submerged in the plots and battles of wits (and occasionally weapons) between Quorn, the priests, and the Ranee.

As is inevitable in a series of independent but related tales, there is much repetition, but the Quorn stories lacked the dynamism of the Jimgrim tales or the historical fascination of the Tros of Samothrace saga. There is a sharp drop-off in quality after the close of the second story, and Quorn's exploits apparently did not go over well in *Adventure*, while its competitor, *Argosy*, was eager for them.[12] On March 9, 1929, the series abruptly shifted over to *Argosy All-Story Weekly*, with *Asoka's Alibi*, serialized in three parts. Over a year later, in May 1930, Quorn returned to *Argosy* in similar installments in *The Affair at Kaligaon*, the best of the later stories, climaxing in the title event in a "holy" city which is a cesspool of immorality, superstition, torture, and priestly depravity, described by Mundy with almost personal vehemence. At the end of 1930, the saga concluded with a novel twice the length of these, *The Elephant Sahib*, serialized in six parts. It was a lesser work, confused in its development, but with a memorable and exciting climax.

One of the supporting characters in the saga, the babu Bamjee, the Ranee's greedy and devious purchasing agent, often unwillingly assisted Quorn and Sankyamuni. Before Mundy could find the key to upgrading the magazine saga to the literary standard necessary for a book, he had to realize that the spotlight needed to be shared with another key character, and the necessary change was provided by recasting Bamjee as Chullunder Ghose, who becomes the dominant figure. With his addition, Sankyamuni is no longer the instigator, as she had been in the magazine series. Unlike the Tros and Jimgrim stories, the Quorn stories were completely rewritten for book form, to such a degree that only the first two Quorn stories are directly traceable. "The Wheel of Destiny" resembles the first few chapters of *The Gunga Sahib*, while "The Big League Miracle" outlines the book's conclusion.

While in the serial, Quorn was a cab driver, in the novel his job is digging graves, an occupation that highlights what was already implicit in the magazine stories: the narrative's underlying assumption is a belief in reincarnation. The fact that the characters seem to have returned so many centuries later, and the arc of the plot leading to the successful reenacting of the legend, are the tools placed in Ghose's conspiratorial hands. He recognizes that culture and custom are paramount over legal niceties: "Anyone who cares may make the laws, if I may cultivate the superstitions."[13] The mixture of the delightful Ghose into the saga of Narada transforms the wholly rewritten Ben Quorn magazine stories into a witty political novel. However, *The Gunga Sahib* is no diatribe; the concern of Mundy and Ghose is not with ends, but means, the methods of acquiring and manipulating power.

Although not especially popular, *The Gunga Sahib* is one of Mundy's near masterpieces, a story wholly unique to his canon. The book effectively distilled the magazine series (and hence was never published separately in this form) while simultaneously becoming an appropriate climax to the saga of Chullunder Ghose. Much of the story was told in dialogue, with Ghose's wise and amusing pronouncements providing an effective forum for Mundy's own disquisitions. With the emphasis on character, Mundy succeeds in making the succession of unlikely events seem plausible.

Chullunder Ghose's last appearance was in *The Elephant Waits*, a short novel in the February 25, 1937 issue of *Short Stories*, and published in the mid–June British edition. Ghose is a much diminished figure, both in appearing briefly as a supporting character — as he was in Grim's earlier Indian exploits— and in having been dismissed from the premiership of Narada. "Am a was-er. Sacked for competence. Too fond of short cuts. Too irreverent of red-tape. Too independent. Too perceptive of stupidity to obey crazy orders. No respect, in fact, for anything but wisdom."[14] Whereas previously each Ghose story had seen him ascend to a new position, the peak of his talents is clearly past. Now he simply hopes to acquire the necessary money to retire, and it is sad and disappointing to see Ghose descend to some rather pedestrian tricks after having scaled the heights of power.

Ghose, the aging intriguer, helps American artist Thwaite Adrian gain access to the palace where wealthy Californian Joan Mornay has been lured to view secret rituals. Adrian does not wish to censor her experiences, but knows there is as much danger here as potential wisdom to be learned, and throughout there is a skeptical attitude toward indigenous "magic," which is explained in an entirely rational manner.

In fact, Adrian is allowed to witness the ceremonies because the Rajah's nephew has killed his uncle and plans to blame the murder on Adrian, as the Western intruder, unless Mornay gives him the rights to her late father's mine. However, Ghose helps Adrian and Mornay to escape via elephant, although the local magicians remain de-facto rulers, as Mundy so often maintained. The combination of themes makes for an effective tale which might, with more rewriting and effort, have been a worthy sequel to *The Gunga Sahib*.

The Elephant Waits was also significant for introducing one of Mundy's most unusual heroic white characters, Thwaite Adrian, a highly-paid American portrait painter who can also use his fists, and has been given a commission to roam India. Mundy was creating an alter ego who was, like himself, an unschooled but nonetheless creative individual, whose adventures combine with the impressions that only an artistic personality would notice. As Mundy explains, "All genuine artists are men of action."[15]

Mundy rewrote *The Elephant Waits*, reducing it to novelette size. This version, entitled "The Night the Clocks Stopped," excised Ghose entirely and shifted Adrian to the center. This is, without doubt, the better of the two works, much more dynamic and imaginative than its predecessor, and gains by the compression. The accelerated pacing makes the plotline more credible, and the characterizations are similarly more focused and convincing. Only the resolution of the trap for Adrian and Mornay comes as too much of a *deus ex machina* to be fully credible.

The Elephant Waits seemed less like a finished, refined work than a sketch for a full-length novel abandoned during composition to simply finish a saleable bit of fiction as quickly as possible. The same could be said of *Solomon's Half-Way House*, a four-part serial in the Canadian biweekly *Maclean's* from August 15 to October 1, 1934, and *Camera!*, a novelette published in the January 6, 1934 issue of *Argosy*.

Camera! was another in Mundy's cycle of stories of the C.I.D. in India, but the central character is an action movie star who gives his fans their money's worth, doing many of his own stunts. Such thinking is hardly a surprise, for Mundy's work was considered for adaptation to the screen using Indian locations. Filmmaking had also been a subsidiary element in *White Tigers*, a novel serialized in two parts in the August 1 and August 15, 1932, issues of *Adventure*.

In *White Tigers*, the subject switched to documentarists, as Mundy creates a big game hunter and filmmaker inspired by, but very different from, Frank Buck. (Buck's catchphrase "bring 'em back alive" became forever attached to his name, and Mundy would satirize it by giving Carl Norwood of *East and West* the nickname "catch-'em-alive-o.") Unlike the well-groomed, smooth-spoken Buck, Mundy's hero in *White Tigers* is a hirsute redhead, who speaks in dialect: Joe Bread. Bread is summoned by the equally metaphorically named Reverend Walter Barking, whose district is being terrorized by two man-eating tigers and asks Bread to kill them. As Bread deduces, Barking's motive for wanting the tigers dead, rather than captured, is to keep his converts and trump a rival religious leader, Padma Sang-jee. Barking is just the kind of missionary whose un–Christian behavior Mundy despises, and Bread decides to thwart him by not only capturing the valuable tigers, who are not only mates but also rare white tigers and in the prime of life, but filming their last moments in the wild.

Mundy's concern with movies at the time was heightened by the most recent screen adaptation of his work. In 1930, as the first major sound film made on location in Africa, Metro-Goldwyn-Mayer produced *Trader Horn*, and after it proved extremely popular, the studios quickly followed it up with other jungle adventures from best-selling books. By August 1931, interest was expressed in filming *The Ivory Trail*, and Carl Brandt sold it to Universal on March 3, 1932.

Mundy's bad luck with the cinema persisted as the movie made from *The Ivory Trail* was transformed and retitled *The Jungle Mystery*, failing to achieve a fraction of the eminence of the Tarzan or Frank Buck films that followed in the wake of *Trader Horn*. *The Ivory Trail* was adapted as a serial, not a feature, a form considered inherently more juvenile and less respectable, and made on a lower budget, without African location photography.[16] After barely two months of preparation, *The Jungle Mystery* went into production in May, 1932, and was quickly completed, with the first chapter going into release on August 5. Mundy's name and *The Ivory Trail* were prominently mentioned with publicity. *The Jungle Mystery* was subsequently released in 1935 as a feature; ironically, while it would be the last Mundy movie produced during his lifetime, it does not survive in any form today.

The movie serial embodies its own specific and endemic characteristics, emphasizing thrills, pace, and low budgets over mood, coherence, detail, history and atmosphere; such elements as probability, logic, and continuity were often irrelevant. These traits were evident as Ella O'Neil, George Plympton, Basil Dickey and George Morgan adapted *The Ivory Trail* into twelve episodes of about 20 minutes apiece. The

Opposite: One-sheet poster for *The Jungle Mystery*.

cast included Tom Tyler and Noah Beery, Jr. as Mundy's heroes Monty (here Kirk Montgomery) and Fred Oakes, and Frank Lackteen as their servant Kazimoto. Philo McCullough, Carmelita Geraghty, and James A. Marcus were Mundy's villains, George Coutlass (played with a heavy accent and makeup), Lady Isobel Saffren Waldon (here renamed Belle Waldron), and Schillingschen (rechristened Boris Shillov), respectively.

Updated to the present, the nationality of the characters is changed and Will Yerkes and the novel's unnamed narrator eliminated. Although retaining much of the plot of *The Ivory Trail*, *The Jungle Mystery* added to the motivations and number of characters found in the original. These include a romantic subplot and a search for a missing fortune hunter; the standard plot device of a woman imperiled allowed her safety to be threatened at every turn by man and beast. The justification for the title is the total creation of the filmmakers, "Zungu," defined only as "half-man, half-ape," who appears at necessary moments to save the heroes and obstruct the villains.

Movie sales could hardly be relied upon for steady income, and in the 1930s Mundy had to return to a form he had given up many years before. In 1917, he had ceased writing short stories in favor of novelettes, serials and books. Longer work not only provided an author greater artistic freedom, with more thorough characterizations and detailed plots, but were also preferred by publishers. However, with the Depression, editors became reluctant to make major publishing commitments.[17] As Dawn recalled, "The book and magazine market didn't have the depression in 1929 — it hit about '33 or '34. That's when your pulps went out of publication, when your bigger magazines fell downhill. Editors got very, very particular."[18]

The changing market forced Mundy to return to short stories as more saleable, involving a difficult change in style that he loathed. As he told Rose Wilder Lane,

> It usually takes me about 10 days to write a short. But my shorts don't sell well. A novelette, of 20 or 30,000 words, takes about a month nowadays, although I used to tear them off in a week.
> Financial worry is my worst enemy, but I suppose that applies to most people. A note due at the bank can throw me into a silent panic in which anything like decent writing is impossible. And I have to write "dry"; as few as two or three cocktails throw me out of my stride for two or three days.
> I find I lack some of the old enthusiasm. The things I burn to write don't interest the magazines; subjects that do interest them, bore me to tears — or rather blasphemy; I'm not given to tears.[19]

In addition to novels, Mundy wrote 25 fictional works in the 1930s. He reached beyond the pages of *Adventure* and *Argosy* into such pulps as *Blue Book* and *Short Stories*, and the inaugural issues of *All Aces* and *Golden Fleece*. He found a new audience in such American Sunday newspaper supplements as *This Week* and *American Weekly*. Mundy increasingly wrote for magazines that were not "pulps" but "slicks," such as *Maclean's* in Canada and the quality magazines *Britannia & Eve* and *The Passing Show* in England; many of his earlier, shorter works continued to be reprinted in Britain.

Most of these stories were of a high calibre, and Mundy did his best work of this length during his last decade; a few even marked new directions, such as "Consistent

Anyhow," "Black Flag," "Speed," "The Bell on Hell Shoal," and "The Avenger." "The Gods Seem Contented," "Companions in Arms," and "The Honorable Pig" dealt with how Englishmen, and Indians, learn to overcome animosities rooted in race. These short stories demonstrated a greater sense of style and ability to handle the form with economical narrative construction, as well as to involve philosophical concepts, than was found in his earlier short stories. Of equal quality were his articles of these years, all of them autobiographical: "A Jungle Sage" and "Watu" for *Adventure*, "Lion Paradise" for *Short Stories* (an abridgement of "On the Trail of Sindbad the Sailor"), and "The Things Men Fear" for *Liberty*. Two brief, occult and ostensibly autobiographical articles of his youth in India appeared, "The Hermit and the Tiger" in the November 1937 issue of *American Cavalcade*, and "Mystic India Speaks" in the December 1938 number of *True Mystic Science*, which promised a later Mundy contribution that never appeared.

Mundy's selection of 10 of his best stories, *The Valiant View*, appeared in England in 1939, the first time a volume had been so created since *Told in the East* in 1920. At the time of his death, and voided as a result, Mundy had several other contracts in England for books to be published after the war. This included a second volume of short stories, and a two volume edition of his "sayings." *The Valiant View* was the third omnibus collection of his works to appear in the 1930s, with the other volumes comprised of compilations of novel-length works, Hutchinson's *All Four Winds* (*King — of the Khyber Rifles, Black Light, Jimgrim*, and *Om*), and *Romances of India*. Mundy only learned of the publication of *Romances of India*, comprising *King — of the Khyber Rifles, Guns of the Gods*, and *Told in the East*, reprinted from the original plates, when he discovered it in a bookstore; it had been arranged by Bobbs-Merrill with Burt without Mundy's knowledge, and only earned him a royalty of six cents a copy.[20]

From 1931–37, the Mundys continued to travel from place to place, never spending as much as a year in any one spot. As Talbot noted, "Unlike King Charles the Second, who had 'no wish to start on his travels again,' I cannot imagine a contenting life that does not include journeys to far-off places; and as my particular type of story seems to call for personal contact with people and things, I shall probably die with my boots on somewhere, someday; and some foreigner will steal my passport in order to beat the quota. Good luck to him...."[21] They considered trailer trips to Africa and India, roaming its Great Highways, as related by *Adventure*. "Perhaps he would never come back — there was so much to see, and learn.... The end of that trailer trip was doubtless to be Talbot Mundy and the Grand Lama conversing about the secrets of immortality no white man had ever learned."[22]

The Mundy's actual travels were more prosaic, as necessitated by working their way out of debt and making car payments. During the Mundy's wedding trip to Mexico, Dawn had taken responsibility for the couple's checkbook, but even with her guidance, there was little change in their often marginal economic existence. When Talbot could see income for the next three months, he considered himself secure.[23]

In 1931, after a few months in Connecticut, the Mundys headed for a winter vacation at a cottage in St. Petersburg, Florida. Natacha Rambova wrote that she had moved to the town of Genova, just outside of the capital city of Palma, on the island of Mallorca. There she was renovating villas and renting them to tourists, and promised Dawn and Talbot that she had just the place for them. So the Mundys repacked, taking their two Pekingese pups, Ping and Babuji, and placed their new Cadillac on board a ship bound from Baltimore to Hamburg, with a stopover in London for Talbot. When they arrived at Palma de Mallorca, Natacha, now age 35, surprised them by introducing her new husband.

She had sailed to the Balearic Islands on board a yacht captained by Alvaro de Urzaiz, a former naval officer, who came from a noble Basque family whose ambitions had fallen with the end of the Spanish monarchy. Although she was now a countess by virtue of her marriage, Natacha and Alvaro avoided both the titles and lifestyle of the aristocracy, going into business together with some of the inheritance received after the death of her stepfather.

The home Natacha and Alvaro had prepared for the Mundys was a few miles up winding dirt roads from Palma, high on a mountain overlooking the Mediterranean a few miles away. The home was modern yet charmingly rustic; each morning a herd of goats went past their gate, providing the day's milk. A local couple lived with the Mundys to take care of the cleaning and cooking.

While on Mallorca, although sales were slow, writing proceeded rapidly, and Mundy finished the first draft of *Thus Spake the Devil*, his only non-fiction book (not published until fifteen years later as *I Say Sunrise*). With its opposition to prevailing philosophical and religious thought, especially as epitomized by the Catholic Church, the book gave rise to many long, earnest, but friendly discussions. Alvaro considered himself a staunch Catholic, a monarchist, and anti–Republican, all positions diametrically opposed to Mundy's convictions.

Meanwhile, Dawn became pregnant. Rents and other costs of living had been rising, rendering the island no longer an inexpensive residence. Then the Spanish Ministry of Finance announced prohibitive taxes on automobiles that affected American and British residents more than elsewhere in the country. Facing a deadline of paying the tax by January 13 or leaving, shortly after Christmas 1932 the Mundys packed up their possessions in the car and placed it on the ferry to Barcelona. Even without the tax, the Mundys would have been compelled to leave Mallorca by subsequent political unrest, with riots the following March causing Francisco Franco to be appointed commander of the military forces in the Balearic Islands.

Driving across Spain to France, the Mundys took a ship to England and finally reached the theosophical clinic in Blackheath. The two doctors there studied ancient and modern forms of healing, despite the pressure of the more orthodox medical community. For two months, the Mundys lived in a small apartment within walking distance of the clinic. Their daughter was stillborn on February 26, with the cause of death given as congenital malformation of the heart. Henrietta was to have been the name of Dawn and Talbot's girl, and he assuaged his grief by beginning a new novel with a heroine of the same name. She is on a quest for the fourth dimension; its nearness may have been a way of expressing the hope that their stillborn child was not so far away.

Despite his amorous life, this was as close as Mundy ever came to being a biological father. Two years before Dawn's pregnancy, Talbot had expressed his feelings

Mundy, Natacha Rambova, and Alvaro de Urzaiz on Palma de Mallorca, 1932. (Courtesy Michael Morris)

about parenthood in a letter to his brother. "Luckily, I have no child — never had one — not even a bastard. Fortune ... spared me that one horrible responsibility. I know I could never screw up the moral courage to neglect him (or her) as my reason, experience, generous impulse and more-or-less modesty argue I should. I would certainly try to instruct and 'educate.' Equally certain I would impose on the child a definite percentage of my own ideas, not one of which is worth a damn, although most of them are quite as good as those of other people."[24] Yet during his years as stepfather to Dick Ames, Mundy was unfailingly kind and indulgent, allowing the teen-ager to successfully develop in his own way.

A welcome respite, blunting the loss of Henrietta, was offered in the invitation to make a long visit to a distant cousin, Major Robert Charles Godfrey Mundy (1874–1940) of Frensham, Surrey. The family were great fans of *Om*, although most of Mundy's other books were perceived as no more than good "money making potboilers" but which remained part of the library for family tradition.[25] Robert and Talbot had met many years earlier in the Boer War or Australia, and Talbot had promoted a manuscript that Robert was writing on a Begum in a letter to Bobbs-Merrill in 1929.[26]

Robert's home was called "The Old House" and occupied over 13 acres, with a butler, several maids, and a half-dozen gardners (it would later be let to Anthony Eden, after the family moved to Europe in the late 1930s). Dawn was struck by the very structured life, with breakfasts at which no one spoke, dressing for dinner with cocktails before the meal, with two kinds of wine, and after dinner drinks. The children lived in the background, but Robert's 10-year-old son Rodney remembered Dawn at this time as tall and thin, with short dark hair, and a cold, almost masculine, personality.

The generosity demonstrated by Robert was in contrast to Talbot's brother, with whom he spent only a single day. Now a Brigadier General, Harold's deteriorating health had compelled him to accept an administrative appointment, and his wife had died that year. (He would remarry in 1936, to a nurse he had met during an illness, Doris May Davies.) It was the first and only meeting for the brothers since they had been teen-agers. Talbot and Harold had been in correspondence for two years, but before then, an antagonism had remained, demonstrated by a direct, unquestionable swipe in *Black Light*, written just prior to the resumption of their contact. The book's hero expressing contempt for a minor colonial official by noting, "He wondered what Cummings' first name was. Probably Percy or Archibald. Or possibly Harold — Joe anticipated an awful kick out of calling him Harold, a name for which, for no earthly reason, he had a fathomless contempt."[27]

Robert's family shared an interest in theosophy and spiritualism, and there was an exquisite drawing room with Chinese decor, which may have influenced Talbot. *Full Moon*, written at The Old House, had an unusually strong Chinese flavor, and the surname Frensham in the novel was certainly a tribute to the area. By summer, Talbot and Dawn were ready to depart; the sojourn had also eased the couple through a difficult emotional and financial time.

Full Moon (published in England under the title *There Was a Door*, from the thirty-first Rubiyat of Omar Khayyam) is a forthright testament of his belief in Indian magic. The plot unfolds with sure dramatic skill, and Mundy spins a gripping narrative that enthralls the reader. Blair Warrender of the secret police is assigned to clear up the mysterious disappearance of Brigadier General David Frensham, despite–or rather because of–the fact he was once nearly engaged to Frensham's daughter, Henrietta. A student of the occult, Frensham was interested in the "Fourth dimension — ancient magic — showers of fish in deserts — sudden appearance of plants and animals on desert islands — Charles Fort's books — disappearance without trace of about a hundred thousand people every year — telepathy — clairvoyance — pretty nearly everything a soldier shouldn't care a damn about."[28]

One of Blair's first stops is to visit the Eurasian Wu Tu, a name meaning Five Poisons. For many years, Wu Tu had been supplying her cleverest women, and sometimes drugs, to Frensham, so he would reveal his knowledge. For the first time, Mundy indicates the British clientele of Wu Tu's activities, always given a more limited, innocent depiction in earlier stories. Mundy had always frequently used houses of ill-repute as settings, but, as Jacques Bergier noted, "the reader who is looking for lewd passages will be disappointed, because it is the 'temple of secrets' aspect of these house, especially, which are of the greatest importance;" they are centers for the exchange of illegal information.[29] Mundy makes no moralistic judgement on Wu Tu herself, or her profession; she is portrayed as employing Hindu widows who prefer selling themselves to the alternative, a life of waiting on their in-laws. Blair has been impressed for years with Wu Tu's intelligence, but, like Yasmini, having learned hypnotism and glutted with the loot of intrigue and influence, Wu Tu now fanatically searches for occult secrets.

Full Moon emerges as the definitive expression of the initiatory motifs in the Mundy canon, and the remainder of the story takes place in a subterranean realm. Crossing narrow ledges, with looming abysses that mean instant death, Blair must learn to master his fears as Wu Tu and another adversary hypnotically create horrifying visions in his mind. As the novel builds toward its conclusion, Blair's weariness increases, induced by hours of sleeplessness. Yet, an ever-increasing alertness is required to fight Wu Tu's thought-suggestion, although Blair finds that each effort to resist Wu Tu's spell strengthens his own self-mastery. She, by contrast, looks ever more aged and weary through the tension of their confrontation.

In the caverns under Gaglajung, amidst the stalagtites, is the ancient secret: an opalescent, smooth, conical crystalline formation in which stands a woman. "The woman was not less than nine feet tall. She stood erect—stark naked—in an attitude of mystic contemplation. She had been turned to stone within the stalagmitic ooze that once dripped from the rocks of the vaulted roof. But the appearance of life still remained. She had woad-blue hair; it fell in a cascade to her knees and over one arm. She was full-breasted, with large feet and hands, and muscled like an athlete. Her legs looked capable of climbing mountains. Her skin was more butter-than ivory-color. It was definitely not a statue. That woman had once lived, moved, had her being."[30]

Blair and Henrietta finally recognize their love, and she tells him that the woman is a hierophant discovered by her father. Henrietta explains to Blair the theory of a whole other world existing in the fourth dimension, beyond the ken of those living only in three dimensions. Her father had studied the Indian rope trick, in which a rope is thrown into the sky and a man climbs up it to disappear in the clouds. Frensham believed that its practitioners had found a way of entering and returning from this fourth dimension. Here is an answer to the question of what happens to the 100,000 people who, the League of Nations reports, disappear every year. They may not die, but may be transported into realms beyond our imagination, at various contact points that become available for entry at certain times under specific conditions. Despite the unusual subject matter, Mundy argues his theme of the fourth dimension so that it is utterly credible within the narrative.

The caverns of Gaglajung contain one of the doors, and it is into this realm that the race of giants departed three-dimensional existence. The giant woman provides the vital clue. To enter the fourth dimension, one must not only be at the exact spot at the appointed time, but be completely nude, a metaphor for leaving behind all ties to three-dimensional life.

Wu Tu, overhearing Henrietta's explanation, strips and within seconds is gracefully whisked from sight. Henrietta wants to go over as well, but Blair keeps her covered to prevent her. She is, like most of Mundy's female characters, willing to cross this threshold into another stage of existence; the male influence holds her back. As Blair and Henrietta prepare to depart, British authorities are sealing the cavern to prevent others finding it.

Full Moon is one of Mundy's most imaginative and original novels, the highlight of his fantasy work of the mid–1930s, a suspenseful classic that ranks with his best efforts. It is unique as perhaps the most intensely mythic and symbolic of all Mundy's work. The romance and the fantasy were ideally mixed, producing a book successful in both areas, with characterizations and a love story that are both convincing. Further, a markedly less wordy style than was typical of Mundy's 1920s fantasies makes *Full Moon* a much more modern book.

In the years since Mundy's last fantasy, *Black Light*, the genre's following and share of the changing literary marketplace had increased, which may have been an impetus for using a form that removed the fetters constraining many of Mundy's earlier stories. The conventions of fantasy allowed Mundy greater latitude for sexual themes in a story, both romantic (Blair and Henrietta) and illicit (Frensham and Wu Tu's women). The novel was ideal for the fantasy audience, but the same ingredients made *Full Moon* accessible to a wide audience, and it was serialized in *The American Weekly*, the first Sunday magazine supplement. Appearing in the Hearst newspapers, *The American Weekly* was guaranteed a circulation of five million, making it one of few reliably profitable magazines during the Great Depression. An editor at *The American Weekly* during this time was the fantasy writer A. [Abraham] Merritt, a veteran lecturer at the Master Institute, influenced by theosophy, and Mundy enthusiast, whose tenure spanned Mundy's contributions to the journal. Merritt especially liked *Full Moon*, and in mid–1937 *The American Weekly* would publish Mundy's later novel *The Thunder Dragon Gate*.[31] *Full Moon* was favorably reviewed in publications from *Amazing Stories* to the mainstream press, where it was recognized as genre literature of the highest quality.[32]

Full Moon was serialized in 14 parts, running from October 28, 1934 to January 27, 1935, a printing which had a different chapter arrangement from the final book publication, and did not contain the sayings prefacing the 24 chapters, purportedly selected from "the nine books of Noor Ali" (a reference never explained in the narrative, and part of the legend of the nine unknown, according to Jacques Bergier).[33] Book publication by Hutchinson and D. Appleton Century took place in March 1935, and in 1990, the story was translated into French by Francis Bourcier from the British version under the title *Il était une porte* by Editions NéO in Paris.

Besides writing a novel in response to Dawn's pregnancy that used his usual themes and locales, Mundy also wrote a short story in a starkly different style and genre, published in the July 15, 1933 issue of the British magazine *The Passing Show*. "The Bell on Hell Shoal" is one of Mundy's few serious love stories, including the role of infidelity and pregnancy in destroying two lovers, and is especially notable for being written in a socially realistic manner. With an epic reach, the story takes place on three continents, in England, India, and the United States, including Florida, where Talbot and Dawn had spent the winter of 1931–32. The title is taken from a real locale, Bell Shoals, near Tampa. "The Bell on Hell Shoal" utilizes a dual narrator, as Joe Molyneux tells a story in which he is of secondary importance. Molyneux is fascinated with bells, and explains that they have characteristics of their own; indeed, in the past, it was customary to sacrifice a living man into the metal when a bell was cast—foreshadowing the coming story.

Molyneux explains how he met the brilliant Ramon, a free spirit and artist. He believes that love is either absolutely free or a form of prostitution. His model, Dorothy, loves him despite his paradoxes and logical refusal to marry her. Molyneux became the couple's best friend, and even secretly falls in love with Dorothy. When Ramon foolishly takes in a British officer on leave, the aptly-named Major Aleck Proudman, his sex appeal and lack of morals make inevitable Dorothy's fall from grace in the Eden she shares with Ramon. When Ramon is informed of Dorothy's pregnancy, he is unable to put into sufficiently convincing words the forgiveness he feels, and she poisons herself.

Receiving Proudman's letter to Dorothy demanding continued favors in exchange for keeping their secret creates an even greater change in Ramon than the loss of Dorothy caused. Ramon gets a job, preparing to cast a bell, near where Proudman is stationed in India. When he comes late at night and pulls a gun, Ramon's fist sends him sprawling into the liquid metal. As Molyneux observed,

> I can't describe it. I can see it now with my eyes open. It was indescribable. The metal leaped up like a mass of liquid flame. It crackled and exploded. All the remaining cartridges in Proudman's automatic burst and sent sprays of the metal squirting up like rockets. Why Ramon wasn't splashed to death, I don't know. Nothing touched him. He stood for a moment outlined like a crimson devil in the glare, and I thought he intended to jump in. But the metal suddenly grew quiet. Ramon seized a hammer and beat furiously on a gong he kept up there for summoning the foundry gang....
>
> Suddenly Ramon shouted "Pour!" in English, and I waited long enough to see the stream of white-hot metal flow into the mould prepared for it. I don't know why I should be fool enough to expect to see bones and buttons. Proudman's body and that bell were one inseparable substance, mixed forever; and I don't know or care where his soul went, supposing he had one.[34]

To escape memories of Dorothy, Ramon joins Molyneux in the United States. There, he is casting a giant bell-buoy that a wealthy patron wants to place on the Florida coast. Ramon disappears the night before the casting; Molyneux finds some tell-tale splashes of hot metal on the wall, but keeps his friend's secret.

While the end is somewhat anticlimactic in its inevitability, it is also required for the final working out of Ramon's Karma, although for once the idea remains entirely unspoken in the tale. Never before "The Bell on Hell Shoal" had Mundy written such a serious love story, or one with fewer illusions. It demonstrated that on occasion Mundy could write such a narrative, in a more modern style; that he did not is probably more a reflection of the marketplace than his abilities as a writer. While the romanticism of *Her Reputation* was typical of Hollywood conventions, there is no hope from the doom implicit in the plot of "The Bell on Hell Shoal;" events follow each other with inescapable logic. Dorothy, Proudman, and Ramon are dead, and Molyneux has lost his friends and can never fill Dorothy's place in his heart. Although one of Mundy's least-known stories, "The Bell on Hell Shoal" is one of his most memorable and unique.

The Mundys returned to America in the summer of 1933. By fall, however, Dawn found that "wanderlust again seized Talbot," and the couple headed to Florida to spend more time on the Gulf Coast, where their stay a year earlier had been interrupted by the sojourn in Europe.[35] On Casey Key, near Osprey, at the end of dirt roads and jungle, they rented a tiny cottage that proved to be dark, short on amenities, and contained cockroaches. As she recalled, "We were living in this shack on the beach with no electricity, gas, or anything else, or running water, between the bay on the back and the Gulf in front — it was beautiful."[36] Encouraged to stay by the location, after giving the place a cleaning they went to the paint store, adding an oriental flavor with a shock of chinese red, jade green, and yellow. A baby grand piano was rented for Dawn's music.

As Dawn noted, "Food simple — I assemble it rather than cook it! Talbot is so good-natured that he doesn't mind how simple it is and that gives me time to do my own work."[37] She began joining Talbot in rising at the quiet, early hour of four A.M., and while he wrote, she typed *Tros of Samothrace* from magazine into book form. They were joined by Rose Wilder Lane, who had been long urging its book publication.

Like Talbot, the 46-year-old Lane was a divorcee who had left high school and lived as a pioneer in the 1890s. In 1919 she coauthored *White Shadows in the South Seas* with Frederick O'Brien, relating how the influence of white settlers and colonialism had been detrimental to the indigenous culture. By 1930, she was collaborating with her mother, Laura Ingalls Wilder, on the series of "Little House" books that related her mother's early years. By the end of the decade, Lane had turned to the increasingly Libertarian political philosophy that would occupy much of her later years. Talbot would tell her, "Your politics are nobody's business, and your religion is worse, but you're a good guy and we like you."[38]

She was suffering from thyroid difficulties, and Talbot believed that sunlight, rest, and the infectious good health of friends would be the perfect cure. Indeed, Lane seemed sympathetic to the Mundy's new belief in the sun's beneficence. They also visited a local group. "We're to play volley ball, two miles down the beach, with some nudists, who are very amusing people — totally broke but quite happy and full of dreams of the millennium."[39] With Lane, the Mundys went into the ocean at midnight, teaching Rose to swim for the first time, and talked philosophy until all hours of the night.

The Mundy's first local friend was Jack Hanna, who was, Talbot wrote to Lane, "deaf, almost dumb, and lacks a leg. But he is (bar none) the best designer in the world of real sea-going small boats. He can think, and he's a good pugnacious, obstinate, opinionated arguer, possessed by a gargantuan contempt for pussy-foot Roosevelt."[40] Boating was Mundy's favorite sport and he always hoped to build or buy a craft in which to live out his nautical dreams, but it was never a luxury he could long afford. As he once remarked, the ideal life, if he could afford it, would be "a yacht large enough to go around the world in with an all–American crew. I would like to make such a yacht a sort of floating headquarters, stopping off where I pleased for as long as I pleased and always drifting back to the yacht to write stories of the adventures I had along the way."[41] In Dawn's words, "We went out on the this great big white sand beach, and with Jack Hanna, plotted the course of this boat, dug a hole where we would steer it from and everything. He laid seaweed along the lines of it.

Talbot and I would go out every night and have a cigarette on our boat!"[42] In *Solomon's Half-Way House*, Mundy's red-haired fictional hero, Jack Hanno, is sailing around the world in his 38 foot ketch, clearly inspired by Mundy's current dreams of travel and a youthful, idealized projection of Jack Hanna.

In the three weeks after Lane's departure, Mundy rewrote *Thus Spake the Devil*, bearing in mind her criticisms and those of Jack Hanna, "and improving the book immensely." By September 1934, after ten months, Talbot found he could not sell stories from Florida, and the Mundys were as broke as beachcombers, awaiting a check from Appleton-Century.[43] The Mundys headed for New York, returning via the shoreline, bringing their dog Babuji and Jack Hanna with them.

With the revised *Thus Spake the Devil* and a new short story in hand, on arriving in New York, gratifying surprises abounded. Carl had sold "Bengal Rebellion" to *Blue Book*, replenishing funds for the moment, and before the end of the year, Dawn would tell Lane that *Tros of Samothrace* has gone into a second edition (it would go into its seventh by 1941).[44] His attorney, Tom MacMahon, was receiving preliminary offers from agents representing all the studios who wanted an option on the movie rights, but Brandt and MacMahon quarreled over who should direct the prospective sale even as it failed to materialize, with Carl urging holding off in the belief that as the book's sales mounted so would the price that could be achieved.

The Mundys returned to the home of Dawn's parents in South Manchester (later renamed simply Manchester), Connecticut, for a winter's work. Mundy had already used the address during his many travels in the three years he had been married to Dawn. Located just outside of Hartford, in central Connecticut, Manchester offered reasonable proximity to New York City, with a drive of several hours enabling quick overnight trips to visit publishers. Talbot knew Connecticut well, having visited many times already while married to Sally, since she had relatives there, and indeed he had wed Rosemary in Stamford in 1913. He found the New England way of life relaxing, although he dreaded the winters.[45]

Dawn's musical talent was inherited from her father, who had a fine singing voice, but had to forfeit such a career after Dawn's birth to go into business. The Conkeys had moved to Manchester at the beginning of the 1920s, where Frank became president and treasurer of "The Conkey Auto Co." Selling and repairing Studebaker Motor Cars, the Conkeys soon bought a home at 27 Pitkin Street, just a short distance down the road from the dealership. However, Frank was naively entangled in bank loans—experiences Dawn never forgot in her own financial dealings. In 1931, the auto business ended, and Frank looked for work; in 1934 and 1935 he was a salesman, but was soon jobless again, and hoped to sell the home. Financially devastated by the Depression, the Conkeys increasingly came to look to their son-in-law for support. At the same time, the Mundys irregular income prohibited buying a home of their own, but he was in a position to help defray expenses for the Conkeys—making living at Pitkin Street a mutually beneficial arrangement. Although not intending such a long stay, the Manchester home was to be the Mundy's base until 1938.

The residence at 27 Pitkin Street was situated on an isolated plot of land, distant from nearby homes with enormous front and back yards and only one neighbor on the block. The three story home with three gables had six bedrooms, providing more than enough space for both families, as well as visitors. The Conkeys and the Mundys lived amicably under the same roof, although Talbot tried to eliminate some of Frank's naiveté at meal time. As Dawn recalled, "My father believed that anybody who was governor, or who was a bank president, was perfect. I remember at the dinner table Talbot used to take huge delight in slamming the Governor of Connecticut, who was suspected of doing things under the table. My father would just straighten up and be horrified; nobody could say anything. Oh dear. [Talbot tried] to knock down some of that trust, and make him see things the way they were."[46] When *The Mystery of Khufu's Tomb* was published in book form in 1935, Talbot would dedicate the book to Frank and Florence Conkey.

Talbot enjoyed having friends over for a chat, entertained reporters, and became known locally through speaking of his adventures to many service clubs such as the Kiwanis.[47] The Mundy's first visitor had been Jack Hanna, and Christmas 1936 included two guests Talbot had taken in despite his own meager circumstances. Meg was a girl the Mundys and Lane had come to know in Casey Key, and after she tried to commit suicide, she was brought up to Connecticut to be talked back into wanting to live again. She stayed almost a year, while Mundy's first American friend came to stay during the fall. Jeff Hanley was out of a job and had a drinking problem, but after drying out with some home life in a strict New England environment found work again. The debt Mundy owed from 26 years earlier was paid, but he hardly thought in those terms. It was the same generosity that had overwhelmed Dick Ames; as Dawn recalled of Talbot, "He would help anybody to his own detriment. We had friends who would say, 'Will you never stop doing these things? You don't have to.' I mean sometimes it's kinder to people to not help them with money, but to help them in some other way — let them learn what they have to learn. He would help them with anything he could.... Talbot was always helping people, and enjoying it thoroughly."[48]

With *Tros of Samothrace* achieving best-seller status, and *Adventure* promising to carry the next series, Mundy had begun to think again of a sequel to *Queen Cleopatra*. He discarded his initial intention of recounting Antony and Cleopatra; two years earlier he and Lane had considered a collaboration on the book, and Talbot believed she could handle it better. He had typically strong and unconventional views on the end of Cleopatra's life. "She did not commit suicide. She was murdered, by the order of that swine Octavian, one of the meanest and pimpliest dogs that ever had a good press."[49]

Instead, Mundy decided to continue the formula he had found commercially successful, focusing on Tros. As Talbot wrote Lane, "It's less than half the length of *Tros*, but contains more fighting to the cubic foot, plus a little more sex, although not enough of that stuff to make you or Dawn blush."[50] As with *Tros of Samothrace*, but unlike *Queen Cleopatra*, Mundy did not attempt historical reconstruction. The continuation of Tros's exploits first appeared as four separate novelettes in *Adventure* from March through October 1935, entitled *Battle Stations*, *Cleopatra's Promise*, *The Purple Pirate*, and *Fleets of Fire*, each prefaced with letters on the period's history; the four were then immediately brought together and published as a large volume collectively titled *Purple Pirate*.[51]

The Conkey home in Manchester still stands today.

Purple Pirate is set following Julius Caesar's assassination as his many would-be successors jostle for power. Cleopatra is ruthlessly trying to retain power despite plots both domestic and Roman, and with Caesar's death, she now emerges as Tros's antagonist. Even though he rescued her from Rome after Caesar's assassination, she becomes angry because he refuses to share her throne or become admiral of her fleet. He stubbornly preserves his independence in order to realize his dream of sailing around a world he believes is round. Once he has confided this secret ambition, she sets a net of circumstance to prevent him and Tros realizes his costly indiscretion. This involves Tros in a series of conspiracies and battles (such as a vivid one amidst the pyramids of Gizeh), as he thwarts the snares she has set but also saves her throne.

One of Tros's tasks requires he capture the Queen's younger, taller, and more beautiful blonde sister, Arsinoe, with whom he falls in love. The fact that comparatively little is known about her offered Mundy the opportunity to make Arsinoe into an important fictional character, in a way he could not with Cleopatra. Unlike Mundy's usual pattern of a woman who is wiser than a man, in *Purple Pirate* it is Tros who teaches Arsinoe. She boldly fights alongside him, and he quickly comes to love her completely, giving her command of his men when he is away, despite her youth and inexperience; she is not yet 18. Symbolizing her transformation from her characterization in *Queen Cleopatra* is Tros giving Arsinoe a new name, Hero. The change of name and its consequences, experiences both Dawn and Talbot had undergone, is hardly accidental in *Purple Pirate*; the book is dedicated to Dawn, the first and only one of his novels to be so prefixed to one of Mundy's wives. Although by taking Hero as his wife, Tros has eliminated Cleopatra's sister as a rival for her throne, the queen turns on him, jealousy ending their friendship.

Royal Egypt is portrayed as a decidedly less spiritual figure than in *Queen Cleopatra*; in *Purple Pirate*, ambition and power become her principal motivations, losing the wise, heroic luster she had displayed in the earlier work. Mundy's views of her had evolved considerably since the altruistic outline of his character he offered to Bobbs-Merrill in 1924, from a woman who only gave herself to the two men she married, Caesar and Anthony, to one who "had her moods.... The fact that Cleo was a high-priestess and an initiate of Philae, seems as important to me as the equally curious fact that she debauched herself, no doubt at Anthony's suggestion, but for her own amusement too.... It shouldn't be left out of the calculation when considering her behavior at the Battle of Actium."[52] *Purple Pirate* portrays a later period in Cleopatra's life, not so much in years as in spirit, when she had been corrupted by the worldly influences already shown undermining her character in *Queen Cleopatra*.[53]

In this second novel of ancient Egypt, Mundy retains his informed facility in dealing with the time.[54] While nearly as critically successful and popular as *Tros of Samothrace*, *Purple Pirate* never acquires the originality of its predecessors. Perhaps the colorful characterization of the villainous Caesar is missed, but the third tale is also not the mighty chronicle of its times which its predecessors had been. *Purple Pirate* has Mundy's occasional irritating habit of reducing some occurrences to monologues, and there are some ellipses and summaries of action, eliding major episodes, that make the novel seem as if it was being rushed to completion or perhaps kept shorter than the subject demanded.

Purple Pirate was popular, going into its sixth edition by 1943. After it, Mundy wrote one last story of ancient Rome, whose title is derived from a phrase for the gladiatorial contests, for an entertainment where pleasure is derived from watching gore and barbarism. *Roman Holiday* appeared in the October 1938 premier issue of *Golden Fleece*, a historical fiction pulp which only lasted nine issues. Like his only other non–Tros story of ancient Rome, *Caesar Dies*, *Roman Holiday* is set in the time of another mad Roman ruler, brilliantly etched by Mundy. In this case it is Caligula, who swears by his own genius. As in *Caesar Dies*, one of the principal supporting characters in *Roman Holiday* is a Christian named Marcia. In this case, she is a woman of true spirit and spirituality, the slave and beloved mistress of Vergilius Cleander, one of Mundy's rare noble Romans in both character and position. Merely a novelette in length, *Roman Holiday* is one of his most captivating works never to appear in hardcover, and a fitting capstone to the saga and innovations he brought to the fictionalization of the ancient world.

Going on the lecture circuit had long been a possible way for Mundy to supplement his income. Not until the mid 1930s, however, did Mundy overcome his resistance to public speaking sufficiently to lecture for the additional public exposure as fiction sold more slowly. Such engagements were particularly frequent during the periods Talbot and Dawn headquartered in Manchester, which provided ready proximity to receptive, major audiences in the northeast. In late 1935, he went on an actual paid lecture tour, and enjoyed it more than he expected; but after deductions for expenses, the speeches did little more than provide a living.

Publicity for the speeches emphasized the most fictional versions of the Mundy past, crediting him with having been a Colonel in the Boer War, Territorial Governor of a province in East Africa, a close friend of Rudyard Kipling, and knowing six African languages fluently, as well as asserting that he was an authority on "African aboriginal and Indian life."[55] Mundy spoke of his colonial experiences in his still noticeably British accent, from his "boyhood in England where as a lad he 'didn't fit,'" emphasizing his time in Africa, typically entitling his remarks "Random Reminiscences of India and Africa" or "The Ivory Trail." "Through his stories of personal experiences and danger, the distinguished author wove a thread of his philosophy of life, the need of a consciousness of being so vast that it can reach to the stars and reduce the troubles and worries of life to a scale where they can be calmly faced and met."[56] Audiences included Kiwanis Club luncheons and women's organization functions; Mundy was able to hold the attention of both genders and various ages.

Despite the success of *Tros of Samothrace* and *Purple Pirate*, and Mundy's lectures, his finances hit a new low. Income from short stories, serials, and novelettes was irregular. Mundy was finished with the last period of his life devoted exclusively to prose; he was about to turn to new outlets for his creativity.

XI

An Audience of Millions, 1936–1940

Throughout the remaining years of his life, Talbot Mundy would be continuously involved with a new market, the motion picture and broadcast media. Not only were his stories considered for film adaptation, but he wrote *East and West* along the narrative formula favored by Hollywood, and was asked to write directly for the screen. However, his greatest success in this vein occurred in an audio medium, not in a visual one, authoring the children's radio series *Jack Armstrong, The All-American Boy*. At a slower pace, he continued his prose output for adults, culminating in *Old Ugly-Face*, which, along with *The Thunder Dragon Gate*, was composed simultaneously with, and inflected by, the radio show.

World events brought Tibet back into the headlines, and in *The Thunder Dragon Gate* and *Old Ugly-Face* Mundy expressed his belief that control of Tibet would be central as the Sino-Japanese war inevitably spread around the globe. Again, as in World War I, his writing served Allied interests, but unlike the acceptance of colonial rule as a temporary necessity in *The Winds of the World*, *King — of the Khyber Rifles*, and *Hira Singh*, Tibet was portrayed as an independent country whose freedom would benefit the West. He accurately fortells Tibet's subjugation by a neighboring power and the resulting exile of its rulers.

Tibet was a land that Mundy had approached while journeying through Sikkim at the end of the 19th century, and he fused these memories with what he had learned subsequently from theosophy and other reading, alluded to in his books. In the ten years since his last novel of the roof of the world, *The Devil's Guard*, Mundy had revised many of his concepts of the land; for instance, his spelling of similar places and phenomena usually differs.

Mundy was probably also inspired to write again of Tibet because of the resounding success of James Hilton's 1933 novel, *Lost Horizon*, soon to have its position as a modern myth cemented by an even more renowned movie version in 1937. Mundy would have been annoyed by the fact that *Lost Horizon*, while purportedly offering a sanctuary informed by Eastern thought, actually has its authority in Christianity. Hilton's High Lama of the Himalayan monastery at Shangri-La (Shambha-la renamed) is a missionary born in Luxembourg. He is also over 300 years old—a magically extended lifespan serving as a variation on the dream of eternal youth, replacing more complex indigenous doctrines such as reincarnation and karma.

However, Mundy began his new Tibetan saga with a misstep, his weakest book of the 1930s. *The Thunder Dragon Gate* was originally published as an eight-part serial in *The American Weekly* from January 24-March 14, 1937, and issued in hardcover shortly thereafter by Appleton-Century in the United States, Huchinson in England, and Ryerson in Canada. The fast moving chain of events and the maze of plots and counterplots turn *The Thunder Dragon Gate* into little more than a standard pulp thriller. It commences in a manner more typical of Sax Rohmer than Talbot Mundy, depicting the menace of the representatives of a clashing, alien Asian culture loose in London. Thö-pa-ga (meaning "time-is-come"), hereditary ruler of the Thunder Dragon Gate, is pursued by several dangerous groups eager to take him home and make him a puppet of their interests. The romance in *The Thunder Dragon Gate* begins as Tom Grayne and Elsa Burbage are secretly married to give her access to his strongbox in case of his death, neither of them able to admit to the other that their mutual feelings extend beyond the stated goal of assisting one another in getting into Tibet.

Despite a grounding in Tibetan mythology and magic, Mundy's plot diminishes the possibility of the more mythic reading he probably desired. Unlike the convincing premise of the fourth dimension in *Full Moon*, the fantasy in *The Thunder Dragon Gate* is muted and less satisfying, concentrating on the "shang-shang," a monster similar to the octopus visualized through hypnosis in Chapter 5 of *Full Moon*. The shang-shang is simultaneously a figure of legend and nightmare—reputedly pursuing its victims into the next world, preventing reincarnation—as well as a rare spider-like creature, over 12 feet in size, captured by the shamans. The cannibalistic shang-shang represent humankind's self-destructive instincts as the world is poised on the brink of another global war.[1]

The Thunder Dragon Gate lacks the necessary depth of character or intellectual motivation; like *The Nine Unknown*, *The Thunder Dragon Gate* suffers from an overabundance of individuals, with so many introduced and reappearing several chapters later as to leave the reader confused. Tom Grayne, Mundy's new hero, has a name which evokes the pseudonym, Mallory Grayson, that Mundy had proposed using on his unpublished philosophical book *Thus Spake the Devil*. As an American, Tom is not precluded by law from entering Tibet, unlike so many other nationalities, and has trained himself to survive there. As one of the Tibetans tells him,

> Tum-Glain, tell us how is it that you, a foreigner, who hadn't the advantage of being born in this blessed beautiful land, nevertheless are so good to be with? Your speak our speech so that it sounds comical, although we understand you, and you understand us. Which is it? Were you one of us in a former life? Were you reborn into some miserable foreign country for your former sins? Or are you a foreigner, too good for your own wretched country, being made ready, because of merit, to be reborn, at the proper time, in this blessed land? If so, better die soon, sooner to be reborn![2]

Lobsang Pun is a figure unlike previous Mundy lamas, pugnacious and irascible, believing a good flogging now is a better punishment than waiting for karma.

Tom admires Pun, even though he had once expelled him into the Tibetan winter with nothing but the prayers of 1100 lamas to ensure his safety. Pun himself spent seven years living as a naked hermit in a cave, subsisting on five grams of raw barley a day. Ten years later, he had tasted all the world's luxuries, seen their effects, and chose to avoid them. More than 60 now, Pun is a force for moral and political order, a foe of Japanese and Russian plots to control Tibet, and ready to engage in international intrigue to advance his country's independence. Pun serves the exiled Tashi Lama, in charge of spiritual law, counterpart of the infant Dalai Lama, whose sphere is civil affairs. In theory the two are equal, while in fact their subordinates battle. When either dies, the other superintends the selection of his successor, a child born at the hour of the late Lama's death, but a council of regents rules until the child comes of age. The recent Dalai Lama, *The Thunder Dragon Gate* asserts, was poisoned by his own faction for being too pro–British and resisting plans to murder the Tashi Lama.

The Thunder Dragon Gate failed to communicate Mundy's knowledge of the East, and his recognition of this fact is evident from his decision to make his next Tibetan novel, its sequel, *Old Ugly-Face*, as challenging a book as he ever wrote. *Old Ugly-Face* appeared in two different versions, as a serial and book. The serial, which ran in the Canadian magazine *Maclean's*, from April 15-May 15, 1938, was the length of one of Mundy's 1920s *Adventure* magazine novels. Character adjustments from *The Thunder Dragon Gate* were already present, and would be more pronounced in the book. Tom is primarily a secret agent, and his colleague Andrew Gunning is introduced; Tom's wife Elsa has had a baby and is left behind, losing the interplay of emotions between her, Andrew, and Tom that will become a significant part of the book with her presence.

Lobsang Pun is given the appellation Old Ugly-Face and is a more heroic figure and a fount of wise sayings. Tom explains that Pun is unbeatable.

> You can kill a mystic.... But there's no way of beating him. A genuine mystic is the most practical man in the world. You can beat any man who believes that death is the end of the road. But Ugly-face doesn't believe in belief. He's a knower. What he doesn't know, he has no use for. He doesn't care a whoop whether you or I understand him. To him it's an absolute fact that he has lived thousands of lives in this world, getting a bit wiser each time. He's so sure, that it bores him to argue about it, that he'll go on incarnating, until at last he doesn't have to any longer, because he'll have learned all that this world can teach him. After that there'll be lots of other worlds. Death means nothing to him. Riches are nothing. Even power is nothing, except as a duty. Ugly-face's duty is to Tibet.[3]

In the serial *Old Ugly-Face*, the plot shifts from the rivalry between the forces of the Dalai and Tashi Lama in *The Thunder Dragon Gate*, to the corruption of the entire Council of Regents in Lhasa by Russian and Japanese agents. Pun, the only Regent faithful to his duty, had barely escaped with his life, and must now lead the assault on the monastery where the Dalai Lama is held by Ram-pa Yap-shi, who will sell the Lama's influence to the highest bidder. Pun leads an army of hermits, mostly "theological students—the everlasting miracle of Tibet—all the stronger for their order, and considered unassailable and holy because of it."[4]

Mundy recognized that the serial formed not so much a complete work as the climax to a novel, and he set out to write the book, incorporating much of the serial but vastly expanding on it. In summer 1938 Mundy was desperately trying to finish the book, but it took another full year to complete, as Dawn recalled.

> He never wrote a book like that before — that all came in longhand. He said, "I cannot do it on the typewriter...." So he started on the outline of that serial, and then it kept getting — he'd get a chapter, and say, "I'll be back to the story tomorrow." But he wasn't — I mean chapter after chapter after chapter, but all in long hand. And that was so different, because he'd always worked directly on the typewriter. I'll bet I retyped those chapters I can't tell you how many times. He was never satisfied, he was a perfectionist then. He was never satisfied with the first draft when it appeared in short hand. And the work went on and on — he did that while he was also doing the radio plays and it was finally completed. He was a very tired man when it was completed; it sort of drained the life out of him.... I know he was disappointed when the first royalties came in — he thought it should be better, he had put so much into it. I love that story — you can read that story again and again and get an awful lot of teaching.[5]

Just as when Mundy wrote *Queen Cleopatra*, his mind was distracted by Liafail and drilling for oil in Mexico, during the writing of *Old Ugly-Face* Mundy was simultaneously concerned with turning out radio scripts, including a long story arc set in Tibet. However, the radio income freed Mundy from the need to rely on magazines, allowing him to spend such a long time preparing a book directly for hardcover publication.

Queen Cleopatra and *Old Ugly-Face* both grew into contemplative books of epic length, but this time Mundy did not allow his publishers to truncate it. Hutchinson wanted to cut *Old Ugly-Face* by 50,000 words without consulting Mundy, but after he threatened to take the book away from them, they finally published the entire text in June 1940; *Old Ugly-Face* had already appeared in the United States in February of the same year. Ironically, after this prelude, the Hutchinson edition was a more definitive text than the American, including some 70 footnotes to the quotations from literary sources. The extent of Mundy's literary background is revealed in passages from the Bible and Shakespeare, and citations including the poetry of Swinburne, Richard Lovelace, Kipling, Goethe's *Faust*, Browning, Milton, Walt Whitman, John Masefield, Virgil, Frazer's *The Golden Bough*; and such other books as Lord Roberts's *Forty Years in India*; a biography of Lord Fisher; *Man, the Unknown*, by Alexis Carrel; *Idea of a University*, by Cardinal Newman; *Essays on Some Controverted Questions* by Huxley; Twain's *A Connecticut Yankee in King Arthur's Court*; and the Tibetan *Book of the Dead* translated by Evans-Wentz.

Mundy asserts that Tibet, Jerusalem, and Russia are where the next war will be decided. With Thö-pa-ga and the Tashi Lama poisoned since the events of *The Thunder Dragon Gate*, the task of saving Tibet must be undertaken again. With the Panchen Lama, the nation's co-leader, having died in exile, "Tibet is not the obvious key, but it's the real key to the control of Asia. And the key to Tibet is the infant Dalai Lama."[6]

Old Ugly-Face carries forward the theme of imperialistic foreign interference in Tibet that had dominated *The Thunder Dragon Gate*, most notably with the character of Von Klaus, a disciple of Hitler who promises a new whirlwind of might making right that shall conquer the world. Unlike the serial version of *Old Ugly-Face*, this time Tom is paid by a U.S. Senator for confidential inside information, and Andrew pays his own way; neither work for the secret service or the State Department. Andrew is careful to point out to Elsa the difference between a secret agent's pursuit of intelligence, and a spy who betrays for thrills and pay—although Tom's information will be misused and fouled once it reaches Washington.

Old Ugly-Face is structured into 63 chapters, of varying length, many of them very short. Few actually begin or end a specific action, usually continuing scenes from the preceding chapter—precisely the style of the radio serial he was writing simultaneously. Hence, many of the book's scenes stretch into numerous chapters, extending well beyond the length of those in his earlier novels, and *Old Ugly-Face* frequently seems to move at a slow pace. With part of Mundy's mind devoted to *Jack Armstrong* and its fast-paced thrills, in *Old Ugly-Face* he indulged in nearly pure philosophy, almost overloading the book with ideas—every religious, political, social, and economic statement that had been bottled up within him for the past several years. Mundy moves away from his usual style by almost draining the typical adventurous elements out of the narrative; for instance, 245 pages pass (of a total of 544; 606 pages in the British edition), before the journey into Tibet actually commences. While an expansive novel that goes beyond generic boundaries, and his most powerful work since *Black Light*, eight years earlier, *Old Ugly-Face* is also overwritten, especially by comparison with *The Devil's Guard*, although the earlier book was much simpler by comparison.

Even in such earlier works as *The Nine Unknown* Mundy relied on spoken interchange back and forth in a manner that almost becomes staccato (especially with the repetition of the word "said"). His style over the years increasingly relied on long conversations about ideas, steadily minimizing the traditional mix with action or the usual brief dramatic exchanges typical of movies. Writing for the radio enhanced Mundy's tendency to convey his ideas predominantly in dialogue rather than narrative, and *Old Ugly-Face* reflects this influence to an unprecedented degree, elaborating his philosophy in a question-and-answer format. (Occasional narrative passages suddenly interrupt, changing the tone, such as Chapter 21.) Whereas *Om* had so skillfully shown his readers the "middle way," in *Old Ugly-Face* Mundy must *tell* his readers, insistently and didactically, since the plot no longer so perfectly illustrates the philosophy. Yet he also expanded to interior monologues, with italicized mystical conversations between the consciousness and higher self, some of which reveal Mundy's awareness of his role as storyteller.

Old Ugly-Face is a bridge to the more disillusioned pattern of subdued heroism, and a fractured, inward-looking narrative, away from the classical, inspiring positivism of books like *Om* and the confines of generic fiction. *Old Ugly-Face* reveals Mundy's style and technique in a state of flux, changing along with the altering standards and expectations of the time, revealing his ability to adjust to a new literary era. Mundy's publishers permit, for the first time, matter-of-fact swearing; Nazi torture methods, and their lineage from inquisition methods, are graphically described; there are several references to the homosexuality of certain minor characters—most notably a child trained as the perfect criminal. As Dawn noted, "*Old Ugly-Face* was much more modern, and something he never attempted before."[7] Nonetheless, critics generally failed to recognize the change, and Mundy continued to be treated as a genre author by critics, who asserted that the philosophy destroyed the story.[8]

Mundy had retained his regard for theosophy, and contact with Point Loma; after his death, Dawn would return several boxes of restricted, esoteric materials which he had been studying.[9] However, the philosophy in *Old Ugly-Face* does not so closely parallel theosophical teachings, but is instead a very personal amalgamation, and one which has never found the devoted following of his other such novels.[10] Nonetheless, the similarity between the epic journey in *Om* and *Old Ugly-Face* is indicated by both ending in the Lama booming "the mystic syllable that leads, like all true music, upward, universe by universe, to an infinity beyond eternity, whence pours all newness—'Aum-m-m-m-m-m-m-m-m-m-m-m-m-m-m-m-m-m-m-m-m-m-m-m-m-m-m-m!'"[11]

As Mundy had in *Black Light*, in *Old Ugly-Face* he attempts to put Eastern ideas into a context that relates them to Christianity, and also reveals its influence during his last years. *Old Ugly-Face* can best be understood as a mystical interpretation of the Bible; as Mundy wrote, "I have taken liberties with the holy name of Jesus, and with the Books of Psalms and lots of other things."[12]

While the characters in *The Devil's Guard* are secondary to events and function largely as symbols, *Old Ugly-Face* is a character-driven book, with the plot firmly in the background. Many of the characters are carried over from *The Thunder Dragon Gate*, but change substantially, and Mundy intended for Elsa, Tom, and Pun to now have a depth and realism equal to any in literature. Elsa is restored to the key position she occupied in *The Thunder Dragon Gate*, but becoming a far more convincing character in *Old Ugly-Face*, an individual who is young and changing, like Amrita of *Black Light* and Arsinoe of *Purple Pirate*. Tom is transformed between the serial and book into a mystic who has seen Lung-gom-pa, "flying lamas," walking through the air. Like another Mundy hero, Jimgrim, he is eager for Tibetan training, and hopes that Old Ugly-Face will accept him as chela, a position to which Elsa also aspires.

Andrew begins as a character who lacks clairvoyant powers, a man of action, but also a modern-day knight pursuing his own grail, trying to overcome a tragedy that occurred in America and disillusioned him. By the conclusion, Andrew has become sensitive to clairvoyance, receiving Elsa's visions—and realizing his love for her.

In *The Thunder Dragon Gate* Nancy Strong was introduced like the Tilgaun schoolteacher Hannah Sanburn in *Om*, or Annie Weems in *Black Light*, as a fiftyish spinster and one of the half-dozen white women to have been to Tibet, arriving when she was 24 and became the mistress of a Tibetan nobleman. In *Old Ugly-Face*, Nancy becomes a considerably more important character, a wise teacher, who has named her cat Akhnaton. She believes human beings evolve *from subconsciousness*, exist *at consciousness*, and move *toward superconsciousness*.[13] "You can't prevent it, any more than the crops can prevent the weather. But you can make hell for yourself if you resist; because evolution breaks the molds of consciousness as the roots of growing trees break rocks. Evolution is a spiritual, irresistible growth — upward and outward from the illusion of solid four-dimensional limited matter."[14]

Nancy is described by one character as "the only genuine Christian I know...."[15] She combines elements of two of Mundy's own female teachers, one from whom he learned personally — Katherine Tingley — and another whose works he had studied — Mary Baker Eddy.'"[16] Elsa believes Nancy is an initiate, but she tells her she is not, and replies to her questions about the Masters by saying "'By their fruits ye shall know them.'"[17] Her didacticism dominates the first half of the book, reshaping Elsa, before Nancy's own teacher for nine years, Old Ugly-Face, takes center stage.

The emphasis shifts from Elsa's qualification in *The Thunder Dragon Gate* as the only woman in the world who can translate ancient Tibetan, to her capacities as a clairvoyant. Nancy Strong asserts that clairvoyance is the means through which news is transmitted throughout Asia, and believes most people are born with the capacity, but are never aware of it. Elsa's character is based on Mundy's friend and fellow author Elsa Barker (1869–1954), an upstairs neighbor while he lived on Staten Island. She had provided "some good instructions" as he put the finishing touches on *Guns of the Gods*.[18] Like Burbage's clairvoyant insights, unexpected, undesired, and irregular, Barker had found she had the gift of "automatic writing." She said that several of her books and volumes of poetry had been written under the influence of deceased individuals who guided her pen.

In part three of the novel appears the man for whom it is named, Lobsang Pun, and the book embellishes considerably on the serial. *Old Ugly-Face* explores the manner in which Elsa, a married woman, begins to love Andrew, and gradually summons the courage to tell Tom that their marriage was a mistake. In a Tibetan cave with Tom the preceding year, Elsa had become pregnant, a thousand miles from help, and begins to fall in love with Andrew when he successfully delivers her child, in the snow, taking her and the baby to a monastery before the infant died. Tom and Elsa had believed they could maintain a Platonic relationship on their journey; but they were disillusioned to discover that the daily process of sharing experiences and confidences inevitably leads to a sexual longing they are unable to resist. The process will repeat itself as Andrew and Elsa make the return. To share warmth and the trouble of unpacking and repacking, Andrew and Elsa share the same blankets in a completely common-sense and asexual manner. The Tibetan headman, Bompo Tsering, believes Tom and Andrew share Elsa in a manner reflecting the polyandrous marriages of his own country.

Just as *The Ivory Trail* told of Mundy's experiences in Africa, and *I Say Sunrise* became an autobiography of his ideas, *Old Ugly-Face* reveals an autobiography of his intuition. This was the first time Mundy had written a book when he was ill (with undiagnosed diabetes), with flagging energy and a physical awareness of his own mortality. In 1936, the death of two of his previous wives, Inez and Rosemary, also reminded him of advancing age. The character pattern in *Old Ugly-Face* had more than a passing resemblance to Mundy's own life, recognizing the inevitable future that awaited he and Dawn. Elsa is like Dawn, a clairvoyant, and her child by Tom / Talbot has died. Mundy's self-identity is largely located in Tom Grayne, preparing to leave his wife to begin a new stage of existence as a chela, just as Mundy knew that he would leave Dawn through his own inevitable death. Talbot may have foreseen the relationship that was developing between himself, Dawn, and their Florida theosophist neighbor, Eric Provost, an aspiring writer who had visited them in Connecticut. Mundy may have seen Eric as "gunning" for Dawn — hence the derivation of Andrew's surname; Dawn would marry Eric shortly after Talbot's death. The nickname "Old Ugly-Face" presents a spiritual teacher in a humorous light, rather than a solemn one, and appealed to Pun for this reason, just as it appealed to Mundy. For the one who has become "Old Ugly-Face" is the aging, gaunt, balding Talbot Mundy, and no other. Pun's nickname is, indeed, a "pun"; Mundy perpetuates a joke on himself in his determination to use this uncommercial title. And it was a resemblance he acknowledged in inscriptions in the book.[19]

By the mid–1930s, colonial India was becoming an identifiable genre of adventure movies enjoying box-office success, with one from each studio: *Clive of India* (1935) at Fox, *The Charge of the Light Brigade* (1936) at Warner Bros., *Storm Over Bengal* (1938) at Republic, *Gunga Din* (1939) at RKO, and from British producer Alexander Korda, the Sabu vehicles *Elephant Boy* (1937) and *Drums* (1938, titled *The Drum* in the U.S.) Paramount's 1934 hit *The Lives of a Bengal Lancer* was the breakthrough that began the cycle, and in the spring of 1936 the company turned to Mundy for a worthy successor by optioning *Rung Ho!*. After the fiasco of *The Black Watch*, Mundy had threatened that "I will never sign a contract that does not stipulate that I shall write the dialogue and that I shall be at least consulted regarding the scenario. Also, I provide the music that goes with the picture. And I must have the right to veto. No more [scenarist John] Stone or Myrna Loy."[20] Paramount asked Mundy to adapt his own novel written 22 years earlier, and he did the work hastily on speculation. The surviving draft submitted is a 59 page treatment, retitled *Fifty-Seven*, referring to the central event, the Sepoy mutiny of 1857. By June, Mundy anticipated leaving for Hollywood.

He sought to give *Rung Ho!* a greater relevance to the 1930s, as India actively sought independence, turning out more of a historical epic than the standard pulp-style adventure tale favored in 1930s cinema. Mundy began his treatment with a "Foreword," and "Theme," each five pages, believing them as important as the story, outlining the historical backdrop and interweaving its complex causes. Indeed this section is the most rewarding and revealing portion of the treatment. In 1857, he reported, India was governed by "the Honorable East India Co., a commercial organization ... whose outrageously anachronistic system produced conditions that brought the rebellion into being."[21] With the British army paid by and answerable to the East India Co., the revolt caught them unprepared and incredulous. "Discontent and disaffection had been brewing for a long time," with the prohibition of suttee a contributing factor; the spark was provided by new army cartridges greased by pig's fat, alienating both Hindus and Moslems."[22] In *Rung Ho!*, Mundy had made clear that even men like Mahommed Gunga, who supported the British, were angered by this action, and priests of all type fanned the sentiment to revolt.

While the outbreak of violence produced atrocities, with many British officers shooting their wives rather than surrender them, Mundy asserts that many other wives were rescued by loyal Indians, and "there was great gallantry on both sides."[23] The Indians, Mundy believed, fought out of patriotism, or in some cases, a hope for "despotic power," yet the suppression of the rebellion was also made possible by those who foresaw that a successful rebellion would result in cruel misgovernment and catastrophic anarchy, and preferred arbitrary British leadership.[24] The rebellion was finally suppressed largely due to the fidelity and personal loyalty of these Indians, who knew how to direct the relatively "innocent" and supposedly naive men who defiantly refused to submit to military tradition and listen to "the stupidity and jealousy of their seniors...."[25] Most British generals and civilians in India in 1857 were over 60 or 70 years of age, and many went mad or died from the shock of the events to come. "They were dyed-in-the-wool reactionaries and, when not incompetent owing to ill health, senile."[26]

This revisionist interpretation had only been tangential in *Rung Ho!*, muted probably because as a new novelist he lacked the stature to assert unpopular notions, and he now expressed his own, more mature views. The few previous films on the rebellion portrayed it far differently than Mundy proposed. Both *The Campbells Are Coming* (1915) and *The Victoria Cross* (1916) show Indian leaders motivated to revolt by the desire to add white women to their harem. Subsequent films avoided the depiction of an actual historical rebellion, preferring a vague temporal setting. Only *The Charge of the Light Brigade* touched on the events of 1857, by portraying a massacre of the British led by a militant Khan.

Traditionally, adventure films began with an action-filled incident, a battle or a skirmish, as had the book. Instead, Mundy begins *Fifty-Seven* with a slow-paced meeting of the elderly council in Peshawar, to which Brigadier General Crawford Byng and his Rajput Rangar Rissaldar Mahommed Gunga have been invited to warn of the coming rebellion and propose military preparations. (In *Rung Ho!*, by contrast, Byng was not named until page 221, and he was a very minor character.) Byng is told, "We have trouble enough as it is with these young squirts of subalterns who are sent out from home with their heads full of fancy notions of their own importance. Damme, sir, this morning's mail brings news that they're sending out Cunningham's son with more introductions and letter of recommendation than if he were a royal bastard! He shall be taught his place, I guarantee you. As for rebellion, Brigadier, I trust you will have the good sense not to interrupt a council meeting again with any such God damned nonsense."[27] The young man referred to is 21-year-old Ralph Cunningham, shortly to arrive in India from England. (In *Rung Ho!* the attitude toward Ralph was of a similar vintage but somewhat more friendly.) His late father once led the famous "Cunningham's Horse," which Mahommed Gunga, despite being told the Rangars are merely disgruntled landowners, hopes to reassemble under the son of the original leader. They will clandestinely subject him to every test the Eastern mind can devise, leaving him only the challenge of facing an eligible woman, a test Mahommed Gunga had avoided in *Rung Ho!*.

Mundy's romance in *Fifty-Seven* was as unconventional as his depiction of the history. Unmarried, upper class English girls were rare at the time in India, and most hoped to catch an eligible, high-ranking officer. However, his heroine was the opposite, and Mundy claimed that both she and his hero are strong-willed, admirable characters: "Her indignation—her natural and in the circumstances quite pardonable hot Scots temper—gets him into serious difficulties that compel him to show the good stuff he is made of."[28] Thrown reluctantly into close association by events, they recognize the virtues in each other's character, admiration at last leading to love.

In Howrah, Reverend Duncan McLean and his daughter Rosemary try to Christianize the indigenous people, but have only one doubtful convert, Joanna, who was much more significant in *Rung Ho!* than in *Fifty-Seven*. The McLeans have concentrated on schooling and abolishing suttee, a practice long outlawed but still favored by Hindus. Rosemary refuses Ralph's advice when a mob threatens them, yet still "arouses his admiration by her sturdy Scots integrity and her contempt for danger."[29] Mahommed Gunga asks his cousin Alwa, a feudal landlord and hereditary chieftain, to protect the McLeans if necessary.

The unfriendly citizenry of Howrah have given the Maharajah's devious younger brother, Jaimihr, an excuse to have Rosemary continuously guarded. Although disliking his attentions, Rosemary hopes to appeal to Jaimihr's better nature, since he pretends to disavow suttee. She is dismayed when both Jaimihr and Ralph have neither the inclination nor resources to interfere with the anticipated burning of Rosemary's young friend Amrita (added from *Rung Ho!*). Rosemary quarrels with Ralph, and Mahommed Gunga's men prevent her from going to the Maharajah to have herself imprisoned in an effort to prevent ritual sacrifice.

When the mutiny breaks out, there is no contingency plan at headquarters, and confusion reigns. Byng is chosen by his fellow officers to oust a senile superior, and hopes to march on Delhi, but he needs to augment the size of his small command. He gives Ralph a triple assignment: gather his father's veterans, prevent the Maharajah of Howrah from joining the rebels, and frustrate Jaimihr's plans to kill his brother and take the throne. Mahommed Gunga is dispatched with Ralph, and given Byng's sword of honor to indicate his trust that he will help Ralph carry out his mission.

When Ralph and Mahommed Gunga arrive at Alwa's stronghold, Ralph and Rosemary remain bitter toward one another; he knows of a letter she wrote after their previous encounter which was widely circulated and sullied his reputation. She resents his commander's air of authority, and Ralph is irritated by her belief that her ideals are superior. Yet Rosemary now is also somewhat ashamed, having realized that he could have done nothing to save Amrita. These events were a reverse of *Rung Ho!*, where Ralph and Rosemary took a nearly instant, if guarded, liking to one another, and had a far more reasonable relationship.

With his word already pledged to the Maharajah, Alwa is unable to follow his natural inclination to help young Cunningham. Sincerely believing that Ralph will lead them to disaster, Rosemary visits Jaimihr in his dungeon, without realizing her treachery. Extracting a written promise to aid the British, end suttee, and help the mission if he takes the throne, she allows him to escape. When the others learn of her action, she proudly displays the promise, like Joan of Arc, while Mahommed Gunga laughs. However, to protect her, and despite what his men know to be the case, Ralph says he ordered her action so that Alwa could keep his promise to the Maharajah. Amazed at his chivalry, she then quietly obeys his request to mend his tunic, mindful that despite all her provocations he has never raised his voice or made one impolite remark to her. (In *Rung Ho!*, this entire episode was treated differently, and was regarded as problematic by Mundy and his British publisher at the time.)

Taking Howrah, with Jaimihr slain, the strengthened Cunningham forces catch up with Byng's column to assist in the march on Delhi. There Ralph again meets the McLeans, and Rosemary offers to help the wounded. She tells Byng that Ralph should have shot her for betrayal, but instead lied for her, like a gentleman; "she is between tears and the most defensive bulwark of her Scottish pride and self critical humor."[30] However, Byng says he has much to do, Alwa and Mahommed Gunga pretend to be distracted, and as her father leaves her carriage, Ralph follows and closes the door behind him. By contrast, in *Rung Ho!*, Mundy emphasizes the personal contest in which Ralph kills Jaimihr, then picks up Rosemary on his horse and kisses her, still bloody from the duel — a far more cinematic climax.

Whatever Mundy's intention and his understanding words in the preface, many incidents are added in the scenario escalating Rosemary's conflicts with Ralph, treating him abominably at every opportunity until the end. One can only speculate how Mundy felt about a character who in *Rung Ho!* had been modeled on his third wife, now rewritten so many years after their bitter divorce. Rosemary is hardly the only problematic characterization in *Fifty-Seven*; with the exception of the treacherous Jaimihr and the loyal Mahommed Gunga, none of the characters are sharply conveyed.

Mundy failed to sort through and condense his cohesive mélange of characters and subplots in *Rung Ho!* to their essentials, with the result that the film treatment seems even more complicated than the literary source. The title itself, *Fifty-Seven*, would hardly be clear or attractive to most audiences. His writing remains literary, not visual, although there are some scenes of impressive and majestic military ritual; his action scenes are only described in the briefest detail. Many of the most cinematic, visual moments were eliminated from the novel, while in their place he tended to add talky, rather muddled scenes. Indeed, his choice of language is more dramatic in the prefatory sections that in the actual treatment, which is told in synopsis form, without his usual colorful, pictorial wording, giving the outline a dull feeling. His occasional passages of dialogue tend to read as speeches, rather than conversation.

Fifty-Seven has much swearing, and Mundy must have known this would be unacceptable dialogue at a time of renewed censorship restrictions. Mundy's depiction of Indians would have been another difficulty, with both the Maharajah and the potential usurper Jaimihr equally ruthless and totalitarian, while England is no better. The concentration on the opposition to suttee paralleled the use of the Kali sect in *Gunga Din*. On the other hand, the unfavorable etching of missionaries would probably have proven palatable, since religion and the devout, of both Christian and Eastern faiths, are often mocked in films of the adventure genre.

The portraits of Alwa and especially Mahommed Gunga would have been most unusual; indigenous people were usually in the background or outright villains. Mundy's tracing of Mahommed Gunga as Ralph's teacher, molding, developing, testing and influencing the young man's character into a leader worthy of his father — and his followers — would have been a complete inversion of the *Gunga Din* archetype.

Considering Mundy had returned from a lengthy visit to England and his family just three years earlier, his attitude toward the British, the military, and the empire was never more virulent. He even departed from the British norm of calling the events of 1857 the "Sepoy mutiny," instead terming it a rebellion, a linguistic distinction reflecting the relative attitudes toward the perception of the Indian desire for independence and self-determination.

Fifty-Seven was ahead of its time, but came surprisingly close to production, and demonstrates that Hollywood's pro–British bias of the time was less a matter of ideology than business. Paramount purchased all film, radio, and audio rights to *Rung Ho!* in perpetuity in November, 1936, and the English censors to whom the scenario draft was submitted only noted the incompetence shown by officials unprepared for the mutiny. However, when a synopsis was submitted to the India Office, they advised against production, as they had an earlier proposal for a British feature set in the same milieu. *Fifty-Seven* even came up in a parliamentary debate on December 7, 1938, in which the Home Secretary explained that the project was considered likely to create bad feeling between Indians and British. Indeed, the censorship was, as pointed out on floor, cleverly constructed so as to deny any official prohibition but to make their views known informally, in this case through the American ambassador, to Paramount.[31] These audiences were a source of considerable box-office power, with the revenues in England and her colonies often making the difference between a picture's profit and loss.

While Mundy and Paramount were laboring on *Fifty-Seven*, 20th Century–Fox, eight years after *The Black Watch*, began a four-year series of aborted attempts to script a remake of *King of the Khyber Rifles*. The project began with fanfare, anticipating a big-budget film, and for the next six years it remained on Fox's production charts, yet never made it to the shooting stage.

The remake was hardly promising for Mundy or his book; one of producer Kenneth MacGowan's first notes read: "The plot of 'King of the Khyber Rifles' is too utterly preposterous to be of any use. It combines the worst features of Ryder [sic] Haggard. But the title is swell and should be retained."[32] To distinguish the new film from *The Lives of a Bengal Lancer*, despite the similar conception, the studio decided to combine a tale of the old Army in India with the new arrival of airplanes on the Afghan frontier. As in *The Black Watch*, Victor McLaglen was again to be starred, as "Mac" King, this time playing an infantryman who must adjust to changing times on the frontier as his Khyber Rifles are disbanded and replaced by the air force. By June, 1936, a treatment was completed by Milton Sperling and Boris Ingster, but the conclusion remained vexing during each draft. The studio decided their India story for 1937 would be *Wee Willie Winkie*, adapted from the Rudyard Kipling story as a Shirley Temple vehicle.

The Mundy adaptation lay dormant until the beginning of 1938, with the hiring of John Balderston, a former playwright who had collaborated on *The Lives of a Bengal Lancer*. However, Balderston's version lacked unity, starting slowly in several different directions, and adding such silly touches as having King become airsick in his first time aloft. King is presented as a thoroughly unlikable, petulant character, without a redeeming feature save bravery, and indeed the title is changed to read simply *Khyber Rifles* or *Khyber Patrol*.

For over a year, no further activity occurred on the project. Finally, in the spring of 1939, it was taken off the shelves and slated for fall production; Boris Ingster was recalled to the project, this time without Sperling. Now titled simply *Khyber Rifles*, "Captain Thomas Boyd" replaces King; the movie was no longer to be touted as an adaptation, and was set in 1920. No more writing occurred until May 1940, when Sam Hellman turned in a new script, replacing many Balderston-Ingster episodes with incidents dropped from earlier scripts, but the characterizations in the script he entitled *Khyber Pass* become muddled.

With the outbreak of World War II, the situation between England and India became increasingly sensitive, making production of a new picture about the colonial situation problematic. Nothing further happened for over a year, until Paramount tried to purchase *King of the Khyber Rifles* as a vehicle to be released in early 1942 for Brian Donlevy, just emerging as a star after playing many supporting heavies. However, Fox considered the offer for only two weeks before deciding the Mundy property was too valuable to dispose of, considering world conditions. Both studios reckoned without the effect of World War II on censorship; suddenly, pictures depicting the status of a colonized country were discouraged as offensive to them.

With his Hollywood contacts fresh, Mundy wrote a novel, *East and West*, calculated to interest filmmakers by using the narrative formula that had achieved the most success for movies set in India. Rather than adventure, this was colonial melodrama; the perils of miscegenation formed the basis of such popular plays and novels brought to the screen as *The Rains Came* and *The Green Goddess*. The dust jackets of both the British and American editions pictured the blond heroine and the dark-skinned Indian; the plot was described on the cover of the dust jacket of the Hutchinson edition as "An exciting and glamorous tale of the clash between a white woman and a coloured man."

East and West, titled in England *Diamonds See in the Dark* (a local saying in the novel that becomes a motif), reworks ideas from several past books around a new central theme. *East and West* merges elements from such Mundy novels as *Guns of the Gods*, *Her Reputation*, *The Red Flame of Erinpura*, and "*C.I.D.*," but in a much inferior manner, and without their literary calibre. As in *Guns of the Gods*, settling a border dispute involves buried treasure — in *East and West*, a diamond mine controlled by the priests. The characterization of the villain, Prince Rundhia, is borrowed from *The Red Flame of Erinpura*, where he was killed by a priest's tiger after poisoning his father, the Maharajah, as part of a plan to exploit the region's oil resources. He is eager to marry an American woman, Deborah, believing it would allow him greater financial control by settling the money on her, outside of a British audit.[33]

In *East and West*, the name Deborah is given to a rich, overbearing American, Mrs. Harding of Aaronville, Ohio (a clear allusion to the corrupt president of that name and state, Warren Harding). She resembles Mrs. Beddington of *Black Light*, rearing her niece, Lynn, with a tyranny of finance that had forced her "to postpone the natural rebellion of youth to" the age of 22.[34] Traveling in India, Lynn partially encourages the lecherous Rundhia's attempt to seduce her as a rejection of the aunt's authority.

Overlaid on this theme is the boundary dispute symbolic of both territory and the rights of an Indian or an Englishman to claim Lynn. British engineer Carl Norwood is threatened, and offered a bribe, by the priests and the Maharajah. Meanwhile, pressed by debt, Rundhia is poisoning his uncle to hasten his demise, so he will be in power before the British Resident reports and the government vetoes his succession. Rundhia tries to also kill Norwood, as a potential rival for Lynn, and to blame his death on the priests, thereby winning the mine for himself.

Only once before had Mundy written a story with a similar theme, *Flame of Cruelty*, appearing in 1929 in *Everybody's Combined with Romance*. These two stories seem inexplicable in the context of Mundy's full canon and his usual celebration of the ways of the East, since his entire oeuvre was in opposition to the precept of "East is East and West is West and never the twain shall meet"—Kipling's phrase quoted on the Appleton-Century dust jacket description of *East and West*. In Mundy's writing, East and West mingle, freely, continuously, and productively, and he portrayed white womanhood as held inviolable by Indians, from Elsa Burbage, or Samding and Amrita reared in the ways of wisdom by Indians in *Om* and *Black Light*, to the wives of officers protected by loyal Sepoys in "For the Salt Which He Had Eaten." When the issue appears in *Om*, and Ommony discovers to his dread that young white orphan girls have been smuggled to India under Samdup's aegis, it turns out they were to provide companions of her own race and age for his niece Samding. Mundy had usually avoided colonial melodrama precisely because it was centered around maintaining the separation of the races, particularly in male-female relationships. Key to explaining *Flame of Cruelty* and *East and West*, cautionary tales so exceptional for Mundy, are the dates. Both were written at times when Mundy was having contact with Hollywood–and the concession on race was not the only shift; *East and West* offers a more positive depiction of both the Resident and his role.

The Conkey home in Manchester gained a radio for Christmas 1934, a decade after its introduction. In addition to the music relished by Dawn and her father, dramatic shows proliferated, and by the end of the decade over 300 different fifteen minute daily serials would be heard. One of these was *Jack Armstrong, the All-American Boy*, the vehicle for General Mills to promote their breakfast cereal, "Wheaties."

As created by actor-writer Robert Hardy Andrews, a prolific figure in early radio drama, the show was descended from over a half-century of dime novel fiction for youth, and emerged with such durable mid–20th century literary heroes as the inventors Tom Swift and Tom Swift, Jr. and the sleuthing Hardy Boys and Nancy Drew. Children were offered idealized heroes sufficiently older to be on the cusp of adulthood, with a large measure of autonomy from supervision, but young enough to still facilitate a ready kinship. This hero solves mysteries and travels to distant lands, using means of transportation such as automobiles, airplanes, and ships, that are normally reserved as symbols of adult status. The characters have no supernatural powers; their tool is knowledge, together with physical agility.

Jack is a high school student in the midwestern town of Hudson, and his best friend is the younger Billy Fairfield. Billy's sister, Betty, was present for female listeners, but was able to take care of herself amidst their adventures. Betty and Billy's uncle, Jim Fairfield, was a former high-ranking army officer who owned an aircraft factory. A cornucopia of knowledge, Uncle Jim frequently took the three teenagers with him on his travels. While serving as the series's authority figure, Uncle Jim was not encumbered with the intrusive disciplinary aspects of parental or teacher authority that would annoy children.

This structure placed Jack in the middle ground between the ultimate adult wisdom of the scientist-explorer Uncle Jim, and the juvenile uncertainty and mistakes of Billy. Hence the listener, while closer to Billy's age, found in Jack the individual he could aspire to become. The youthful audience might be reassured that even when Billy made errors, it was possible to outgrow them, since it was Jack's maturity and judgement that was most often on display, making him the *de facto* leader — even as Uncle Jim had the final word.

Jack Armstrong debuted July 31, 1933, and would continue on the air for another 17 seasons. As scripted by Andrews, Lee Knopf, and Irving J. Crump, *Jack Armstrong* quickly outgrew sports tales centered around Hudson High, and sent Jack hero traveling; different backgrounds increased the variety of story possibilities (and could obscure a rehashing of a familiar narrative). The title phrase, "Jack Armstrong, the All-American Boy," initially devised to emphasize the athletic connection, came to increasingly connote an all-around American who embodied the best national ideals no matter what country he was in.

An average day's 15-minute script was eight pages in length, including roughly 250 lines, and 150 exchanges of dialogue. Six of the minutes were consumed by the opening credits and advertising, with the announcer often touting a current promotional tie-in for the series, a product whose partial cost was a number of Wheaties box-tops. Radio premiums had begun to be used nationally in 1931, and frequently the *Jack Armstrong* narrative would highlight a premium.

Despite the impression that might be gleaned from a single episode, serial structure was far from random. The frequent mini-crises and cliffhangers often concluding each show provided the illusion of constant movement, and listeners who heard it in serial form each day absorbed what seemed a near-constant whirlwind of action. Such scriptwriting required meticulous organization to relate a story arc that tells a near-epic tale one small bit at a time. Individual broadcasts took place in real time, with the only ellipsis occurring between episodes — presenting each show as if it were a glimpse into the daily life of Jack and his friends. Incidents are often repetitious (such as the buried treasure motif), and much of the dialogue and even whole episodes consist largely of recapitulations of what had happened up to that point. Plotlines move at a glacial pace despite fast moving incidents, with a single story often lasting months, only encompassing periodic climaxes. Characters left behind would reappear in new combinations (a technique already used in Mundy's Jimgrim and Tros stories).

Children's stories would hardly seem a possible outlet for Mundy's talents as a writer, yet it was a bully pulpit. His audience was larger and more impressionable than achieved by all his previous writing: the pre-adolescent youth of America, predominantly boys, open to word of far horizons. The staggering sales of the premiums reveal the extent of the depth of the cultural penetration of *Jack Armstrong*, and Mundy, into the life of American youth.

Dawn recalled his initial reaction to the idea of the show. Talbot asked her to read the previous scripts before he did, to tell him what she thought. By the end of the third script she felt nauseous, telling him, "You can't write this kind of trash, it is absolutely impossible, no way!" The program had to be filled with educational tips, and in addition came a list of all the "can't do's" dictated by the sponsor. Talbot read these injunctions first. Two of the stipulations were that there was to be no religion and no philosophy, together with network injunctions against use of the supernatural or superstition, that might arouse fear in listeners. Dawn recalled, "You tell Talbot 'don't,' and you hoist the red flag for the bull. So then he read the scripts, and said, 'Well, I think I can handle this.'" Through geography, which had already been part of his prose, Mundy easily fulfilled the pedagogical essentials, as Jack traveled the globe, encountering different habitats, animals, and peoples. Then Mundy turned breaking the remaining rules into a personal challenge, infusing the show with his own, theosophical perspective, a fact that was never spotted by the sponsor.[35]

Jack Armstrong took its first summer hiatus from April 24, 1936, to August 28, shifting from the CBS to the NBC-Red Network, and Mundy was announced as the show's writer when it resumed on August 31, heard weekdays from 5:30 to 5:45, making a minimum of about 170 separate broadcasts annually. Publicity announced that the show's return would have Jack Armstrong traveling to India, Tibet, China, the Himalayas, and the Gobi Desert — a clear reflection of the motifs of Mundy's adult fiction. Publicity for the show occasionally noted Mundy as its writer, with advertisements describing him as a world traveler and explorer, sometimes claiming that he had hunted tigers in India, fought savages in Africa, and was with King Feisal during the World War.

Jack Armstrong gained Mundy a steady, predictable job for the first time, and considering the broadcast output of the last four years of his life makes it as prolific as any period of his writing. He authored some 700 scripts, roughly 5500 printed pages (three times the length of the entire Tros saga), almost 120 hours of airtime. There were enough plots to make the equivalent of at least nine novels: Far East (fall 1936), Africa (spring 1937), Egypt (1937–38), Zanzibar shipwrecks (fall 1938), the Dorjes and the Iron Keys of India (1938–39), Mayan temple (1938–39), Tibet (spring 1939), West Indies (fall 1939), and Easter Island (1940). Unfortunately, only four of the actual shows survive, but together with other artifacts it is possible to reconstruct much of this enormous output.

Mundy's first known radio adventure began with a flight aboard the China Clipper to Manila, then on by boat to Shanghai where Uncle Jim has been given a jade talisman, key to an ancient city buried in the Gobi Desert (a resonance with *Jimgrim*). By mid September, 1936, 150,000 listeners sent in a boxtop and three cents for a dragon talisman (inscribed in Mandarin with the saying "Whoever owns me owns the key to the house of treasure") and a chart game map of Jack's wanderings in the East. The game resembles the radio serial, as Jack crosses the border of Tibet, going south and east through India, flying to Rangoon, Burma and the Malay States, taking a tramp steamer to Borneo, before returning to the Philippines. The first *Jack Armstrong* serial both reflected the novel he was composing at the time, *The Thunder Dragon Gate* (one of the show's characters, Su-li Wing, would be recast as a spy in the novel), as well as his experiences in southeast Asia, a part of his life he had never previously fictionalized.

For his next sequence, beginning in January 1937, Mundy decided to borrow directly from one of his past novels. *The Ivory Trail* had already proven adaptable to serial form with *The Jungle Mystery*, and its nonfiction basis had been the foundation for many of Mundy's recent lectures. Ascertaining the radio version's plot is possible from combining such sources as his only surviving *Jack Armstrong* script, and the adaptation of the overall sequence in Whitman's 1937 Big Little book, *Jack Armstrong and the Ivory Treasure*, by Leslie J. Daniels, Jr. Over 225,000 "Moviescope" premiums were sold, with one of the five 35 mm. filmstrips ostensibly showing photos taken by Jack on his Ivory Patrol Expedition in Africa.

Considering the updating of the story, his audience, and that *The Jungle Mystery* had already changed the antagonist's nationality from German to Russian, it is hardly surprising that Mundy eliminates the theme of Teutonic colonial oppression found in *The Ivory Trail* in favor of new antagonists. The radio's Kazimoto is a loyal friend but hardly the pillar of courage presented in the novel. Opening in Brazil, Uncle Jim arranges for Ali to be freed from the villainous Alonzo Lopez's plantation, and Ali thanks him with an ivory ring given him by Tippoo Tib.

Jack, Billy, Betty, and Uncle Jim's first sight of an African village is Matadi, in the Belgian Congo where they meet the silent magician Booloola. Booloola purportedly knew Tippoo Tib and where he buried the map of the place where the elephants go to die; Tib was killed for taking some of the ivory for himself. Flying the seaplane *Silver Albatross* up the Congo River, Uncle Jim lands only to be ambushed by a Belgian hydroplane from which Lopez emerges. Jack tackles Lopez to prevent him from beating Booloola with a stick, and Kazimoto assists while Billy cheers from the sidelines.

Lopez is taken aboard the *Silver Albatross* as Uncle Jim navigates by Booloola's directions to a lost city in the jungle where Lopez believes Tib's map has been secreted. Menacing pygmies are turned into friends to help the search. In the wild, Jack begins to use his "mercy gun," armed with bullets that merely put an animal to sleep, rather than killing it. Their use became not only a way to minimize killing in a show directed at youth, but for Mundy to inculcate a new generation with a different attitude toward wildlife than he had practiced 30 years earlier. Mundy even includes a mystical element to amplify this theme, for Booloola is known as a Bwana of Beasts, for the influence he holds over wild animals and his ability to speak to them; hence Booloola's nickname "Elephant Man."

While searching a cave, they find the map, showing the Mountains of the Moon, Lake Victoria, and the unknown "Castle That Shouts." Booloola steals the map, but Jack already has a mental copy in his mind. Stopping at Kisumu, Lopez disappears during the night, having disabled the *Silver Albatross*. Jim's old friend Sheik Mohammed invites him to join them in his camp near Mount Elgon.

Mohammed shows Jim a much more complex parchment map, and when the Sheik is abducted by Lopez, Booloola leads Jack to the Rocks That Shout, their angles causing sounds like a crowd of people as the wind whips across them. A landslide traps them and crushes Lopez; Booloola deliberately blocked the way into the elephant's graveyard to protect it. Mohammed explains that Booloola mistrusts all whites, believing all are merciless in the quest for wealth. In that way his switching

Cover art of a Big Little Book reflecting the novel it retold, *The Ivory Trail*.

of sides, a useful serialization device for extending the narrative, is explained altruistically; Booloola meant to keep anyone from finding the map, and joined whoever would advance that purpose of his own. Jack tells Booloola that the wealth would not be exploited for private gain but to preserve the elephants, and he will serve on a government commission to control the fund.

After a season lasting 34 weeks, the last show was April 23, 1937, with a summer hiatus until September 27, when Jack returned to the airwaves. He was searching for Captain Hughes, one of the original 1933 characters on the show. The trek led Jack, Billy, Betty, and Uncle Jim to Egypt, where they are trapped in the Cave of the Mummies and join the Camel Corps to outwit tomb robbers among the pyramids.

A gift from Sheik Mahmoud of a special whistling ring saves Jack. It contained the symbols of long life, good luck, and secret power, with the Ick bird ("and Lotus mean the glorified being in the sky") in one corner, and the image of Osiris ("the sun god source of life and judge of the dead") on one side, and the Ankh ("means secret power") on the reverse side, popularizing these ancient symbols with new twists for modern listeners. The ring was the January 1938 premium, with a code sheet of the whistle signals used on the program, and attracted orders from three-quarters of a million listeners.

After a 30 week season, *Jack Armstrong* went off the air during the summer of 1938, from April 22, and returned on September 26, 1938. Going to the coast of Zanzibar, Jack helps Uncle Jim as he recovers valuable art objects from a ship sunk by pirates in the Indian ocean. Jack learns deep-sea diving, rescues the marooned crew, and leads the recovery of Uncle Jim's vessel, taken by the pirates. A contest was held to help name the pet monkey of Kazimoto, and nearly 400,000 entries were received.

Jack and his friends, having helped a grateful Nate Pierson find his father's buried treasure chest, are given a key found inside. It proves to be from Karachi, carved from a meteorite of iron, and the details of the sequence are in the second "Better Little Book" based on the show, *Jack Armstrong and the Mystery of the Iron Key*, published by Whitman in August 1939. There are echoes of *Jimgrim* and *The Nine Unknown*, and to a lesser degree *Om* and *Full Moon*, in the naming and conspiracy of the Dorjes and their Thirteen Keys, their use of electricity, and the meteorite. *Jack Armstrong and the Mystery of the Iron Key* also demonstrates the degree to which Mundy completely overcame all the show's injunctions against the supernatural and science fiction.

The dirigible *Golden Secret*, built by Uncle Jim, is sold to his old friend, the Rajah of Rawal Doon, and Jack has to put down a mutiny led by one of the Rajah's crew, Kamaran Khan. (This name was reminiscent of Kurram Khan in *King — of the Khyber Rifles*, and used in the 1934 short story "The Gods Seem Contented," while the airship's commander, Captain Doughty, is named for the friend that Sir Francis Drake hanged who was the subject of "Consistent Anyhow.")

Jack takes a meteorite of iron from Khan which interacts strangely with their key, periodically emitting a whining buzz sound when Uncle Jim holds it over his head, while becoming quiet when he lowers it. The Maharajah is terrified by the key; it is one of the Keys of the Thirteen Dorjes, meaning lightning bolts, a secret organization conspiring to seize control of India. The Maharajah bought the dirigible because airplanes have been unable to fly over the Dorje stronghold. He assigns his groom, Sidiki, to look after the Americans; a comical fellow who pretends not to know English, he proves valiant and resourceful.

The Dorjes have some mysterious way to control electricity along with a type of radio communication. The metal originates from the crater of a meteor from another world that emits strange rays, part electricity, part radioactive, drawing lightning from the clouds which is absorbed and given off in pulsating waves. Jack causes the rocks above the meteorite, loose from the vibrations, to tumble in and cover it under tons of earth. With the Dorjes defeated, the Maharajah gives Jack the remaining 11 keys to take back to America so that scientists can learn the secret of their power. He also offers a share of the Dorje's treasure, but they refuse it, preferring it be returned to the Indians from whom it was stolen.

Returning home to Hudson, Jack next joins an airplane race to Rio de Janeiro. On the return, one of the planes is captured by a gang with a base in an underground city in the jungle, and Betty and another girl are taken captive. Jack finds the secret "Phantom" submarine hideout of Captain Quinto, a soldier of fortune, who plans a revolution from his base beneath a Mayan temple. In the show, Jack, Billy, and Uncle Jim find Betty and her friend by using a "Hike-O-Meter" to guide them through the labyrinth of winding passages and tunnels; in February, 1939, a "Hike-O-Meter" premium received over 650,000 requests in just over a week. Eventually, twice that many were sent out — a ratio of one for every seven young Americans.[36]

This proved to be Mundy's only opportunity to fictionalize Mayan culture, the subject of a planned novel since living at Point Loma; Yucatan was to be one of the stops for Tros on his projected round-the-world voyage.[37] Mundy's theosophical understanding of the sights he had seen in Mexico in 1924 were crystallized in an article written upon his return, "The Maya Mystery — Yucatan," in which he stated that the best way to understand this civilization was through *The Secret Doctrine*.[38] Talbot was intrigued by the Mayan myth that their ancestors had come over the ocean from the East, but did not believe the Mayas were simply derivative of Egypt. Instead, in accord with Blavatsky, Mundy thought that the cultural and artistic similarities between the Mayas and the Egyptians were a result of both deriving from a previous, unknown continent, before known history — Atlantis. William Gates, a widely-published specialist on Mayan culture, had similar persuasions and had come many years before to head the Point Loma School of Antiquity, which became a center of Mayan research. At the end of 1925 Tingley had suggested to Kenneth Morris that he also write on pre–Columbian America.[39] Finishing the first draft over the next four years, eventually the book would be published posthumously as *The Chalchiuhite Dragon* (and, in an interesting connection with *Om*, "Chalchiuhite" means "jade").[40]

By now, Talbot was writing *Jack Armstrong* scripts nearly every evening, year-round. His labors were rewarded as being "tops on the air," with an audience of nine million children, and the next best a distant second.[41] As Dawn recalled, "He had a desk and I had a desk — we had this long table — and he would sit on one side of it, and I was on the other, and dictate to me. I think I acted as a mirror because if he said something that was going in the script and I didn't like it, I showed it in my face and he would say, 'Wait a minute.'"[42] He even played solitaire while composing the scripts.

In the spring of 1939, Jack delivers, all the way from America, an ancient manuscript stolen from the Great Grand Lama of Tibet. The sequence reveals how steeped Mundy was in the setting, simultaneously composing *Old Ugly-Face*. Uncle Jim lands the Flying Fortress, with Jack, Betty, and Billy, amidst storms in the high Tibetan plateaus. Their crew leaves them stranded, but fortunately they encounter Taliesan, who is in the service of the Lama. Taliesan nicknames Betty "Chenresi;" in Mundy's novels, Chullunder Ghose receives this comparison, while in *Tros of Samothrace*, Taliesan had been the high priest of the Druids (and supposed author of many of the sayings added for hardcover publication of the novel in 1934). Aviation fuel is obtained in this remote spot from bandits who robbed a China-bound camel caravan; Taliesan convinces them that by giving him the gas, they may acquire "what is known as merit," and the Lama authorizes forgiveness.

While on the roof of the world, Jack encounters incredible sights, and the monks display the ability to read the thoughts of others and perform feats of strange magic. The promotion was a torpedo flashlight, in three different colors, and 6.6 million were given away with the purchase of two boxes of wheaties.

The last program of the 31-week season, heard on April 28, 1939, is again steeped in the religion and philosophy that was supposedly prohibited, and embodies all that Mundy sought to accomplish in writing *Jack Armstrong*. As in *Old Ugly-Face*, the dialogue is filled with texture and pith, not just the simple exchanges expected in a program of this type.

The episode begins with Jack, Billy, and Betty, in the words of the narrator, "facing Taliesan at the top of a stairway hewn from solid rock, in the mysterious palace of the Great Grand Lama of Tibet. Do you hear the temple bells blown by the wind, on the roofs of buildings that are hidden by white fog through which the sun shines dimly?" Outside, Uncle Jim has just landed the Flying Fortress on the frozen snow. Jack is bursting with questions for Taliesan about who the Grand Lama is and how he knew they had "the happy-blessed-secret-sacred-Sanskrit-parchment-scroll" (all one word in Tibetan). Taliesan tells them "We Tibetans believe that his holiness-the-lotus-born-great-grand-lama is the greatest ruler in all the world, whose greatness resides in his intelligence. His intelligence is so great that he is able to know clairvoyantly and by telepathy whatever he wishes to know." Taliesan is a jolly man, who sings, and laughs at the many questions of Jack, Billy, and Betty with a demeanor more reminiscent of Kris Kringle than a solemn sage, evoking Lobsang Pun. The alliteration and rhythm in such wording accentuates the cultural distinction of the Tibetans while not alienating an American listener.

Jack and the Fairfields will be the first Westerners to ever see the Great Grand Lama, breaking all precedent by admitting them into his presence for "one blessed, happy, destiny-creating minute." His holiness has recognized their sterling character, although preferring to call it higher intelligence, rather than Jack's term, a "hunch." (With such equating of concepts, Mundy's script places Eastern concepts in a Western vernacular.) Taliesan explains that no interpreter will be necessary; as the most intelligent man in the world, the Lama speaks any language he pleases. The door opens magically before them, and as they enter, Betty quietly remarks on the Lama's advanced age, and his beautiful eyes. He is grateful for Jack returning the scroll.

> Jack, I thank you, and I ask you to take my blessing to your country, my special blessing. Tell the boys and girls of the United States that this world is theirs, and they shall use it as they will, and as they are, so shall their world become. If they have hearts of gold, a glorious new golden age awaits us all. If they are brave, they shall find a world full of chivalry. If they are honest, they shall neither fear poverty nor need to beg their bread. All riches are theirs if they are honest. If they are kind to one another, so that kindness overflows like blessed water in a thirsty desert, they shall save the whole world from malice, even meanness, and the war, tearing its heart. Take that message to the boys and girls of the United States.

As the Lama intones "Om mani padme om," Jack promises to proudly convey the message. The Lama's message is safely non-sectarian and motivational, ostensibly building self-esteem, and with a strong socially conscious component suitable for a time of waning Great Depression and looming war. Yet it also encompasses the concept of karma and personal responsibility, and is a type of prayer, removing any aura of "otherness" in the Lama's faith to allow it to seem directly relevant to American youth of the day.

Jack asks Taliesan to tell the Lama that he will spend the rest of his life trying to live that message. Before making a segue to the Wheaties commercial, the announcer further drives the point home by telling the boys and girls listening that he hopes they got every word of the Great Grand Lama's message that Jack is bringing home. "The world is yours, said the Great Grand Lama, and you can make of the world what you will."

Wheaties cereal boxtop advertisement reflects the occult element Mundy added to *Jack Armstrong*.

After a summer "vacation," like the school holidays for the show's young listeners, Jack returned on September 25, 1939, hunting for pirate treasure buried in the West Indies. (While pirates might seem a motif of *Jack Armstrong* otherwise foreign to Mundy's writings, his short stories "Christening Cannon Rock" and "Black Flag" had proved his ability to handle this type of adventure.) Jack uses a new kind of flashlight to send signals in Morse Code — and the "Safety Signal Light Kit" became the October 1939 promotion, sent to 200,000 listeners for a dime and a Wheaties boxtop.

Recovering the treasure, a grateful Cuban government gives a huge diamond to Uncle Jim, which he takes back to Hudson. Jack and his friends are followed when they depart on a 10,000 mile trip to test a new airplane. When they land in Egypt, Uncle Jim produces a "Magic Answer Box," which, when held in the hand, suggests whether the holder is truthful or not. Mundy, who necessarily was involved in the creation of premiums, had objected to a device originally envisioned as a sort of lie-detector, to determine whether children were truthful, when it was under consideration as a test premium. Eventually the idea was adapted instead into the "Magic Answer Box" and advertised as a type of game, decorated with a scarab, ankh, and pyramids to create an Egyptian motif. The "Magic Answer Box" became the premium early in 1940, with over 600,000 orders sent in by listeners.[43]

Jack and the Fairfields meet "the Babu," who serves as a source of humor and causes many importunities, while also advancing the narrative. In all of these respects, the Babu of *Jack Armstrong* resembles the similarly-nicknamed Chullunder Ghose. The radio character's dialogue is amusing, and reminiscent of Ghose's speech, such as describing himself as "this miserable Babu."

Flying across the Pacific to Easter Island gives Jack and Billy time to examine the chest entrusted to Uncle Jim to take to America by the Prince of Lan Dor Ling, who believed that the chest's contents were unique in all the world. Inside are 13 statuettes, the size of bowling pins, each made of solid gold, which Uncle Jim believes are sculptures of ancient kings that came from Easter Island some 50,000 years ago. Billy points out that the statuettes resemble no human being who ever lived, with such a long neck and strangely-shaped ears. (The idea is similar to the set of 32 gold plates, made by an Eastern artist and depicting the initiates of an occult group of which the Biblical Moses was a member, in *Moses and Mrs. Aintree*.) Jack notices how the statuettes resemble the huge stone statues on Easter Island, which "nobody has every explained to anyone's satisfaction." He suspects those on Easter Island are either enlarged copies of the statuettes, or the statuettes are miniatures— despite coming from Lan Dor Ling, on the other side of the world.

The tone of the Easter Island episode of *Jack Armstrong* is completely different from the Tibetan episode or the Congo River script. Whereas the visit with the Lama was contemplative and thought-provoking, and the Congo River script full of action, the Easter Island one is full of quick, short exchanges of dialogue as a new juvenile narrative begins. Instead of the intricate cadences of the Tibetans, the Easter Island emphasizes the boys' slang-ridden dialogue, full of interjections.

Within the guise of a treasure chest, Mundy creates a program more deeply occult in its content than the Tibetan episode, which in its invocation of Buddhist doctrine had still relied on a recognized regional faith. In the Easter Island episode, Mundy's speculations are far more subtle, stated in an off-hand manner. He openly propagandizes for theosophical theories of pre-history and the ancient origins of humanity and culture, long before the establishment of modern civilization. The full implications of the dating of the statues and their discovery on the other side of the Pacific would only be realized by adults, listening carefully, but would be accepted uncritically by children.

These episodes also share a key motif with Mundy's fiction, the centrality of non-white characters. Through the presence of Kazimoto and Booloola on the Congo River, or the Babu, Mundy adds culturally contrasting figures. Admittedly, Kazimoto and the Babu provide some humor. However, Booloola and the Babu also have motivations and objectives of their own; they are trickster figures like Chullunder Ghose who are neither servile nor menacing. Similarly, Taliesan had served as a representative of another part of the Eastern culture in the Tibetan episode, mediating the almost-unapproachable wisdom of the Grand Lama.

In Mundy's recasting of the characters, Billy and Betty represent the skeptics and the doubters, the naive everyman. Uncle Jim remains the wise mentor, the sage guiding the initiate, Jack. However, Mundy's innovation is to make Jack a young version of Athelstan King, Jimgrim, or Tros, who gains wisdom on his odysseys in the remote regions of the world, uncovering occult mysteries.

Despite the unusual elements Mundy was able to inject into *Jack Armstrong*, Mundy believed that he had prostituted himself by stooping to write the "grossly commercial" series, according to Jack Marshall, a local Anna Maria resident. Marshall recalled visiting at the time of the show.

> I went over late one afternoon just before five o'clock when *Jack Armstrong* would come on the radio.
>
> Everyone gathered in the living room around the radio. Mundy's mother-in-law, who was younger than he was, would bring in the script for that day's episode, so he could check it. He had a contract that the producer could not change any of the wording.
>
> Everyone became still when the announcer said, "Jack Armstrong, the All-American boy." No one said a word the entire time and Mundy sat with his ear close to the radio and his head hanging down. After it was over he just sat there for a long time, then would raise his head and look around, and say:
>
> "God, what tripe!"[44]

When Talbot died, he was about to begin a five-year contract on the show, and only two more scripts in the current sequence remained to be completed, according to Dawn. "We had discussed it, I knew where he was going, so I wrote the four agents in Chicago and said I would like to try and do it, and I did it. I'm sure I had help doing it: the conversations [Talbot and I] had had. I knew his way of phrasing things because I think we had done 750 scripts before that and so I was able to complete the series and have it broadcast."[45] Many years later, Wyatt Blassingame corroborated her recollection, saying she had asked him to help her finish the season.[46] The final episode of the Easter Island sequence, the last "Mundy" broadcast to survive, seems unusually compressed and full of action, with a near-frantic pace.

The Mundys last vacation was a summer in Virginia Beach in 1937. He had hoped to go to a number of European countries, and visit such figures as Professor Wincenty Lutoslawski in Poland. Lutoslawski, author of *Preexistence and Reincarnation* (1928) and other books, had begun a correspondence, the two exchanging volumes by one another. Lutoslawski, who was not a theosophist, sought testimonies from other writers "that each of us has lived in human shape many times and that we reap now what we have sown ages ago."[47] Talbot was impressed with the Pole's learning, and in turn, Lutoslawski reviewed Mundy's works and wanted to translate them into Polish.

However, the Mundys delayed a European trip until the next year; and by then war had overtaken any such plans. Only the second choice of a trip around the entire United States seemed a possibility. So the Mundys drove some 10,000 miles during the 12 months from mid–1938 to mid–1939, stopping at road camps, groups of small rental cottages that were the equivalent of motels at the time.

Stomach problems had been bothering Talbot's health for years. In 1934, as Dawn told Rose Wilder Lane from Manchester, he had the most severe recurrence of intestinal problems that struck unpredictably during their travels. Talbot remained in the hospital for 10 days, with treatments to be stretched out for several months. In 1936, he had abruptly quit smoking after a fit of coughing. He had habitually used a tin of Luckies, 50 cigarettes a day, and, as he noted, "Dawn (God pity her) smokes Spuds."[48] (Dawn remained a heavy smoker to the end of her long life.) Within another two years, his weight had declined from 205 pounds to 150, and the good-humor that was so typical of his nature was no longer so evident, as Dawn noticed. "He was a very vital person. I never saw him really moody except when he was coming down ill and didn't know it; and then he was moody when reading all the terrible things that were happening in Europe prior to the war, and that upset him very much."[49] Talbot's once round face became drawn and lean, and those meeting him believed him to be a man in his 70s—while Dawn had retained her youthful appearance, so that the disparity in their ages was widely regarded as much greater than in fact it was. By early 1937, the Mundys had known that his sister was ill with a form of diabetes, but did not connect the malady to his own condition; a Connecticut physician had noticed no problems.

Moving to Florida, Dawn hoped that a change to a warmer, more relaxing locale than the northeast might improve his health. As well, she was looking for a good home for her parents in their retirement. Talbot preferred an area on the ocean, and Jack Hanna advised the Mundys to rent a home he had found on the Gulf Coast, but north of Casey Key. Anna Maria was a five-mile island that is the northernmost part of a key located at the southern mouth of Tampa Bay, a half-hour drive from the nearest large town. The upper part of the island was populated by several hundred people, with the middle uninhabited, and the lower end of the key a resort. Resembling Point Loma, Anna Maria is a wind-swept, sunny strip of land isolated from the mainland and along a bay. At night, the lights are dim from the shore, and the white-tipped breakers, the moon, and the glistening of the pinkish white coral sand provide the only reflection under the light panoply of stars. Like Casey Key, during the summer the ocean temperature rises to bath-level.

During a 1920s Florida boom, Alvin I. Albinson, a Swede from Minnesota, had built one of the largest residences on the island, "the house of seven gables," in the English Tudor style, at No. 1 Beach Avenue.[50] (The lot that once contained the Mundy home was subdivided in the 1990s into a development to eventually include six large residences.) Picture windows overlooked the beach, and the rhythmic roaring of the surf was readily audible indoors during the night. Beach is a short, dead-end street that leads directly into the white sandy shore, and the Mundys frequently went swimming in the morning and walked along the beach at night.

The Mundys were not close to the community in Anna Maria; indeed, they were comparative Bohemians. Talbot again took up his hobby of amateur photography; he assembled the necessary equipment and darkroom whenever he could afford it.

The last publicity photograph of Mundy, his health undermined by diabetes.

An 11-year-old girl reportedly went through their trash on one occasion, examining some of the discarded photos, and was startled to find several nude studies of Dawn. This was Peggy Blassingame, daughter of Wyatt and Gertrude Blassingame, who were the Mundys closest neighbors, living two blocks south (with only one unoccupied house between them) in a much simpler home.[51] Blassingame was also a writer, and quickly became a fast friend of the Mundys, although Blassingame had read no more than "The Soul of a Regiment."[52]

After a month in the new home, Dawn's parents came down for the Thanksgiving and Christmas season, deciding to sell their Manchester residence. The four-bedroom house had enough room for them, as well as visitors, including Talbot's nephew Peter Gribbon, Harold's son, who died in the Merchant Navy during the coming war. A local couple employed as houseman and cook lived over the garage and completed the household. Albinson sold the home to the Mundys early in 1939, for around $13,000 (Blassingame, by contrast, had spent about $2500 for his home).[53] Like the last time Mundy had bought a home, at the end of 1924 in Point Loma, he promptly went into debt making renovations.

To cover the expenses, Talbot had to obtain life insurance as extra collateral toward a mortgage. What was expected to be a routine physical with a local general practitioner discovered the cause of Talbot's long-standing malady: a blood test indicated he was on the brink of a diabetic coma. Dawn recalled that Talbot had to

The "House of Seven Gables," at No. 1 Beach Avenue in Anna Maria, Florida, the final Mundy home. (Courtesy Anna Maria Historical Society)

overcome his horror of hypodermic needles. "From then on he had to have insulin every day, and I had to give it to him. I had never handled a hypodermic needle either, but I learned very quickly. So he was a lamb about that. I fixed recipes for breakfast, lunch, and dinner, and I weighed it on that little gram scale. I learned about diabetes, I read books about diabetes.... Do you know we had to go home from the doctor's office to the *Encyclopædia Britannica* to look up what it was?"[54] Diabetes had been a contributing factor in his father's death, and took the life of Talbot's sister Daisy in September 1939, shortly after recognition of his own condition. Three months later, he had begun to recover.

The Mundys obtained most of their news via the radio; Talbot listened to the 7:30 radio programs from Europe each morning, and tuned in to the frightening broadcasts of Adolf Hitler's speeches. While a couple of Mundy's early 1920s *Adventure* novels mentioned Benito Mussolini in a laudatory manner, Mundy compensated for this initial receptiveness by denouncing fascism in all its forms. During the depression, he was troubled by its potential rise in America, and he wrote virulently against Hitler from the outset, warning friends and publishers of the threat of another European war. He was far more aware than his brother and other associates in England. "He could see it coming," Dawn recalled, and those who naively hoped for peace "bothered him terribly."[55]

Mundy had also been concerned since 1919 with the rise of communism, and believed America must oppose it. Nonetheless, Mundy had supported the Republican cause in the Spanish Civil War, partly because of his opposition to fascism, and Dawn recalled one of the few incidents to ever make him truly angry. "There was a picture on the front of the *New York Times* magazine of the Pope at the time, blessing the bombs that fell. Things like that made Talbot mad. Then he could use four-letter words vehemently — he had no use for that sort of thing."[56]

Despite extreme fatigue, Mundy spent his last evening, August 5, 1940, in lively fashion. As Dawn recalled, "He had a beautiful last day — that is in my heart. It was a Sunday, and we walked down the beach; a hurricane had gone by. In the morning he had said, 'I've never been so tired.' I said, 'Let's take a vacation. We don't have to start writing scripts again for a month.' That's the one thing that still gives me heat waves when I think about it. Tomorrow we were going to decide to take a vacation."[57] The evening was spent with the Blassingames, Mundy telling them literary lessons he had learned, punctuated with gestures of his thin hand as he leaned back. Wyatt recalled, "They brought over an ancient, yellow, small, male dog (I can't remember the breed) to see if it would mate with a small mongrel I owned that was in heat. Nothing happened between the dogs, but the four of us — Dawn and Talbot, my wife and I — drank a good bit of whiskey and Talbot was in fine fettle, one story after another. Sometime around midnight they took their dog and walked back home."[58] In Dawn's words, "When we came back you could see the sky with the moon behind the clouds, and I said, 'Now how do you feel?' and he said, 'I feel much better — I feel fine.'"[59] The next morning Peggy Blassingame went over to the Mundys to practice on their piano. Dawn met her at the door and told her she couldn't play that morning, and she'd be over later to explain — there were few telephones on the island. "She came, told us that she had awakened that morning, got up, turned on the radio to the news, and told Talbot to wake up. He had died in his sleep."[60]

As Mundy had written, "The experience called death is a change of consciousness," and Wyatt remarked that Talbot firmly believed in the transmigration of souls. "If he awoke before he died, and knew he was going to die, then he wasn't afraid — he was excited about this something new that was going to happen to him."[61] Fifteen years earlier, Talbot had remarked, "What problems life presents — and we here for no purpose but to solve the puzzle! The reward? The privilege of disentangling, if we can, more complicated ones. No doubt we need a rest when the mortician steps in...."[62] Talbot Mundy's body was taken to St. Petersburg for cremation. The funeral was short and private, with only a few local friends; Wyatt Blassingame read the 23rd and 19th psalms, which had figured so prominently in *Old Ugly-Face*.

XII

Legacy

The years after Talbot Mundy's death have found him far from forgotten. Successive generations of readers have discovered Mundy's writing with a passion at least equal to the appreciation given him while he was alive. In conclusion, I will offer a survey and evaluation of the themes and motifs common to all his work.

While Mundy received long obituaries in the *New York Times* and many American journals, including those around Bradenton, few of these tributes gave serious attention to his writing. His passing was almost completely overlooked by the London *Times* and other British periodicals; Mundy had become a man who wrote for his adopted land and its readers, not those of the country of his birth. This may have been the reason that Talbot's brother Harold did not learn of his passing until Dawn responded to his routine letter to Talbot some months later. With the outbreak of war in 1939, Harold had volunteered to form and command a Home Guard Battalion for the local defense of Dover and Folkestone, and these efforts contributed to his own death at the end of 1944.

Dawn presented a will to the Manatee Court dated September 18, 1931, bequeathing any property to her, and appointing her sole executrix. Probate did not begin until 1942 and was completed two years later, with the estate declared insolvent and without assets. Bill Cox and Walter S. Hardin appraised Mundy's literary estate on behalf of the court in 1942 and declared it to be of no value, with all contracts voided by Mundy's death. Their inventory of material published in the United States and England, some of it under the name of Walter Galt, included 47 books, 130 novelettes and short stories, and 23 articles. The inventory does not include the unpublished manuscript of what became *I Say Sunrise*, and most intriguing is the mention of four unpublished novelettes.

In the year after Mundy's death, two new novelettes did appear. First was "The Night the Clocks Stopped," published in the March 1941 edition of *Adventure*. His last published original story, *Odds on the Prophet*, appeared in the August 10, 1941 issue of *Short Stories* and was one of his least significant, reading as if it were salvaged from his files.

By the time that *Odds on the Prophet* appeared, 10 months after Talbot's death, Dawn had married Eric Provost, who had helped her on the mortgage arrangements as the estate was settled. Dawn remained at the home on Anna Maria until her marriage, then moved to nearby Whitfield Estates, where she finally had the family she had hoped for, a son and daughter.

Dawn retained a sympathetic regard for theosophy in the subsequent years, and her friendship with Natacha Rambova continued until Natacha's death in 1966.[1] Dawn remained in Florida until 1973, when, widowed a second time, she moved to Morgan Hill, California, where she passed away in 1988.

The renaissance of literary interest in Talbot Mundy began when a friend of his, the British publisher Alan Dakers, inquired about his unpublished philosophical manuscript, resulting in the posthumously published *I Say Sunrise*. It was initially authored in 1932, while living in Mallorca, as *Thus Spake the Devil* under the pseudonym of Mallory Grayson. Failing to interest a publisher at the time, Mundy rewrote the book for a British concern while living at Casey's Key in the summer of 1934. However, the book was not considered the "Talbot Mundy" type of manuscript and it was rejected again, lying dormant for the next six years.

Finally, Dawn told her husband, "I think you have tried to cover too many subjects and have missed finding your focal point. What you're really trying to say is not coming in — you've got too much clutter all around it, your own personal antipathies. You should go through it and let those go." He told her to edit it and then show it to him. This was the very night before he died. Dawn said she "had the most fantastic experience" when she began six weeks later. "I had the whole tome, the whole book, and I started reading it, and I started typing. And I would come to a place, and I'd say in myself quietly, 'I can't do anything about this, I'm going to cut this piece out. I don't like it, it doesn't belong here...!' It was as if I had contacted a river flowing by and as long as I was working on that manuscript I'd get feedback: 'Now you're not going to cut that bit, I like that!' 'Yes I am — I don't like that bit.' All right, that is how it came down to a little book, *I Say Sunrise*."[2] Because of the subjectivity of her selections, what finally appeared must be regarded as hardly a definitive, unbiased text.

The fragments which are bequeathed as *I Say Sunrise* leave a controversial, occasionally solemn, although ultimately optimistic masterpiece. Although Alan Dakers believed the book was still too vehement, it was already down to under 200 pages and Dawn would cut no more; it was published in 1947. Dakers selected the title by choosing the final sentence from the Preface, which Dawn had left untouched; it was also foreshadowed by a line from one of his *Theosophical Path* articles, "The grandeur that Theosophy reveals is like the sunrise."[3]

Despite the temptation to regard *I Say Sunrise* as Mundy's final testament, because of the editing and the prior date of its writing, that honor must be reserved for *Old Ugly-Face*, although there is also much in common between the volumes. Mundy places his teaching in a Christian context, believing his readers would be most familiar with this more Western perspective.

I Say Sunrise is different from the poems and sayings in his novels, and even his articles in *The Theosophical Path*, with their rhetorical composition. Mundy often makes seemingly radical statements as the premise of a chapter, then uses portions of the Bible, especially psalms and sayings, to support his points. While emulating their style, he rephrases scripture to indicate how their original meanings validate many of his assertions. By the end, the reader understands such seeming conundrums as unto him who hath, shall more be given in a completely new way—Mundy suggests it means wisdom, which he defines as true affluence, not monetary wealth.

Proposing an appeal to wisdom — as differentiated from knowledge — in place of God, *I Say Sunrise* is essentially a manifesto of Mundy's personal religious philosophy.[4] At the same time, the church was one of the principal targets, and Dawn said the book "brought forth all of his strong dislikes of bureaucracy, lawyers, doctors, and the Catholic Church;" it is full of his disdain for ecclesiasticism for impeding true spirituality.[5]

At Point Loma, Mundy had written that "if all pain is imaginary, human beings nonetheless imagine it, and suffer," but his interest in Christian Science had resurfaced during his marriage to Dawn, who believed that he had the power to physically heal her when the need was urgent.[6] As Mundy wrote to Wincenty Lutoslawski, "It is my belief that if Theosophy and Christian Science could be blended, that would be a great step forward in the evolution of human consciousness."[7] Mundy found H.P. Blavatsky and Mary Baker Eddy to be complementary, attacking the same problem from opposite directions, despite the opposition of their organizations to one another. Mundy believed Eddy's insights into the illusion of "mortal mind" needed the work of Blavatsky and a knowledge or reincarnation to become complete.[8] *I Say Sunrise* reveals Eddy and Blavatsky to have been the most important influences on Mundy; spiritualism is only mentioned to be denounced briefly.

The result is a sometimes uneasy synthesis, without the unity of his *Theosophical Path* articles. Situating Blavatsky and Eddy as the heroines of *I Say Sunrise*, Mundy was well aware that one or the other, and more likely both, were bound to provoke negative reactions; indeed, this was his purpose. He explained that he used this device to remind his readers of their own preconceptions and often spontaneous reactions to unfamiliar ways of thought. Rather than being imprisoned by prejudices, he encourages open-mindedness and thinking for oneself. Silence is necessary to create a quiet place in which to think, without the well-meaning interference of friends, and "argument is merely an effort at self-justification."[9]

However, Mundy thereby allows much of the power of his own thoughts to be diffused by many reader's doubts of his sources, prejudice indeed obscuring his message. Had he based his assertions purely on his own experiences of "mystic thought and practice," rather than such controversial authorities, *I Say Sunrise* probably would have won more approval.[10] But Mundy was unwilling to lose the opportunity to show that "our prejudices are the bars of our dungeons" or to fail to acknowledge Blavatsky and Eddy as his own principal guides.[11]

As he had written to Lutoslawski, "I affirm that Herbert Spencer, McTaggart, Bradley, and Bertram Russell have, as you describe it, a 'very insufficient understanding of Reality.' All of them set forth to find the Real by dissecting the unreal, like the students in a morgue."[12] Mundy divides consciousness between the personality, that dies, and the individual that is indestructible and without dimension. Life, he writes, is the eternal evolution of consciousness, where all experience takes place, away from materiality toward wisdom, which is the source of happiness.

He wrote modestly in *I Say Sunrise*, urging his reader not to take his words or examples dogmatically, but only as helpful illustrations to stir consciousness. *I Say*

Sunrise is addressed, not to the successful, but to those who have also known sorrow, grief, despair, and shame, to the point that suicide seems attractive. The volume seeks to prove that from failure comes the best time to start appreciating and exploring the adventure of existence. The book was enlightened with the thinking of the adventurer: "Everything begins now. Forget yesterday. Leave yesterday to bury itself in its own mistakes. It is always Now."[13]

As his most ambitious, intense book, *I Say Sunrise* is "a metaphysical classic," beautifully written and powerfully conceived, and, though less obvious, a marvel of organization, all the more surprising considering its revision.[14] It is a remarkable book, leaving little doubt as to his own genius as a writer and philosopher. The book is filled with insight, such as "No fact has ever meant exactly the same to any two people, because no two people have ever been in exactly the same stage of evolution."[15] "You can't 'have' an idea. You can't 'get' one. Ideas *Are*. You can become conscious of them."[16] *I Say Sunrise* was reviewed in the theosophical journal of the time and John Cowper Powys agreed to publicly endorse the book, writing Alan Dakers that he found it so "extremely enthralling that I've practically read it through at a go.... I warrant you'll be soon getting rid of all yours already printed. I rejoice in— and wholly and entirely agree with— the *enjoyment* method and practice and principles in this book."[17] While probably too iconoclastic, eclectic, and individual an effort ever to evoke widespread attention, the book is popular and has been in print almost continuously since publication.

Along with bringing out the American edition of *I Say Sunrise* in 1949, Milton F. Wells of Philadelphia also issued intelligent versions of *The Devil's Guard* in 1945 (hoping to start an Oriental Book Club) and *Old Ugly-Face* in 1950. The latter was the first Mundy book in English to include a thoughtful literary appreciation, by Clyde B. Clason, who also wrote stories of the Far East. Only two years earlier, the first fanzine article about Mundy had appeared, Darrell C. Richardson's "Talbot Mundy: Oriental Mystic" in the Fall 1948 issue of *Fantasy Commentator*. Otherwise, the only other posthumous Mundy publications had been a single reissue of *King— of the Khyber Rifles* by Grosset & Dunlap in 1942, which sold over 6000 copies, along with occasional reprints of short stories, including "The Soul of a Regiment" by *Adventure* in 1950, 1954, and 1970.

Wells died while planning more Mundy reissues, but the seed he had planted blossomed elsewhere. In 1951, the widely-read genre reprint magazine *Famous Fantastic Mysteries* colorfully reprinted *The Grey Mahatma*, followed by *Full Moon* in 1953, heralding Mundy's emerging classic status in fantasy literature. These editions benefitted from Virgil Finlay's graphic illustrations, among the best accompaniment his work ever received. Mundy fared less well in 1953, when Royal Book's oversize paperbacks issued five of his stories, often paired within the same volume with incompatible stories by different authors. Not only did Royal covers rely on women in distress, not to be found in the books, but Mundy's titles were changed as well: *The King in Check* became *Affair in Araby*, *W.H.* (in its first American book edition) became *The Queen's Warrant*, *Jimgrim* became *Jimgrim Sahib*, and *The Ivory Trail* was turned into *Trek East*, with all the poems eliminated (*Full Moon* was also included in the series).

Ironically, the centerpiece of the Mundy renaissance also had the least resemblance to his work, a movie of *King— of the Khyber Rifles*. Empire adventure movies were reaching a new peak of popularity during the decade after World War II, with many set in India given the added interest in the country due to the climax of the struggle for independence and the division with Pakistan. The new films in this cycle, whether produced in England or Hollywood, never thoughtlessly adopted the unconditional support for British rule of the pre–World War II era, and offered critiques of colonialism.

In early 1951 20th Century–Fox recalled owning the rights to the Mundy novel. Studio chief Darryl Zanuck, regarding the title *King— of the Khyber Rifles* as "sensational," telephoned producer Frank P. Rosenberg and assigned him to create a new narrative. Rosenberg perused the scripts using the title written from 1936–40, and quickly realized their drawbacks. He proposed moving the story back to the 19th century with a social consciousness strain. Zanuck appreciated the combination of a subtle "message" while still subsuming it beneath "a showmanship picture" that would be "a boxoffice proposition."[18]

First Walter Doniger, then Niven Busch, worked on scripts, Busch conceiving a hero during the mutiny who is a half-caste, the son of a British father and Indian mother, but falls in love with a young English woman. By the end of the year, Rosenberg still believed he did not have an adequate story, and asked Harry Kleiner, a 35-year-old contract writer at Fox, to prepare a treatment.

Although ostensibly unfamiliar with the Mundy book, Kleiner's three treatments, written from late December, 1951, through early January, 1952, had more resemblance to the novel than any of the other material written for this version of *King of the Khyber Rifles*. A number of Busch and Doniger ideas are used, but in an entirely new framework. The ultimate film began to take shape in Kleiner's final treatment, which removed many of the Mundy-style incidents involving caves and disguise to instead emphasize the regimental milieu, and how a half-caste British officer is reconciled to the father of the English girl who loves him.

Six months passed until the contract writer team of Ivan Goff and Ben Roberts were assigned to *King of the Khyber Rifles*, and spent from August 1952 developing a story line and fine-tuning the script, constantly rewriting dialog. Goff, born in Australia, grew up amidst the lore of the British empire and developed most of the narrative line. He was familiar with Mundy's novels and at least examined it as a source for ideas.

Goff, as well as Rosenberg, was particularly concerned with the history, and the background of 1857 began to emerge as the linchpin of the story. Free of distracting comic relief, *King of the Khyber Rifles* is essentially the story of one man, exploring King's personal difficulties as he tries to find his own social position in a world polarized between native and Anglo, creating a conflict truly unique to its time and place.

The most intriguing shared element between Mundy's book and the final movie is a character of Eurasian ancestry, but it is shifted from Yasmini (who is eliminated entirely) to King. In the movie, having King fall in love with a British girl provides an opportunity for exploring racial attitudes in a colonial setting. Visiting the fort along the Khyber Pass, as unlikely as this would be, is the daughter of the commanding officer, Susan Maitland, who falls in love with the "half-caste" King.

Fox's directing "King" was appropriately assigned to *King of the Khyber Rifles*. Henry King had little input at the subsequent story conferences; his usual fascination for history simply left him in this instance, and he never looked at the Talbot Mundy novel.[19] Yet *King of the Khyber Rifles* won him the award of the Screen Directors Guild for the year. He plays down the scenes of conflict throughout, emphasizing character and beliefs over action, pacing the picture slowly in a realistic fashion, with equally slow editing.

By May, "Ty" Power, Fox's long standing leading star, especially in adventure pictures, and Henry King's close friend, had been, as expected, set for the lead in *King of the Khyber Rifles*. Power looked older than his 40 years, giving the role of Captain King a restrained, quietly brooding quality that verged on a lack of emotion.

Contract player Terry Moore pursued the role of Susan Maitland assiduously in order to be cast opposite Power, and imbues her part with a naive sense of puppy-love, in contrast to Power's quiet maturity. "Moore had nothing at all," Ivan Goff recalled. "It was very bad casting, because she should have been an aristocratic British girl, from a very fine family, and she should be as British and regal as it would be possible to be, which then makes the fact of her falling in love with the half caste all the more unheard of, and that could have been conveyed just with different casting, really, instead of a cute little blonde."[20]

King of the Khyber Rifles was well produced, on a $3 million budget, although without any sense of extravagance or lavish quality; some critics regarded its scale, budget and cast size as inadequate to the subject.[21] Zanuck was enthusiastic about using Lone Pine, California, in place of India; Lone Pine was 240 miles north of Hollywood in the shadow of the Sierra Nevada range. The nearby mountain passes substituted well, the purported Himalayan mountain peaks even impressing Mundy's widow Dawn as authentic.[22]

The movie was shot in the bright, full hues of Technicolor over three months with temperatures around 110 degrees. The decision had been made by April, 1953, to photograph in Fox's new widescreen process, CinemaScope, making it the fourth Fox production to utilize the anamorphic lens. Rather than using CinemaScope simply to display an abundance of action, Henry King emphasized the landscape of the "Indian" setting, frequently situating Mount Whitney in the background.[23]

Rosenberg selected Bernard Herrmann to write the score and his music was primarily in the background and almost imperceptible; there were exotic, foreign themes used in the titles, but these never appeared as battle or marching music. Widely touted as Fox's Christmas release, *King of the Khyber Rifles* became a box-office hit, and is still popular on television today.

King of the Khyber Rifles opens with colorful, lively footage of cavalry on the gallop beneath the credits, with the caption, "India—1857—the hundredth year of British rule." The forces of Kurram Khan (Guy Rolfe) hide among the rocks, attacking a British column led by Captain Alan King. A dissident Indian, Ahmed, provides them a moment's warning and a few minutes later, Lt. Heath's force comes to their relief. (Ahmed was played by Frank Lackteen; he had been cast as Kazimoto in the 1932 Mundy film, *The Jungle Mystery*.) While King rescues one of his men, Heath

Locale, the widescreen to reveal it, and Mundy's source novel figure in this advertisement.

(John Justin), an elitist, stands by indolently, warning him of native treachery. From the outset, with this dialogue, *King of the Khyber Rifles* establishes both the sheer stupidity of British thinking (in the mistrust of Ahmed) as well as the unrepentant racism underlying it.

The British fort along the Khyber Pass is first seen in a fanciful fashion, with Susan Maitland riding her horse as bagpipes play in the noonday sun. King explains to her father that Ahmed's brother was tortured, and in revenge he betrayed Kurram Khan, and would now "like to eat the British salt and join his cousins in the Khyber Rifles." As Maitland, 43-year-old Michael Rennie brought his usual dignity and a stern military rectitude to the role.

In town, King visits the father who adopted him; the families of both his parents disowned them when they married. In a scene eliminated in most prints, Hamid Bahra (Maurice Colbourne) looks back on how he reared him alongside his own son, Hassan, who, King learns, has adopted the name Kurram Khan to lead the rebellion.

Because of his racial status, King is given command of the unruly Afridi Khyber Rifles, a regiment of undisciplined Sepoys. He has accepted the racial snobbery and is accustomed to being snubbed by his fellow officers, but the treatment angers Susan.

Susan continues to pursue King, insisting on accompanying him to Peshawar, and they must flee to the desert where some of Kurram Khan's men try to take her hostage. When they are reported missing, Maitland is clearly fearful of more. He sends out several search parties, and when they are finally located, King is shown clutching the faint Susan possessively, as if to confirm the worst racial fears—although his behavior with her has been entirely that of a gentleman.

The first half of *King of the Khyber Rifles*, with Susan the principal other character, drags from insufficient suspense; this lack of balance becomes especially noticeable with prints which delete the Hamid Bahra scene. In the words of the *New Yorker*, "When Mr. Power is mooning over Miss Moore, the film is a terrible nuisance, but when he gets to charging around the hills of India, things pick up considerably."[24] The second half, by contrast, centers around Kurram Khan, his camp, and the conflict with the Khyber Rifles over their firearms.

Meanwhile, Baird's patrol has been captured by Kurram Khan, and King impersonates a deserter to gain access to his foster brother, and he is warily welcomed. Sneaking up while Kurram Khan is asleep, the memory of childhood friendship prompts King to hesitate a fatal second, and, captured, Khan personally spares King—promising that the slate is wiped clean and their next meeting will be as enemies.

Maitland's punkah-wallah spreads the word that the bullets for the new, longer-range Enfield rifles, which must be bitten to load, have been greased with pig's fat. With the Sepoys driven to open resistance, King acts as a mediator for the British by demonstrating his disbelief in the gossip, and Ahmed leads the men in following him.

However, by the time they arrive at the cliff behind Kurram Khan's encampment, King's men have resolved not to use the rifles, but offer to follow him with their knives. The surprise night attack succeeds, and the Khyber Rifles memorably return to the fort in a loose column, wounded, bloody and exhausted. Soon they are

248   XII. Legacy

Advertising art in the Mexican lobbycard of *King of the Khyber Rifles*, with inset of Tyrone Power as Alan King and Terry Moore as Susan Maitland.

back at maneuvers, observed approvingly by Maitland and Susan. King has overcome native and English suspicions to be recognized as a hero and establish not just his equality within the fort, but his eligibility to marry Susan.

King is in a unique position; his half-caste status, negotiating between British and Indian with a knowledge of both, is no longer a drawback, and has enabled the victory to take place. The imperial conflict shown is between sons of India, whether Kurram Khan and his men or King, Ahmed, and the Khyber Rifles.

King of the Khyber Rifles evades the central question of the desire for Indian independence through depicting Kurram Khan as far more ruthless than the flawed British presence. Khan is fighting the occupation from a desire to rule India himself, a convention by which adventure films justify a colonial presence. Simultaneously, this unique setting of an Indian outpost at the time of the mutiny offers King the only possible world where he can win recognition for his own merits. Alan King is recognized as the role-model from the outset, but the stress is not simply on his courage, but more on the different nature of the challenges he must face in living daily with prejudice all around him. Only in India is he able to partake of both sides of his ancestry, following in his father's military footsteps while enjoying the association with his mother's forebears. *King of the Khyber Rifles*, like Mundy's writing, shows East and West meeting, and mingling through the adventure, both in the personal ancestry of King, and uniting a couple representing both worlds.

King of the Khyber Rifles has been criticized, justifiably, as scarcely a version of the novel, only taking, out of context, the mixed race theme, the name Kurram Khan, and one line regarding building an empire in India. And yet it is, unquestionably, the work with which Talbot Mundy's name is most widely connected today, and its plot is often attributed to him. This is not so problematic; Mundy himself had used the device of the young King raised alongside an Indian who becomes an adversary when he leads a rebellion, as the preface to *Jungle Jest*. The resemblances between *King of the Khyber Rifles* and Mundy's own unproduced 1936 movie treatment, *Fifty-Seven*, are remarkable. Both are tales of the Sepoy rebellion, analyzing fictional portions of the conflict as analogous to the whole and offering unusual love stories. They note the incidents regarding the rifles and how the younger officers better grasp the rebellion and overcome it. Despite relative inexperience, an ancestral connection enables a newcomer to have an instinctive understanding of India, better able to recognize and handle the disturbance than more senior officers. Both heroes are disliked by fellow officers, even ostracized, but they earn the respect and following of their native regiments.

Dawn Mundy Provost was living in Sarasota, Florida, when she heard the news of the proposed remake on July 31, 1951, the 20th anniversary of her wedding to Talbot. Bobbs-Merrill had been in contact with her occasionally since 1944, regarding copyright renewals, a matter not handled by Brandt & Brandt, and occasional reprints. The original contract for *The Black Watch* gave 20th Century–Fox exclusive motion picture rights throughout the world forever, and although there was nothing in the original 1928 contract to prevent the studio from filming the novel a second time, they decided to pay her a "technical assignment" of $2,000 to guarantee those rights. Under the 1928 contract's stipulation of a 50 percent commission to Bobbs-Merrill, the publisher kept half of that fee. However, they did persuade the studio to limit the television clause to the screening of the film, so that any broadcast rights for another version would revert to her.

Dawn sent her correspondence with Bobbs-Merrill over the movie rights to Murray Segal, a New York lawyer, asking for information. "The next thing I knew, I had sued these people," she said.[25] Segal maintained that the original sale of the work applied only to the original contract, and that the remake of the film was a separate matter because a new copyright was in effect, replacing the one under which rights were first sold.[26] After six months of inactivity, Bobbs-Merrill hoped Dawn would drop the case, but 20th Century–Fox joined them as co-defendant and she faced the combined battery of experienced attorneys of two large corporations. Bobbs-Merrill pointed out that they, not Dawn or Brandt & Brandt, had renewed the copyright on *King— of the Khyber Rifles*, and that they had arranged with the Gilberton Company for a superb comic version of the novel for the esteemed "Classics Illustrated" series, which sold over a half million copies and appeared in many languages.[27]

By contrast, Brandt & Brandt's Bernice Baumgarten, whom Mundy had called "the little bitch," and who once told John Marquand that *The Late George Apley* was not worth finishing, had sold reprint rights for *King–of the Khyber Rifles* to Universal Publishing under a contract which allowed for re-writing of the novel.[28] Universal issued the book in their notorious Beacon Books paperback line, revised to include numerous passages of soft-core erotica. Although promising to indicate the work was modernized, instead it was published under Mundy's name as the "Uncensored edition."

The case of *Provost vs. Bobbs-Merrill* finally came to trial in New York in April 1955, after the movie had been made and released. Dawn expected the trial to last a week, but instead waited five weeks in the wintry city as the case was delayed. The chief lawyer for the defendant believed that although the fraud charge might have been withdrawn from the jury, and the case against 20th Century–Fox dismissed, the negligence charge was more difficult to defend against, and a compromise verdict or appeal by Dawn of an adverse verdict might be possible.[29] Dawn finally agreed to a settlement in which Bobbs-Merrill paid $2,000 to her attorney for expenses, and believed she had "the satisfaction of having them admit that they had not done right by me."[30]

Meanwhile, fan interest in Mundy increased. He received literary recognition in 1953 in *333 — A Bibliography of the Science-Fantasy Novel*. Two years later, Bradford M. Day compiled the first bibliography of Mundy's work, a groundbreaking publication; after asking for additional new information in a 1974 issue of *Pulp*, a revised version appeared in Day's 1978 *Bibliography of Adventure: Mundy, Burroughs, Rohmer, Haggard*.

In 1958 and 1959, respectively, Gnome Press, a fantasy reprint publisher, reissued *Tros of Samothrace* and *Purple Pirate*, cementing the growing reputation of the Tros books as among his most popular in the years since Mundy's death. *Queen Cleopatra* was given its first paperback printing in 1959 by Ace Books, keeping it in print throughout the 1960s — once with a cover resembling Elizabeth Taylor, as seen in the unrelated 1963 film, *Cleopatra*.

From 1967 to 1971, Mundy's writing was brought to the attention of a new generation of receptive readers by Avon's publication of a series of widely sold mass market paperbacks of *Om — The Secret of Ahbor Valley*, *The Nine Unknown*, *The Devil's Guard*, and *Jimgrim*. *Queen Cleopatra* and *Purple Pirate* were also included, and *Tros of Samothrace* was divided into four shorter novels, *Tros*, *Helma*, *Liafail*, and *Helene*, along the lines of the original serialization format in *Adventure*. Unfortunately, unlike the four Grim novels, these Tros versions were given rather lurid covers, especially the version put out by Tandem Press of London. In 1968, in London, Cedric Chivers published hardcover editions of *Om — The Secret of Ahbor Valley* and *Tros of Samothrace*. *King, of the Khyber Rifles* was published in England by Tom Stacy in 1973. That same year, Centaur published the small paperback, *Caesar Dies*, the first American book version of this story. The timing was ideal, presenting Mundy to the "sixties" generation, for whom the very occult beliefs and anti-colonialism that had once diminished his popularity made him timely.

Mundy was also remembered on the continent. A translation of *Guns of the Gods* into Italian, entitled *Il Tesoro de Sialpore*, was printed in 1944, with a preface by Claudio Montalbano, the first appearance of a Mundy book in any language to include a critical perspective. Thanks to theosophists, *Om — The Secret of Ahbor Valley* appeared as *Om — Het Geheim van de Ahbor Vallei* in the Hague in 1984. Due to the interest of Jacques Bergier, who wrote of Mundy in a chapter in his 1970 book, *Admirations*, several Mundy novels appeared in France. *The Nine Unknown* was translated as *Les neuf inconnus* in 1972; the 1930 Louis Postif translation of *Om* as *L'Oeuf de Jade* was reprinted in 1980; and *Full Moon* was translated under its British title, *There Was a Door*, as *Il était une porte* in 1990. Bergier's appreciation was the first major critical analysis of Mundy's oeuvre, ironic in that such a tribute did not emerge from either the land of his birth or his adopted home.

In 1977 Zebra Books issued a mass market softcover edition of *Tros of Samothrace* divided into three volumes; *Purple Pirate* and *Queen Cleopatra* were included separately. The ultimate insult, however, was perpetrated when all were headlined "Heroic fantasy in the tradition of Robert E. Howard." Not only was this a generic misnomer, but a historical one as well. Mundy was one of the many authors Howard learned from, but did not imitate, and it is doubtful Mundy ever read the younger writer. Fortunately, Zebra's reprints of these volumes eliminated the caption. However, the resurgence of interest in Howard did advance Mundy; a fanzine for Howard enthusiasts, *Amra*, carried L. Sprague de Camp's appreciation, "Mundy's Vendhya," in 1970 (reprinted in *The Blade of Conan*, a 1979 anthology.) The June 1979 issue of *The Dragon* magazine published a "Dungeons and Dragons" gaming option for classic heroes from literature, in which the altruistic Tros, committed to religious ideals, is sent on missions by the priests of Samothrace and the Greek goddess of wisdom, Athena.

The next Mundy reprint was, on the surface, almost inexplicable; a severely edited version of *Black Light* in 1978 for Barbara Cartland's short-lived "Library of Ancient Wisdom." Cartland did not follow through on her intention to so treat other Mundy books, including *The Nine Unknown*, although her version of *Black Light* did contain portions of the poems and sayings only previously seen in the British edition.

By the 1970s, Mundy had become regularly mentioned in books on mysticism, pulp magazines, film, fantasy literature, or adventure, but often falsely describing him as a Kiplingesque Anglophile, interchangeable with his predecessor.[31] Publisher Donald M. Grant's 1978 reprint of *King— of the Khyber Rifles*, with an introduction, was an elegant edition accompanied for the first time in hardcover form by all of the dark, other-worldly drawings of Joseph Clement Coll from their original serialization in *Everybody's* magazine. Grant followed this with a compilation in 1983 of *Talbot Mundy, Messenger of Destiny*, including mountains of bibliographic information and biographical essays, and contributions by Mundy's widow, Dawn, and fantasy writers Darrel Crombie and Fritz Leiber. Unfortunately, much of the information was unverified or incomplete; Grant also published *The Last Adventurer*, a biography by Peter Berresford Ellis, who concentrated on Mundy's marital and business failings at the expense of literary analysis. Ellis relied largely on the Bobbs-Merrill correspondence at Indiana University, first utilized back in 1967 in a publishing history of *The Ivory Trail* that appeared in *The Indiana University Bookman* by a professor at the institution, Louis E. Lambert. Grant's three publications represented the pinnacle of several decades of enthusiasm for Mundy among fantasy fandom, but the shortcomings of these books demonstrated the inherent limitations of this approach, and the need for new methodologies to properly account for Mundy's enduring legacy. Reflection of the old tendencies continued to appear in an article by Richard Dalby for the November 1990 issue of the British magazine *Book and Magazine Collector*.

The task of a deeper examination of Mundy's significance was undertaken in succeeding years by a number of hands, and by the 1980s, exciting, fresh developments were taking place. Everett F. Bleiler wrote several detailed and opinionated chapters on Mundy in his books on supernatural fiction and science fiction in 1983, 1985, and 1990. Similarly, analyses of other Mundy books began to appear in such new references as Magill's *Survey of Modern Fantasy Literature* in 1983. Three issues of *The Fantasy Collector* from 1990–1992 discussed Mundy, and I merged an account of the central aspect of Mundy's experience and writing in "Philosophy Into Popular Fiction: Talbot Mundy and the Theosophical Society," an article in the summer 1985 issue of *Southern California Quarterly*.

A variety of theosophical journals, especially *The Eclectic Theosophist*, issued by Point Loma Publications, a San Diego firm formed by veterans of the Tingley-Purucker era, reprinted excerpts from *Om — The Secret of Ahbor Valley*, Mundy's articles in *The Theosophical Path*, and occasional literary appreciations of his work. The first critical edition of a Mundy work appeared with Point Loma Publications's 1993 edition of *Om — The Secret of Ahbor Valley*, with an introduction by Peter Berresford Ellis (left over from the 1980 edition), and my own new afterword (based on some of my articles for *The Eclectic Theosophist*). The cover illustration was from one of Nicholas Roerich's paintings of a Tibetan monastery, and marked the first time that the ideally appropriate match of Mundy's writing and Roerich's art had ever been made. In 1998 Mundy moved onto the world wide web in the first significant manner in a site assembled by R.T. Gault, providing not only bibliographic background but also a number of insightful articles on various aspects of his writing. Sadly, the site and Gault's writing on Mundy was brought to an end by his untimely death.

In 1983, two Mundy devotees, writer-director Philip Kaufman and producer Steve Roth, announced that they believed the time was right to bring to the screen a mystical hero like Mundy's Grim, with Kaufman to script and direct a series of large scale action pictures, with the first to be released in the summer of 1985 by Tri-Star. The Indiana Jones movies were then popular, and Kaufman had been given partial script credit for the original in the series, *Raiders of the Lost Ark* (1981). However, after the commercial failure of Kaufman's highly-touted *The Right Stuff* (1983), Tri-Star withdrew as the backer of *Jimgrim vs. the Nine Unknown*. Whatever possibility there might have been for its production ended when Kaufman became typecast as a director of intelligent erotica with *The Unbearable Lightness of Being* (1988), *Henry and June* (1990), and *Quills* (2001).

Kaufman wrote, "My own screenplay went beyond (or around) the *Jimgrim*, *Nine Unknown* and *Devil's Guard* books."[32] His 134 page script used the framework of the quest towards Tibet in search of Elmer Rait lifted from *The Devil's Guard*, along with a sprinkling of incidents from *The Nine Unknown*, and a climax similar to *Jimgrim*. Changes, many of them inexplicable, are made in Grim and his followers. Grim's motives are vastly diminished, and friendship is labeled his religion. Only Chullunder Ghose and Narayan Singh remain as presented in the book, but outside the period of the original stories their representation of old and new India is lost. As introduced by Ghose, Athelstan King is the granddaughter of the hero played in the movie by Tyrone Power, and the former lover of both Grim and Rait. Perhaps in recognition of the fact that ill-informed critics would invariably label the movie a knock-off of *Lost Horizon*, Kaufman adds a referential level by making filmmaking itself a key theme, as he would in his later *Rising Sun* (1993).

Without a movie, the possibility of a major 1980s Mundy publishing revival also stalled. Carroll & Graf added *Om — The Secret of Ahbor Valley* and *King — of the Khyber Rifles* to their mass market paperback list. At the end of the decade, *Black Light* was reprinted in paperback, but while it contained the entire book, unlike the Cartland edition, it was from the Bobbs-Merrill edition and so lacked all the introductory sayings and poems that she had included from the Hutchinson text. In 2001, the same publisher, the occult-oriented Ariel Press, also issued a reprint of *Caves of Terror*. Ariel's 1991 compilation of reviews, *Books of Light*, covered *I Say Sunrise*, *Om*, and *King — of the Khyber Rifles*. In 1995, Mark Jaqua collected Mundy's *Theosophical Path* articles — a dream advanced in the 1970s by Iverson Harris, Katherine Tingley's former secretary — into an original softcover book, *The Lama's Law*, published by Isis Books.

In 1999, Mark Wheatley combined *The "Iblis" at Ludd* and *The Seventeen Thieves of El-Kalil* into a new volume entitled *Jimgrim and the Devil at Ludd*, the first in a planned series that never came to fruition. Wheatley provided color art, with line drawings by Frank Cho, creating the first Mundy book since Joseph Clement Coll to be fully and appropriately illustrated throughout its text. I provided an introduction on Mundy and the Middle East in the volume, published in Baltimore by Legendary Library.

In 2001, Wildside Press reprinted a series of Mundy novels overseen by Alan Rodgers, using online web texts as the basis for fresh typesetting. The titles included *Rung Ho!*, *King — of the Khyber Rifles*, *Hira Singh*, *The Ivory Trail*, *The Eye of Zeitoon*, *Guns of the Gods*, *Told in the East*, and *Om*. *The Winds of the World* included my own introduction on Yasmini and the feminist themes in Mundy's writing.

* * *

Talbot Mundy admitted having read *Boy's Own Paper*-type writers during his childhood, but many other influences were at work. He outlined his planned summer reading in 1920 as "Homer's *Oddysey* [sic] and *Iliad*, a lot of Shakespear [sic], as much of Swinburn [sic] as I can swallow, Meredith's *Drama of the Crossways* (for the seventh time), and a considerable quantity of Kipling."[33] The literature he discussed was far afield from his own specialty. Among those whose work he reviewed include H.H. the Ranee of Sarawak's *A Star Fell* and Lord Dunsany, whose plays and fantasy he admired. In *The Theosophical Path*, he discussed H.G. Wells's *Men Like Gods* and L.P. Jacks's *Legends of Smokeover*; William J. Long's *Mother Nature*; and the concept of historical cycles in Kenneth Morris, Sir William Matthews Flinders Petrie's *Revolutions of Civilization*, and Oswald Spengler's *Der Untergang des Abendlandes*. He once wrote facetiously that poetry is the only material worth reading, although an unfulfilling regimen; his other favorites were works of philosophy, metaphysics and travel. "I believe that the apex of exquisite enjoyment is, for instance, reading Kant or John Wesley and shooting their arguments all to pieces."[34]

Kipling and Haggard had clearly set the traditions of the empire adventure by the time Mundy began writing, but he wrote his publishers that he was "sick" of being compared to them.[35] Mundy could be more accurately said to combine the strengths of both without the weakness of either. Yet precisely because Mundy is a more modern writer in his attitudes than either of those predecessors, he is neglected by scholars looking for a convenient paradigm of dominant popular literature infused with colonial sentiment.

Although Mundy met and corresponded with Kipling, there is more of a resemblance to Haggard, since he was also influenced by theosophy. Beyond Haggard's apparently magical occurrences, Mundy heightens the believability of the supernatural by supplying the indigenous religious background. Mundy is not only more modern in terms of content, but superior in form as well, as one critic noted: "He has a better sense of character, his plots are much tighter, and his style is smoother."[36]

Mundy tended to reveal character through action; as he wrote, "Deeds being the result of character, it is inevitably only character that really counts; but character is weighed by deeds, whose quality depends entirely on the motive that provides their impulse."[37] When asked by Arthur Hoffman what element of writing was most vital, Mundy replied, "I am afraid that abstract ideas are the important points of a story to me. I don't care so much about a character as *why* he does so and so. I like to know his mental arguments and all about his motives."[38] Such protagonists as Ommony, Strange, Quorn, Tros, Warrender, Adrian, Will Halifax, "Gup" McLeod, Tom Grayne, and Andrew Gunning are all men of decidedly mixed attributes, full of self-doubt, questions, and uncertainty. Rather than following a flag, such heroes as Grim and Tom Grayne follow their own beliefs, Kagig's "the sporting instinct," and a spiritual quest, that leads men like King and Ommony to become outcasts from their own kind.

Mundy is most successful in creating believable, multi-dimensional women, with Yasmini, Joan Angela Leich, Henrietta Frensham, Wu Tu, and Elsa Burbage, and Indians and Tibetans like Ranjoor Singh, Hira Singh, Narayan Singh, Chullunder Ghose, the Gray Mahatma, Tsiang Samdup, and Lobsang Pun. With such novels as *Hira Singh*, *Guns of the Gods*, and later *Om*, he shifted from adventure's authorial voice of a male imperialist to cast indigenous people and women in the forefront. Even his white male heroes questioned the colonial ethic, respects in which he was far ahead of his contemporaries.[39]

Frequently Mundy characters undergo exhausting physical ordeals, groping their way through a dark cave filled with unseen enemies, representing the dangers of fear and the unconscious. His heroes survive these literal "caves of terror" as a form of initiation, opening secrets to those who endure the passage in *King— of the Khyber Rifles*, *Cock o' the North*, and *Full Moon*.[40] A mystical experience brings them face to face with their innermost selves, resulting in metaphysical meditations on the soul and the meaning of existence. These novels, along with such others as *Caves of Terror*, *The Devil's Guard*, *Black Light* and *The Thunder Dragon Gate*, could well be termed surreal or symbolic adventures. Fantasy became steadily more dominant in Mundy's most serious novels; for him, it allowed presenting psychic phenomena, and the theosophical ideas of the "Ancient Wisdom," as an occult science of the past.

As he once exclaimed in a letter to Bobbs-Merrill that dismayed his publisher, "When writing, the plot and adventure are to me mere pegs on which to hang my preachment!"[41]

Unfortunately, far too much of Mundy's talent went into churning out fiction for a living, leaving too little time for his more literary and philosophical novels.[42] Yet Mundy was a superb craftsman, whose narratives are skillfully constructed and deftly told.[43]

His style is simultaneously breezy and pungent, full of epigrams and laden (but never leaden) with meaning. Attention to timing, tone, feel, mood, and atmosphere, including the olfactory senses, contribute enormously to all Mundy's stories, whatever the region — not only the fantasy and Roman novels inspired by the Point Loma experience, but also to the tales of adventure in India that were the staple of his commercial output.[44] He was able to describe locales and foreign beliefs with a convincing touch of authenticity, combining knowledge from other books, popular legends, and his own travels and friendships with a vivid imagination, leaving the reader unable to discern what was fact and what was fiction.[45]

Mundy pushed the idea of adventure to its limit within the popular literature of the time, and he provides a key link from the revisionism of Joseph Conrad to subsequent authors, such as Ernest Hemingway and André Malraux, who declared the death of adventure. Like Malraux, especially in *Man's Fate*, Mundy is concerned with justifying his character's existence through converting their beliefs into actions, searching for meaning in the events leading to death. In life experiences, and in the structuring of his novels, Mundy was most akin to Joseph Conrad. However, unlike Conrad, Mundy's theosophical convictions kept him hopeful of the possibilities of human nature; even *Caves of Terror* found human goodness not evident in Conrad's *Heart of Darkness*.

Mundy's stories were not primarily about action, courage, or even geographical travel; rather he stresses intrigue, although he wrote that it was merely incidental.[46] At his best, Mundy had a mind capable of developing extremely complex, convoluted plots. A reviewer describing *Guns of the Gods* noted that "Intrigue in Mr. Mundy's dictionary means a complex winding of tiny threads, so multiplex, so interwoven, that one takes off one's hat to the author for being able ... to keep them apart and to keep them together. No reader possibly could. But he needn't bother. He can read along happily and gradually the pattern becomes clear."[47] Throughout his literature, Mundy had a fascination with the mechanics and dynamics of power politics, on the personal and territorial level, that gave a sophistication to his work, providing insight into the practice of statecraft and the machinations of the priestly class. He analyzed the ways in which power is manipulated, whether by Caesar and Cleopatra or by such fictional figures as Yasmini and Chullunder Ghose.

Because of the extensive veins of fantasy and intrigue, the topicality of Mundy's writing is apt to be unrecognized, but book reviews and commentary in magazines indicate that Mundy was received through the filter of his times. Much of this element may be lost on modern readers; for instance, *Jungle Jest* would seem merely an imagined reserve with its forest and junglis, for a reader unaware that it was spawned by newspaper accounts of the Moplah revolt. Acknowledging Mundy's engagement with the issues of his own time, and with history, is no less vital than recognizing the theosophical roots of his fantasy.

Mundy held strong political as well as spiritual views. He had a personal loathing for the British social establishment he had rebelled against and fled as a youth, making him egalitarian by nature and an opponent of all class and caste systems. Never partisan, at first Mundy fervently supported Franklin D. Roosevelt and the New Deal, admiring the President's fearlessness, then found him too cautious. Finally, Mundy turned more conservative toward the end of the decade. While having no sympathies of a Socialist nature, Talbot was always generous with whatever money, time or friendship he could give, and never let an opportunity pass to help others; friends and relatives were nearly always living with the Mundys.

The key political issue in Mundy's writing is colonialism. During nearly all of his career, most of the conceptions of the East in popular literature were stereotypes that today are the relics of an imperial mindset. Dominant were Edgar Rice Burroughs' Tarzan, the noble savage who is, of course, actually a white Englishman, and Sax Rohmer's Fu Manchu, expressing the widespread fear of the Far East as a strange, unknown place, threatening to overthrow Anglo global dominance. Mundy's challenge to Rohmer and his ilk was evident early on; in 1922, he wrote, "We're taught to regard colored people as the agents of the enemy of man. Our missionaries go out to convert them, lest the heathen in their blindness overwhelm the world in another chaos any old night. They've educated us, these missionaries have, into believing things that aren't so; and we commit the indecency, in consequence, of being astonished when a man with colored skin acts 'white.'"[48]

Pro-colonial and anti-colonial views were not unusual among individuals Mundy knew, but he grew to increasingly detest the "white man's burden" attitude.[49] He opposed imperialism wherever he saw it, whether Russia in the "Dick Anthony of Arran" series, German cruelty in Africa in *The Ivory Trail*, Ottoman atrocities in *Hira Singh* and *The Eye of Zeitoon*, Anglo-French blocking of Arabia's nascent desire for self-government, and the danger of revived German and Japanese dominion over Tibet in the 1930s in *The Thunder Dragon Gate* and *Old Ugly-Face*. He followed the argument's logical conclusion. While simultaneously nationalistic regarding his homeland, especially when war in Europe was underway or threatened, he also loathed its imperial tendency. As early as 1919, he wrote "On the part of [England] it has been unfortunate but true that every time she placed her foot on foreign territory she made it her own. Territorial expansion has seemingly been her doctrine."[50]

His articles for *The Theosophical Path* allowed a forum for freely expressing his anti-colonial views without concern for the editorial opinion of commercial magazines. While lauding America's liberation of Cuba as the first time any nation had taken such an action, he also criticized Theodore Roosevelt's seizure of Panama as immoral.[51] Yet, he points out, when American intervention might save such beleaguered nations as Armenia or Tibet from foreign domination, the United States responds with apathy.

The Rome of Mundy's historical novels is clearly an imperial power whose corrupting influence palpably harms all those it touches, both without and within. Tros of Samothrace, with his wish to sail around the world, is its antithesis: "Caesar stood for all that Tros loathed: Interference with men's liberties, imposition of a foreign yoke by trickery and force of arms, robbery under the cloak of law, vice and violence, lies gilded and painted to resemble truth."[52] It was precisely Mundy's adverse portrayal of Rome, the foundation of much of Western civilization, including the historical rationale for colonialism, that caused such outrage on the initial publication of the Tros series. By the 1930s, there was nothing subtle about Mundy's attitude, as in this passage about a train in India from *The Thunder Dragon Gate*. "All the fancy novelties—cool air — ice water — glare-proof glass— a better dining car than any prewar king ever had — lots too many men to ask if you needed anything. White man's burden hell, it was a white man's shocking waste of other people's money, grudgingly, not too politely shared with the duskier gentry who were taxed to pay for the extravagance."[53] Similarly, Chullunder Ghose is eager to serve the princess Sankyamuni, less from shared ideology than the cheerful desire to "see her buck the British government!"[54]

Mundy's curiosity about indigenous culture and beliefs led him to the sympathetic investigation of Eastern teachings that replaced adventure's traditional preference for exoticism. Mundy's view was simultaneously realistic and atmospheric, and he wrote of the region's people and customs on their own terms, without condescension, either liberal or reactionary. Mundy presented characters from both sides, the colonized and the colonizers, even in the secret service. Nor did he take the other extreme; his whites and natives were never easily separable into heroes and villains, or vice versa, with some of each race in both categories, and many others who embodied a measure of both aspects.

Mundy acknowledged in a letter to *Adventure* readers that *The Devil's Guard* was a direct challenge to Western assumptions of philosophical and spiritual superiority.

> For a century or two (two seconds in eternity) we [the West] have been powerful and have subdued the greater portion of the globe. Our energy is indisputable, and our mechanical inventions are superior to anything the world has known at any time of which we have an undisputed record....
>
> It may not harm us to remember that we are a minority of the world's inhabitants, and that there are races much more numerous than ours, who have attained — in the fields of literature, philosophy, sculpture, painting and government — to heights we have not yet reached....
>
> My point is that we are hoodwinked, possibly, by the success of our material achievements to the point where we believe we know it all and consequently think the races we have overwhelmed are superstitious, ignorant, incapable and unheroic fools.
>
> I challenge that peculiarly modern viewpoint.

His belief in the cycles of history and the rise and fall of nations led him to a different conclusion, one that was not positive for the West. "When man or nation takes the attitude that 'what I think I know is good enough for me,' then it is time to sound the requiem and look for who shall next appear on the horizon."[55]

For the 10 years from the mid–1920s to the mid–1930s, Mundy remained poised on the brink of greatness, never quite breaking through — the result, not of a lack of ability, but of an unsteadiness in applying himself, as reflected in the tumult of his personal life, whether his divorces or the hiatus of the Mexican oil venture. The same inconstancy can be found in his literature. In a pattern that undercut his critical reception, Mundy was unable to stay with a single goal or subject for more than a few years at a time, although he would sometimes return to a topic later, prompted by such events as the intrigue surrounding a new Dalai Lama.

Mundy never subscribed fully to one mode of thought, going from one tradition to another, taking whatever he found useful and integrating it into his own philosophy, rather than becoming a strict adherent. Because of the range of influences and traditions his canon reveals, Mundy's work is to a large degree unique and original—and remains so to this day. At the same time, he did influence many younger writers, most of whom acknowledged the debt, such as Marion Zimmer Bradley, Clyde Clason, Jeremy Lane, Ganpat, Daniel Easterman, E.O. Foster, Robert E. Howard, Fritz Leiber, A. Merritt, H. Warner Munn, E. Hoffman Price, Andre Norton, and L. Sprague de Camp. In 2002, with *The Peshawar Lancers*, S.M. Stirling became the first author to write a book using a number of characters with the same names as those in the Mundy oeuvre.

In retrospect, Mundy can be seen as the most influential and enduring, if not the best-selling, writer of Eastern adventure of his day. He has not been regarded as literary enough for those who might have otherwise examined his work more carefully, reflecting an ingrained suspicion of an author whose works often first appeared in the "pulps," albeit the best of them.[56] Nor has he been swept up in the appreciation accorded other more typical writers of the same era, whether the hard-boiled detectives of the pulp *Black Mask*, or the posthumous cult enjoyed by Robert E. Howard. Moreover, fueled by his theosophical beliefs, Mundy's writing had a moralistic tone, decrying the "realism" of modernist literature of his time, with its approbation for portrayals of life as either full of ambiguity or nihilistic.[57] Together, this combination of divergent factors has deprived Mundy of the literary recognition he deserves.[58]

Mundy realized he had to write so that he could be appreciated on two seemingly contradictory levels. On the one hand, he offered philosophical parables, but also could be appreciated, in the words of one contemporary critic, for "that rare instinct which gives us just what we want, mystery danger, unknown lands, [and the] occult realism of Eastern thought."[59] Few, if any, other authors have so successfully reconciled such apparently contradictory ingredients, the philosophy melding persuasively into his fiction.[60] He knew that he could best convey his views through the means of metaphor and allegory, and that, in the words of later commentators, a "deeply understood occultism" could be made digestible for a large audience by following the tradition of teaching "the uninitiated the mystic truth as myths and fantasy."[61] He sought to translate Eastern ideas into a Western idiom through his own experience in the far-flung corners of the world, and the aid of the theosophical influence.

While this strain gave Mundy a steady, reliable group of readers, it also kept him from reaching the universal popularity he might have achieved had he been content to become simply an entertainer for a larger audience with its traditional, conservative view of world politics and belief in the Judeo-Christian heritage.[62] This was widely recognized in his own time; editor A.A. Proctor introduced the serialization of *Jimgrim* in *Adventure* by noting that Mundy presents ideas which are at the least novel and challenging, and frequently inflammatory, provoking some of the most vigorous debates in the magazine.[63]

There is no answer to such criticism; it all depends on whether Mundy's digressions are to one's taste. I find no self-indulgence; Mundy has turned his creativity toward issues of vital, enduring importance. As Pervin Mistry has noted, the "second time you read [Mundy] with a new insight and yet the adventure remains. I enjoy his books even after I know the outcome, the end, the true characters."[64] Hence, it is not simply the adventure or fantasy, or even the unique descriptions of distant locales, that his won Mundy a place in the literary constellation. It is, rather, his teaching, and because of this he will always remain a controversial writer, one with a devoted but necessarily limited following.

> Enjoy life. Enjoy Existence. The worse the hell in which you find yourself, the more good you can do. But the only good you can do anywhere, at any time, in any circumstances, is to summon Wisdom to direct your thinking. Then think. And then *do.*—Talbot Mundy, *I Say Sunrise.*

Appendix A: Books by Talbot Mundy

(in order of first appearance, including magazine form)

The Soul of a Regiment
Rung Ho!
The Winds of the World
King — of the Khyber Rifles
Hira Singh (UK: *Hira Singh's Tale*)
The Ivory Trail (reissued as *Trek East*)
The Eye of Zeitoon
Guns of the Gods
Jimgrim and Allah's Peace
Jimgrim and the Devil at Ludd
The Seventeen Thieves of El-Kalil
The Lion of Petra
The Woman Ayisha
The Lost Trooper
The King in Check (reissued as *Affair in Araby*)
The Mystery of Khufu's Tomb
Caves of Terror
Jungle Jest
The Nine Unknown
Her Reputation (UK: *The Bubble Reputation*)
The Marriage of Meldrum Strange
The Hundred Days
Om — The Secret of Ahbor Valley (UK: *Om*)
Tros of Samothrace (reissued as *Tros, Helma, Liafail, Helene* and *Lud of Lunden, Avenging Liafail, The Praetor's Dungeon*)
The Devil's Guard (UK: *Ramsden*)
Caesar Dies
The Red Flame of Erinpura
When Trails Were New
Queen Cleopatra
W.H. (reissued as *The Queen's Warrant*)
Cock o' the North (UK: *Gup Bahadur*)
Black Light
Jimgrim (reissued as *Jimgrim Sahib*)
"C.I.D."
The Gunga Sahib
Full Moon (UK: *There Was a Door*)
Purple Pirate
The Thunder Dragon Gate
East and West (UK: *Diamonds See in the Dark*)
Old Ugly Face
I Say Sunrise

Anthologies

Told in the East (1920)
All Four Winds (1933)
Romances of India (1936)
The Valiant View (1939)
The Lama's Law (1995)

Appendix B: Chronological List of Original Publications of Talbot Mundy's Work

Note: As indicated, some material appeared under Mundy's pseudonym "Walter Galt"; a few of these were reprinted under the Talbot Mundy by-line. All journals are published in the United States unless otherwise noted; bibliographic information is provided for book reprints by authors other than Mundy. Serializations of Mundy books after hardcover publication are not included.

1896
Month & day unknown, *Answers* (GB), title unknown.

1911
Feb, *The Scrap-Book*, 11 (369–384), "A Transaction in Diamonds" (reprinted in *Corner Magazine* [GB], May 1926). **Apr**, *Adventure*, 1 (1097–1103), "Pig Sticking in India." **Jun**, *All Story*, 20 (243–251), "The Lady and the Lord." **Jul**, *Adventure*, 2 (497–504), "Single-Handed Yachting." **Jul**, *All Story*, 20 (485–491), "Kitty Burns Her Fingers." **Aug**, *Adventure*, 2 (651–657), "The Phantom Battery" (reprinted in *The Grand* [GB], Sep, 1912; *Fantastic Collector*, Apr/May 1991). **Aug**, *All Story*, 20 (635–640), "Vengeance Is Kitty's." **Aug**, *Cavalier*, 9 (530–538), "Jansen and Jansen — Twins." **Sep**, *All Story*, 21 (171–177), "Cornelia's Englishman." **Sep**, *The Scrap Book*, 12 (363–369), "Sentence of Death." **Oct**, *The Scrap Book*, 12 (492–496), "The Fire Cop." **Nov**, *The Scrap Book*, 12 (760–764), "An Offer of Two to One." **Dec**, *Adventure*, 3 (281–287), "The Blooding of the Ninth Queen's Own" (reprinted in *The Grand* [GB], Aug 1912; *Best Stories of All Time*, Apr 1927). **Dec**, *All Story*, 21 (683–689), "Kitty and Cupid."

1912
Jan, *Adventure*, 3 (409–419), "For Valour." **Feb**, *Adventure*, 3 (609–615), "The Soul of a Regiment" (cover illustration by David Robinson) (reprinted in *The Grand* [GB], Mar 1912; *Adventure*, Apr 1917; *Theosophical Path*, Jun 1925; *Adventure*, Nov 1935; *Adventure*, Nov 1940; *Adventure*, Nov 1950; *Adventure*, Oct 1954; *Adventure*, Jun 1970; *Short Stories* [GB], May 1981; and in the books *The Soul of a Regiment*; A.S. Hoffman, ed., *Adventure's Best Stories — 1926*; *My Best Adventure Story*, 1934; *The Valiant View*; and *The Lama's Law*). (686–690) "The Goner?" ("by Walter Galt") (reprinted in *Pall Mall Magazine* [GB], Aug 1912 as "by Talbot Mundy"). **Feb** 10 *Cavalier*, 12 (359–368), "Christening Cannon Rock." **Mar.**, *Adventure*, 3 (803–813),

"The Chaplain of the Mullingars (reprinted in *Pall Mall Magazine* [GB], Jun 1912; and in *The Valiant View*). **Apr**, *Adventure*, 3 (1024–1028), "W. Mayes — The Amazing." **May**, *Adventure*, 4 (16–24), "The Queen — God Bless Her!" (reprinted in *London Magazine* [GB], Jan 1913; *Boy's Journal* [GB], 4 Oct 1913). (64–66), "Francis Bannerman — A Man of Mystery and History" ("by Walter Galt"). **Jun**, *Adventure*, 4 (348–358), "The Second Rung" ("by Walter Galt"). (364–368), "T.C. Ansell — Adventurer." **Jul**, *Adventure*, 4 (437–445), "The Cowards" (reprinted in *Best Stories of All Time*, Jun 1927). (553–559), "Elephant-Hunting For a Living" ("by Walter Galt") (reprinted in *Pall Mall Magazine* [GB], Feb 1913 as "by Talbot Mundy"). (633–634), "The Camp-Fire" (Letter: "At the time of the famous Jameson..."). **Aug**, *Adventure*, 4 (19–29), "The Payment of Quinn's Debt" (reprinted in *Best Stories of All Time*, Aug 1927) (abridged as "Quits!," *London Magazine* [GB], Jun 1913) (153–162), "Dorg's Luck" ("by Walter Galt"). **Sep**, *Adventure*, 4 (3–10), "In Winter Quarters" (reprinted in *The Grand* [GB], Dec 1912; *Newnes Summer Annual* [GB], 2 Nov 1916). **Oct**, *Adventure*, 4 (135–147), "Across the Color Line" ("by Walter Galt"). (182–191), "The Man Who Saw" (reprinted in *The Grand* [GB], Mar 1913, and in the book, Mike Ashley, ed., *The Mammoth Book of Sword and Honor*, 2000). **Nov**, *Adventure*, 5 (3–10), "Honor." (66–77), "Love and War" ("by Walter Galt") (reprinted in *The Grand* [GB], Oct 1913). **Dec**, *Adventure*, 5 (19–30), "Rabbit" (reprinted in *London Magazine* [GB], Feb 1913). (135–149), "The Top of the Ladder" ("by Walter Galt"). (224), "The Camp-Fire" (Letter: "When Lord Roberts of Kandahar..."). **Dec**, *Everybody's*, 27 (744–756), "The Pillar of Light" (Illustrations by Charles B. Falls) (reprinted as "Climate and Conditions: A Red Sea Rhapsody," *Pall Mall Magazine* [GB], Apr 1913; *Theosophical Path*, Sep and Oct 1925 [in two parts]; and in *The Valiant View* and *The Lama's Law*). **Dec**, *Cassell's Magazine of Fiction* (?), "Ikey Hole's Luck" (probably reprinted as "Payable to Bearer," *Cavalier*, 28 Dec 1912). **Dec** 28, *Cavalier*, 23 (709–730), "Payable to Bearer" (probably a reprint of "Ikey Hole's Luck").

1913

Jan, *Adventure*, 5 (26–36), "Three Helios" (abridged in *Strand Magazine* [GB], Jul 1913). **Feb**, *Adventure*, 5 (15–27), "One Year Later" ("by Walter Galt"). (184–187), "A Low-Veldt Funeral." **Mar**, *Adventure*, 5 (186–218), "For the Salt Which He Had Eaten" (reprinted as "The Empty Saddle" in *The Storyteller* [GB], Jun 1913; and as "For the Salt Which He Had Eaten" in *Told in the East* and *Romances of India*). **Apr**, *Adventure*, 5 (3–14), "Private Murdock's G.C.M." (reprinted in *The Storyteller* [GB], Jul 1913). **Apr**, *McClure's*, 40 (36–45), "Making £10,000" (Illustrated by Clarence F. Underwood) (abridged as "Sulphur's National," *Strand Magazine* [GB], Apr 1913). **May**, *Adventure*, 6 (179–217), "The Guzzler's Grand Prix." **Jun**, *Adventure*, 6 (3–10), "At Maneuvers." (221), "Lost Trails" (Letter searching for old friends: "Talbot Mundy wishes to hear from the two following..."). **Jul**, *Adventure*, 6 (171–211), "Hookum Hai" (reprinted in *Told in the East* and *Romances of India*). **Aug**, *Adventure*, 6 (143–158), "The Closed Trail of William Walker." **Aug**, *Everybody's*, 29 (181–196), "From Hell, Hull and Halifax" (Illustrated by Charles Sarka) (reprinted in *Pearson's* [GB], Dec 1913). **Sep**, *Adventure*, 6 (3–43), "The Letter of His Orders." **Oct**, *Adventure*, 6 (163–176), "In a Righteous Cause." **Nov**, *Adventure*, 7 (64–75), "An Arabian Night" (reprinted in *Told in the East* and *Romances of India*, and as "One Arabian Night" in *The Valiant View*). **Dec**, *Adventure*, 7 (126–140), "The Tempering of Harry Blunt" (reprinted in *The Storyteller* [GB], Jul 1916).

1914

Jan, *Adventure*, 7 (3–34), "A Soldier and a Gentleman." **Jan**, *Everybody's*, 30 (42–54), "Burberton and Ali Beg" (Illustrated by Adolph Treidler) (reprinted in *New Magazine* [GB], Aug 1914; *Argosy* [GB], Aug 1927). **Feb**, *Adventure*, 7 (92–125), "For the Peace of India" (Part 1, of 3; concludes April, 1914) (reprinted as *Rung Ho!*). **Mar**, *Adventure*, 7 (161–195), "For the Peace of India" (Part 2, of 3). **Apr**, *Adventure*, 7 (126–162), "For the Peace of India" (Part 3, of 3); **Jun**, *Adventure*, 8 (163–176), "The Gentility of Ikey Blumendall" (reprinted in *The Storyteller* [GB], Jun 1914; *Best Stories of All Time*, Oct 1927) (excerpted in *Adventure*, Sep 1914). **Jul**, *Adventure*, 8 (3–42), "Gulbaz and the Game". **Aug**, *Adventure*, 8 (3–25), "Dick Anthony of

Arran — The Sword of Iskander" (cover illustration). **Sep**, *Adventure*, 8 (63–89), "Foul of the Czar." (182–183), "Nothing Doing" ("by Walter Galt"). **Oct**, Adventure, 8 (193–218), "Go, Tell the Czar!" **Nov**, *Adventure*, 9 (126–157), "King Dick." **Dec**, *Adventure*, 9 (62–96), "The Lancing of the Whale."

1915

Jan, *Adventure*, 9 (107–142) "Disowned!" **Feb**, *Adventure*, 9 (178–216), "No Name!" **Mar**, *Adventure*, 9 (97–130), "On Terms" (reprinted in *The Storyteller* [GB], Jul 1915). **Apr**, *Adventure*, 9 (85–99), "MacHassan Ah" (reprinted in *The Storyteller* [GB], Jun 1915, and *Told in the East, Romances of India* and *The Valiant View*). **May**, *Adventure*, 10 (49–60), "A Temporary Trade in Titles." **Jun**, *Adventure*, 10 (127–138), "The Dove with a Broken Wing" (reprinted in *New Magazine* [GB], Oct 1915; *The Storyteller* [GB], Nov 1937). **Jul**, *Adventure*, 10 (106–126), "The Winds of the World" (Part 1, of 3; concludes Sep 1915) (cover illustration by James Reynolds) (reprinted in *Royal Magazine* [GB], Dec 1915–Jan 1916; and as *The Winds of the World*). **Aug**, *Adventure*, 10 (151–173), "The Winds of the World" (Part 2, of 3). **Sep**, *Adventure*, 10 (153–180), "The Winds of the World" (Part 3, of 3). (221), "The Camp-Fire" (Letter: "Camp-Fire pen-picture of *Adventure's* editor..."). **Nov**, *Adventure*, 11 (127–139), "The Return of Billy Blain" ("by Walter Galt").

1916

Jan, *Adventure*, 11 (160–171), "Billy Blain Eats Biscuits" ("by Walter Galt"). **Jan**, *The Storyteller*, 1 [GB] (?), "Sam Bagg of the Gabriel Group" (reprinted in *Saturday Evening Post*, 11 Mar 1916; *Argosy* [GB], Apr 1934). **Feb**, *Adventure*, 11 (183–192), "A Drop or Two of White" (reprinted in *Golden Book*, Sep 1925). (96–106), "Billy Blain's Onions and Garlic" ("by Walter Galt"). (213–214), "Tucker's Tongue" (reprinted in *Fantastic Collector*, Oct 1992). **May**, *Everybody's*, 34 (548–570), "King, of the Khyber Rifles" (Part I, of 9; concludes Jan 1917) (reprinted as *King, of the Khyber Rifles/King — of the Khyber Rifles*, included in *All Four Winds*). **Jun**, *Everybody's*, 34 (738–760), "King, of the Khyber Rifles" (Part 2, of 9). **Jul**, *Everybody's*, 35 (97–118), "King, of the Khyber Rifles" (Part 3, of 9). **Aug**, *Everybody's*, 35 (224–246), "King, of the Khyber Rifles" (Part 4, of 9). **Sep**, *Everybody's*, 35 (352–374), "King, of the Khyber Rifles" (Part 5, of 9). **Oct**, *Everybody's*, 35 (479–499), "King, of the Khyber Rifles" (Part 6, of 9). **Nov**, *Everybody's*, 35 (608–626), "King, of the Khyber Rifles" (Part 7, of 9). **Dec**, *Everybody's*, 35 (608–626), "King, of the Khyber Rifles" (Part 8, of 9). **Dec 28**, *The Dial*, 61 (575–576), "America and the Great War" (Book review of *The New Map of Africa, 1900–1916* by Herbert Adams Gibbons).

1917

Jan, *Everybody's*, 36 (98–111), "King, of the Khyber Rifles" (Part 9, of 9). **Feb 22**, *The Dial*, 62 (135), "Life on the Veld" (Book review of *From the Heart of the Veld* by Madeline Alston). **May**, *Adventure*, 14 (166–179) "The Damned Old Nigger" (reprinted as "That Darned Old Nigger," *New Magazine*, Jun 1917, and as "The Damned Old Nigger" in *The Valiant View*). **Jun 2?**, *Bangor Daily Commercial*, [Maine] (?), "Talbot Mundy, An Author Who Has Hunted In Jungle." **Oct 18**, *Adventure*, 15 (3–42), "Hira Singh's Tale" (Part 1, of 4; concludes 3 Dec 1917) (reprinted as *Hira Singh / Hira Singh's Tale*). **Nov 3**, *Adventure*, 15 (110–131), "Hira Singh's Tale" (Part 2, of 4). **Nov 18**, *Adventure*, 15 (79–100), "Hira Singh's Tale" (Part 3, of 4). **Dec 3**, *Adventure*, 15 (156–177), "Hira Singh's Tale" (Part 4, of 4).

1918

Aug 18, *Adventure*, 18 (34), "Blighty." **Jun**, *Everybody's*, 38 (109–110), "Patriotism and the Plow-Tail." **Dec 3**, *Adventure*, 19 (3–20), "Oakes Respects an Adversary."

1919

Jan 1, *Adventure*, 20 (157–173), "America Horns In." **Feb 18**, *Adventure*, 20 (157–174), "Jackson Tactics." (178), "The Camp-Fire" (Letter to A.S. Hoffman regarding democracy and the character "Monty": "Don't consider my feelings; I simply haven't..."). **Mar** 18, *Adventure,* 20 (3–34), "Heinie Horns into the Game." **Apr** 3, *Adventure,* 21 (178–183), "The Camp-Fire" (Autobiographical letter: "It happens very seldom in a man's life that he..."). **Apr** 18, *Adventure,* 21 (3–37), "The End of the Bad Ship Bundesrath." **May** 3, *Adventure,* 21 (67–94), "On the Trail of Tippoo Tib" (Part 1, of 6; concludes 18 Jul 1919) (reprinted as *The Ivory Trail*) (Two of the poems anthologized in Robert Frothingham, ed., *Songs of Adventure,* 1926). **May** 18, *Adventure,* 21 (64–94), "On the Trail of Tippoo Tib" (Part 2, of 6). **May** 25 (6), "The New York Times America as Protector of Armenia." **Jun**, *The Crescent,* 10 (17–31), "The Real Red Root." **Jun** 3, *Adventure,* 21 (69–98), "On the Trail of Tippoo Tib" (Part 3, of 6). **Jun** 18, *Adventure,* 21 (72–101), "On the Trail of Tippoo Tib" (Part 4, of 6). **Jul** 1, *The Christian Science Monitor* (3), "Letters: The Duty to Armenia." **Jul** 3, *Adventure,* 21 (62–83), "On the Trail of Tippoo Tib" (Part 5, of 6). **Jul** 18, *Adventure,* 21 (107–128), "On the Trail of Tippoo Tib" (Part 6, of 6). **Sep** 3, *Adventure,* 22 (3–58), "The Shriek of Dûm." **Sep** 18, *Adventure,* 22 (174–175), "The Sayings of Hell-Fire Smith Done Into Polite English." **Oct** 18, *Adventure,* 23 (3–54), "Barabbas Island." **Nov** 14, (18), *New York Globe and Commercial Advertiser,* "Letter to the Editor: Armenians in Jerusalem."

1920

Jan 18 *Adventure,* 24 (3–58), "In Aleppo Bazaar." **Feb**, *Romance,* 1 (3–55), "The Eye of Zeitun" (Part 1, of 2; concludes Mar 1920) (reprinted, with poems added to Chapters 3, 5, 7, and 10, as *The Eye of Zeitoon*). (188–190), "The Meeting Place" (Letter on Armenians to editor James Shelby Hamilton: "The good Armenian needs no bush. We have..."). **Feb** 9, *Jerusalem News,* 1 (2), "Italy in Strike Time." **Feb** 10, *Jerusalem News,* 1 (2), "England After the War" (Part 1, of 4; concludes 13 Feb 1920). **Feb** 11, *Jerusalem News,* 1 (2), "England After the War" (Part 2, of 4). **Feb** 12, *Jerusalem News,* 1 England (2), "After the War" (Part 3, of 4). (2), "Lord Astor of Cleveden" (unsigned). **Feb** 13, *Jerusalem News,* 1 (1), "Lord Dunsany" (Part 1, of 2; concludes 14 Feb 1920). (2), "England After the War" (Part 4, of 4). **Feb** 14, *Jerusalem News,* 1 (2), "Lord Dunsany" (Part 2, of 2). **Feb** 16, *Jerusalem News,* 1 (1), "Mespot." **Feb** 17, *Jerusalem News,* 1 (1), "America After the War" (Part 1 of 5 part serial, numbered as 4 [sic]; concludes 23 Feb 1920). **Feb** 18, *Jerusalem News,* 1 (2), "America After the War" (Part 1 continued, of 4). **Feb** 19, *Jerusalem News,* 1 (2), "America After the War" (Part 2, of 4). **Feb** 20, *Jerusalem News,* 1 (2), "America After the War" (Part 3, of 4). **Feb** 23, *Jerusalem News,* 1 (2), "America After the War" (Part 4, of 4). **Mar**, *Romance,* 1 (21–74), "The Eye of Zeitun" (Part 2, of 2). **Mar** 2, *Jerusalem News,* 1 (2), "Elizabeth." **Mar** 6, *Jerusalem News,* 1 (2), "Ready Rhino." **Mar** 13, *Jerusalem News,* 1 (2), "The American Rattlesnake." **Mar** 26, *Jerusalem News,* 1 (2), "Candles." **Mar** 27, *Jerusalem News,* 1 (2), "Shooting Foxes." **Apr** 5, *Jerusalem News,* 1 (2), "Baboons." **Apr** 25, *Des Moines Register* (4E), "How Talbot Mundy Came to Write" (reprinted as "Mundy an Exception Among Maine Writers," *Bangor Herald,* 2 Oct 1920).

1921

Mar 3, *Adventure,* 28 (3–27), "Guns of the Gods" (Part 1, of 5; concludes 3 May 1921) (reprinted as *Guns of the Gods*). **Mar** 18, *Adventure,* 28 (102–125), "Guns of the Gods" (Part 2, of 5). **Apr**, *Delineator,* 98 (10–11), "Oh, Jerusalem!" (rewritten as "Jerusalem," *Theosophical Path,* Feb 1923). **Apr** 3, *Adventure,* 29 (92–120), "Guns of the Gods" (Part 3, of 5). **Apr** 18, *Adventure,* 29 (115–137), "Guns of the Gods" (Part 4, of 5). **May** 3, *Adventure,* 29 (111–134), "Guns of the Gods" (Part 5, of 5). **Jun**, *Brentano's Book Chat,* 1 (36–37), "A Land Where Romance Reigns" (reprinted as "India: Paradise of the Imaginative Story-Teller," *New York Tribune,* 21 Aug 1921). **Jun**, *The Crescent,* 11 (35–48), "Peter from Paradise Bend." **July** 18, *Adventure,* 30 (174), "The Camp-Fire" (Letter to A.S. Hoffman regarding "Yasmini": "No, she's not an historical character. I once saw..."). **Nov** 10, *Adventure,* 31 (3–56), "The Adventure at El-Kerak (rewritten as the first part of *Jimgrim and Allah's Peace*). **Dec** 10, *Adventure,* 32 (3–51), "Under the Dome of the Rock (rewritten as the second part of *Jimgrim and Allah's Peace*). (174–175), "The Camp-Fire" (Letter regarding the characters "Jimgrim" and "Narayan Singh": "The chief difficulty about these stories...").

1922

Jan 10, *Adventure*, 32 (3–61), "The 'Iblis' at Ludd" (reprinted in *Jimgrim and the Devil at Ludd*). **Feb** 20, *Adventure*, 33 (3–56), "The Seventeen Thieves of El-Kalil" (reprinted as *The Seventeen Thieves of El-Kalil* and in *Jimgrim and the Devil at Ludd*). (176), "The Camp-Fire" (Letter introducing *The Seventeen Thieves of El-Kalil*: "The first non–Moslem since crusaders' times to be..."). **Mar** 20, *Adventure*, 33 (3–71), "The Lion of Petra." (182–183), "The Camp-Fire" (Letter introducing *The Lion of Petra*: "Petra, in Arabia, was practically unheard of for..."). **Apr** 20, *Adventure*, 34 (3–77), "The Woman Ayisha" (reprinted as *The Woman Ayisha* and as Part 2 of *The Hundred Days and the Woman Ayisha*). **Apr** 30, *Adventure*, 34 (180–181), "The Camp-Fire" (Letter on the history of the Anglo-Saxon race: "One of the most wonderful things in the world is..."). **May** 30, *Adventure*, 34 (3–80), "The Lost Trooper" (reprinted as *The Lost Trooper*). **Jul** 10, *Adventure*, 35 (3–67), "The King in Check" (reprinted as *The King in Check*). (174–175), "The Camp-Fire" (Letter introducing *The King in Check*: "I have avoided the charge of propaganda, which..."). **Aug** 10, *Adventure*, 36 (3–55), "A Secret Society." (178), "The Camp-Fire" (Letter introducing *A Secret Society*: "In the very nature of things no government that..."). **Sep** 10, *Adventure*, 36 (3–63), "Moses and Mrs. Aintree." (177–179), "The Camp-Fire" (Letter on the Ark of the Covenant: "I must begin by apologizing for the delay in..."). **Sep** 30, *Adventure*, 36 (180–181), "The Camp-Fire" Letter regarding anti–British sen-timent in Mundy stories: "Your letter makes good reading, and I hope that..."). **Oct** 10, *Adventure*, 37 (3–78), "Khufu's Real Tomb" (reprinted as *The Mystery of Khufu's Tomb*). (176–177), "The Camp-Fire" (Letter introducing *Khufu's Real Tomb*: "This story is founded not on one fact but on..."). **Nov** 10, *Adventure*, 37 (3–79), "The Grey Mahatma" (Reprinted as *The Grey Mahatma/Caves of Terror*) (reprinted in *Famous Fantastic Mysteries*, Dec 1951). Dec 10 *Adventure*, 38 (3–71), "Benefit of Doubt" (reprinted as Book One of *Jungle Jest*).

1923

book: *Fiction Writers on Fiction Writing*, edited by A.S. Hoffman (Bobbs-Merrill) (30–31, 69–70, 164–165, 225, 255, 280, 303, 326, 356–357, 382, 401, 421). **Jan** 10, *Adventure*, 38 (3–70), "Treason" (reprinted as Book Two of *Jungle Jest*). (181–182), "The Camp-Fire" (Letter introducing *Treason*: "This story, the second I have placed in Moplah..."). **Feb**, *Theosophical Path*, 24 (123–135), "Jerusalem" (reprinted in *The Lama's Law*) (rewritten from "Oh, Jerusalem!" *Delineator*, Apr 1921). **Mar** 20, *Adventure*, 39 (60–84), "The Nine Unknown" (Part 1, of 5; concludes 30 Apr (reprinted as *The Nine Unknown*). **Mar**, 30 *Adventure*, 39·(87–115), "The Nine Unknown" (Part 2, of 5). **Apr** 10, *Adventure*, 40 (85–120), "The Nine Unknown" (Part 3, of 5). **Apr** 20, *Adventure*, 40 (126–140), "The Nine Unknown" (Part 4, of 5). **Apr** 30, *Adventure*, 40 (117–140), "The Nine Unknown" (Part 5, of 5). (180–183), "The Camp-Fire" (Letter to David R. Cummins with further discussion of *Khufu's Real Tomb*: "Dear Mr. Cummins: Your very interesting..."). **May**, *Theosophical Path*, 24 (499–500), "An Appreciation of Kenneth Morris" (reprinted in *The Lama's Law*) **May** 30 *Adventure*, 40 (183), "The Camp-Fire" (Letter to George Castor Martin: "It is difficult to answer because I have no books..."). **Aug**, *Theosophical Path*, 25 (109), "History" (poem) (reprinted as "Evolution" in *0m*, and in *The Lama's Law*). **Aug** 10, *Adventure*, 42 (3–70), "Diana Against Ephesians" (reprinted as Book Three of *Jungle Jest*). (177–178), "The Camp-Fire" (Letter introducing *Diana Against Ephesians*: "This story is placed in an imaginary native state..."). **Sep**, book: *Her Reputation/The Bubble Reputation* (Bobbs-Merrill). **Sep**, *Theosophical Path*, 25 (232), "A Nemesis" (poem) (reprinted in *The Lama's Law*). (250–252), "Universal Brotherhood" (reprinted in *The Lama's Law*) (excerpted as "A Teaspoonful of Earth," *Sunrise*, Jul 1957). **Oct**, *Theosophical Path*, 25 (343–347), "Brotherhood or League?" (reprinted in *The Lama's Law*). **Oct** 10, *Adventure*, 43 (3–72), "The Marriage of Meldrum Strange" (reprinted as *The Marriage of Meldrum Strange*). (180), "The Camp-Fire" (Letter introducing *The Marriage of Meldrum Strange*: "Having grown a little tired of always seeing the..."). **Nov**, *Theosophical Path*, 25 (451), "Unsung As Yet" (poem) (reprinted in *The Lama's Law*). (457–463), "The King Can Do No Wrong" (reprinted in *The Lama's Law*). **Dec,** *Theosophical Path,* 25 (550–559), "The Turning Tide": Two Recent Books — A Review (Book Review of H.G. Wells's *Men Like Gods* and L.P. Jacks's *The Legends of Smokeover*) (reprinted in *The Lama's Law*). **Dec 10,** *Adventure,* 44 (3–69), "Mohammed's Tooth" (reprinted as *The Hundred Days*).

1924

Jan, *Theosophical Path,* 26 "Universal." (5–9) (reprinted in *The Lama's Law*) (excerpted as "Until the Stars Grew Pale," *Sunrise,* Feb 1965). **Feb,** *Theosophical Path,* 26 (132–142), "Mother Nature": A Review of a Book by William J. Long. **Feb 4,** *San Diego Union* (10), "Talbot Mundy Says San Diego Has Opportunity to Set Pace For This Glorious West Coast" (reprinted in *Theosophical Path,* Mar 1924). **Mar,** *Theosophical Path,* 26 (218–225), "Miscarriage of Justice" (reprinted in *The Lama's Law*) (excerpted as "The Utter Certainty of Law," *Sunrise,* Jul 1965). **Mar 2,** *San Diego Union* (?), "Well-Known Writer Predicts Brilliant Career for San Diego Artist; Reviews His Paintings" (reprinted in *Theosophical Path,* Apr 1924). **Mar 23,** *San Diego Union* (8), "Writer Comments Presentation of 'The Eumenides' at Point Loma" [sic] (reprinted as "Students of Lomaland Give Wonderful Interpretation of the 'The Eumenides' at Greek Theater," *Theosophical Path,* May 1924). **Apr,** *Theosophical Path,* 26 (332–340), "Sincerity" (reprinted in *The Lama's Law*). (357), "The Lama's Law" (poem) (reprinted in *Om; Eclectic Theosophist,* May-Jun 1984; and in *The Lama's Law*). (370), "Eastern Proverb" (reprinted as "From the Book of the Sayings of Tsiang Samdup," preceeding Chapter 5 in *Om*; and in *The Lama's Law*). **May,** *Raja Yoga Messenger,* 20 (127–129), "Some True Stories About Wild Animals." *Theosophical Path,* 26 (429), "Hope (poem) (reprinted without title preceeding Chapter 26 in *Om*; and in *The Lama's Law*). (443–450), "Hope" (reprinted in *Eclectic Theosophist,* Winter 1994, and in *The Lama's Law*). **Jun,** *Theosophical Path,* 26 (515), "From the Book of the Sayings of Tsiang Samdup." (515–524), "Blackmail" (reprinted in *The Lama's Law*) (excerpted as "Flapdoodle," *Eclectic Theosophist,* 15 May 1974, and "Thoughts to Remember —," *Theosophia,* Fall 1978). (574), "Fata Virumque Cano" (poem) (reprinted in *The Lama's Law*). **Jun 4,** *San Diego Union* (9), "Katherine Tingley Again Gives "The Eumenides" Before Large Audience in Greek Theater (reprinted in *Theosophical Path,* Jul 1924). **Jul,** *Theosophical Path,* 27 (15), "Oyez!" (poem) (reprinted in *The Lama's Law*). (25–33), "Another's Duty Is Full of Danger" (reprinted in *The Lama's Law*). **Aug,** *Theosophical Path,* 27 (112–118), "I Will and I Will Not" (reprinted in *The Lama's Law*). (157), "Chant" (poem) (reprinted as "Chant Pagan" in *Om*; and in *The Lama's Law*). **Oct 10,** *Adventure,* 49 (53–85), "Om" (Part 1, of 6; concludes 30 Nov 1924) (reprinted as *Om / Om–The Secret of Ahbor Valley;* included in *All Four Winds*). (181–183), "The Camp-Fire" (Letter introducing *Om*: "*Om* explores two fields that have been hitherto untouched...") (reprinted in *Theosophical Path,* Feb 1925; *Eclectic Theosophist,* Nov-Dec 1980). **Oct 20,** *Adventure,* 49 (104–133), "Om" (Part 2, of 6). **Oct 30,** *Adventure,* 49 (108–135), "Om" (Part 3, of 6). **Nov 10,** *Adventure,* 49 (100–130), "Om" (Part 4, of 6). **Nov 20,** *Adventure,* 49 (73–99), "Om" (Part 5, of 6). **Nov 30,** *Adventure,* 49 (130–155), "Om" (Part 6, of 6) (portion excerpted in Joseph Head and S.L. Cranston, *Reincarnation: An East-West Anthology,* 1961). **Dec,** *Theosophical Path,* 27 (573–578), "The Maya Mystery — Yucatan (Illustrated with photographs) (reprinted in *The Lama's Law*).

1925

Jan, *Theosophical Path,* 28 (37–41), "An Answer to Correspondents" (reprinted in *The Lama's Law*). (93–94), "Reviews of 'The Wine of Life,' Katherine Tingley's Forthcoming Book" (reprinted as "Preface" in Tingley's book, *The Wine of Life,* 1925). **Jan 20,** *Adventure,* 50 (178), "The Camp-Fire" (Letter on hunger as the source of crime: "No nation that has enough food to go around..."). **Feb,** *The Frontier,* 1 (103–108), "On the Trail of Sindbad the Sailor" (excerpted as "Lion Paradise," *Short Stories,* 10 Aug 1932). **Feb,** *Theosophical Path,* 28 (136–142), "As to Writing and Reading" (reprinted in *The Lama's Law*). **Feb 10,** *Adventure,* 51 (3–59), "Tros of Samothrace" (rewritten as part one of *Tros of Samothrace*). (179–180), "The Camp-Fire (Letter introducing *Tros of Samothrace:* "I have followed Caesar's Commentaries as closely..."). **Apr,** *Theosophical Path,* 28 (338–346), "As to Success and Failure" (reprinted in *The Lama's Law*).

Apr 10, *Adventure*, 52 (3–63), "The Enemy of Rome" (rewritten as part two of *Tros of Samothrace*). May, *Theosophical Path*, 28 (428–435), "A Beginner's Concept of Theosophy" (reprinted in *The Lama's Law*) (excerpted as "Like the Sunrise," *The Eclectic Theosophist*, Mar-Apr 1985). Jun 10, *Adventure*, 53 (3–66), "Prisoners of War" (rewritten as part three of *Tros of Samothrace*). (175–176), "The Camp-Fire" (Letter introducing *Prisoners of War*: "What appeals to me most about this period of…"). Jul, *Raja Yoga Messenger*, 21 (168), "True Drama, The Soul's Interpretator." Jul 10, *Adventure*, 53 (181–183), "The Camp-Fire" (Letter to Arthur D. Howden Smith on the Tros stories: "The difficulty of answering Mr. Smith lies chiefly…"). Jul 30, *Adventure*, 53 (175–178), "The Camp-Fire" (Letter to the editor on the Tros stories: "There are some redoubtable antagonists to answer…"). Aug 20, *Adventure*, 54 (1–67), "Hostages to Luck" (rewritten as part four of *Tros of Samothrace*). (173–175), "The Camp-Fire" (Letter introducing *Hostages to Luck*: "There is a host of people who accept the word of…"). Oct 10, *Adventure*, 55 (3–73), "Admiral of Caesar's Fleet" (rewritten as part five of *Tros of Samothrace*). Dec, *Theosophical Path*, 29 (514–526), "As to Capital Punishment" (reprinted in *The Lama's Law*). Dec 10, *Adventure*, 56 (3–74), "The Dancing Girls of Gades" (rewritten as part six of *Tros of Samothrace*).

1926

Jan, *Theosophical Path*, 30 (16–20), "Apology" (reprinted in *The Lama's Law*) (excerpted as "How Is a Story Written?," *Eclectic Theosophist*, Jul-Aug 1980). Feb 10, *Adventure*, 57 (66–101), "The Messenger of Destiny" (Part 1, of 3; concludes 28 Feb 1926) (rewritten as part seven of *Tros of Samothrace*). Feb 20, *Adventure*, 57 (104–129), "The Messenger of Destiny" (Part 2, of 3). Feb 28, *Adventure*, 57 (114–138), "The Messenger of Destiny" (Part 3, of 3). Jun 8, *Adventure*, 58 (37–63), "Ramsden" (Part 1, of 5; concludes 8 Aug 1926) (rewritten as *The Devil's Guard/Ramsden*). (178–181), "The Camp-Fire" (Letter introducing *Ramsden*: "Let me begin by saying once and for all that this…"). Jun 23, *Adventure*, 58 (112–137), "Ramsden" (Part 2, of 5) (Saying preceeding Chapter 7 reprinted as "Guarded Secrets," *Golden Book*, Dec 1926). Jul 8, *Adventure*, 58 (114–138), "Ramsden" (Part 3, of 5). Jul 23, *Adventure*, 58 (115–141), "Ramsden" (Part 4, of 5). Aug 8, *Adventure*, 58 (108–126), "Ramsden" (Part 5, of 5). Oct 23, *Adventure*, 60 (132–195), "The Falling Star" (reprinted as *Caesar Dies*).

1927

Jan 1, *Adventure*, 61 (114–188), "The Red Flame of Erinpura"(reprinted as *The Red Flame of Erinpura*). Sep, *San Diego Magazine*, 3 (3, 46), "Talbot Mundy on Civilization, Art and San Diego."

1928

book: *The Great Horn Spoon* by Eugene Wright (Bobbs-Merrill) [dust jacket endorsement]. Oct 27, *Argosy All-Story Weekly*, 198 (726–749), "When Trails Were New" (Part 1, of 6; concludes 1 Dec 1928) (cover illustration by Alta Graef) (reprinted as *When Trails Were New*). (861), "Argonotes: When Trails Were New" (Letter introducing *When Trails Were New*: "In the spring of 1832 Black Hawk, who was…."). Nov 1, *Adventure*, 68 (2–19), "The Wheel of Destiny" (cover illustration by L.J. Cronin). Nov 3, *Argosy All-Story Weekly*, 199 (68–88), "When Trails Were New" (Part 2, of 6). Nov 10, *Argosy All-Story Weekly*, 199 (243–261), "When Trails Were New " (Part 3, of 6). Nov 15, *Adventure*, 68 (2–19), "The Big League Miracle." Nov 17, *Argosy All-Story Weekly*, 199 (380–401), "When Trails Were New " (Part 4, of 6). Nov 24, *Argosy All-Story Weekly*, 199 (516–537), "When Trails Were New " (Part 5, of 6). Dec 1, *Adventure*, 68 (156–178), "On the Road to Allah's Heaven." Dec 1, *Argosy All-Story Weekly*, 199 (692–713), "When Trails Were New" (Part 6, of 6). Dec 6, *New York Times* (32), "Letter to the editor: Triumvirate of Mayors."

1929

book: *A Curious Life*, by George Wehner (Horace Liveright) (5–13), "Introduction." Jan 1, *Adventure*, 69 (2–26), "Golden River." Feb, book: *Queen Cleopatra* (Bobbs-Merrill) (Two chapters reprinted in Allan Barnard, ed., *Cleopatra's Nights*, 1950). Feb 1, *Adventure*, 69 (156–179), "A Tucket of Drums." Feb 2, *Argosy All-Story Weekly*, 201 (145–163), "Ho for London Town!

(Part 1, of 4; concludes 23 Feb 1929) (cover illustration by Alta Graef) (reprinted as *W.H./The Queen's Warrant*). **Feb** 9, *Argosy All-Story Weekly*, 201 (339–360), "Ho for London Town!" (Part 2, of 4). **Feb** 15, *Adventure*, 69 (156–180), "In Old Narada Fort." **Feb** 16, *Argosy All-Story Weekly*, 201 (518–538), "Ho for London Town!" (Part 3, of 4). **Feb** 23, *Argosy All-Story Weekly*, 201 (697–717) "Ho for London Town!" (Part 4, of 4). **Mar** 9, *Argosy All-Story Weekly*, 202 (5–23) "Asoka's Alibi" (Part 1, of 3; concludes 23 Mar 1929) (cover illustration by Paul Stahr). **Mar** 16, *Argosy All-Story Weekly*, 202 (211–230), "Asoka's Alibi" (Part 2, of 3). **Mar** 23, *Argosy All-Story Weekly*, 202 (391–406), "Asoka's Alibi" (Part 3, of 3). **Apr**, *Theosophical Path*, 36 (302–303), "I Have Risen" (reprinted in *The Lama's Law*). **Apr** 27, *Argosy All-Story Weekly*, 203 (150–165), "By Allah Who Made Tigers" (Part 1, of 3; concludes 11 May 1929) (cover illustration by Paul Stahr). (285), "Argonotes: The Moslem Mullah" (Letter regarding Mullahs in relation to *By Allah Who Made Tigers*: "The Mohammedans have no priesthood...."). **May** *Everybody's combined with Romance*, 2 (2–43), "One Egyptian Night" (cover illustration). (174), "Talbot Mundy" (autobiographical letter) (reprinted as "The Men Who Make the Argosy," *Argosy*, 24 May 1930). **May** 4, *Argosy All-Story Weekly*, 203 (343–358), "By Allah Who Made Tigers" (Part 2, of 3). **May** 11, *Argosy All-Story Weekly*, 203 (515–532), "By Allah Who Made Tigers" (Part 3, of 3). **Jun** 30, *New York Times* (VIII, 4), "An Author's Characters." **Jul**, Theosophical Path, 36 (361–362), "Spiritual Man is Eternal: There Are No Dead!" (reprinted as "The Art of Dying Daily," *Eclectic Theosophist*, Sep-Oct 1981) (excerpted as "Death and the Actor and the Stage," *Eclectic Theosophist*, Jul-Aug 1983). **Aug**, *Everybody's Combined with Romance*, 2 (20–58), "Flame of Cruelty" (cover illustration by Duncan McMillan). **Sep** *Theosophical Path*, 36 (402), "Hail and Farewell!" (reprinted in *The Lama's Law*). **Oct** 1, *Adventure*, 72 (76–104), "The Invisible Guns of Kabul" (Part 1, of 5; concludes 1 Dec 1929) (cover illustration by Hubert Rogers) (reprinted as *Cock o' the North/Gup Bahadur*). **Oct** 15, *Adventure*, 72 (58–88), "The Invisible Guns of Kabul" (Part 2, of 5). **Nov**, *Theosophical Path*, 36 (539–548), "Three Signs of the Times: Kenneth Morris— Flinders Petrie — Spengler." **Nov** 1, *Adventure*, 72 (152–181), "The Invisible Guns of Kabul" (Part 3, of 5). **Nov** 15, *Adventure*, 72 (44–70), "The Invisible Guns of Kabul" (Part 4, of 5). **Dec** 1, *Adventure*, 72 (56–83), "The Invisible Guns of Kabul" (Part 5, of 5). **Dec** 7, *Saturday Evening Post*, 202 (12, 234, 237), "Random Reminiscences of African Big Game."

1930

Feb 1, *Adventure*, 73 (62–74), "Consistent Anyhow." **Feb** 11, *New York Times* (26), "Letter to the editor: The Result of Cynicism. **May** 24, *Argosy*, 212 (436–452), "The Affair at Kaligaon" (Part 1, of 3; concludes 7 Jun 1930) (cover illustration by Paul Stahr). **May** 31, *Argosy*, 212 (626–643), "The Affair at Kaligaon" (Part 2, of 3). **Jun** 7, *Argosy*, 212 (795–813), "The Affair at Kaligaon" (Part 3, of 3). **Oct**, book: *Black Light* (Bobbs-Merrill) (Reprinted in *All Four Winds*). **Nov** 15, *Adventure*, 76 (3–27), "King of the World" (Part 1, of 7; concludes 15 Feb 1931) (cover illustration by Hubert Rogers) (rewritten as *Jimgrim/Jimgrim Sahib*, included in *All Four Winds*). (184–185), "The Camp-Fire" (Letter introducing *King of the World*: "In real life *Grim* was an American officer attached....") (reprinted as "Preface" in first Century edition of *Jimgrim*). **Dec** 1, *Adventure*, 76 (128–154), "King of the World" (Part 2, of 7). **Dec** 6, *Argosy*, 217 (145–163), "The Elephant Sahib" (Part 1, of 6; concludes 10 Jan 1931) (cover illustration by Paul Stahr). **Dec** 13, *Argosy*, 217 (342–359), "The Elephant Sahib" (Part 2, of 6). **Dec** 15, *Adventure*, 77 (78–104), "King of the World" (Part 3, of 7). **Dec** 20, *Argosy*, 217 (529–543), "The Elephant Sahib" (Part 3, of 6). **Dec** 27, *Argosy*, 217 (692–710), "The Elephant Sahib" (Part 4, of 6).

1931

Jan 1, *Adventure*, 77 (84–109), "King of the World" (Part 4, of 7). **Jan** 3, *Argosy*, 217 (840–859), "The Elephant Sahib" (Part 5, of 6). **Jan** 10, *Argosy*, 218 (113–127), "The Elephant Sahib" (Part 6, of 6). **Jan** 15, *Adventure*, 77 (72–102), "King of the World" (Part 5, of 7). **Feb** 1, *Adventure*, 77(92–115), "King of the World" (Part 6, of 7). **Feb** 5, *Adventure*, 77 (69–96), "King of the World" (Part 7, of 7). **May** 1, *Adventure*, 78 (2–11), "Black Flag" (reprinted in *Famous Pulp*

Classics, 1975). **Aug** 1, *Adventure*, 79 (2–13), "The Man on the Mat." **Oct** 1, *Adventure*, 80 (2–13) "The Babu" (rewritten as "Milk of the Moon," *Passing Show* [GB], 30 Apr 1932; *Argosy*, 17 Sep 1938; and reprinted as "Impudence Is Art," *Britannia & Eve* [GB], May 1939). **Nov** 15, *Adventure*, 80 (2–17), "The Eye-Teeth of O'Hara" (cover illustration by Robert W. Amick) (reprinted in the books *The Valiant View*, and Martin H. Greenberg and Charles G. Waugh, eds., *Loaded for Bear*, 1990).

1932

Jan 1, *Adventure*, 81 (2–18), "Case 13" (reprinted in *Britannia and Eve* [GB], Aug 1932). **Mar** 1, *Adventure*, 81 (2–23), "Chullunder Ghose the Guileless" (reprinted as "Innocent, Noncombatant and Guileless" in *The Valiant View*). **Mar** 15, *Adventure*, 82 (111–122), "A Jungle Sage." **Apr** 1, *Adventure*, 82 (52–63), "Watu." **Apr** 30, *The Passing Show* (GB) (?), "Milk of the Moon" (reprinted in *Argosy*, 17 Sep 1938, and as "Impudence is Art," *Britannia and Eve* [GB], May 1939) (rewritten from "The Babu," *Adventure*, 1 Oct 1931). **Jun**, book: *"C.I.D."* (Hutchinson). **Aug** 1, *Adventure*, 83 (26–52), "White Tigers" (Part 1, of 2; concludes 15 Aug 1932). **Aug** 15, *Adventure*, 83 (94–117), "White Tigers" (Part 2, of 2).

1933

Feb, book: *The Gunga Sahib* (Hutchinson). **Jun** 14, *Argosy*, 239 (54–65), "The Man from Poonch" (reprinted in *Britannia and Eve* [GB], Aug 1933; and in *The Valiant View*) (abridged in *The Thriller* [GB], 30 Mar 1935). **Jul** 15, *The Passing Show* (GB) (?), "The Bell on Hell Shoal" (reprinted in the book, *My Most Exciting Story*, 1936). **Aug**, *Adventure*, 87 (2–15), "Red Sea Cargo" (copyrighted under the title "In the Red, Red Sea"). **Dec** 12, *The Christian Science Monitor* (16), "Letters to The Christian Science Monitor: Restraint Appreciated."

1934

Jan 6, *Argosy*, 243 (4–36), "Camera!" (cover illustration by Paul Stahr). **Jan** 20, *The Christian Science Monitor* (16), "Letters to The Christian Science Monitor: 'Bar the Bar.'" **Feb** 10, *Liberty*, 2 (30–31), "The Things Men Fear." **Mar** 14, *The Christian Science Monitor* (WM13), "Over the Editor's Desk: Japan." **Jul** 25, *The Christian Science Monitor* (WM6), "Renaissance: The Hope of Hollywood." **Aug** 15, *Maclean's* (Canada), 47 (3–5, 38–40), "Solomon's Half-Way House" (Part 1, of 4; concludes 1 Oct 1934) (Illustrated by John F. Clymer). **Sep** 1, *Maclean's* (Canada), 47 (18–20, 39–40), "Solomon's Half-Way House" (Part 2, of 4). **Sep** 15, *Maclean's* (Canada), 47 (20–22, 55), "Solomon's Half-Way House" (Part 3, of 4). **Sep** 15, *Argosy*, 249 (61–72), "The Gods Seem Contented"(reprinted in the book, *My Best Thriller*, 1935). Oct book: *Tros of Samothrace* (Hutchinson) (xi–xiii) "Foreword" (reprinted in *Fantastic Collector*, Apr/May 1991). **Oct** 1, *Maclean's* (Canada), 47 (18–20, 32), "Solomon's Half-Way House" (Part 4, of 4). **Oct** 28, *The American Weekly* (1, 16, 18, 22), "Full Moon" (Part 1, of 14; concludes 27 Jan 1935) (cover and interior illustrations) (rewritten as *Full Moon/There Was a Door*, reprinted in *Famous Fantastic Mysteries*, Feb 1953). **Nov** 4, *The American Weekly* (20, 22, 23), "Full Moon" (Part 2, of 14). **Nov** 11, *The American Weekly* (14, 16, 20), "Full Moon" (Part 3, of 14). **Nov** 18, *The American Weekly* (14, 16, 23), "Full Moon" (Part 4, of 14). **Nov** 25, *The American Weekly* (17, 19), "Full Moon" (Part 5, of 14). **Dec** 2, *The American Weekly* (16, 18, 22), "Full Moon' (Part 6, of 14). **Dec** 9, *The American Weekly* (16, 18), "Full Moon" (Part 7, of 14). **Dec** 16, *The American Weekly* (16, 18), "Full Moon" (Part 8, of 14). **Dec** 23, The *American Weekly* (15, 17), "Full Moon" (Part 9, of 14). **Dec** 30, *The American Weekly* (14, 16), "Full Moon" (Part 10, of 14).

1935

Jan, *Blue Book*, 60 (4–15), "Bengal Rebellion" (Illustrated by John Richard Flanagan) (slightly rewritten as "Ill Wind," *Britannia and Eve* [GB], Aug 1935; *The Grand* [GB], May 1937) **Jan** 6, *The American Weekly* (14, 15), "Full Moon" (Part 11, of 14). **Jan** 13, *The American Weekly* (14, 15, 17), "Full Moon" (Part 12, of 14). **Jan** 20, *The American Weekly* (17, 18), "Full Moon"

(Part 13, of 14). **Jan** 27, *The American Weekly* (18, 20), "Full Moon" (Part 14, of 14). **May** 1, *Adventure*, 92 (2–56), "Battle Stations" (rewritten as part one of *Purple Pirate*). (118–119), "The Camp-Fire" (Letter introducing *Battle Stations*: "The basis of my story, 'Battle Stations....'"). **May** 5, *This Week* (9–10, 15), "Speed" (Illustrations by Karl Godwin) (reprinted in *Novel* [GB], Nov 1936). **Jun** 15, *Adventure*, 92 (2–57), "Cleopatra's Promise" (rewritten as part two of *Purple Pirate*). (117–119), "The Camp-Fire" (Letter introducing *Cleopatra's Promise*: "I wonder how many people who read...."). **Aug** 15, *Adventure*, 93 (2–54), "The Purple Pirate" (rewritten as part three of the book *Purple Pirate*). (117–118), "The Camp-Fire" (Letter introducing *Purple Pirate*: "Roman charioteers were almost without..."). **Oct** 1, *Adventure*, 93 (2–58), "Fleets of Fire" (rewritten as part four of *Purple Pirate*). (116–117), "The Camp-Fire" (Letter introducing *Fleets of Fire*: "From earliest times until the days when...").

1936

Apr, *Forum and Century*, 95 (195), "To the Editor." **May-Jun**, *All Aces*, 1 (6–58), "The Wolf of the Pass." **Dec**, *Britannia & Eve* [GB], 13 (40–43, 148–155), "The Princess" (Illustrated by Edward Osmond) (rewritten as "The Piping Days of Peace," *Maclean's*, 1 Jun 1937).

1937

Jan 24, *The American Weekly* (1, 14, 17–20), "The Thunder Dragon Gate" (Part 1, of 8; concludes 14 Mar 1937) (cover and interior illustrations) (reprinted as *The Thunder Dragon Gate*). **Jan** 31, *The American Weekly* (18, 19, 22, 23), "The Thunder Dragon Gate" (Part 2, of 8). **Feb** 7, *The American Weekly* (19, 23–26), "The Thunder Dragon Gate" (Part 3, of 8). **Feb** 14, *The American Weekly* (16, 20, 22, 24–26), "The Thunder Dragon Gate" (Part 4, of 8). **Feb** 22, *The American Weekly* (18–22), "The Thunder Dragon Gate" (Part 5, of 8). **Feb** 25, *Short Stories*, 158 (14–60), "The Elephant Waits" (cover illustration) (reprinted in *Short Stories* [GB], Mid-Jun 1937; *Short Stories* [US], Feb 1959) (rewritten as "The Night the Clocks Stopped," *Adventure*, Mar 1941). **Feb** 28, *The American Weekly* (16, 18, 20, 21), "The Thunder Dragon Gate" (Part 6, of 8). **Mar** 7, *The American Weekly* (18, 20, 26, 29), "The Thunder Dragon Gate" (Part 7, of 8). **Mar** 14, *The American Weekly* (18, 26, 28, 29), "The Thunder Dragon Gate" (Part 8, of 8). **May** 16, *This Week* (20, 32), "The Avenger' (copyrighted under the title "The Sirdar's Oath"). **Jun** 1, *Maclean's* (Canada), 50 (7–9, 41–44), "The Piping Days of Peace" (Illustrated by Ralph Coleman) (reprinted in the book, *My Best Spy Story*, 1938) (rewritten from "The Princess," *Britannia & Eve* [GB], Dec 1936). **Aug** 15, *This Week* (4, 20), "The Treacherous Road" (Part 1, of 4; concludes 5 Sep 1937) (Illustrated by Marshall Frantz). **Aug** 22 *This Week* (7, 20, 27), 'The Treacherous Road" (Part 2, of 4). **Aug** 29, *This Week* (7, 11), "The Treacherous Road" (Part 3, of 4). **Sep** 5, *This Week* (12–13), "The Treacherous Road" (Part 4, of 4). **Nov**, book: *East and West / Diamonds See in the Dark* (Appleton-Century). **Nov**, *Adventure*, 98 (105–113), "Companions in Arms." **Nov**, *American Cavalcade*, 1 (79–80), "The Hermit and the Tiger."

1938

book: *Radio Continuity Types*, ed. Sherman Paxton Lawton (Boston: Expression Co.) (50–56), "Jack Armstrong, the All-American Boy, Episode No. 893." **Apr** 15, *Maclean's* (Canada), 51 (7–9, 34–44), "Old Ugly Face" (Part 1, of 3; concludes 15 May 1938) (Illustrated by Ralph Pallen Coleman) (rewritten as *Old Ugly-Face*). **May** 1, *Maclean's* (Canada), 51 (20–22, 43–49), "Old Ugly Face" (Part 2, of 3). **May** 15, *Maclean's* (Canada), 51 (20–22, 28–32), "Old Ugly Face" (Part 3, of 3). **Oct**, *Golden Fleece*, 1 (2–42), "Roman Holiday" (cover and illustrations by Harold Delay) (reprinted in *Pulp Vault*, 1990). **Dec**, *True Mystic Science*, 1 (14–16, 63), "Mystic India Speaks."

1939

book: *The Valiant View* (n.p.), "Foreword" (reprinted in *Fantastic Collector*, Apr/May 1991). book: *The Valiant View* (237–256), "The Honourable Pig."

1940

Feb, book: *Old Ugly-Face* (Appleton-Century) (rewritten from "Old Ugly Face," *Maclean's* magazine serial, 15 Apr-15 May 1938). **Jun** 15, *Saturday Review*, 22 (15), "Great Idea" (Book review of H.H. The Ranee of Sarawak's *A Star Fell*).

1941

Mar, *Adventure*, 104 (8–32), "The Night the Clocks Stopped" (rewritten from "The Elephant Waits," *Short Stories*, 25 Feb 1937). **Aug** 10, *Short Stories*, 176 (8–61), "Odds on the Prophet."

1947

Nov, book: *I Say Sunrise* (Andrew Dakers).

Chapter Notes

Chapter I

1. William Bolitho, *Twelve Against the Gods: The Story of Adventure* (New York: Reader's Club, 1941), 174.
2. Peter Berresford Ellis, *The Last Adventurer* (West Kingston, RI: Donald M. Grant, 1984), 23.
3. Dawn Mundy Provost, interview with the author, April 1, 1980.
4. TM, "'Mother Nature': A Review of a Book by William J. Long," *The Theosophical Path*, 26 (February 1924), 142.
5. TM, Author's questionnaire, p. 1, Bobbs-Merrill mss.
6. TM, "'Mother Nature,'" 133–134.
7. *The Times*, June 14, 1893, p. 5; TM, Author's questionnaire, p. 1.
8. TM, "The Camp-Fire," *Adventure* (July 3, 1925), 178.
9. "Rugby Scholarships," *The Times*, June 14, 1893, p. 5.
10. TM, "Autobiography," in "The Camp-Fire," *Adventure*, 21 (April 1, 1919), 178–183, reprinted in Donald M. Grant, *Talbot Mundy, Messenger of Destiny* (West Kingston, RI: Donald M. Grant, 1983), 16.
11. TM, letter to D.L. Chambers, March 27, 1924, Bobbs-Merrill mss.
12. Ellis, 33–34.
13. "Mundy, Sandbagged, Robbed, Tells Past," *The World*, October 4, 1909, p. 14.
14. "The Men Who Make the Argosy: Talbot Mundy," *Argosy*, 212 (May 24, 1930), 573. Although his reminiscences never identified his benefactor, Mundy was called home to work for the husband of his mother's sister, his uncle William Sharpe, on an estate in Bardney, in the northern half of England near Nottingham. Ellis in Grant, 37; Ellis, 35. The length of time between Mundy's return from Germany and his departure for India has been estimated at closer to three years by Ellis. This is not only totally out of character for the young Talbot, but is contradicted by the quote cited, which Mundy placed distinctly in chronology between his arrival from Germany and his first trip to India.
15. TM, "Autobiography," in Grant, 18.
16. TM, "Brotherhood or League?," *The Theosophical Path*, 25 (October 1925), 345–346. The same article reports similar results in Assam, when he saw a railroad contractor order wheelbarrows to carry the dirt from the construction site previously carried in baskets on the worker's heads; they would only handle the barrows in the same manner.
17. Archie Kilpatrick, "Talbot Mundy Is Dead, Writer, Resident Here," *Manchester Evening Herald*, August 6, 1940, p. 2.
18. TM, "Autobiography," reprinted in Grant, 18.
19. TM, "Mystic India Speaks," *True Mystic Science*, 1 (December 1938), 16, 63. Portions of this incident, as well as some autobiographical and much fictional material, were incorporated into the short story "The Man on the Mat."
20. TM, letter to Wincenty Lutoslawski, May 1, 1938, p. 1, Janina Lutoslawski Collection; B.K., "Point Loma's Lure Induces World-Traveled Author to Stay Here and Establish His Permanent Home," *The San Diego Union*, February 15, 1925, p. 9; TM, Letter to "The Camp-Fire" on the Ten Lost Tribes of Israel, *Adventure*, 36 (September 10, 1922), 178.
21. TM, "Mystic India Speaks," 15.
22. TM, letter to Rose Wilder Lane, June 25, 1934, p. 2, RWL mss.
23. TM, "Autobiography," reprinted in Grant, 20. *Adventure* habitually abbreviated swearing with the requisite number of dashes.
24. TM, "Autobiography," reprinted in Grant, 21.
25. A.S. Hoffman, *Adventure*, 2 (February 1912).
26. TM, "Autobiography," reprinted in Grant, 21. Ellis believes Mundy never saw the conflict, but in fact his evidence does not prove this. Although there are no government records that mention his involvement in the Boer War, Mundy may have been using an alias, since his description of leaving India already indicates possible legal difficulties, and he would use several aliases in subsequent years in Africa. He may certainly have been in a supporting role in the conflict, not actually in the military, but close enough to the action for it to make a lasting impression; fifteen years later his poor eyesight would render him ineligible for World War I. Mundy did learn tales of the combat that would

serve him well in providing background to some of his early short stories, such as "The Cowards," "Rabbit," and "Three Helios," and such articles as "Tucker's Tongue" and briefer tales in *Adventure* magazine's "Camp-Fire" section in July and December 1912. Whether a military veteran or not, the idea of Mundy as having been in the Boer War occupied a large place in the conceptions of those who knew him.

27. Ellis, 38; Ellis in Grant, 50–51. The birthday recollection comes from a cousin and contemporary of Mundy's, Mrs. May Nicholson, interviewed 78 years after the fact. Curiously, she recalled Mundy leaving that Autumn, which would coincide with Mundy's own memory of six months at home; Ellis, meanwhile, points to Mundy's next departure as occurring in March 1901. See Ellis, 42 and Grant, 51. Mundy places himself in India during at least part of 1900 in "An Author's Characters," *New York Times*, June 30, 1929, pp. VIII, 4.

28. *The Times*, August 1, 1903, p. 8. Ellis alternately gives her age as a year younger than Mundy (Grant, 52) or a year older (Ellis, 44).

29. TM, "Autobiography," reprinted in Grant, 21.

30. Kilpatrick, 2.

31. TM, "A Jungle Sage," *Adventure*, 82 (March 15, 1932), 113.

32. TM, "Autobiography," reprinted in Grant, 22.

33. TM, "Random Reminiscences of African Big Game," *Saturday Evening Post*, 202 (December 7, 1929), 12, 234.

34. TM, "Random Reminiscences of African Big Game," 234.

35. Kilpatrick, 2.

36. Marguerite Mooers Marshall, "Treasure of Tippoo Tib, 100,000,000 Pounds Ivory, Awaits Finder in Africa," *New York Evening World*, 60, no. 21, 169, undated newspaper clipping in Talbot Mundy Promotional File, Bobbs-Merrill mss.

37. TM, "Autobiography," reprinted in Grant, 23. He fictionalized the experience in chapters 6–9 of *The Ivory Trail*.

38. W.R. Foran, letter to A.S. Hoffman, November 4, 1960, A.S. Hoffman Collection, Pennsylvania State University. The letter was perhaps prompted by the fact that Foran, also a contributor to *Adventure*, had far less literary success than Mundy.

39. TM, *I Say Sunrise* (Philadelphia: Milton F. Wells, 1949), 8–9. He placed the incident in a fictional context in *The Ivory Trail* (Indianapolis: Bobbs-Merrill, 1919), 307.

40. TM, letter to Rose Wilder Lane, June 25, 1934, p. 2, RWL mss.

41. TM, "Some True Stories About Wild Animals," *Raja Yoga Messenger*, 20 (May 1924), 36; TM, "Watu," *Adventure*, 82 (April 1, 1932), 60–63.

42. TM, "A Jungle Sage," *Adventure*, 82 (March 15, 1932), 117.

43. TM, "A Jungle Sage," 118, 119.

44. TM, "A Jungle Sage," 117.

45. *The Times Law Reports*, v. 24 (1907–1908), 160; "Wife's Divorce," *The Times*, May 6, 1908, p. 18; "Gribbon v. Gribbon," *The Times*, May 9, 1908, p. 5; "Gribbon v. Gribbon," *The Times*, May 11, 1908, p. 3.

46. *The Times*, June 28, 1899, p. 13. The complete trial is covered in *The Times*, 1899: June 21, p. 4; June 24, p. 18; June 28, p. 13; July 1, p. 17; December 14, p. 15; December 15, p. 4; December 16, pp. 3–4; December 20, p. 15; December 21, p. 15. See also "Former Mrs. Craven in Poverty Here," *New York Times*, October 8, 1909, p. 11.

47. "'Lady Mundy' on Trail of Robbers," *The New York Herald*, October 3, 1909, p. II-6, quoted in Complaint 9668–1921, Supreme Court, New York County, Inez Morton Mundy against New York Herald Company, December 7, 1909.

48. Provost, interview.

49. "Thugs' Victim Found Dying," *The Sun*, October 2, 1909, p. 1.

50. "Thugs' Victim Found Dying," 1; "'Lady Mundy' on Trail of Robbers," II-6.

51. "Thugs' Victim Found Dying," 1.

52. "Blackjacked, Former British Officer Dying," *New York Evening Journal*, October 2, 1909, p. 5.

53. Amended Answer, Supreme Court, New York County, Inez Morton Mundy against New York Herald Company, February 11, 1910.

54. "Former Mrs. Craven in Poverty Here," *New York Times*, October 3, 1909, p. 11.

55. "Mundy, Sandbagged, Robbed, Tells Past," *The World*, October 4, 1909, p. 14. "Thugs' Victim Found Dying," 1.

56. Complaint 9668–1921, Supreme Court, New York County.

57. Answer 1948–1912, Supreme Court, New York County, Talbot Miller Mundy against Cunliffe Owen, pp. 1–2.

58. Kilpatrick, 2.

59. Summons and Complaint 1947–1912, Supreme Court, New York County, Talbot Miller Mundy against Cunliffe Owen, April 28, 1910, p. 2; Summons and Complaint 1948–1912, Supreme Court, New York County, Inez Morton Mundy against Cunliffe Owen, April 26, 1910, p. 2.

60. Summons and Complaint 1948–1912, Supreme Court, New York County, Talbot Miller Mundy against Cunliffe Owen, p. 2; Summons and Complaint 1948–1912, Supreme Court, New York County, Inez Morton Mundy against Cunliffe Owen, p. 2.

61. Answer 1948–1912, Supreme Court, New York County, Talbot Miller Mundy against Cunliffe Owen, p. 1.

62. Summons and Complaint 1948–1912, Supreme Court, New York County, Talbot Miller Mundy against Cunliffe Owen, April 28, 1910, p. 1; Summons and Complaint 1948–1912, Supreme Court, New York County, Inez Morton Mundy against Cunliffe Owen, April 26, 1910, p. 1. Mundy used the venue of a boxing story of Billy Blain, "The Goner?," appearing in the February 1912 issue of *Adventure*, to fictionalize his immigrant arrival in New York City. "The trip across the ocean was one of the greatest events of Billy's life," but after being passed by the physicians at Ellis Island, he is slated

for deportation when the board of examiners learns he has no job waiting for him, or even a skill beyond boxing." Walter Galt, "The Goner?," *Adventure*, 3 (February 1912), 688. Mundy had even fewer abilities. The story continues, "But there are people on Ellis Island who are not quite so particular as the examining board — big Irish guards, for instance, who love any one who can fight and are sincerely sorry for any kind of 'white man' whose fate it is to be cooped up in a detention room with forty or fifty unwashed men who are 'not white.'" Galt, "The Goner?," 688. They obtain a second hearing before the board, and Blain's deportation order is revoked when they learn that Billy gave more than half his money to a female passenger who needed it to be allowed to land. Once in New York, Billy wanders to the West Side to search for a temporary job, and initially supports himself at menial jobs.

63. "Suffragist in Bellevue," *New York Times*, January 20, 1913, p. 2.

64. Provost, interview.

65. Provost, interview.

66. "The Men Who Make the Argosy: Talbot Mundy," *Argosy* (May 24, 1930), 573.

67. A.S. Hoffman, *Adventure*, February 1912, inside front cover; Elmer Davis, "A Loss to Fiction," *The Saturday Review of Literature*, 22 (August 17, 1940), 8; Wyatt Blassingame, letter to Peter Ellis, March 18, 1978, p. 1, carbon in Anna Maria Historical Society; Robert Lloyd Davis, letter to the author, December 2, 1996, p. 1; Jan Zilliacus, letter to the author, October 1997, p. 1.

68. Wyatt Blassingame, letter to Lurton Blassingame, quoted in "Camp-Fire," *Adventure* (November 1940), 113.

69. Provost, interview.

70. "Mundy an Exception Among Maine Writers."

71. "The Men Who Make the Argosy: Talbot Mundy," *Argosy*, 212 (May 24, 1930), 573; "Talbot Mundy Joins Ince Staff," *The Silver Sheet* [*Scars of Jealousy*], March 1923], 16; "Mundy Novels to be Ince 'Specials,'" *The Silver Sheet* [*Soul of the Beast*, May 1923], 19.

72. TM, Letter to H.H. Howland, December 23, 1918, p. 1, Bobbs-Merrill mss.; "Talbot Mundy Joins Ince Staff," 16; "Mundy Novels to be Ince 'Specials,'" 19; "County Club to Hear Talbot Mundy," undated newspaper clipping, Richards Ames collection. He probably wrote other, now-forgotten articles for the city dailies, including sports coverage and book reviews. Other output may have included "turnovers," dull 1000-word articles printed on two pages and culled from reference sources — since he turned to such essays when he had to quickly write material to fill *Jerusalem News* in 1920.

73. Kilpatrick, 2; TM, letter to Sinclair Lewis, April 7, 1914, p. 1, Beinecke Rare Book and Manuscript Library, Yale University.

74. Among those who appeared in *Adventure*, many for the first time, were Octavus Roy Cohen, Gouverneur Morris, Damon Runyon, and T.S. Stribling. "No. 1 Pulp," *Time*, 26 (October 21, 1935), 40.

See also "*Adventure* is 25 Years Old," *Publishers Weekly*, 128 (November 2, 1935), 1667; "Adventure: Dean of the Pulps Celebrates Its Silver Jubilee," *News-week*, 6 (October 26, 1935), 23, and Darrell C. Richardson, "Talbot Mundy: Oriental Mystic," *Fantasy Commentator*, 2 (fall 1948), 291; Arthur Sullivant Hoffman, "Camp-Fire," *Adventure*, 15 (October 18, 1917), 181; Grant, 121; Ron Goulart, *Cheap Thrills* (New Rochelle, NY: 1972), 30–42; Robert Kenneth Jones, *The Lure of Adventure* (Starmont House, 1989).

75. "Talbot Mundy Joins Ince Staff," 16; "Mundy Novels to be Ince 'Specials,'" 19; "County Club to Hear Talbot Mundy."

76. A.S. Hoffman, "The Camp-Fire," *Adventure*, 30 (September 3, 1921), 180.

77. TM, letter to D.L. Chambers, December 13, 1925, p. 2, Bobbs-Merrill mss.

78. TM, "The Soul of a Regiment," *Adventure*, 3 (February 1912), 609.

79. A.S. Hoffman, "The Camp-Fire," *Adventure*, 14 (July 1917), 184.

80. TM, "Autobiography" in "The Camp-Fire," *Adventure*, 21 (April 1, 1919), reprinted in Grant, 26.

Chapter II

1. TM, letter to Wm. C. Bobbs, December 17, 1921, p. 4, Bobbs-Merrill mss.; "The New Books: Fiction," *Saturday Review of Literature*, 1 (November 29, 1924), 330; Clyde B. Clason, "Foreword: Talbot Mundy — An Appreciation" in TM, *Old Ugly-Face* (Philadelphia: Wells & Shakespeare, 1950), vii; Bradford M. Day, *Talbot Mundy Biblio* (New York: Science-Fiction and Fantasy Publications, 1955), 1; Nirmal Singh Dhesi, "Mundy's 'Om' a Psychic or Spiritual Journey," *The Eclectic Theosophist*, No. 77 (September-October 1983), 8. See also "Story of East Pictures Way of Life," unidentified newspaper clipping, Richards Ames collection.

2. TM, *Rung Ho!* (New York: Charles Scribners's Sons, 1914), 185.

3. TM, *Rung Ho!*, 110.

4. "Talbot Mundy's Stirring Romance of India," *New York Times Book Review*, March 29, 1914, pp. 144–145; "One Hundred Books for Summer Reading," *New York Times Book Review*, June 14, 1914, p. 276; *New York Sun*, quoted in *Rung Ho!* Promotional Materials, Bobbs-Merrill mss.; "History and Adventure," *The Athenaeum, Supplement*, no. 4521 (June 20, 1914), 874; F.S. Hoppen, letter to TM, May 19, 1914, Scribner Archives, Princeton University; *The Times Literary Supplement*, August 23, 1917.

5. They were the only one of the three publishers to request a change in the novel. Cunningham and the McLeans trick Jaimihr by offering to release him and support him over the Maharajah, and to sell Rosemary in marriage, in trade for a portion of the treasure, a bargain which they had no intention of keeping. The chief editor at Cassell's called this a "hateful scheme," saying treachery was unnecessary and out of character for the principal white

characters. Instead, the editor suggested Rosemary seem to sacrifice herself, so Cunningham, as the hero, is not "smirched with dishonour." Newman Flower, Chief Editor, letter to James B. Pinker, November 5, 1913, Scribner Archives, Princeton University. Mundy agreed to rewrite the section, saying, "Candidly, and without shame, I have to confess that I don't like this last section, with the possible exception of the last chapter — which, too, might be improved. It lacks the 'punch' that it is meant to have, and gives the impression of having been written in a hurry." TM, letter to F.S. Hoppen, December 12, 1913, Scribner Archives, Princeton University. Mundy switches the story awkwardly as Rosemary suddenly takes pity on Jaimihr, with little motivation. Taking Jaimihr water, Ralph orders her to release him after he promises to aid the British, in return for which she pledges to marry Jaimihr. Scribners was pleased, "although it does not seem to me perhaps to move quite as rapidly as it did before. Still, it saves the missionary from disgrace and perhaps removes a shadow from the hero, and that is probably a good thing." F.S. Hoppen, letter to TM, January 8, 1914, p. 2, Scribner Archives, Princeton University.

6. TM, letter to H.H. Howland, June 10, 1919, Bobbs-Merrill mss.

7. TM, "The King Can Do No Wrong," *The Theosophical Path*, 25 (November 1923), 457.

8. TM, "Foreword," in *Tros of Samothrace* (London: Hutchinson, 1934), xiii.

9. TM, letter to D.L. Chambers, November 21, 1924, p. 2, Bobbs-Merrill mss. Many readers typed out the sayings, such as A.C. Henderson, whose manuscript copy survives at the University of Texas at Austin. The "sayings" were recognized in their time and enhanced Mundy's reputation; for instance, the president of the University of Illinois used one from *The Devil's Guard* on his 1928 Christmas card to 50 fellow university presidents. D.L. Chambers, letter to TM, December 13, 1928, Bobbs-Merrill mss.

10. TM in "Mundy Praises Kipling, but Says He Isn't Like Him," 2.

11. Provost, interview.

12. Dawn Mundy Provost, "Talbot Mundy," in Grant, 80.

13. Robert Lloyd Davis, letter to the author, December 2, 1996, p. 1.

14. Provost, interview.

15. TM to D.L. Chambers, July 27, 1916, p. 2, Bobbs-Merrill mss.

16. TM, letter to D.L. Chambers, April 3, 1922, p. 3, Bobbs-Merrill mss.

17. TM, "Kitty Burns Her Fingers," *All-Story*, 20 (July 1911), 486.

18. "A Story of India," *New York Times Book Review*, December 16, 1917, p. 555; excerpted in *Herald* (Washington, D.C.), December 30, 1917, clipping in *The Winds of the World* publicity file, Bobbs-Merrill mss.

19. TM, "An Author's Characters," *New York Times* (June 30, 1929), X4. The memory of this incident stayed with Mundy through the years, and eight years after this description, in one of his last novels, *East and West*, Mundy fictionalized this same incident, in a novel unrelated to Yasmini. TM, *East and West* (New York: D. Appleton-Century, 1937), 17–19.

20. TM, *Guns of the Gods* (Indianapolis: Bobbs-Merrill, 1921), 7.

21. TM, *Guns of the Gods*, 3.

22. TM, *Guns of the Gods*, 249.

23. TM, *The Winds of the World*, 222.

24. TM, "Gulbaz and the Game," *Adventure*, 8 (July 1914), 42.

25. TM, "An Author's Characters," p. X4.

26. R.T. Gault, "About *King — of the Khyber Rifles* and Talbot Mundy," unpublished essay, March 2000.

27. "India Truly Loyal, Says Lord Hardinge," *New York Times* (May 20, 1916), 1.

28. "Intrigue in India," Springfield, Massachusetts *Republican*, January 3, 1918, clipping in *The Winds of the World* publicity file, Bobbs-Merrill mss.

29. TM, *The Winds of the World* (Indianapolis: Bobbs-Merrill, 1917), 135.

30. *New York Tribune*, December 15, 1917, clipping in *The Winds of the World* publicity file, Bobbs-Merrill mss. *The Winds of the World* was received differently upon its publication in book form in the United States and England. In England, it was Mundy's first book since *Rung Ho!*, and regarded as a new story of India, published by Cassell & Co. in 1916, with *King, of the Khyber Rifles* appearing from Constable & Co. in July of the following year. In the United States, by contrast, publication by Bobbs-Merrill of *The Winds of the World* followed the appearance of *King — of the Khyber Rifles* in book form. *The Winds of the World* was discussed by American critics as a sequel — although of course it had been written before *King — of the Khyber Rifles*, and its events took place prior to that novel.

31. TM, *The Winds of the World*, 323.

32. TM, "An Author's Characters," p. X4. Some of the settings had also been conjured for some time; at the end of 1914, Rosemary had exhibited a painting entitled "Khinjan."

33. TM, "An Author's Characters," X4.

34. TM, letter to Bobbs-Merrill, August 7, 1916. The novel was also serially syndicated in newspapers of almost every state. New York Supreme Court, New York County, Summons and Complaint 4907–1919, p. 20. *King — of the Khyber Rifles* was the first — and only — Mundy story given elaborate illustrations during its magazine publication, from which a few were selected for the book edition. The artist, Joseph Clement Coll, a pen-and-ink specialist, had a flair for the picturesque and dramatic, and captured the story's fantastic dimension. Although Coll's illustrations did not attract praise from reviewers, nonetheless, Coll and Mundy must have been considered a good match by Bobbs-Merrill, for their subsequent book publications of *The Winds of the World*, *Hira Singh*, and *The Ivory Trail* all included about a half-dozen Coll illustra-

tions especially commissioned for the books. *New York Tribune*, December 15, 1917, clipping in *The Winds of the World* publicity file, "*King— of the Khyber Rifles*," *New York Globe*, December 23, 1916, clipping in *King— of the Khyber Rifles* files, Bobbs-Merrill mss. Another method of illustrating Mundy books was tried with *The Eye of Zeitoon*, but when it proved a commercial failure, Coll was brought back to illustrate another Yasmini novel, *Guns of the Gods*, in 1921. Coll's subsequent death from appendicitis at age 41 seemed to remove the necessity Bobbs-Merrill had felt to illustrate Mundy's novels. Scribner had rejected even the idea of an illustration on the title page to *Rung Ho!* when Mundy suggested Charlie Falls, who had prepared several covers for his stories in *Adventure* as well as drawings for "The Pillar of Light" for *Everybody's*. TM, letter to Messrs. Scribner, August 4, 1913, p. 1, Scribner Archives, Princeton University.

35. H.H. Howland, letter to TM, February 17, 1917; cover ad, *The Bookseller Newsdealer & Stationer*, 45 (December 1, 1916), and other advertisements, Bobbs-Merrill collection. There was a major embarrassment in the first edition, when Talbot's first name was misspelled on the title page as "Talbott."

36. "Brings $150,000 Film Suit," *New York Times*, February 22, 1919, p. 5.

37. TM, *King— of the Khyber Rifles* (Indianapolis: Bobbs-Merrill, 1917), 1.

38. "Intrigue and Adventure in New Romance of India," *Philadelphia North American*, December 23, 1916, clipping in *King— of the Khyber Rifles* files, Bobbs-Merrill mss.

39. TM, "Hope," *The Theosophical Path*, 26 (May 1924), 446.

40. King has been completely misunderstood by such critics as Jeffrey Richards, who saw in him a typical representative of the British Raj, a "moustached, square-jawed, eagle-eyed and resourceful" secret agent in "the great game." Richards, *Visions of Yesterday* (London: Routledge and Kegan Paul, 1973), 28. Some reviewers compared the character of King to Kipling's Strickland in the "Plain Tales." "In India," *The Sunday Call* (Newark, N.J.), December 24, 1916, clipping in *King— of the Khyber Rifles* files, Bobbs-Merrill mss.; "*King— of the Khyber Rifles*," *The Indianapolis News*, January 20, 1917, clipping in *King— of the Khyber Rifles* files, Bobbs-Merrill mss.

41. *The Milwaukee Sentinel*, January 15, 1917, clipping in *King— of the Khyber Rifles* files, Bobbs-Merrill mss.

42. *The Times Literary Supplement*, August 23, 1917; "*King— of the Khyber Rifles*," *New York Tribune*, January 13, 1917, clipping in *King— of the Khyber Rifles* files, Bobbs-Merrill mss.; "Books and Authors," *Grand Rapid News*, undated clipping in *King— of the Khyber Rifles* files, Bobbs-Merrill mss. *The Bookman* review compared *King— of the Khyber Rifles* to Stewart Edward White's *The Leopard Woman*, while the review in the *Grand Rapid News* compared it to Flora Anna Steele. *The Bookman*, 44 (February 1917), 648, *King— of the Khyber Rifles* files, Bobbs-Merrill mss.; "Books and Authors," *Grand Rapid News*, undated clipping in *King— of the Khyber Rifles* files, Bobbs-Merrill mss. The *New York Tribune*, reviewing *The Winds of the World*, would also compare it to Steele, along with Kipling and Maud Diver. *New York Tribune*, December 15, 1917, clipping in *The Winds of the World* publicity file, Bobbs-Merrill mss. Among the competitive books with the same locale published simultaneously were Will Levington Comfort's *The Last Ditch*. "Quick, Spirited Tales," *Chicago Herald*, December 23, 1916, clipping in *King— of the Khyber Rifles* files, Bobbs-Merrill mss.

43. "Intrigue and Adventure in New Romance of India," *Philadelphia North American*, December 23, 1916, clipping in *King— of the Khyber Rifles* files, Bobbs-Merrill mss.

44. TM, quoted in Greensboro (N.C.) *Daily News*, December 20, 1916, clipping in *King— of the Khyber Rifles* files, Bobbs-Merrill mss.

45. TM, *King— of the Khyber Rifles*, 371.

46. "Books and Authors," *Grand Rapid News*, undated clipping in *King— of the Khyber Rifles* files, Bobbs-Merrill mss.

47. Quoted in ad no. 649, *King— of the Khyber Rifles* files, Bobbs-Merrill mss.

48. "The Camp-Fire," *Adventure*, 35 (July 20, 1922), 178.

49. TM, letter to Elsa Barker, July 15, 1921, Stephen Michaluk Collection. Talbot's hope that royalties from *Guns of the Gods* would soon liquidate his debt to Bobbs-Merrill company proved futile; after initial promise, further advertising was not boosting lagging sales. Not until 1923 would royalties on the book bring in more than $2000 from Bobbs-Merrill. Monthly Statement to TM, April 28, 1924, Bobbs-Merrill mss. The situation was no more encouraging in England, with just over 2,000 copies sold by the end of 1922. Statements December 31, 1921, June 30, 1922, December 31, 1923 and June 30, 1924, *Guns of the Gods* Talbot Mundy in account with Hutchinson & Co., Curtis Brown mss.

50. Claudio Montalbano, "Prefaeione" (trans. by Lucy Rapillo) in T. Mundy, *El Tesoro di Sialpore*, traduzione a cura di Alfredo de Donno (Roma: Apollon, 1944), xi.

51. *Bulletin* (July 9, 1921), clipping in *Guns of the Gods* publicity file, Bobbs-Merrill mss.

52. Clipping in *Guns of the Gods* publicity file; Bobbs-Merrill mss.

53. TM, *Guns of the Gods*, 282.

54. TM, *Caves of Terror* (London: Hutchinson, 1932), 172.

55. TM, *Caves of Terror*, 35.

56. TM, *I Say Sunrise*, 65, 102.

57. Deposition of Estella B. Winslow, August 14, 1923, p. 2, Mundy vs. Mundy, Case 18130.

58. TM, letter to Rose Wilder Lane, April 24, 1934, p. 2, RWL mss.

59. TM, "Case 13," *Adventure*, 81 (January 1, 1932), 3.

60. TM, "England After the War," Part 2, *Jerusalem News*, No. 54 (February 11, 1920), 2.

61. "Writer of Short Stories Tells Long One," *Reno Evening Gazette*, August 20, 1923, p. 2.
62. TM, letter to D.L. Chambers, July 27 1916, p. 2, Bobbs-Merrill mss.
63. TM, *I Say Sunrise*, 91, 102.
64. TM, *I Say Sunrise*, 64–65.

Chapter III

1. "Talbot Mundy," publicity, rear flap of dust jacket in Appleton-Century editions.
2. TM, letter to H.H. Howland, December 23, 1918, Bobbs-Merrill mss.
3. TM, letter to Howland, September 5, 1919, Bobbs-Merrill mss.
4. TM, letter to H.H. Howland, March 12, 1919, Bobbs-Merrill mss.
5. TM, "The Real Red Root," *The Crescent*, 10 (June 1919), 17.
6. A.S. Hoffman, "The Camp-Fire," *Adventure*, 8 (July 1914), 218.
7. TM, letter to D.L. Chambers, July 27, 1916, p. 2, Bobbs-Merrill mss.
8. William Almon Wolff, "Norway, America!" *Everybody's*, 38 (January 1918), 73.
9. A.S. Hoffman, "The Camp-Fire," *Adventure*, 15 (Mid-October, 1917), 182.
10. TM, letter to H.H. Howland, October 2, 1918, p. 1, Bobbs-Merrill mss.
11. TM, letter to D.L. Chambers, December 13, 1925, pp. 2–3, Bobbs-Merrill mss.
12. "Says Indian Corps Left Proud Record," *New York Times* (December 31, 1915), 2; "British Recognize Claims of India," *New York Times* (May 22, 1916), 2; Basanta Koomar Roy, "When India Fights for England," *The Independent* (New York), 82 (April 19, 1915), 105. For a modern and very different perspective on Indian participation, see Jeffrey Greenhut, "The Imperial Reserve: The Indian Corps on the Western Front, 1914–15," *The Journal of Imperial and Commonwealth History*, 12 (October 1983), 54–73.
13. TM, *Hira Singh* (Indianapolis: Bobbs-Merrill, 1918), 24.
14. "Indian Troops Eluded Their Turkish Jailers," *New York Times*, July 11, 1915, II:2. In fact, the clipping in the book was not from the *New York Times*, but another newspaper; the wording of the *New York Times* article is similar but slightly different.
15. Basanta Koomar Roy, "When India Fights for England," *The Independent* (New York), 82 (April 19, 1915), 107; G.A. Natesan, ed., *The Indian Review War Book* (Madras: G.A. Natesan & Co., 1915), 265; "Indians Astonish By Cavalry Feats," *New York Times* (April 17, 1915), 3; "India Truly Loyal, Says Lord Hardinge," *New York Times* (May 20, 1916), 1; W.G. Tinckom-Fernandez, "India Fights for England," *Asia*, 17 (October 1917), 636.
16. "Hira Singh," *The Times Literary Review*, June 27, 1918, p. 300.
17. TM, letter to H.H. Howland, December 23, 1918, p. 2, Bobbs-Merrill mss.
18. TM, letter to D.L. Chambers, September 1, 1925, p. 2, Bobbs-Merrill mss.
19. Deposition of Arthur S. Hoffman, August 14, 1923, p. 2, Mundy vs. Mundy, Case 18130, Washoe County, Nevada. Shortly after the Mundys moved to Norway in 1914, Parke Hanley and Miss Mary E. Curtis, subsequently Mrs. Hoffman, were house guests. Deposition of Arthur S. Hoffman, August 14, 1923, p. 2, Mundy vs. Mundy, Case 18130, Washoe County, Nevada.
20. Deposition of Arthur S. Hoffman, August 14, 1923, pp. 3–4, Mundy vs. Mundy, Case 18130; Deposition of Charles G. Bond, August 14, 1923, p. 2, Mundy vs. Mundy, Case 18130, Washoe County, Nevada.
21. Deposition of Arthur S. Hoffman, August 14, 1923, p. 3, Mundy vs. Mundy, Case 18130, Washoe County, Nevada.
22. Deposition of Mary Hoffman, August 14, 1923, Mundy vs. Mundy, Case 18130, Washoe County, Nevada.
23. Deposition of Arthur S. Hoffman, August 14, 1923, pp. 2, 4, Mundy vs. Mundy, Case 18130, Washoe County, Nevada.
24. "Writer of Short Stories Tells Long One," 2.
25. "Mrs. Mundy Witness in Divorce Action," *Nevada State Journal*, August 22, 1923, p. 8.
26. Hoffman continued, "He numbered women as well as men among his friends and acquaintances and in the course of his work was of course thrown with both sexes, but with the exception of reports of [Rosemary's] jealousy I have never heard even a breath of scandal against him. During the dozen years I've known him, even when he was unmarried, I have never heard of his having an affair with a woman, or, except for [Rosemary], heard of even any gossip of this nature.... In matters of sex he is one of the cleanest-minded men I have ever known." Deposition of Arthur S. Hoffman, August 14, 1923, p. 4, Mundy vs. Mundy, Case 18130, Washoe County, Nevada.
27. Provost in Grant, 86.
28. David Edwin Mann, letter to the author, September 3, 1998. She later met Dawn Mundy, and passed along her enthusiasm for the author to her son. Mann inherited from his mother Mundy's copy of *Isis Unveiled*, given to her by another Mundy acquaintance, and which presently is in the author's collection.
29. "Writer of Short Stories Tells Long One," 2.
30. TM, letter to Harriette Mundy, January 12, 1921, pp. 2–3, exhibit U, Mundy vs. Mundy, Case 18130, Washoe County, Nevada.
31. "Writer of Short Stories Tells Long One," 2.
32. "Writer of Short Stories Tells Long One," 2.
33. Deposition of Mrs. Mary Hoffman, August 4, 1923, p. 2, Mundy vs. Mundy, Case 18130, Washoe County, Nevada.
34. TM, "Oakes Respects an Adversary," *Adventure*, 19 (December 3, 1918), 3.
35. TM, letter to H.H. Howland, November 7, 1918, p. 2, Bobbs-Merrill mss.

36. TM, *The Ivory Trail* (Indianapolis: Bobbs-Merrill, 1919), 84.
37. TM, letter to H.H. Howland, April 2, 1919, p. 1, Bobbs-Merrill mss. See also "Watu," *Adventure*, 82 (April 1, 1932), 52–53.
38. TM, *The Ivory Trail*, 221.
39. TM, *The Ivory Trail*, 201–202.
40. TM, *The Ivory Trail*, 404.
41. TM, *The Ivory Trail*, 353.
42. Fred F. Fleischer, Letter in "The Camp-Fire" on propaganda and *The Ivory Trail*, *Adventure*, 42 (April 20, 1923), 183.
43. "The Ivory Trail," *New York Times Book Review*, July 13, 1919, p. 355.
44. Bobbs-Merrill publicity, *The Ivory Trail* publicity file, Bobbs-Merrill mss.
45. "Mission Board Told of Turkish Horrors," *New York Times*, September 17, 1915, www.cilicia.com/armo10cnyt19150917.html.
46. TM, letter to Mr. Bobbs, October 18, 1919, Bobbs-Merrill mss.
47. D.L. Chambers to TM, June 8, 1920, p. 1, Bobbs-Merrill mss. In the United States, sales of *The Eye of Zeitoon* brought Mundy a royalty payment of around $2300, but had then slowed to a trickle. Such poor sales were especially disappointing considering the popularity of the previous "Up-and-Down-the-Earth-Tales" book, *The Ivory Trail*, but Mundy was disillusioned with the book even before publication; in November 1919 he wrote Sally Ames that he regarded it as "a very bad book." TM to Sally Ames, November 13, 1919, p. 6, Richards Ames collection.
An unusual approach was taken to illustrating Bobbs-Merrill's edition of *The Eye of Zeitoon*. Dwight Franklin created wax figurines of the characters against realistic backgrounds, which were then photographed in color. Franklin was a sculptor who sold most of his work to the Metropolitan Museum of Art. He would later be recognized as a pioneer in developing the modern diorama technique, with historical reconstructions at the Museum of the City of New York, the Naval Academy Museum, and elsewhere. Franklin was also an expert on weapons and dress whose articles appeared in many publications into the 1960s. Mundy was enthusiastic about Franklin's work, believing that these expensive illustrations and his frequently vague poems (which had not appeared in the *Romance* serialization) would be major selling points. Sadly, he was wrong at least regarding Franklin's four illustrations, and the Bobbs-Merrill campaign built around them failed dismally: the plaster casts proved too difficult to be shipped for display without suffering damage.
48. Curtis Brown to Howland, April 15, 1920, Curtis Brown mss.

Chapter IV

1. Passport, June 22, 1920, Ames collection.
2. Richards Ames, letter to P.B. Ellis, undated "Questions and Answers," p. 1, Ames collection.
3. Richards Ames, interview with the author, September 1, 1984. Talbot wrote Sally that Mrs. McQueen was inspiring a character in one of his stories. "Q goes later into *All Manner of Men* under the cognomen of Hepzibah! You'll all recognise her. Even her own husband will." TM to STA, excerpt from undated letter, 1919, Ames collection. Nothing further is known of *All Manner of Men*; it is probably the work of which Mundy wrote to Bobbs-Merrill "that is partly experiment and perhaps may not materialise just yet." TM, letter to H.H. Howland, September 11, 1919, p. 2.
4. W.D. McCrackan, *The New Palestine* (Boston: Page, 1922), 1, 47–49.
5. McCrackan, *The New Palestine*, 54.
6. Although in the light of World War II, Anglo-American partnership seems a natural and expected part of foreign policy, it had not been so in the first years of the 20th century. The participation of the United States in World War I had not been widely accepted domestically, and anti-British sentiment, much of it remaining from the American Revolution, still ran high. Indeed, the War of 1812 was remembered as having taken place only a century earlier. Nor was England eager to accept the growing role of the United States as a world power, and World War I had marked the first occasion that Britons and Americans had fought together, rather than in opposition. One of the Anglo-American Society's achievements was Sir George Watson's 20,000 pound endowment of the Prince of Wales chair in American History, Literature, and Institutions, a rotating position to promote such studies in all British universities. Similar programs and scholarships appeared in the United States. The Society also raised statues of Lincoln and Washington in London and Manchester, and arranged celebrations of the tercentenary of the voyage of the *Mayflower*. "Barnard's Statue of Lincoln," London *Times*, January 30, 1919, p. 5; London *Times*, June 18, 1919, p. 15; "Anglo-American Relations," London *Times*, June 27, 1919, p. 7; "Propaganda in Palestine," *New York Times*, October 25, 1919, p. 9; "The Anglo-American Society," London *Times*, September 20, 1919, p. 6; "To Make America Known to Britons," *New York Times*, December 6, 1919, p. 11; "England and America," *New York Times*, December 8, 1919, p. 14; "American Studies," London *Times*, December 11, 1919, p. 10; "Anglo-American Unity," London *Times*, January 2, 1920, p. 13.
7. McCrackan, *The New Palestine*, 1636–37, 290.
8. Mrs. Richards Ames, interviews with the author; McCrackan, *The New Palestine*, 41.
9. McCrackan, *The New Palestine*, 3, 36.
10. McCrackan, *The New Palestine*, 36–37, 290.
11. McCrackan, *The New Palestine*, 282.
12. Sarah Ames, letter to TM, January 14, 1920, p. 1, Ames collection.
13. "Adventure Writer Here," Unidentified New York City newspaper clipping, Bobbs-Merrill mss.
14. TM, Letter to "The Camp-Fire" on the history of the Anglo-Saxon race, *Adventure*, 34 (April 30, 1922), 180–181; TM, Letter to "The Camp-Fire"

on the Ark of the Covenant, *Adventure*, 36 (September 10, 1922), 177–179; TM, Letter to "The Camp-Fire" in reply to George Castor Martin, *Adventure*, 40 (May 30, 1923), 183.

15. Arthur Hoffman deposition, August 14, 1923, p. 2, Mundy vs. Mundy, Case 18130, Washoe County, Nevada.

16. "Writer of Short Stories Tells Long One," p. 2. For instance, since Christian Science offered a lay ministry, one of Mundy's teachers in the faith was the wife of a local butcher, but Rosemary became jealous.

17. TM, letter to Harriette Mundy, January 25, 1920, p. 5, exhibit q, Mundy vs. Mundy, Case 18130, Washoe County, Nevada.

18. Sarah Ames, letter to TM, January 14, 1920, p. 2, Ames collection.

19. W.C. Bobbs, royalty statement memo to H.H. Howland, October 16, 1919, Bobbs-Merrill mss.

20. TM, letter to Sarah Ames, December 3, 1919, pp. 1–2, Ames collection.

21. TM, "Lord Dunsany," *Jerusalem News*, No. 56 (February 13, 1920), 2.

22. TM, "England After the War," Part 3, *Jerusalem News*, No. 55 (February 12, 1920), 2; TM, "England After the War," Part 4, *Jerusalem News*, No. 56 (February 13, 1920), 2.

23. TM, letter to Harriette Mundy, January 18, 1920, pp. 3b-4, Mundy vs. Mundy, Case 18130, Washoe County, Nevada.

24. TM, letter to Harriette Mundy, January 29, 1920, Mundy vs. Mundy, Case 18130, Washoe County, Nevada.

25. McCrackan, *The New Palestine*, 203–204.

26. McCrackan, *The New Palestine*, 28–33.

27. TM, letter to Harriette Mundy, February 8, 1920, p. 3, exhibit M, Mundy vs. Mundy, Case 18130, Washoe County, Nevada.

28. McCrackan, *The New Palestine*, 40.

29. TM, letter to Sarah Ames, February 13, 1920, p. 3, Ames collection.

30. TM, letter to Harriette Mundy, February 28, 1920, p. 3, Mundy vs. Mundy, Case 18130, Washoe County, Nevada.

31. TM, letter to Harriette Mundy, February 28, 1920, p. 1, Mundy vs. Mundy, Case 18130, Washoe County, Nevada.

32. Harriette Mundy, letter to TM, April 9, 1920, pp. 2, 3, 5, exhibit B-1, Mundy vs. Mundy, Case 18130, Washoe County, Nevada.

33. TM, letter to Harriette Mundy, February 28, 1920, pp. 2–3, Mundy vs. Mundy, Case 18130, Washoe County, Nevada.

34. TM, "Jerusalem," *The Theosophical Path*, 24 (February 1923), 130, 127–128.

35. TM, "Jerusalem," 129.

36. McCrackan, *The New Palestine*, 125.

37. Norman and Helen Bentwich, *Mandate Memories, 1918–1948* (London: The Hogarth Press, 1965), 25.

38. TM, *I Say Sunrise*, 77–78; TM, "Jerusalem," 130; Mrs. Richards Ames, interviews.

39. Richards Ames, interview.

40. McCrackan, *The New Palestine*, 304, 306, 310; TM, letter to W.C. Bobbs, April 19, 1920, p. 2, Bobbs-Merrill mss.

41. McCrackan, *The New Palestine*, 39.

42. TM, letter to W.C. Bobbs, April 19, 1920, p. 2, Bobbs-Merrill mss.

43. Malcolm B. Russell, *The First Modern Arab State: Syria Under Faysal, 1918–1920* (Minneapolis: Bibliotheca Islamica, 1985), 131.

44. Philip Mattar, *The Mufti of Jerusalem* (New York: Columbia University Press, 1988), 16.

45. TM in "The Camp-Fire," *Adventure*, 35 (July 10, 1922), 174; Documents in Sally Ames scrapbook, Ames collection; TM, letter to W.C. Bobbs, April 19, 1920, p. 2, Bobbs-Merrill mss.

46. TM, *The King in Check*, 189.

47. TM in "The Camp-Fire," *Adventure*, 35 (July 10, 1922), 174.

48. A.S. Hoffman in "The Camp-Fire," *Adventure*, 39 (February 20, 1923), 184.

49. "Feisal Drops Recognition Plan; Appeals to Wilson to Aid Arabs," *New York Times*, April 5, 1920, p. 17.

50. Russell, 197.

51. "Riots in Jerusalem," *New York Times*, April 8, 1920, p. 17.

52. Mattar, 16.

53. "Ten Killed in Jerusalem," *New York Times*, April 9, 1920, p. 25.

54. TM, entry in Sarah Ames diary, "Hebron — Easter Sunday," Ames collection.

55. "The Nebi Musa Riots in Jerusalem," *Jerusalem News*, April 7, 1920, pasted clipping in Ames collection.

56. TM in "The Camp-Fire," *Adventure*, 32 (December 10, 1921), 176.

57. TM, entry in STA diary, "Hebron — Easter Sunday," Ames collection. Bailey was the model for the British officer De Crespigny in *The Seventeen Thieves of El-Kalil*, *The Lion of Petra*, and *The Lost Trooper*, an identification possible because of parallel descriptions of their actions in Sally and Talbot's Jerusalem diary and a later *Adventure* "Camp-Fire" letter.

58. Bentwich, 37.

59. McCrackan, *The New Palestine*, 300, 23.

60. TM, "Foreword," in *Tros of Samothrace*, xiii.

61. Taysir Jbara, *Palestinian Leader Hajj Amin Al-Husayni* (Princeton, NJ: Kingston Press, 1985), 33.

62. TM, unlabeled entry in Sarah Ames diary, Ames collection.

63. TM, entry in STA diary, "Thursday, April 8th," Ames collection. The accuracy of his account is more than attested to by the fact that it was given by Talbot in Sally's diary, which remained in her keeping both during and after their marriage, and in the years following their divorce and Mundy's death. While there are marginal emendations elsewhere in the diary from both Sally and Dick, clearly dating from much later years, there are no marks on these pages. Considering that Sally was present at the meeting, and had more than sufficient motivation in the three decades she lived after their divorce

64. W.D. McCrackan, letter to Sarah Ames, May 15, 1920, p. 2, Ames collection.
65. TM, letter to Sarah Ames, undated [1921], Ames collection.
66. Mrs. Richards Ames, interviews.
67. TM, letter to Harriette Mundy, June 26, 1920, p. 1, exhibit R, Mundy vs. Mundy, Case 18130, Washoe County, Nevada.
68. McCrackan, *The New Palestine*, 358.
69. McCrackan, *The New Palestine*, 318, 317.
70. "Wm. D. McCrackan, Author, Dies Suddenly," *New York Times*, June 4, 1923, 19.
71. Anthony Verrier, ed., *Agents of Empire: Anglo-Zionist Intelligence Operations 1915–1919 — Brigadier Walter Gribbon, Aaron Aaronsohn and the NILI Ring* (London: Brassey's, 1995).
72. TM, letter to Sarah Ames, undated ["Wednesday," 1921], p. 1, Ames collection.
73. April 9, 1923, answer (of defendant, Harriette Mundy); April 24, 1923, reply (of plaintiff, TM), Mundy vs. Mundy, Case 18130, Washoe County, Nevada.
74. Monthly Statement to TM, April 28, 1924, Bobbs-Merrill mss.
75. Richards Ames, interview.
76. TM, letter to Sarah Ames, March 28, 1921, p. 2, Ames collection; TM, letter to Sarah Ames, April 1, 1921, p. 1, Ames collection.
77. TM, *The Mystery of Khufu's Tomb* (New York: Appleton-Century, 1935), 133.
78. TM in "The Camp-Fire," *Adventure*, 33 (March 20, 1922), 183.
79. TM, *Jimgrim* (New York: Century, 1931), 55; TM in "The Camp-Fire," *Adventure*, 32 (December 10, 1921), 174.
80. TM in "The Camp-Fire," *Adventure*, 33 (March 20, 1922), 182–183. Mundy dedicated the American edition of *Jimgrim and Allah's Peace* to "Jimgrim, whose real name, rank, and military distinctions, I promised never to make public."
William Peacock and P.B. Ellis have asserted that Jimgrim was actually based on one John D. Whiting. Ellis, 128. Whiting was an American who was born around 1884, whose upbringing in Jerusalem was of an intensely Christian nature. He remained devout throughout his life, and married Grace Spofford in 1909. Learning to speak several Arabic dialects, Whiting was a man of scholarly inclinations, an amateur archeologist and geographer. For twenty-five years, from 1914–1939, Whiting wrote detailed photographic articles on Middle East archeology and Bible history for *National Geographic Magazine*, and occasionally contributed to other periodicals as well.
In 1917 he was asked to join British Field Intelligence under General Wyndham Deedes, securing the rank of captain but maintaining his United States citizenship. A 1950 autobiographical book on the family and the American colony in Jerusalem by Whiting's sister-in-law, Bertha Spafford Vester, was entitled *Our Jerusalem*. "He had traveled all over Palestine on foot, on donkey and horseback, and by carriage. No non-Palestinian knew the country so intimately as John. His knowledge of every by-path, well, and spring of water was invaluable to General Allenby's troops in their advance north and east." Bertha Hedges Vester, *Our Jerusalem; An American Family in the Holy City, 1881–1949* (Garden City, NY: Doubleday, 1950), 264.
By 1920, Whiting had become one of the most hospitable members of the American colony and Jerusalem, and he was known to all the members of the delegation; his family appeared in Mundy's photo album of the trip. McCrackan, *The New Palestine*, 303. Mrs. Vester described a man valuable in intelligence for his knowledge of the people and region, not as an adventurer.
81. Richards Ames, interview. Mundy was not able to take advantage of an opportunity to interview Lawrence in London because he could not stop there on the return trip. Richards Ames, letter to TM, November 3, 1920, p. 2, Ames collection.
82. TM, *The King in Check*, 190.
83. Paul Zweig, *The Adventurer* (Princeton: Princeton University Press, 1974), 229.
84. TM, letter to Sarah Ames, undated ["Monday morning," April, 1921], p. 2, Ames collection.
85. TM, *The Lost Trooper* (London: Hutchinson, 1931), 72.
86. TM in "The Camp-Fire," *Adventure*, 36 (August 10, 1922), 178.
87. A.S. Hoffman, "The Camp-Fire," *Adventure*, 39 (February 20, 1923), 183.
88. TM, *Jimgrim and Allah's Peace* (London: Hutchinson, n.d.), 17.
89. TM, *The Lost Trooper*, 53.
90. A.S. Hoffman, "The Camp-Fire," *Adventure*, 39 (February 20, 1923), 184.
91. TM in "The Camp-Fire," *Adventure* 35 (July 10, 1922), 174–175; Hutchinson spring 1933 catalog in TM, *The Gunga Sahib* (London: Hutchinson, 1934), 18.
92. TM in "The Camp-Fire," *Adventure*, 35 (July 10, 1922), 174–175.
93. TM, letter in "The Camp-Fire," *Adventure*, 36 (August 10, 1922), 178; TM, *A Secret Society*, 14.
94. McCrackan, *The New Palestine*, 8–11.
95. "The Tutankhamun business has been over done," wrote D.L. Chambers in a letter to TM, May 1, 1924, Bobbs-Merrill mss.
96. TM, letter to Wincenty Lutoslawski, May 1, 1938, p. 2, Janina Lutoslawski Collection.
97. TM, letter to "The Camp-Fire," *Adventure*, 37 (October 10, 1922), 177.
98. TM, *The Mystery of Khufu's Tomb*, 3–12.
99. TM, *The Mystery of Khufu's Tomb*, 182. One episode, where Zegloush and his allies are given a thrashing by British officers, seems to be a throwback to imperialism but was, instead, based on an actual occurrence. "A wealthy American girl was abducted during the time I was in Egypt; the motive was said to be blackmail, but the culprits were caught in the act and 'put through it' by the British, there being more than one reason at the time,

including the lady's own expressed wish, why punishment, if any, should be administered without publicity." TM, letter to "The Camp-Fire," *Adventure*, 37 (October 10, 1922), 176.

100. "The Camp-Fire," *Adventure*, 35 (July 20, 1922), 178.
101. "The Camp-Fire," *Adventure*, 40 (May 20, 1923), 178.
102. TM, letter to D.L. Chambers, October 16, 1922, p. 1, Bobbs-Merrill mss.
103. TM, letter to H.H. Howland, November 14, 1922, p. 2, Bobbs-Merrill mss.
104. D.L. Chambers, letter to L.E. Pollinger, April 24, 1922, Curtis Brown mss.
105. TM, letter to H.H. Howland, November 14, 1922, p. 2, Bobbs-Merrill mss.
106. TM, letter to D.L. Chambers, February 21, 1925, Bobbs-Merrill mss.

Chapter V

1. B.K., 9.
2. Robert Wernick, "Where You Went if You Really Had to Get Unhitched," *Smithsonian*, 27 (June 1996), 64–73.
3. TM, letter to Sarah Ames, Christmas 1921, pp. 1–2, Ames collection.
4. TM, letter to D.L. Chambers, April 19, 1922, p. 2, Bobbs-Merrill mss.
5. TM, *The Mystery of Khufu's Tomb*, 82.
6. TM in "The Camp-Fire," *Adventure*, 36 (September 10, 1922), 177–80.
7. TM, letter to Wm. C. Bobbs, December 17, 1921, p. 4, Bobbs-Merrill mss.
8. *Adventure*, 40 (May 20, 1923), 178. See also Grant, 147.
9. TM in Stanley Kunitz and Howard Haycraft, *Twentieth Century Authors* (New York, 1942), p. 997.
10. TM, Letter to "The Camp-Fire" on the history of the Anglo-Saxon race, *Adventure*, 34 (April 30, 1922), 180–181; TM, Letter to "The Camp-Fire" on the Ark of the Covenant, *Adventure*, 36 (September 10, 1922), 177–179; TM, Letter to "The Camp-Fire" in reply to George Castor Martin, *Adventure*, 40 (May 30, 1923), 183.
11. Readers were also especially interested if the Ark of the Covenant would retain its ability to kill anyone who touched it. Mundy was skeptical of this, believing it took someone with the knowledge of Moses or the Israelitish priests to give it this power. The priests, he noted, who inherited Moses's knowledge "gradually let it dwindle into superstition until it finally became mere legend. TM, Letter in "The Camp-Fire" on the Lost Tribes of Israel, *Adventure*, 36 (September 10, 1922), 177–178. His letters on the lost tribes of Israel and kindred matters refer to some of the books that may have been his formative reading in the occult. Those cited include William Skene's *The Coronation Stone* (1869), Bishop Allen's *Judah's Sceptre and Joseph's Birthright*, Willis's *The Ten Lost Tribes*, and A.A. Beauchamp's magazine *The Watchman of Israel*. He may have even been introduced to the subject by Beauchamp, whom he describes as a Boston bookseller and friend with an infinite knowledge of the subject. On prophecy, he read Redding's *Curious Causes*, *The Three Churches*, and *Mysteries Unveiled*. Another book Mundy had recently read was Edward Schure's *The Great Initiates* (1889), which he described as throwing "more light on ancient miracles and the men who 'made' them than anything else I have found." TM, Letter in "The Camp-Fire" on the Lost Tribes of Israel, *Adventure*, 36 (September 10, 1922), 177–178. This book, in turn, may have refined his ideas for his next occult novel, *The Nine Unknown*.

12. TM, letter to David R. Cummins in "The Camp-Fire," *Adventure*, 40 (April 30, 1923), 182–183.
13. TM, letter to STA, Christmas 1921, Ames collection.
14. TM, letter to Sarah Ames, December 14, 1921, p. 2, Ames collection.
15. Quoted in TM, letter to Wm. C. Bobbs, December 17, 1921, p. 3, Bobbs-Merrill mss. It was an idea compatible with the content of his books.
16. TM, letter to D.L. Chambers, January 26, 1921, p. 3, Bobbs-Merrill mss.
17. D.L. Chambers, letter to TM, March 27, 1924, Bobbs-Merrill mss.
18. D.L. Chambers, letter to L.E. Pollinger, March 21, 1922, Curtis Brown mss.
19. TM, letter to D.L. Chambers, July 11, 1922, p. 2, Bobbs-Merrill mss.
20. TM, letter to D.L. Chambers, July 11, 1922, pp. 1–2, Bobbs-Merrill mss.
21. TM, letter to Mary Converse, January 15, 1924, p. 3, Bobbs-Merrill mss.
22. Malcolm R. Henderson, letter to the author, November 27, 1995, p. 1.
23. L. Sprague De Camp, "Mundy's Vendhya," *Amra*, 2 (September 1970), 18.
24. Jacques Bergier, *Admirations* (Paris: Christian Bourgois Editeur, 1970), 303; chapter translated by Evelyn Copeland.
25. TM, *The Mystery of Khufu's Tomb*, 15–16.
26. TM, *The Hundred Days and The Woman Ayisha* (New York: The Century Co., 1931), 70.
27. TM, *The Hundred Days and The Woman Ayisha*, 63.
28. "The Hundred Days," *Times Literary Supplement* (January 30, 1930), 80.
29. Jan Zilliacus, letter to the author, October 1997.
30. Laurence Trimble, "Motion-Picture Dogs and Others," *The Saturday Evening Post*, 201 (February 2, 1929), 104.
31. Jan Zilliacus, letter to the author, October 1997.
32. TM, letter to D.L. Chambers, March 10, 1922, p. 2, Bobbs-Merrill mss.
33. Richards Ames, letter to P.B. Ellis, April 19, 1979; TM, letter to D.L. Chambers, March 10, 1922, p. 2, Bobbs-Merrill mss.
34. TM, letter to D.L. Chambers, April 3, 1922, p. 1, Bobbs-Merrill mss.

35. TM, "'Mother Nature': A Review of a Book by William J. Long," 137.
36. TM, letter to D.L. Chambers, April 10, 1924, p. 1, Bobbs-Merrill mss.
37. Richards Ames, interview.
38. TM, Letter to "The Camp-Fire" on *Diana Against Ephesians*, *Adventure*, 42 (August 10, 1923), 177–178.
39. TM, *Jungle Jest* (New York: Century, 1932), 293.
40. See Mundy's three letters to "The Camp-Fire" in *Adventure* regarding Ommony: 38 (January 10, 1923), 181–182; 42 (August 10, 1923), 177–178; 43 (October 10, 1923), 180.
41. *Times Literary Supplement*, September 10, 1931, p. 685.
42. TM, *Jungle Jest*, 125.
43. TM, letter to "The Camp-Fire" on *Treason*, *Adventure*, 38 (January 10, 1923), 181.
44. TM, *Jungle Jest*, 160.
45. TM, *The Marriage of Meldrum Strange*, *Adventure*, 43 (October 10, 1923), 3.
46. Iverson L. Harris, letter to P.B. Ellis, August 12, 1978, p. 2, Ames collection; Richards Ames, interview.
47. Richards Ames, interview.
48. TM, letter to D.L. Chambers, January 25, 1924, p. 3, Bobbs-Merrill mss.
49. *The White Panther*, directed by Alvin J. Nietz, was ready by October 1923, and remained in release through at least the spring of 1924. The picture no longer survives, so it is only through contemporary reviews that *The White Panther* can be judged. *Film Daily*, January 27, 1924, p. 10; *Harrison's Reports*, February 16, 1924, p. 26; *Variety*, January 31, 1924; Mary Kelly, "The White Panther," *Moving Picture World*, 66 (February 9, 1924), p. 487; George T. Pardy, "Here's Good Entertainment," *Exhibitor's Trade Review*, 15 (March 1, 1924), 27.
50. Box 43, Business File, Financial Papers, Ince Estate, Thomas H. Ince Corporation, 1924–1926, Picture Costs and Residual Value at December 31, 1924; Box 43, Business File, Financial Papers, Miscellany, 1917–1928, n.d., Thomas H. Ince Motion Picture Productions including all Pictures Released Prior to Jan. 1st, 1924, Ince Collection, LC.
51. Carbons of letter of understanding of January 5, 1923 to Mundy, and contract of January 19, 1923, Box 42: Business File—Employment contracts—Misc. employees; Minutes of Regular Meeting of Board of Directors, February 1, 1923, Box 39: Business File—Corporate Records—Thomas H. Ince Corp.; Thomas H. Ince Papers, Manuscript Division, Library of Congress.
52. "Elaborate Specials Planned by Thomas H. Ince for Coming Year," *Moving Picture World*, 62 (June 9, 1923), 506.
53. Bradley King contracts file (signed as Josephine Miller), Box 42: Business File—Employment contracts; Box 17: Production file: Her Reputation; Thomas H. Ince Papers, Manuscript Division, Library of Congress.
54. Carbons of letter of understanding of January 5, 1923 to Mundy, and contract of January 19, 1923, Box 42: Business File—Employment contracts—Misc. employees, Thomas H. Ince Papers, Manuscript Division, Library of Congress.
55. Carbons of letter of understanding of January 5, 1923 to Mundy, and contract of January 19, 1923, Box 42: Business File—Employment contracts—Misc. employees, Thomas H. Ince Papers, Manuscript Division, Library of Congress.
56. Jane Wray is also listed in some credits as Jane Miller, and may have been related to director Wray; apparently she had little experience, looking at the camera according to one reviewer. McElliott, "Ye Gods! How May M'Avoy Suffers in *Her Reputation*," *News*, December 21, 1923, clipping from Lloyd Hughes scrapbook in Rose Library, Lincoln Center for the Performing Arts. However, the child actress Jane Wray is certainly not Bradley King, as Ellis believes, and King and director Wray would not marry until five years later. Ellis, 135–136.
57. This summary is based primarily on a two-page summary on legal size paper found in the *Her Reputation* file in the Academy of Motion Picture Arts and Sciences Margaret Herrick Library, and a script of intertitles in Box 17: Production file: Her Reputation; Thomas H. Ince Papers, Manuscript Division, Library of Congress.
58. Provost, interview.

With Ince's death, Bradley King began free-lancing for various studios, and she was a frequent guest from 1925–1927 at Mundy's Point Loma home where Larry spent much of his time. She easily made the transition to writing for sound films at the end of the 1920s. In 1928, she married the director of *Her Reputation*, John Griffith Wray, who had divorced his actress wife a few months earlier. Less than a year later, having just completed his first "talkie," Wray died of appendicitis, leaving King his estate of $100,000.

A year later, in Honolulu to develop a screen epic based on the ancient peoples of Hawaii, she met George Hiram Boyd. Although King was raised as a Catholic (and her mother a Quaker), this marriage was conducted by Rev. Ernest Holmes, Divine Science Minister of the Institute of Religious Science—better known as "Science of Mind." King promoted interest in adapting Mundy's stories for the screen at the studios where she worked during the 1930s. Writing steadily through 1937 on a variety of genres, she then found it impossible to create as her husband had lost her entire fortune of $400,000 in failed investments, and refused to work. In 1940, she divorced Boyd, and returned to screenwriting in 1947 for one final film. Subsequently, she vanished from the film industry, and not even the date of her death is known.

59. TM, letter to Rose Wilder Lane, June 25, 1934, p. 1, RWL mss.
60. TM, *Her Reputation* (New York: Bobbs-Merrill, 1923), 323.
61. Bradley King, *News*, scenario, shot 52, Box 17: Production file: Her Reputation; Thomas H. Ince Papers, Manuscript Division, Library of Congress.
62. TM, *Her Reputation*, 265.

63. TM, *Her Reputation*, 234.
64. Carbon of contract of January 19, 1923, Box 42: Business File — Employment contracts — Misc. employees, Thomas H. Ince Papers, Manuscript Division, Library of Congress; Richards Ames interview. Mundy wrote to the Theosophical Society on Ince studio stationary in March, a letter printed as "An Appreciation of Kenneth Morris," *The Theosophical Path*, 24 (May 1923), 499–500. "Elaborate Specials Planned by Thomas H. Ince for Coming Year," 506, indicates Mundy was still at the studio.
65. King had written an adaptation of *Scars of Jealousy* (another by Lambert Hillyer, who also directed *Scars of Jealousy*, was used instead), which included extensive background incorporating Longfellow's themes. She portrayed how the Acadian's land was ceded to England and they were forced to search for a new home, even finding they were rejected in New Orleans when it is taken over by Spain. Hillyer's prologue simply began in France under Louis XV before shifting to the modern Cajans [sic]. Box 26, Production File, Rudd, Anthony E., *Scars of Jealousy*, N.D., Ince Collection, LC.
66. Box 34, Business File, Administrative card file, n.d., Ince Collection, LC.
67. TM, letter to D.L. Chambers, March 10, 1922, p. 2, Bobbs-Merrill mss.
68. Box 36, Business File, Assignments and Rights, By Title, The Last Frontier, 1923–1926, Memorandum of Agreement between Thomas H. Ince Corp. and Courtney Ryley Cooper, April 10, 1923, Ince Collection, LC.
69. TM, letter to D.L. Chambers, January 25, 1924, p. 3, Bobbs-Merrill mss.
70. See George T. Pardy, "*Her Reputation*," *Exhibitors Trade Review*, 14 (October 20, 1923), 956; Edwin Schallert, "Heroine Appeals," *Los Angeles Times*, October 15, 1923, clipping from Lloyd Hughes scrapbook in Rose Library, Lincoln Center for the Performing Arts; "Garrick," *Duluth News*, October 15, 1923, clipping from Lloyd Hughes scrapbook in Rose Library, Lincoln Center for the Performing Arts; "'*Her Reputation*'—With May MacAvoy and Lloyd Hughes," *Harrison's Reports*, October 27, 1923, p. 171; "May M'Avoy Gives Spanish Dances in Newspaper Drama," *Washington Post*, November 5, 1923, clipping from Lloyd Hughes scrapbook in Rose Library, Lincoln Center for the Performing Arts; "May McAvoy as the Heroine in '*Her Reputation*' at Rialto," unidentified newspaper clipping, October 6, 1923, clipping from *Her Reputation* file in Rose Library, Lincoln Center for the Performing Arts; "Newspaper Contest Ties Up with '*Her Reputation*,'" *Motion Picture News*, December 8, 1923, p. 2677; "Reviews: *Her Reputation*," *Exhibitors Herald*, September 8, 1923, p. 49.
71. Box 43, Business File, Financial Papers, Miscellany, 1917–1928, n.d., Thomas H. Ince Motion Picture Productions including all Pictures Released Prior to Jan. 1st, 1924, Ince Collection, LC.
72. T.M., "Introduction" in Mundy, *Her Reputation* (New York: Bobbs-Merrill, 1923), n.p.
73. Sisk, "*Her Reputation*," *Variety*, September 27, 1923.
74. "Talbot Mundy Loses Divorse [sic] Suit After Fight of Over Year," *Nevada State Journal*, August 28, 1923, p. 8.
75. Answer, April 9, 1923, pp. 2–3, Mundy vs. Mundy, Case 18130, Washoe County, Nevada.
76. Reply, April 24, 1923, p. 3, Mundy vs. Mundy, Case 18130, Washoe County, Nevada.
77. Answer, April 9, 1923, Mundy vs. Mundy, Case 18130, Washoe County, Nevada.
78. Reply, April 24, 1923, p. 3, Mundy vs. Mundy, Case 18130, Washoe County, Nevada.
79. "Refuses Divorce to Mundy," *The New York Times*, August 28, 1923, p. 2.
80. "Mrs. Mundy Witness in Divorce Action," *Nevada State Journal*, August 22, 1923, p. 8; "Religion to Blame for Mundy Split Says Wife," *Reno Evening Gazette*, August 22, 1923, p. 3.
81. "Well Known Author Tells of Troubles in District Court," *Nevada State Journal*, August 21, 1923, p. 8; "Mundy Case Ended; Decision Monday," *Nevada State Journal*, August 24, 1923, p. 8; "Talbot Mundy Loses Divorse [sic] Suit After Fight of Over Year," 8; "Author is Denied Divorce by Bartlett," *Reno Evening Gazette*, August 27, 1923, p. 8.
82. TM, letter to Harriette Mundy, February 1, 1920, exhibit N, n.p., Mundy vs. Mundy, Case 18130, Washoe County, Nevada.
83. "Well Known Author Tells of Troubles in District Court," 8.
84. "Mundy Prolific Letter Writer," *Reno Evening Gazette*, August 21, 1923, p. 3; Cf. "Mundy Contest Is About Ended," *Reno Evening Gazette*, August 23, 1923, p. 4.
85. TM, "Payable to Bearer," *The Cavalier*, 23 (December 28, 1912), 712.
86. "Well Known Author Tells of Troubles in District Court," 8; "Writer of Short Stories Tells Long One," *Reno Evening Gazette*, August 20, 1923, p. 2.
87. "Mundy Prolific Letter Writer,"3; Richards Ames, letter to P.B. Ellis, March 10, 1979, p. 4, Ames collection.
88. Ruth E. Hermann deposition, August 14, 1923, Mundy vs. Mundy, Case 18130, Washoe County, Nevada.
89. "Mrs. Mundy Witness in Divorce Action," *Nevada State Journal*, August 22, 1923, p. 8.
90. "Mrs. Mundy Witness in Divorce Action," 8.
91. "Mrs. Mundy Witness in Divorce Action," 8.
92. "Mrs. Mundy Witness in Divorce Action," *Nevada State Journal*, August 22, 1923, p. 8.
93. "Religion to Blame for Mundy Split Says Wife," 3.
94. "Mrs. Mundy Witness in Divorce Action," 8.
95. "Religion to Blame for Mundy Split Says Wife," *Reno Evening Gazette*, August 22, 1923, p. 3.
96. "Mundy Divorce Case Goes Into 3rd Day," *Nevada State Journal*, August 23, 1923, p. 8.
97. "Mundy Contest Is About Ended," *Reno Evening Gazette*, August 23, 1923, p. 4; "Mundy Case Ended; Decision Monday," *Nevada State Journal*, August 24, 1923, p. 8.

98. "Talbot Mundy to Leave for London Next Week," *Nevada State Journal*, August 25, 1923, p. 4.

99. "Talbot Mundy Denies He Is Going to India," *Nevada State Journal*, August 25, 1923, p. 4.

100. "Talbot Mundy Loses Divorse [sic] Suit After Fight of Over Year," 8.

Chapter VI

1. Emmett A. Greenwalt, *California Utopia: Point Loma: 1897–1942* (San Diego: Point Loma Publications, 1978), 1; this is the definitive history of Tingley's endeavors. For a complete account of the Theosophical movement, see Bruce Campbell, *Ancient Wisdom Revived* (Berkeley, 1980).

2. Leah Leneman, "The Hindu Renaissance of the Late 19th Century," *History Today*, 30 (May 1980), 24; Charles Samuel Braden, *These Also Believe: A Study of Modern American Cults and Minority Religious Movements* (New York, 1949), p. 255. See also Campbell, 165.

3. Greenwalt, 18–19.

4. Paul Kagan and Marilyn Ziebarth, "Eastern Thought on a Western Shore," *California Historical Quarterly*, 52 (winter 1973), 5; Greenwalt, 204. The Point Loma group was not the only Theosophical organization existing in California in the 1920s. The Adyar society had two nearby colonies in southern California, one in Krotona that ended in 1922, and another later in the Ojai Valley near Santa Barbara, both intended to facilitate the emergence of the teacher Krishnamurti. Between these groups there was a lack of fraternization, indeed hostility, echoed by Mundy. He described Tingley's faction as "the original Theosophical Society," and would urge readers of Blavatsky's works to only use those editions published by Point Loma, saying those Besant's group put out "contain additions and emandations which, I think, mislead the enquirer." TM, letter to D.L. Chambers, February 7, 1924, p. 1, Bobbs-Merrill mss.; TM, letter to Miss E. Griffin, September 7, 1930, Stephen Michaluk collection.

5. Richards Ames, letter to P.B. Ellis, December 20, 1978, p. 1–2, Ames collection.

6. Greenwalt, 210.

7. Boris de Zirkoff, letter to Iverson L. Harris, quoted in Harris, letter to P.B. Ellis, July 10, 1978, pp. 2–3, Point Loma Publications archive.

8. Richards Ames, letter to P.B. Ellis, March 10, 1979, p. 4, Ames collection.

9. TM, "A Beginner's Concept of Theosophy," *The Theosophical Path*, 28 (June 1925), 429–430.

10. Greenwalt, 48. For a feminist interpretation of Point Loma, see Evelyn A. Kirkley, "'Starved and Treated Like Convicts': Images of Women in Point Loma Theosophy," *The Journal of San Diego History*, 43 (winter 1997), 2–27. For an examination of the contrasting attitudes toward women articulated by the Adyar theosophical group, whose doctrines Mundy opposed, see Joy Dixon, "Ancient Wisdom, Modern Motherhood: Theosophy and the Colonial Syncretic," in Antoinette Burton, ed. *Gender, Sexuality and Colonial Modernities* (New York: Routledge, 1999), 193–206, and Joy Dixon, *Divine Feminine* (Baltimore: Johns Hopkins, 2001).

11. TM, "As To Capital Punishment," *The Theosophical Path*, 29 (December 1925), 523, 595.

12. TM in "Reception to Colonel Arthur L. Conger," *The Theosophical Path*, 34 (January 1928), 86.

13. Reminiscence of Mrs. Louise Savage in Iverson L. Harris, letter to P.B. Ellis, August 12, 1978, p. 4, Ames collection.

14. Greenwalt, 135.

15. TM, letter to D.L. Chambers, February 5, 1924, p. 1, Bobbs-Merrill mss.

16. W. Emmett Small interview; W. Emmett Small, note to Iverson L. Harris, May 10, 1978, pp. 1–2, Point Loma Publications archive.

17. Recorder, "Theosophical Items of Interest: 27th Anniversary of Chicago Convention Celebrated," *The Theosophical Path*, 28 (March 1925), 290.

18. W. Emmett Small, "Foreword," in G. de Purucker, *Fundamentals of the Esoteric Philosophy* (San Diego: Point Loma Publications, 1990), xiv.

19. Greenwalt, 129–132; Reginald Poland, "The Divinity of Nature in the Art of Maurice Braun," *The Theosophical Path*, 34 (May 1928), 476; TM, "Well-Known Writer Predicts Brilliant Career for San Diego Artist; Reviews His Paintings," *The San Diego Union*, March 2, 1924, p. 10; reprinted in *The Theosophical Path*, 26 (April 1924), 405–407.

20. TM, "Blackmail," *The Theosophical Path*, 26 (June 1924), 518.

21. TM, "Miscarriage of Justice," *The Theosophical Path*, 26 (March 1924), 222.

22. TM, "A Beginner's Concept of Theosophy," *The Theosophical Path*, 28 (June 1925), 434.

23. A number of other occasions where he spoke are noted. His speeches were recounted or reprinted in "Of Wild Animals in Africa," *Raja-Yoga Messenger*, 20 (January 1924), 25–27, and TM, "Universal," *The Theosophical Path*, 26 (January 1924), 5–9. He spoke at the May 8, 1924 anniversary of the death of H.P. Blavatsky; see Observer, "White-Lotus Day Celebration at the International Theosophical Headquarters Point Loma, California, May 8, 1924," *The Theosophical Path*, 27 (July 1924), 36–43. He addressed the anniversary of the acceptance of Tingley's leadership of the Society, February 18, 1925; see Recorder, "Theosophical Items of Interest: 27th Anniversary of Chicago Convention Celebrated," *The Theosophical Path*, 28 (March 1925), 289–290. Mundy was a featured speaker at a special reception for a San Diego convention of the State Disabled Veterans of the World War and the War-Mothers of California, on May 15, 1925; see "The Screen of Time — Mirror of the Movement: War Veterans and War Mothers in Lomaland," *The Theosophical Path*, 29 (July 1925), 98–100. He spoke at Tingley's birthday celebration on July 6, 1925; see "The Screen of Time — Mirror of the Movement: Tributes to Katherine Tingley," *The Theosophical Path*, 29 (September 1925), 298–299. He gave one of the tributes upon the death of Fred J. Dick on May 27, 1927. *The San Diego Union*, May 28, 1927, reprinted in "The

Screen of Time — Mirror of the Movement: Theosophical Society Pays Tribute to Memory of F.J. Dick," *The Theosophical Path*, 33 (July 1927), 98–100. His last recorded address was during a reception to Colonel Arthur L. Conger held by Tingley at her residence on November 4, 1927 (Conger became Leader of the Society in 1942); see Recorder, "The Screen of Time — Mirror of the Movement: Reception to Colonel Arthur L. Conger," *The Theosophical Path*, 34 (January 1928), 81–86.

24. "I remember that his accent seemed very English to my young ears." Robert Lloyd Davis, letter to the author, December 2, 1996, p. 1.

25. "Of Wild Animals in Africa," 25.

26. Greenwalt, 13.

27. "Talbot Mundy Says San Diego Has Opportunity to Set Pace for This Glorious West Coast," *The San Diego Union*, February 4, 1924, p. 10; reprinted in *The Theosophical Path*, 26 (March 1924), 300–301. TM, "Writer Comments Presentation of 'The Eumenides' at Point Loma," *The San Diego Union*, March 23, 1924, p. 8; reprinted as "The Screen of Time — Mirror of the Movement: Students of Lomaland Give Wonderful Interpretation of 'The Eumenides' at Greek Theater," *The Theosophical Path*, 26 (May 1924), 503–504; and TM, "Katherine Tingley Again Gives 'The Eumenides' Before Large Audience in Greek Theater," *The San Diego Union*, June 4, 1924, p. 9; reprinted in *The Theosophical Path*, 27 (July 1924), 100–101.

28. Greenwalt, 103–104.

29. Iverson Harris, letter to P.B. Ellis, July 24, 1978, pp. 1–2, Point Loma Publications archive.

30. Greenwalt, 108.

31. Iverson L. Harris, letter to P.B. Ellis, July 24, 1978, pp. 1–2; Lucie Moljin, letter to Katherine and Iverson L. Harris, August 18, 1978, Point Loma Publications archive.

32. TM, "An Answer to Correspondents," *The Theosophical Path*, 28 (January 1925), 37–39. See also Greenwalt, 7; William Q. Judge, *The Ocean of Theosophy* (Los Angeles: United Lodge of Theosophists, 1915), vi, 1–13, 153–154; Robert S. Ellwood, Jr., *Alternative Altars: Unconventional and Eastern Spirituality in America* (Chicago, 1979), 120–121.

33. A.S. Hoffman, quoted in TM, letter to D.L. Chambers, April 18, 1924, p. 2, Bobbs-Merrill mss.

34. D.L. Chambers, letter to TM, April 24, 1924, Bobbs-Merrill mss.

35. Richards Ames, letter to P.B. Ellis, undated "Questions and Answers — Also Incidentals," Ames collection.

36. Austin Adams, "Austin Adams Gives Highest Praise to New Book by Mundy," unidentified San Diego newspaper clipping, Richards Ames Collection. Mundy had gained the latest information on the Ahbors directly from Sven Hedin the previous year, during the explorer's visit to Point Loma. The two volume 1910 edition of Hedin's book, *Overland to India*, was part of Mundy's personal library. Later, when Hedin became a Fascist sympathizer, Talbot wrote to his brother that "I can't understand how a man of Sven Hedin's intelligence could seriously believe in the tripe that the Nazis think is philosophy." TM, letter to W.H. Gribbon, June 4, 1940, Gribbon mss., reprinted in Ellis, 143.

37. TM, *Om* (Indianapolis: Bobbs-Merrill, 1924), 89–90.

38. Adams.

39. TM, *Om*, 363.

40. TM, "Another's Duty Is Full of Danger," *The Theosophical Path*, 27 (July 1924), 25. R.T. Gault noted that the Tibetan name "Samding" is a very good one for a female chela (almost unheard of in Tibetan religion), since it is the name of a monastery/nunnery in south central Tibet, not run by a lama but an abbess.

41. G. de Purucker, "'Om, the Secret of Ahbor Valley,' by Talbot Mundy: An Appreciation," *The Theosophical Path*, 27 (December 1924), 607; "Talbot Mundy's 'Om' Much Appreciated," *The Theosophical Path*, 28 (April, 1925), 391.

42. Talbot Mundy to Katherine Tingley, November 1924 in Mundy, *Om: The Secret of Ahbor Valley* (Indianapolis, 1924), notation in copy at the Theosophical University Library, Altadena, California.

43. TM, Letter to "The Camp-Fire" introducing *Om*, *Adventure*, 49 (October 10, 1924), 181–183; reprinted in *The Theosophical Path*, 28 (February 1925), 194–197 and *The Eclectic Theosophist*, No. 61 (November-December 1980), 1–3.

44. "*Om*," *Milwaukee Evening Telegram* (February 22, 1925), clipping in Ames collection.

45. TM, *Om*, 371. Similarly, Morris wrote that "the deepest truths of religion and philosophy had their first recording for the instruction of the peoples, not in the form of treatise, essay, or disquisition, but as epics, sagas, [and] stories," while Purucker also taught that legends, myths, and fairy tales were far from mere stories, but had their origin in the secret wisdom Blavatsky had outlined. Douglas A. Anderson, "Introduction," in Kenneth Morris, *The Dragon Path* (New York: TOR, 1995), 10; G. de Purucker, *Fundamentals of the Esoteric Philosophy* (San Diego: Point Loma Publications, 1990), 547–548.

46. Cian Draoi, "Book Reviews," *Dublin Magazine*, 2 (May 1925), 683.

47. Claire Walker, "Book Reviews," *The Eclectic Theosophist*, No. 78 (November December 1983), 9, reprinted from *Journal of the Academy of Religious and Psychical Research*, July 1983.

48. Pervin Mistry, "An Appreciation of 'Om,'" *The Eclectic Theosophist*, No. 73 (January-February 1983), 10; TM, letter to D.L. Chambers, January 8, 1924, Bobbs-Merrill mss.

49. D.L. Chambers, letter to TM, January 12, 1924, Bobbs-Merrill mss.

50. A.S. Hoffman, quoted in TM, letter to D.L. Chambers and H.H. Howland, April 17, 1924, p. 1; TM, letter to D.L. Chambers, May 2, 1924, p. 1, Bobbs-Merrill mss.; Clyde B. Clason, "Foreword: Talbot Mundy — An Appreciation" in TM, *Old Ugly-Face* (Philadelphia: Milton F. Wells, 1949), vii; Christmas Humphreys, "Book Reviews," *The Eclectic Theosophist*, No. 66 (November-December 1981), 5, reprinted from *Buddhism in England*; TM, letter

to D.L. Chambers, May 2, 1924, p. 1, Bobbs-Merrill mss.

51. Martin Green, *Dreams of Adventure, Deeds of Empire* (New York: Routledge & Kegan Paul, 1979), 271; TM, letter to D.L. Chambers, May 2, 1924, p. 1, Bobbs-Merrill mss.

52. A.S. Hoffman, "The Camp-Fire," *Adventure*, 49 (October 10, 1924), 181.

53. B.K., "Point Loma's Lure Induces World-Traveled Author to Stay Here and Establish His Permanent Home," *The San Diego Union*, February 15, 1925, p. 9.

Mundy hoped to add Theosophical visual accompaniment to the text, unsuccessfully proposing pen-and-ink illustrations for alternate chapters by Leonard Lester. TM, letter to D.L. Chambers, May 2, 1924, p. 2, Bobbs-Merrill mss. Lester was an artist who had become a follower of Tingley in the 1890s and would remain at Point Loma until her death. Greenwalt, 132–133. One of his unique etchings, in the style of Reginald Machell, was used as the first of the two dust jackets Bobbs-Merrill issued for *Om*.

54. TM, letter to D.L. Chambers, March 26, 1925, p. 2, Bobbs-Merrill mss.

55. TM, letter to W.C. Bobbs, June 21, 1925, p. 1, Bobbs-Merrill mss

56. B.K., 9; Walker, 8.

57. "The Way of Life," *Manchester City News*, April 25, 1925, reprinted in *The Theosophical Path*, 28 (June 1925), 602.

58. "Miscellaneous Headquarters Notes," *The Theosophical Path*, 27 (December 1924), 603; "Talbot Mundy's New Book 'Om,'" *The Theosophical Path*, 28 (January 1925), 92; "'Om' Delights Everyone," *The Theosophical Path*, 28 (February 1925), 185–186; "The Wine of Life," *The Theosophical Path*, 28 (February 1925), 192; "More Words of Praise for 'Om,'" *The Theosophical Path*, 28 (March 1925), 284; "Talbot Mundy's 'Om' Much Appreciated," *The Theosophical Path*, 28 (April 1925), 391; "The Way of Life," *The Theosophical Path*, 28 (June 1925), 602, reprinted from *Manchester City News*, April 25, 1925; "'Om,'" *The Theosophical Path*, 29 (August 1925), 200; "News from Nurnberg," *The Theosophical Path*, 33 (October 1927), 386.

59. For an example of how *Om* was used with the children of Point Loma, see Aunt Esther, "Our Brothers of Forest and Veldt," *Raja-Yoga Messenger*, 22 (September 1926), 233–234.

60. Katherine Tingley in "Miscellaneous Headquarter Notes," *The Theosophical Path*, 27 (December 1924), 603.

61. TM, telegram to H.H. Howland, October 11, 1924, Bobbs-Merrill mss. For instance, one that Mundy forwarded to Bobbs-Merrill was from R. Mitchell Brown, letter to TM, June 14, 1925, Bobbs-Merrill mss.

62. TM, letter to D.L. Chambers, November 21, 1924, p. 2, Bobbs-Merrill mss.

63. TM, "An Answer to Correspondents," 37.

64. TM, letter to H.H. Howland, Labor Day, 1924, p. 4; Mary Converse to TM, March 9, 1925; Bobbs-Merrill mss.

65. TM, letter to H.H. Howland, January 10, 1925; H.H. Howland, letter to TM, February 9, 1925, Bobbs-Merrill mss. The incident was used as publicity by the publisher, sent out to newspapers where, for instance, it was picked up in the *New York Post*. Mary Converse, Publicity, letter to TM, March 9, 1925, Bobbs-Merrill mss.

66. For example, see "New in Paperback: Fiction," *Washington Post Book Watch*, 107 (May 13, 1984), 20. It was published for the first time in a paperback edition in 1962 by Crown Publishers in "The Xanadu Library," a series of classics of imaginative writing. (Amusingly, the cover title misspelled "Ahbor" as "Abhor," but the frontispiece of Mundy and the plates were otherwise taken from the McKinlay, Stone and Mackenzie imprint.) Five years later, in 1967, *Om* was published again in paperback in the United States, by Avon Books, and in England, Cedric Chivers reprinted a hardcover edition in 1968. The Theosophical Press first published *Om* in 1931, and Point Loma Publications, founded by former members of the Society, reprinted the book in 1980, and again in 1993. A mass market paperback was issued in 1984 by Carroll & Graf. In 2000, it was published in an elegant edition by The Reincarnation Library. French and Dutch editions of *Om* were also reprinted, in 1980 and 1984 (by a Theosophical group), respectively.

67. TM, "Apology," *The Theosophical Path*, 30 (January 1926), 19.

68. "Talbot Mundy's 'Om' Much Appreciated," 391; TM, "Apology," *The Theosophical Path*, 30 (January 1926), 19–20.

69. Richards Ames, letter to P.B. Ellis, undated "Questions and Answers—Also Incidentals," Ames collection.

70. D.L. Chambers, letter to TM, October 29, 1925; D.L. Chambers, letter to TM, November 6, 1925, Bobbs-Merrill mss.

71. TM, letter to J. Creswell, April 8, 1927, Ames collection.

72. TM, Letter in "The Camp-Fire" introducing Ramsden, *Adventure*, 58 (June 8, 1926), 178–181.

73. "Books and Reprints: Fiction," *The Times Literary Supplement* (September 16, 1926), 617.

74. TM, *The Devil's Guard* (Indianapolis: Bobbs-Merrill, 1926), 199.

75. TM, *The Devil's Guard*, 323.

76. TM, *The Devil's Guard*, 12. Equally significant inspirations may have been William McGovern's *To Lhasa in Disguise*, which was being simultaneously serialized, and press coverage of Alexandra David-Neel's journey. R.T. Gault, "Talbot Mundy and the Search for Shambhala," http://ditch.midtnn.net.mundsham.htm.

77. Pervin Mistry, "The Devil's Guard by Talbot Mundy," *The Eclectic Theosophist*, No. 86 (March-April 1985), 10.

78. TM, *The Devil's Guard*, 170.

79. TM, *The Devil's Guard*, 169.

80. TM, Letter in "The Camp-Fire" introducing Ramsden, 180.

81. Carty Ranck, "Adventurers and Detectives,"

New York Herald Tribune Books, November 21, 1926, p. 2.

82. "The Camp-Fire: The Fiction Vote," *Adventure* (April 1, 1928), 186.

83. TM, *The Red Flame of Erinpura*, *Adventure*, 61 (January 1927), 137.

84. TM, *The Red Flame of Erinpura*, 136.

85. TM, *The Red Flame of Erinpura*, 156.

Chapter VII

1. Richards Ames, interview; TM, letter to Julian Bobbs, May 12, 1925, p. 2, Bobbs-Merrill mss.

2. Mortgage Guaranty Company, letter to W.C. Bobbs, June 4, 1925, p. 1, Bobbs-Merrill mss

3. Richards Ames, interview.

4. B.K., 9; TM, letter to William C. Bobbs, April 29, 1925, p. 3, Bobbs-Merrill mss.

5. W. Emmett Small, interviews with the author.

6. Richards Ames, interview; TM, letter to Sarah Ames, March 12, 1920, p. 2, Ames collection.

7. Richards Ames, interview.

8. TM, letter to Rose Wilder Lane, April 24, 1934, pp. 1–2, RWL mss.

9. Richards Ames, interview.

10. Jan Zilliacus, letter to the author, October 1997, p. 2.

11. Richards Ames, letter to P.B. Ellis, December 20, 1978, p. 2, Ames collection.

12. Richards Ames, interview.

13. "Book List: Standard Theosophical Literature," *The Theosophical Path*, 28 (March 1925), back cover. The book's purity of thought and deeply literary style made *Om* ideal for wholesale adoption by Point Loma, while *The Devil's Guard*, thematically similar but different in tone, was never accorded such an official reception.

14. Douglas A. Anderson, "Introduction," in Kenneth Morris, *The Dragon Path* (New York: TOR, 1995), 16.

15. TM, letter to "The Camp-Fire" on hunger as the source of crime, *Adventure*, 50 (January 20, 1925), 178.

16. TM, letter to "The Camp-Fire" on hunger as the source of crime, *Adventure*, 50 (January 20, 1925), 178.

17. TM, letter to D.L. Chambers, October 16, 1922, p. 1, Bobbs-Merrill mss.

18. TM, letter to H.H. Howland, November 14, 1922, p. 1, Bobbs-Merrill mss.

19. TM, Letter in "The Camp-Fire" on the Lost Tribes of Israel, *Adventure*, 36 (September 10, 1922), 178–179.

20. TM, Letter in "The Camp-Fire" introducing *Ramsden*, *Adventure*, 58 (June 8, 1926), 178.

21. Kenneth J. Zahorski and Robert H. Boyer, *Lloyd Alexander, Evangeline Walton Ensley, Kenneth Morris: A Primary and Secondary Bibliography* (Boston: G.K. Hall, 1981), pp. 163–266. Morris's fictional books are *The Fates of the Princes of Dyfed* (1914), its sequel, *Book of the Three Dragons* (1930), and an anthology of his short stories, *The Secret Mountain and Other Tales* (1926). Just as many publications have appeared posthumously, including the fiction anthologies *Through Dragon Eyes* (1980), *The Dragon Path* (1995), and the novel *The Chalchiuhite Dragon* (1991). A series of his articles was gathered as *Golden Threads in the Tapestry of History* (1975).

22. "Theosophical Items of Interest: An Appreciation of Kenneth Morris," *The Theosophical Path*, 24 (May 1923), 499–500; TM, "Three Signs of the Times: Kenneth Morris—Flinders Petrie—Spengler" *The Theosophical Path*, 37 (November 1929), 539–548; Kenneth Morris, "'Queen Cleopatra': by Talbot Mundy," *The Theosophical Path*, 36 (May 1929), 330, reprinted in *The Eclectic Theosophist*, No. 93 (May-June 1986), 8.

23. W.E. Small in Helynn Hoffa, "Editor's Introduction" in Kenneth Morris, *Through Dragon Eyes* (La Jolla, CA: West Anglia Publications, 1980), 2–3.

24. TM, Letter in "The Camp-Fire" on the Lost Tribes of Israel, *Adventure*, 34 (April 30, 1922), 181.

25. TM, Letter to "The Camp-Fire" introducing *Hostages to Luck*, *Adventure*, 54 (August 20, 1925), 174.

26. Joseph Campbell, *The Hero of a Thousand Faces* (Princeton: Bollingen, 1949), 198–199.

27. Fritz Leiber, "The Glory of Tros," in Grant, 171–173.

28. The original magazine stories correspond to these chapters in the book version of *Tros of Samothrace*: *Tros of Samothrace*, chapters 1–14, *The Enemy of Rome*, chapters 15–26, *Prisoners of War*, chapters 27–37, *Hostages to Luck*, chapters 38–51, *Admiral of Caesar's Fleet*, chapters 52–66, *The Dancing Girls of Gades*, chapters 67–81, and *The Messenger of Destiny*, chapters 82–87, 88–92, and 93–96. Late 1960s-early 1970s paperback reprints by Avon in the United States and Tandem in England divided *Tros of Samothrace* into four parts, following the original division with *Tros*, *Helma*, and *Liafail* each containing two of the novels, except for *The Messenger of Destiny*, which was kept separate and intact as *Helene*. An American paperback printing of the 1970s ignored the original magazine divisions and split *Tros of Samothrace* into three volumes, *Tros of Samothrace—Lud of Lunden*, *Avenging Liafail*, and *The Praetor's Dungeon*.

29. "He told them better, but here some of them are," Talbot wrote in a copy of the fifth edition of *Tros of Samothrace* sent to Harold in July 1937; inscription in copy in Stephen Michaluk Collection.

30. Louise Maunsell Field, "Cleopatra's Throne," *New York Times* (27 October 1935), 7.

31. TM, *Tros of Samothrace* (New York: D. Appleton-Century, 1934), 260.

32. Jane Spence Southron, "'Tros of Samothrace' and Other Recent Works of Fiction," *New York Times Book Reviews* (October 14, 1934), 6.

33. TM, Letter to "The Camp-Fire" introducing *Tros of Samothrace*, *Adventure*, 51 (February 10, 1925), 179.

34. TM, Letter to "The Camp-Fire" introducing *Tros of Samothrace*, *Adventure*, 51 (February 10, 1925), 179.

35. Leiber in Grant, 171–173; TM, *Tros of Samothrace*, 14.

36. TM, Letter to "The Camp-Fire" introducing *Hostages to Luck*, *Adventure*, 54 (August 20, 1925), 174.

37. TM, "Foreword," *Tros of Samothrace* (London: Hutchinson, 1934), xi.

38. TM, Letter to "The Camp-Fire" on the Tros series, *Adventure*, 53 (July 30, 1925), 176–178.

39. Grant, 152, 155, 122.

40. For instance, note the veiled allusion in Alfred Tressider Sheppard, *Art and Practice of Historical Fiction* (London: Humphrey Toulmin, 1930), 115–116. See also William C. Weber, "*Tros of Samothrace*," *New York Herald Tribune Books* (November 18, 1934), 22, and Elmer Davis, "Caesar's Turn," *The Saturday Review of Literature*, 11 (October 27, 1934), 241. Correspondents included Professor Arthur G. Brodeur of the University of California and Dr. H.E. Eggers of the University of Nebraska, and authors Hugh Pendexter and Arthur D. Howden Smith; Elmer Davis wrote two letters and years later reviewed *Tros of Samothrace* in book form. Brodeur had simultaneously coauthored with Farnham Bishop a book on the waning Roman influence in Britain, *The Altar of the Legion*. In addition to professional historians, amateurs also made their views known: readers from all over the country sent in detailed and often knowledgeable letters, and fifteen were printed, from Clements Heaton, Frank R. Whitzel, James Hathaway, L.S. Hughes, H.G. Patterson, R.E. Briggs, Arthur C. Temmis, John H. Tyree, H.W. Chapman, John W. Anderson, Curtis Bunce, E.S. Pladwell, O.A. Fanwell, Neil Martin, and A. Gray.

41. One such editorial was reprinted by editor Hoffman in "The Camp-Fire," *Adventure*, 53 (July 10, 1925), 177–178. Mundy's letters all appeared in "The Camp-Fire," *Adventure*, 51 (February 10, 1925), 179–180; 53 (June 10 1925), 175–176; 53 (July 10, 1925), 181–183; 53 (July 30, 1925), 175–178; 54 (August 20, 1925), 173–175. Mundy's own views in retrospect on the controversy were expressed in a superb three-page "Foreword" to Hutchinson's British first edition of *Tros of Samothrace*, a "Foreword" which has only appeared in America in *The Fantastic Collector*, No. 229/230 (April/May 1991), n.p.

42. Elmer Davis, "A Loss to Fiction," *The Saturday Review of Literature*, 22 (August 17, 1940), 8. For more recent comments on *Tros of Samothrace* see also *Fantastic Universe*, 11 (March 1959), 106–107; Ron Goulart, *Cheap Thrills* (New Rochelle, NY: Arlington House, 1972), 36, and Leiber in Grant, 171–173.

43. "Heroic Adventure," *The Christian Science Monitor, Weekly Magazine Section* (October 31, 1934), 12; Jane Spence Southron, "'Tros of Samothrace' and Other Recent Works of Fiction," *New York Times Book Reviews*, October 14, 1934, p. 6.

44. D.L. Chambers, letter to TM, January 30, 1924, p. 1, Bobbs-Merrill mss.

45. D.L. Chambers, letter to TM, August 25, 1925, p. 1, Bobbs-Merrill mss.

46. D.L. Chambers, letter to TM, March 27, 1924, Bobbs-Merrill mss.

47. Bobbs-Merrill, letter to TM, August 14, 1925, Bobbs-Merrill mss.

48. Rose Wilder Lane, letter to TM, March 19, 1929, p. 1, Bobbs-Merrill mss.

49. Reprinted in publicity, "What the Reviewers Are Saying of *Tros of Samothrace* by Talbot Mundy," quotations which were featured on the back of the dust jackets of many of Mundy's post-1934 Appleton-Century novels.

50. Floyd C. Gale, "Galaxy's Five Star Shelf," *Galaxy*, 18 (February 1960), 165.

51. Leiber, 172. Leiber extends the comparison to imply that the Tros saga was to the 1930s what J.R.R. Tolkien's fantasies were to the 1960s, a more nebulous point.

52. TM, *Caesar Dies* (London: Hutchinson, 1934), 215, 217–218.

53. Davis, "A Loss to Fiction," 8. See also the reviews in the *Times Literary Supplement*, No. 1700 (August 30, 1934), 590 and *Locus*, No. 166 (October 23, 1974), 6.

54. D.L. Chambers, letter to TM, June 19, 1928, pp. 2–3, Bobbs-Merrill mss.

55. TM, *I Say Sunrise*, 111.

56. TM, letter to Rose Wilder Lane, June 12, 1934, p. 4, RWL mss.

57. Inscription in copy of the first edition of *The Ivory Trail* in Stephen Michaluk Collection.

58. Greenwalt, 102.

59. TM, *W.H.* (London: Hutchinson, 1931), 11–12.

60. TM, *W.H.*, 11–12.

61. TM, *W.H.*, 26–27.

62. TM, *W.H.*, 26–27.

63. TM, *W.H.*, 74; Ellis in Grant, 28.

64. TM, *W.H.*, 119–120.

65. TM, *W.H.*, 256.

66. TM, letter to D.L. Chambers, February 5, 1924, p. 2, Bobbs-Merrill mss.

67. Morris, "'Queen Cleopatra': by Talbot Mundy," 330.

68. TM, letter to D.L. Chambers, February 19, 1925, p. 2, Bobbs-Merrill mss.

69. TM, letter to Rose Wilder Lane, April 24, 1934, pp. 4–5, RWL mss.

70. D.L. Chambers, letter to TM, July 23, 1928; D.L. Chambers, letter to TM, June 19, 1928, pp. 1–2, Bobbs-Merrill mss.

71. TM, letter to D.L. Chambers, March 22, 1924, Bobbs-Merrill mss.

72. TM, letter to Mitchell S. Buck, March 22, 1929, p. 1, Stephen Michaluk Collection.

73. TM, *Queen Cleopatra* (Indianapolis: Bobbs-Merrill, 1929), 291.

74. Promotional reel, *Queen Cleopatra*, Bobbs-Merrill mss.

75. D.L. Chambers, letters to L.E. Pollinger, March 28, 1929 and September 10, 1929, Curtis Brown mss.

76. D.L. Chambers, letter to L.E. Pollinger, March 28, 1929, Curtis Brown mss.; D.L. Chambers, letter to L.E. Pollinger, September 10, 1929, Curtis Brown

mss.; D.L. Chambers, letter to TM, May 6, 1929, p. 2, Bobbs-Merrill mss. Mundy could not be consoled when Bobbs-Merrill, Arthur Hoffman, and Konrad Bercovici said the 7400 copies sold by May "was not bad." D.L. Chambers, letter to TM, May 14, 1929, p. 2; TM, letter to D.L. Chambers, May 10, 1929, p. 4, Bobbs-Merrill mss. The contrast is evident in the reviews in the *New York Times* (February 17, 1929), 7, 25; the *New York Herald Tribune Books* (May 12, 1929), 10; and the London *Times* (April 18, 1929), 317.

77. TM, letter to D.L. Chambers, February 17, 1929, p. 2, Bobbs-Merrill mss.

Chapter VIII

1. Richards Ames, letter to P.B. Ellis, March 10, 1979, pp. 2–3, Ames collection.
2. Richards Ames, interview; Richards Ames, letter to P.B. Ellis, March 10, 1979, pp. 2–3, Ames collection.
3. Richards Ames, interview.
4. Richards Ames, interview; Richards Ames, letter to P.B. Ellis, March 10, 1979, pp. 2–3, Ames collection; TM, letter to D.L. Chambers, August 30, 1927, Bobbs-Merrill mss.; Iverson L. Harris, letter to Richards Ames, July 2, 1978, Ames collection; Iverson L. Harris, letter to P.B. Ellis, April 20, 1978, Point Loma Publications Archive; Iverson L. Harris, letter to P.B. Ellis, August 12, 1978, p. 3, Ames collection; W. Emmett Small, "Foreword," in G. de Purucker, *Fundamentals of the Esoteric Philosophy* (San Diego: Point Loma Publications, 1990), xiii; W. Emmett Small, "G. de Purucker's 'Fundamentals of the Esoteric Philosophy,'" *The Eclectic Theosophist*, No. 116 (March-April 1990), 1–2.
5. TM, "Oakes Respects an Adversary," *Adventure*, 19 (December 3, 1918), 3. See also Charles W. Hamilton, *Early Day Oil Tales of Mexico* (Houston: Gulf, 1966).
6. TM, letter to Mr. Scott, undated, pp. 1–2, Stephen Michaluk Collection.
7. TM, letter to Mr. Scott, undated, p. 2, Stephen Michaluk Collection; Richards Ames, letter to P.B. Ellis, March 10, 1979, p. 2, Ames collection.
8. TM, letter to Mr. Scott, undated, p. 2, Stephen Michaluk Collection; Richards Ames, letter to P.B. Ellis, undated "Questions and Answers— Also Incidentals," Ames collection.
9. TM, letter to D.L. Chambers, August 30, 1927, p. 2, Bobbs-Merrill mss.; TM, letter to Mr. Scott, undated, pp. 1, 3, Stephen Michaluk Collection.
10. Richards Ames, interview.
11. Mrs. Richards Ames, interviews.
12. Recorder, "Theosophical Items of Interest: Leader Plans 1926 European Crusade," *The Theosophical Path*, 30 (April 1926), 378–379.
13. Recorder, "Theosophical Items of Interest: Leader's 1926 Lecture-Tour Under Way," *The Theosophical Path*, 30 (May 1926), 502.
14. "The Screen of Time— Mirror of the Movement: Katherine Tingley in Europe," *The Theosophical Path*, 31 (July 1926), 96.
15. TM, letter to D.L. Chambers, August 30, 1927, Bobbs-Merrill mss.
16. Richards Ames, interview; Richards Ames, letter to P.B. Ellis, March 10, 1979, p. 2, Ames collection.
17. Richards Ames, interview.
18. TM, letter to Mr. Scott, undated, p. 2, Stephen Michaluk Collection.
19. D.L. Chambers, letter to Sally Mundy, December 13, 1927, Bobbs-Merrill mss.
20. Julian Bobbs, memo to D.L. Chambers, September 16, 1927, Bobbs-Merrill mss.
21. Iverson L. Harris, letter to P.B. Ellis, August 12, 1978, p. 3, Ames collection; Richards Ames, interview; Richards Ames, letter to P.B. Ellis, undated "Questions and Answers," p. 2, Ames collection.
22. Richards Ames, interview.
23. Richards Ames, letter to P.B. Ellis, March 10, 1979, p. 3, Ames collection; Iverson L. Harris, letter to P.B. Ellis, August 12, 1978, p. 3, Ames collection; Cancelled checks and check-stubs of Talbot Mundy, Ames collection.
24. Richards Ames, interview.
25. Richards Ames, letter to P.B. Ellis, March 10, 1979, p. 3, Ames collection.
26. Richards Ames, interview.
27. TM to Sarah Mundy, excerpt from undated letter, Ames collection.
28. Lillian J. Cramer, letter to Iverson L. Harris, July 4, 1978, Point Loma Publications archive.
29. Lilla Worthington, letter to TM, March 24, 1932; Lilla Worthington, letters to Mrs. Sarah T. Mundy, May 31 and July 22, 1932, Ames collection.
30. Boris de Zirkoff, letter to Iverson L. Harris, quoted in Harris, letter to P.B. Ellis, July 10, 1978, pp. 2–3, Point Loma Publications archive.
31. Provost in Grant, 75–76.
32. Provost in Grant, 76.
33. Provost in Grant, 81.
34. Provost, interview.
35. Provost, interview; Provost in Grant, 76–79.
36. TM, "Speed," *This Week* (May 5, 1935), 9.
37. Later, Larry's granddaughter would be named Dawn. With the stock market crash the next year, many of Larry's investments were lost, and MacDonald Island was one of the few he was able to keep. Independent production dried up further; it had already been three years since his last movie. Henceforth, he exclusively trained animals, especially "seeing-eye dogs" for the blind, which was his passion. "Laurence Trimble Dies," *The New York Times*, February 10, 1954, p. 29; Jan Zilliacus, letter to the author, October 1997, p. 3. Eventually he remarried in 1941, to Marian Blackton, the daughter of one of the early film pioneers who had once employed him.
38. TM, letter to D.L. Chambers, February 1, 1929, Bobbs-Merrill mss.
39. Provost, interview.
40. TM, letter to Wincenty Lutoslawski, May 1, 1938, p. 2, Janina Lutoslawski Collection.
41. Archie Kilpatrick, "Talbot Mundy Is Dead, Writer, Resident Here," *Manchester Evening Herald*,

August 6, 1940, p. 2. Like most Americans, he opposed prohibition, having described it as a political impossibility as early as 1920 in the *Jerusalem News*. TM, "America After the War: Part 3," *Jerusalem News*, No. 62 (February 20, 1920), 2.

42. TM, letter to D.L. Chambers, December 30, 1928, p. 5, Bobbs-Merrill mss.
43. TM, letter to D.L. Chambers, May 12, 1929, p. 2, Bobbs-Merrill mss.
44. TM, letter to D.L. Chambers, March 12, 1929, Bobbs-Merrill mss.
45. TM, letter to D.L. Chambers, December 30, 1929, Bobbs-Merrill mss.
46. TM, letter to D.L. Chambers, December 13, 1925, Bobbs-Merrill mss.; "The Camp-Fire: The Fiction Vote," *Adventure* (April 1, 1928), 186.
47. TM, letter to D.L. Chambers, December 13, 1925, p. 2–3, Bobbs-Merrill mss.
48. Jan Cohn, *Creating America: George Horace Lorimer and the Saturday Evening Post* (Pittsburgh: University of Pittsburgh Press, 1989), 192–193. Mundy's old friend Sinclair Lewis also believed that the standardizing influence of the *Post* inhibited originality and emphasized materialism. Cohn, 174.
49. TM, letter to D.L. Chambers, December 30, 1928, p. 5, Bobbs-Merrill mss.
50. TM, letter to D.L. Chambers, February 17, 1929, p. 1, Bobbs-Merrill mss.
51. TM, letter to D.L. Chambers, March 4, 1929, p. 1, Bobbs-Merrill mss.
52. TM, letter to Rose Wilder Lane, April 24, 1934, pp. 4–5, RWL mss.
53. TM, letter to D.L. Chambers, March 16, 1929, p. 1, Bobbs-Merrill mss.
54. TM, telegram to Mina Kersey, September 23, 1929, Bobbs-Merrill collection.
55. TM, *Cock o' the North* (Indianapolis: Bobbs-Merrill, 1929), 17.
56. TM, *Cock o' the North*, 13.
57. TM, *Cock o' the North*, 15.
58. TM, *Cock o' the North*, 192.
59. D.L. Chambers, letter to TM, November 12, 1929, Bobbs-Merrill mss. Fox did, however, consider the Jimgrim stories for McLaglen. TM, letter to D.L. Chambers, May 17, 1929, p. 1, Bobbs-Merrill mss.
60. TM, "An Author's Characters," *New York Times*, June 30, 1929, Part VIII, p. 4; Sid., "The Black Watch," *Variety*, May 15, 1929.
61. Provost, interview.
62. TM, letter to John Curtis, May 23, 1929, p. 4, Bobbs-Merrill mss. See also praise of Lewis in reviews, such as "The Black Watch Is Feature of Fox," unidentified newspaper review clipping, Museum of Modern Art files.
63. TM, letter to John Curtis, May 23, 1929, p. 2, Bobbs-Merrill mss.
64. TM, letter to John Curtis, May 23, 1929, p. 5, Bobbs-Merrill mss.
65. Some have mistakenly quoted this line to say that "it is better to be a woman in the arms of a white man than to be a goddess to thousands of natives." Never in any version of the script or the final film did the line acquire this additional element of racism as well as its sexism. See William K. Everson, "Forgotten Ford," *Focus on Film*, No. 6 (spring 1971), 17, and Jeffrey Richards, *Visions of Yesterday* (London: Routledge & Kegan Paul, 1973), 128.
66. Tag Gallagher, *John Ford — The Man and His Films* (Berkeley: University of California Press, 1986), 498.
67. Gallagher, *John Ford — The Man and His Films*, 498.

Chapter IX

1. Robert Florey, letter to Jack Spears, September 24, 1972, Author's collection.
2. Michael Morris, *Madam Valentino* (New York: Abbeville Press, 1991), 1974.
3. George Wehner, *A Curious Life* (New York: Horace Liverwright, 1929), 190, 326–327. In 1926, "H.P.B." Publishers, distributing through Orient Exchange of New York (a publisher of the books of Blavatsky and A.P. Sinnett), had issued *The One Way*, "by Teachers in the Spirit World through George B. Wehner as Medium to A Group of Detroit Students."
4. TM, letter to D.L. Chambers, December 30, 1928, Bobbs-Merrill mss.; Morris, 190.
5. Provost, interview.
6. Wehner, *A Curious Life*, 13.
7. TM, *The Elephant Waits, Short Stories*, 158 (February 25, 1937), 17; TM, "The Night the Clocks Stopped," *Adventure*, 104 (March 1941), 11.
8. TM, letter to D.L. Chambers, November 15, 1928; TM, letter to D.L. Chambers, November 25, 1928; D.L. Chambers, letter to TM, June 19, 1928, pp. 1–2, Bobbs-Merrill mss.
9. TM, "Introduction," in Wehner, *A Curious Life*, 8–9.
10. Provost in Grant, 80; Provost, interview.
11. Talbot Mundy to "G. de P.," October 9, 1929 in Wehner, *A Curious Life*, inscription in copy at the Theosophical University Library, Altadena, California, 920.9 W.
12. Provost, interview.
13. TM, letter to Rose Wilder Lane, April 24, 1934, p. 4, RWL mss.
14. W. Emmett Small, letter to the author, March 5, 1996, p. 2.
15. Dennis E. Berge in Iverson L. Harris, "Reminiscences of Lomaland: Madame Tingley and the Theosophical Institute in San Diego," *Journal of San Diego History*, 20 (summer 1975), 7.
16. Provost, interview.
17. Morris, 197.
18. Garabed Paelian, *Nicholas Roerich* (Sedona, AZ: Antiquarian Educational Group, 1974), 84.
19. Paelian, 84.
20. Jacqueline Decter, *Messenger of Beauty: The Life and Visionary Art of Nicholas Roerich* (Rochester, VT: Park Street Press, 1997).
21. R.T. Gault, "Talbot Mundy and the Search for Shambhala," http://ditch.midtnn.net.mundsham.htm.

22. L.V. Mitrokhin, "N.K. Roerich: A Great Explorer of the East," in *Nicholas K. Roerich 1874–1974* (Simla: Himaachal Pradesh, 1975), 43–45.
23. Mitrokhin, 45–46.
24. Provost, interview.
25. Mitrokhin, 47.
26. Provost in Grant, 86.
27. Robert Lloyd Davis, letter to the author, December 2, 1996, pp. 1–2.
28. Provost, interview.
29. TM, *Old Ugly-Face* (New York: D. Appleton-Century, 1940), 131. In *I Say Sunrise*, Mundy would comment that spiritualism is a part of the "pool" of human subconsciousness, in which memories may be stirred like echoes, which, however, have no value, despite deceiving many people looking for proof of an afterlife in the form of personalities rather than individual, reincarnated souls. TM, *I Say Sunrise*, 170–171. Among the group that had been part of the seances with Wehner, only Scott, who had known Wehner since the early 1920s, continued to defend him, joining silent serial queen Ruth Roland in a February 1931 attempt to summon the spirit of Rudolph Valentino at the offices of the *Los Angeles Herald*. R.T.M. Scott, "Valentino's 'Spirit' Tells of His Death," *Los Angeles Herald*, February 17–18, 1931; Wehner, *A Curious Life*, 182–183. Wehner would return to acting, and gave exhibits of his art in New York later in the 1930s before writing on the American Indian and China. As Dawn circumspectly described Wehner in 1980, using modern vernacular, "He turned out to be a bit of a weirdo, even in today's 'gay' company." Provost, interview.
30. TM, letter to D.L. Chambers, May 10, 1929, p. 3, Bobbs-Merrill mss.
31. Bobbs-Merrill, statement to TM, April 19, 1931, Bobbs-Merrill mss.
32. TM, *Black Light* (London: Hutchinson, 1930), 167. See also the saying on astrology facing chapter 9 in TM, *Black Light*, 91.
33. D.L. Chambers, letter to TM, January 15, 1930, Bobbs-Merrill mss.
34. TM, *I Say Sunrise*, 33.
35. Malcolm R. Henderson, letter to the author, March 8, 1996, p. 1.
36. "Austin Adams Gives Highest Praise to New Book by Mundy."
37. TM, *Black Light*, 84.
38. "Teachers in the Spirit World through George B. Wehner as Medium to A Group of Detroit Students," *The One Way* (New York: "H.P.B." Publishers, 1926).
39. TM, *I Say Sunrise*, 53.
40. Malcolm R. Henderson, letter to the author, February 26, 1996, p. 3.
41. Malcolm R. Henderson, letter to the author, March 8, 1996, p. 1.
42. TM, "Consistent Anyhow," *Adventure*, 73 (February 1, 1930), 74.
43. TM, "Consistent Anyhow," 62.
44. TM, letter to D.L. Chambers, May 10, 1929, p. 4, Bobbs-Merrill mss.
45. TM, letter to D.L. Chambers, May 4, 1929, p. 2, Bobbs-Merrill mss.
46. TM royalty statement, June 4, 1930, Bobbs-Merrill mss.
47. D.L. Chambers, letter to L.E. Pollinger, September 10, 1929, Curtis Brown mss.
48. TM, letter to D.L. Chambers, January 31, 1930, p. 1, Bobbs-Merrill mss.
49. TM, *Old Ugly-Face*, 237.
50. Robert Lloyd Davis, letter to the author, April 3, 1997, p. 1.
51. D.L. Chambers, letter to TM, July 31, 1928; D.L. Chambers, letter to TM, August 27, 1928, p. 2, Bobbs-Merrill mss.
52. Correspondence, December 1926, Curtis Brown mss.
53. Stephen Birmingham, *The Late John Marquand* (Philadelphia: J.B. Lippincott, 1972), 66.
54. Millicent Bell, *Marquand, an American Life* (Boston: Little, Brown, 1979), 275; Birmingham, 65. Biographers of John Marquand, another Brandt & Brandt client at this time, have written extensively of the firm's influence; see the indices of Birmingham and Bell. After Carl's death in 1957, his wife and his children took charge of the agency, which still represents Mundy's interests to this day. Bell, 416–417.
55. John Marquand in a 1945 letter to Jack Briggs, in Bell, 121. See also Birmingham, 130.
56. Marquand in Bell, 349.
57. Statements of October 30, 1930 and May 8, 1931, from Curtis Brown Ltd. to Bobbs-Merrill, Curtis Brown mss.
58. Provost, interview.
59. TM, letter to W.H. Gribbon, August 5, 1939, in Ellis, 220–221.
60. R.L. Pollinger, letter to D.L. Chambers, March 15, 1930, p. 1, Curtis Brown mss.
61. TM, letter to Wm. C. Bobbs, December 17, 1921, p. 4, Bobbs-Merrill mss.
62. Unsigned carbon of letter from Bobbs-Merrill to Mr. Curtis Brown, February 14, 1930, Curtis Brown mss.
63. "Black Light," *Times Literary Supplement*, November 27, 1930, p. 1016.
64. Anthony Rud, "Handshake," *Adventure*, 68 (November 1, 1928), 185.
65. Nicholas Roerich, *Shambhala* (New York: Frederick A. Stokes, 1930), 32.
66. "Jimgrim: Talbot Mundy Invades the Realm of Dreamland," *Boston Transcript*, April 29, 1931, p. 3.
67. TM, *Jimgrim* (New York: Century, 1931), 241.
68. TM, *Jimgrim*, vii, viii.
69. Bergier, *Admirations*, 286; Introduction in "The Camp-Fire," *Adventure*, 76 (November 15, 1930), 183.
70. Susanne Howe, *Novels of Empire* (New York: Cambridge University Press, 1949), 128.
71. Inscription in copy of *Jimgrim* in Robert Lloyd Davis Collection.
72. Clyde B. Clason, "Foreword" in TM, *Old Ugly-Face* (Philadelphia: Wells & Shakespeare, 1950), vii; *Times Literary Supplement*, May 7, 1931, p. 369.

73. Robert Lloyd Davis, letter to the author, December 2, 1996, p. 1.
74. Morris, 198; Decter, 99.
75. Provost in Grant, 89.

Chapter X

1. TM, *Old Ugly-Face*, 13.
2. TM, *The Gunga Sahib* (New York: D. Appleton-Century, 1934), 12.
3. TM, *The Gunga Sahib*, 47.
4. TM, "*C.I.D.*" (New York: Century, 1932), 76.
5. TM, "Milk of the Moon," *Argosy* (September 17, 1938), 27.
6. TM, *The Gunga Sahib*, 46.
7. TM, "*C.I.D.*," 235.
8. TM, "*C.I.D.*," 213.
9. TM, *The Gunga Sahib*, 2.
10. TM, *The Gunga Sahib*, 51.
11. TM, "The Big League Miracle," *Adventure*, 68 (December 15, 1928), 2.
12. TM, letter to D.L. Chambers, May 4, 1929, p. 1, Bobbs-Merrill mss.
13. TM, *The Gunga Sahib*, 58.
14. TM, *The Elephant Waits*, *Short Stories*, 158 (February 25, 1937), 24.
15. TM, "The Night the Clocks Stopped," *Adventure*, 104 (March 1941), 25.
16. Universal serials were made for an average cost of $125,000 or less. Roy Kinnard, *Fifty Years of Serial Thrills* (Metuchen, NJ: Scarecrow, 1983), 133. At least a momentary scene from *The Jungle Mystery* with Noah Beery is visible in *Tim Tyler's Luck* (1937); Tyler goes to Africa in search of his father, abducted to use his knowledge to locate a cache of ivory. Chapter 4 of *Tim Tyler's Luck* was even titled *The Ivory Trail*.
17. Cohn, 224.
18. Provost, interview.
19. TM, letter to Rose Wilder Lane, April 24, 1934, p. 3, RWL mss.
20. Bernice Baumgarten of Brandt & Brandt, letter to D.L. Chambers, November 4, 1936; Bobbs-Merrill, letter to Baumgarten, November 12, 1936, Bobbs-Merrill mss.
21. "The Men Who Make the Argosy: Talbot Mundy," *Argosy* (May 24, 1930), 573.
22. *Adventure* (November 1940), 118.
23. Majorie Kinnan Rawlings, letter to Chuck Rawlings, Nov. 11, 1933, pp. 2–3, University of Florida Libraries; TM, letter to Rose Wilder Lane, June 25, 1934, p. 1, RWL mss.
24. TM, letter to Walter Harold Gribbon, September 2, 1931, in Ellis in Grant, 47–48.
25. Rodney Mundy, letter to the author, September 21, 1995.
26. TM, letter to D.L. Chambers, November 29, 1929, Bobbs-Merrill mss.
27. Talbot Mundy, *Black Light*, 161.
28. TM, *Full Moon* (New York: D. Appleton-Century, 1935), 284.
29. Bergier, *Admirations*, 202.
30. TM, *Full Moon*, 202.
31. Darrell C. Richardson, "Talbot Mundy: Oriental Mystic," *Fantasy Commentator*, 2 (Fall 1948), 291.
32. "A Very Fine Fantastic Adventure Story," *Amazing Stories*, 10 (December 1935), 134; "Hindustan Adventure," *The New York Times Book Review* (April 28, 1935), 22.
33. Bergier, *Admirations*, 298.
34. TM, "The Bell on Hell Shoal," in *My Most Exciting Story* (London: Faber & Faber, 1936), 350.
35. Provost in Grant, 100.
36. Provost, interview.
37. Dawn Mundy, letter to Rose Wilder Lane, June 25, 1934, p. 2, RWL mss.
38. TM, letter to Rose Wilder Lane, July 7, 1935, p. 2, RWL mss.
39. TM, letter to Rose Wilder Lane, April 24, 1934, p. 5, RWL mss. Lane brought with her John Turner, a young man whom she regarded as a son. He had knocked on her door a year earlier asking for food, and she provided him with a home while he attended high school. She later sent him to a military institute, on a European trip, and a semester at Lehigh University before they had a falling out in 1939.
40. TM, letter to Rose Wilder Lane, June 25, 1934, p. 3, RWL mss.
41. "Mundy an Exception Among Maine Writers," *Bangor Herald*, October 2, 1920, Bobbs-Merrill mss.
42. Provost, interview.
43. TM, letter to Rose Wilder Lane, September 18, 1934, p. 1, RWL mss.
44. Dawn Mundy, letter to Rose Wilder Lane, December 10, 1934, pp. 4–5, RWL mss.
45. "Talbot Mundy, 61, Prominent Author, Dies in Florida," *Hartford Daily Courant*, August 6, 1940, p. 4; TM, letter to W.H. Gribbon, July 26, 1937, in Ellis, 213.
46. Provost, interview.
47. "Talbot Mundy, 61, Prominent Author, Dies in Florida," 4; Kilpatrick, 2.
48. Provost, interview.
49. TM, letter to Rose Wilder Lane, April 24, 1934, pp. 4–5, RWL mss.
50. TM, letter to Rose Wilder Lane, July 7, 1935, p. 1, RWL mss.
51. All of these letters appeared in "The Camp-Fire" section of *Adventure* in the same issue carrying the accompanying novel: 92 (May 1, 1935), 118–119; 92 (June 15, 1935), 117–119; (August 15, 1935), 117–118; (October 1), 116–117.
52. TM, letter to D.L. Chambers, March 22, 1924, p. 3, Bobbs-Merrill mss.; TM, letter to Rose Wilder Lane, June 12, 1934, pp. 1–4, RWL mss.
53. For a contrasting view, see P. Schuyler Miller, "The Reference Library," *Astounding Science Fiction*, 62 (January 1959), 146.
54. Louise Maunsell Field, "Cleopatra's Throne," *New York Times* (27 October 1935), 7. See also William C. Weber, "*Purple Pirate*," *New York Herald Tribune Books* (October 27, 1935), 22; "The New Novels: Tros Again," *The London Times Literary*

Supplement (January 4, 1936), 13; Donald Colpitts, *The Spur*, 57 (January 1936), 32; Floyd C. Gale, "Galaxy's Five Star Shelf," *Galaxy*, 18 (February 1960), 165.

55. "Novelist Mundy Kiwanis Speaker," undated newspaper clipping, Richards Ames collection.

56. "Youth Hostel Movement Is Indorsed by Talbot Mundy World Traveler and Author," undated newspaper clipping, Richards Ames collection.

Chapter XI

1. E.C. Beckwith, "Tibetan Adventure," *The New York Times* (April 18, 1937), 26. See also C.A. Brandt, "In the Realm of Books," *Amazing Stories* (December 1937), 134.

2. TM, *The Thunder Dragon Gate* (New York: D. Appleton-Century, 1937), 274. A couple, Tom and Doris Grayne, had appeared in *Full Moon*, but that Tom Grayne was a bookish, eccentric man.

3. TM, *Old Ugly-Face*, *Maclean's*, 51 (May 1, 1938), 21; See also TM, *Old Ugly-Face* (New York: D. Appleton-Century, 1940), 467–468.

4. TM, *Old Ugly-Face*, *Maclean's*, 51 (May 15, 1938), 22.

5. Provost, interview.

6. TM, *Old Ugly-Face*, 50.

7. Provost, interview.

8. William C. Weber, "*Old Ugly-Face*," *New York Herald-Tribune Review of Books*, February 25, 1940, p. 12; Jane Spence Southron, "Mystery in Tibet," *New York Times Book Reviews*, February 25, 1940, p. 20. Such evaluations continue in Everett F. Bleiler, *The Guide to Supernatural Fiction* (Kent, OH: Kent State University Press, 1983), 378, and Everett F. Bleiler, *Supernatural Fiction Writers—Fantasy and Horror*, Vol. 2 (New York: Charles Scribner's Sons, 1985), 850.

9. John Van Mater, Theosophical Library, 1979 interview.

10. Pervin Mistry, letter to the author, September 7, 1989.

11. TM, *Old Ugly-Face*, 510, 544.

12. TM, letter to W.H. Gribbon, August 5, 1939, quoted in Ellis, 220.

13. TM, *Old Ugly-Face*, 171.

14. TM, *Old Ugly-Face*, 99.

15. TM, *Old Ugly-Face*, 75.

16. Dawn also agreed with the Tingley-Strong comparison in Provost, interview.

17. TM, *Old Ugly-Face*, 225.

18. TM, letter to H.H. Howland, undated [January 1921], Bobbs-Merrill mss; TM, letter to Elsa Barker, July 15, 1921, courtesy Paul Dobish, Jr., presently in Stephen Michaluk Collection.

19. Note inscription by Mundy in just such a manner to Alvin Albinson in a copy of *Old Ugly-Face* offered for sale online in 2001, presently in Stephen Michaluk Collection.

20. TM, letter to John Curtis, May 23, 1929, p. 7, Bobbs-Merrill mss.

21. *Fifty-Seven*, based on the novel *Rung Ho!*, by Talbot Mundy (mss.), (n.p.). The manuscript was examined in 1989 in The Book Sail bookstore courtesy of John McLaughlin, prior to its sale to an unknown party. This summary follows Mundy's own wording as closely as possible.

22. TM, *Fifty-Seven*, (b).

23. TM, *Fifty-Seven*, (d).

24. TM, *Fifty-Seven*, (b, g-h).

25. TM, *Fifty-Seven*, (c, h).

26. TM, *Fifty-Seven*, (g); TM, *Rung Ho!*, 40.

27. TM, *Fifty-Seven*, (2–3).

28. TM, *Fifty-Seven*, (i).

29. TM, *Fifty-Seven*, (7).

30. TM, *Fifty-Seven*, (46).

31. *Parliamentary Debates (Hansard) Official Report*, December 7, 1938, pp. 1273–1274, 1307–1309; British Board of Film Censors, Scenarios 1936, 150, British Film Institute; Jeffrey Richards, *The Age of the Dream Palace: Cinema and Society in Britain 1930–1939* (New York: Routledge, 1989), 143–144; "'Lucknow' Film Ban Sensation," *Daily Film Renter*, June 12, 1938, reprinted in Dorothy B. Jones, *The Portrayal of China and India on the American Screen, 1896–1955* (Cambridge: Center for International Studies, Massachusetts Institute of Technology, 1955), 66–67.

32. Kenneth MacGowan to Darryl F. Zanuck, Inter Office Correspondence, March 31, 1936, Twentieth Century–Fox collection, University of Southern California Special Collections Library.

33. The same year Mundy wrote *East and West*, 1937, he had authored an article, "The Hermit and the Tiger," about his youthful experiences around Mount Abu that had formed part of the basis for *The Red Flame of Erinpura*. Youthful memories also created an interesting touch in the second chapter of *East and West*, where Mundy fictionalizes the incident which he said gave him the idea for Yasmini: a carriage crashes, revealing a beautiful, unveiled woman, who looked straight at him, unabashed, and laughed. TM, *East and West*, 17–19. *East and West* even includes a reference to Gulbaz from the 1914 novelette "Gulbaz and the Game."

34. TM, *East and West*, 28.

35. Provost, interview.

36. Fred L. King, *Jack Armstrong Encyclopedia* (Macon, MO: 1984), 8. A related tie-in showed how to use the "Hike-O-Meter" as part of an outdoor game covering a mile distance searching for treasure, illustrated with a modern setting but the face of a classic buccaneer.

37. Provost, interview.

38. TM, "The Maya Mystery—Yucatan," *The Theosophical Path*, 27 (December 1924), 573–578.

39. Douglas A. Anderson, "Afterword," in Kenneth Morris, *The Chalchiuhite Dragon* (New York: TOR Books, 1991), 284.

40. Dainis Bisenieks, "Introduction," in Kenneth Morris, *The Fates of the Princes of Dyfed* (North Hollywood: Newcastle Publishing, 1978), v.

41. TM, letter to W.H. Gribbon, June 7, 1939, in Ellis, 220.

42. Provost, interview.

43. King, 8. Even then, instructions noted that the

box does not give true answers every time—failing to explain that it functioned by a strip of cellophane that curled in response to the heat of a thumb placed over the side of the box.

44. Jack Marshall in Kent Chetlain, "'Henry Aldrich House' really 'Jack Armstrong House,'" *The Islander*, October 20, 1977, p.2.

45. Provost, interview.

46. Wyatt Blassingame in Kent Chetlain, "'Henry Aldrich House' really 'Jack Armstrong House,'" p. 2. Ironically, for the year immediately after Mundy's death, much of the *Jack Armstrong* programs survive, as Jack goes to the Philippines on the trail of Professor Loring and uranium. The plot had to incorporate a "Dragon's Eye Ring" already tested in the spring as a fall 1940 premium, and which would have been a centerpiece in whatever new serial Mundy was planning at the time of his death. Mundy's mystical interest and exploration of the unknown and Eastern beliefs was substituted by Strong with the appeal of modern science, especially the burgeoning field of atomic power.

47. Printed card of Wincenty Lutoslawski, Janina Lutoslawski Collection.

48. TM, letter to Rose Wilder Lane, July 2, 1934, p. 5, RWL mss.

49. Provost, interview.

50. Dennis Ecklund, "Old Sayler Home has Colorful History," *The Islander*, January 17, 1985, pp. 1–3, copy in Anna Maria Historical Society files; address given in letter from Carl Brandt to TM, November 30, 1938, facsimile in Grant, 100.

51. Wyatt Blassingame in Kent Chetlain, "'Henry Aldrich House' really 'Jack Armstrong House,'" p. 23.

52. Wyatt Blassingame, letter to P.B. Ellis, March 18, 1978, p. 1, carbon in Anna Maria Historical Society.

53. Warren Hosmer in Kent Chetlain, "Henry Aldrich Author Lived in Gulf View Subdivision," *The Islander*, October 6, 1977, p. 2; Wyatt Blassingame in Kent Chetlain, "'Henry Aldrich House' really 'Jack Armstrong House,'" 23.

54. Provost, interview.

55. Provost, interview. Among the Mundy's guests in Anna Maria was the writer George Fielding Elliot and his wife Sally, and doubtless many of the conversations centered on the global situation. Elliot had written for pulp magazines, but was also an expert in national defense, an area in which he would acquire a leading reputation during the coming war and afterwards.

56. Provost, interview. By contrast, his friend, Natacha Rambova, had come to know Franco as the best hope against the communist tendencies of the left. Still in Mallorca in 1936, Natacha found herself under Republican bombardment. Dismayed by the wealthy, indolent class, she was also in danger from many of her communist neighbors, and was irate at the favorable international press coverage they received, when the fighting she witnessed placed them in the worst light. When she tried to stop retaliations against civilians which the church did nothing to stop, she had to be smuggled to France at the end of 1936 through Franco's intervention, and she and Alvaro eventually divorced.

57. Provost, interview.

58. Wyatt Blassingame, letter to P.B. Ellis, March 18, 1978, p. 2, carbon in Anna Maria Historical Society.

59. Provost, interview.

60. Wyatt Blassingame, letter to P.B. Ellis, March 18, 1978, p. 2, carbon in Anna Maria Historical Society.

61. TM, *I Say Sunrise*, 133; Wyatt Blassingame, letter to Lurton Blassingame, quoted in "Camp-Fire," *Adventure* (November 1940), 120.

62. TM, letter to H.H. Howland, March 17, 1925, p. 2, Bobbs-Merrill mss.

Chapter XII

1. Among twenty-five bequests for $78,000 in Rambova's 1965 will, she left Dawn and her family $2500, mentioning a project on which Dawn was then collaborating with Mildred Orick.

2. Provost, interview.

3. TM, "A Beginner's Concept of Theosophy," *The Theosophical Path*, 28 (May 1925), 434.

4. TM, *I Say Sunrise*, 82.

5. Provost in Grant, 95; TM, *I Say Sunrise*, 125.

6. TM, "'Mother Nature': A Review of a Book by William J. Long,"140; Provost in Grant, 83.

7. TM, letter to Wincenty Lutoslawski, May 1, 1938, p. 1, Janina Lutoslawski Collection.

8. TM, *I Say Sunrise*, 93.

9. TM, *I Say Sunrise*, 185.

10. Anthony Boucher and J. Francis McComas, "Recommended Reading: Reprints and Reissues," *Magazine of Fantasy and Science Fiction*, 1 (fall 1950), 83.

11. TM, *I Say Sunrise*, 100.

12. TM, letter to Wincenty Lutoslawski, March 11, 1938, p. 2, Janina Lutoslawski Collection.

13. TM, *I Say Sunrise*, 120–121.

14. *Books of Light* (Columbus, OH: Ariel, 1991), 22.

15. TM, *I Say Sunrise*, 84.

16. TM, *I Say Sunrise*, 156.

17. A. Copeland, *Theosophical Forum*, 27 (July 1949), 437–439; John Cooper Powys, letter to Alan Dakers, January 28, 1948, University of Michigan Special Collections Library.

18. Conference Notes, Darryl Zanuck, April 6, 1951, Twentieth Century–Fox collection, University of Southern California Special Collections Library; Frank Rosenberg, interview with the author, July 20, 1987.

19. Henry King, interview with the author, January 28, 1981.

20. Ivan Goff, interview with the author, October 30, 1987.

21. Thomas Wood, "Set Engulfs Landscape: Tyrone Power to Battle In Khyber Pass (Calif.)," unidentified newspaper clipping, New York Public Library, Lincoln Center, Billy Rose Theater Collection.

22. Provost, interview.
23. "New Films," *Newsweek*, 43 (January 11, 1954), 80; William Whitebait, "The Movies," *New Statesman and Nation*, 47 (April 17, 1954), 502; Penelope Houston, "CinemaScope Productions," *Sight and Sound*, 23 (April-June 1954), 198. With the background landscapes also serving to fill the wide screen, *King of the Khyber Rifles* would be received as the best picture yet made in the process, the first whose action fully justified a wide screen. John McCarten, "The Current Cinema," *New Yorker*, 29 (January 2, 1954), 51.
24. John McCarten, "The Current Cinema," *New Yorker*, 29 (January 2, 1954), 51.
25. Provost, interview.
26. "Inside Stuff—Pictures," *Variety*, July 16, 1952.
27. D.L. Chambers, letter to Pincus Berner, March 9, 1951, Bobbs-Merrill mss.
28. TM, quoted in Dawn Mundy, letter to Rose Wilder Lane, October 27, 1934, p. 4, RWL mss.
29. Pincus Berner, letter to Ross Baker, April 29, 1955, Bobbs-Merrill mss.
30. Provost, interview.
31. Franz Rottensteiner, *The Fantasy Book* (New York: Collier, 1978), 103.
32. Philip Kaufman, letter to the author, April 25, 1988.
33. TM, letter to Miss Laura Elliott, January 5, 1920, Bobbs-Merrill mss.
34. TM in Arthur Sullivant Hoffman, ed., *Fiction Writers on Fiction Writing* (Indianapolis: Bobbs-Merrill, 1923), 421.
35. TM, letter to D.L. Chambers, February 19, 1925, Bobbs-Merrill mss.; TM in "Mundy Praises Kipling, but Says He Isn't Like Him," *Pittsburgh Press*, October 24, 1934, p. 2.
36. Rottensteiner, 103.
37. TM, "Blackmail," *The Theosophical Path*, 26 (June 1924), 522.
38. TM in Hoffman, ed., *Fiction Writers on Fiction Writing*, 8, 326.
39. L. Sprague De Camp, "Mundy's Vendhya," *Amra*, 2 (September 1970), 19.
40. Mircea Eliade, *No Souvenirs* (New York: Harper & Row, 1977), 2.
41. TM, letter to William C. Bobbs, December 17, 1921, Bobbs-Merrill Collection.
42. Richardson, 292.
43. Clyde B. Clason, "Foreword" in TM, *Old Ugly-Face* (Philadelphia: Wells & Shakespeare, 1950), vii; Everett F. Bleiler, *The Guide to Supernatural Fiction* (Kent, OH: Kent State University Press, 1983), 379.
44. Darrell Crombie, "Ghosts Walk...," in Grant, 117.
45. Mundy discusses this ambiguity in his article, "An Authors Characters," *New York Times* (June 30, 1929), Sec. VIII, p. 4.
46. Everett F. Bleiler, *Supernatural Fiction Writers—Fantasy and Horror*, Vol. 2 (New York: Charles Scribner's Sons, 1985), 847; TM, letter to Mary Converse, January 15, 1924, p. 2, Bobbs-Merrill mss.
47. I.W.L., "*Guns of the Gods*: A Talbot Mundy Romance of the Mystic East," *Boston Transcript*, July 9, 1921, Bobbs-Merrill mss.
48. TM, *A Secret Society*, *Adventure*, 24 (August 10, 1922), 43–44.
49. Robert Lloyd Davis, letter to the author, April 3, 1997, p. 1.
50. TM, "America as Protector of Armenia," *New York Times*, May 25, 1919, p. 6.
51. TM, "America as Protector of Armenia," 6; TM, "America After the War: Part 2," *Jerusalem News*, No. 61 (February 19, 1920), 2.
52. TM, *Tros of Samothrace*, 251.
53. TM, *The Thunder Dragon Gate*, 134.
54. TM, *The Gunga Sahib*, 226.
55. TM, Letter in "The Camp-Fire" introducing *Ramsden*, *Adventure*, 58 (June 8, 1926), 181.
56. Elmer Davis, "A Loss to Fiction," *The Saturday Review of Literature*, 22 (August 17, 1940), 8; Lawrence Durrell, *Assays* (Santa Barbara, CA: Ross-Erikson, 1961), 122; Peter S. Prescott, "American Samurai," *Newsweek*, July 5, 1982, p. 72.
57. TM, "As to Writing and Reading," *The Theosophical Path*, 28 (February 1925), 142.
58. Davis, "A Loss to Fiction," 8.
59. B. Virginia Lee, "Books and Writers," *Overland Monthly*, 83 (August 1925), 306.
60. Clyde B. Clason, "Foreword" in TM, *Old Ugly-Face*, vii.
61. Boucher and McComas, 83; Pervin Mistry, letter to the author, July 3, 1986.
62. For instance, Everett Bleiler condemns Mundy for nagging, bombastic exhortations, and L. Sprague De Camp decries the interruption of the action "by long, moralistic lectures." David Drake calls Mundy unreadable, "an incredibly sluggish writer who was able to make the most exciting events boring by the creaking delays by which he approached them." David Drake, letter to the author, March 25, 1980.
63. A.A. Proctor, "The Camp-Fire," *Adventure*, 76 (November 15, 1930), 183.
64. "From Letters Received," *The Eclectic Theosophist*, No. 94 (July-August 1986), 12.

Index

Ace Books 250
"Across the Color Line" (1912) 18, 263
Admiral of Caesar's Fleet (1925) 268
Adventure 9, 17–19, 21–24, 33–34, 39, 47–48, 50–52, 54–56, 63, 77, 80–81, 83, 87–88, 90–92, 94, 99, 101, 120, 124, 126, 132, 136, 138, 140, 147, 158–159, 181, 185–186, 193–194, 196, 199, 208, 238, 240, 243, 257, 259
The Adventure at El-Kerak (1921) 77, 81, 265
Adventure's Best Stories — 1926 135, 262
The Affair at Kaligaon (1930) 158, 194, 269
Affair in Araby (retitling of *The King in Check*)
Africa 8–14, 54–57, 196–198, 228–229, 235
Agents of Empire 74
All Aces 100, 198
All Four Winds 178, 199
All Manner of Men 279
All Story 18, 29, 144
Allen, Dawn, 155–157, 168–172, 175–176, 183–184, 188, 198, 200–202, 219, 231, 235, 239, 240–242, 249–250, 278
"America After the War" (1920) 265
"America and the Great War" (1916) 264
"America as Protector of Armenia" (1919) 57, 265
"America Horns In" (1919) 10, 54, 264
American Cavalcade 199
"The American Rattlesnake" (1920) 265
Ames, Richards 60–61, 65, 67, 70–74, 77, 101, 113, 126, 133–135, 153–155
Ames, Sarah Teresa 60, 62, 65,
68–75, 89, 92, 94, 110, 113, 132–133, 151, 153–155, 188, 280–281
Anglo-American Society 61, 72, 279
"Another's Duty Is Full of Danger" (1924) 122, 267
"An Answer to Correspondents" (1925) 125, 267
Answers 6, 262
Anti-semitism 67
"Apology" (1925) 268
"An Appreciation of Kenneth Morris" (1923) 266
"An Arabian Night" (1913) 60, 150, 263
Argosy 108, 144, 158–159, 191, 194–195
Ariel Press 253
Armenia 57–59
"Armenians in Jerusalem" (1919) 265
The Aroma of Athens 119–120
"The Art of Dying Daily" (reprint of "Spiritual Man Is Eternal: There Are No Dead!")
"As to Capital Punishment" (1925) 136, 268
"As to Success and Failure" (1925) 267–268
"As to Writing and Reading" (1925) 267
Asoka's Alibi (1929) 158, 194, 269
Astor, Lady Nancy 43, 64
"At Maneuvers" (1913) 23, 263
Australia 9
"An Author's Characters" (1929) 158, 164, 269, 276
"The Avenger" (1937) 199, 271
Avenging Liafail (volume of *Tros of Samothrace*)
Avon Books 186, 250, 287, 288

"Baboons" (1920) 10, 265
"The Babu" (1931) 190–191, 269
"Bar the Bar" (1934) 270
Barabbas Island (1919) 57–58, 63, 77, 265
Barker, Elsa 218
Battle Stations (1935) 208, 271
"A Beginner's Concept of Theosophy" (1925) 268
Bel Geddes, Norman 158
"The Bell on Hell Shoal" (1933) 199, 204–205, 270
Benefit of Doubt (1922) 89, 99–101, 266
"Bengal Rebellion" (1935) 207, 270
Bercovici, Konrad 158, 290
Bergier, Jacques 95, 187, 204, 250–251
Besant, Annie 285
"The Big League Miracle" (1928) 158, 193–194, 268
"Billy Blain Eats Biscuits" (1916) 18, 264
"Billy Blain's Onions and Garlic" (1916) 18, 264
"Black Flag" (1931) 158, 199, 234, 269–270
Black Light (1930) 42, 93, 119, 124, 158, 168, 172, 176–180, 184, 188, 192, 199, 202, 204, 216–217, 225, 253–254, 261, 269
The Black Watch 3, 162–167, 219, 223, 249, 291
"Blackmail" (1924) 267
Blassingame, Wyatt 225, 235, 237, 239
Blast see *Down and Bugle Blast*
Blavatsky, H.P. 44–45, 112–113, 115, 117, 123, 135, 144, 168–169, 242
Bleiler, Everett F. 252
"Blighty" (1918) 264
"The Blooding of the Ninth Queen's Own" (1911) 18, 262
Blue Book 198, 207
Bobbs-Merrill 34–36, 39, 42–43, 50, 55, 63, 74, 77, 83,

87–88, 93–94, 101, 120–121, 124, 126, 141, 150, 160, 162, 164, 169, 176–178, 181, 184, 199, 201, 249, 250–251, 276–277, 279
Boer War 8, 9, 22, 211, 273–274
Book reviews by Mundy *see* "America and the Great War"; "Great Idea"; "Life on the Veld"; "'Mother Nature': A Review of a Book by William J. Long"; "Reviews of 'The Wine of Life,' Katherine Tingley's Forthcoming Book"; "The Turning Tide: Two Recent Books— A Review"
Brandt & Brandt 168, 183, 196, 207, 249, 292
Braun, Maurice 118
Britannia and Eve 198
"Brotherhood or League?" (1923) 266
Brown, Curtis 184
The Bubble Reputation (UK title for *Her Reputation*)
"Burberton and Ali Beg" (1914) 99, 263
Burroughs, Edgar Rice 256
Burt, A.L. 93, 104, 185, 199
Burton, Sir Richard 79
By Allah Who Made Tigers (1929) 158, 269

"C.I.D." (1932) 131, 185, 189–191, 193, 253, 261, 270
Caesar Dies (1926) 142–143, 185, 210, 250, 261, 268
Caesar's Commentaries 140
Camera! (1934) 195, 270
"Candles" (1920) 265
Carroll & Graf 253, 287
Cartland, Barbara 251, 253
"Case 13" (1932) 270
Cassell's 25, 29, 275–276
Caves of Terror (1922) 29–30, 41–42, 87, 89–91, 95–96, 123, 126, 128–131, 135, 179, 243, 253–255, 261, 266
Cedric Chivers 256, 287
Centaur Press 143, 250
Century Co. 97, 184–185; *see also* D. Appleton-Century
Chandos-Pole case 14–15
"Chant" (1924) 267
"The Chaplain of the Mullingars" (1912) 23, 262–263
Charles Scribner's Sons 34, 275–276
China 8, 227
"Christening Cannon Rock" (1912) 234, 262
Christian Science 42–44, 53, 64, 66, 110, 113, 242, 280

"Chullunder Ghose the Guileless" (1932) 95, 127–128, 130, 191, 270
Clarke, Charles G. 158
Clason, Clyde B. 243, 258
Classics Illustrated 249
Cleopatra (retitled *Queen Cleopatra*)
Cleopatra's Promise (1935) 208, 271
"Climate and Conditions: A Red Sea Rhapsody" (reprint of "The Pillar of Light")
"The Closed Trail of William Walker" (1913) 22, 263
Cock o' the North (1929) 26, 42, 93, 159–160, 179, 181, 253, 261, 269
Coll, Joseph Clement 251, 276–277
"Companions in Arms" (1937) 199, 271
Conkey, Frank and Florence 188, 207–208, 237
Conkey, Theda *see* Allen, Dawn
Connecticut 43, 60, 199, 208
Conrad, Joseph 2, 255
"Consistent Anyhow" (1930) 158, 181, 199, 230, 269
"Cornelia's Englishman" (1911) 262
"The Cowards" (1912) 23, 274, 263
Craven, Inez 14–16, 43, 55, 110, 181, 218
The Crescent 46
Crime 136–137, 291
A Curious Life (1929) 169, 176, 268

D. Appleton-Century 142, 184–185, 204, 213, 225, 289
Dakers, Alan 241, 243
Dalby, Richard 252
"The Damned Old Nigger" (1917) 52, 264
The Dancing Girls of Gades (1925) 268
Davis, Elmer 26, 51, 140–141, 143, 149, 154, 158, 175–176, 187, 289
Day, Bradford, M. 250
"Death and the Actor and the Stage" (excerpt of "Spiritual Man Is Eternal: There Are No Dead!")
De Camp, L. Sprague 251, 258, 296
The Delineator 77
The Devil's Guard (1926) 26, 93, 102, 112, 119, 124, 126–131, 159, 174, 186, 189, 212, 216–217, 243, 252, 254, 257, 261, 268, 276, 288

The Devil's Own (retitled *Her Reputation*)
Diamonds See in the Dark (UK title of *East and West*)
Diana Against Ephesians (1923) 101, 266
Dick, Fred J. 92, 285–286
Dick Anthony of Arran: The Sword of Iskander (1914) 27–29, 263–264
Disowned! (1915) 27, 264
Doniger, Walter 3, 244
"Dorg's Luck" (1912) 18, 263
Doty, Douglas Z. 162
Doubleday, Page, and Co. 135
"The Dove with a Broken Wing" (1915) 264
Down and Bugle Blast 158
Drake, David 296
A Drama with Music 157, 176
"A Drop or Two of White" (1916) 52, 264
"Dungeons and Dragons" 251
"The Duty to Armenia" (1919) 265

East and West (1937) 42, 185, 191, 196, 212, 224–225, 261, 271, 276, 294
Easter Island 234–235
"Eastern Proverb" (1924) 267
Eddy, Mary Baker 44–45, 53, 64, 66, 123, 169, 242
Egypt 57, 83, 87, 92, 147–150, 205, 208–210, 229, 234
"Elephant-Hunting for a Living" (1912) 10, 263
The Elephant Sahib (1930–31) 158, 194, 269
The Elephant Waits (1937) 195, 271
Eliade, Mircea 168
Eliot, George Fielding 295
"Elizabeth" (1920) 10, 145, 147, 265
Elizabeth I (Queen of England) 143–147
Ellis Island 16
"The Empty Saddle" (reprint of "For the Salt Which He Had Eaten")
"The End of the Bad Ship Bundesrath" (1919) 10, 54–55, 265
The Enemy of Rome (1925) 268
England 5–7, 14, 64, 143–147, 171, 201–202
"England After the War" (1920) 64, 265
Evangeline 106, 284
Everybody's 34–35, 48, 98, 251, 277
Everybody's Combined with Romance 88, 150, 158, 225

"Evolution" (reprint of "History")
The Eye of Zeitoon (1920) 26, 46, 55, 57–60, 77, 90, 138, 183, 253, 256, 261, 265, 277, 279
The Eye of Zeitun (reprinted as *The Eye of Zeitoon*)
"The Eye-Teeth of O'Hara" (1931) 270

The Falling Star (reprinted as *Caesar Dies*)
Falls, Charles G. 277
Famous Fantastic Mysteries 243
Fantasy Commentator 243
"Fata Virumque Cano" (1924) 267
Feisul 68–69, 82–83
Feminism 29–31, 42–45, 96, 105, 122–123, 147–149, 157, 160–161, 166, 168, 179, 193, 202–203, 209–210, 217–218, 253, 254
Fiction Writers on Fiction Writing (1923) 158, 266
Fifty-Seven 3, 219–225, 249, 294
Films 22–23, 89, 97–98, 101–109, 162–167, 196–198, 207, 219–225, 101–106, 196–198, 208, 219–225, 252–253, 283
Finley, Virgil 243
The Fire-Cop (film) 22–23
"The Fire Cop" (story, 1911) 22, 262
Flame of Cruelty (1929) 158, 225, 269
"Flapdoodle" (excerpt of "Blackmail")
Fleets of Fire (1935) 208, 271
Florida 206, 236–238
For the Peace of India (retitled *Rung Ho!*)
"For the Salt Which He Had Eaten" (1913) 24–25, 77, 162, 225, 263
For Valor (film) 22
"For Valour" (story, 1912) 22, 262
Foran, W.R. 12, 274
Ford, John 163, 166
Foul of the Czar (1914) 27, 264
Fox Films 162, 291
"Francis Bannerman—A Man of Mystery and History" (1912) 22, 263
Franklin, Dwight 279
"From Hell, Hull and Halifax" (1913) 263
"From the Book of the Sayings of Tsiang Samdup" (1924) 267
Full Moon (1934–35) 26, 42, 124, 185, 189, 202–204, 213, 230, 243, 251, 254, 261, 270–271, 294
Fussell, Joseph H. 117

Galt, Walter 5, 18, 22, 240, 275
Garden City Publishing 135
Gates, William 231
Gault, R.T. 252
"The Gentility of Ikey Blumendall" (1914) 67, 263
Germany 6–7, 49, 56
Gnome Press 250
"Go, Tell the Czar!" (1914) 27, 264
"The Gods Seem Contented" (1924) 199, 230, 267
Goff, Ivan 3, 244
Golden Fleece 198, 210
"Golden River" (1929) 158, 193, 268
"The Goner?" (1912) 18, 262, 274–275
Grand Mufti of Jerusalem 71–72
Grant, Donald M. 35, 251
Grant, Leslie 35, 158
The Great Horn Spoon (1928) 268
"Great Idea" (1940) 272
The Grey Mahatma (reprinted as *Caves of Terror*)
Gribbon, Harold 5, 36, 74, 176, 202, 240
"Guarded Secrets" (saying from *The Devil's Guard*)
Gulbaz and the Game (1914) 29–31, 42, 263, 294
The Gunga Sahib (1934) 185, 189, 190–195, 270
Guns of the Gods (1921) 26, 29–30, 39, 42, 77, 93, 130, 183, 189, 191, 193, 199, 218, 224, 250, 253–255, 261, 265, 277
Gup Bahadur (UK title for *Cock o' the North*)
"The Guzzler's Grand Prix" (1913) 18, 263

Haggard, H. Rider 19, 38, 79, 148, 254
"Hail and Farewell!" (1929) 269
Hanley, Jeff 17, 79, 208
Hanna, Jack 206–207, 236
Hedin, Sven 117, 286
"Heinie Horns into the Game" (1919) 10, 54, 265
Helene (volume of *Tros of Samothrace*)
Helma (volume of *Tros of Samothrace*)
Her Reputation (book, 1923) 42, 93, 104–105, 108–109, 204, 224, 261, 266
Her Reputation (film) 102–106, 108, 135
"The Hermit and the Tiger" (1937) 199, 271, 294
Herrmann, Bernard 245
Hira Singh (1917) 26, 31, 33, 49–52, 57, 80, 90, 253–256, 261, 264, 276, 278
Hira Singh's Tale (reprinted as *Hira Singh*)
"History" (1923) 266
Ho for London Town! (reprinted as *W.H.*)
Hoffman, Arthur Sullivant 18–19, 21, 47–48, 52–53, 58, 63, 120–121, 124, 126, 132, 154, 183, 278
Hollywood, California 97, 101–109, 162–167, 196–198, 207, 219–225, 244–250, 283
"Honor" (1912) 23, 263
"The Honourable Pig" (1939) 199, 271
Hookum Hai (1913) 24, 77, 263
"Hope" (article, 1924) 36, 267
"Hope" (poem, 1924) 267
Hostages to Luck (1925) 268
"How Is a Story Written?" (excerpt from "Apology")
"How Talbot Mundy Came to Write" (1920) 265
Howard, Robert E. 251, 258
Humor 144
The Hundred Days (1923) 42, 82, 96–97, 185, 261, 267
The Hundred Days and The Woman Ayisha see *The Hundred Days* and *The Woman Ayisha*
Hutchinson 59, 88, 90, 93, 94, 101, 108, 126, 142–143, 159–160, 178, 183–185, 199, 204, 213, 215

"I Have Risen" (1929) 170, 269
I Say Sunrise (1947) 44, 119, 179, 200, 207, 240–243, 259, 261, 272
"I Will and I Will Not" (1924) 267
The "Iblis" at Ludd (1922) 78, 81, 253, 266
"Ikey Hole's Luck" (1912) 67, 263
"Ill Wind" (slightly rewritten from "Bengal Rebellion")
Illustrations 243, 251, 253, 276–277, 279
"Impudence Is Art" (reprint of "Milk of the Moon")
"In a Righteous Cause" (1913) 263
In Aleppo Bazaar (1920) 57, 63, 77, 265

"In Old Narada Fort" (1929) 158, 193, 269
"In the Red, Red Sea" see "The Red Sea Cargo"
"In Winter Quarters" (1912) 23, 263
Ince, Thomas H. 3, 101–102, 105–106, 108, 115
India 7–9, 23–25, 29–42, 49–51, 89–91, 94–96, 99, 121–131, 160–167, 188–194, 205, 219–225, 227, 230, 278
"India: Paradise of the Imaginative Story-Teller" (reprint of "A Land Where Romance Reigns")
"Innocent, Noncombatant and Guileless" (reprint of "Chullunder Ghose the Guileless")
The Invisible Guns of Kabul (reprinted as *Cock o' the North*)
"Italy in Strike Time" (1920) 265
The Ivory Trail (1919) 10, 26, 55–57, 63, 87, 144, 196, 198, 211, 218, 228, 243, 251, 253, 256, 261, 265, 276, 279

Jack Armstrong and the Ivory Treasure 228
Jack Armstrong and the Mystery of the Iron Key 230
Jack Armstrong, the All-American Boy 3, 10, 138, 183, 212, 216, 225–235, 294–295
"Jack Armstrong, the All-American Boy, Episode No. 893" (1938) 271
"Jackson Tactics" (1919) 10, 54, 264
"Jansen and Jansen—Twins" (1911) 262
"Japan" (1934) 270
Jaqua, Mark 108
"Jerusalem" (1923) 77, 266
Jerusalem News 61–62, 64–65, 67–69, 70–72, 74, 275, 291
Jimgrim (1930–31) 158, 185–187, 189, 199, 230, 243, 250, 252, 259, 261, 269
Jimgrim and Allah's Peace 77–78, 185, 261
Jimgrim and the Devil at Ludd 82, 253, 261; see also *The "Iblis" at Ludd* and *The Seventeen Thieves of El-Kalil*
Jimgrim Sahib (retitling of *Jimgrim*)
Jimgrim vs. The Nine Unknown 253–254
Jungle Jest 101, 185, 249, 255, 261; see also *Benefit of Doubt*; *Diana Against Ephesians*; and *Treason*

The Jungle Mystery 196–198, 228, 245, 293
"A Jungle Sage" (1932) 12, 199, 270

"Katherine Tingley Again Gives 'The Eumenides' Before Large Audience in Greek Theater" (1924) 267
Kaufman, Philip 252
Khufu's Real Tomb (reprinted as *The Mystery of Khufu's Tomb*)
King, Bradley 102, 104, 106, 135, 283, 284
King, Henry 3, 245
"The King Can Do No Wrong" (1923) 266–267
King Dick (1914) 27, 264
The King in Check (1922) 68, 78–79, 82–83, 138, 185, 243, 261, 266
King of the Khyber Rifles (1953 film) 3, 26, 154, 160, 162, 211, 219, 235, 243–249, 296
King — of the Khyber Rifles (novel, 1916–17) 26, 29, 31, 33–36, 39–41, 46, 49, 88–90, 102, 141, 155, 160–162, 164–167, 184, 199, 224, 243–249, 250–251, 253–254, 261, 264, 276–277
King of the World (rewritten as *Jimgrim*)
Kipling, Rudyard 1, 7, 211, 254, 277
"Kitty and Cupid" (1911) 18, 262
"Kitty Burns Her Fingers" (1911) 18, 262
Kleiner, Harry 5, 244
Kublai Khan 184

"The Lady and the Lord" (1911) 18, 262
The Lama's Law (book) 118, 253, 261
"The Lama's Law" (poem, 1924) 267
Lamb, Harold 184
Lambert, Louis E. 251
The Lancing of the Whale (1914) 27, 264
"A Land Where Romance Reigns" (1921) 40, 265
Lane, Rose Wilder 42–43, 141, 148, 159, 206, 293
Lawrence, T.E. 78–79
Leiber, Fritz 142, 251, 258
Lester, Leonard 287
The Letter of His Orders (1913) 33, 34, 189, 263
Lewis, Mitchell 164
Lewis, Sinclair 17, 291
Liafail 139

Liafail (volume of *Tros of Samothrace*)
Liberty 199
"Life on the Veld" (1917) 264
"Like the Sunrise" (excerpt of "A Beginner's Concept of Theosophy")
The Lion of Petra 78, 81–82, 261, 280
"Lion Paradise" (excerpt from "On the Trail of Sinbad the Sailor") 199
"Lord Astor of Cleveden" (1920) 64, 265
"Lord Dunsany" (1920) 64, 253, 265
The Lost Trooper (1922) 78–79, 82, 87, 185, 261, 266, 280
"Love and War" (1912) 18, 263
"A Low-Veldt Funeral" (1913) 263
Loy, Myrna 163–164, 219
Lud of Lunden (volume of *Tros of Samothrace*)
Lutoslawski, Wincenty 84, 236, 242

"MacHassan Ah" (1915) 60, 77, 264
Machell, Reginald 117, 287
Maclean's 54, 195, 198, 214
Maine 47–48, 53–54, 60
"Making £10,000" (1913) 18, 263
Malaysia 8, 227
Malraux, Andre 255
The Man from Jupiter (retitled *Black Light*)
"The Man from Poonch" (1933) 270
"The Man on the Mat" (1931)158, 181, 270, 273
"The Man Who Saw" (1932) 23, 24, 270
Marquand, John P. 292
The Marriage of Meldrum Strange (1923) 101, 185, 189, 261, 266
"Masterpieces of Oriental Mystery" 93
"The Maya Mystery—Yucatan" (1924) 230–231, 267
McClure's 18
McCrackan, William Denison 61–62, 67, 72, 74, 77
McGovern, William 287
McGuinness, James Kevin 162–163
McKinley, Stone & McKenzie 93
McLaglen, Victor 162, 165–167, 223
McLaughlin, Josephine see King, Bradley

McQueen, Elizabeth L. 60–61, 63, 72, 279
Merritt, A. 204, 258
"Mespot" (1920) 265
The Messenger of Destiny (1926) 141, 251, 268
Mexico 132, 152–154, 188
Middle East 54, 60–88
"Milk of the Moon" (1932) 191, 270
"Miscarriage of Justice" (1924) 267
Mohammed's Tooth (reprinted as *The Hundred Days*)
Moore, Terry 245
Moplah Revolt 99–100, 255
Morris, Kenneth 113, 126, 136–137, 172, 231, 253, 286, 288
Moses and Mrs. Aintree (1922) 78, 101, 234, 266
"The Moslem Mullah" (1929) 269
"'Mother Nature': A Review of a Book by William J. Long" (1924) 267
Mundy, Dawn *see* Allen, Dawn
Mundy, Robert Charles 201–202
Mundy, Rosemary *see* Strafer, Harriett Rosemary
Mundy, Sally *see* Ames, Sarah Teresa
"Mundy an Exception Among Maine Writers" (reprint of "How Talbot Mundy Came to Write")
Murfin, Jane 98
The Mystery of Khufu's Tomb (1922) 42, 78, 83–88, 96, 150, 185, 208, 261, 266, 281–282
"Mystic India Speaks" (1938) 8, 199, 271

Nazimova, Alla 168
"A Nemesis" (1923) 266
New Earth News 63–64
New York City 14–17, 54, 158, 168, 170, 172–174, 181, 188, 207
New York Times 158
News (retitled *Her Reputation*)
Next Week (retitled *Jimgrim*)
The Night the Clocks Stopped (1941) 195, 240, 272
The Nine Unknown (1923) 93–95, 126–128, 130–131, 189, 213, 216, 230, 250, 261, 266
Niven, Busch 244
No Name! (1915) 27, 264
Norton, Andre 258
"Nothing Doing" (1914) 106, 264

"Oakes Respects an Adversary"
(1918) 9, 54, 152, 264
Odds on the Prophet (1941) 88, 240, 272
"Of Wild Animals in Africa" 10, 285
"An Offer of Two to One" (1911) 18, 262
"Oh, Jerusalem!" (1921) 77, 265
Old Ugly Face (book, 1940) 8, 42, 119, 124, 212, 214–219, 231, 239, 241, 243, 261, 272, 294
Old Ugly Face (serial, 1938) 214–215, 271
Om (1924; reprinted as *Om — The Secret of Ahbor Valley*) 8, 26, 42, 93, 112, 119–131, 135, 178–181, 183, 185–186, 188, 199, 216–217, 225–226, 230–231, 250–254, 256, 261, 267, 287, 288
On Jimgrim's Beat 88
On Terms (1915) 264
"On the Road to Allah's Heaven" (1928) 158, 193, 268
"On the Trail of Sindbad the Sailor" (1925) 10, 199, 267
On the Trail of Tippoo Tib (reprinted as *The Ivory Trail*)
"One Arabian Night" (reprint of "An Arabian Night")
One Egyptian Night (1929) 88, 150, 158, 269
"One Year Later" (1913) 18, 263
"Oyez!" (1924) 267

The Passing Show 191–198, 204
"Patriotism and the Plow-Tail" (1918) 48, 264
"Payable to Bearer" (reprint of "Ikey Hole's Luck")
"The Payment of Quinn's Debt" (1912) 23, 263
Pendexter, Hugh 47, 53, 87, 289
The Peshawar Lancers 258
"Peter from Paradise Bend" (1921) 46–47, 265
"The Phantom Battery" (1911) 18, 23–24, 262
"Pig Sticking in India" (1911) 7, 262
"The Pillar of Light" (1912) 60, 135, 263
"The Piping Days of Peace" (1937) 88, 271
Point Loma, California 101, 111–154, 170, 172, 217, 242
Point Loma Publications 252
Polynesia 9, 48–49
Positif, Lewis 167
Power, Tyrone 245, 253
Powys, John Cooper 243
The Praetor's Dungeon (volume of *Tros of Samothrace*)
"The Princess" (1936) 88, 271

Prisoners of War (1925) 268
"Private Murdock's G.C.M." (1913) 263
Prohibition 291
Provost, Dawn Mundy *see* Allen, Dawn
Provost, Eric 219, 240
Provost vs. Bobbs-Merrill 248–250
Pulp 250
Purple Pirate (book) 26, 42, 132, 138, 142, 185, 188–189, 208–210, 217, 250–251, 261
The Purple Pirate (magazine novelette, 1935) 208, 271
Purucker, Gottfried de 116–117, 119, 125, 136, 152, 170–171, 286

"The Queen — God Bless Her!" (1912) 23, 263
Queen Cleopatra (1929) 26, 112, 132, 138, 142, 144, 147–151, 157, 159–160, 169, 208–210, 215, 250–251, 261, 268
The Queen's Warrant (retitling of *W.H.*)
"Quits!" (abridgement of "The Payment of Quinn's Debt")

"Rabbit" (1912) 23, 263, 274
Radio Continuity Types (1938) 271
Rambova, Natacha 158, 168–169, 171–172, 175–176, 188, 199, 201, 241, 295
Ramsden (rewritten as *The Devil's Guard*)
"Random Reminiscences of African Big Game" (1929) 10, 158, 211, 269
"Ready Rhino" (1920) 10, 265
"The Real Red Root" (1919) 46, 265
"Reception to Colonel Arthur L. Conger" 286
The Red Flame of Erinpura (1927) 112, 119, 130–131, 185, 189–191, 224, 261, 268, 294
"The Red Sea Cargo" (1933) 88, 270
"Renaissance: The Hope of Hollywood" (1934) 270
Reno, Nevada 89, 92, 94, 97–98, 109–111, 136
"Restraint Appreciated" (1933) 270
"The Result of Cynicism" (1930) 269
"The Return of Billy Blain" (1915) 18, 264
"Reviews of 'The Wine of Life,' Katherine Tingley's Forthcoming Book" (1925) 267
Reynolds, Paul 35, 183

Richardson, Darrel 243
Robert M. McBride Co. 184
Roberts, Ben 244
Roerich, Nicholas 168, 174–175, 186, 188, 252
Rohmer, Sax 2, 256
Roman Holiday (1938) 132, 142, 210, 271
Romances of India 199, 261
Rosenberg, Frank P. 3, 244, 255
Roth, Steve 252
Royal Books 243
Rugby 2, 6, 49
Rung Ho! (1914) 24–26, 34, 42, 48, 90, 219–223, 253, 261, 263, 276, 277
Ryerson Press 213

Sabatini, Rafael 19
"Sam Bagg of the Gabriel Group" (1916) 48–49, 264
San Diego, California 101, 119, 125, 151
San Diego Union 119, 152
Saturday Evening Post 48, 151, 158–160, 162, 177, 291
"The Sayings of Hell-Fire Smith Done Into Polite English" (1919) 13, 106, 265
Scars of Jealousy 106, 284
Scherr, Amy Lay Hull 144
Scott, R.T.M. 158, 292
The Scrap Book 17, 18, 22, 54
"The Second Rung" (1912) 18, 263
A Secret Society (1922) 78–79, 83, 266
"Sentence of Death" (1911) 18, 262
Sepoy Rebellion of 1857 17–18, 23, 24–25, 219–223
The Seventeen Thieves of El-Kalil (1922) 78, 82, 185, 261, 266, 280
Shakespeare, William 144–146
"Shooting Foxes" (1920) 53, 265
Short Stories 93, 195, 198–199, 240
The Shriek of Dûm (1919) 57, 63, 77, 265
"Sincerity" (1924) 267
Sindicato de Desarrollo Liafail, S.A. 151–154
"Single-Handed Yachting" (1911) 22, 262
"The Sirdar's Oath" *see* "The Avenger"
A Soldier and a Gentleman (1914) 29–31, 42, 102, 263
Solomon's Half-Way House (1934) 10, 54, 195, 207, 270
"Some True Stories About Wild Animals" (1924) 10, 119, 267
Songs of Adventure (1919) 265

"The Soul of a Regiment" (1912) 21–23, 77, 90, 135, 243, 261, 262, 263
Spain 199–200, 239, 295
Speeches 119, 153, 210–211, 275, 285–286
"Speed" (1935) 156, 199, 271
"Spiritual Man Is Eternal: There Are No Dead!" (1929) 170, 269
Spiritualism 168–170, 175–176, 292
Staten Island, New York 74–75, 218
Steele, Kathleen 9, 13
Stirling, S.M. 258–259
Stone, John 162
Stone of Scone 139
Strafer, Harriette Rosemary 43–44, 52–53, 63, 65–66, 74–75, 109–111, 113, 161, 218, 278
Strongheart 98–99
"Students of Lomaland Give Wonderful Interpretation of the 'The Eumenides' at Greek Theater" (reprint of "Writer Comments Presentation of 'The Eumenides' at Point Loma [sic]")
"Sulphur's National" (abridgement of "Making £10,000")
The Sword of Iskander see *Dick Anthony of Arran: The Sword of Iskander*

"T.C. Ansell—Adventurer" (1912) 22, 263
"Talbot Mundy" (1929) 269
"Talbot Mundy, an Author Who Has Hunted in Jungle" (1917) 264
"Talbot Mundy on Civilization, Art and San Diego" (1927) 268
"Talbot Mundy on 'Om'" (reprint of letter to "The Camp-Fire," *Adventure*, October 10, 1924) 267
"Talbot Mundy Says San Diego Has Opportunity to Set Pace for This Glorious West Coast" (1924) 267
Tandem Press 250
Tasmania 9
"A Teaspoonful of Earth" (excerpt of "Universal Brotherhood")
"The Tempering of Harry Blunt" (1913) 263
"A Temporary Trade in Titles" (1915) 106, 264
"That Darned Old Nigger" (reprint of "The Damned Old Nigger")

The Theosophical Path 77, 112, 118–119, 121–123, 125, 130, 135–136, 150, 153, 158, 170–171, 241–242, 252–253, 256
"Theosophical Society Pays Tribute to Memory of F.J. Dick" 285–286
Theosophy 111–153, 170–172, 241–243
There Was a Door (UK title for *Full Moon*)
"The Things Men Fear" (1934) 10–11, 199, 270
This Week 198
"Thoughts to Remember—" (excerpt of "Blackmail")
"Three Helios" (1913) 23, 263, 274
"Three Signs of the Times: Kenneth Morris—Flinders Petrie—Spengler" (1929) 171, 269
The Thunder Dragon Gate (1937) 42, 185, 188, 204, 212–214, 217–218, 227, 254, 256–257, 261, 271
Thus Spake the Devil (retitled *I Say Sunrise*)
Tibet 8, 120, 128, 172–174, 212–219, 227, 228, 231–234, 286
Tingley, Katherine 45, 113–115, 117, 119, 123, 125–126, 133, 135–136, 152–153, 169–171, 212–219, 231, 285
"To the Editor" (1936) 271
Told in the East 24, 77, 162, 199, 253, 261
"The Top of the Ladder" (1912) 18, 263
"A Transaction in Diamonds" (1911) 10, 17, 54, 262
The Treacherous Road (1937) 271
Treason (1923) 99–101, 266
Trek East (retitling of *The Ivory Trail*)
"Tributes to Katherine Tingley" 285
Trimble, Larry 97–99, 106, 135, 155–156, 290
"Triumvirate of Mayors" (1928) 268
Tros (paperback volume of *Tros of Samothrace*)
Tros of Samothrace (book) 26, 112, 132–133, 137–142, 147, 149–150, 185, 208–210, 231, 235, 250–251, 261, 267–268, 288–289
Tros of Samothrace (magazine novelette, 1925) 267
"True Drama, the Soul's Interpretator" (1925) 268

True Mystic Science 190
"Tucker's Tongue" (1916) 264, 274
"A Tucket of Drums" (1929) 103, 158, 268
"The Turning Tide: Two Recent Books—A Review" (1923) 267
20th Century-Fox 223–224, 244, 249–250; *see also* Fox
"27th Anniversary of Chicago Convention Celebrated" 285

Under the Dome of the Rock (1921) 66, 77, 79, 81, 87, 91, 265
"Universal" (1923) 119, 266, 285
"Universal Brotherhood" (1923) 119, 266
"Unsung as Yet" (1923) 266
"Until the Stars Grew Pale" (excerpt of "Universal")
"Up-and-down-the-Earth Tales" 58, 81
"The Utter Certainty of Law" (excerpt of "Miscarriage of Justice")

Valentino, Rudolph 168–169

The Valiant View (1939) 60, 185, 191, 199, 261, 271
"Vengeance Is Kitty's" (1911) 18, 262

"W. Mayes—The Amazing" (1912) 22, 263
W.H. (1929) 132, 143–147, 185, 243, 268–269
"War Veterans and War Mothers in Lomaland" 285
"Watu" (1932) 12, 199, 270
Webber, Theda Conkey *see* Allen, Dawn
Wee Willie Winkie 223
Wehner, George 168–169, 170–171, 175–176, 268, 291, 292
"Well-Known Writer Predicts Brilliant Career for San Diego Artist; Reviews His Paintings" (1924) 267
Wells, Milton F. 243
Wheatley, Mark 253
"The Wheel of Destiny" (1928) 158, 193–194, 268
When Trails Were New (book, 1928) 106–108, 158, 185, 261, 268
"When Trails Were New" (letter, 1928) 108, 268

"White-Lotus Day Celebration at the International Theosophical Headquarters Point Loma, California, May 8, 1924" 285
The White Panther 101, 162, 283
White Tigers (1932) 196, 270
Whiting, John D. 281
Wildside Press 253
The Winds of the World (1915) 26, 29, 31–33, 35, 49–51, 80, 90, 189, 211, 253, 261, 264, 276–277
The Wine of Life (1925) 136, 267
The Wolf of the Pass (1936) 100, 271
The Woman Ayisha (1922) 78, 82, 97, 185, 261, 266
Wray, John Griffith 108
"Writer Comments Presentation of 'The Eumenides' at Point Loma [sic]" (1924) 267

Young, Collier 183

Zanuck, Darryl F. 244–245
Zebra Books 251, 288
Zionism 66–68, 74

www.ingramcontent.com/pod-product-compliance
Lightning Source LLC
Chambersburg PA
CBHW080909040526
R18240100001B/R182401PG44116CBX00014B/3